The Macroeconomics of Developing Countries

Endorsements

Most macroeconomic analyses of developing countries either assumed that developed country macroeconomics provided an adequate toolkit, or focused on stabilisation and structural adjustment. This excellent new textbook develops a macroeconomic analysis specifically focused on the special features of developing countries and thus allows students and policy-makers to understand short-run and long-run macroeconomic policy-making to promote development and economic stability.

Stephan Klasen, Professor of Economics, Gottingen University

The difference between the macroeconomics of the developed and developing countries is not merely the fact that they are focussed on aggregate demand and aggregate supply respectively. Over the years, it has become clear that both types of economies have to concern themselves with demand and supply conditions, albeit with differences in depth. What must distinguish the models of these different economies is the stylisation of their underlying structures and institutions and their overall concerns. The author argues that the structural and institutional features of developing countries must have a bearing on the macroeconomics applied to them. Issues of poverty, equality agrarian change must be accorded higher priority in the models for developing countries. Although the book is based on a structuralist-Keynesian approach, it extensively and fairly discusses other schools of thought, making this lucid book highly recommendable as a textbook.

Thandika Mkandawire, Professor of African Development,
London School of Economics

Professor Andrea Cornia's textbook on the Macroeconomics of Development is the outcome of many years of teaching and interaction with development economists. This outstanding text emphasizes in particular how developing countries' economic structures generate different macroeconomic dynamics vs. that of developed countries—in his own words, how the missing, incomplete and dualistic markets that characterize developing countries affect the behavior of economic agents. I also find particularly interesting the relations between economic liberalization and inequality, which brings into this book another field in which Professor Cornia has made outstanding contributions—the analysis of worldwide inequality trends.

José Antonio Ocampo, Professor, Columbia University

Macroeconomics was developed in, and for, industrialized countries. It cannot simply be transplanted for use in developing countries, because causation, relationships and outcomes, which shape analysis, diagnosis and prescription, depend upon the institutional setting rather than the analytical structure of models. Andrea Cornia has produced a masterful and comprehensive textbook explaining heterodox approaches to the macroeconomics of development, highlighting structural differences that characterize developing economies while recognizing the diversity among them. It begins with a primer on standard macroeconomics, to analyze alternative long-term growth models and short-run macro-management models. It also discusses specific macroeconomic challenges or dilemmas faced by developing economies that affect growth, poverty and inequality. The careful treatment and lucid exposition make for a reader-friendly text, brought to life with real-world examples and supportive evidence across countries. This book, which will enable students to understand, to learn, and to question, is a most valuable contribution the literature on the subject.

Deepak Nayyar Emeritus Professor of Economics, Jawaharlal Nehru University, New Delhi, and former Vice Chancellor, University of Delhi

I wish that Andrea Cornia had written this book a quarter-century ago. A sensible development macro text was essential then, and is even more important now. This book should be the go-to text all around the world.

Lance Taylor, Arnhold Professor Emeritus of Economics, New School for Social Research

The Macroeconomics of Developing Countries

An Intermediate Textbook

GIOVANNI ANDREA CORNIA

OXFORD
UNIVERSITY PRESS

OXFORD
UNIVERSITY PRESS

Great Clarendon Street, Oxford, OX2 6DP,
United Kingdom

Oxford University Press is a department of the University of Oxford.
It furthers the University's objective of excellence in research, scholarship,
and education by publishing worldwide. Oxford is a registered trade mark of
Oxford University Press in the UK and in certain other countries

First Edition published in 2020

Published in the United States of America by Oxford University Press
198 Madison Avenue, New York, NY 10016, United States of America

British Library Cataloguing in Publication Data
Data available

Library of Congress Control Number: 2019953281

ISBN 978–0–19–885667–2

DOI: 10.1093/oso/9780198856672.001.0001

Dedicated to Jeannie, Marco, and my students

Preface

This textbook has been written over the last several years for the first-year Italian and foreign master students who followed my classes of development macroeconomics at the University of Florence. The idea of turning my teaching notes into a textbook began to take shape during the fall 2010 term I spent on sabbatical at Nuffield College, Oxford, and was then pursued systematically during the half sabbatical year I spent at UNICEF-IRC, Florence, in 2016. This volume draws on the fast growing (but still limited) literature in this area and, in part, on my research. This textbook does not aim at being a Handbook of Macroeconomics which covers every possible topic in this area and which generally exceeds thousands of pages.[1] It does not aim either at being a Manual of Development Macroeconomics, discussing all possible mechanisms of macroeconomic adjustment and growth.[2] Likewise, the approach followed emphasizes less the recent developments of macroeconomic theory for advanced countries, such as the micro-based dynamic stochastic general equilibrium models for which there is not yet a general consensus concerning their usefulness in formulating macroeconomic policy and for which we refer the interested reader to the relevant literature. It focuses instead on theoretically sound and testable models that help to define a response to the real-life macroeconomic challenges and dilemmas faced in the developing economies. In these countries, economic structures and institutional problems affect long-term growth, short-term macroeconomic equilibrium, employment and inequality far more than in the advanced economies. In doing so, and unlike other macro textbooks that specialize either on demand-management or long-term growth, this volume deals with both demand-side models of determination of the income level over the short term and on supply-side macro models of potential growth over the long term.

The volume is in four parts. The first presents an overview of the main topics and models covered in a standard introductory course of macroeconomics for the developed countries. I must emphasize that this part could be enlarged substantially by adding topics and models but that, at the same time, it is necessary to be selective to accommodate space restrictions. There are two main reasons behind the (apparently surprising) inclusion of Part I in this volume. The first is that not all students following classes of development macroeconomics have taken a course in advanced undergraduate or intermediate macroeconomics for the developed countries. There is, therefore, a need to familiarize these students with the basic concepts and the related literature, so as to broadly equalize the starting points of all students of a given class in this area. The second, and by far most important, reason for including Part I in a textbook of development macroeconomics is

[1] For instance, the textbook by J. B. Taylor and H. Uhulig *Handbook of Macroeconomics*, Vol. 2B (North Holland, 2016) is 1370 pages long.

[2] For instance, although the volume by Agénor and Montiel (1999, and subsequent editions) does not cover long-term growth issues and focuses mainly on middle-income developing countries, it is 800 pages long. The interested reader is referred to this and similar manuals when restrictions on space in this textbook do not permit the discussion of some specific topics to be included.

that the conclusions arrived at by macroeconomic models for the developed countries differ in several cases from those discussed in Parts II and III when using broadly similar models. These similar models, however, reflect the structural and institutional characteristics of developing countries and incorporate equations (for production, consumption, savings, investment, import, exports, and money demand) describing the agents' behaviour in low-income nations characterized by missing, incomplete, and dualistic markets. This is a central message of this textbook that underscores the differences in results when using similar models for economies at different stages of development. The straight application to developing countries of models inspired by the reality of advanced economies may thus lead to wrong conclusions.

Part II discusses the main differences in structural conditions between developed and developing countries that justify the construction of alternative models for the latter group. Obviously, the developing countries are a heterogeneous group in terms of size, development stage, and economic structure, and there is a need to allow for exceptions (such as China on the one side and the microeconomies of the Pacific Islands on the other). Yet, a number of common features distinguishes the majority of developing countries from the advanced ones. For this reason Part II focuses on a number of structural archetypes of developing economies that capture the reality of many low-income countries, and develops for each of them an alternative long-term growth model. Among the structural differences that distinguish the developing countries, particular emphasis is placed on the problems caused by dependence on land and natural resources, supply rigidities in agriculture, dualistic markets and a large informal sector, fast population growth (still common in some developing regions), and a weak external sector for both trade and finance. The major institutional differences between developed and developing countries are also discussed in Part II.

In turn, Part III discusses short-term demand management models reflecting the economic and institutional conditions prevailing in developing countries. Before doing so, we reformulate the basic behavioural equations that enter the demand side models determining the level of income over the short term. As noted above, these models show that the conclusions about single or multiple equilibria reached in developing countries may differ from those derived on the basis of the standard models for the developed countries. In addition, Part 3 discusses a few models (for the traded versus the non-traded sector and for dependent economies) that deal with problems still facing groups of developing countries, but that are now of less concern in most advanced ones.

Finally, Part IV discusses the impact of the macroeconomic reforms that have been introduced during the last thirty years in the developing countries. This part focuses on issues of macroeconomic stabilization and structural adjustment, internal and external liberalization, and their impact on inequality, growth, and poverty. The latter issues have taken centre stage in the global development debate after the launch of the strategy of the Millennium Development Goals (MDGs) and, more recently, of the Sustainable Development Goals(SDGs). While the MDG strategy has generated positive results, its macroeconomic approach has not been spelled out in clear terms, let alone theorized in a formal way. In the absence of a clear pro-poor and pro-growth macroeconomic strategy, there is therefore a risk that wrong macroeconomic policies and sudden shocks may derail progress towards the SDGs and similar initiatives which might be achieved by means of social policies. Reaching the SDGs by 2030 thus requires not only the adoption of progressive social and sectorial policies but also of a macroeconomic framework that ensures stable and equitable growth while contributing directly to the eradication of poverty over the medium term.

As noted with a mixture of realism and bonhomie by Taylor (1983, Acknowledgements): "Most scholarly books are pastiches of other people's works. This one is no exception and draws heavily on studies by people from different parts of the world". This is true also for this volume, but with a twist. Indeed, the theoretical approach it follows is deliberately eclectic. Although the overall slant of Parts II, III, and IV is structuralist–Keynesian, the textbook also discusses approaches developed by other schools of thought. In this way, rather than offering a consistent treatment of development problems from a Keynesian, monetarist, neoclassical, or structuralist perspective, the textbook presents a discussion of alternative (and at times conflicting) approaches to development macroeconomics in order to offer the student a toolkit of theoretical instruments that she may use in different country situations. In addition, the discussion of the various models is placed as far as possible in the historical context that led to their development. And when the literature allows it, their econometric robustness is also reviewed, and so is the political economy of the various models.

To the instructor

While this textbook is primarily pitched at senior undergraduates and master level students of development macroeconomics, Part I may be suitable for students of graduate programmes of public policy, public economics, and international development, especially for those on terminal masters courses who may have taken no courses or only a short course of standard macroeconomics. At the same time, the instructor of a development macroeconomic class may choose to drop Part I or some sections of it whenever the need is felt. In turn, instructors and students focusing on more advanced research-intensive degrees in development economics may benefit from focusing on Parts II and III of the textbook. Those who wish to deepen their knowledge in these areas are referred to the relevant literature. Finally, Part IV offers a discussion of key policy issues and models that are highly relevant in developing countries but less so in the advanced ones. Part IV could therefore constitute a module of a broader course of development economics or development policies. The issues covered in Part IV, in particular, concern the design and impact of mainstream and pro-poor macroeconomics, stabilization and structural adjustment, and the relation between inequality, growth, and poverty.

I hope the students, instructors, and readers interested in the macroeconomics of developing countries find the articulation and eclecticism of this textbook useful, as well as the discussion in the same volume of both short-term demand management problems and long-term growth issues. I hope that the attempt to show how, given differences in economic structures, behaviours, and institutions, the same model may lead to different conclusions in the developing versus the developed countries will also be of interest. I likewise hope that readers will value the inclusion of accounting, institutional, and growth problems that are still central in developing countries but are less so in the advanced ones.

Acknowledgments

The preparation of this textbook has benefited from the detailed and constructive criticism received from three anonymous referees who read the initial proposal for this manuscript. Their comments encouraged me to reshape the structure of the volume, add two chapters, fill gaps in existing chapters, and expand chapters that required additional explanations. My most sincere and heartfelt thanks also go to a number of colleagues who teach development macroeconomics. They went through the initial manuscript thoroughly, shared with me additional material, and suggested in a frank way changes, additions, and shifts in emphasis. I would like to thank in particular Jean Luis Combes and Simone Bertoli (University of Auvergne at Clermont Ferrand), Stephan Klasen (University of Gottingen), José Antonio Ocampo (Columbia University and Central Bank of Colombia), and Francesco Volpi (University of Florence). Other colleagues shared with me useful material and/or found time to discuss different parts of the manuscript. I would like to mention in particular Francois Bourguignon (Paris School of Economics), Sheetal Chand (independent expert and former IMF staffer), Marco Dardi and Vinicio Guidi (University of Florence), Roberto Frenkel (University of Buenos Aires and CEDES), Gerry Helleiner (University of Toronto), Raghbnedra Jha (Australian National University), Richard Jolly (IDS, Sussex University), Bruno Martorano (University of Maastricht), Deepak Nayyar (Jawaharlal Nehru University, New Delhi and former Vice-Chancellor, University of Delhi), Mario Domenico Nuti (University of Tor Vergata, Rome), Frances Stewart (Oxford University), Finn Tarp (University of Copenhagen), Lance Taylor (New School for Social Research, New York), and Elisa Ticci (University of Siena). The ideas, constructive criticism, and material provided by these colleagues and the three anonymous reviewers helped me sharpen the initial proposal and the overall articulation of the volume. Any remaining gaps, errors, and inaccuracies are obviously only mine.

Finally, I would like to thank the PhD students in development economics of the University of Florence who helped me to update some of the tables and figures presented in this textbook. I would like to mention in particular Luca Bortolotti. I am also indebted to the Department of Economics and Business Management of the University of Florence for granting me, in 2016, a half year sabbatical and for smoothing the administrative procedures for the preparation of this volume. In this regard, Barbara Napolitano deserves a special mention. I would also like to thank the publisher, Oxford University Press, which demonstrated considerable understanding as successive deadlines were trespassed, and for the overall encouragement shown for the project. Last but not least, I would like to thank Robert Zimmermann for his help in editing and formatting this textbook.

Giovanni Andrea Cornia

Florence, July 2019

Contents

PART IV. SPECIFIC MACROECONOMIC PROBLEMS FACED BY DEVELOPING COUNTRIES

List of Figures

List of Tables

PART I

CONTEXT AND INSTRUMENTS OF STANDARD MACROECONOMICS

An Overview

1

Genesis, Context, Focus, and Accounting Relations of Standard Macroeconomics

This chapter discusses the field of investigation and the main issues analysed by short-term and long-term macroeconomics in the now advanced economies, the set of accounting relations used to describe the functioning of the macroeconomy and to measure its performance, and the context and historical evolution of macroeconomic theory during the last two centuries.

1.1 Genesis and Focus of Macroeconomics

Field of investigation and historical genesis

Contrary to microeconomics, which analyses the supposedly rational, individualistic, and self-interested behaviour of the single consumer, investor, entrepreneur, worker, and so on, macroeconomics focuses on the functioning of the economic system taken as a whole by studying the aggregate behaviours of the main groups of agents or of their representative agents.

The economy is treated as if it were constituted by only one productive sector. However, a few macro models discussed in this volume include two or three broad sectors characterized by different behaviours, that is, the formal and informal sectors, the traded and non-traded sectors, and the imports, exports, and non-tradeable sectors. The study of macroeconomics also assumes that economic decisions can be represented through aggregate functions concerning consumption, savings, capital outlays, money demand, and so on. Most often, such functions refer to the whole economy and deliberately ignore the individual characteristics of different groups of consumers, producers, and other types of economic agents. Also, in this case, there are some exceptions. Although many of these macroeconomic relations take inspiration from microeconomics, as discussed in this volume, aggregate macroeconomic behaviours are not necessarily the summation of the *ex ante* rational microeconomic behaviours of individuals or groups of individuals such as wage-earners, farmers, or rentiers.

For its analysis, macroeconomics uses macro prices that refer to the economy as whole, that is, the wage rate, the exchange rate, the interest rate, and the inflation rate. The most commonly utilized policy tools used to influence such variables are the monetary, fiscal, exchange rate, and debt management policies. In recent times, however, the macroeconomic toolkit has included other policy instruments, such as financial and banking regulation which was considered until recently part of financial economics and, in any case, outside the remit of macroeconomic policy. Given the enthusiasm for financial

The Macroeconomics of Developing Countries: An Intermediate Textbook. Giovanni Andrea Cornia, Oxford University Press (2020).

DOI: 10.1093/oso/9780198856672.001.0001

deregulation which prevailed until the 2008 sub-prime crisis, the macroeconomic regulation of financial transactions was seen as an intrusion in the supposedly efficient functioning of financial markets. But in view of the severe macro shocks generated by the financial sector since 2008, it is now generally accepted that the regulation of the financial sector is part of the remit of macroeconomics.

As for its genesis, the study of macroeconomics can be divided into two broad areas of analysis, the first with important historical antecedents, while the second is around 80 years old. One can thus broadly divide the field of investigation into:

a) supply-side macroeconomics of potential growth over the long term;
b) demand-side macroeconomic models of determination of the level of income over the short term;
c) the interaction between short- and long-term macroeconomics;
d) a representation of the functioning of the macroeconomy.

Supply-side macroeconomics of potential growth over the long term

Such a branch of macroeconomics studies the growth of the potential output and the evolution of income distribution over the long term (30–50 years or more). Supply-side macroeconomics emphasizes the accumulation of stocks of production factors, that is, natural resources, farmable land, physical capital, labour, human capital, technology, public infrastructure, and several other factors, the relationship between the stocks of production factors and the level of potential output, the growth impact of a population increase, and the dynamics of long-term growth and income distribution.

The topic of long-term aggregate growth has important historical roots as it has been widely discussed in the eighteenth and nineteenth centuries by classical economists such as Malthus, Ricardo, Marx, Mills, and Smith. However, it received less attention during the century preceding the Great Depression of 1929–36, a period during which the dominant schools of thought focused mainly on the allocative efficiency of what were seen then as limited and slowly increasing stocks of production factors. In the post-World War II period, the issue of aggregate growth has been vigorously reconsidered—if with a different slant—first by Keynesian economists and interventionist governments and institutions such as the Soviet Gosplan and the Indian Planning Commission. The latter used the Mahalanobis model (an extension of the Harrod Domar model to two or four sectors), or some of its variants, to design various five-year plans to formulate long-term growth strategies. Nevertheless, it was mainly the neoclassical economists who re-discovered supply-side macroeconomics. Starting from the Cobb–Douglas production function and similar functions, new growth models were developed, such as those of Swan–Solow, Mankiw–Romer–Weil and, more recently, the endogenous growth models of the new growth theory. The Unified Growth Theory discussed in Chapter 2 is a further attempt to reconcile the conclusions of long-term models emphasizing different variables.

Specific issues analysed by long-term supply-side macro models are economic growth and income distribution. In the analysis of such topics, one aims in particular to explain, among others, the following five phenomena: why during the last two centuries GDP per capita increased 10–50 times (or even 50–300 times) in some countries, while it barely rose in other nations; the acceleration of GDP per capita growth since the English agricultural and industrial revolution of the seventeenth and eighteenth centuries while—before then—growth had remained close to zero for centuries; the Chinese miracle and the African stagnation of the last two decades of the twentieth century; the persistence of large differences in GDP per capita among groups of countries (e.g. those of Europe and Africa) while, at the same time, the economic distance between European countries has broadly vanished; the rise of income inequality in most developed and developing countries over 1980–2000, while in the twenty-first century there was a cross-country divergence in inequality trends among countries; and so on.

The gradual refinement of the classical and neoclassical growth models and of the subsequent development of the endogenous growth theory allowed macro growth models to incorporate new production factors such as human capital and technology which had been theorized at the microeconomic level. Yet, many relevant growth factors (population structure, income distribution, international trade, environmental sustainability, incentives, and several others[1]) are seldom included in aggregate growth models, possibly because of the difficulties encountered in rigorously defining these concepts and in deriving the general mathematical properties of growth models when the number of explanatory variables increases.

Demand-side macroeconomic models of determination of the level of income over the short term

The second branch of macroeconomics, demand-side macroeconomics, studies the formation of the nominal and/or real level of GDP and its fluctuations (the business cycle) over the short–medium term. It has a more recent history. Until about 80 years ago, the neoclassical economists (who enjoyed great favour in those days) believed that markets always cleared and in this way reached Pareto-efficient allocative results. In their view, there was no need to study the aggregate behaviour of markets or—even worse—to interfere with their functioning through policy interventions. This laissez-faire position was, however, discredited by the Great Depression of 1929–36 during which, in spite of the free play of market forces, a dramatic and unexpected fall of GDP took place, bringing with it a large increase in unemployment, capital idleness, and poverty. Faced with such a massive crisis, the analyses of the allocative efficiency of markets and the accumulation of

[1] The list of production factors has grown over time even though economic modelling has not always embodied them in formal models because of problems of data availability. Environmental capital has long been recognized as an essential element of sustainable development. One also has to recall the increasingly more frequent use of the concept of social capital, that is, the totality of relationships of trust, cooperation, and solidarity existing between citizens and firms of a given area. Microeconomic studies have shown that social capital reduces transaction costs, improves cost-effectiveness at both the micro and macro level and reduces income inequality. In this connection, it is worth recalling the book by American sociologist Richard Putman (1993) who showed how the Italian regions with greater social capital enjoyed not only a better quality of life but also higher economic efficiency. In addition, major psychological studies (such as the famous US Head Start Programme) have shown that labour productivity, poverty, and social outcomes are influenced by the workers' emotional capital, that is, their degree of self-confidence, diligence, ambition, and ability to communicate with others, qualities that are all mostly transmitted within cohesive families and communities (Currie and Thomas, 1995). Such individual characteristics are weakened when persistent social discrimination or exogenous shocks—such as wars, natural calamities, and protracted recessions—erode the social fabric of a nation and of its economy.

stocks of production factors turned out to be of no help. Nobody could explain why, despite the huge amount of underutilized production factors, the economy continued to shrink for almost a decade.

Faced with the failure of the classical and neoclassical analyses, John Maynard Keynes and his colleagues worked out a new theory of income formation over the short term (up to 3–5 years), a period of time during which the stocks of production factors and prices were considered to remain broadly constant. The new theory posited that the price system and the market are not always capable of coordinating the decisions of different agents. In this new approach, aggregate demand—properly manipulated by the policymaker—plays a central role in keeping real output as close as possible to potential output. Keynes' (1936) *General Theory of Employment, Interest and Money* thus represents, from several viewpoints, the first systematic attempt to analyse the cyclical fluctuations of GDP and the formation of its equilibrium level over the short term as a problem of lack or excess of aggregate demand. In the past such fluctuations were attributed to bad weather or other random shocks. Several other, at times conflicting, approaches to short-term demand-side macroeconomics have been developed since the 1960s and are briefly illustrated in a quasi-chronological perspective in the following pages.

Thus, short-term demand-side macroeconomics studies the business cycle. In particular, it focuses on the mechanisms that determine the GDP equilibrium level over the short term, which GDP components (such as private consumption, investment, and so on) increase, which stagnate over the business cycle, and whether inflation is accelerating or not. It also studies whether GDP fluctuations over the short and medium term prevent a complete and profitable utilization of production factors (land, capital stock, and labour); whether the fundamental conditions for macroeconomic equilibrium are respected; or whether the internal or external deficits are so large that they require the adoption of stabilization policies. It also analyses whether the income distribution between capital and labour is fair or not and why it may change over the business cycle. For each of these phenomena, macroeconomics relies on behavioural functions that aim to explain such developments, and it analyses the impact of alternative policy measures aiming to reduce macroeconomic imbalances.

Interaction between short- and long-term macroeconomics

Obviously, these two branches of macroeconomics are not disconnected. For example, while it is true that the equilibrium level of income over the short term depends on the level of aggregate demand, the long-term level of potential output is influenced by a composition of the aggregate demand itself during the various short-term periods that constitute the long term. In this regard, the relation $K_t = K_{t-1}(1 - \delta) + I_t$ shows that the physical capital stock K_t, which is one of the key arguments of the long-term production function.[2] also depends on I_t (investments) which is a key component of short-term aggregate demand. The same relation can be written for human capital, that is, $HC_t = HC_{t-1}(1 - \omega) + NG_t$, in which the stock of human capital at time t (HC_t) depends

[2] Similar relations between stock and flows can be developed for all the other production factors except for land and natural resources, the amount of which is broadly fixed (see Part III).

on its past value minus its ω fraction of skilled workers who are retiring, dying, or migrating, plus the wave of new graduates (NGs) entering the labour force at time t. Likewise, expansionary aggregate demand policies may affect the debt/GDP ratio and so influence the future debt sustainability. Therefore, a good short-term macroeconomics should pay attention to the composition of the increase in aggregate demand. If its rise consists mainly of investments in machinery, research, training, and human capital formation (and is not accompanied by a loss of natural capital and environmental resources), one will expect a rise in aggregate demand and the equilibrium level of income over the short term, as well as an expansion of the production possibilities frontier over the long term. An example of such an approach is the strong investment in renewable energies and green growth promoted in the United States by the Obama administration in the aftermath of the 2008 recession that was caused by the sub-prime financial crisis.

If little attention is paid to the composition of aggregate demand, a short-term fiscal stimulus may lead to a short-to-medium term stagnation in physical investments and human capital formation, reducing in this way the potential and effective growth of GDP over the long term. This occurs when the short-term demand stimuli focus on private expenditure on consumption goods and public expenditure on transfers, while the public investments on infrastructure, human capital formation, and research stagnate.

Representation of the functioning of the macroeconomy

The functioning of the macroeconomy can be represented by identifying the transactions that take place among its three main actors, that is, the private sector (which includes households, firms, and the financial sector), the public sector, and the rest of the world (namely the foreign sector). These interact in various ways described by the relationships of the System of National Accounts (SNA). Such interactions can be summarized in a diagram of macroeconomic flows.[3]

Burda and Wiplosz's figure shows for instance that: firms pay wages to households and taxes to the government; the state receives taxes on profits realized by firms and the income and consumption of households; the state provides social transfers to the household sector and purchases goods and services from the firms; the households receive social transfers from the state and wages from the firms, and—at the same time—purchases goods from the firms to which they supply labour and savings through the financial market; the rest of the world purchases goods from the country considered and provides it with goods for the production process or final consumption; moreover, the rest of the world supplies to or receives savings from the country considered; and so on.

These flows of goods, services, taxes, savings, etc. refer to a given lapse of time (a month, a quarter, a year) and are expressed at current prices, that is, prices that in most cases change over time. For this reason, macroeconomics also analyses the evolution and impact of changes in four key macroeconomic prices, that is, the average price of goods that is often proxied by the consumer price index (CPI). The CPI summarizes the evolution of the prices of consumer goods, that is, (CPI_{t+1}/CPI_t). The CPI is often used to proxy the

[3] See for instance Figure 2.2. in Burda and Wiplosz (1997).

inflation rate. However, the index which more accurately measures the inflation rate is the change in the GDP price deflator $[\text{DeflY}_{t+1}/\text{DeflY}_t]$. Obviously, since private consumption represents 70–80 percent of GDP, there is a close relationship between these two indicators of changes in the price level. The other three key macro prices are the price of labour (the wage rate); the user price of money (the interest rate); and the price of the national currency (the exchange rate). It must be remembered here that in developing countries the exchange rate used, $e^{nc/\$}$, represents the amount of national currency (nc) that needs to be paid for one US dollar or other reference currency (such as the yen, pound, or euro). In contrast, in the developed countries—which generally have a strong currency—the exchange rate $e^{fc/Euro}$ is the amount of foreign currency (fc) received for one unit of domestic currency, such as the euro (or yen, dollar). For instance, the euro exchange rate with the US dollar at the time of writing is 1.15, meaning that one needs 1.15 dollars to buy one euro.

Demand-side macroeconomics studies the effect of changes in the macro prices described above on aggregate consumption, private investment, saving, imports, and the management of aggregate demand by the policymaker. Through appropriate interventions (e.g. a rise in public expenditure on infrastructure, or a reduction of the interest rate), the policymaker may increase aggregate demand and boost national production until the current GDP gets as close as possible to the potential GDP, that is, the amount of goods and services that can be produced under conditions where there is full utilization of labour, land, equipment, and other production factors.

Macroeconomic interventions (such as a rise in public expenditure) must, however, be sustainable over both the short and long term. Yet, their effects vary considerably depending on the way such interventions are financed, that is, through bond emissions, international loans, seignorage, or an increase in money supply. These alternative financing approaches have, in other words, to ensure that the key macroeconomic aggregate balances indicated hereafter retain sustainable values. Such key aggregate balances include: the balance of payments (exports minus imports, plus invisibles, plus net capital movements); the public deficit (the difference between total government revenue and public expenditure); the public debt (domestic and foreign) as a share of GDP; and the private debt as a share of GDP (the 1997 Thai crisis has shown that this imbalance can cause a crash of the exchange rate and a financial collapse); the rate of inflation; and (more recently) an adequate regulation of the financial sector.

The choice of the best policy interventions can thus be represented as a problem of constrained maximization, where the policymaker tries to raise GDP as close as possible to the production possibilities frontier by manipulating aggregate demand, while making sure that the five macroeconomic constraints just mentioned are broadly respected. For instance, the Maastricht Treaty has introduced several constraints to the economic policies of EU members which, in the attempt to maximize output, should not exceed sustainable thresholds. These thresholds include 3 per cent for the structurally adjusted budget deficit, 60 per cent for the public debt/GDP ratio, and 2 per cent for core inflation. Nonetheless, there is no consensus on the precise values these constraints should take.

Whenever the conditions concerning the sustainability of long-term development are not respected, the economy may incur costs in terms of a slackening of growth, instability, and loss of credibility. For example, in most countries persistent large deficits in the balance of payments raise the exchange rate and may lead to a difficult-to-control series of devaluations. In turn, a large budget deficit may lead to a rise in inflation or in the interest rate. Likewise, an excessive accumulation of public debt may cause capital flights, a dollarization of the economy, and a credibility crisis. The policymaker must thus maximize the level of GDP while respecting the above constraints.

1.2 Macroeconomic Accounting Relationships: A Reminder

The System of National Accounts (SNA) is a set of accounting relations which measure the main economic activities recorded in a country over a certain period of time (generally one year). The SNA has been developed by the UN Statistical Commission and has been adopted worldwide. It draws its inspiration from the work of Sir Richard Stone, a Cambridge economist who was a contemporary and friend of Keynes. In fact, the SNA was developed to represent in a consistent accounting framework the concepts expressed by Keynes (1936) in the *General Theory* and to test empirically its conclusions. We take for granted here the basic concepts of the SNA, that is, GDP, GNP, GNP and GDP deflators, consumption deflator (that is, the consumer price index or CPI), investments, and so on, and focus only on the main accounting relations which represent the functioning of the aggregate economy.

Accounting relations concerning GDP formation, uses and distribution

The formation of GDP is obtained by adding all final sales (FS) of goods and services, after excluding the intermediate sales as indicated in (1.1):

$$Y = \Sigma_j FS_j \tag{1.1}$$

or as the sum of the value added of all sectors (as in (1.2)), which corresponds to the difference between the sum of gross sectorial productions X and the sum of intermediate inputs X_{hi} acquired by sector i from all sectors h.

$$Y = \Sigma_i VA_i = \Sigma_i (X_i - \Sigma_h X_{hi}) = \Sigma_i X_i - \Sigma_i \Sigma_h X_{hi}, \tag{1.2}$$

The distribution of GDP among production factors before taxes and transfers, that is also called primary distribution of income (or distribution of market income) can be written as follows:

$$Y = W + R + I + \Pi + SE \tag{1.3}$$

It corresponds to the sum of wages (W), rents (R), interests (I), profits (Π), and self-employment income (SE). The last term includes a high share of mixed incomes obtained from the joint use of labour and capital, as in the case of small firms operating in the informal sector. These primary incomes (before transfers and taxes) are received by both families and firms.

At this point, the government carries out a series of income transfers (TR) (in parallel with taxation and the collection of social security charges, a topic discussed in greater detail in

Chapter 17) as it provides subsidies to households in the form of child allowances, unemployment benefits, non-contributory pensions, antipoverty subsidies, sick pay, and so on. The government also provides production and export subsidies to firms. These are banned by the WTO in the market economies, but they are still important in several developing and developed countries, as in the case of the slowly declining farm subsidies in the OECD. The overall gross disposable income (YDG) of families and firms is then equal to the following:

$$YDG = Y + TR \tag{1.4}$$

How do households and firms use their income? The answer is that they spend it, save it, or use it to pay taxes to the government. In symbols:

$$YDG = C + S + T \tag{1.5}$$

where C refers to consumption, S to savings, and T to taxes. In particular, households consume C, save S^h, and pay taxes T^h to the government, while firms save S^f and pay taxes T^f to the government, so that $S = S^h + S^f$ and $T = T^h + T^f$.

As a result, household net disposable income YDN^h (often indicated as YD in abbreviated form) is equal to the following:

$$YDN^h = YDG^h - T^h = C^h + S^h \tag{1.5a}$$

Finally, the uses of GDP by households, firms, governments, and the rest of the world by type of aggregate expenditure can be written as follows:

$$YDN = C + G + I + X - M \tag{1.6}$$

where the terms on the right hand side represent private consumption C, public expenditure G, investment expenditure I, exports X, and imports M. Given their small size, changes in inventories are included in the investments I.

Accounting relations concerning the balance of payments

The balance of payments (BP) is equal to the sum of the current account balance (CA) and capital account balance KA. CA includes the trade balance (X − M), that is, the outflow minus the inflow of goods, as well as the invisible balance that summarizes transactions on services, tourism, net royalties and returns on foreign investments, inflows/outflows of migrant remittances, international aid, and unilateral transfers. In turn, $KA = KI - KO$ is the difference between capital inflows KI and outflows KO. It includes inflows and outflows of Foreign Direct Investments (FDI), bank loans, portfolio flows, and derivatives of short- and long-term maturity. The algebraic sum of the net positions of the current and capital account balances (a surplus or a deficit) corresponds to the variation of the foreign exchange reserves (ΔRES) deposited at the central and the commercial banks as shown in (1.7):

$$CA + KA - \Delta RES = 0 \quad \text{or } CA + KA = \Delta RES \tag{1.7}$$

In case the CA deficit is greater than the KA surplus, over the medium term there will be pressure to reach a situation in which CA = KA. as otherwise sooner or later it will no longer be possible to reduce RES, which in several non-oil developing countries is chronically low and, which practical experience suggests, should never fall below 90 days of imports. CA generally has a positive sign in developed countries and a negative sign in the developing ones, but this is no longer true for several Asian emerging economies. KA generally has a negative sign for developed countries (that are exporting capital) and a positive one for developing ones. However, for almost two decades, this rule has not applied to the United States, China, and other Asian or oil-producing economies. The United States, for instance, has for many years recorded massive trade deficits estimated at 6–7 per cent of its GDP. In turn, for years China, other East Asian economies, and the oil economies have recorded large current account surpluses.

Thus, in terms of the sign and value of their CA and KA one can distinguish four typical situations applying to different types of countries:

(a) Countries with a negative CA and a positive KA. These are the typical poor countries that need to import essential goods for their development (machinery, energy, and wage goods) and that compensate their current account deficit with an inflow of various types of private capital and aid flows coming from abroad.

(b) Countries with a positive CA and negative KA. These are the typical advanced economies, such as Germany, Japan, and Italy, as well as the Asian emerging economies and the OPEC countries that have the capacity to export high-value manufactured goods or energy and that consequently realize a surplus in their current account balance, CA. These countries generally invest their CA surplus in developing countries in the form of FDI, or in the financial sector of the United States, United Kingdom, and other nations in search of financial returns higher than those they can obtain domestically, or anywhere that is convenient as part of their industrial policy aimed at strengthening their high-tech sector.

(c) The United States. In spite of being highly developed, this country has recorded a negative CA balance and a positive KA balance for a long time. The same situation has been observed—on a smaller scale—in the United Kingdom, as London is the biggest financial market in Europe, and in Spain where the development of the real estate sector has benefited from the inflow of large amounts of foreign capital. The situation of the United States requires some clarification. Its large and positive KA means that the country absorbs an enormous amount of world savings. These are mostly placed in financial instruments (and less in industrial assets), as US$ Treasury Bills are considered a safe asset. Before the collapse of the Dow Jones in 2008, a substantial part of the incoming foreign savings originated from private citizens who purchased, through intermediaries, US Treasury Bills and other financial instruments in the American Stock Exchange with the hope of earning high returns and preserving the value of their assets. However, since the 2008 crisis, thc inflow of capital into the US has originated almost exclusively from the central banks of China, Japan, South Korea, and the OPEC countries. It is not clear, though, how long this huge macroeconomic imbalance can last, and there has been talk of a possible 'hard landing' of the dollar with a consequent loss of its fundamental role in the international payments system.

(d) China. Since the beginning of its mercantilist development strategy in 2000, the country has recorded massive CA surpluses that in 2007 reached 10 per cent of its GDP. At the same time, it has also recorded a KA surplus, mainly due to the inflow of FDI in selected manufacturing and services sectors. Portfolio inflows are not permitted. The net effect of persistent KA and CA surpluses has been a rapid accumulation of currency reserves (ΔRES) that are mostly invested in US$ Treasury Bills. In June 2014 such reserves reached an all-time high of US$3.99 trillion. This trend began to moderate after 2007, and the CA surplus fell to 1.8 per cent of GDP in 2016, to 1.3 per cent in 2017, and to even smaller percentages in 2018.

Large global balance of payments disequilibria (that is, huge surpluses in some countries and deficits in others) are a major source of exchange rate instability and—at the same time—feed speculative capital flows from surplus countries to the main financial centres (Wall Street, the City of London, Singapore, Shangai, and Hong Kong). This encourages speculative short-term investments in risky financial assets, a trend that has been shown to increase instability and lead to financial crises.

On the basis of identity (1.6), the relation between CA and the economy can be written as follows:

$$CA = X - M = Y - (C + I + G) = Y - A, \tag{1.8}$$

in which the variable 'absorption' (A) represents the resources utilized in the domestic economy in the form of private consumption, investments, and public expenditure. This relation shows that the difference between Y and A is equal to the value of the current account balance, CA. This is an important relation that is often used to suggest that—whenever $X < M$ (and $CA < 0$)—a reduction of the current account deficit requires absorption to be cut. This entails reducing public expenditure, private consumption, or investments through a restrictive monetary policy (e.g. a rise in interest rates) which would reduce C and I, or a contractionary fiscal policy aimed at reducing public expenditure, G.

As a matter of course, the adjustment of CA might be achieved by trying to influence its direct determinants, that is, M and X. In this case, measures aimed at boosting exports and restraining imports should and could be adopted. Among these measures, the devaluation of the exchange rate, export subsidies, the reimbursement of VAT to exporters, import duties and quotas, as well as other non-tariff barriers play an important role. It should be noted, however, that these measures generate asymmetric effects depending on the economic structure of each country, and in particular, depending on the price elasticities of the demand for imports and supply of exports. In developing countries the effectiveness of devaluation is disputed, and is analysed in detail in Chapters 5 and 14.

Another way of representing *ex post* the position of the current account balance is to equalize (1.5) and (1.6), obtaining:

$$C + S + T = C + G + I + X - M \tag{1.9}$$

that after simple manipulations can be written as:

$$(S - I) + (T - G) = (X - M) \tag{1.9a}$$

where it appears that a negative CA is equal to the sum of the household savings gap ($S - I < 0$) and the fiscal gap ($T < G$). Relation (1.9a) links, in other words, the expenditure balance of the three main macroeconomic actors: the private sector, the government, and the rest of the world. Relation (1.9a) does not, however, establish a direction of causality between these three gaps (see Chapter 14).

Accumulation and macro financial account

The accumulation account evaluates the stock of net wealth at the end of each accounting period. It is broken down in two parts, the first covers financial assets and liabilities, and the second non-financial assets. According to the SNA (2008) Standards, the total assets and liabilities can be disaggregated as follows: fixed assets (housing, inventories, valuables); non-produced assets (natural resources such as land, forestry, rivers); contracts, leases, and licences; and financial assets and liabilities (monetary gold and SDRs, currency and deposits, loans, equity and shares in equity funds, insurance pensions and standardized schemes, financial derivatives, other accounts receivable).

The financial assets account has been defined by a group of international organizations (the IMF, World Bank, OECD, and European Commission), under the guidance of the United Nations Statistical Division. It includes the balance of the financial transactions (net acquisition of financial assets minus repayments of liabilities) broken down by instrument for the economy as a whole or for the following agents: non-financial corporations, financial corporations, government, households, non-profit institutions, and the rest of the world. Since their creation in the 1990s, the financial assets accounts, and more broadly the accumulation account, have represented an important part of the overall SNA. The sub-prime crisis of 2008 and the macroeconomic shock it caused in terms of losses of real output and fall in asset prices has given a new impulse to the production of information on financial flows and stocks. The 2008 SNA Standards include many important new features and initiatives such as a quarterly release of figures on financial stock and flows by G-20 countries. The basic relation is as follows:

$$\text{Stock of Assets}_t - \text{Stock of assets}_{t-1} = \text{Asset Flow}_t \qquad (1.10)$$

where Asset Flow_t depends on the algebraic sum of the destruction of physical assets due to natural disasters plus the value of net asset transactions, plus other changes in the volume of assets-liabilities, plus assets' revaluation or devaluation. During periods of fast economic growth, the value of housing (the main component of household wealth for all wealth quintiles, and up to 60 percent of the total for the richest quintile, see Figure 1.1) rises sharply (Figure 1.2) while during financial crises it collapses and leads to a decline of GDP, owing to a large downfall in asset prices, a rise in non-performing loans, foreclosures, and bank failures. All these changes strongly impact the macroeconomy, starting from a contraction of the finance, insurance, and real estate sectors which is then transmitted to the rest of the economy, as observed since 2007 in the United States, United Kingdom, Ireland, Belgium, Spain, and other countries (Figure 1.2). The economies unaffected by the financial contagion of these countries may in turn be hit by a real contagion—that is, a decline of imports, tourism, capital outflows, and so on between themselves and the countries suffering a financial crisis.

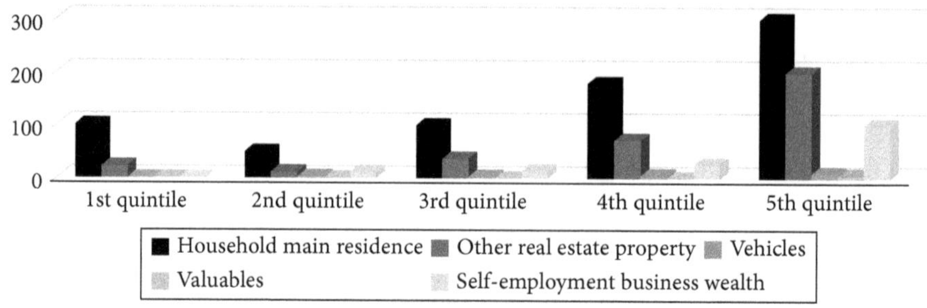

Figure 1.1 Net portfolio by wealth quintile and type of asset (euro 000s), average of Euro area
Source: Elaboration on ECB Statistics (2016)

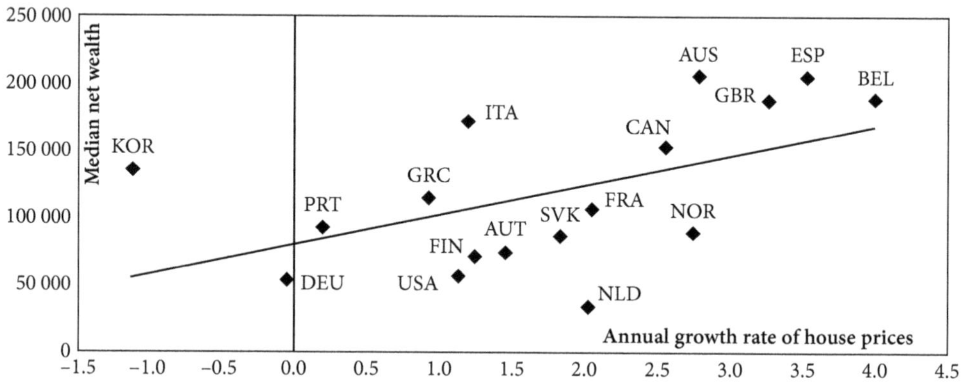

Figure 1.2 Median wealth and change in house prices, 2010 or latest available year, 2005 US dollars
Source: OECD (2015)

In advanced economies, fluctuations in asset values are therefore a main source of macroeconomic instability: in boom periods they cause an inflationary 'wealth effect' and overcapacity creation, while, as just noted, when the housing bubble is punctured, the economy over-contracts. Similar effects are observed for financial assets, whose values fluctuate even more than housing values over the short term, but whose aggregate value is generally lower (with the exception of the United States) than that of non-financial assets (Figure 1.1). After taking into account eventual statistical discrepancies due to differences in data sources, the aggregate change over time in financial accounts must reflect the difference between savings and investments corrected for capital inflows and changes in the nominal value of the financial assets over the prior year.

$$\Delta \text{ Fin Acc}_t = (S - I)_t \tag{1.11}$$

1.3 Measurement of National Account Aggregates

The theoretical definition of the economic aggregates mentioned above (final sales, value added, consumption, investments, profits, assets, and so on) is fairly clear, although difficulties may still arise in trying to solve some remaining conceptual problems. In contrast, the practical measurement of macroeconomic aggregates is rather complex and expensive. Hereafter are mentioned briefly the procedures generally followed to deal with the most common problems encountered in the measurement of macroeconomic aggregates.

Of course, to solve these measurement problems, the Central Statistical Offices (CSOs) could launch large sample surveys. However, their prohibitive cost reduces the applicability of this approach. For this reason, CSOs generally rely on indirect estimation methods, using administrative data routinely gathered by government agencies for other purposes, as in the case of the indexes of industrial and agricultural production (collected by the relevant ministries on the basis of sectoral samples); of tax revenue data (collected for tax purposes by the ministry of finance, allowing estimation of part of the income distribution); and of foreign trade statistics (bills of entry, collected trade duties, etc.—used to produce aggregate measures of imports and exports). Relying on administrative statistics is not satisfactory when dealing with countries with a sizeable informal economy that escapes the controls of the public administration (see Chapter 8).

Ensuring the consistency of the macro aggregates estimated through routine statistics produced by different branches of the public administration becomes even more complicated if the dimension of the formal sector varies significantly in only a few years. This is the case, for example, for the former socialist countries during their transition to the market economy of the 1990s and 2000s.[4] More generally, it should be underscored that the informalization of the economy (and the related national accounts problems) are growing in several developed and developing countries. This is due to the diffusion of sub-contracting and home-work (due to mounting international competition from low-wage economies), the liberalization of the labour market resulting from explicit policy choices, the structural decline of the traditional formal sector (manufacturing) and the growth of inherently informal activities (private services, craftsmanship) facilitated by the spread of low-cost data processing equipment.

As already noted, GDP can be measured in three different ways, that is, by focusing on its production, uses, and distribution accounts. The risk is that, in the end, one may get three diverging valuations of GDP. It is therefore necessary to ensure that these three estimates are consistent with each other. The problem is generally solved by first calculating the value of GDP on the production account side (or—more rarely—on the uses account side). This result is then used as the total value of GDP in the uses and distribution accounts.

For example, in the estimation of the uses of GDP, the national CSOs rely on international trade statistics to calculate X and M which are generally fairly reliable, even though unrecorded shuttle and informal trade may at times be sizeable. Likewise, investments, I, are estimated on the basis of the data on the production and imports of equipment and the volume of industrial constructions which require the issuance of a building licence. In turn, the government expenditure data (obtainable from the budget accounts and their revisions) are used to estimate G. In this way, if we adopt the estimation of GDP obtained from the production side, C might be calculated by difference, that is, $C = Y - I - (X - M) - G$. To double check the reliability of such an estimate, one can use the data on final sales supplied by producers' associations which offer an alternative estimate of C. Alternatively, whenever the indirect estimate of C is considered reliable, one may determine I as a residual.

[4] The estimate of production of the informal sector can be carried out on the basis of studies of energy consumption. In the transition economies (less so in Africa), the consumption of electricity strongly correlated with the level of economic activity and was therefore used to estimate changes in the level of GDP.

In developed countries, the calculation of the GDP on the production side is obtained by adding the value added of each sector (see Section 1.2). The agricultural value added is estimated by the farmers' associations or, sometimes, by satellites which monitor the growth of the biomass and several crops. The industrial production and value added of big industrial companies (a few thousands in the case of Italy) is assessed firm by firm through questionnaires. The last component of total production is that originating from the small and medium-sized enterprises (SMEs) and the informal sector. In this case, the value of production and the value added are computed on a sample of firms on which the public administration carries out detailed sectorial studies. In turn, the added value of the public sector corresponds by definition to the wage bill paid by the state to its employees, while the value added of the private services sector is calculated on the basis of the data provided by business associations and through indirect methods.

1.4 Evolution of Theoretical Approaches to Short-term Macroeconomics: A Bird's-eye View

While supply-side macroeconomic theory has a long history, demand-side macroeconomics is more recent. Hereafter we discuss its evolution during the last century, as this branch of macroeconomics has witnessed a series of important theoretical advances generated by classical macroeconomics, the Keynesian and New-Keynesian schools (with additional insights emphasizing structuralist macroeconomics in developing countries), and the new classical macroeconomics. The number of theoretical contributions grew in importance during the decades after the Great Recession. Alternative theoretical explanations of the functioning and crises of the macroeconomy most often co-existed, despite differences in their basic hypotheses, formulation, and approach. At times, such new formulations attempted to improve on the shortcomings of former theories. This has not led, however, to a linear, orderly, and unified evolution of macroeconomic theory. The quasi-chronological order in which these new advances are presented in the following subsections should not give the impression of a gradual convergence of alternative views towards a generally accepted model. Differences between the Keynesian, monetarist, and structuralist schools have co-existed and will likely continue to co-exist in the future. Be that as it may, the main macroeconomic schools of thought of the last hundred years (most of them are also discussed in the subsequent chapters) are presented in a quasi-chronological way, although some of them were developed in parallel with or even earlier than theories discussed later on in this book.

Classical macroeconomics

Traditional nineteenth-century classical macroeconomics originated from the study of the business cycle and monetary theory, which was mainly based on Fisher's (1911) quantitative theory of money and his famous exchange equation $MV = PY$. Fisher's theory argued that monetary factors did not affect the level of real output but only inflation. For instance, an increase in money supply (M) would be expected to raise prices (P) without affecting the level of output (Y). In this view, money is neutral, and it does not impact the real output level which depends exclusively on the accumulation of production factors such as labour, capital, and technology. Early business cycle theories also focused on the impact of weather changes on the then dominant agricultural sector. These partial equilibrium theories did not capture general equilibrium effects, as the markets for goods and money were analysed separately and their interaction was ignored.

Keynesian macroeconomics

Keynes criticized classical macroeconomics and developed a general theory that described the whole economy in terms of macroeconomic aggregates rather than of its individual microeconomic components. Modern macroeconomics can thus be said to have begun with the publication in 1936 of Keynes's *General Theory of Employment, Interest and Money*, a work that offers a comprehensive theoretical framework and set of accounting relations resting on new concepts such as aggregate demand, preference for liquidity, multiplier effect, increase in household savings, and firms' investment avoidance during recessions. Keynes's ideas contradicted the assumption of classical macroeconomists that markets always find an optimal clearing while in reality they reach sub-optimal equilibria characterized by high joblessness. In this way, Keynes was able to explain involuntary unemployment and recessions. The Keynesian models brought together for the first time the markets for money and goods into a general equilibrium framework.

Keynesian macroeconomics also proposed measures (that is, the fine-tuning of aggregate demand by means of fiscal and monetary policies) to achieve economic stability and full employment. For instance, during downturns, government should increase public expenditure to purchase excess goods and employ idle labour. The effects of public spending are amplified by the Keynesian multiplier; newly employed workers would spend their wages, which would percolate through the economy, while firms would invest to respond to this increase in demand and take up unutilized capacity. Keynes did not, however, lay out an explicit theory of inflation, as early Keynesian models assumed that wages and other prices were fixed over the short term. This assumption caused little concern in the 1950s when inflation was low and stable, but started posing problems from the mid-1960s when inflation rose in the United States and other OECD countries. As a response to such criticism and to model inflation, later Keynesians developed the Phillips curve and its various refinements in which inflation is inversely related to the level of unemployment.

The neoclassical synthesis

Meanwhile, starting from the late 1930s, the work of neo-Keynesians (including Sir John Hicks, the father of the IS-LM model) led to the neoclassical synthesis that combines Keynes's macroeconomics with neoclassical microeconomics. It provided micro foundations for a few components of Keynesian theory (such as the consumption and investment functions) and combined Keynesian macroeconomics with general equilibrium theory. The latter assumes that individual markets interact with one another, and that a set of equilibrium prices exists under assumptions such as perfect competition, no externalities, and perfect information. Samuelson (1947) provided much of the microeconomic basis for this synthesis, while the neo-Keynesians formulated their theories by means of formal mathematical models. The synthesis explicitly tackles the problems of a lack of market clearing and unemployment by attributing such results to downward sticky nominal prices and wages that fail to adjust to changes in supply and demand, so as to offset an increase in unemployment. However, some neo-Keynesians opposed the neoclassical synthesis, criticized the concept of Walrasian equilibrium, and worked instead on the development of disequilibrium models, or of models of non-Walrasian general equilibrium characterized by queues and quantity rationing rather than price clearing.

The revival of monetarism

In the 1960s Milton Friedman and his colleagues at the University of Chicago developed an alternative to the then dominant Keynesian macroeconomics. Their alternative explanation emphasized the role money played in determining inflation and the business cycle. Monetarism had a huge influence in the 1970s, 1980s, and 1990s, in both the United States and the UK (especially under the Reagan and Thatcher administrations), and in those developing countries which had to borrow from the International Monetary Fund (IMF) and the World Bank during the years of structural adjustment. In fact, this school of thought became dominant in countries such as Chile and Mexico whose leading macroeconomists had been trained at the University of Chicago or other fresh water universities. According to the monetarist approach, monetary variables (money supply, the interest rate, money velocity, and the mechanisms of monetary transmission) are considered the main determinants of changes in both the business cycle and inflation. In this approach, the policy instruments of choice also changed, and targeting money supply replaced, to a large extent, changes in the interest rate and fiscal policy.

The most telling example of the implementation of monetarist policies was offered in 1979 by the US Federal Reserve Chairman Paul Volcker who, to tackle an inflation running at 20 per cent a year, raised the policy rate by ten points over a short period of time, tightened the money supply, and brought inflation down quickly. Such a policy, however, caused a severe recession both in the United States and worldwide, with huge negative effects in terms of growth, unemployment, poverty, and social conditions. The crisis reduced monetarism's popularity and generated a wave of criticism towards the IMF, which was seen as the enforcer of this approach in developing countries. Yet, monetarism demonstrated the influence of changes in money supply and other monetary variables on the real economy, although it became less credible after the early 1980s when the once-stable money velocity began to move erratically in the United States. The monetarist simple, single-equation models and non-statistical analysis of the data lost out to the simultaneous-equation models used by neo-Keynesians, so that their influence declined among both central bankers and academics.

New classical macroeconomics

In a 1976 article, Robert Lucas (and, later, other economists of the Chicago School) levelled a major criticism at Keynesian economics on the basis of the concept of rational expectations.[5] Traditional Keynesian forecasting models were in fact based on statistical correlations between aggregate historical data and relied on adaptive expectations that assume that agents will behave in the future as suggested by the parameters of equations estimated on past data. Yet, according to Lucas, such an approach is unable to replicate the complexity of the agents' microeconomic decisions, as their behaviour may be modified by new or unexpected circumstances and policy changes, which the agents take into account on the basis of all information available. The new classical macroeconomics assumes that, when considering what decisions they need to take, the agents elaborate all the information at their disposal in an optimal way, without making systematic errors. This implies that the impact of economic policies cannot assume a systematic neglect or misunderstanding of their effects by consumers, investors, exporters, and other agents, particularly if the current and future economic circumstances differ substantially from those of the past due to structural breaks and the fact that a new policy is itself perceived as a structural break. The Lucas critique does not imply that people have perfect foresight, but that their forecasting errors are random variables with zero mean and serially uncorrelated errors. For instance, economic agents would, on average, anticipate inflation and adjust to higher prices before a monetary stimulus could boost employment and output, thus reducing or offsetting the impact of the announced monetary policy. A recent example of the failure of Keynesian interventions based on adaptive expectations is given by the expansionary fiscal policies adopted in Japan in the 1990s in response to the recession caused by the collapse of a huge housing bubble. Rather than increasing spending following a government fiscal stimulus, households reduced their propensity to consume in order to save income for what they expected to be a risky future, possibly characterized by the collapse of Japanese banks burdened by high levels of non-performing loans. For all these reasons, Lucas argued that Keynesian empirical models would not be as stable as models based on microeconomic foundations and rational expectations. The empirical evidence seems to suggest that rational expectations work to some extent in case of announced policy interventions, less so in the case of un-announced measures.

The new classical macroeconomics culminated in the development of the real business cycle (RBC) theory of Kydland and Prescott (1982). The RBC theory assumes a homogeneous population featuring representative households or dynasties, with general market clearing occurring at all dates, and fluctuations driven exclusively by changes in technology and supply shocks, and not by demand changes as argued by the Keynesians. This approach is based on dynamic stochastic general equilibrium (DSGE) models that attempt to explain aggregate growth and the impact of monetary, fiscal, and other policies on the basis of macro models founded on the microeconomic decisions of representative households, firms, governments, and central banks in the fields of consumption, savings, investment, labour supply and demand, and money supply. The terms dynamic and stochastic refer to the focus not only on equilibrium at one point in time (as in the Walrasian model), but also at how the economy evolves over time around a long run trend. This reflects an intertemporal equilibrium that adjusts in response to random shocks

[5] Sachs and Larrain (1993, 39–40) have discussed the way households, firms, and the government make intertemporal choices by formulating expectations about the future values of incomes, prices, demand, employment, and other variables. They refer in this regard to the work of psychologists and economists and distinguish between static, adaptive, and rational expectations.

such as technological discoveries (the most recent ones being oil fracking and smart robots), unexpected fluctuations in key prices (e.g. energy and metals), or exogenous changes in the global economy. DSGE models are based on basic relationships common to several other models such as: households and firms maximize the discounted expected value of future utility streams by choosing plans of consumption, labour supply, investment, and production extended to an infinite horizon under constraints describing the way real wealth and physical capital accumulate. Utility and production functions are of the Cobb–Douglas type found in many macroeconomic models. In the RBC models, however, the equilibrium is an equilibrium of plans, that is, an equilibrium through time of all the relevant price–quantity variables. Shocks may be temporary or permanent: all of them affect the actual path of the economy but only the latter affect the long-run steady state to which the economy converges. Policy constraints (such as the Maastricht criteria), and policy rules in the fiscal and monetary areas, may be introduced in the model to predict under rational expectations their temporary and permanent effects on the equilibrium path. Thus, by specifying preferences (what the agents want), technology (what they can produce), and institutions (the rules that guide the agents' interactions) and by maximizing intertemporally, DSGE models predict what is actually produced, traded, and consumed, and how these variables evolve over time in response to shocks and changes in rules and institutions.

As DSGE models start from microeconomic principles, instead of relying on past correlations, they are technically more difficult to develop and solve and must therefore abstract from sectoral details and include fewer variables than the usual forecasting models. In addition, DSGE models have been criticized for their excessive reliance on the assumption of complete and frictionless markets that makes them unable to describe complex fluctuations under real-life conditions of incomplete markets and strong frictions. For instance, Gregory Mankiw, Chief of the US Council of Macroeconomic Advisers, 2003–05, suggested that the research carried out by the new classical macroeconomic school had little influence on the macroeconomists in charge of policymaking and macroeconomic decisions. In particular, standard DSGE models failed to foresee the financial crisis of 2007–10, that was, in contrast, accurately predicted by scholars such as Minsky (1986) and Schiller (2000). This is because the DSGE models did not incorporate key issues such as financial market frictions, asset bubbles, and the possibility of systematic mistakes in forecasting due to lack of information and ignorance about the nature of the random processes driving the economy. Other economist, in turn, criticized the idea that the whole economy can be thought of as a single infinitely lived representative agent or dynasty carrying out a rational long-term plan, occasionally disturbed by unexpected shocks, to which she adjusts in a consistent way. As noted by Mankiw (2006), given the difficulty of constructing accurate DSGE models, most central banks still rely on traditional macroeconometric models for short-term forecasting.

A final point of contention concerns the microeconomic foundations of the aggregate macroeconomic behaviours posited by the new classical macroeconomics. Aggregate trends, in fact, do not necessarily correspond to the sum of rational microeconomic behaviours of all individuals, since these often derive from choices made without being informed about the decisions of other individuals or collective bodies (the state, the global market, etc.). In fact, no theory is entirely micro-founded or macro-founded, the key problem being how to model the micro–macro relations between these two levels. For instance, a microeconomic foundation of the game-theoretic type may help to explain how it is that choices which are rational at the individual level may add to up inefficient social outcomes. For instance, as noted by Chand (2004), unemployment may rise when labour is willing to work at prevailing or even lower wages but firms are not willing to hire because they are uncertain that they will be able to sell the extra output produced. This is a chicken and egg problem. If more workers are hired, they would increase total demand and firms as a group would benefit: therefore, they should be willing to hire more labour. However, individually each firm ignores whether other firms will also act in the same way.

In this case, while all unemployed workers are ready to work at low wages, the uncertainties faced by firms concerning the volume of market sales and the recruitment of workers (whose wages would feed market demand), give rise to a sub-optimal situation whereby, although firms want to increase their profits and workers are willing to work, unemployment remains high and the volume of production low. This coordination problem cannot find a solution through the market (which aggregates individual decisions) but instead needs a government stimulus to aggregate demand aimed at minimizing the reciprocal uncertainties about the behaviours of the main agents, in this way solving the coordination failure of multiple microeconomic decisions.

Structuralist macroeconomics

Structuralist macroeconomics posits that the state of institutions and real economic structures (supply rigidities, absence of key markets, unfavourable export/import structure, the importance of the food and mining sector, and so on) affect economic outcomes and macroeconomic equilibrium (Taylor 1983) and the adjustment mechanisms developing countries have to follow to adjust to crises (Taylor 1987). The new classical economics was developed having in mind the United Kingdom, the United States, and a few other advanced economies. Even for these economies, the model's assumptions entail a high degree of abstraction which generally ignores the existing institutions and economic structures. Their inclusion may invalidate, at least in part, its conclusions. The strong assumptions of the new classical macroeconomics are even less a good fit for the situation of poorer countries. Such assumptions (and in parenthesis the reality of developing countries) may be tentatively summarized as follows (see also Ocampo et al., 2009): (a) the distribution of assets is a given and rewards merit and effort (history, geography, and institutions determine the distribution of assets); (b) economic behaviour can be depicted by a representative agent who is self-interested, rational, and maximizing (there are conspicuous heterogeneities and behavioural differences between agents who do not necessarily behave according to standard rationality); (c) prices are set by demand and supply relations and reflect the scarcity of goods (prices are set by the mark-up rule or by exploitative production relations influenced by discriminatory social norms); (d) perfectly competitive markets are price-clearing and ensure a Pareto-efficient allocation of resources (in most cases markets are cleared by quantity adjustments or queues). Since markets always clear, 'getting the prices right' becomes a necessity (such measures have generated mixed results and raised inflation, and need to be introduced after a close scrutiny of their likely effects); (e) all present/future markets exist and are efficient and independent from each other (many of them—starting from those for credit, insurance, and incentive goods—are missing or interlocking, as in the case of credit and output markets in rural India); (f) the structure of the economy does not influence the output level (a rigid supply of wage goods, a key dependence on imported inputs, and export of income inelastic and price elastic primary commodities do affect the output level and its distribution) (Taylor 1983, 5); (g) in most mainstream models, institutions. that is, the rules of the game, such as laws, property rights, and contract enforcement mechanisms are given, stable, non-discriminatory and do not affect economic outcomes (institutions evolve and do affect the output level and its distribution); (h) inflation is due to changes in money supply (inflation is mainly caused by structural rigidities and distributive conflicts); (i) wages are set by demand and supply relations (in several sectors wages are set institutionally); (j) there are perfect domestic substitutes for all imported goods (there are no domestic substitutes for imported capital goods and many intermediate inputs); (k) monetary and other macroeconomic policies do affect inflation and instability but not long-term growth which depends on the accumulation of stocks of production factors (money and financial variables may affect sharply the real side of the economy); and so on.

The roots of structuralist macroeconomics are to be found in Keynesian, institutionalist, and structuralist thinking. It is Keynesian because it emphasizes the demand side of growth. It is institutionalist because—especially in developing countries—institutions condition in an important way the achievement of growth (see Chapter 12). It is structuralist because economic structures, such as the composition of output (for example in terms of traded versus non-traded goods, importables versus exportables, and primary commodities versus manufactured goods) and the adjustment mechanisms to reach equilibrium in these sectors affect overall growth and income distribution. It must be pointed out, however, that there is no such thing as a single structuralist macroeconomic model, although several components recur in structuralist models for countries with different characteristics, such as agricultural economies with a rigid food supply, commodities exporters, oil exporters, economies with a high population growth or a large informal sector, and so on. These models are analysed in detail in Part 2.

As shown in the following chapters, it is important to stress that structuralist macroeconomics comes to conclusions about policy prescriptions and their impact that often differ substantially from those generated by the DGSE, neoclassical, and—especially—monetarist models that constituted the theoretical basis of the Washington Consensus policies of the 1980s and 1990s. As noted in Taylor (1987), Bresser Pereira (2011) and Cornia (2014) differences over policy prescriptions concern exchange rate regimes, fiscal and monetary policy, taxation, prudential regulation of the domestic banking and financial sector, the modalities of adjustment, and the impact of all this on output, employment, and income distribution.

1.5 Concluding Remarks

This introductory chapter has circumscribed the field of investigation of long-term and short-term macroeconomics, and discussed the interaction between the two branches of this discipline. It has also discussed the national accounts relationships that are needed to measure macroeconomic performance and econometrically test the validity of alternative models. At the same time, it has reviewed the main accounting problems encountered in the measurement of the macroeconomic aggregates and the solutions adopted to overcome them. Finally, to place the discussion of the following chapters in a broad theoretical framework, the chapter has provided an overview of the main macroeconomic theories (classical, Keynesian, neoclassical, monetarist, new classical, and structuralist) that have inspired policymaking over the short term—and, to some degree, the long term—during the last century. It is important to underscore that such theories often offer radically different interpretations of the determinants of growth and macroeconomic equilibrium.

References

Bresser Pereira, L.C. (2011), 'An Account of New Developmentalism and its Structuralist Macroeconomics', *Brazilian Journal of Political Economy*, 31 (3): pp. 493–502.

Burda, M. and C. Wyplosz (1997), *Macroecoomics: A European Text*, 2nd edn, Oxford: Oxford University Press.

Chand, S. K. (2004), 'Macroeconomics: Which Way Now? Old versus New Styles', *Nordic Journal of Political Economy*, 30: pp. 11–26.

Cornia, G. A. (2014), 'The New Structuralist Macroeconomics', in G. A. Cornia and F. Stewart (eds), *Towards Human Development: New Approaches to Macroeconomics and Inequality*. Oxford: Oxford University Press.

Currie, J. and D. Thomas (1995), 'Does Head Start Make a Difference?', *American Economic Review*, 85 (3): pp. 341–57.

European Central Bank (2016), Assets Paper n. 18 (December). Frankfurt. European Central Bank.

Fisher, I. (1911), *The Purchasing Power of Money: Its Determination and Relation to Credit, Interest, and Crises*. New York: Macmillan.

Keynes, J. M. (1936), *The General Theory of Employment, Interest, and Money*. Basingstoke: Palgrave Macmillan.

Kydland, F. and E. Prescott (1982), 'Time to Build and Aggregate Fluctuations', *Econometrica*, 50 (6): pp. 1345–70.

Lucas, R. E. Jr (1976), 'Econometric Policy Evaluation: A Critique', *Carnegie-Rochester Conference Series in Public Policy*, 1: pp. 19–46.

Mankiw, G. (2006), *Principles of Macroeconomics*. Nashville, TN: Southwestern College Publications.

Minsky, H. (1986), *Stabilizing an Unstable Economy*, New Haven, CT: Yale University Press.

Ocampo, J. A, C. Rada, and L. Taylor (2009), *Growth and Policy in Developing Countries: A Structuralist Approach*. New York: Columbia University Press.

OECD (2015), *In It Together: Why Less Inequality Benefits All*, Paris: OECD Publishing.

Putnam, R. D. (1993), *Making Democracy Work: Civic Traditions in Modern Italy*, Princeton, NJ: Princeton University Press.

Sachs J. D. and F. B. Larrain (1993), *Macroeconomics in the Global Economy*, Washington, DC: Pearson.

Samuelson, P. A. (1947), *Foundations of Economic Analysis*. Harvard Economics Studies Series, 80. Cambridge, MA: Harvard University Press.

Schiller, R. (2000), *Irrational Exuberance*, 3rd edition. Princeton, NJ: Princeton University Press.

Taylor, L. (1983), *Structuralist Macroeconomics: Applicable Models for the Third World.* New York: Basic Books.

Taylor, L. (1987), *Varieties of Stabilization Experiences: Towards Sensible Macroeconomics in the Third World.* UNU-WIDER Series in Development Economics. Oxford: Oxford University Press

United Nations (2008), *System of National Accounts 2008*, New York: United Nations.

Suggested further reading

Blanchard, O. (2009), *Macroeconomics*, 5th edition. Upper Saddle River, NJ: Prentice Hall.

Minsky, H. P. (1986), *Stabilizing an Unstable Economy.* New Haven, CT: Yale University Press.

Wickens, M. (2012), *Macroeconomic Theory: A Dynamic General Equilibrium Approach*, 2nd edition. Princeton, NJ: Princeton University Press.

2

Long-term Supply-side Macro Models of Potential Growth

This chapter discusses the nature, main features, and immediate and underlying causes of long-term growth. It also reviews the origins of income differences among world citizens by making reference to colonial history, pre-existing feudal institutions in today's low-income countries and the differences in growth rates between developed and developing countries. It subsequently discusses the Harrod–Domar model, two neoclassical exogenous growth models, two endogenous growth models, and Unified Growth Theory.

2.1 Long-term Growth: A Recent Phenomenon, still Poorly Understood

Economic growth is a recent phenomenon (Figure 2.1). Until the seventeenth and eighteenth centuries, GDP per capita and population size remained broadly constant. Growth was imperceptible and, as a matter of fact, the economy was characterized by a stable stationary state. In numerous economies of the developing world, which were bypassed by modern technological improvements and the spread of international trade, this stationary state lasted till forty years ago and, in some cases, it is still common, as in Central Africa. The persistence of a stable GDP or of its slow growth explains the attention reserved for so many years to allocative problems: if GDP per capita does not grow, then collective welfare should be maximized by way of a better allocation of the available resources. With the advent of the agricultural revolution (in the eighteenth century), and the subsequent industrial revolution (starting with the invention of the steam engine followed by the combustion engine in the eighteenth–nineteenth centuries), GDP per capita began a slow but steady rise, despite important cyclical fluctuations. In the leading countries, the growth rate of GDP per capita rose gradually from 0.2 per cent a year (in the Netherlands, 1580–1820), to 1.2 per cent (in England, 1820–90), to 3.4 per cent (in the United States, 1870–1950), to 5–6 per cent (in Europe from the mid-1950s to the mid-1970s), and to 8–9 per cent in China between 1978 and 2016.

Despite these changes in economic leadership, over the last forty-five years the growth of world GDP per capita did not accelerate but oscillated between 1.30 and 1.84 per cent a year (Table 2.1). During the structural adjustment years of the 1980s and 1990s the growth of world GDP slowed down in relation to the previous decade, not only in the mature economies but everywhere else with the exception of the Asian Tigers, China, and—since 1991—India. Nonetheless, during the 2000s and particularly during the period 2002–12 growth accelerated in Latin America, sub-Saharan Africa, and the Middle East that benefited from the rapid growth of Chinese imports of primary commodities.

The Macroeconomics of Developing Countries: An Intermediate Textbook. Giovanni Andrea Cornia, Oxford University Press (2020).

DOI: 10.1093/oso/9780198856672.001.0001

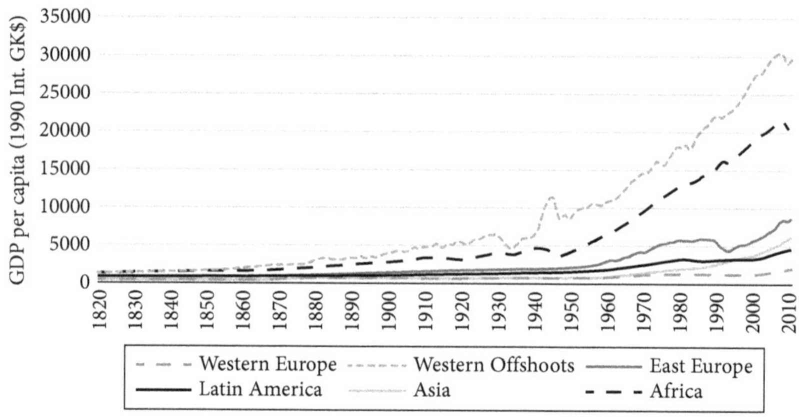

Figure 2.1 Evolution of average GDP per capita, selected regions, 1820–2000
Source: Own calculations on data of the Maddison Project database, 2013 version. University of Groningen

Table 2.1 Per capita GDP growth rate by region, 1971–2015

Region	1971–80	1981–90	1991–2000	2001–10	2011–15
World	1.84	1.30	1.34	1.63	1.51
North America	2.17	2.27	2.16	0.76	1.41
Latin America	3.52	−0.59	1.46	2.04	1.07
Europe	2.61	2.09	1.97	1.10	0.71
Former Soviet Union	2.16	1.34	−4.01	5.48	1.45
Asia	2.85	3.64	2.33	3.84	3.78
East Asia	3.11	4.05	2.58	4.13	4.00
China	4.36	7.70	9.41	9.94	7.33
South Asia	0.83	3.08	3.26	5.35	5.03
Oceania	1.20	1.60	1.84	1.55	1.48
Middle East	3.42	−1.03	1.77	2.47	1.69
Africa	1.35	−1.25	−0.15	2.83	0.76
North Africa	3.03	−0.45	0.95	2.71	−0.65
Sub-Saharan Africa	0.81	−1.54	−0.50	3.08	1.49

Source: Own elaboration on the ERS International Macroeconomic Dataset.

2.2 Stylized Facts about the GDP Growth Phenomenon

Pace of growth

From a historical perspective, the growth rate of individual countries has differed markedly. Each period is, in fact, characterized by rapid growth in one or more leading countries that play the role of global growth engine, and by weaker economic activity in other regions. As suggested by the rise of the BRICS (Brazil, Russia, India, China, and South Africa), the world economy is at the moment characterized by a multitude of growth poles (United States, China and the other East Asian economies, and India), while Europe and several developing countries have entered a period of slow growth (Table 2.1) as underlined by the literature on growth slowdowns and meltdowns.

The growth acceleration recorded during the last century in Europe was due to a constant increase of the stock of production factors. The amount of farmable land

Table 2.2 Mean annual growth rate of productive capital stock, selected countries, 1913–1987

Country	1913–50	1950–73	1973–87
France	1.21	6.37	3.69
Germany	1.06	7.71	2.68
Japan	3.59	10.21	6.65
United States	1.69	3.84	2.59

Source: Burda and Wyplosz (2003).

remained practically constant but the number of workers rose by 1–2 per cent a year. The capital stock, in contrast, grew almost always at a faster rate (Table 2.2). This means that the production process became ever more capital-intensive and, as a result, the stock of capital per industrial worker and the equipment per hectare of farmable land have constantly increased over time. The situation is similar in selected (mostly Asian) developing countries which have recently recorded a rapid rise in their stocks of production factors.

Pattern of growth

Another key aspect concerns the sectors that drive growth. Based on the experience of the now developed countries, Rostow (1960) described the evolution of the growth pattern into five stages. In the initial stage the economy is dominated by a low-yielding subsistence agriculture and a limited understanding of science and technology. During the second phase, GDP growth accelerates in parallel with the development of education, technology, and rising returns to the land. Industrialization starts to develop following a diversification of the demand for consumer goods. The third and crucial phase is that of take-off. This stage is characterized by important organizational changes, in particular in the industrial sectors that enjoy sizeable economies of scale and continuous technological improvements that are less common in agriculture and the personal services sector. This phase is followed by a drive to industrial maturity with still high growth rates led by continuous if gradually decelerating technological innovation and an expansion of the tertiary sector. Finally, the fifth and final stage is the age of mass consumption where all or most citizens enjoy a high standard of consumption that is spread evenly (see Section 2.5). Having said that, it must be immediately pointed out that not all developed and, especially, developing countries followed this development path. The main exceptions are the many small economies that continue to rely on tourism, tertiary activities, and outmigration (such as Haiti and El Salvador); the economies that have not yet enjoyed a Green Revolution; and the rising number of fast-growing primary commodity producers, such as the OPEC countries and diamantiferous Botswana, where the mineral riches have driven growth since the beginning and still do so. However, the historical evidence shows that commodity-driven growth lasts only a few decades and that it either turns into growth lead by manufacturing and knowledge or is characterized by stagnation, economic decline, and high inequality over the long term. Indeed, on average, countries endowed with natural resources grow less rapidly than those with no resources, a phenomenon labelled in the literature as 'the curse of natural resources'; this is discussed in Chapter 5.

Growth instability and the business cycle

Stability is an important aspect of the growth process and one that deserves particular attention. In fact, where credit markets are incomplete and consumers and firms are credit constrained, unstable growth generates a lower level of individual and collective well-being than a more stable growth pattern with the same mean. This conclusion can be demonstrated formally whenever the collective and individual welfare functions are concave. While in the past the main sources of instability were different types of climatic shocks (a bad monsoon in India or Bangladesh or a drought in the Sahel), during the 1980s and 1990s growth instability increased in middle-income developing and transitional economies as a consequence of a long series of financial, currency, and banking crises (Tables 2.3 and 2.4). This phenomenon has abated since 2006–07, while instability increased in the United States and Europe as those areas were hit by the devastating sub-prime and sovereign debt crises. Improvements in regulatory policies in the 2000s in Latin America explain the greater stability and absence of notable financial crises in this

Table 2.3 Average standard deviation of GDP per capita growth rate, 1960–2016

Country group	1960–70	1971–81	1982–90	1991–2005	2006–16
Low income	4.69	6.13	4.26	4.15	3.17
Middle income	3.82	4.42	5.43	4.66	3.42
High income	2.26	2.71	1.87	1.80	2.48
All countries	3.82	4.64	4.30	4.02	3.18

Note: The standard deviations for the country groups were obtained by calculating the standard deviations of all country, which were then aggregated by means of the simple arithmetic average.

Source: Own elaboration on World Development Indicators, World Bank, Washington, DC.

Table 2.4 Percentage of countries recording negative growth of GDP per capita, 1971–2015

	1971–80	1981–90	1991–2000	2001–10	2011–15
North America	0	0	0	0	0
Latin America	9	53	12	9	12
Western Europe	3	6	17	3	20
Former Soviet Union	17	25	100	0	8
East Asia	0	24	12	6	6
South Asia	29	14	14	0	0
Oceania	40	30	10	0	20
Middle East	29	50	14	14	36
North Africa	20	40	40	0	40
Sub-Saharan Africa	40	61	48	13	15

Source: Own elaboration on the ERS International Macroeconomic Dataset.

region, while sustained investments in irrigation and flood control reduced the variability of agricultural output and GDP in South and South East Asia.

Growth financing and the volatility of financial markets

A theme of growing macroeconomic importance concerns the functioning of the financial sector that includes banks, the stock exchange, the foreign exchange market, and the market for financial instruments such as derivatives and synthetic products like mortgage-backed securities. Financial markets play a key role in channelling the savings of families, firms, and the rest of the world to the real economy so as to stimulate capital accumulation and GDP growth. Efficient financial markets also facilitate the policymaker's task of supporting aggregate demand and GDP growth during downturns. For instance, governments may borrow from the financial markets through the issuance of securities in order to be able to finance the increase in public expenditure needed to stimulate aggregate demand. More than other measures of monetary policy, the supply of credit to the economy is critical in determining the level of output and employment. Yet, financial variables and exchange rates have for a long time been less stable than the real ones (Table 2.5).

One of the reasons for growing economic instability is that during the last two decades, the financial sector has increasingly focused on asset trading, that is, trading within itself old and new financial assets with contracts which have increasingly taken the form of speculative instruments. In this way, the supporting role of the financial sector to the real economy has weakened while its instability has increased (Figure 2.2). Thus, to the extent that a steady volume of credit to the real economy is key for macroeconomic growth, an

Table 2.5 Coefficient of variation of selected macroeconomic variables, 1975–1994

	France	Germany	United Kingdom
Real GDP growth	1.20	1.38	1.94
Inflation rate	0.57	0.51	0.64
Currency devaluation/appreciation	−7.35	2.31	−6.94
Nominal interest rate	0.27	0.40	0.28
Investment rate (I/GDP)	0.09	0.10	0.07

Note: the coefficient of variation is the standard deviation divided by the mean.
Source: Burda and Wyplosz (2003).

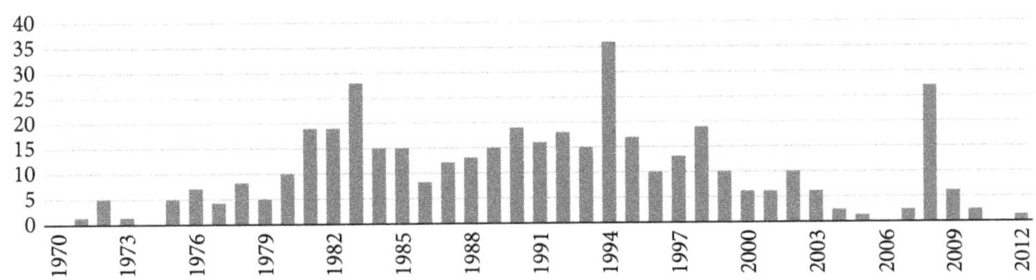

Figure 2.2 Number of systemic banking and financial crises by year of onset, 1970–2012
Source: Laeven and Valencia (2012)

Table 2.6 Trends in domestic financial liberalization and capital account openness, 1982–2010

Region	1982–90	1991–97	1998–2002	2002–10
Index of domestic financial liberalization				
South America	5.1	6.8	6.9	7.7
Central America and Mexico	6.7	7.3	7.5	8.4
Sub-Saharan Africa	4.5	5.1	6.6	7.4
Middle East and North Africa	3.6	4.6	5.8	6.5
South Asia	4.7	5.6	6.4	7.4
East and South East Asia	5.9	6.9	6.6	8.2
China and Vietnam	0.0	2.9	4.6	8.0
Eastern Europe and Central Asia	0.5	3.2	7.4	8.7
Advanced economies	7.6	8.2	8.6	8.8
Kaopen index of capital account openness				
South America	−0.78	−0.17	0.76	1.00
Central America and Mexico	−0.84	0.29	1.18	1.67
Sub-Saharan Africa	−0.91	−0.82	−0.59	−0.56
Middle East and North Africa	−0.64	−0.35	0.02	0.36
South Asia	−1.29	−0.74	−0.93	−0.90
East and South East Asia	0.85	0.96	0.50	0.57
China and Vietnam	−1.73	−1.31	−1.07	−1.00
Eastern Europe and Central Asia	−1.84	−0.53	0.01	0.65
Advanced economies	0.83	1.89	2.28	2.32

Note: The index of domestic financial liberalization ranges between 0 and 10, where 10 corresponds to complete liberalization. The Kaopen index ranges between −2.5 (closed capital account) and 2.5 (completely open capital account).

Source: Author's compilation on the basis of the 2011 version of the Economic Freedom Dataset of the Frazer Institute (https://www.fraserinstitute.org/economic-freedom/dataset) and of 'The Chinn and Ito Index, a *de jure* measure of financial liberalization' http://web.pdx.edu/~ito/Chinn-Ito_website.htm (2011 version).

effective regulation of the financial sector becomes essential to promote real growth and prevent financial crises. Despite this, during the last two decades, financial markets have become the source of bubbles, inflationary pressures, and high volatility, as demonstrated by the high variance (σ/m) of the financial variables when compared with the real ones, even during years of relative tranquility. Financial markets also have a strong influence on macro-prices such as the interest rate and the exchange rate which, in their turn, influence positively or negatively the growth of GDP beyond the effects of the macroeconomic stimuli of aggregate demand introduced by the policymaker.

In its attempt to push up GDP and employment levels, the policymaker not only has to avoid causing the macroeconomic imbalances mentioned in Section 1.3, but must also try to curb the booms-and-busts of financial markets. Over time, the attainment of this objective has become increasingly more complex because of the deregulation of domestic financial markets which began in the 1980s and the increasing openness of the capital account (Table 2.6).

Growth and income inequality

The debate over growth and income inequality is split in two parts. The first concerns the inequality of the distribution of income per capita among world citizens. This can be exactly decomposed into between-country and within-country inequality. In this regard, Bourguignon and Morrisson (2002) showed that world income inequality was already high in the early nineteenth century (Table 2.7, last column) and that it steadily increased until 1970, to level off and decline thereafter (Figure 2.3). These authors have also shown that until the period 1910–1929 the main sources of global inequality among world citizens were (a) within-country income inequality due to colonial or feudal rule prevailing at that time within the developing countries and (b) the limited development of social security and redistribution in Europe and the Western offshoots, that is, USA, Canada, New Zealand, Australia, Argentina, and Chile. The inequality between countries played a much smaller role in explaining global inequality. Since 1910–1929, however, world inequality increased due to a rise of inequality between country groups (Table 2.7, second column). This was explained by the industrialization and comparatively rapid growth recorded by Europe and the Western offshoots, and the very slow growth (0.2 per cent a year) registered in populous Asia and other developing regions. For instance, between 1820 and 1950 Europe recorded cumulative growth of 400 per cent, while India and China recorded, respectively, cumulative growth of 10 and 17 per cent (Bourguignon and Morrisson, 2002)).

However, as shown by Figure 2.3, world income inequality has declined in the 1990s and 2000s because of a rapid fall of between-country inequality driven by fast growth in the

Table 2.7 Decomposition of world income inequality[a] into within-country and between-country inequality, 1820–1992

	Inequality within-country groups	**Inequality between-country groups**	**Total world inequality**
1820	0.370	0.053	0.422
1850	0.374	0.011	0.485
1890	0.393	0.217	0.610
1910	0.399	0.269	0.669
1929	0.356	0.334	0.690
1950	0.303	0.472	0.775
1970	0.304	0.518	0.823
1992	0.332	0.495	0.827

Note: [a] Inequality is measured through the mean logarithmic deviation.
Source: Adapted from Bourguignon and Morisson (2002).

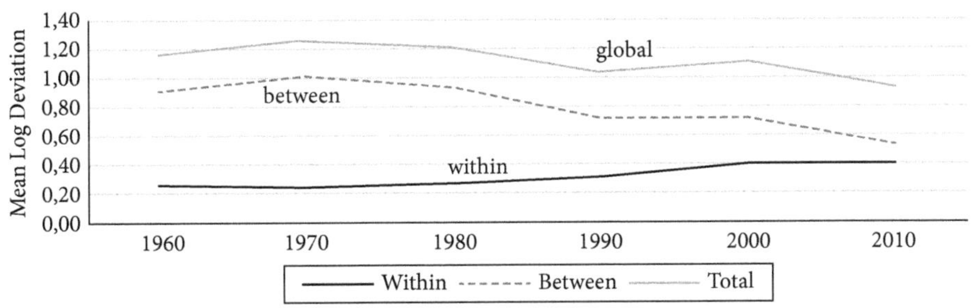

Figure 2.3 Global, within-country and between-country income inequality
Source: Adapted from Bourguignon and Morisson (2002)

Asian economies (see Table 2.1). This has reduced the relative economic distance between the citizens of the advanced nations and those of the emerging and some developing countries. Meanwhile, within-country income inequality has recorded a rise since 1970 in several developed and developing economies, as argued hereafter.

Indeed, the second aspect of the current inequality debate concerns the trends in the distribution of income within countries. As shown in Table 2.8, in 69 per cent of the 105 countries with adequate time series between 1980 and 2000 for the Gini coefficient it worsened. This phenomenon obviously affected all transition economies (which moved from a socialist distributive rule to a market rule), but also the OECD countries, two-thirds of the countries of Africa and Latin America, and even various Asian economies such as South Korea, Taiwan, and Singapore which in the past had recorded rapid but egalitarian growth. The causes of such a trend are discussed in Chapter 17.

It must be noted, however, that the 2000s have been characterized by a divergence in within-country inequality trends: on the one side, most countries in Latin America and a few in South East Asia and sub-Saharan Africa recorded declines in within-country income inequality while the remaining regions registered a greater number of inequality increases than declines (Table 2.8). The inequality decline observed in many Latin American countries between 2002 and 2015 is an encouraging real-life example of how public policies helped to reduce social polarization and offers a policy blueprint that may be emulated by other developing regions (Cornia, 2014).

Growth convergence

One aspect of the growth process linked to the evolution of between-country inequality concerns the long-term convergence of GDP per capita among nations with different initial values of GDP.[1] In this respect, the empirical evidence suggests that economies whose GDP per capita has reached US$30,000–40,000 are likely to experience a growth slowdown, while—beyond a given threshold—growth tends to accelerate in countries with lower income per capita. In some models, the slackening of growth in mature economies is explained by the law of decreasing returns to the capital per worker (see Section 2.7). There are, however, other structural factors which contribute to this phenomenon, such as the gradual shift of consumer demand towards private and public services, that is, sectors in which the economies of scale are modest or non-existent. Moreover, it is probable that, at high income levels, the utility function of many citizens assigns decreasing value to income and an increasing value to rest and leisure or—in other words—to the consumption of immaterial goods such as a clean environment, art, culture, meditation, and spending time with one's family and friends. At high income levels, these activities consume a good proportion of people's time and entail a gradual reduction in the supply of labour for the production of material goods. A fourth factor which contributes to slackening growth in mature societies is the ageing of the population, and the consequent

[1] The equation used to test the hypothesis about convergence among countries is generally written as follows: $\Delta y_{(t,t+n)}/y_t = a - b \log y_t + c[X_t] + \varepsilon$, where y_t is the GDP per capita in the initial year of the $(t,\ t+n)$ period analysed, b is a parameter measuring the speed of convergence (the greater it is, the quicker the countries with a low GDP per capita catch up with the high-income countries), X_t is a vector of factors that might influence growth, a is a constant term, and ε a random error.

Table 2.8 Trends in the regional Gini coefficients of per capita household income, 1980–2010

Inequality trend	OECD	European transition economies	Asian transition economies	Latin America	Middle East and North Africa	South-East Asia	South Asia	Sub-Saharan Africa	World
	Broad period 1980–2000								
	1980–2001	**1990–8**	**1980–2000**	**1980–2002**	**1980–2000**	**1980–95**	**1980–2000**	**1980–95**	**1980–99**
Rising	14	24	2	14	2	5	3	9	73 (69%)
No change	1	0	1	1	3	0	0	2	8 (8%)
Falling	6	0	0	3	3	2	2	8	24 (23%)
Total	21	24	3	18	8	7	5	19	105 (100%)
Broad period 2000–2010									
	2000–10	**1998–2010**	**2000–09**	**2002–10**	**2000–07**	**1995–2009**	**2000–10**	**1995–2007**	**2000–10**
Rising	9	13	2	2	4	3	4	7	44 (41%)
No change	4	5	1	1	0	0	1	1	13 (12%)
Falling	8	6	0	15	4	4	0	13	50 (47%)
Total	21	24	3	18	8	7	5	21	107 (100%)

Note: Countries have been assigned to the rising, no change, or falling inequality groups on the basis of an analysis of the trend of their Gini coefficients and of the difference between the initial and final Gini for the two sub periods, that is, 1980–2000 (or closest available year) and 2000–2010 (or closest available year).

Source: Cornia and Martorano (2012).

rise in medical, caring, and pension costs that reduces the volume of productive investments (Vos et al., 2008).

Overall, a greater co-variation of growth rates and convergence in GDP per capita has been recorded among countries of the same region, as in the European Union. In this case, we speak of 'club convergence'. The traditional view of this phenomenon has been summarized by Obstfeld and Rogoff as follows:

> Baumol, Blackman, and Wolf (1989) argue that, if an observer looked in turn and separately at countries, first with low, then medium, and then high income, he would observe a convergence inside each group. However, this does not tell us why it is not possible to see any absolute convergence among the different groups.
>
> (Obstfeld and Rogoff 1996, 456)

However, as already noted, Figure 2.3 shows that since around 1990 the faster growth recorded in several large developing countries such as China reduced between-country inequality and so increased the cross-country convergence of GDP per capita, thus contradicting the above conclusions of Obstfeld and Rogoff that were based on an earlier period of time. More research on the new inequality trends, their determinants, and their implication for convergence is therefore needed.

2.3 Is GDP Growth the only Overarching Economic and Social Objective?

In high income economies especially, the exclusive and continuous search for rapid GDP growth is being questioned by some authors as an appropriate development strategy. While in Burundi, Bangladesh, and Bolivia, there is an obvious need to increase the incomes of large sections of the population, it is not equally obvious that this is the case in societies where average GDP per capita has reached US$40,000 a year. Beyond such a threshold, the marginal utility of money is smaller than at lower levels of GDP per capita. While in rich societies as well there are substantial pockets of poverty and unemployment which require the creation of more jobs and the allocation of greater resources to social protection, the single-minded search for a higher GDP per capita may not increase human well-being. As argued by Amartya Sen, a higher GDP per capita only marginally improves life expectancy, morbidity, education, personal security, and the cleanliness of the environment. This is particularly true if faster GDP growth is not accompanied by a socially acceptable income distribution, and an adequate supply of public goods. Thus, in this view, it is not the pace of growth that matters but its environmental sustainability and equity, as emphasized for instance by the literature on green-growth, and pro-poor growth. Likewise, given the present state of technology, especially in the field of nonrenewable energy, the search for rapid GDP growth per se may cause negative environmental externalities which reduce current and future growth itself as well as human well-being. In other words, growth needs to be environmentally sustainable. In industrialized countries, in particular, the critique of GDP growth has also been articulated by social scientists and movements focusing on ecological economics, anti-consumerist ideas, and (at times) anti-capitalist and

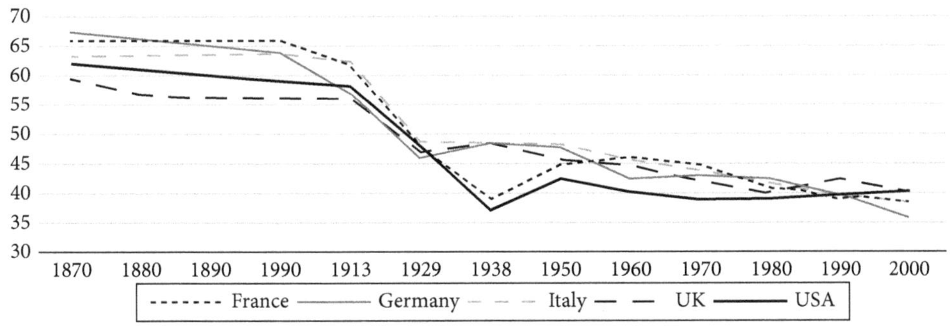

Figure 2.4 Duration of the working week of full time workers employed outside agriculture
Source: Elaboration on 'The Decline of Working Hours per Year after the Industrial Revolution', https://ourworld in data.org'working-hours/

anti-globalization views on the assumption that de-growth in the rich North would make room for faster growth in the poor South. De-growth thinkers (Latouche, 2009) advocate for the downscaling of production and consumption in the rich North and for sharply limiting advertising which creates in less-educated individuals induced needs that do not improve well-being per se but only help to raise their consumption standards to those of the reference group, the élites. Key to the concept of de-growth is the idea that reducing consumption in the rich part of the world does not require individual martyrdom and a decrease in well-being. Rather, it would maximize happiness and well-being by sharing work, consuming and polluting less, and avoiding wasting resources, while devoting more time to science, family, culture, and community.

Some of these views about changing attitudes about work and GDP growth were aired in Keynes's 1930 pamphlet on 'The economic possibilities for our grandchildren' (see *http://www.econ.yale.edu/smith/econ116a/keynes1.pdf*) in which he foresaw that, thanks to continuous technological gains and the law of compounded interest rates, at the end of the twentieth century people would work 15–20 hours a week, as their higher hourly output would allow them to satisfy all their needs by working substantially less.[2] As a matter of fact, in most OECD countries the length of the average working week has declined substantially since then, although it has not reached the 15–20 hours predicted by Keynes.

Figure 2.4 shows that—at least in Italy, France, Germany, the United Kingdom, and the United States—the biggest decline (from around 65 hours a week to about 50) occurred between 1820 and 1930, while the fall between 1930 and 2000 was from about 50 to 35–40. The United States is an exception, as from 1938 to 2000 it recorded a small increase in weekly working hours (Figure 2.4).

A comparison with Japan for the period 1980–2006 (Figure 2.5) confirms that the United States is an outlier, as discussed by Stiglitz in Piga and Pecchi (2008). While in

[2] In his 1930 essay, Keynes expressed optimism about the economic future despite the onset of the Great Depression. He imagined that, by 2030, the standard of living would be dramatically higher. People, liberated from want (and without the desire to consume for the sake of consumption) would work no more than 15 hours a week, devoting the rest of their time to leisure and culture. In Piga and Pecchi (2008), leading contemporary economists consider what Keynes got right in his essay—the rise in the standard of living, for example—and what he got wrong—such as a much shorter working week and consumer satiation. The contributors to Piga and Pecchi (2008)—who include four Nobel laureates in economics—point out that Keynes neglected the problems of distribution and inequality, underestimated the immaterial rewards of professional work, and could not foresee the influence of wealth, advertisement, and consumerism in creating new needs.

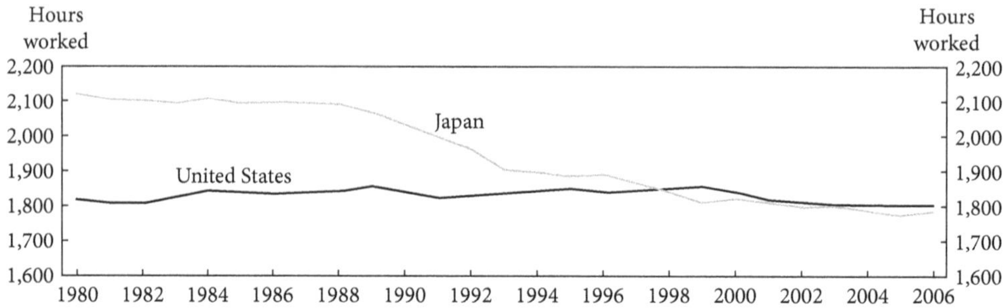

Figure 2.5 Average number of hours worked per year, Japan and the United States, 1980–2006
Source: Fleck (2009)

Japan the number of hours worked per year dropped by 340 hours, there was no change in the United States. In this country, where the pressure of advertisement and consumerism is possibly the greatest, in 2006 people worked on average as many hours as in 1980, and possibly more hours per week today than during Keynes' time. Recent OECD data confirm a steady decline in the working week in Europe and stability in the United States., In Germany in 2017, 300,000 workers started an experimental working 28-hour week.

2.4 Underlying Causes of Long-term Growth: A Taxonomy of the Main Theories

The literature makes a distinction between immediate (or proximate) causes and underlying (or deep) causes of growth.[3] Among the first are a number of factors, most of which will be discussed in detail in the subsequent chapters, such as the availability of fertile land, natural resources, labour, physical capital, innovation, technical progress, economies of scale, human capital, public infrastructure, social and emotional capital, income and wealth distribution, demographic trends, and so on. These production factors are universally recognized as key determinants of growth, offering an indication of potential output growth. Why then, if they are so important, do countries that were similar at the beginning of the growth process accumulate vastly different stocks of these factors? Theories that rely on the immediate causes of growth do not shed a great deal of light on the growth phenomenon. There is therefore a need to find deeper explanations that emphasize the role of underlying causes. This will allow cross-country differences in growth over the long term to be identified. Five explanations are put forward in the literature concerning the underlying causes of growth: luck, geography, institutions, culture, and the persistence of early evolutionary advantages. These are briefly reviewed hereafter to give the student an overall perspective of the debate on long-term growth.

[3] See, for instance, Acemoglou (2009).

Luck

The first explanation emphasizes the role of luck, meant as favourable external shocks (for instance, a long-term rise in a country's export prices), strong cooperation among economic agents, or the presence of a charismatic and visionary leader (Acemouglu, 2009). This may be especially true in autocratic countries, such as China or Uzbekistan, while in th democratic countries, constitutional checks and balances often limit the power of even charismatic leaders. Given a set of possible multiple equilibria, luck pushes some countries towards a higher GDP per capita equilibrium and other countries, with similar structural characteristics but no charismatic leader and stagnant prices of their exports, towards a lower GDP per capita equilibrium.

Geography

A second family of underlying causes of long-term growth—already emphasized in the past by Montesquieu and vigorously put forward recently by the New Economic Geography School—suggests that the physical, ecological, and geographical environment of a country has a major influence on its rate of growth. This view emphasizes the role of physical factors (such as access to the sea, distance from the coast, presence of navigable rivers, physical obstacles such as mountain ranges, and distance from international markets, that is, all variables which have an impact on transport costs and the access to internal as well as international markets). Second, this approach also highlights the impact of morphological and climatic factors (temperature, precipitation, humidity, and soil fertility) which influence the choice and efficiency of production technologies, especially in agriculture. Lastly, geographical considerations underscore the importance of the healthiness of the environment (influenced by the presence or absence of infection vectors which spread malaria, Ebola, trypanosomiasis, and other tropical diseases that reduce the productivity of workers and shorten their life expectancy).[4] In summary, isolation, high transport costs, limited access to markets, underdeveloped production techniques, and an unhealthy environment, would explain the slow growth of numerous developing countries, as these factors have a direct and immediate effect on labour productivity. One may therefore claim that underdevelopment in some tropical countries can be partly explained by the negative effects of their location and by two main ecological handicaps: low agricultural productivity and a high burden of disease. Other scholars claim that geography affects development indirectly through historical channels, such as the effects of prehistoric geographic and biological conditions on the onset and spread of agriculture and animal domestication, and the effects of crops and germs on population settlements (Diamond, 1997).

[4] Gallup and Sachs (2001) argued that in sub-Saharan Africa, malaria alone reduced the growth rate of GDP by 2.6 per cent a year. Similarly, in a study of the impact of HIV-AIDS on the economic performance of sub-Saharan Africa, Cornia and Zagonari (2007) found that GDP growth could decline by up to 1.3 per cent a year in countries with HIV-AIDS infection rates greater than 20 per cent.

Institutions

A third family of underlying causes of growth are a country's collective institutions and the organizations that have to ensure their enforcement. The term 'institutions' is rather difficult to define since it has several meanings (see Chapter 11). This volume refers to both political institutions (democracy or autocracy, different forms of government, constitutions, and legal systems) and economic institutions (property rights, norms on market entry-functioning-exit, and types of contracts) and assumes that different institutions generate diverging incentives to boost production, market exchange, and accumulation.

Certain types of institutions, for example, stimulate innovation, investment, human capital formation, the solution of collective problems, and the reduction of transaction costs. These institutions are supported by organizations (among which the judiciary and the police stand out) which must ensure that the legal norms are enforced. In several developing and transitional economies, and a small number of developed ones, such institutions are missing or incomplete owing to coordination problems among interest groups, conflicts between social classes, and disagreements about the distribution of resources. Frequently, poorly developed institutions (like *latifundia* or unregulated monopolies) that retard overall growth generate huge benefits for a small elite, keeping the economy in a state of low level equilibrium.

Culture

Another group of underlying causes of growth focuses on the role of culture, of which religion is an important component. According to this explanation, different social, ethnic, and religious groups differ in their principles, preferences, duties, and behaviours which all influence economic performance. The work that best expresses this viewpoint is Max Weber's 1905 book on *The Protestant Ethic and the Spirit of Capitalism*. Weber argues that in the eighteenth century, the greater industrialization of Central Europe was mostly due to the Protestant Reform and the spread of Calvinism, while Catholicism, which prevailed in Southern Europe, was a deterrent to capitalist development. The convergence in average GDP per capita between Protestant and Catholic countries that took place in Europe during the second half of the twentieth century demonstrates the fallacy of this hypothesis. A second example was offered in the 1960s and 1970s by Indian scholars who coined the concept of 'Hindu rate of growth of GDP' (a low 2–3 per cent a year), imputing the past lacklustre growth of India to the inborn principles of Hinduism. This religion promotes meditation, a search for transcendence, asceticism and renunciation of material goods, the segmentation of society into castes, and the endurance of injustice in this life in the hope of reincarnation in a better social class. However, the acceleration of growth that has taken place in India since 1991, most of the time under the leadership of the Nationalist-Hinduist BJP Party (which places a strong emphasis on Hindu values) also shows the limits of this explanation. Similar arguments have been put forward recently in the United States by those who argue that only some immigrant groups—Cubans, Mormons, Jews, Iranians, Nigerians, Indians, and Lebanese—are likely to succeed due to their cultural traits such as a superiority complex, a tradition of group insecurity, and an ability to control impulses.

Data on the success of any group which has been effectively assimilated and schooled over a few generations in American society show that these claims too are groundless.

Persistence of early evolutionary advantages

An extensive, if preliminary, body of evolutionary literature and empirical work focuses on the effects on contemporary income growth of distant historical variables such as the ancestral traits of current population that have been transmitted across generations (Spolaore and Wacziarg, 2013). Such traits are biological (via genetic or epigenetic transmission) and cultural (via behavioural or symbolic transmission).[5] An important issue is whether historically transmitted traits have affected development through their direct impact on productivity or, indirectly, by facilitating the diffusion of productivity-enhancing innovations across populations.

The evidence shows that Neolithic advantages in technology still persist in modern societies because of an ancient genetic distance between pairs of populations (Spolaore and Wacziarg, 2013, 343). After correcting for possible changes in ancestry, those who used more advanced technologies in 1000 BC are still technologically ahead. Regression analysis by Putterman and Weil (2010) found that technology adoption in AD 1500, but also as far back as in 1000 BC, is a significant predictor of income per capita and technology adoption today. One may wonder whether it is the historical legacy of geographic *locations* or of the *populations* currently inhabiting them that matters more for contemporary economic outcomes. These authors show that it is population groups rather than location that matters, especially in places that experienced a long history of state centralization and an early adoption of animal domestication and settled agriculture.

Development differences across countries would thus depend on their 'genetic distance', that is, a summary measure of differences across a range of neutral genes based on each population's ancestral composition. While the effects of genetic distance point to the importance of an intergenerational link, they do not provide evidence of the direct effect of specific genes or genetically transmitted traits on income or productivity. Rather, genetic distance captures differences in traits that are transmitted vertically from one generation to the next through a variety of biological and cultural mechanisms, as well as through the interactions of gene-culture coevolution. For instance, when migrating to the New World, populations brought with them traits that carried the seeds of their economic performance. Using new data on European settlements during colonization, the literature shows that European ancestry offered a strong development advantage. Europeans carried with them general education, scientific and technological knowledge, access to international markets, and the capacity to create institutions, ideologies, values, and social norms.

The key point of this explanation is that human traits are important for comparative development performance, quite apart from the effects of the geographic and institutional factors discussed above. Similarity, historically rooted traits facilitate communication and learning, and hence the adoption, diffusion, and adaptation of technologies. In contrast, differences in traits across populations hinder the flow of technology, goods, and people,

[5] Epigenetics is the study of heritable changes in gene function that do not involve changes in the DNA sequence.

create barriers that retard development, may generate mistrust—and even racial or ethnic discrimination—hindering interactions between populations that could result in a quicker diffusion of productivity-enhancing innovations to the rest of the world. However, traits persistence does not mean perfect persistence and there is still room for development policies to reduce barriers and accelerate the spread of ideas and innovations across populations, especially in the context of an increasingly globalized world where barriers to the diffusion of ideas may rapidly decline.

2.5 Classical Development Theory: A Reminder of its Main Insights

This section provides a summary of key insights and models part of the Classical Development Theory that has dominated development thinking in the post-colonial period. The inclusion of such topic in this textbook is justified by the search for completeness and by the importance the ideas emanating from this analytical tradition have had in the construction of the formal long-term growth models discussed in Sections 2.6 to 2.8. At the same time, the brevity and non-formal treatment of Classical Development Theory in what follows is justified for three reasons. To start with, space restrictions suggest keeping it to a few pages. Second, such theories are generally discussed in courses on development economics (see for instance Dutt and Ros, 2008) and not in textbooks of development macroeconomics. In addition, while several of these ideas are still relevant from a historical perspective, some of them have lost their influence on policy formulation, as they have proven to be factually incorrect. The economic challenges faced today by developing countries have changed with the spread of liberalization and globalization and equally important demographic and technological changes. Finally, the specialized literature offers a detailed and rigorous treatment of the main models part of Classical Development Theory (see for instance Part 2 of Ros, 2013) to which students and instructors particularly interested in this debate are referred.

Linear stages of growth

In the 1950s and early 1960s some theorists viewed the process of development as a sequence of historical stages. This view was popularized by Rostow (1960). Building on the historical development pattern of the then advanced countries, he suggested that the transition from underdevelopment to development would pass through the five stages mentioned in Section 2.2. The decisive stage is the take-off, through which developing countries were expected to transit from an underdeveloped to a developed stage. Increasing the rate of investment was considered to be essential to induce per capita GDP growth. Every country therefore needed to mobilize domestic savings and raise investments to reach a pre-established rate of growth of GDP. If domestic savings were not sufficient, foreign savings had to be mobilized (see the gap models discussed in Chapter 10) so as to reach a total saving rate of at least 10–15 percent. The main weakness of such models lies in their simplifying assumptions. A single production function is assumed for all countries and every economy is supposed to pass through the same stages of development. Yet, the development process is actually nonlinear (Chenery and Syrquin 1975) as countries have followed distinct development paths, leapfrogged some stages of development, or become locked into a particular stage, for example countries caught in low level equilibrium poverty traps. From a political economic perspective, Rostow's theory has been seen by some as a sort of anti-communist manifesto meant to encourage poor countries to follow capitalist over socialist development approaches, and as a justification for the large amounts of Western aid provided to them in the early decades after independence.

Structural change and growth: the Lewis model

During the 1960s and early 1970s, many economists described the development process in terms of a structural reallocation of labour from subsistence agriculture to the modern sector. Perhaps the most important example of this approach is the Lewis (1954) model. Lewis's path-breaking analysis assumes a two-sector economy comprising a low productivity subsistence agriculture that does not use reproducible capital, but only unskilled labour and a fixed amount of land. Due to the assumption of the law of diminishing marginal returns to the land, the improvement of agriculture is given low priority in relation to that placed on the modern sector that includes manufacturing, plantations, mines, and modern services. The wage rate in the modern sector should equal the marginal productivity of labour that rises with an increase in capital per worker. However, in most cases, given the existence of a huge level of 'surplus labour' in agriculture, the manufacturing wage remains constant despite an increase in capital accumulation, labour productivity, and profits. In agriculture, the wage rate is given by a social norm ensuring the subsistence of workers.

All profits realized in the modern sector are reinvested therein, so that the sector experiences an increase in capital stock per worker, marginal productivity of labour, and labour demand. As noted, in agriculture, part of the workforce (the surplus labour), is assumed to have zero marginal productivity and can therefore be transferred to the industrial sector without causing a drop in output. In turn, the surplus labour is attracted to the manufacturing sector by the higher wages offered. With workers moving from the subsistence to the capitalist sector, the economy-wide output and productivity increase. In this way, the agricultural product remains unchanged while the industrial output grows.

Once all surplus labour has been transferred to the modern sector, any further shift of workers from agriculture causes an increase in its marginal productivity and agricultural wages and a slowdown in industrial profits and labour demand. Eventually, the wage rates in agriculture and manufacturing will equalize, as workers leave the agricultural sector for the manufacturing sector, increasing marginal productivity and wages in agriculture whilst slowing their rise in manufacturing. As the marginal product of labour and wages in agriculture equal those of manufacturing, no further enlargement of manufacturing takes place as there is no longer a monetary incentive to move to that sector.

Expansion of the modern sector with self-sustaining growth and employment facilitate the structural transformation from a traditional subsistence economy to a more modern developed economy. Yet, capital accumulation does come to an end at some point, that is, when a steady capital accumulation in the modern sector absorbs all of the rural labour surplus. This can occur at an early stage if capital accumulation increases faster than any population growth in agriculture. Yet, the increase in the size of the industrial sector relative to the subsistence sector may turn the domestic terms of trade against the capitalist sector, as, according to this model, the amount of available land is fixed and, as a result of diminishing returns to the land. This would subsequently force the capitalists to pay the urban workers a higher wage that absorbs a greater share of the output in order to keep their product wage constant (see Chapter 6). Likewise, if the subsistence sector adopts improved production techniques, the level of subsistence wages will rise, in turn forcing an increase in the capitalist wage. As a result, the surplus of the capitalist sector and the rate of capital accumulation will decline. Finally, although the productivity of the capitalist sector remains unchanged, its workers may demand increased wages (e.g. because of unionization) that will affect both capitalist and subsistence wages, and reduce the rate of capital accumulation.

The Lewis model has been the object of a number of criticisms. From a historical perspective, some of its assumptions have not always been proven valid, as in the case of an infinitely elastic supply of rural surplus labour, and of the proportional rate of expansion of capital accumulation in the modern sector. Another criticism has focused on the possible loss of crops linked to the transfer of agricultural labour during the peak harvesting season. Likewise, the model underestimates the impact of a rapidly growing rural population and workforce on food surpluses, the price of food, capitalist profit share, the real wage rate, and overall employment opportunities.

From a policy perspective, the Lewis model has nurtured a view of development that neglects investments in agriculture and the need to increase food output and yields, that is, changes that preceded or accompanied industrialization, as recently observed in post-1978 China and Bangladesh. If some of the profit made by the capitalists is not devoted to agricultural development, the process of industrialization may be jeopardized by increases in food prices and nominal wages. Greater investment in agriculture may thus stabilize food supply, food prices, and wages. A model that describes endogenously such a scenario is that by Fei and Ranis (1964), in which investing part of the modern sector profit in agriculture improves its productivity, increases the supply of food, and contains the rise in manufacturing wages. In contrast, as argued in Chapter 6, a rigid food supply increases its price and money wages in manufacturing, thus making the development of that sector more problematic.

Another criticism concerns Lewis' assumption that the capitalists' marginal propensity to save is close to one, although it has been observed that an increase in conspicuous consumption frequently accompanies an increase in profits, so that the total increment of savings and investments will be lower than the increment in profits. Finally, the transfer of unskilled workers from agriculture to industry is usually regarded as smooth and costless, but this is not the case in practice because of the heterogeneity of agricultural and industrial workers. Industry requires labour with specific types of skills, in turn requiring investment in education and skill formation. Such a process is neither smooth nor inexpensive.

Externalities, learning by doing, and increasing returns in the Lewis model

The Lewis model assumes a constant returns to scale technology in the modern sector. But this may not always be the case. Nurske and other economists have tried to overcome this limitation and examined the sources of increasing returns to scale in the modern sector and their growth implications within the context of the Lewis model. Increasing returns can be internal or external to the modern sector firm. They may arise when the activities of other firms in the same or adjacent sectors favourably affect the production conditions of the firm considered (see also the next subsection on coordination failures). For instance, consider the training of skilled industrial workers by firms which are then unable to appropriate all the benefits of this activity, as the trained workers move to different firms. This generates positive externalities for the receiving firms—that they may experience increasing returns thanks to the improved skills of workers without incurring the expense of their training. In addition, increasing returns may also arise from learning-by-doing. In this case, the experience and knowledge accumulated by workers due to a protracted engagement in directly productive activities allows them to increase output more than is proportionate for any increase in the scale of production, given the same capital per worker. Increasing returns can also be generated by efficiency wages (these are higher than equilibrium wages) that improve the health and nutrition of workers as well as their productivity. Finally, increasing returns seem to be closely associated with the phase of rapid industrialization of a country, that is, when the scale of production rises rapidly and generates a decline in the unit cost of production due to the introduction of Fordism and workers' greater specialization in each phase of the production process. Thus, beyond a minimum scale of production, an increase in output may be associated with increasing returns to labour. According to Kaldor (1967), as a result of such organizational changes, the growth rate of labour productivity increases in line with the rate of growth of output, as suggested by Verdoorn's law. An analysis of a sample of forty-four countries over the period 1970–2008 shows that a 1 per cent increase in the growth of output requires only a 0.35 per cent increase in employment while the remaining 0.65 per cent is due to the growth of productivity for the reasons given above (Ros, 2013). In addition, employment growth in industry also tends to raise the rate of productivity growth in other sectors. The evidence of Verdoorn's law provides additional support for the view that an acceleration in growth in middle-income countries is based on the complementarity between increasing returns and an elastic labour supply. In the context of the Lewis model, increasing returns raise the marginal productivity of labour (given the same capital per worker) and so accelerate the absorption of surplus labour from agriculture, offsetting in this way a possible increase in surplus labour due to population growth.

Coordination failures and the Big Push theory

The theory of coordination failures was first elaborated by Rosenstein-Rodan (1943), Nurkse (1953), and others, and has attracted new interest in the 1990s. The basic insight is that the market may fail to achieve coordination among complementary activities and firms. Indeed, when complementarities exist among different sectors and companies, returns on one firm's investment depend crucially on investments in other sectors and in public goods. This is particularly true in underdeveloped countries that have to progress from scratch and so require large amounts of investment to embark on the path of economic development. In such situations, an incremental, market-coordinated investment programme is likely to be inefficient and needs to be replaced by selective government interventions to ensure a minimum level of complementarity among private investments. According to the proponents of such an approach, optimal coordination was to be ensured through a Big Push—a public-led massive investment programme—which could facilitate the realization of complementarities in the economy. The need for a Big Push was justified by three indivisibilities and the tackling of these was expected to generate positive externalities for all firms.

The first concerns production indivisibilities. Efficient production and increasing returns require not only an optimum size of firms (especially in basic industries), but also investment in natural monopolies such as power, transport, and communications which are essential for the functioning of firms engaged in directly productive activities. Even today, the limited rural and peri urban industrialization in low-income countries is often due to lack of electricity, water, and roads. Investments in natural monopolies are sizeable, cannot be imported from abroad, and generally need to precede those in directly productive activities. Therefore, heavy initial investment in public goods (30 to 40 per cent of total investment undertaken by developing countries every year) is needed. Production indivisibilities are also observed when some firms generate positive externalities by training workers who may then work for other firms.

Second, there is indivisibility in the supply of savings. High levels of investment require a corresponding high level of savings. Countries cannot always rely on foreign aid, as important investments in different sectors has to be carried out several times in the course of economic development. Hence, the savings rate needs to be increased following the increase in investment and income, regardless of the sector that, in every period, will benefit from the aggregate increase in savings. If decisions are coordinated and investment is carried out at the same time, all investors are better off. In contrast, a bad equilibrium may arise if firms in some sectors have pessimistic expectations, are reluctant to invest, realize few savings and consequently fail to coordinate their business with that of other firms. Coordination failures therefore lead to an equilibrium outcome inferior to a potential situation in which savings are increased and are optimally allocated. The latter situation would make all agents better off.

Third, there is an important complementarity of demand. In a closed economy, domestic firms supply inputs to each other while their workers purchase a proportion of the consumer goods produced by other firms. In part, this overcomes the inefficiency of too narrow a domestic market that is observed in developing countries characterized by low purchasing power. In a closed economy, modernization and increased efficiency in a single industry has no impact on the economy as a whole since the output of that industry may fail to find a domestic outlet. Thus, it requires a large number of industries to be set up simultaneously so that people employed in one industry consume the output of other industries. The situation may be different in an open economy as the output of the new firms may replace former imports or possibly find outlet markets abroad by exporting part of their output (Ros, 2013, ch. 9). Indeed, with the spread of foreign trade since the 1980s, several small–medium sized developing economies have specialized in few sectors where they have a comparative advantage while the world market has become the principal outlet of their output. But there are exceptions, as in the case of economies with very low price and income elasticities of export demand or whose international terms of trade fluctuate excessively.

The state-coordinated Big Push approach lost favour when it transpired that the developing countries run by a centrally planned system experienced slow growth. However, development economists have recently emphasized again the problem of complementarities necessary for successful development to take place, underscoring once more that a firm's productivity depends not only on its own internal efficiency and general economic conditions, but also on the actions of other firms, infrastructure, and public goods. Thus, if the market mechanism does not work, it is important to emphasize the active roles of central and local governments in helping to coordinate the move of firms from a bad to a good equilibrium. However, in recent times, the theory of coordination failures has been criticized for its strong emphasis on the role of the state. It is argued that governments may be ineffective and may choose a bad policy that could push an economy into a bad equilibrium for years to come. Moreover, the policies recommended by coordination failure models often lack details of how the government would coordinate the economy.

2.6 Exogenous Growth: The Harrod–Domar Model

The Harrod–Domar Model is a simple but influential model of post-Keynesian inspiration, based on independent articles respectively published by the two authors in 1939 and 1946. The model links the short and long term, but has been also used extensively to explore long-term growth, as is done in this chapter. In the Harrod–Domar model, the growth rate of GDP per capita depends on two principal variables, the savings rate and the capital–output ratio (a proxy of production technology), and on two additional variables, the population growth rate and the rate of amortization of physical capital. Like its predecessors—the Feldman's model used for the Soviet Plan, or its subsequent extensions to more sectors (such as the Mahalanobis model used by the Indian Planning Commission in the 1950s and 1960s)—such models have been the work-horse of the first growth models of Keynesian-interventionist inspiration. In India, for example, the Planning Commission developed a Harrod–Domar-like model with two or four sectors, with the objective of providing a rational justification of the government's decision to raise the savings rate, M1/GDP, M2/GDP, and the rate of capital accumulation in the heavy industry sector. The Harrod–Domar model reflects contextual characteristics that are peculiar to the time and place during which it was theorized. For example, growth appears totally independent from labour supply, an assumption that suited the pre- and immediate post-war conditions of the now advanced economies (and of most of today's developing countries) characterized by a large reserve army of unemployed or underemployed workers. This assumption, however, became more problematic in the mid-1950s, when the economies of North and Central Europe started to suffer from a growing labour shortage. The model also assumes constant returns to capital, a hypothesis that has turned out to be unrealistic in almost all advanced countries where the increase in capital stock per worker generated decreasing returns, as shown by the Solow model and the literature on endogenous growth. The hypothesis may be plausible, however, in poor economies where capital accumulation is still low, and decreasing returns to capital have yet to set in, particularly if the new investments take the form of capital widening rather than capital deepening.

Growth of GDP

In a closed economy without current public expenditure—given Y, C, S, I (GDP, public and private consumption, savings and public and private investments)—the national accounts imply that $Y_t = C_t + I_t$ and $S_t = I_t$. Let us remember now the basic equation which describes the accumulation of capital stock, that is, $K_{t+1} = K_t(1 - \delta) + I_t$ and introduce the following concepts:

Saving rate: $s = S_t/Y_t$, from which one can derive $S_t = sY_t$
Capital–output ratio: $v = K_t/Y_t$, from which one can derive $K_t = vY_t$
Growth rate of the economy: $g = (Y_{t+1} - Y_t)/Y_t$

Substituting S_t in lieu of I_t in the capital stock equation and remembering that $K_t = vY_t$ and that $S_t = s\,Y_t$, one obtains the following relations:

$$K_{t+1} = K_t(1 - \delta) + S_t \tag{2.1}$$

$$vY_{t+1} = vY_t(1 - \delta) + sY_t \tag{2.2}$$

$$Y_{t+1} - Y_t = Y_t(s/v - \delta) \tag{2.3}$$

$$g = s/v - \delta \tag{2.4}$$

where $g = (Y_{t+1} - Y_t)/Y_t$. Equation (2.4) shows that the growth rate of GDP (g) is equal to the savings rate s (that is assumed to be constant) divided by the capital–output ratio (v, also assumed to be constant) minus the amortization rate (δ)· In this relation, g grows for an increase of s and decreases for a rise of v (the capital–output ratio which proxies the capital intensity of production) and δ, the amortization rate, which is equal to the inverse of the duration of the physical capital. The shorter is the duration of physical capital, the lower is the GDP growth rate.

Let us now imagine three prototypical economies. In an OECD country, s oscillates between 18 and 22 per cent, while v varies between 2.5 and 3 (with higher values in heavy industry), and δ is on average 5–6 per cent. With these values, the yearly growth rate of such a country is $g = 20/2.5 - 6 = 2$ In contrast, in a low-income and low-saving African economy, s is at most 10–12 per cent, v is 1.5–2 and the amortization rate is 4, so that $g = 12/1.5 - 4 = 4$ In turn, in the Chinese economy the sum of public and private savings rate s is 40–45 per cent, while v is around 3 and δ is 5. Consequently $g = 45/3 - 5 = 10$ In this model, the variable which varies most is s, while v varies less but still affects g in an important way.

Growth of GDP per capita

Let us define the population growth rate $P_{t+1} = P_t(1 + n)$ where n is its yearly growth rate, and y_{t+1} the GDP per capita Y_{t+1}/P_{t+1}. To derive the determinants of the growth rate of GDP per capita ($g^\wedge$), one starts from relation (2.2), $vY_{t+1} = vY_t(1 - \delta) + sY_t$, and then divides all its terms by P_t, obtaining:

$$vY_{t+1}/P_t = vY_t(1 - \delta)/P_t + sY_t/P_t = vYy_t(1 - \delta) + sy_t \tag{2.5}$$

By multiplying the left hand side by P_{t+1}/P_{t+1} one then obtains

$$vy_{t+1}P_{t+1}/P_t = vYy_t(1-\delta) + sy_t \tag{2.6}$$

At this point, by dividing equation (2.6) by $y_t v$ one obtains

$$y_{t+1}/y_t P_{t+1}/P_t = (1-\delta) + s/v \tag{2.7}$$

Now, given that $y_{t+1}/y_t = 1 + g\hat{}$ and that $P_{t+1}/P_t = 1 + n$ it is possible to write:

$$s/v = (1 + g\hat{})(1 + n) - (1 - \delta) \tag{2.8}$$

$$s/v = 1 + g\hat{} + n + g\hat{}n - 1 + \delta \tag{2.9}$$

$$s/v = g\hat{} + n + g\hat{}n + \delta$$

and given that $g\hat{}n$ tends to 0, as both terms are very small, one obtains the growth rate of GDP per capita, that is:

$$g\hat{} = s/v - \delta - n \tag{2.10}$$

As it is to be expected, the model shows that the GDP per capita growth rate is equal to the GDP growth rate minus the population growth rate[6] except for the term $g\hat{}n$ (an infinitesimal of higher order that tends to zero because it is the product of two small numbers). In the advanced and European transition economies, n ranges between 0 and 0.5 per cent (Table 2.9). In the developing countries and extra-European transition economies n ranges between 1.5 and 4 per cent A numerical example with parameters for middle-income countries, using equation (2.10) shows that $g\hat{}$ is 3 per cent:

$$g\hat{} = 20/2.5 - 5 - 2 = 3 \tag{2.11}$$

This model emphasizes the need to increase the savings rate, as it is assumed that savings fully transform themselves into investments with no friction. An ample literature has thus developed on the mobilization of urban, rural, and foreign savings. The smooth transformation of savings into investment is a hypothesis with some theoretical plausibility but it is far apart from the reality of developing countries with a chronic negative foreign exchange gap (X − M) and S ≠ I (see Chapter 13). A second way to increase the GDP or GDP per capita growth rate consists in decreasing the capital–output ratio *v*, thus boosting capital efficiency. Yet, if the technology is imported from countries adopting capital-intensive production techniques, this turns out to be difficult. At any rate, in the 1960s and 1970s (less so at the present time) there has been an important debate (especially in India) on how to develop appropriate technologies, that is, technologies which are less

[6] As a general rule, the growth rate of the ratio A/B is equal to the growth rate of A minus the growth rate of B.

Table 2.9 Capital–output ratio, savings rate, and population growth in selected developed countries, 1913–1987

Country	Capital–output ratio				Savings rate (percent)	Population growth rate (per cent)
	1913	1950	1973	1987	1981–7	1990
France	1.64	1.68	1.75	2.41	—	0.5
Germany	2.25	2.07	2.39	2.99	20.0	0.2
Japan	1.01	1.80	1.73	2.77	27.0	0.2
United Kingdom	1.03	1.10	1.73	2.02	18.5	0.3
United States	2.91	2.26	2.07	2.30	19.0	0.8

Source: Maddison (1991) for the first variable, Burda and Wyplosz (2003) for the second; and own estimates for the third.

capital-intensive and more labour-intensive, but limited results have been achieved in this area so far. Another way to raise the growth of GDP and GDP per capita is to pay greater attention to the maintenance of the existing equipment. This would raise its physical life and consequently reduce the amortization rate δ. Yet, in several developing countries the human capital to do this is often inadequate—such countries lack specialized technicians with a good knowledge of what are usually imported technologies. Lastly, a decline in the population growth rate n helps to increase the growth rate of GDP per capita (see Chapter 7).

Dynamic properties

The Harrod–Domar model enjoys some important dynamic properties. The first is that it allows for perpetual growth. In fact, taking the example of equation (2.11), if the initial level of GDP per capita at time t was US\$1,000, at time $t + 1$ it would be $US\$1,000\ (1 + 0.03)$ In the second year it would become $US\$1,000\ (1 + 0.03)^2$ and in the n-th year it would be $US\$1,000\ (1 + 0.03)^n$ This means that the GDP per capita would go on growing at 3 per cent every year regardless of its initial level. Second, given different initial GDP per capita, even assuming that different countries have identical values for s, v, δ, and n there never will be convergence in their GDP per capita (in contrast, this is one of the key results of Solow's model), even though there is convergence in growth rates. Both results depend on the fact that the production process is characterized by constant returns to scale.

Poverty traps

The Harrod–Domar model can help to illustrate the persistence of poverty traps at low levels of GDP per capita, known in the literature as 'low level equilibrium poverty traps', that is, situations of widespread and persistent poverty, as observed for decades in Africa and South Asia and in centuries past in Europe. Equation (2.10) in fact shows that given a low savings rate s (typical of economies with a low GDP per capita and shallow financial markets), a high growth rate of population n, and technological dependence from abroad (that raises v), the GDP per capita growth rate tends to approach zero or be negative. For instance, if $s = 9$, $v = 3$, $\delta = 2$ and $n = 3$, the growth rate of GDP per capita would be $12/3 - 2 - 3 = -1$ per cent. With the new emphasis from the Sustainable Development Goals on eradicating poverty, the Harrod–Domar model may therefore offer a first rough tool to identify strategies for getting out of poverty by acting on s, n, and v. Historically, policymakers have mainly tried to raise average GDP per capita above the poverty line over the long term by raising the saving rate, as observed in the Former Soviet Union or in developing countries with a strong urban bias. This objective was achieved by increasing forced savings, that is, by squeezing wages and reducing agricultural prices and farmers' incomes so as to let the capitalists, landowners, and the state raise the savings rate. Less attention was paid to v, which was very high in the former socialist economies of Europe in particular, as their choice of techniques was very capital-intensive.

In a non-coercive political environment, however, the right-hand side variables of the Harrod–Domar model are strictly endogenous. Indeed, the savings rate s tends to change in line with the level of GDP per capita and of its growth rate (as well as, of course, of other variables—see Chapter 13). This means that both s and g are endogenous to the level of GDP per capita. In turn, s varies in relation to the level and distribution of GDP per capita and to the composition of savings. In autocratic political regimes, high public savings can raise the overall savings rate s even if income per capita is low, as observed in the former Eastern European socialist economies, and in today's China. The population growth rate n is also endogenous, as it also depends on GDP per capita, since a rise in the latter reduces the necessity of begetting children who are expected to provide free labour and support their parents in old age (see Chapter 7). Here, too, n depends on other variables, but one cannot ignore its relation with GDP per capita. Finally, the capital–output ratio v depends on the relative price of production factors (that over the long term depends on n and s), and for this reason it is also endogenous. Indeed, if n is high, it is likely that (in those sectors characterized by a choice of techniques) v may be low, reflecting a more labour-intensive factor mix. In brief, the endogeneity of variables s, n, and v makes it more difficult to start the growth process. At low levels of GDP per capita, s is low, and n and v are high, a situation that often leads to the persistence of the low level equilibrium poverty traps mentioned above.

How then can one estimate correctly g^ when keeping in mind the endogeneity of s, v, and n? To do so, one has to develop models which include truly exogenous variables (determined by the decisions of the policymaker) that influence the level of s, v, and n. One may, for instance write—as a simple illustrative example—the following three equations model (where for simplicity v and δ are assumed to be exogenous).

$$\begin{array}{llll}
1. & (y_{t+1} - y_t)/y_t = s/v - \delta - n & 1a & (y_{t+1} - y_t)/y_t = s/v - \delta - n \\
2. & n = -ay_t - bSS_t + cGini_t & 2a & n = -ay_{t+1} - bSS_t + cGini_t \\
3. & s = dy_t + eM2_t - fGini_t & 3a & s = dy_{t+1} + eM2_t - fGini_t
\end{array} \qquad (2.11a)$$

where the first equation is the growth rate of GDP per capita generated by the Harrod–Domar model, and the second and third explain n and s by means of fully exogenous variables such as the public spending on social security and family planning (SS), the volume of liquidity and bank deposits of the economy (M2), and the Gini index of income inequality. These variables are influenced by public policies and therefore can be considered quasi-exogenous. Variables a, b, c, d, e, and f are parameters to be estimated econometrically. In the left-hand versions of equation (2.11a) this three-equation system can be solved by substitution, that is, by inserting into equation 1 the results of equations 2 and 3 that can be easily solved as y_t and the exogenous variables are known. This allows y_{t+1}, to be determined, and therefore $g\hat{} = (y_{t+1} - y_t)/y_t$. In contrast, in the right-hand versions of the above three equation system, g^, n, and s are all unknown and need to be simultaneously determined (note that in this case, n and s depend on y_{t+1}, which is unknown, and not on y_t, which is known). Such a system therefore needs to be solved with matrix algebra which allows the values of g^, s, and n to be computed simultaneously on the basis of the values of the exogenous variables SS, M2, and Gini. All this means that private savings should be mobilized (and M2 increased) through the creation of a capillary banking infrastructure, an egalitarian income distribution, and adequate incentives. It also means reducing the total fertility rate through public health and social security measures (SS) which reduce n and thus increase GDP per capita g^.

2.7 Exogenous Growth: The Solow Model

Historical background

The 1950s, 1960s, and part of the 1970s (a period that may be labelled the second golden age of capitalism) featured not only a rise in capital accumulation but also a rapid development of technical knowledge and a quick re-absorption of unemployment As a result it also witnessed a marked acceleration of economic growth in the developed and some developing countries. Due to mounting labour shortages, the formulation of the growth process provided by Harrod–Domar-type models was becoming increasingly inadequate. Under such circumstances, it became obvious that explaining the long-term growth of the output level Y required taking into account all the factors employed in the production process, that is, labour L, land T, capital K, and technical progress TP. In symbols:

$$Y = f(T,K,L,TP) \tag{2.12}$$

Basic features of the Solow model

Given this situation, in 1956 Robert Solow (and independently from him Trevor Swan) proposed a model where aggregate output Y_t is explained by a production function of the Cobb–Douglas type in which agricultural land (T) is ignored, as it was no longer important in an economy dominated by industry and services. The extensive version of the Solow model takes the form:

$$Y_t = A_t K_t^{\alpha} L_t^{(1-\alpha)} \quad \text{with } 0 < \alpha(=0.25 - 0.40) < 1 \tag{2.13}$$

where A_t is an index of technical progress ($A_t = A\ (1+\lambda)^t$) which grows over time at an exogenous constant annual rate λ, K_t and L_t are the stocks of capital and labour, α and $(1-\alpha)$ are parameters meant to measure the elasticities with which the product grows in relation to a unitary increase in K and L. The marginal productivity of capital (MPK) and labour (MPL) are the partial derivatives of function (2.13) with respect to K and L, that is:

$$MPK = \delta Y/\delta K = \alpha A K^{(\alpha-1)} L^{(1-\alpha)} = (\alpha A K^{\alpha} L^{1-\alpha})/K = \alpha Y/K \qquad (2.14)$$

$$MPL = \delta Y/\delta L = (1-\alpha) A K^{\alpha} L^{-\alpha} = (1-\alpha) Y/L \qquad (2.15)$$

from which in can be inferred that—if the production factors are paid according to their marginal productivity MPK and MPL—the capital share and wage share of the aggregate output are:

$$MPK^{*}K = \alpha(Y/K)K = \alpha Y \qquad (2.16)$$

$$MPL^{*}L = (1-\alpha)Y/L,L = (1-\alpha)Y \qquad (2.17)$$

where, in the end, $(1-\alpha)$ and α (the parameters of production function (2.13)) also represent the shares of the national income Y received by capital owners and labourers, which remain constant over time, independent from the relative quantities of the production factors used.

Summing up, the main characteristics of the Solow model can be summarized as follows:

- The mathematical formulation of equation (2.13) (i.e. a homogeneous function of degree one) implies that the sum of its exponents is equal to one. Such a function therefore exhibits constant returns to scale, which means that when all production factors increase by x per cent, output increases by x per cent as well. This property is not trivial and requires that the scale of production is sufficiently big to operate in the most efficient part of the costs schedule. In short, we have constant returns to scale for the production factors taken as a whole, but declining returns to scale of capital and labour taken individually. In the latter case, this means that a given percentage increase in capital per worker yields a less than proportional increase in output per worker.
- The marginal productivity of labour (MPL) and capital (MPK) are positive but concave as α and $(1-\alpha)$ are smaller than one· This means that with increased inputs of a single factor, the output rises less than proportionally. In symbols:

$$\delta Y/\delta K > 0, \quad \delta Y/\delta L > 0 \quad \text{but} \quad \delta^2 Y/(\delta K)^2 < 0, \quad \delta^2 Y/(\delta L)^2 < 0 \qquad (2.18)$$

  which confirms there are decreasing returns to scale to either factor taken alone. From this derives the endogeneity of the capital–output ratio.
- If one assumes a competitive market and that factors are remunerated according to their marginal productivity, α e $(1-\alpha)$ represent the fair remuneration of production factors.

Solow's model can also be written in intensive (or compact) form. If one neglects for a moment the contribution of technical progress A_t, divide everything by L_t, and remember that $y_t = Y_t/L_t$ and $k_t = K_t/L_t$, then equation (2.13) can be transformed into a function where the output per worker y_t depends on the capital per worker k_t elevated to α·· As α is smaller than one, we obtain a function with decreasing returns to an increase in the capital per worker.

$$y_t = k_t^{\alpha} \text{ or, after re-introducing } A_t \tag{2.19}$$

$$y_t = A_t k_t^{\alpha} \tag{2.19a}$$

Solow's decomposition of the relative contribution to growth of each production factor

Equation (2.13) lists the factors that in the Solow model explain growth but it does not specify what their respective contribution to growth is. To answer this question, one starts again from equation (2.13), and then transforms it into logs, obtaining:

$$\log Y = \log A + \alpha \log K + (1 - \alpha) \log L \tag{2.20}$$

By totally differentiating equation (2.20) in relation to time, one obtains the following expression:

$$\Delta Y/Y = \Delta A/A + \alpha(\Delta K/K) + (1 - \alpha)(\Delta L/L) \quad \text{or} \quad \mathbf{g} = \boldsymbol{\lambda} + \alpha\mathbf{k} + (1 - \alpha)\mathbf{l} \tag{2.20a}$$

where the lower case letters in bold indicate the growth rates over time of GDP (**g**), technical progress (**λ**), capital stock (**k**), and labour force (**l**). As noted, the parameters α and (1 − α) are the output elasticities of capital and labour. This equation summarizes the contributions to production originating from an increase in capital, labour, and total factors productivity due to improvements in production technologies or to a better deployment of existing equipment.

While the growth rate of GDP (**g**), capital inputs (**k**), and labour inputs (**l**) are measurable, $\boldsymbol{\lambda} = \Delta A/A$ cannot be measured, as it depends on very many different microeconomic innovations. As a result, **λ** is derived by difference as follows: $\boldsymbol{\lambda} = \mathbf{g} - \alpha\mathbf{k} - (1 - \alpha)\mathbf{l}$ Technical progress is thus obtained as a residual. The interesting finding of empirical studies on the OECD countries for which such growth decomposition was carried out is that capital and labour accounted for a relatively modest share of overall growth, a finding that is ascribed to a not-clearly specified 'technical progress'. For example, an analysis of Solow on the United States assigned more than 80 per cent of the overall growth realized over 1900–49 to technical progress. And a study by Denison (1974) on the United States over 1929–69 attributed 45 per cent of overall growth to technical progress, while in the European countries such estimated values ranged between 33 and 60 per cent (Table 2.10).

Solow-type growth decompositions carried out for different periods and countries have come to different conclusions about what drives growth. All this suggests that the growth

Table 2.10 Results of the Solow decomposition for selected European countries, 1913–1987

	France	Germany	Holland	United Kingdom
Gross national product	2.6	2.8	3.0	1.9
Growth of production factors	1.1	1.4	2.0	1.2
Residual (technical progress)	1.5	1.4	1.0	0.7

Note: the values in the table are average annual growth rates.

Source: Burda and Wyplosz (2003).

Table 2.11 Contribution of production factors to GDP growth, various regions, 1960s and 1970s

Country	λ	K	L	Growth pattern
United States	60	40		Intensive growth
Western Europe	40	60		Fairly intensive growth
Asian Tigers	35	40	35	Fairly extensive growth
Soviet Union	20	55	25	Very extensive growth
China	25	45	30	Fairly extensive growth

Note: The values are percentage shares.

Source: Compilation of studies cited in the text and author's conjectures for China.

factors and the pattern of growth have varied substantially across countries and over time (Table 2.11). For instance, the studies of OECD countries mentioned in the previous paragraph suggest that, especially in the interwar period, growth was mainly driven by productivity gains made possible by rapid technical progress. In contrast, the Soviet Union adopted an extensive growth pattern where the rise in output was mainly due to a massive transfer of rural labour and previously inactive female workers into industry, and to strong capital accumulation achieved by suppressing wages. This meant, however, that growth slowed when all labour reserves were exhausted and households started complaining loudly about the slow increase of private consumption due to a continued allocation of a high share of national income to investment in machinery. This slowdown in growth was due to limited domestic innovation (except in the military sector) and the lack of micro-economic incentives to absorb imported foreign technology. Young (1994) and others have argued that even the mythical Asian Tigers (Taiwan, South Korea, Hong Kong, and Singapore) adopted an extensive pattern of growth during the 1960s and 1970s, meaning that their rapid GDP growth was achieved mainly thanks to a strong capital accumulation, and less—as is usually argued—to a rise in the efficiency of utilization of productive resources (see Chapter 7). The growth of output per capita averaged 6–7 per cent a year from the 1960s till the 1990s as in such countries participation rates, educational levels, and investment rates rose rapidly while there were large intersectoral reallocations of labour, with non-agricultural and manufacturing employment growing one and half to twice as fast at the aggregate working population thanks to the demographic dividend. However, the growth of output per effective worker in the non-agricultural sector averaged 3–4 per cent per year that is, a value that is fairly similar to those recorded by the OECD and Latin American economies over equally long periods of time.

This situation changed, however, in subsequent decades when the Asian Tigers continued to grow at a sustained rate thanks to rapid technical progress. The situation of Western Europe has been an intermediate one but, as shown in Table 2.9, in this region also the capital stock grew rapidly over the period 1950–73. In turn, the recent growth acceleration of China was driven by investment rates of up to 45 per cent of GDP and by the massive transfer of rural labour into manufacturing. This was somewhat similar to that recorded among the Asian Tigers in the 1960s and 1970s.

It is important to underscore that the high value of the residual attributed to technical progress is partly a statistical artefact which may depend on the underestimation of the growth of production factors (it is easier to measure outputs than inputs), the omission of other variables which boost growth such as human capital (see Sections 2.8 and 2.9), and the *ex ante* exclusion of the impact of growing economies of scale, given that equation (2.13) assumes constant returns to scale. Another possible source of overestimation of the impact of technical progress is intersectoral allocative changes, that is the shift of resources towards sectors with higher productivity, but such a phenomenon cannot be captured in an aggregate model. Once these statistical biases are taken care of, what is left is the percentage improvement of growth due to technical progress *strictu sensu*.

Overall, the Solow growth decomposition had the effect of casting water on the fire of the then dominant capital fundamentalism which singled out the accumulation of machinery and equipment as the main source of growth in industrialized countries, a conclusion which was then transferred with only limited adaptations to the developing countries. All this suggests that capital accumulation is certainly necessary—especially as most technical progress is embodied in new capital goods, and would not generate its effect without an adequate level of investment—but that there are other factors which contribute to growth in an important way.

Dynamic properties of the Solow model: the case of growth without technical progress

What is the growth rate generated by Solow's model over the short term and the long term? To answer this question we start anew from the intensive form of the model:

$$y_t = k_t^{\alpha} \tag{2.21}$$

that is, a relation where the output per worker ($y_t = Y_t/L_t$) grows as a function of the capital per worker ($k_t = K_t/L_t$) As previously pointed out, since α is smaller than one, the output per worker grows less than proportionally in relation to an increase of the capital per worker, thus confirming the law of decreasing returns to capital investment. Naturally, the rise of K_t/L_t depends on the saving rate per capita. This influences the total accumulation of capital which, in turn, determines the trend of the capital per worker k_t in equation (2.21). In this regard, the model plausibly assumes that the savings per worker σ are a constant fraction s of the output per worker y, that is $\sigma = s\ y$ Let us now ask what is the investment per capita i necessary to keep constant the capital stock per worker. It is equal to the investment which compensates the reduction of k caused by its amortization d plus the rate of increase of the working population n as, without additional investments,

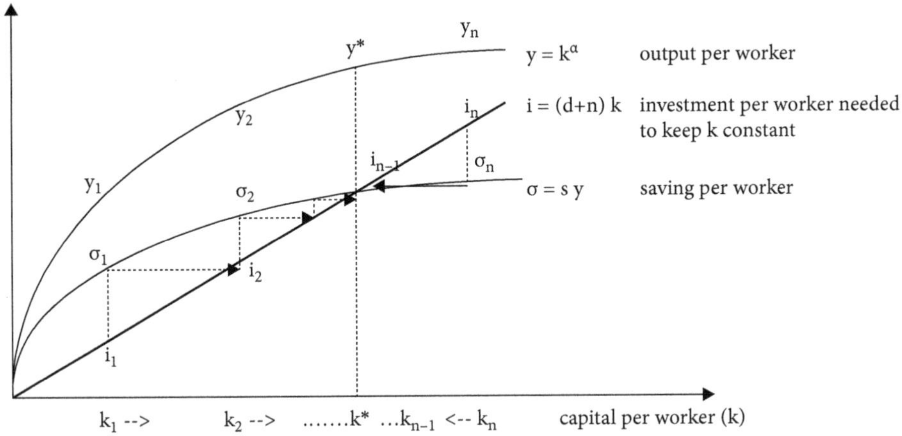

Figure 2.6 Growth and convergence towards the steady state in the Solow model with no technical progress

the growth of the labour force would reduce the capital per worker (the model assumes that all labour is employed).

For any k, then, the investment per capita required to maintain constant the capital stock per worker, and therefore output per capita, will be equal to $(n + d)k$ Let us now represent all this in Figure 2.6.

The schedule $y = k^{\alpha}$ describes how output per worker increases as a function of the capital per worker.[7] The second concave schedule reflects the savings per worker and is nothing other that the s fraction of the output per worker. In turn, the straight line represents the total amount of investments necessary to keep constant the capital stock per worker k. The i schedule thus rises as a linear function of k. Let us summarize in equation (2.21a) the main relationships of the Solow model with no technical progress in absolute terms (equations on the left-hand side) and on a per-worker basis (equations on the right-hand side):

$$\begin{array}{ll} Y = K_t^{\alpha} L_t^{(1-\alpha)} & y = k^{\alpha} \\ S = sY & \sigma = sy \\ I = S \equiv \Delta K & i = \sigma \equiv \Delta k \\ L_t = (1+n)L_{t-1} & \end{array} \qquad (2.21a)$$

What is the dynamic behaviour of this model? Let us suppose that the economy has an initial capital stock per worker k_1: this generates an output per worker y_1 and savings per worker σ_1 that are bigger than i_1. The current saving per worker is thus sufficient to finance a higher investment per worker i_2 that allows the capital stock per worker to rise to k_2 and produce an output y_2 which generates savings per worker σ_2 greater than i_2, and this permits the financing of an investment i_3, which allows the capital per worker to be increased to k_3, and so on. This process will continue until k reaches k^* in an endogenous

[7] This relation is concave, and as a consequence it exhibits decreasing returns. It is derived from the Cobb–Douglas function, where the returns to scale are constant for a rise in all factors, but decreasing for an increase in a single factor.

way. In contrast, if we start from capital per worker $k_n > k^*$, the investment needed to keep k constant is greater than the savings σ_n and consequently the capital stock will drop to k_{n-1} which will be sufficient to produce y_{n-1}, and so on. Thus, even though the initial k is higher than k*, sooner or later, the former will converge to k*. Regardless of the starting conditions, the economic system will thus steadily converge to the capital per worker k* where the equilibrium $i = \sigma$ is stable and generates a 'steady state output per worker' y* which remains constant over time.

From this, it follows that, in the steady state, growth:

$$\Delta y^*/y^* = 0 \text{ and } \Delta Y/Y = n \tag{2.22}$$

Moreover, as in the steady state, $k^* = (K/L)^*$ and $y^* = (Y/L)^*$ remain constant, the numerators and denominators of these fractions (that is, K, X, and L) have to grow at the same rate, which means that, in the steady state, the growth rates of K, L, and Y are identical (Figure 2.6).

Dynamic properties of the Solow model: the case of growth with technical progress

Let us now repeat the same analysis by including the technical progress, in order to illustrate in an intuitive way its impact on long-term growth. We will start from the general relation $y_t = A_t k_t^{\alpha} = A\ (1+\lambda)^t k_t^{\alpha}$ Since A_t grows every year at an exogenously given rate $\lambda > 0$, technical progress has the effect of shifting upwards every year the y schedule by an amount equal to λ. This means that—under conditions of steady state growth—y* will grow each year at a rate λ. At the same time, given the assumption that the working population increases every year at a rate n, Y increases at the same rate as the labour force plus the rate of technical progress (Figure 2.7). In symbols:

$$\Delta y^*/y^* = \lambda \text{ or } \Delta Y/Y = g = n + \lambda \tag{2.23}$$

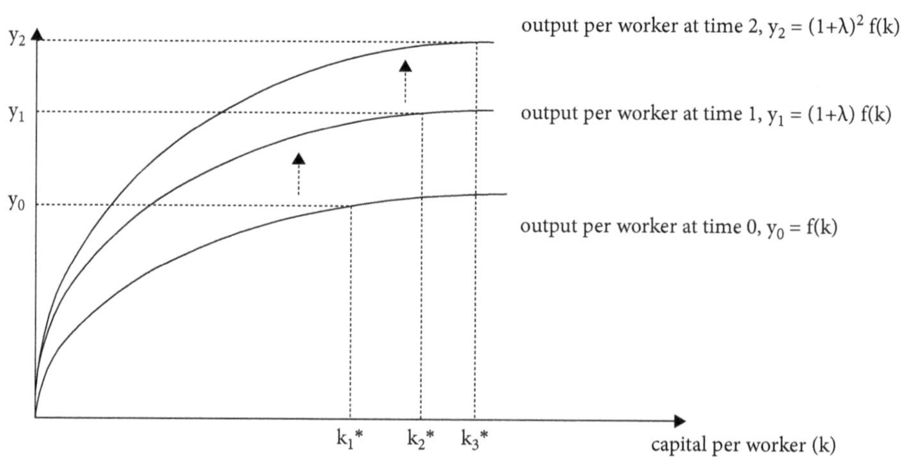

Figure 2.7 Growth in the Solow model with technical progress

In short, the Solow model shows that, once the steady state is reached, output grows at the same rate as the workforce plus the rate of technical progress, while output per worker (y) grows at the rate of technical progress λ, a situation broadly observable in current day Europe. And, as noted above, in the absence of technical progress, Y (and, with some simple transformations, GDP) grows only at the rate n, while y and GDP per capita remain constant. As a matter of course, this result is achieved over the long term, which may be very distant. These are, of course, strong and counter intuitive conclusions, since—at least over the last fifty years—similar situations have rarely been verified—even in developed countries. However, the Solow model also tells us that when k lies on the left of the steady state capital per worker k^*, the growth rate of output per worker is positive and that output per worker is greater than n (or $n + \lambda$ if technical progress is included). To conclude, as the steady state is still far away, countries can grow at a faster rate before reaching it.

Effect of a rise in the savings rate

Let us now examine the effect of a rise in the savings rate on the growth of output per worker, remembering that in the Harrod–Domar model this leads to a permanent increase in the growth rate. In this regard, Figure 2.8 shows that a rise in the saving rate has a level effect, that is an effect on the savings schedule which shifts upwards (since $s_2 > s_1$) thus allowing the steady state capital per worker to rise from k^* to k^{**}. This, in turn, allows a higher output per worker $y^{**} > y^*$ to be achieved.

During this period, the growth rate of output per worker ($\Delta y/y$) accelerates, starting from its previous steady state growth rate of zero. However, once k^{**} is reached, which allows a higher output per worker y^{**} to be produced, its growth rate $\Delta y/y$ will once again be equal to zero and $\Delta Y/Y$ to n. In short, a rise in the savings rate generates three effects: to start with, the short-term growth rate of output per worker accelerates; in turn, over the long term the growth rate remains constant at zero. Finally, in the long term, the level of output per worker will be higher than that obtainable with a lower savings rate (Figure 2.8). To conclude, the savings rate does not influence the long-term steady state growth rate because of the endogenous adjustment of the capital per worker that, in this model, is endogenous and with decreasing returns.

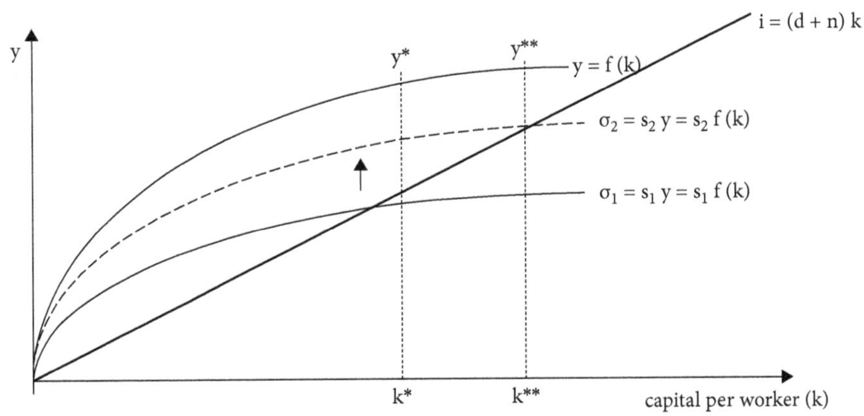

Figure 2.8 Effect of an increase in the saving rate in the Solow model

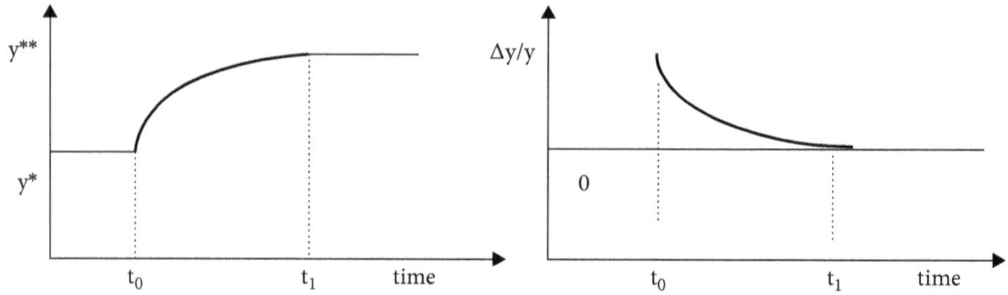

Figure 2.9 Effects on the steady state growth rate of a rise of the saving rate in the Solow model

Graphically, the temporal effects of a rise in s on y and Δy/y might be represented as follows. At time t_0, we are in a situation of steady state growth y^*. If s increases, k rises as well and allows a growing y to be produced despite the decreasing returns to capital per worker. This process goes on until a new steady state with output per worker $y^{**} > y^*$ is reached (Figure 2.9). At this point, the output per worker becomes constant once again, while its growth rate, which experienced a sudden rise in the short term, falls to zero.

Before closing, let us point out that changes in n and d generate effects similar (or opposite) to those illustrated in the case of a rise in the savings rate s, that is: (a) a rise (fall) in the growth rate y over the short term if n and d drop (increase); (b) the new steady state growth rate remains constant at zero, (c) an upward shift of the output per worker (when d and n decrease) and a downward shift (when d and n increase).

Optimal savings and golden rule

The aforesaid analysis has shown that an increase in the savings rate s raises the capital per worker and leads to a steady state in which the level of output per worker—and after a simple transformation also GDP per capita—is higher than those of the previous steady state. This analysis might paradoxically lead us to think that, in order to reach the highest steady state y^*, it would be desirable that the savings rate reaches 100 per cent! However, in this case, everything would be re-invested and nothing consumed. For example, in the case of fast growing China, the savings rate is equal to some 45 per cent of GDP while the remaining 55 per cent is used for public and private consumption; in most OECD countries public and private consumption absorbs about 75 per cent of GDP. Is it therefore convenient in terms of national well-being to raise the saving rate to a very high level? The answer is no, since the citizens' objective is to maximize their consumption, not output or investment. What, then, is the optimal savings rate (and, as a result, the optimal capital stock per worker) which maximizes consumption per capita? To answer this question we define consumption per worker c as the difference between output per worker y and investment per worker i, that is:

$$c = y - i = f(k) - (d+n)k \tag{2.24}$$

Now, before solving this maximization problem algebraically, Figure 2.10 illustrates three cases in which s is low (left panel), medium (central panel), and high (right panel). For simplicity, we omit the symbols of the variables. In the first case, the consumption per capita $(y - i)$ is a high share of y, which is, however, low due to low investment. In the last case, consumption per

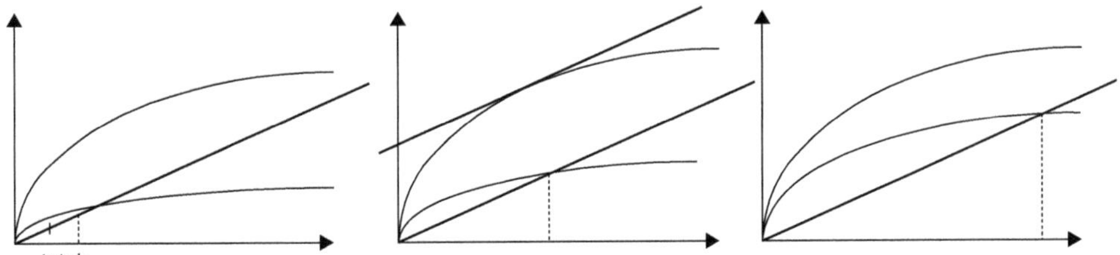

Figure 2.10 Consumption per worker in the case of low, medium, and high saving rates in the Solow model

capita c is a low share of output per worker which, however, is high because of the high savings rate. In the middle case, s is in between these two extremes. Graphically, it is easy to see that the optimal savings rate is the one which leads to a steady state where the tangent to the output per worker schedule is parallel to the $(i + d)k$ schedule (central case). Thus, in order to maximize steady state consumption, the policymaker should boost the savings rate in the left-hand (low s) case and reduce it in the right-hand (high s) case.

The algebraic solution of this problem entails the maximization of the difference function described in (2.25). This requires computing the derivative of the difference function $c = y - i$ and to equalize it to zero. In symbols:

$$\begin{aligned} &\max c = \max(y - i) = \max[f(k) - (d+n)k] = 0 \\ &\max c = [f(k) - (d+n)k]' = 0 \qquad \text{which yields} \qquad (2.25) \\ &f'(k) - (d+n) = 0 \quad \text{that can also be written as} \quad f'(k) = (d+n) \end{aligned}$$

Now, recalling that in the steady state $s\,f(k) = (d + n)k$ and that this expression can be transformed in $s\,f(k)/k = (d + n)$, one can substitute in the right-hand side of equation (2.25) (bottom line) the term equivalent to $(d + n)$ just obtained, that is, $f'(k) - s\,f(k)/k = 0$, which can also be written as $f'(k) = s\,f(k)/k$. From this one can derive the optimal value of s (symbolized by s^{**}), that is:

$$s^{**} = [k^{**}f'(k)]/f(k) \qquad (2.25a)$$

Now, $f'(k)$ is the marginal productivity of capital per worker that, if multiplied by k^{**}, represents in this model the fair remuneration of the capital per worker in the steady state, that is, αy. By dividing this by $f(k) = y$, one obtain $s^{**} = \alpha y/y$, which gives $s^{**} = \alpha$

This expression shows that the optimal savings rate s^{**} which maximizes consumption in the steady state is equal to the capital share (α) of the output per worker (see also equations (2.16) and (2.17)). In real life, in both developing and developed countries, α depends not only on the marginal productivity of capital but also on its scarcity, on the segmentation of credit markets, the over-supply of labour and market structures and social norms that increase α regardless of its productivity, as noted by Phelps (1961)[8] and recently by Piketty (2014). In developing countries, where the asset distribution is highly concentrated, capital markets are dualistic, excess labour supply widespread, full employment a chimera, and labour bargaining institutions nearly absent, the golden rule offers an elegant

[8] 'To underlie the implausibility of the results of the Golden Rule', in his 1961 article Pelphs describes the Golden Rule of Capital Accumulation as a 'Fable for Growthmen'.

but mostly irrelevant solution to the choice of the optimal savings rate, as the model on which such a solution is derived is based on unrealistic assumptions.

Implications of the Solow model for convergence

The model has important implications in terms of long-term trends of output per worker across countries with different initial levels of GDP per capita and output per worker.

Let us examine first the implications for unconditional convergence (that is, in output per worker). In this regard, the Solow model predicts that countries with different levels of initial capital and output per worker, but with the same savings rate s, amortization rate d, workforce growth rate n, and growth rate of technical progress λ (knowledge is assumed to circulate freely and at zero cost among countries) will converge in the long term to the same steady state level of capital per worker k^* and output per worker y^* (Figure 2.6). The reason for this conclusion is the decreasing returns of capital per worker. This means that, countries which in the initial conditions have an output per worker lower than that of countries with a higher initial capital per worker will experience faster growth rates until they gradually approach the same steady state growth y^*. In conclusion, if the above assumptions are true, the convergence in the output per worker supposes the existence of an inverse relation between the initial output per worker (and GDP per capita) and their growth rate.

What does the empirical evidence show in this respect? The above conclusion has been tested several times, in most cases without success (see footnote 1 on the formulation of the convergence test). Econometric tests on wider samples little affected by selection bias have actually denied the Solowian conclusion about unconditional convergence, or accepted it for only some groups of fairly similar countries (e.g. those of the OECD). Yet, the recent rapid GDP growth recorded in China, India, Vietnam, and even a few African and Latin American countries tends to support more than before the conclusions of the Solow model in terms of unconditional convergence.

Let us now examine the conditional convergence, or convergence in growth rates of output per worker and, after a simple transformation, in GDP per capita. In this analysis, the unrealistic hypothesis about the equality of the rates of saving, amortization, and workforce growth among different countries are abandoned. This means that, with differences in these rates, the various countries will reach different steady states. If one, however, continues to accept the hypothesis that technology is a sort of international public good that circulates at no cost among countries, technical knowledge will in the end be the same everywhere, and all countries will converge to a growth rate λ, even though at different levels of output per worker. In this case, then, output per worker and GDP per capita will be different but their growth rates will be identical. However, even this hypothesis has not been successfully tested (see Table 2.1.).

Advantages and limitations of the Solow model

In some respects, the Solow model gets closer to reality but in other respects it gets far from reality. Among its improvements, one must note the endogenization of the capital–output ratio that was constant and exogenously given in the Harrod–Domar model. This ratio varies, in fact, according to the level of capital per worker and the parameter α of the production function. The model also introduces the concept of technical progress and captures some of its correlations with the growth process. However, the Solow model explains a modest part of the variance in growth rates observed across countries. Moreover, it predicts the cessation of growth of output per worker in advanced societies due to decreasing returns to capital per worker, while this phenomenon is not often observed in reality or—when it is observed—it is mainly explained by population ageing, the tertiarization of the economy, and other factors discussed in Section 2.1.

Another important limitation of the model concerns the treatment of technical progress that is assumed to be exogenously given, while in real life it depends on the decisions about investment in education, research, innovation, and so on made by households, firms, and the state. Moreover, in the analysis of convergence, the model assumes the same technology for all countries, which means that technology circulates freely among nations while in real life this does not happen because of domestic factors (low education and capability to absorb imported technologies at the local level) and restrictive international laws on patents which have been reinforced by the Trade Related International Property System (TRIPS) agreement. Finally, the Solow model ignores important factors which are discussed in subsequent models or that until now have not been included in long-term aggregate models, as is the case of incentives, international trade, and so on.

2.8 The Enlarged Exogenous Solow Model of Mankiw–Romer–Weil

The novelty of this model consists in the explicit introduction into the Solow model of human capital, a production factor that varies considerably among the developed countries and, even more so, between the developed and the developing countries. As the empirical literature has demonstrated, growth is in fact highly contingent on a country's level of human capital. A review of the literature by Klasen (2003) shows, for instance, that growth of any variety is higher in countries with adequate human capital, as many of the returns to growth are dependent on this production factor. It must be noted that various developing countries in Africa, Central America, and South Asia lag behind massively in this area. This helps to explain their low income per capita. The fundamental hypothesis is that part of the unexplained regression residual in the Cobb–Douglas function with two production factors is due to improvements in the quantity and quality of education of the workforce and not only to technical progress. Convinced of the veridicality of this idea, Mankiw, Romer, and Weil develop a new production function:

$$Y_t = AK_t^{\alpha}HC_t^{\gamma}L_t^{\beta} \quad \text{where} \quad 0<\alpha,\beta,\gamma<1 \quad \text{and} \quad \alpha+\beta+\gamma=1 \tag{2.26}$$

where the new factor HC measures the human capital accumulated until time t, that is, the average number of years of education of the workforce. Alternative estimates of the parameters α, β, and γ are reported in Table 2.12.

In the Mankiw–Romer–Weil (1992) model, a Solow-type decomposition of equation (2.26) takes the form:

$$\Delta Y/Y = \Delta A/A+\alpha(\Delta K/K)+\beta(\Delta L/L)+\gamma(\Delta HC)/HC \text{ or } \mathbf{g} = \boldsymbol{\lambda} + \alpha\mathbf{k} + \beta\mathbf{n} + \gamma\mathbf{hc} \tag{2.27}$$

where the lower case letters in bold are the growth rates over time of output (**g**), the capital per worker (**k**) the technical progress (**λ**), the labour force (**n**), and the human capital (**hc**). It is evident that the mysterious residual assigned to technical progress $\Delta A/A$ (λ) will be

Table 2.12 Parameters of the enlarged Cobb–Douglas production function for selected country groups

Parameters	Non-oil developing country	Middle-income developing country	OECD
Mankiw–Romer–Weil (*1992*)			
Physical capital (α)	0.31	0.29	0.14
Human capital (γ)	0.28	0.30	0.37
Labour (β)	0.41	0.41	0.49
Technical progress (λ)	1.30	1.80	2.00
Islam (1996)			
Physical capital (α)	0.68	0.69	0.54
Human capital (γ)	0.23	0.13	0.11
Labour (β)	0.09	0.18	0.35
Technical progress (λ)	1.10	1.20	1.90

Source: Cornia et al. (1998).

smaller than the one obtained in the original Solow decomposition, as in this formulation output growth also depends on investment in human capital. Indeed, if $\Delta A/A$ is ignored, and remembering that $\beta = 1 - \alpha - \gamma$ (see Table 2.11) and that $\Delta L/L = n$, equation (2.27) can be written after a series of simple manipulations as

$$\mathbf{g}^* = \alpha\mathbf{k}^* + \gamma\mathbf{hc}^* \tag{2.28}$$

where the bold lower case letters with an asterisk indicate rates of growth per worker. Equation (2.28) indicates that the growth rate of output per worker $\mathbf{g}^*$ (and with small transformations, of the growth of GDP per capita) depends on the growth rate of physical capital per worker ($\mathbf{k}^*$), and on the growth rate of human capital per worker ($\mathbf{hc}^*$).[9] The importance of this formulation is that, by introducing the growth rate of human capital, one can verify empirically the convergence in income levels per capita among countries which start the development process with different capital per worker k and GDP per capita. If this is true, one can conclude that what prevents several developing countries from converging to the growth rate of the developed countries is an insufficient accumulation of human capital due to inadequate public spending on education (especially technical education). It also indicates low investment in education by families that are unable to finance the private cost of education, or that are not well informed of its economic and social benefits. This is an important conclusion that has strongly influenced the success of the development policies followed for five decades in East Asia and more recently in South East Asia and selected Latin American countries.

Equation (2.26) is a production function with constant returns for all the factors taken together (as $\alpha + \beta + \gamma = 1$) Returns are, however, decreasing for each production factor considered on its own, and decreasing also for a joint rise of K and HC as the sum of their parameters is smaller than one. If we drop for the moment technical progress and labour, the function can be written as:

[9] The economists Barro and Lee have produced quinquennial time series over 1960 to 2010, for about 100 countries, illustrating the average number of years of education of the workforce (seewww.barrolee.com/)

$$Y_t = K_t^{\alpha} HC_t^{1-\alpha} \tag{2.29}$$

This production function has constant returns to K and HC taken together, thus suggesting that a continuous improvement in human capital may compensate for the decline of returns on physical capital. Consequently, in advanced economies where unskilled labour is no longer widely utilized in the production process, investment in human capital that is complementary to those in machinery generates perpetual growth.

What is the dynamic behaviour of this model? To answer this question, we suppose that economic agents save both to accumulate physical capital and to invest in human capital. In symbols we can write:

$$K_{t+1} - K_t = sY_t, \text{ and } HC_{t+1} - HC_t = qY_t \tag{2.30}$$

where s is the savings rate to invest in physical capital and q the expenditure on human capital. It is possible to show that over the long term Y_t, K_t and HC_t grow at the same rate which depends on s and q. To do so, we introduce the variable r = HC/K, that is, the ratio of human capital to physical capital. By manipulating the first expression of equation (2.30), that is by dividing both terms on the right and the left by K_t, and then substituting in lieu of Y_t its value $K_t^{\alpha} HC_t^{1-\alpha}$ we obtain:

$$(K_{t+1} - K_t)/K_t = sK_t^{\alpha} HC_t^{1-\alpha} K_t \tag{2.31}$$

from which one can derive the growth rate of the capital stock **k** as follows:

$$\mathbf{k} = s(K_t^{\alpha}/HC_t^{\alpha})(HC_t/K_t) = sr^{-\alpha}r = sr^{1-\alpha}$$

The second expression of equation (2.30) can be manipulated in the same way, thus obtaining:

$$(HC_{t+1} - HC_t)/HC_t = q(K_t^{\alpha} HC_t^{1-\alpha})/HC_t$$

$$\mathbf{hc} = q(K_t^{\alpha} HC_t^{1-\alpha})/HC_t = q[K^{\alpha}/HC^{\alpha}] = qr^{-\alpha} \tag{2.32}$$

It is also possible to show (demonstration omitted) that over the long term the growth rates of output, physical capital, and human capital (**g**, **k**, and **hc**) are the same and that consequently **g** = **k** = **hc** From this, it follows that

$$\mathbf{k} = \mathbf{hc} \text{ from which it follows that } sr^{1-\alpha} = q\, r^{-\alpha} \text{ and that } r = q/s \tag{2.33}$$

Now, in order to calculate the growth rate of output (**g**) we substitute q/s in lieu of r in relation (2.31):

$$\mathbf{k} = sr^{1-\alpha} \tag{2.34}$$

$$\mathbf{k} = s(q/s)^{1-\alpha}$$

$$\mathbf{k} = s^{\alpha} q^{(1-\alpha)}$$

and since **k** = g, it follows that

$$g = s^{\alpha}q^{(1-\alpha)} \tag{2.35}$$

which means that the output growth rate depends on the investment rate in both physical and human capital. For instance, if the savings rate for productive investment is 12 per cent, the expenditure on secondary and tertiary education 4 per cent, and α is ½, then g = 3.4x × 2 = 6.8 per cent. In contrast, in Solow's model with no technical progress, the growth of output per worker was zero and aggregate growth was equal to the growth rate of the labour force n. Moreover—in terms of convergence—the differences existing between s and q lead to differences in growth rates (and not only, as in the Solow model, to different levels of output per capita, with identical growth rate equal to n or n + λ). Summing up:

- the Mankiw et al. (1992) model generates perpetual growth, as in the Harrod–Domar model, even though K and HC taken singularly continue to exhibit decreasing returns. But the model exhibits constant returns if the two variables are taken together.[10]
- Even if they have identical investment rates in physical and human capital, countries with lower initial values of output per worker and GDP per capita will not converge to the output per worker and GDP per capita of more advanced countries, as in the latter the decreasing returns to K are offset by the rising stock of HC.
- The model predicts conditional convergence in growth rates if poor developing countries accumulate HC and K at rates similar to those of the developed countries (see above).
- Growth is endogenous since it depends on q and s—both internal to the model—and not oly on n and λ which are given exogenously in the Solow model.

2.9 Endogenous Growth Models

The modelling improvements of the 1960s and 1970s brought about by the exogenous growth theory left two major issues unanswered. The first concerns the nature and determinants of technical progress or innovation. This is a multifaceted variable that empirically accounts for a large share of long-term growth in exogenous growth models (see Table 2.11). The micro-founded endogenous growth theory confirms that investments in knowledge and innovation are significant contributors to economic growth, together with the positive externalities and spillover effects generated by an overall knowledge-based economy, and thus tries to endogenize it. Innovation exhibits several characteristics of a quasi-public good (non-rivalry and non-excludability). It may lead to market failure due to the erosion of the incentives of its private producers who bear all the costs of its production but are unable to fully internalize all the benefits of their investment because of the non-excludability of knowledge.

[10] The hypothesis of constant returns for K and HC taken together is no longer valid when we introduce a third production factor such as labour. In this case, the conclusions of the model are closer to those of the Solow model.

But innovation and externalities can be made excludable if the state grants monopoly rights to its producers. However, monopolies are bad for welfare and efficiency because they generate a deadweight loss in the economy, as prices are higher than marginal costs. However, the literature on the economics of ideas suggests that it is the possibility to make profits, and thus to set a markup over marginal costs, that creates incentives for the R&D sector to produce more ideas and innovations. Indeed, in the innovation sector, while firms must bear a sunk cost for product development, their outlay can be compensated with monopoly rents. This means, that there is a trade-off between short-run welfare losses and long-run growth gains. In deciding antitrust policies, the regulator has to weigh the deadweight losses against the incentive to innovate and grow. But, innovation and long-run growth also depend on other public measures, such as the promotion of education and the allocation of subsidies to research and development, that is, measures that increase the incentive to innovate. In extreme cases, the state may bear the entire cost of developing general purpose open source technologies. Thus, according to the endogenous growth theory, the rate of growth of an economy depends to a large extent on policy measures that facilitate innovation by firms.

The second issue left unanswered by the exogenous growth models concerns the origins of increasing returns to scale. While exogenous growth models assume constant or decreasing returns to scale, in several sectors there is ample evidence of the existence of increasing returns. These may derive from an increase in the scale of production (as suggested by Verdoorn's law), research spillovers, product differentiation, learning-by-doing, and increasing specialization of labour across a growing variety of activities producing innovation inputs that raise the productivity of labour and capital. The conclusions of these analyses may influence the public policy stance towards the organization of production, industrial policy, and innovation policies. The following two subsections present two (of the many) models developed by the endogenous growth theory.

The Romer model of monopolistic competition with rents as a reward to innovation

As noted, in the Solow model, the rate of technical progress λ is assumed exogenously. This is, of course, a major simplification. In contrast, in the Romer (1990) model the stock of technical progress (or knowledge, or innovation) is only in part the result of learning externalities among individual firms. It is mainly the result of endogenous decisions by firms and of public policies. Consequently, it varies from one firm to another and, more importantly, from one country to another according to the decisions taken by governments and firms in the field of technology, education, and subsidies to research and development. Differences in these areas would explain the observed cross-country variations in GDP growth rates and the lack of convergence discussed above (see Section 2.6). The econometric testing of such hypotheses is, however, quite complex and the results remain unsatisfactory.

In this model, technology is generated through the explicit allocation of resources to its production by firms which respond to market incentives, and less through technological spillovers across firms, or the creation by the government of positive externalities for the economy as a whole (this last point is not discussed here). Let us assume that an economy has a given stock of human capital HC that can be used for the production of final consumer goods or for generating new knowledge, for example for the production of new intermediate inputs (machines and equipment) and for a better utilization of the existing inputs. Based on this, one can write the following aggregate production function:

$$Y_t = A_t^{\gamma} K_t^{\alpha} (uHC_t)^{(1-\alpha)} \tag{2.36}$$

where

$$A_t = A_{t-1}[1 + a(1 - u)HC_{t-1}] \tag{2.37}$$

where it appears that a fraction u of the human capital stock HC_t is used for the direct production of goods and services while the fraction $(1-u)$ is used for the production of knowledge A_t, which increases accordingly, and so raises the total efficiency of production factors due an increase in A_t given an efficiency parameter a. Let us assume as well that the capital stock rises according to the traditional hypothesis $\Delta K = sY$. It is clear that in such a model, a high u increases the efficiency of production while a low u tends to increase the level of knowledge as a function of innovation, boosting future income and consumption. Who then determines the value of u and $(1 - u)$? The answer will be either the government—if knowledge is developed by the public sector—or firms. Concerning the latter, the use of patents is rendered necessary to convince them to invest in research (a heated debate is still underway on what type of incentives are needed to promote research in the private sector, and on the duration of patents). Without the granting of patents, firms would have little incentive to innovate owing to the non-excludability of innovation. As seen earlier, in the real world, technology does not circulate freely across countries, as suggested in the exogenous growth models. The Romer model assumes realistically temporary monopolies, a condition that may allow for monopolistic competition among firms but that entails the violation of the hypothesis of perfect competition. In this model, the stock of knowledge increases continuously and endogenously as a function of $1 - u$ and HC. Countries and firms that invest more in human capital formation have a greater possibility of raising HC, a condition that implies—in order to benefit from the productivity-increasing positive effects generated by research activities—that other countries and firms must pay a monopoly rent. However, any such monopoly rent is compensated by the increasing returns generated by the adoption of the new technologies. Local firms will assess the convenience of paying a monopoly rent to the producers of innovation or engage in monopolistic competition by themselves investing in innovation as illustrated by Aghion and Howitt (1998) in the next subsection.

Aghion and Howitt's model of Schumpeterian creative destruction

Aghion and Howitt's model dwells on the Schumpeterian idea that growth is a process of creative destruction in which new, better-quality, products with increasing returns in production replace obsolete goods characterized by mature products and decreasing or constant returns to scale. The model attempts to endogenize two key drivers of the growth process, that is, continuous technical progress and growing differentials in returns to the scale of production. Given a number of hypotheses, the model allows conclusions to be drawn that are quite different from those of the exogenous growth theory. On the normative side, although current innovations generate positive externalities for future research, they also impose negative externalities on the current producers of innovation, due to the possibility of patents-copying by new innovators. This patent-copying increases if excessive *laissez-fare* is allowed, and it will lead to a new wave of innovations by other firms that have benefited from the prior discoveries of other firms.

The model abstracts from capital accumulation, and the economy is made up of firms each of which is endowed with one unit flow of labour L. Output of the consumption good y depends on the input of an intermediate good x (i.e. research leading to innovation) and on a technology parameter A according to the relation

$$y = Ax^{\alpha}(\text{with } 0 < \alpha < 1) \tag{2.38}$$

Innovation consists of the invention of a new type of intermediate good that annually raises the technology parameter A by a constant factor $\gamma\cdot$ As in the Romer model, each firm's human capital can be used to produce final goods or an intermediate good such as innovation. The firm that first succeeds in innovating can monopolize the intermediate sector until it is replaced by a new innovator; the current invention facilitates other firms to begin working on the next innovation, because of a business-stealing effect and the related negative externality affecting the first monopolist. The first firm to innovate makes all previous intermediate or consumption goods qualitatively obsolete, as the prior innovation circulates freely without monopoly protection.

The amount of labour devoted to research by the innovating firm is determined by the arbitrage condition

$$w_t = kV_{t+1} \tag{2.39}$$

where t is the number of innovations that have occurred so far, w the wage rate of an hour of work in manufacturing, V_{t+1} is the expected discounted payoff of the $(t+1)^{th}$ innovation (that is, the expected value of an hour of research), and k the probability that such innovation takes place. The arbitrage equation and labour market equation are the basis of the Schumpeterian approach. In turn, the value of V_{t+1} is determined by the asset equation:

$$rV_{t+1} = \pi_{t+1} - kn_{t+1}V_{t+1} \tag{2.40}$$

which states that the expected income generated by a licence on the $(t+1)^{th}$ innovation during a unit time interval is equal to the profit flow π_{t+1} attainable by the $(t+1)$ innovation minus the expected capital loss that occurs when the first innovator is replaced by a new innovator. The first innovator is not supposed to do any more research and product development as all other firms have cost-free access to the innovation she paid for. The first innovator therefore loses V_{t+1}, as the economy is characterized by a steady flow of new research. The probability that new research will lead to new discoveries is given by k n_{t+1}, which rises with the probability k that a new discovery will take place and by the amount of skilled labour n_{t+1} allocated to research and development. The shorter the likely duration of the endogenous but unpatented monopoly profits, the smaller the payoffs to innovate. Aghion and Howitt (1998, 60) show that under these conditions the average steady-state growth rate of output g is:

$$g = \lambda n^\wedge \ln \gamma, \tag{2.41}$$

where $\gamma > 1$ is the constant annual rate at which new research raises the technology parameter A_t of equation (2.38), λ is the productivity of R&D in manufacturing (i.e. the probability it will lead to new innovation) and n the amount of labour used in research.

Although they are all getting closer to reality in some respects, these models ignore fundamental growth factors. New endogenous growth models have continued to crop up focusing on various structural characteristics of the economy and society, on how the latter interplays with growth via the effects of organizations and social capital, institutions, market structure and imperfections, externalities, the introduction of general-purpose technologies, trade, government policy, the effect of legal norms on the agents' incentives to engage in knowledge producing activities, income distribution, and political economy (Aghion and Howitt, 1998). As this is a field that is expanding in many different directions, the general conclusions on steady-state growth and convergence are difficult to theorize. It is even more difficult to observe the theory in practice given the multitude of models analysed and the complexity and diversity of the mathematical techniques used and of the pathways analysed (Aghion and Howitt, 1998).

The econometric evidence in favour of endogenous growth therefore remains in doubt. The theoretical predictions of endogenous growth models have not generally been confirmed by the empirical evidence that speaks much more for the Solow and Mankiw et al. models (Aghion and Howitt, 1998; Agenor, 2005). In addition, contrary to the predictions of endogenous growth models, the industrialized countries have been converging towards a common growth rate over the long run, despite different policies towards innovation (Evans, 1996). This makes this author argue that either endogenous growth models are fundamentally flawed, or that the effects they predict are relatively unimportant.

The endogenous unified growth theory

The different long-term growth models of Keynesian and neoclassical (either exogenous or endogenous) inspiration that have tried to explain long-term growth and convergence come to diverging conclusions while leaving a large part of output growth unexplained in econometric tests. Does this mean that the nature of growth has changed so much over time, and that the divergence in conclusions is due to the selection of samples covering different periods and countries? Or that the various models focused only on the last 50–100 years and are unable to really explain secular growth? In particular, it appears that traditional endogenous growth theory was satisfied with accounting for empirical regularities of the growth process in developed economies over the last hundred years, but was not able to explain the qualitatively different empirical findings that characterized the growth process over longer time horizons in both developed and developing economies.

The unified growth theory (UGT) of Galor (2011), is an endogenous growth theory that (with some exceptions) offers a consistent and integrated explanation of centuries-long processes of development. It was developed to deal with the inability of traditional endogenous models to explain key empirical regularities and differences in growth rates and processes of individual economies, particularly during the transition from the era of Malthusian stagnation (that characterized most development paths) to the modern era of sustained economic growth.

UGT attaches considerable importance to population dynamics and innovation. It is constituted by a single dynamic framework that starts from an initial stable Malthusian equilibrium which—due to the evolution of latent state variables (such as population and induced technical innovation)—ultimately evolves endogenously, leading in this way to a transitional take-off of growth before the system gradually converges to a modern steady-state growth equilibrium.

The Malthusian state is characterized by slow technological progress and rapid population growth that eats into part of the benefits of technological progress. In contrast, in the era of modern growth, technological progress does not encourage population growth but human capital accumulation, which further spurs technological progress. In brief, the theory captures in a single analytical framework the main characteristics of the process of development during the Malthusian stagnation that characterized most of human history, the escape from such a Malthusian trap, the emergence of human capital formation in the process of development, the onset of the demographic transition, the origins of the contemporary era of sustained economic growth, and the divergence in income per capita across countries.

UGT suggests that the transition from stagnation to growth was an inevitable byproduct of the process of development that was accelerated by the pace of technological progress. This progress eventually stimulated a demand for human capital formation by the industrial sector, triggered a demographic transition, thus enabling economies to convert a larger share of the fruits of factor accumulation and technological progress into the growth of income per capita.

The UGT approach can be modelled in a simplified way following Galor (2014):[11] the economy produces one homogeneous good, there is only one factor of production (labour) that is measured in efficiency units, while land is a fixed production factor. In the Malthusian phase there is a minimum subsistence constraint $C > C_m$ (i.e. consumption per capita must exceed a minimum threshold C_m), while the effect of an increase in income Y is to raise the price of food and to cause a drop in land productivity due to decreasing returns of land following increasing applications of labour. Output per capita fluctuates around a constant level in the long-run reflecting diminishing returns to labour. The efficiency units of labour evolve endogenously as a result of the household's decisions about the number of their children and the level of their human capital, given the subsistence consumption constraint indicated above.

The output produced in period t is

$$Y_t = H_t{}^{\alpha}(A_t T)^{1-a} \tag{2.42}$$

where H_t represents the efficiency units of labour, A_t the level of technological development, and T the (fixed) amount of land. Output per worker at time t is

[11] See Galor's lectures of 2014 at Brown University (Lecture II AEA2014 UGT and Comparative Development, Brown University, 2014), https://www.brown.edu/Departments/Economics/Faculty/Oded_Galor/pdf/Galor-Lecture2-AEA2014-handout.pdf.

$$y_t = h^{\alpha}{}_t x_t{}^{1-\alpha} \tag{2.43}$$

where the low case variables are those in equation (2.42) divided by the number of workers.

According to the UGT, in the earlier stages of development, a rise in population and labour supply L_t positively affects technological progress by triggering an induced technical innovation, as an increase in L_t raises A_t via a greater demand for and supply of innovation, a greater division of labour, and other innovation-enhancing processes. All this triggers an increase in the demand for human capital (HC) and affects the growth rate of technological progress (λ), HC_t human capital formation via education E_t and L_t population size. Technological progress is given by

$$\lambda_{t+1} = (A_{t+1} - A_t)/A_t = f(E_t, L_t) \tag{2.44}$$

entailing that an increase in education E_t raises A_{t+1} and its rate of increase λ_{t+1}. Educated individuals have an advantage and an incentive to adopt and promote new technologies, as education has a positive if diminishing effect on technological progress while it avoids obsolescence of HC in a changing technological environment. The increase in the rate of technological progress raises the demand for human capital which permits individuals to better cope with the changes in the technological environment. The introduction of more advanced production techniques is skills-biased in the short-run, although the nature of the technology can be skills-biased or skills-saving in the long run. The human capital of an individual who joins the labour force in period t + 1 is as follows:

$$hc_{t+1} = f(e_{t+1}, \lambda_{t+1}) \tag{2.45}$$

where the first term is the individual education level (determined by parental investment, subject to their subsistence constraint, in period t), and λ_{t+1} the rate of technical progress.

In the early part of the second phase of industrialization, the income effect dominates and there is a moderate demand for human capital. Population growth and human capital formation increase. In the later part of the industrialization phase, the substitution effect dominates, as there is a significant demand for human capital, so that population growth declines and human capital formation increases further. In this model, the utility function of individuals shows a trade-off between the quantity and quality of the children they beget, subject to the subsistence consumption constraint C_m.

In brief, the Malthusian interaction between technology and population leads to an acceleration of technological progress that increases industrial demand for human capital formation that leads to a decline in fertility rates and further technological progress, and a decline in population growth. Technological progress, human capital formation, and a decline in population growth lead to sustained economic growth. Variations in countries' timing of the take-off has significantly contributed to the divergence in income per capita in the past two centuries, which explains the origins of vast and persistent differentials of income per capita across countries. Country-specific characteristics that affected the take-off include, according to Galor (2014), the conditions affecting technological progress, that is: policies to protect intellectual property rights; the stock of knowledge within a society; the propensity of a country to trade; technological diffusion, specialization, and technological progress via learning by doing; a negative attitude toward knowledge creation and diffusion (as the anti-scientific Inquisition of the past); the composition of interest groups in society; incentives to block or promote technological innovation (as in the case of the Luddites and landowners); and cultural and genetic diversity. A wider spectrum of traits are more likely to contain those complementary to the adoption of new technologies: the abundance of natural resources complementary to industrialization; the ability of individuals to afford the cost of education and forgone earnings; the extent of human capital formation; the availability, accessibility, and quality of public education (due to policy choices and pressures of interest groups); the cultural and religious composition of society; attitudes towards education; the availability, quality, and desirability of education; the stock of knowledge in society; the productivity of human capital; the skill-intensity of production and its effect on the demand for human capital; the effect of geography on health (measured for instance by the incidence of malaria and hookworm); the composition of religious groups within a society and their positive attitude towards literacy (as in Judaism and Protestantism); and the social status associated with education.

Although very comprehensive and spanning centuries of economic development, UGT still does not seem to fit the reality of several countries, such as those of the Sahel and Central Africa. These areas have been trapped for centuries, and are still trapped today, in near-Malthusian low-level equilibria characterized by no or little 'induced technical innovation' following growing land scarcity that, according to Galor (2014), should have been stimulated by a rapid population increase. In these countries, rapid population growth has led to the cultivation of land with poor fertility that is affected by frequent weather shocks, resulting in recurrent famines and internal and foreign emigration. In this sense UGT suggests (perhaps too optimistically) that the transition from stagnation to growth is an inevitable byproduct of population growth and the process of development, as theorized in the field of agricultural innovation by Boserup and Hayami and Ruttan (cited in Chapter 6). In addition, UGT does not place a great emphasis on the growth-retarding role of institutions (such as *latifundia* or educational institutions favouring mainly the children of the elites, as observed for instance in Latin America) in countries exhibiting a high concentration of income, physical assets and human capital. Indeed, according to Galor, the size and composition of the population and its interaction with an accelerated pace of technological progress ultimately raise the importance of education in coping with a rapidly changing technological environment. The assumption that a rise in industrial demand for educated workers brings about significant reductions in fertility rates is another component of this theory. However, this assumption has not been validated for the last half century in large parts of sub-Saharan Africa that suffer from a stalled demographic transition (Chapter 7), a situation that according to this model may explain the slow long-term growth in income per capita observed in these countries. Under normal conditions, the increase in industrial labour demand enables a larger share of the gains from factors accumulation and technological progress to be diverted to the enhancement of human capital formation and income per capita, paving the way for the emergence of sustained economic growth. But, as noted, there are many exceptions.

The UGT theory further explores the dynamic interaction between human evolution and the process of economic development. It advances the hypothesis that the forces of natural selection have played a significant role in the evolution of the world economy from stagnation to growth. The Malthusian era shaped the composition of the population as well. This formulation gets closer to the debate on the underlying causes of long-term development discussed by Spolaore and Wacziarg (2013) in Section 2.4. Finally, the UGT sheds light on the divergence in income per capita across the world during the past two centuries. It identifies the factors that have governed the transition from stagnation to growth and have thus contributed to the observed worldwide differences in economic development (see above). All these factors have been discussed in isolation by various theories, and the merit of UGT is to remind us of the persistent effects that variations in historical and prehistorical conditions have had on the subsequent composition of human capital and economic development (Spolaore and Wacziarg, 2013).

2.10 Comparing the Features and Predictions of the above Models

Table 2.13 compares the main features and conclusions of the models discussed in this chapter and their applicability to the developed and developing countries. It is interesting to note that the key production factors emphasized by each model vary considerably with the possible exception of physical capital, and so do the conclusions concerning the duration of growth that is perpetual in the Harrod–Domar and Mankiw et al. models, but that stops in the Solow model once the steady state is reached.

2.11 Concluding Remarks

By historical standards, economic growth is a relatively new phenomenon that is still only partially understood. Trying to comprehend such a complex phenomenon requires paying attention not only to its pace, but also to its composition, stability, financing, and inequality, that is, features that have been evolving markedly over time because of changes in technology, demography, political institutions, and other factors. These features of the growth process have attracted different degrees of attention by economists. As a result, alternative paradigms (emphasizing capital accumulation, human capital, technical progress, and so on) have dominated the theoretical explanations of economic growth in specific periods of time. At the same time, the locus of fast growth has shifted from Europe, to North America and, more recently, to Asia—and these are notably regions with different cultural, institutional, and political characteristics that have affected the nature of their long-term development patterns.

Alternative explanations and formal models of long-term growth have been developed, including those proposed by the classical development theory, and by exogenous, endogenous, and unified growth models. These alternative models appear to explain the growth process in specific country situations but not under all circumstances. Therefore, the formal analyses discussed in this chapter seem to suggest that the main conclusions derived are model- and context-specific. Furthermore, despite the important theoretical advances of the last three decades, the available econometric evidence does not support the view that the latest theoretical models offer a more satisfactory fit of the data. In particular, despite substantial progress, endogenous growth theory has not yet managed to replicate econometrically the observed development trajectories or to incorporate in its formulation factors that in the empirical debate are considered important for growth, as for example finance and institutions.

Table 2.13 Comparison between various growth models

Features and conclusions	*Harrod Domar*	*Solow*	*MRW*	*Romer*	*Aghion-Howitt*	*UGT*
Production factors	Physical capital	Physical capital, labour, technical progress (exogenous)	Physical capital, human capital, labour, technical progress (exogenous)	Physical capital, human capital, labour, technical progress (endogenous)	Various factors	Labour, induced technical innovation, and human capital
Returns to scale	Constant	Decreasing for both factors	Constant in HC and K taken together	Increasing	Increasing	Increasing
Dynamic properties	Perpetual growth	Steady state growth	Perpetualgrowth	Steady state depends on effective monopoly rights	Growth depends on incentives to innovate	Long-term growth depends on population and innovation
Cross country convergence in output per worker	Constant distance	Unconditional convergence. (if n, s, d, λ are equal)	No convergence	Not discussed	Not applicable	Depends on long list of country circumstances
Cross country convergencein growth rates	Convergence	if λ is equal in all countries	if s and p are the same in developed and developing countries	Not applicable	Not applicable	Expected over the long term if countries follow right policies
Relevance	Realistic in poor countries; does not capture growth slowdown in the rich ones	Fits better the situation of mature economies, but statistical fit is poor	Fairly realistic for both developing countries and developed countries	Gets pretty close to reality of developed countries, less to that of developing countries	Mainly applicable to advanced countries	Useful attempt to capture long term dynamics using demographic and technology variables

References

Acemoglu, D. (2009), *Introduction to Modern Economic Growth.* Princeton, NJ: Princeton University Press.

Agenor, P. R.(2005), 'The Macroeconomics of Poverty Reduction', *The Manchester School,* 73 (4): pp. 369–434.

Aghion, P. and P. Howitt (1998), *Endogenous Growth Theory.* Cambridge, MA: MIT Press.

Bourguignon, F. and C. Morisson (2002), 'Inequality among World Citizen', *The American Economic Review,* 92(4): pp. 727–44.

Burda, M. and C. Wyplosz (2003), *Macroeconomics: A European Text.* 2nd edition. Oxford: Oxford University Press.

Chenery, H. and M. Syrquin (1975), *Patterns of Development, 1970–1975,* A World Bank Research Publication. New York: Oxford University Press.

Cornia G. A. (2014a), *Falling Inequality in Latin America: Policy Changes and Lessons,* Oxford: Oxford University Press.

Cornia, G. A. and B. Martorano (2012), 'Development Policies and Income Inequality in Selected Developing Regions, 1980–2010', *UNCTAD Discussion Paper* 210, Geneva: UNCTAD.

Cornia, G. A. and F. Zagonari (2007), 'The HIV-AIDS impact on the rural and urban economy, in Cornia G. A. (ed.) *AIDS, Child Wellbeing and Public Policy.* Florence: UNICEF-ICDC.

Cornia, G. A., J. Honkkila, R. Paniccià, and V. Popov (1998), 'Investment Behaviour, Population Structure and Long-term Growth in Eastern Europe and Russia', *MOCT-MOST,* n.1.

Denison, E. (1974), *Accounting for United States Economic Growth 1929–1969,* Washington, DC: The Brookings Institute.

Diamond, J. (1997), *Guns, Germs and Steel: The Fates of Human Societies,* New York: Norton & Company.

Dutt, A. and J. Ros (2008), *International Handbook of Development Economics.* Cheltenham: Edward Elgar.

Evans, P. (1996), 'Using Cross-Country Variances to Evaluate Growth Theories', *Journal of Economic Dynamics and Control,* 20: pp. 1027–1049.

Fei, J. C. H. and G. Ranis (1964), *Development of the Labour Surplus Economy: Theory and Policy,* a Publication of the Economic Growth Centre, Yale University.

Fleck, S. E. (2009), 'International Comparisons of Hours Worked: An Assessment of the Statistics', *Monthly Labor Review* (May), Washington, DC: Bureau of Labor Statistics.

Gallup, J. and J. Sachs (2001), 'The Economic Burden of Malaria', *American Journal of Tropical Medicine and Hygiene,* 64 (1 supplement): pp. 85–96.

Galor, O. (2011), *Unified Growth Theory.* Princeton, NJ: Princeton University Press.

Galor, O. (2014), Lecture II UGT and Comparative Development, Brown University, https://www.brown.edu/Departments/Economics/Faculty/Oded_Galor/pdf/Galor-Lecture2-AEA2014-handout.pdf

Kaldor, N. (1967), *Strategic Factors in Economic Development.* The Frank W. Pierce Memorial Lectures at Cornell University, October 1966, Ithaca, New York: Cornell University.

Klasen, S. (2003), 'In Search of the Holy Grail: How to Achieve Pro-Poor Growth?' in B. Tungodden and N. Stern *(eds)*. *Towards Pro Poor Policies.* Proceedings from the Annual Bank Conference on Development Economics-Europe. Washington, DC: World Bank.

Latouche, S. (2009), *Farewell to Growth*, Cambridge: Polity Press.

Lewis, A. W. (1954), Economic Development with Unlimited Supply of Labour, *The Manchester School*, 22: pp. 139–191.

Maddison, A. (1991), *Dynamic Forces in Capitalist Development: a Long-Run Comparative View.* New York. Oxford University Press.

Mankiw, N. G., D. Romer, and D. N. Weil (1992), 'A Contribution to the Empirics of Economic Growth', *Quarterly Journal of Economics*, 107 (2): pp. 407–437.

Nurske, R. (1953), *Problems of Capital Formation in Underdeveloped Countries.* Oxford: Oxford University Press.

Obstfeld, M. and K. Rogoff (1996), *Foundations of International Macroeconomics*, Cambridge, MA: The MIT Press.

Phelps, E. (1961), 'The Golden Rule of Accumulation: A Fable for Growthmen', *The American Economic Review*, 51 (4): pp. 638–43.

Piga, G. and L. Pecchi (2008), *Revisiting Keynes: Economic Possibilities for Our Grandchildren*, Cambridge, MA: MIT Press.

Piketty, T. (2014), *Capital in the XXI Century*, Cambridge, MA: Harvard University Press.

Putterman, L. and D. N. Weil (2010), 'Post-1500 Population Flows and the Long-Run Determinants of Economic Growth and Inequality', *Quarterly Journal of Economics* 125 (4): pp. 1627–82.

Romer, P. M. (1990), 'Endogenous Technological Change', *Journal of Political Economy*, 98 (5) part 2: pp. 71–102.

Ros, J. (2013), *Rethinking Economic Development, Growth and Institutions*, Oxford: Oxford University Press.

Rosenstein- Rodan, P. (1943), 'Problems of industrialization in Eastern and South-Eastern Europe', *Economic Journal*, 53: pp. 202–11.

Rostow, W. W. (1960) *The Stages of Economic Growth: a noncommunist manifesto.* Cambridge, MA: Cambridge University Press.

Solow, R. M. (1956), 'A Contribution to the Theory of Economic Growth', *Quarterly Journal of Economics*, LXX: pp. 65–94.

Spolaore, E. and R. Wacziarg (2013), 'How Deep Are the Roots of Economic Development?', *Journal of Economic Literature*, 51 (2): pp. 325–69.

Valencia, F. and L. Laeven (2012), *Systemic Banking Crises database: an Update*, Washington, DC: International Monetary Fund.

Vos, R., J. A. Ocampo, and A. L. Cortez (2008), *Ageing and Development.* London and New York: Zed Books, published in association with the United Nations.

Young, A. (1994), 'Confronting the Statistical Realities of the East Asian Growth Experience: On the Tyranny of Numbers'. Washington, DC: NBER Working Papers No.4680, National Bureau of Economic Research.

Suggested further reading

Diamond, J. (1997), *Guns, Germs and Steel: The Fates of Human Societies*, New York: Norton & Company.

Galor, O. (2011), *Unified Growth Theory*. Princeton, NJ: Princeton University Press.

Piga, G. and L. Pecchi (2008), *Revisiting Keynes: Economic Possibilities for Our Grandchildren*. Cambridge, MA: MIT Press.

Ray, D. *Development Economics*. Princeton, NJ: Princeton University Press.

3

Demand-side Models of Short-term Income Formation

This chapter discusses the main behavioural equations that are part of the Keynesian aggregate demand model, and the IS-LM, AS-AD, and Mundell–Fleming models that study the formation of the level of income and its fluctuations over the short term due to exogenous or policy shocks.

3.1 The Consumption Function

All demand-side macroeconomic models are based on: (a) an accounting framework derived from the System of National Accounts (SNA) which includes the variables that influence the decisions of the economic agents and the policymaker; (b) behavioural relationships that show how decisions about investment, consumption, etc. are taken by economic agents; (c) exogenous policy variables such as the interest rate, money supply, compulsory reserve ratios, taxes, public expenditure, exchange rates, import tariffs, and so on; (d) equilibrium conditions (named also closure rules) which reconcile the choices made by economic agents by means of macroeconomic identities. In this section we shall discuss point (b).[1]

In the macroeconomic models used in developed countries (and, *mutatis mutandis*, in developing countries) for forecasting purposes and for simulating the impact of economic policies, a few behavioural relations play a central role. Among them it is necessary to consider explicitly the functions which describe the equilibrium in the goods and money markets, that is, the relationships of consumption, investment, and money demand. For instance, the impact of fiscal policy on aggregate demand crucially depends on the characteristics and properties of the consumption function. In its turn, alternative specifications of the money demand function may affect the impact of monetary policy.

The Keynesian current income hypothesis

This relation tries to explain the trend of private consumption of a representative agent and, by implication, aggregate consumption, which is the principal component of aggregate demand. At both the microeconomic and—by aggregation—the macro level, it suggests that households' current disposable income per capita (YD_t) is the main determinant of per capita consumption (C_t) that is:

[1] See Chapter 4 of Sachs and Larrain (1993) for a comprehensive discussion of alternative private consumption models.

The Macroeconomics of Developing Countries: An Intermediate Textbook. Giovanni Andrea Cornia, Oxford University Press (2020).

DOI: 10.1093/oso/9780198856672.001.0001

$$C_t = a + b\, YD_t \tag{3.1}$$

where $0 < b < 1$ $(b \cong 0.7 - 0.9)$ and where 'a' is the minimum level of consumption when disposable income equals zero. People finance such minimum consumption by borrowing, receiving gifts, or selling their assets. 'b' is the marginal propensity to consume which remains constant for every level of YD_t. By dividing both sides of (3.1) by YD_t we obtain $C_t/YD_t = a/YD_t + b$, that is the average propensity to consume which diminishes when YD_t rises. In most developed countries the marginal and average propensity to consume have risen during the last fifty years, mostly owing to the spread of consumer credit and payment by instalments which relieve the household from the necessity of saving before buying durable goods.

This formulation is rather simple but is still frequently used. Yet, it can be criticized for several reasons. First of all, in this model consumption (and hence the well-being of households) fluctuates in parallel with disposable income, while it is well-known that the households have a strong preference for smoothing their consumption stream over time, or for raising it gradually at an annual rate $\Delta C/C$, by consuming less than allowed by their current disposable income in good years and more during difficult times. In such a framework, consumption smoothing is therefore also influenced by expectations about the household's future income, but this effect is not captured by the Keynesian model.

Second, relation (3.1) ignores the role played in consumption decisions by the interest rate and access to financial markets. The latter can, in fact, allow an intertemporal reallocation of part of the current consumption. For instance, if the interest rate rises over time faster than the household's time preference (called also social discount rate—see later), the consumer may decide to postpone some of its current expenditure because in the future it will be able to consume not only the delayed expenditure but also the interest earned on it. Third, the Keynesian consumption function does not always generate a good statistical fit, especially for some social groups. For example, this function overestimates the consumption of working age households (who save part of their current income for their old age) and underestimates the consumption of pensioners (who spend part of their savings in their old age) and of the youth (who may borrow to finance current consumption). Fourth, its mathematical formulation does not allow the inflection points of the aggregate consumption trend to be easily replicated. Given all this and the large regression residual unaccounted for by YD_t, the literature has tried to explain the time trend of aggregate consumption on the basis of more realistic hypotheses.

The life-cycle income hypothesis

This aggregate theory of consumption elaborated by Nobel Laureate Franco Modigliani is micro founded and was developed as an answer to the previously mentioned critiques of the current income hypothesis. It suggests that people plan their consumption and saving decisions over their expected lifetime, including both their young adulthood (from age 18 to 25) and their old age (over 65 years). Before the age of 18 people are considered to be dependent on their family. The hypotheses on which this formulation rests are: (a) people have credible expectations about their future incomes and average life expectancy, a fairly plausible hypothesis—on average—in an advanced economy;

(b) people can shift their income backward and forward over time by resorting to the financial markets, that is, by saving for their old age or taking out a student or mortgage loan during their young adulthood; (c) people want to maintain a constant or gradually increasing consumption level during their lifecycle and abhor large year-to-year fluctuations in their consumption level; (d) all wealth possessed by the household is consumed during its lifecycle as there is no intention of leaving any inheritance to heirs. In view of this, the basic relation of this model can be expressed as follows:

$$C_t = c\ WR_t + b\ YL_t \tag{3.2}$$

This expression indicates that current consumption at time t depends on WR_t (real wealth) and YL_t (the average lifetime income from work, capital income, or social transfers) and on c and b which are the propensities to consume out of WR_t and YL_t. For the analytical derivation of this relation, let us suppose that a person lives NL years and that of these years she will work WL years and spend NL – WL years in old age, without receiving a pension (a not too unlikely event in the United States and other countries—but a rare event in Europe). If we ignore WR for a moment, and imagine that the person would like to make arrangements to enjoy the same average yearly consumption (C*) for the rest of her life years (NL – T), then yearly consumption C* will be equal to:

$$C^*(NL - T) = YL^*(WL - T) \tag{3.3}$$

$$C^* = (WL - T)/(NL - T)\ YL^* \quad \text{or} \quad C^* = bYL^*$$

where YL* is the average lifetime annual income over the remaining working life (WL – T) and b is (WL – T) / (NL – T). If, besides the income from work YL, the person can count on some accumulated wealth, WR, she will also consume part of that in order to generate an additional uniform consumption stream during her entire lifecycle. If, for instance, at moment T the person in question owns an amount of wealth WR and assumes that she will be able to count on a labour income YL in the future for WL – T years, then her annual consumption C will be:

$$C^* = WR/(NL - T) + YL(WT - T)/(NL - T) \tag{3.4}$$

which can be written as

$$C^*_t = c\ WR_t + bYL^*_t \quad \text{where } c = 1/(NL - T) \text{ and } b = (WL - T)/(NL - T) \tag{3.4a}$$

This approach (as well as the one illustrated below) can be further enriched by introducing rational (rather than adaptive) expectations about future incomes, unexpected risks and the possibility that, even in developed countries, households may face liquidity constraints (Besley, 1993).

No doubt, the life-cycle hypothesis presents some improvements with respect to the Keynesian formulation. In fact, it is consistent with consumption smoothing, it takes into account the demographic structure of the population, and it allows the impact of wealth on consumption to be considered. However, in spite of all this (and of improving the econometric fit of the data), it also presents some limitations: (a) it ignores changes over time in the interest rate. This may not generate large effects over the lifecycle, but it might explain backward and forward shifts of part of consumption over the short term; (b) it assumes that individuals will not pass any wealth to the next generation, a fact that is uncommon in numerous cultures where the transfer of wealth to heirs is a common code of behaviour; (c) it assumes that the future income streams, YL, are predictable, while the recent labour market liberalization has entailed a rise in their volatility in developed countries.

The permanent income hypothesis

Theorized by Milton Friedman, the permanent income model starts from the observation that income fluctuates considerably over time and that agents—who aim to maintain their consumption flow in as stable a state as possible over time—adjust their current consumption to the possibilities of long-term consumption, where the latter depends on the permanent income (YP). In symbols:

$$C_t = b\ YP_t \tag{3.5}$$

But how are we to measure permanent income? In practice, owing to the fluctuations of income streams, current income (YD) is disaggregated into permanent income (YP) and transitory income (YT). A first method for estimating YP is to consider it equal to (3.6):

$$YP_t = YD_{t-1} + \theta\ (YD_t - YD_{t-1}) \tag{3.6}$$

where $0 < \theta < 1$. This relation shows that permanent income varies less than current income, as the second term on the right-hand side (that represents a rise or fall of income during the last year) is multiplied by $\theta < 1$. In this relation, the parameter θ is a measure of how the consumer evaluates the rise/fall of income observed during the last period as a temporary or permanent change. In this regard, the following two points have to be noted: (a) θ tends to diminish (and so do, as a result, YP_t and C_t) if the consumer predicts on the basis of rational or adaptive expectations that the income increase $YD_t - YD_{t-1}$ is in part or totally transitory; (b) YP_t and C_t are increasingly smaller/bigger than YD_t the bigger the increase (decrease) of current income over the last period $(YD_t - YD_{1-t})$. At any rate, by substituting into (3.5) the value of YP_t given by (3.6) one obtains:

$$C_t = b[YD_{t-1} + \theta\ (YD - YD_{t-1})] = bYD_{t-1} + b\theta YD_t - b\theta YD_{t-1} \tag{3.7}$$

from which one obtains

$$C_t = b\theta\ YD_t + b(1-\theta)\ YD_{t-1} \tag{3.8}$$

where b is the short-term marginal propensity to consume from the current income derived from the Keynesian model, which is clearly greater than $b\theta$ (as $\theta < 1$), which is the long-term propensity to consume derived by Friedman's model. In practice, the permanent income hypothesis suggests that, if $(YD_t - YD_{t-1}) > 0$, consumption

Table 3.1 Comparison of three models of private consumption

Features	Keynesian model	Modigliani model	Friedman model
Main hypothesis	Consumption depends on current income	Consumption depends on life-cycle income and wealth	Consumption depends on permanent income
Formulation	$C = a + b\ YD$	$C = c\ WR + b\ YL$	$C = b\theta YD + b(1-\theta)\ YD_{t-1}$
Meaning of the parameters	a = minimum consumption b = marginal propensity to consume out of current income $C/YD = a/YD + b$ average propensity to consume	c = average propensity to consume wealth b = average/marginal propensity to consume out of the average life-cycle income	θ = prudential coefficient (falls in line with the variability of YD) b = average/marginal propensity to consume out of permanent income
Comments	For the USA, Kuznets found C/YD: 1869–98 = .867; 1884–1913 = .867; 1904–33 = .879	C rises/falls in case of exogenous shocks on WR (wealth effect) as during today's crisis	Adjustments: C rises (falls) more slowly, the smaller is θ; C rises (falls) more slowly the smaller is $(YD - YD_{t-1})$
Comparison among parameters	b (Keynes) > b (Modigliani) in case of wage earners b (Keynes) < b (Modigliani) in case of students/pensioners b (Keynes) > bθ (Friedman)		

Note: The econometric estimates of the parameters a, b, c, and θ can be carried out on: (a) aggregate yearly time series of income, wealth, and consumption. In this case the value of the estimated parameters reflects their average for the period; (b) cross-sections of individuals or households at one point in time. This makes it possible to measure the parameters accurately over the short term (but not the long term), (c) panel data (individual or household data observed over several years, for instance all the years of the period 2001–10). The choice of the estimation method depends on the objective of the estimates, i.e. whether they have been carried out for forecasting or simulation purposes over either the short or the long term.

increases during the current year more slowly than in the case of the current income hypothesis during the first year. In contrast, if $(YD - YD_{1-t}) < 0$, current consumption declines less sharply than in the current income model. Table 3.1 presents a comparison of the features of the three consumption models just discussed.

A general neoclassical formulation of the consumption function

The three consumption models discussed above neglect the impact of the interest rate (ρ) and of the time preference rate (α). Modern consumption functions of neoclassical derivation summarize several of the properties already examined (in particular those illustrated by the life-cycle theory) but take also into account the impact of these two variables. The basic version of the general model postulates a representative household that defines an intertemporal consumption plan which maximizes its utility over the entire lifecycle subject to its intertemporal budget constraint. The model assumes no uncertainty about future income flows (as in case of perfect foresight), and constant interest and time preference rates.

Given these hypotheses, the representative household calculates the present value of the resources R which can be spent on consumption during its lifecycle. Such resources are given by the household initial wealth WR_0 and the value of future income streams YD_t discounted at the present time with ρ, that is,:

$$R = WR_0 + YD_0 + YD_1/(1+\rho) + YD_2/(1+\rho)^2 + \ldots + YD_t/(1+\rho)^t + \ldots + YD_n/(1+\rho)^n \quad (3.9)$$

$$R = WR_0 + \Sigma_t YD_t/(1+\rho)^t \quad (t = 0, n) \quad (3.10)$$

At the same time, the sum of life-cycle consumption should respect the budget constraint, that is:

$$C = C_0 + C_1 + \ldots. + C_t \ldots.. + C_n \leq R \quad (3.11)$$

The representative household then calculates the overall utility of life-cycle consumption by discounting the utility of future consumption flows with the time preference rate α:

$$U(C) = U(C_0) + U(C_1)/(1+\alpha) \ldots + U(C_t)/(1+\alpha)^t \ldots + U(C_n)/(1+\alpha)^n = \sum_i U(C_t)/(1+\alpha)^t \quad (3.12)$$

The solution of the problem consists in finding the consumption path which maximizes $U(C) = \sum_t U(C_t)/(1+\alpha)^t$ while respecting the condition $C \leq WR_0 + \sum_i YD_t/(1+\rho)^t$. The first order condition ($\delta U/\delta C = 0$) of this maximization problem is given by the Euler equation (demonstration omitted) which defines the equivalence between the marginal utilities at time t and t + 1, that is

$$U'(C_{t+1}) = [(1+\alpha)/(1+\rho)]\, U'(C_t) \quad \text{or} \quad [U'(C_{t+1})]/[U'(C_t)] = (1+\alpha)/(1+\rho) \quad (3.13)$$

If we now consider the case in which the utility function of private consumption takes a logarithmic form, that is, $U(C_t) = \ln C_t$, then $U_t' = 1/C_t$ (as the first derivative of $\log C_t$ is $1/C_t$). By substituting this result in expression (3.13) one obtains:

$$1/(C_{t+1}) = [(1+\alpha)/(1+\rho)]\, 1/(C_t) \quad \text{or} \quad (C_{t+1}) = (1+\rho)/(1+\alpha)C_t \tag{3.14}$$

where the second expression indicates that the representative household will distribute equally its consumption over its lifetime. Consumption will thus not depend on the current income but on initial wealth WR_0 and the vital income. Yet, in this case, the consumption path is influenced by the ratio between the interest rate and the time preference rate. Equation (3.14) plausibly suggests that a high interest rate, ρ, leads to an increase in future consumption in comparison to the current one, as some current income is saved to earn a high interest. In this case, the growth rate of consumption g will be:

$$g = C_{t+1}/C_t - 1 = (1+\rho)/(1+\alpha) - 1 \tag{3.15}$$

For example, if $\rho = 7$ per cent, while $\alpha = 5$ per cent, consumption will grow every year by $(1.07/1.05 - 1 = 1.9$ percent). In contrast, where there is a high time preference rate, α (typical of low income households), the representative family tends to anticipate current consumption compared with future consumption. Finally, if $\alpha = \rho$ we shall have perfect consumption smoothing, in which annual consumption does not change over the entire lifecycle.

Equation (3.15) obviously assumes the absence of liquidity constraints, and the possibility of shifting resources intertemporally, as in the life-cycle model. A second issue regards the time horizon over which this consumption smoothing takes place. As already noted when discussing the permanent income model, even in developed countries households are increasingly unable to assume no uncertainty over a long time horizon and to formulate plausible expectations about their future income streams. This has become particularly true during the recent years of increasing volatility and labour precariousness.

3.2 The Investment Function

Over the last two decades, investments absorbed $12 - 15$ per cent of GDP in the poorest African and Asian economies and up to 45 per cent of GDP in China, with the majority of countries exhibiting ratios of around $18 - 25$ per cent. Investments do not represent the most important component of aggregate demand but they do exhibit the greatest variability and at the same time a strong correlation with the long-term growth of GDP. Total investments are generally disaggregated into: (a) machinery and equipment used in the production process (if we divide these two terms by GDP we obtain the equipment ratio), (b) investment in industrial buildings, offices, and residential buildings, and (c) investment in inventory ΔS. For example, in Argentina, in 2007 the equipment/GDP ratio was equal to 8 per cent and the buildings/GDP ratio was 14 per cent, while investment in inventory was negligible. Investment can be carried out by the private sector (domestic and foreign) and the public sector. The models discussed hereafter focus on the private sector and do not explain well the trend in public investment that may play a key role in capital accumulation, as in today's China.

The accelerator approach

This non-neoclassical investment function assumes that the optimum capital stock is strictly proportional to the output level (Y) and that this relation is stable over time. In this framework, a rise of Y from Y_{t-1} to Y_t generates a rise in net investments ($NI = K_t - K_{t-1}$) according to the formula below where v represents the capital/output ratio:

$$\text{given that } K_{t-1} = vY_{t-1} \text{ and } K_t = vY_t \tag{3.16}$$

$$K_t - K_{t-1} = v(Y_t - Y_{t-1})$$

$$NI_t = v\ \Delta Y_t \quad \text{while} \quad I_t = v\ \Delta Y_t + \delta K_{t-1}$$

In this formula, net investments at time t (NI_t) are equal to the capital–output ratio (v) multiplied by the increase in production (ΔY_t). To obtain the gross investments (I_t), it is necessary to add amortization at the rate δ of the capital stock of the previous year, that is, δK_{t-1}. Since v oscillates between 3 and 4, an increase in output tends to generate a rise in net investment 3 – 4 times larger than that of Y, which means that it accelerates the demand for investment goods. Symmetrically, a decrease in Y, heavily depresses the demand for investment goods. For example, if GDP drops by 1 per cent, the demand for investment goods drops by 3 – 4 per cent, contributing in this way to the volatility of the business cycle.

However, other factors help to explain the strong variability of investments. Among them, the uncertainty which characterizes the expectations about future production levels and the overall volatility of the time period in which—once it is decided what the optimum capital stock is—new investments ought to be realized. The empirical data show in fact that private investments follow the rise in production expectations with long time lags. A third factor might be the uncertainty about the investment plans of other companies or competing countries. And to conclude, even in developed countries, private investment is often substantially influenced by the level of public investment either through the direct effect that these generate on aggregate demand, or through the impact they have on externalities that raise the marginal productivity of private capital.

The optimal capital stock approach

This is a model of neoclassical inspiration in which the optimal capital stock K^* depends on the usage cost of capital (cu) and the expected level of production (Y) estimated on the basis of the current production and future production plans, as shown in equation (3.17).

$$K^* = f\ (cu, Y) \tag{3.17}$$

Obviously, given a production level Y, firms will invest until the usage cost per invested unit of capital is lower than or equal to the marginal productivity of capital (MPK). The usage cost of capital includes the interest rate r—considering that firms need to borrow at this rate to carry out new investments—plus the annual amortization δ per unit of capital).

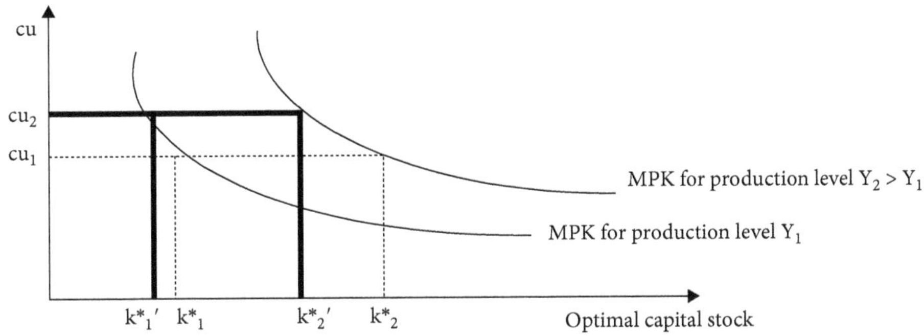

Figure 3.1 Determination of the optimal level of the capital stock

In turn MPK determines the marginal rate of return on investment. In formal terms, the equilibrium condition can be written as follows:

$$\mathrm{MPK} = r + \delta \tag{3.18}$$

A few more variables can be added to this formulation. To start with, r is the nominal interest rate and, in periods of inflation, it is possible that this rate will not be raised (at least not immediately) to keep the nominal cost of money constant. In contrast, it is likely that firms will immediately (or after a short delay) increase the sale price of the goods produced with new investment, in line with the expected inflation rate (π^*), in this way boosting the MPK at current prices. At the same time, if firms have to pay taxes t proportional to their gross returns, the net MPK will decline. Last, if technical progress should occur—thus boosting the output obtainable with the same capital stock—the MPK would grow at the rate λ. With all these changes, the equilibrium condition becomes:

$$\mathrm{MPK}(1 - t)\,(1 - \lambda) = r - \pi^* + \delta \tag{3.19}$$

A final consideration concerns the impact of changes in the output level Y on the demand for K^*. Obviously, its increase (represented graphically by the shift of the production schedule Y_1 to Y_2 (Figure 3.1) will shift the MPK schedule upwards, given that for each level of capital stock this will be combined with a greater amount of labour, shifting the demand of capital from K^*_1 to K^*_2. At the same time, a surge in the usage cost of capital from cu_1 to cu_2 will reduce the optimal capital stock, and consequently the demand for new investment. In Figure 3.1, for example, given a production level Y_1, an increase of the usage cost of capital from cu_1 to cu_2 will shrink the optimal capital stock to $K^*_1{}'(K^*_2{}'$ in the case of production level Y_2) as Y_1 will be produced with more labour-intensive techniques.

The role of other explanatory variables

Other explanatory variables are at times included in the investment function of developed countries. The first is the level of profits or sales of firms (global sales are not too dissimilar from Y), which influence the expectations of future production levels and consequently the desired level of capital stock. Second, a rise of the ratio between the stock market value and the replacement cost of the capital stock (equal to their book value multiplied by the deflator of investment goods)—a ratio called in the literature 'Tobin's q'—has a boosting effect on investment in countries (such as the United States and UK) where the stock market plays an important role in the financing of investments. In most countries the stock market value of a firm generally differs from its book value, as it incorporates information on its future profitability. This information is derived from the analysis of investments plans and technological discoveries, estimates of future market demand, and so on. A high q means that the value the market assigns to the future flows of profits discounted at the present time is higher than the replacement cost of investment. This suggests high profitability for firms and thus should generate an incentive to increase investment, capital stock, and production.

3.3 The Money Demand Function

Money demand is always expressed in real terms (MD/P)—that is, it is calculated as the nominal demand for money divided by a price index such as the GDP Deflator or CPI. This entails that the stock of real money demand does not vary when the nominal money mass grows at the same speed of the inflation rate. Money demand (meant as M1, that is, currency plus liquid deposits) is the sum of money demanded for current transactions, and for precautionary and speculative reasons. A first reason to demand money is to pay for every day's current transactions. The necessity of holding cash or liquid bank deposits is attributable to the fact that the families' wages (generally received once a month) are not synchronized with the expenditures for current consumption items that take place every day or every week (Figure 3.2).

The best indicator of the volume of current transactions is the total sales, even though, as a matter of fact, in most models these are often proxied by GDP. In developed countries, the elasticity of money demand due to an increase in GDP, is low (0.1–0.2) over the short term, but about 1.2 over the long term.

A second reason for holding liquid cash balances is on account of precautionary measures. This is relevant when one faces uncertainties about future payments, the need

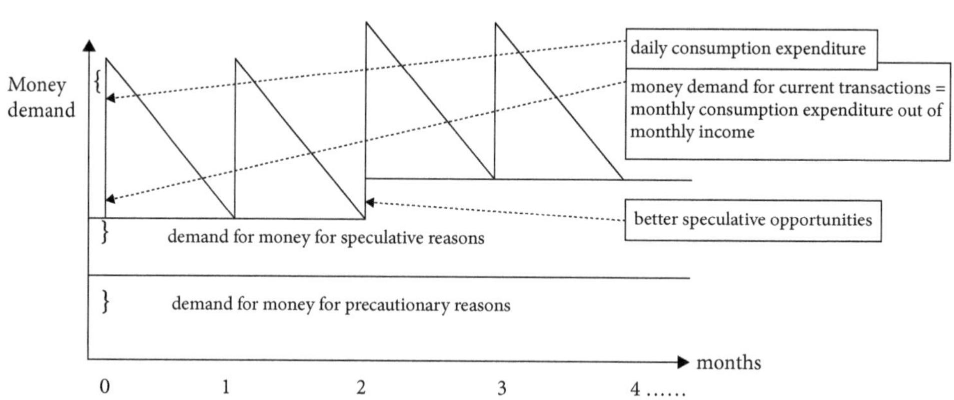

Figure 3.2 Change over time in the demand for money by component

to finance contingent expenses (e.g. for consumer durables), or to ensure against a high earnings variability. Holding cash is also useful to avoid the high cost of illiquidity, that is, the interest paid on overdrafts or the cost of converting savings or other assets (e. g. real estate property) into cash or liquid deposits. Such conversion costs include: time costs, communication costs (e.g. for mailing, phone, and fax), notaries/contractual costs, and taxes, as well as fees and incidental penalties. Third, money is also held in liquid form for speculative purposes, that is, in view of the possibility of making lucrative investments rapidly. These speculative opportunities may change over time, as shown in Figure 3.2 as an example at the start of the third month.

The demand of money for precautionary and speculative purposes is influenced by the interest rate on savings accounts and the opportunity cost borne to maintain liquid funds. Needless to say, if the interest rate on deposits is high, families have to endure a high cost to keep money in liquid form. For example, in 1994, M1 in Germany was equal to 25 per cent of GDP. In that year, the interest rate on saving accounts was 5 per cent, which means that the opportunity cost endured by all those holding liquid money balances was equal to 1.25 per cent of GDP. This opportunity cost explains the high negative elasticity of money demand in relation to an increase in the nominal interest rate. The latter has been estimated at 3.7 per cent on average for the OECD countries, but can reach values of 7 – 8 per cent.

By virtue of all this, traditional models of money demand for developed countries include among their explanatory variables the real income (proxied by Y), the nominal interest rate on deposits r (as a proxy of the opportunity cost borne to keep money in liquid form), and the transaction costs tc met to transform non-liquid assets into cash. The higher the value of these variables, the higher is the quota of financial assets that people will maintain in liquid form. Summing up, the money demand function takes the form:

$$MD/P = f\ (Y, r, tc) \tag{3.20}$$

It is important to note that an interest rate rise has not only a negative impact on money demand but also a positive effect on money velocity (V). In fact, given Fisher's exchange relation $VM = YP$ (see Section 1.4),$V = YP/M$. After substituting in lieu of M the right-hand side of equation (3.20), money velocity becomes $V = YP/f\ (Y,\ r,\ tc)$ which shows that if r increases, V accelerates. In simple terms, when the interest rate rises, holding large money balances in cash becomes expensive, and the monetary mass circulates more rapidly to cover all current transactions.

Finally, it is important to underscore that in this formulation inflation does not affect real money demand. In fact, one speaks of money neutrality since (moderate) inflation does not affect real transactions, which means that what families really care about is the purchasing power of real money, not its nominal value. If P grows, then the nominal demand for money will rise in the same way, on condition that Y, r, and tc remain unchanged. Naturally, things may change if the increase in inflation pushes the monetary authorities to raise the nominal interest rate so as to keep the real rate constant. It is also clear that the neutrality of money is valid within a certain interval of the inflation rate, such as the one observed in most cases during the last fifty years in developed countries. As we shall see, the situation is different in developing countries characterized by high inflation, instability, and low credibility of monetary authorities. Under these circumstances, high inflation and instability lead to a decrease in the demand for domestic money, dollarization, and the simultaneous use of two currencies (see Chapter 13).

3.4 The Keynesian Model of Aggregate Demand

In the *General Theory* Keynes manifested all his scepticism about the prescriptions of neoclassical economics, which—as we saw earlier—explained the formation of income on the basis of the stocks of production factors and technology. With these stocks unchanged, in 1933 GDP was 30 per cent lower than in 1929, while one-quarter of the workforce was unemployed. According to Keynes, the GDP contraction was due to a lack of aggregate demand, not to an insufficient supply potential.

Standard analysis

The Keynesian analysis focuses on equilibrium in the goods market. It assumes fixed prices that are sticky over the short term. It defines the concept of planned expenditure E (also called aggregate demand, or AD), that is the sum of the monies households intend to spend on consumption goods (C), that firms intend to invest in buildings and equipment (I), and the government intends to spend on public services and transfers (G). Equation (3.21) defines in symbols the planned expenditure in a closed economy, while equation (3.21a) also includes net exports $NX = X - M$ (exports–imports) and measures the planned expenditure in the case of an open economy:

$$E = C + I + G \tag{3.21}$$

$$E = C + I + G + NX \tag{3.21a}$$

The components of planned expenditure are defined as follows: $C = c\,(Y - T^*)$,[2] where the last term in the parenthesis is equal to disposable income YD, that is, gross income Y minus a given amount of taxes T^* (as indicated by the asterisk). c is the marginal propensity to consume. Also I^* and G^* are given. In the case of an open economy, NX is the net exports that are equal to the exogenous exports X^*, minus the imports $M = M^* + mY$. M^* represents the autonomous imports that are independent from the income level and mY the imports proportional to the level of Y, given the import coefficient m. In a closed economy, this model includes only one behavioural relationship, while in an open economy there are two. After introducing into equations (3.21) and (3.21a) the functions for private consumption and imports just mentioned, these equilibrium relations can be rewritten in closed and open economies, respectively, as follows:

$$E = c(Y - T^*) + I^* + G^* = [I^* + G^* - cT] + cY \tag{3.22}$$

[2] The consumption function can also be written as $C = c\,(1 - t)Y$ where t is the direct tax rate (e.g. 20 per cent, or 0.20).

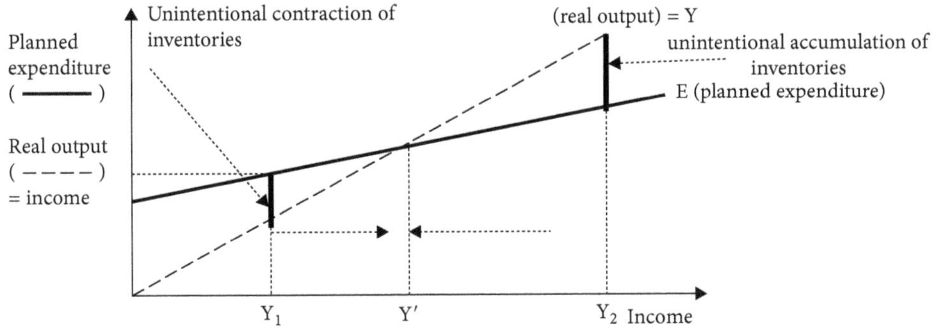

Figure 3.3 Keynesian cross and the equilibrium level of income

$$E = c(Y - T^*) + I^* + G^* + X^* - M^* - mY = [I^* + G^* - cT + X^* - M^*] + (c - m)Y \tag{3.22a}$$

Both equations are growing functions of Y, with positive intercept $(I^* + G^* - cT^*)$ or $(I^* + G^* - cT^* + X^* - M^*)$, that are the autonomous components of the planned expenditure, and with slope c in the case of a closed economy and $(c - m)$ in an open economy. The economy is in equilibrium when planned expenditure E intersects the schedule 'real output produced = income distributed' (see Section 1.2 on the national accounts for the production and distribution of GDP). We have equilibrium when $E = Y$ (Figure 3.3).

If the real output is at the Y_2 level, higher than the equilibrium level, aggregate demand is insufficient to absorb all output, and firms accumulate inventories unintentionally. They will therefore fire some workers and reduce production, a decision that lowers Y until it reaches the equilibrium level Y'. The opposite is true if the economy starts from the income level Y_1, which is lower than the planned expenditure, a situation that causes an involuntary drop in the level of inventories. Firms will therefore increase the level of output and employment so that the planned expenditure grows until it reaches the equilibrium level of income Y'. In conclusion, the Keynesian cross allows us to determine the equilibrium level of income over the short term, given I^*, G^*, T^*, c, and m. Indeed, as shown by equations (3.23) and (3.23a), in equilibrium the following relations hold true, where the ratios $1/(1 - c)$ and $(1/1 - c + m)$ are the Keynesian multipliers in closed and open economies, respectively.

$$Y = E \tag{3.23}$$

$$Y = [I^* + G^* - cT^*] + cY = [1/(1 - c)]\ [I^* + G^* - cT^*]$$

$$Y = E \tag{3.23a}$$

$$Y = [I^* + G^* - cT^* + X^* - M^*] + (c - m)Y = [1/(1 - c + m)]\ [I^* + G^* - cT^* + X^* - M^*]$$

Impact of an increase in public expenditure

Relations (3.23) and (3.23a) define the equilibrium level of income Y' (Figure 3.4) in a closed and open economy. It is not obvious, however, that the income level Y' ensures full

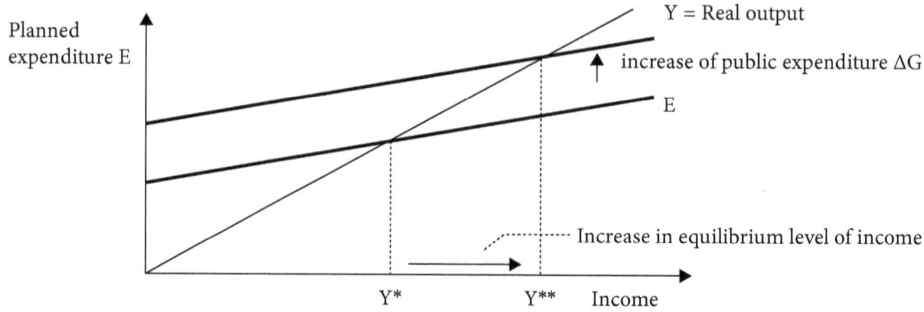

Figure 3.4 Keynesian cross, increase in public expenditure and the multiplier

employment, which was the main preoccupation of Keynes and his colleagues. Indeed, given the average productivity per worker π, the labour demand, LD, generated by Y' is equal to $LD = Y'/\pi$. The latter may be smaller than the labour supply LS, in this way causing involuntary unemployment $U = LS - LD$. If that is the case, Y' is an under-employment equilibrium.

To solve this unemployment problem (which was extremely marked during the Great Depression, and then reappeared during the crisis of 2008–12 in Europe) the policymaker may decide to increase public expenditure (one of the components of autonomous demand) by ΔG so as to increase employment. Let us examine the impact of such a decision on the national income Y and employment level LD. There are two ways to do this, the first is geometric and the second algebraic. Let us start with the first. If the policymaker increases G^*, the planned expenditure E in Figure 3.4 shifts upward by ΔG for any level of income Y.

As shown by Figure 3.4, the public expenditure increase ΔG generates a greater increase in the income level ΔY, as its equilibrium level rises from Y' to Y''. In fact, in a closed economy, a rise in ΔG triggers an increase of private consumption equal to $c\Delta G$ which determines a further rise of the national income by the same amount, which in turn causes an increase of private consumption equal to $c^2\Delta G$, and so on. In this way, the overall increase in ΔY following the rise of ΔG will be equal to:

$$\Delta Y = \Delta G + c\Delta G + c^2\Delta G + c^3\Delta G + \ldots.\ c^n\Delta G = \Delta G(1 + c + c^2 + \ldots.\ c^n) \quad (3.24)$$

which is the product of ΔG for an arithmetic sequence with initial value 1 and rate of increase c whose sum is equal to $1/(1 - c)$. We can thus write that $\Delta Y = \Delta G/(1 - c)$ where—as noted—$1/(1 - c)$ is the Keynesian multiplier in a closed economy. A similar process takes place in an open economy (simple demonstration omitted). Relations (3.25) and (3.25a) therefore describe the Keynesian multiplier in a closed and open economy, respectively:

$$\Delta Y/\Delta G = 1/(1 - c) \quad (3.25)$$

$$\Delta Y/\Delta G = 1/(1 - c + m) \quad (3.25a)$$

What is the value of such multipliers? For instance, if in equation (3.25) c is equal to 0.75, the multiplier will be equal to $1/(1-0.75) = 4$ and so generate a rise in national income Y four times greater than the increase in G. Obviously, the greater c is, the higher the increase in the equilibrium level of national income in relation to the increase in public expenditure. As $m > 0$, the open economy Keynesian multiplier is smaller, because part of the fiscal stimulus generates an increase in imports, which have no effect on domestic production and employment. For instance, if $m = 0.25$ (which means that imports are a quarter of national income) the value of the multiplier will be equal to $1/(1-0.75+0.25) = 2$. This means that the impact on production, national income, and employment will be smaller than in a closed economy.[3]

With the algebraic method, we add to the constant (the autonomous component of aggregate demand in (3.23) and (3.23a) the increase of public expenditure ΔG which will raise the equilibrium level of income by $\Delta Y = 1/(1-c)\,\Delta G$ in a closed economy, and $\Delta Y = 1/(1-c+m)\,\Delta G$ in an open economy, while the decline in unemployment (U) will be equal to $[1/(1-c)\,\Delta G]/\pi$ and to $[1/(1-c+m)\,\Delta G]/\pi$.

Effect of a tax cut

The policymaker may decide to support the level of income and employment by means of tax cuts rather than by means of an increase in public expenditure (see Table 3.3). Equations (3.22) and (3.22a) show that a tax cut generates, for any level of income Y, a rise in consumption and planned expenditure equal to $c\Delta T$ (Figure 3.5). The decrease in tax revenue will be financed by the government in ways that are discussed later on.

In this case, the initial surge in consumption by $c\Delta T$ provokes an income increase of an equal amount which causes a further rise in consumption equal to $c^2\Delta T$ and so on, so

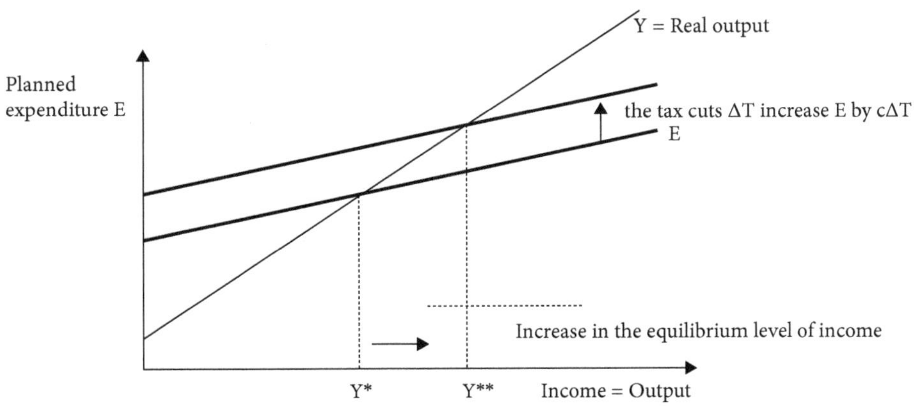

Figure 3.5 Keynesian cross, tax cuts, and the multiplier

[3] This explains the recurrent protectionist appeals to 'buy American', 'buy Spanish', etc. issued by governments of countries which fear that the effect of a domestic fiscal stimulus leaks out via an increase in imports. Because of this, an increase of protectionist practices occurred on a massive scale in the aftermath of the Great Depression of 1929 – 36.

that the overall income rise will be equal to $\Delta Y = c\Delta T + c^2\Delta T + c^3\Delta T + \ldots c^n\Delta T = \Delta T(c + c^2 + \ldots c^n) = \Delta T\, c/(1 - c)$, from which we infer that the Keynesian multiplier of tax cuts in a closed economy (as in (3.26)) and by analogy (simple demonstration omitted) in open economy (as in (3.26a)) are equal to:

$$\Delta Y / -\Delta T = c/(1 - c) \tag{3.26}$$

$$\Delta Y / -\Delta T = c/(1 - c + m) \tag{3.26a}$$

If, as in the case of a closed economy, $c = 0.75$, the Keynesian multiplier $\Delta Y/\Delta T$ is equal to $0.75/(1 - 0.75) = 3$, from which it follows that—since c is constant—$\Delta Y/\Delta T < \Delta Y/\Delta G$, as $c\,(1 - c) < 1/(1 - c)$.[5] In the case of an open economy, as discussed above ($c = 0.75$, $m = 0.25$), the Keynesian multiplier of tax cuts is $\Delta Y/\Delta T = 0.75/(1 - 0.75 + 0.25) = 1.5$.

Let us summarize in Table 3.2 the value of the Keynesian multipliers due to an increase in public expenditure and a tax cut in a closed and open economy. We add, for the sake of completeness, the case in which the consumption function is written as $C = c(1 - t)\,Y$, in which private consumption is the product of the marginal propensity to consume c multiplied by the after-tax disposable income $(1 - t)Y$ instead of the gross disposable income Y (a decision that reduces the planned expenditure and the multiplicative effect of budget operations).

Table 3.2 Comparison between the Keynesian multipliers of ΔG and $-\Delta T$ in a closed and open economy, with two alternative specifications of taxation

	Closed Economy		**Open economy (consumption function with fixed taxes T*)**		**Open economy (consumption function with taxes proportional to Y : $T = (1 - t)\,Y$**
$\Delta Y/\Delta G$	$1/(1 - c)$	>	$1/(1 - c + m)$	>	$1/[1 - c\,(1 - t) + m]$
	∨		∨		∨
$\Delta Y/-\Delta T$	$c/(1 - c)$	>	$c/(1 - c + m)$	>	$c/[1 - c\,(1 - t) + m]$

Table 3.2 summarizes the values of the Keynesian multipliers in cases of fiscal expansion and tax cuts in both closed and open economies and provides a comparison of their size. As for the values of c, m, and t, their range of variation is generally the following: $c = 0.6 - 0.9$; $m = 0.1 - 0.6$ (the smaller an economy, the higher its m; extreme cases tend to be re-exporting economies such as Hong-Kong and Singapore where $m = 2$, but in these examples a rise in M is accompanied by a rise of X, which was instead taken as constant in the prior model); $t = .01 - 0.2$ where t is the income tax rate.

[4] $(c + c^2 + \ldots c^n)$ is an arithmetic sequence with initial value and rate of increase c, the sum of which is equal to $c/(1 - c)$.

[5] This condition is always validated empirically given that $(0 < c < 1)$, except for the estimations of c inspired by life-cycle consumption theory (see in Section 2.1 the subsection 'A general neoclassical formulation of the consumption function') which includes wealth among the determinants of consumption. As a result, for instance, in the United States c reached the value of 1.03 during the 1990s. This violation of the received theory can be explained on the basis of the accounting rules used in the computation of disposable income (Y), which does not normally include the capital gains, unless these are realized. If, in contrast, the disposable income also includes the unrealized capital gains, then condition $0 < c < 1$ would not be necessarily verified.

Conditions for the success of an expansionary fiscal policy

A first condition for the success of an expansionary fiscal policy concerns the size of the parameters c, m, and t that determine the value of the Keynesian multiplier. The *ex ante* analysis of their values helps to inform the policymaker about the potential effect of a fiscal expansion or tax cut. For instance, in the case of an open economy with taxes expressed as a function of income, the condition for the success of an increase in public spending (i.e. that the level of income rises more than the fiscal stimulus) is as follows:

$$1/[1 - c(1 - t) + m] > 1 \tag{3.27}$$

$$1 > 1 - c(1 - t) + m \quad \text{that can be reduced to} \quad c(1 - t) > m$$

Condition (3.27) shows that the success of an increase in public expenditure depends on the fact that the marginal propensity to consume net of the income tax rate must be greater than the import coefficient. This condition may not be met in an economy with a medium-low c (0.7), high income taxes (0.4), and strong international trade integration ($m = 0.5$). In this case, condition (3.27) would not be verified and the Keynesian multiplier would be equal to 0.87, which means that the increase in national income Y would be less than the fiscal stimulus. This is because an important part of the latter would be absorbed by taxes and imports that displace an increase in domestic production. This is not uncommon in developing countries where there are no domestic substitutes for several imported goods, leading in this way to the paradoxical result that—as noted—the equilibrium level of income rises by less than the value of the fiscal stimulus.

A second condition for the success of an expansionary fiscal policy is that the increase in planned expenditure can be satisfied with existing but underutilized domestic production factors such as labour, equipment, and intermediate inputs. For instance, the fiscal stimulus may raise labour demand (LD) in this way causing a fall in the unemployment rate U below the NAIRU (the non-accelerating inflation rate of unemployment—estimated in the United States at around 4.5 per cent). As suggested by the Phillips curve, a decline of unemployment below such a natural rate may cause an increase in nominal wages and inflation. In this regard, the expectations about future increases in wages and incomes play an important role in determining future inflation. But, how do inflation expectations form? Most are based on rational expectations. One talks in this case of a prolongation of the Phillips curve based on rational expectations (Besley 1993).

The same phenomenon may occur if the under-utilization rate of the capital stock falls below 10–15 per cent (a threshold similar to the NAIRU for equipment and machinery), or if there are—as frequently observed in developing countries—supply bottlenecks in key sectors such as steel, glass, cement, and other intermediate inputs. These materials originate from sectors where production takes place in very large plants, so that the investment function is strongly nonlinear, a fact that entails that—once full capacity utilization of the existing plants is reached—it is impossible to increase output by only moderate amounts. In developing countries, the same problem also arises in terms of the ability to import essential intermediate inputs for the domestic production. In such cases, fiscal expansion leads to the expected higher equilibrium income only if the level of foreign reserves is high enough and, in any case, if it is higher than the canonical alarm threshold of ninety days of

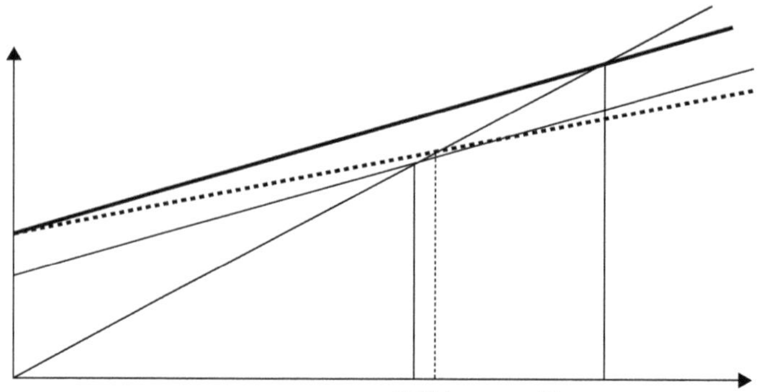

Figure 3.6 Keynesian cross: impact of a fiscal expansion accompanied by a drop in the marginal propensity to consume

imports. This will allow the additional imports—made necessary by the fiscal stimulus—to be paid for. If the currency reserves are lower than such a threshold, the central bank may start rationing access to foreign exchange. Whenever these four above conditions are not met, a fiscal stimulus may generate an increase in inflation or a worsening of the trade balance.

Another precondition for the success of fiscal expansion, is that the marginal propensity to consume, c, does not decline and the import coefficient, m, does not increase. This requires that the policy process be represented by a top-down interaction between the policymaker and the consumers, entrepreneurs, and other agents whose behaviours are not modified by the introduction of new measures. However, success of the fiscal policy is not assured in cases where there is strategic interaction between the policymaker and the agents, who may change their behaviour in response to the introduction of new measures. For instance—as observed in Japan in the 1990s—an increase in public expenditure, meant to stimulate a stagnant economy, generated a decline of the marginal propensity to consume, c. Indeed, households increased their precautionary savings to cover possible future income/asset losses caused by the default of the domestic banks which had accumulated large non-performing loans due to the puncturing of a large speculative bubble in the real estate sector. Figure 3.6 shows that—under such circumstances—an increase in public expenditure ΔG does not raise the equilibrium level of income to Y_2 but only to Y_2' owing to a decline of c.

Another condition for the success of a fiscal stimulus concerns its effect on the macro balances. This depends *inter alia* on the way the short-term budget deficit entailed by the fiscal expansion is financed, that is, via monetary emissions, the issuing of state bonds, or international borrowing. In the first case, beyond a tolerable threshold of 2–3 per cent of GDP (Agénor and Montiel, 1998), the benefits of raising public spending may be eroded by a rise in inflation which—beyond a given threshold—harms growth. If the budget deficit is financed with the issuance of treasury bonds, the rise in public debt/GDP may be offset by a GDP growth acceleration and a rise in tax revenue. This is due to the surge in growth and the positive medium-term effect of improved human capital and infrastructure, with the effect that the budget deficit and public debt/GDP ratio may not rise. In this case, the fiscal expansion finances itself. Yet, if growth does not accelerate enough over the medium term (due to the low quality of public spending, lack of complementary inputs, or a worsening of the global economy) a debt-financed increase in public spending may generate problems of medium-term growth sustainability and intergenerational equity. Indeed, if the public debt/GDP ratio rises beyond a sustainable level, the government may be forced to cut public spending in the future or raise taxes to cover mounting debt servicing costs. Such Ricardian equivalence, rediscovered by Barro, is, however, rarely verified empirically. Finally, covering the deficit with foreign loans denominated in hard currency may be risky, as it exposes a country to possible rises in the dollar interest rate and spread for country risk as well as to a possible devaluation of the domestic currency. Such a scenario has often been associated with financial crises (see Chapter 10 for more details).

Differences in doctrinal orientation among scholars and policymakers also affect the likelihood of the adoption of expansionary fiscal policies during recessions. Since the late 1990s, the austerity school has opposed fiscal expansion during recessions based on four theoretical arguments. The first is the conviction that fiscal contraction can be expansionary (see Giavazzi and Pagano, 1996, cited in Nuti, 2014). Their paper argues on the basis of a panel of OECD national data that closing the budget deficit via higher taxes and/or lower expenditure could be expansionary, especially if the tightening consisted of spending cuts. These would trigger an increase in private consumption within one year thanks to the promotion of private sector-led growth, increasing confidence, lowering borrowing costs, and a weaker currency. A second related argument is that, with fiscal consolidation, government expenditure would no longer crowd out private investment via an increase in interest rates on state bonds leading to a surge in interest rates on private loans., In addition, Barro-type Ricardian equivalence between government expenditure and future higher taxes is also invoked, although there is very little empirical evidence to support such a hypothesis. On this view, when government expenditure is funded by borrowing, economic agents discount the future payments of higher taxes that they anticipate will have to pay to service a future higher debt. Further support for austerity was provided by Reinhart and Rogoff (2010). On the basis of a dataset of forty-four countries spanning roughly 200 years, and including over 3,700 annual observations covering a wide range of political systems, institutions, and exchange rate arrangements, these authors found that the relationship between government debt and real GDP growth was weak for debt/GDP ratios below 90 per cent. Above that level, median growth rates fell by 1 per cent, and average growth by considerably more.

However, the idea of expansionary fiscal contraction has been subjected to many criticisms on both theoretical and empirical grounds (see Nuti 2014 for details). The IMF (2010), for instance, found that austerity (also referred to as fiscal consolidation) typically reduces output and raises unemployment in the short term, especially if it occurs simultaneously across many countries. In addition, Ostry et al. (2016) argue that it is difficult to see whether fiscal consolidation produces the hoped for results in terms of growth, while it is clear that it is associated with an increase in inequality that these authors claim has a negative effect on growth. In turn, the Reinhart and Rogoff idea of a critical 90 per cent threshold of the debt/GDP ratio was criticized by Irons and Bivens (2010), who argued that causation runs from slow growth to debt accumulation, and not vice versa. Meanwhile, in replicating the analysis of Reinhart and Rogoff (2010), using the full set of original data, Herndon et al. (2013) found that such results depend on the selective exclusion of countries such Australia, Nez Zealand, and Canada. In the post-World War II period, these three countries recorded high GDP growth despite a very high debt/GDP ratio. When these countries were included in the sample, the average real GDP growth rate for countries with a public debt/GDP ratio of over 90 per cent was actually 2.2 per cent, and not 0.1 per cent.

In recent years, whether and for how long a fiscal stimulus should be introduced to sustain the equilibrium level of income during a crisis has still been hotly debated in countries affected by the sub-prime and sovereign debt crises which began in 2007 and lasted at least until 2015. As noted, the Keynesian school argues that, if well designed (that is, if they entail an increase in productive investments), the fiscal stimulus and an accommodating monetary policy can raise GDP and tax revenue while keeping the budget deficit and debt/GDP ratio in check. A comparison between the fiscal and monetary policies followed between 2008 and 2014 in the United States (where Keynesian policies dominated) and the European Union (which adopted an austerity stance) shows more favourable results in the former than in the latter.

Besides impacting long-term growth (except if only unproductive expenditures are cut), over the short term a fiscal contraction also causes a short-term downward shift in aggregate demand and the equilibrium level of income, and a rise in unemployment. Furthermore, while the spread may go down because of the lower budget deficit, the debt/GDP ratio may increase due to the decline in GDP, while the decline in revenue implied by the contraction often widened the budget deficit. The extent of the GDP decline due to public expenditure cuts and tax increases is another issue of contention. The Keynesian multipliers discussed above (Table 3.3) should work with equal intensity during expansions and contractions, only their sign is opposite.[6] But, in practice, the components of the Keynesian multiplier (c, t, m) as well as other factors (political credibility, the evaluation of rating agencies, and the market sentiment about the reforms being carried out) that affect their levels vary over the business cycle, and can be greater in periods of recession than periods of expansion.

A turning point in the discussion on fiscal consolidation has emerged following the recent upward revision of the magnitude of fiscal multipliers during consolidation. Blanchard and Leigh (2013) recognized that the recessionary effect of the fiscal cuts recommended by the IMF in 2010–12 (the phase of austerity that followed the IMF 2009 expansionary stance) was underestimated because of the low negative value predicted for the fiscal multipliers. In their words (see their abstract):

> We find that, in advanced economies, stronger planned fiscal consolidation has been associated with lower growth than expected, with the relation being particularly strong, both statistically and economically, early in the crisis. A natural interpretation is that [the negative] fiscal multipliers were substantially higher than implicitly assumed by forecasters. The weaker relation in more recent years may reflect in part learning by forecasters and in part smaller multipliers than in the early years of the crisis.
>
> (Blanchard and Leigh, 2013, abstract)

[6] These conclusions apply in Keynesian models, but not in neo-Keynesian ones in which a fiscal stimulus is offset by a drop in private investment due to the'crowding out effect' of the issuing of state bonds at high interest rates needed to finance the fiscal expansion. The values of the multipliers depends therefore on the specification of the model used.

With higher than expected negative fiscal multipliers during fiscal consolidation, the developing countries and some developed ones (Greece *in primis*) had to put up with sharp deflationary policies that lowered aggregate demand, investment, consumption, and revenue generation further than originally predicted. The result was that the budget deficits widened again, as trying to achieve an illusory fiscal adjustment meant that various rounds of fiscal cuts that severely depressed the economy had to be implemented (for more details see Chapters 16 and 18).

During the recession of 2008–09 fiscal policy varied widely across countries, partly because of differences in initial debt/GDP ratios, and partly due to differences in the doctrinal orientations of the incumbent governments. In any case, the majority of governments adopted expansionary policies which, unsurprisingly, raised public debt/GDP ratios. In Ireland this ratio grew by some 30 points in just a year. As one can see from Table 3.3, during 2009–10 Italy, Germany, UK, and Japan introduced modest fiscal stimuli while the opposite was true in the United States, Argentina, Russia, and, especially, China and South Korea. The fiscal mix between tax cuts and increased spending also varied greatly. In contrast, the second phase of the crisis—2010–2013/2014—saw a dominance of austerity policies in the European Union which lead to a decline in domestic aggregate demand and GDP. Only the countries whose exports grew rapidly were able to sustain a positive, if modest, GDP growth.

Table 3.3 Extent of fiscal stimulus in selected countries during the crisis of 2008–2009

Country	Total fiscal stimulus (% of GDP)	Tax cut share(%)	Spending share (%)
Italy	0.3	33.3	66.7
Germany	1.4	68.0	32.0
United Kingdom	1.5	56.0	44.0
Japan	2.3	30.0	70.0
United States	5.7	36.5	63.5
Argentina	6.0	8.5	91.5
Russian Federation	6.4	31.3	68.7
Korea, Republic	10.2	2.9	97.1
China	13.1	0.0	100.0

Source: UNCTAD (2011).

3.5 The IS-LM Model

The Keynesian cross model discussed in this chapter illustrates the formation of the equilibrium level of income focusing on the goods market while neglecting the money market, disregarding in particular the level of the interest rate r. The IS-LM model solves this problem by attempting to determine the level of income that ensures a simultaneous equilibrium on the goods and money markets. The model assumes fixed prices and a closed economy.

The goods market and the derivation of the IS (investment-saving) schedule

The analysis of the Keynesian cross assumed that the planned investments are fixed. However, this is not a realistic hypothesis given that beyond the autonomous investment I_0, investments

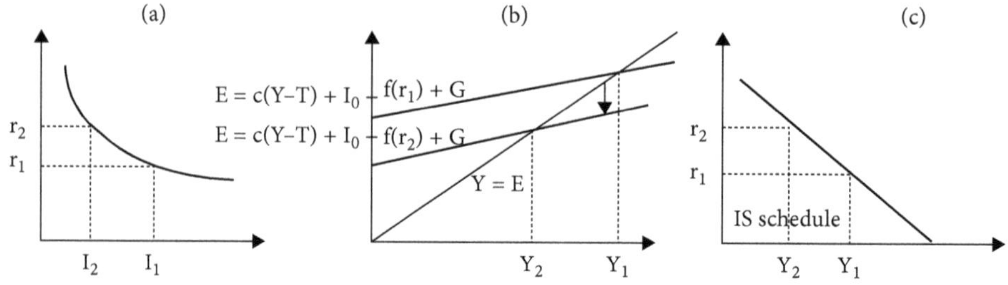

Figure 3.7 Derivation of the IS schedule: relationship between r, I and Y

depend on the interest rate r (see Chapter 1 and Figure 3.7(a)). We can therefore write that $I = f(I_0, r)$. From this it follows that a change in the interest rate affects the level of investments and, thus, of the planned expenditure.

Such a modification causes a change in the income level Y. For instance, let us suppose that the interest rate rises from r_1 to r_2. In this case—as shown by Figure 3.7a, beyond the autonomous component I_0, investments diminish from I_1 to I_2. This means that the planned expenditure will fall (as shown in Figure 3.7b) from $[c(Y - T^*) + I_0 + f(r_1) + G^*]$ to $[c(Y - T^*) + I_0 + f(r_2) + G^*]$ and that the income level drops from Y_1 to Y_2. This relation is summarized in Figure 3.7c where—given a fixed public expenditure G—the IS illustrates the relation between interest rate and equilibrium income, Y, based on the investment function and the Keynesian cross. Thus, the IS represents the equilibrium relation between interest rate and income level.[7]

Impact of fiscal policy on the IS schedule

We now examine the impact on the IS schedule of a fiscal policy that raises public expenditure by ΔG or cuts taxes by ΔT. For any given interest rate r, an increase of G pushes up the planned expenditure schedule and leads to a higher income level Y, which means that—*ceteris paribus*—the IS schedule shifts to the right. The same occurs less markedly if the fiscal policy consists of tax cuts of the same amount. In algebraic terms (see footnote 7), an increase ΔG or tax cut ΔT raise the constant term of the IS without affecting its slope, thus causing a rightward shift of the IS. Symmetrically, the IS shifts leftward whenever public expenditure is cut or taxes raised.

[7] The IS schedule can also be derived in algebraic terms. Let us start from the Keynesian cross in which we have, as usual, the two equations E = Y and E = planned expenditure in which beyond the 'autonomous component' I_0, investments are a negative function h of r, that is, $E = c(Y - T^*) + I_0 - hr + G^*$. By equalizing the two above relations one obtains $Y = c(Y - T^*) + I_0 - hr + G^*$, which can be rewritten as $r = (G^* + I_0 - cT^*)/h - [(1-c)/h]\,Y$, i.e. the closed economy IS. In an open economy one has $Y = c(Y - T^*) + I_0 - hr + G^* + NX\,e^{nc/\$}$ where NX are the net exports in dollars and $e^{nc/\$}$ the exchange rate, i.e. the amount of national currency needed to buy one dollar. In the two-dimensional plane (r,Y) this relation becomes $r = (G^* + I_0 - cT + NX\,e^{nc/\$})/h - [(1-c)/h]\,Y$, which is the open economy IS.

The money market and the derivation of the LM schedule

The LM (liquidity-money) schedule is derived from the equilibrium in the money market. The theory of liquidity preference constitutes the basis of such relation. Let us consider first the demand for money, then the money supply and finally the equilibrium in the money market. As discussed in Section 3.3, the economic agents show a clear preference for liquidity, as they need cash for current transactions, to insure themselves against the uncertainty of future outlays, to avoid the high costs of transforming non-liquid assets into liquid assets in case of illiquidity, and to take advantage of new speculative investment opportunities. Holding large liquid money balances, however, entails an opportunity costs equal to the forgone interest received by depositing such monies in an interest-bearing account. The interest rate thus measures the opportunity cost borne by the agents to keep the financial assets in liquid form. Obviously, if the interest rate rises, the opportunity cost will rise and the demand for money will fall. The opposite occurs if the interest rate falls. One can thus write the function of demand for real money (nominal money divided by the CPI) as follows:

$$MD/P = f(r) \tag{3.28}$$

In turn, the real money supply (MS/P) depends on decisions of the central bank about the nominal money supply (MS) and the appropriateness of the price level P, which in this model is assumed to be fixed. This means that nominal and real money supply remain constant if the interest rate varies. Figure 3.8 describes real money demand and supply as a function of r.

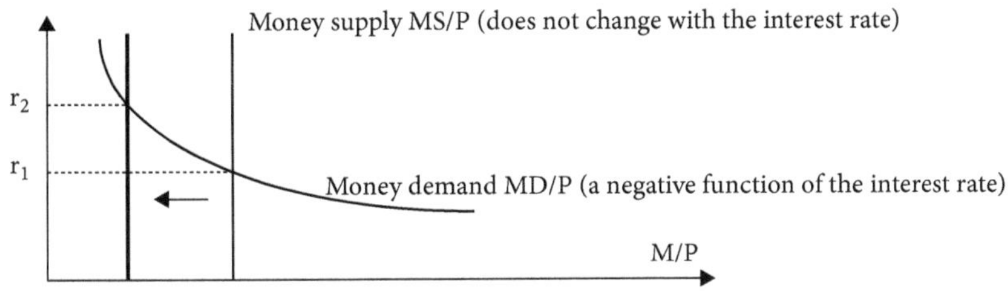

Figure 3.8 Real money demand and supply and the interest rate

In Figure 3.8, the money market equilibrium is found in the correspondence of the nominal interest rate r_1. However, if the central bank reduces money supply[8] (corresponding to a leftward shift of MS/P), the nominal interest rate rises to r_2.

[8] Money supply is given by the monetary base H multiplied by the money multiplier mm. There are five ways to expand the monetary base H: (a) printing money (now forbidden in most countries; yet, until 1993 the Bank of Italy was allowed to monetize up to 14 per cent of the budget deficit of the government by crediting its current account); (b) voluntary or compulsory purchases by the central bank of new issues of state bonds; (c) open market operations, that is, central bank purchases of bonds on the secondary market, injecting in this way liquidity into the economy while increasing its bonds portfolio. In recent years, this operation, named quantitative easing, has been applied on a massive scale in the United States and the European Union; (d) cash advances by the central bank to commercial banks against promissory notes (or bonds) given as guarantee; (e) money creation from abroad. This occurs when the central bank purchases foreign exchange in the currency market (in exchange for domestic currency), or converts into domestic currency (via the commercial banks and the Foreign Exchange Bureau) the

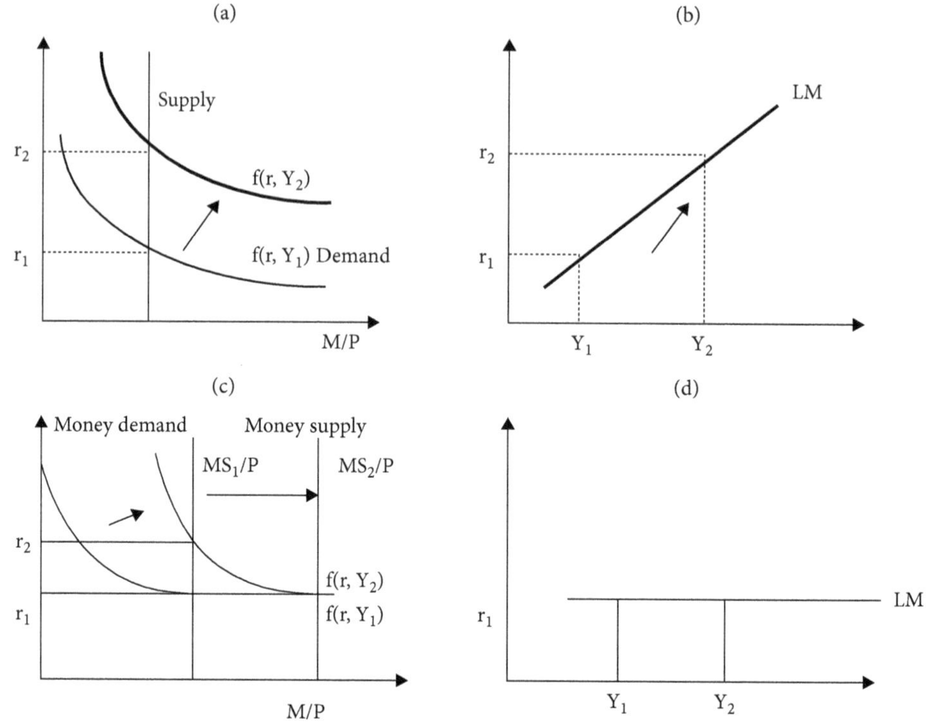

Figure 3.9 Derivation of the LM schedule due to an increase in the income level

Let us examine now what happens to the interest rate when the level of income rises, a change that increases the demand for money. Indeed, if the income level rises from Y_1 to Y_2, there will be an increase in the volume of transactions economic agents carry out, and therefore their demand for money will rise. This raises the interest rate for any given level of money supply as shown by Figure 3.9a.

The LM schedule (Figure 3.9b) summarizes the relationship that exists between the income level, demand for money, and the interest rate. Each point on this schedule represents the equilibrium on the market for real money balances, which occurs when the money supply M/P equals the demand for money (Figure 3.9a). Given that the demand for money can be written as $MD = l_0 + l_1Y - l_2r$, and that money supply MS/P is determined by the exogenous decisions of the central bank, then in equilibrium the LM can be written as $MS/P = l_0 + l_1Y - l_2r$ which can be transformed into $r = [l_0 - MS/P]/l_2 + [l_1/l_2]Y$.

However, it is possible that—given an increase in the level of income—the central bank will not keep the money supply constant but will rather increase it, so as to prevent a surge in the interest rate from r_1 to r_2 (as in Figure 3.9a) that it feels may prove detrimental for the economy. In this case, the central bank raises the money supply so as to reach the

surpluses of the trade balance and capital account balance. In addition, for any given monetary base H, the central bank can increase money supply by increasing the money multiplier (mm), i.e. by lowering the compulsory reserve ratios (rr) of commercial banks at the central bank and cutting the discount rate (r_d) paid by the latter to cash their promissory notes.

desired level of the interest rate. In the extreme case (Figure 3.9c) the stock of money is increased from MS_1 to MS_2, that is, to a level that leaves the level of interest rate unchanged (Figure 3.9d), despite the increase in income from Y_1 to Y_2. The LM will therefore be flat as the interest rate remains at r_1 regardless of the shift in income from Y_1 to Y_2. This is obviously an extreme case, and it is likely that in most cases the central bank will accept some increase in the interest rate but by less than that shown in Figure 3.9b. The LM would therefore be upward sloping but in a less pronounced way than in Figure 3.9b.

Impact of monetary policy on the LM schedule

Let us suppose that the central bank decides to reduce nominal money supply from MS_1 to MS_2 and that therefore the real money supply falls from MS_1/P to MS_2/P. Figure 3.10 shows that this causes a shift of the vertical MS/P schedule to the left and a rise of r, assuming that the income level Y remains constant. Thus, given the same level of income, the interest rate will rise, and this is true for any level of Y, which means that the LM will shift upwards (or to the left). Algebraically, we can see that in the LM equation $r = [l_0 - MS/P]/l_2 + l_1/l_2 Y$ a reduction of MS/P raises the value of the constant term $[l_0 - MS/P]/l_2$ without changing the slope (l_1/l_2) of Y.

Figure 3.10 shows, therefore, that a contraction of the nominal money supply triggers a leftward shift of the LM. Symmetrically, an increase in money supply triggers a rightward shift.

Combining the IS and LM schedules in the IS-LM model

At this stage, we have developed both components of the IS-LM model that—as just described—consists of two equations representing all possible combinations of r and Y which satisfy the equilibrium conditions on the goods market (equation 3.29) and on the market for money balances (equation 3.30):

$$\text{IS:}\quad r = (G^* + I_0 - cT^*)/h - [(1 - c)/h]Y \tag{3.29}$$

$$\text{LM:}\quad r = [(l_0 - MS/P)/l_2] + (l_1/l_2)Y \tag{3.30}$$

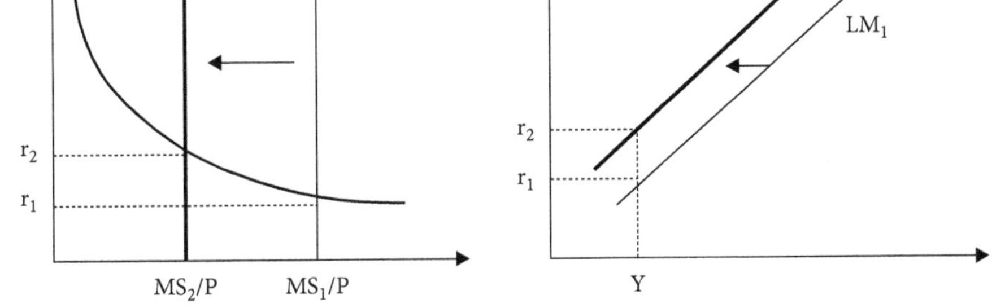

Figure 3.10 Impact of the reduction of money supply on the interest rate and the LM schedule

In this model, fiscal policy (consisting of changes in G* and/or T*) and monetary policy (proxied by shifts in MS) are exogenous, that is, modifiable by the policymaker, while the price level P is assumed to be constant. The simultaneous equilibrium in the goods and money markets is found in the correspondence of the values Y* and r* (Figure 3.11).[9]

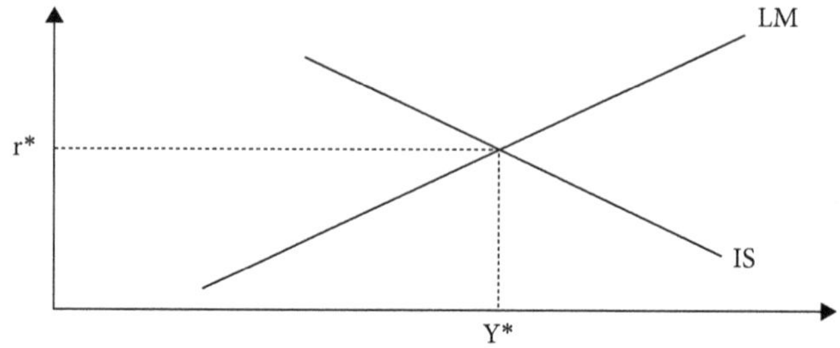

Figure 3.11 Equilibrium in the IS-LM model

This analytical framework can be used to study various kinds of problems such as the short-term fluctuations of national income (Y), or to simulate the effects of fiscal and monetary policies (via changes in G, T, and MS), or to study the effect of endogenous shocks which affect the components of aggregate demand (private consumption and investments) not controlled by the policymaker.

Impact of fiscal policy on the income level and interest rate

Let us first examine a change in fiscal policy (that is simulated on the IS). In the Keynesian cross (Figure 3.12a), a rise in public expenditure G leads to a rise of the equilibrium level of income for every level of the interest rate r. In Figure 3.12b, the IS schedule identifies all points in which Y and r are in equilibrium. For instance, before the increase in public expenditure ΔG, the equilibrium income Y_1 corresponded to the interest rate r_1. Now, given the same interest rate $r_{1,}$ the effect of a rise in public expenditure ΔG leads to an income increase of $\Delta Y = \Delta G\, 1/(1-c)$, which raises the income level to $Y_2 = Y_1 + \Delta G\, 1/(1-c)$. The entire IS schedule thus shifts from IS_1 to IS_2. This shift is described in Figure 3.12c, which also includes the LM schedule. The inclusion of the latter shows that in the IS-LM framework the rightward shift of the IS leads to an increase of the equilibrium level of income that is smaller than that identified by the shift of the IS, and to a rise of the interest rate. Indeed, the surge in Y triggered by the fiscal expansion causes an upward shift in the money demand schedule (see Figures 3.9c and 3.12c) that raises the interest rate, which in turn reduces the investment demand. A similar, if less pronounced effect, is observed for a tax cut ΔT = ΔG, with the difference that in Figure 3.12a this raises the equilibrium level of income by $c/(1-c)$ instead of $1/(1-c)$.

[9] With algebra, the equilibrium level of income Y* is obtained by equalizing the right-hand sides of equations (3.29) and (3.30) and then solving for Y. In symbols: $(G^* + I_0 - cT^*)/h - (1-c)Y^*/h = (l_0 - MS/P)/l_2 + l_1/l_2 Y^*$ that can also be written as $Y^* [l_1/l_2 + (1-c)/h] = [(G^* + I_0 - cT^*)/h - (l_0 - MS/P)/l_2]$ or $Y^* = [(G^* + I_0 - cT^*)/h - (l_0 - MS/P)/l_2]/[l_1/l_2 + (1-c)/h]$.

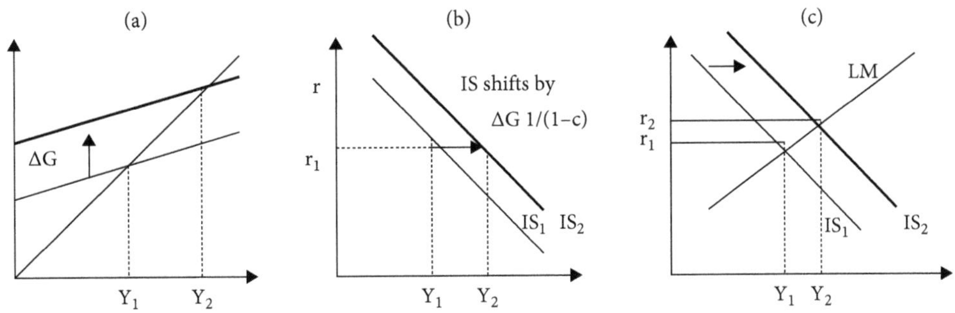

Figure 3.12 Impact of a public expenditure rise on the income level and interest rate in the IS-LM model

The algebraic solution of this policy change is even simpler. Indeed, given the initial equilibrium level of income $Y_1 = [(G^* + I_0 - cT^*)/h - (l_0 - MS/P)/l_2]/[l_1/l_2 + (1-c)/h]$, and a fiscal expansion of ΔG, the new equilibrium level of income grows to $Y_2 = [(G^* + \Delta G + I_0 - cT^*)/h - (l_0 - MS/P)/l_2]/[l_1/l_2 + (1-c)/h]$, and thus its increase is ΔY (from Y_1 to Y_2) $= [(\Delta G)/h)]/[l_1/l_2 + (1-c)/h]$.

Impact of monetary policy on the income level and interest rate

Let us examine now the effect of an increase in nominal money supply from M_1 to M_2. Given that P is assumed to be fixed, this measure will also entail an increase in the real money supply from M_1/P to M_2/P which shifts rightward and lowers the interest rate from r_1 to r_2 (Figure 3.13a). As seen above, this interest rate drop shifts the LM schedule rightwards (Figure 3.13b), given that—for every Y—the corresponding interest rate will be lower due to the increase in money supply. By combining in Figure 3.13c this rightward shift of the LM with the IS schedule (which did not move), one obtains an equilibrium level of income $Y_2 > Y_1$ and an interest rate $r_2 < r_1$. The opposite effects (a rise in the interest rate and a fall in income level) are observed in the case of a reduction of the nominal money supply.

The algebraic solution follows the approach delineated above. Indeed, given the initial income equilibrium, a monetary expansion ΔMS leads to a new equilibrium income:

$$Y_1 = \left(\frac{G^* + I_0 - cT^*}{h} - \frac{l_0 - \frac{MS}{P}}{l_2}\right) \Big/ \left(\frac{l_1}{l_2} + \frac{1-c}{h}\right) \quad (3.31)$$

$$Y_2 = \left[\frac{G^* + I_0{}^*cT^*}{h} - \left(l_0 - \frac{\frac{MS+\Delta MS}{P}}{l_2}\right)\right] \Big/ \left(\frac{l_1}{l_2} + \frac{1-c}{h}\right)$$

which increases the second term of the constant (which is however negative), so that the constant of the LM schedule declines.

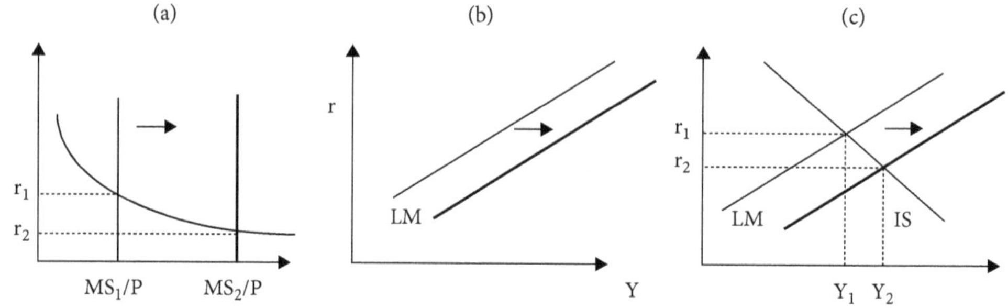

Figure 3.13 Impact of an increase in money supply in the IS-LM model

Interaction between monetary and fiscal policy

If the policymaker simultaneously introduces changes in the monetary and fiscal policies, these will mutually affect each other. Also in developing countries, monetary policy is generally in the hands of the central bank (that is more or less independent from the treasury and the prime minister),[10] while fiscal policy is formulated by the government, in particular by the ministry of finance.

Let us now suppose that the government decides to raise taxes, and examine how the income level and interest rates are affected by such a change (Figure 3.14). The tax increase reduces the level of planned expenditure and leads—given a constant LM—to a lower level of national income (Figure 3.14a) that drops from Y_1 to Y_2 while the interest rate falls from r_1 to r_2. In this case, the central bank has kept money supply unchanged, and therefore the LM also remains unchanged.

Let us now suppose that—given such a tax increase—the central bank decides to keep the interest rate at the initial level r_1 (Figure 3.14b) so as to avoid inflationary pressures. To reach this objective, it must reduce money supply by an adequate amount. Such a measure causes a leftward shift of the LM. In this way, the interest rate does not fall, but the income contraction is accentuated in relation to the prior case, that is, from Y_1 to Y_3 rather than to Y_2. In contrast, if the central bank wants to avoid the tax increase leading to a drop in the levels of income and employment, it must increase money supply, with the effect that the LM shifts to the right (Figure 3.14c). This means that a situation is reached where the income level is unchanged but the interest rate falls to r_3. Despite the lack of change in the income level, there are other important changes worth noting. The overall policy package (increase in taxes, reduction of interest rates) implies, in fact, a change in the uses of GDP. On the one side, the higher taxation of families depresses their consumption level but, on the other side, the reduction of the interest rate stimulates investment by firms.

In conclusion, the discussion in this section shows that the final impact of fiscal policy depends on the nature of the accompanying monetary policy adopted by the central bank,

[10] There are several models of central bank that are more or less independent from the political authority. During the post-World War II period, the most independent central bank has traditionally been the Bundesbank, which has been completely independent from the government as far as monetary policy is concerned. In contrast, the Bank of England has until recently been institutionally obliged to consult on monetary policy with the Chancellor of the Exchequer. The mainstream view sees in the independence of the central bank a guarantee for the development of a rational monetary policy uninfluenced by pressures of interest groups and political parties. However, this point is still hotly debated.

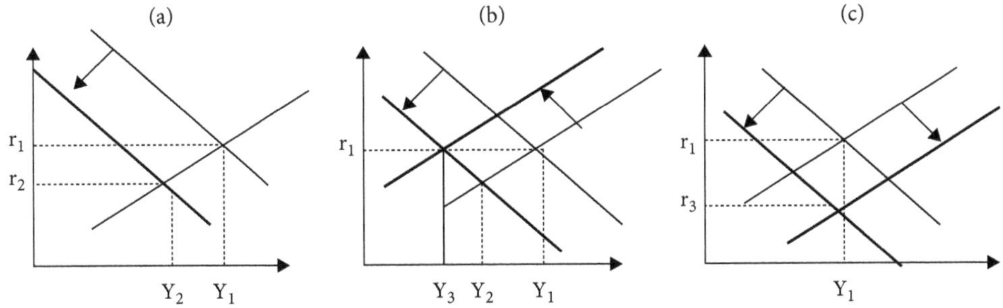

Figure 3.14 Impact of a combination of monetary and fiscal policies in the IS-LM model

that is, whether the latter keeps money supply constant (and thus leaves unchanged the interest rate), reduces it, or augments it (so as to keep constant the income level). In general terms, when assessing the impact of a policy, it is necessary to consider how this may influence the stance of other policies.

Exogenous shocks in the IS-LM model

Such shocks are not due to policy decisions but to endogenous factors that can affect the IS or the LM. Among the factors that influence the IS, there are changes in expectations that affect the components of planned expenditure, for example, sudden waves of euphoria or panic which affect private investments in equipment and housing. A panic wave can reduce the level of investments and overall planned expenditure and cause a leftward shift in the IS schedule. The opposite can occur if there is a sudden spread of optimistic expectations. In addition, private consumption can shift upward or downward following changes in expectations that will affect the marginal propensity to consume—as observed in Japan in the 1990s, and in the United States and the EU during the more recent crisis. An improvement in expectations (due for instance to the wealth effect caused by a steady rise of the stock market) tends to shift the IS schedule rightward and determine a higher equilibrium level of income. Shocks to the LM schedule can originate from endogenous changes in money demand, due for instance to the desire of households to increase their liquidity for speculative purposes. In this case, a growing demand for funds causes an upward shift of the money demand schedule, and so triggers an increase in the interest rate that generates a leftward shift of the LM, which in turn pushes up the interest rate.

Summing up, various kinds of endogenous or exogenous shocks (common in developed countries, and even more so in developing countries) lead to shifts in the IS and LM schedules and thereby help to explain short-term fluctuations in the national income. Monetary and fiscal policy can try to offset such shocks through the play of automatic stabilizers or the timely use of discretionary countervailing policies.

3.6 The AD-AS Model of Aggregate Demand and Supply

Until now, determination of the equilibrium income level has assumed that prices do not change over the short term, so that—given any change in money supply, tax rates, and public expenditure—any demand increase (decrease) transforms itself into supply increases (decreases) at the existing price level. This means neglecting inflation—that is the variation in the overall price level from one year to the next—while we know that inflation has represented—especially in the 1980s and 1990s—one of the main concerns of macroeconomists and policymakers. This is true in both developed countries and—as we shall see in Chapter 14—developing countries. It is therefore necessary to introduce inflation into the analysis of the determination of the income level over the short term, and to develop a formal model in which the level of production and the price level are simultaneously determined.

Derivation of the AD schedule from the IS-LM model

In order to draw the aggregate demand (AD) schedule, it is important to examine what happens in the IS-LM framework when a change in the price level occurs, recalling that this variable appears only in the denominator of the real money supply. In this equation, when the nominal money supply is constant at M*, an increase in the price level from P_1 to P_2 leads to a reduction of the real money supply from M^*/P_1 to M^*/P_2 and to an increase in the interest rate (Figure 3.15a). Furthermore, a rise in the price level causes a leftward shift of the LM curve from LM (P_1) to LM (P_2) because, for each income level, a lower money supply determines an increase in the interest rate. In the IS-LM model, a leftward shift of the LM curve entails a drop in the equilibrium level of income and an increase in the interest rate (see Figure 3.15b). Thus, an increase in the price level leads to a fall in the real money supply that generates an increase in the interest rate that, in turn, causes a leftward shift of the LM curve. The new LM curve intersects the IS curve in correspondence of a lower level of income Y_2. For these reasons, there is a negative relationship between the price level and the income level, and therefore the AD curve has a negative slope.

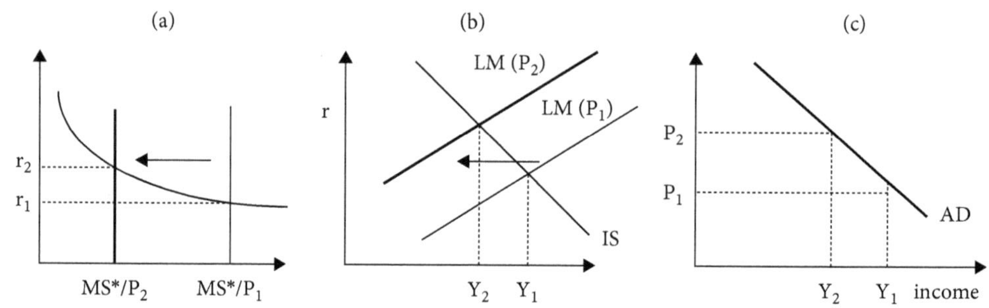

Figure 3.15 Impact of a price increase in the IS-LM model and derivation of the aggregate demand schedule AD

In summary, the AD schedule identifies the combinations of price and production levels for which there is a simultaneous equilibrium in the goods market and the money market. AD is, therefore, neither a microeconomic demand schedule that indicates, for instance, the demand for shoes at a given price, nor the aggregate planned expenditure schedule discussed at the end of Section 3.5. Algebraically, the AD schedule is obtained by setting the equilibrium between IS and LM, as shown in equation (3.31b):

$$\frac{G + I_0 - cT}{h} - \frac{1-c}{h}Y = \frac{l_0 - \frac{MS}{P}}{l_2} + \frac{l_1}{l_2}Y \tag{3.31b}$$

From this one can derive equation (3.31c), in which P is a function of Y:

$$P = \frac{1}{\frac{l_2}{MS}\left(\frac{l_0}{l_2} - \frac{G+I_0-cT}{h}\right)} + \frac{1}{\frac{l_2}{MS}\left(\frac{1-c}{h} + \frac{l_1}{l_2}\right)Y} \tag{3.31c}$$

from which it appears that an increase in Y (to be found in the denominator of the second right-hand side term) causes a fall in P, since the slope of Y, that is, $[(1-c)/h + l_1/l_2]$, is positive (given that c, h, l_1, $l_2 > 0$ and that $c < 1$).

Slope and shifts of the AD schedule

As noted, the AD schedule is negatively sloping. Let us now examine what determines its gradient.[11] This depends on the equations for the IS and LM that determine the AD and ensure equilibrium in the markets for goods and money balances for any given price level. The slope of AD depends in particular on the following parameters:

- The marginal propensity to consume of the function $C = c\ (Y - T)$ where $c > 0$. The higher the value of c, the greater the inclination of AD and the consumption multiplier, and therefore the larger the shift of the IS caused by a change in either T or G. Depending on the direction of the IS shift, different equilibrium points are reached in both the IS-LM model and the AD schedule.
- The parameters of the investment function $[I = I_0 - h\ r]$ where $h > 0$. The higher the value of h (the elasticity of the demand for investment in relation to the interest rate), the greater the variation in investment demand determined by a unitary variation of r, the flatter the IS schedule, and the steeper the AD schedule.
- The parameters of the money demand function $MD = l_2 Y - l_1 r$ (with l_1, $l_2 > 0$) indicate the extent of the variation of MD with respect to a change in Y and r. The higher the value of l_2, the steeper the slope of the AD schedule. In turn, the higher the value of l_1, the lower the money demand with respect to a unitary increase of r, the flatter the money demand curve, and the flatter the AD slope.

Thus, the inclination of AD depends on the values of c, h, l_1, and l_2. Generally speaking, it can be noted that the AD curve is flatter (a) the lower is the responsiveness of the money demand l_1 in relation to level of income Y; (b) the greater is the sensitivity h of investment demand with respect to the interest rate; (c) the greater is c and, by implication, the Keynesian multiplier; (d) the smaller is the responsiveness of money demand l_2 with respect to the interest rate.

Let us examine now what factors cause a shift of the AD schedule. As illustrated in (Figure 3.15), the AD schedule is derived from the IS-LM model, and therefore the

[11] Space limitations do not allow a longer discussion. For further details see, among others, chapters 4 and 5 of Dornbush and Fisher (1985).

factors that cause shifts in the AD consist in changes in monetary and fiscal policy (discussed above) as well as endogenous shocks that cause a shift of the IS and LM curves and alter the equilibrium level of income. For example, expansionary fiscal or monetary policies determine a rightward shift of the AD curve, while restrictive measures shift it to the left.

To conclude, one can summarize this discussion by noting that the AS-AD model provides a general theory of aggregate demand. The income level shifts arising in this model from price changes cause a shift along the aggregate demand curve, AD, while variations in the income level (keeping P constant) entail a leftward or rightward shift of the whole AD curve. Therefore, the aggregate demand schedule, AD, fluctuates in line with policy interventions affecting money supply, government spending and taxation, and endogenous shocks that influence the demand for investments and private consumption.

Derivation and shifts of the aggregate supply AS schedule

The AS schedule identifies the amount of output that firms are willing to offer for any given price level. In this sense the macro supply schedule is similar to a micro supply schedule. Thus, the higher the price of output, the greater the quantity of goods firms are willing to supply. However, this result depends on the dynamics of the prices of goods to be sold relative to the cost of production factors, in particular the cost of labour, that is, a production factor that has been in short supply for decades in developed countries.[12]

The slope of the aggregate supply (measured by its elasticity $\Delta AS/AS{:}\Delta P/P$) depends on the assumptions made about the functioning of the factors market. In the Keynesian approach, the labour market is not in equilibrium, involuntary unemployment is high, and wages are constant. Thus, an increase in labour demand does not involve any increase in wages because the labour supply schedule is infinitely elastic (that is, is parallel to the x-axis (Figure 3.16a). This means that any demand increase will be met by an equivalent rise of aggregate supply without any pressure on wages and production costs. In contrast, the neoclassical aggregate supply schedule is completely vertical (that is, it is completely rigid) and the quantity of goods supplied does not change with the level of prices. This is due to the fact that the labour market is always characterized by full-employment thanks to constant adjustments in the level of wages. Hence, since all workers are employed, when

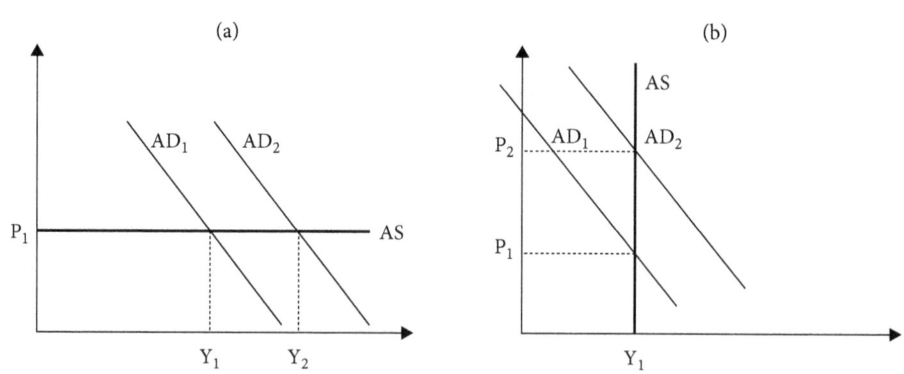

Figure 3.16 Keynesian and neoclassical aggregate supply schedules

[12] For the mathematical formulation of the supply schedule see Section 3.7.

faced with an increase in the price of final goods, firms will offer higher wages in order to attract workers already employed by other firms without being able however to achieve an overall increase in employment and output. Thus, an increase in demand will not lead to an increase in output but to proportional increases of wages and prices (see Figure 3.6b).

In the advanced countries, the functional form of the aggregate supply curve $P = f(Y)$ (its inverse is: $Y = g(P)$) takes the following form:

$$P = a\ w\ (1 + z) \tag{3.32}$$

or, considering that in equation (3.32) $w = w_{-1}\ [1 + (\varepsilon Y/Y^* - 1)]$, one obtains:

$$P = a(1 + z)w_{-1}[1 + (\varepsilon Y/Y^* - 1] \tag{3.32a}$$

where Y is the output level, Y^* is the potential output under full employment conditions (assuming a 8-hour working day and equipment utilization of 85 per cent), a is the average number of working hours per unit of output (that is, a measure of productivity), z represents the mark-up (the profit rate charged by firms over total production costs), w_{-1} is the lagged wage and ε is a parameter that reflects the trade-unions' bargaining power. This equation is suitable for developed countries and it is grounded in the Phillips curve given that the price level (inflation) depends on the tightness of the labour market (proxied by Y/Y^*) and the wage rate. In case we include explicitly the cost of intermediate inputs (raw materials, energy, and semi-finished inputs), the price per unit of output and the aggregate supply schedule AS would take the following form:

$$P = a\ w(1 + z) + \lambda P_m \tag{3.33}$$

that can also be written

$$P = \frac{a(1 + z)}{1 - \lambda p_m} w_{-1}\left[1 + \left(\frac{\varepsilon Y}{Y^*} - 1\right)\right] \tag{3.33a}$$

where $\lambda\ p_m < 1$ is the amount of imported raw materials or semi-finished goods per unit of output, P_m is their cost per unit of output and p_m (P_m/P) is the price of the primary commodities or intermediate inputs relative to the price of the final good.

Given relation (3.33a), one may ask which factors can cause a shift in the AS schedule (Figure 3.17). Holding Y^* constant, the AS shifts to the left to AS′ (implying a loss of efficiency as it produces the same amount of output Y^* at a price $P' > P$) if there is an increase of p_m (the relative price of primary commodities), z (the mark-up), or a (which signals that more hours of work are needed to produce a unit of output, implying that the productivity of labour worsens). The AS schedule shifts to the right to AS″ (which indicates an increase in efficiency) when a, z, and p_m decrease.

AD-AS equilibrium, exogenous shocks, and the impact of policy interventions

Once we have derived the AS and AD schedules, the equilibrium level of income and prices can be simultaneously determined.

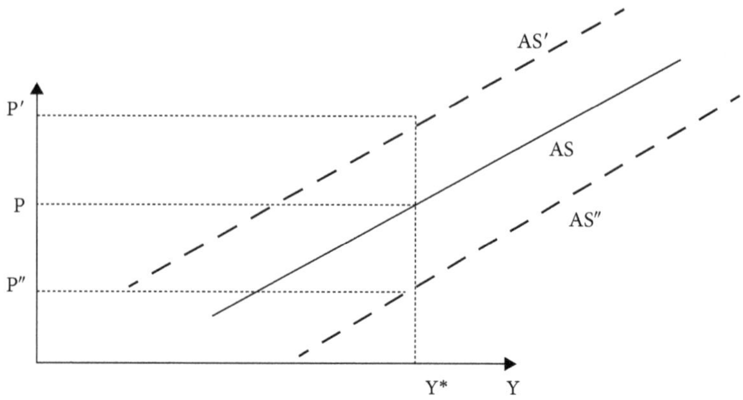

Figure 3.17 Shifts of the AS schedule

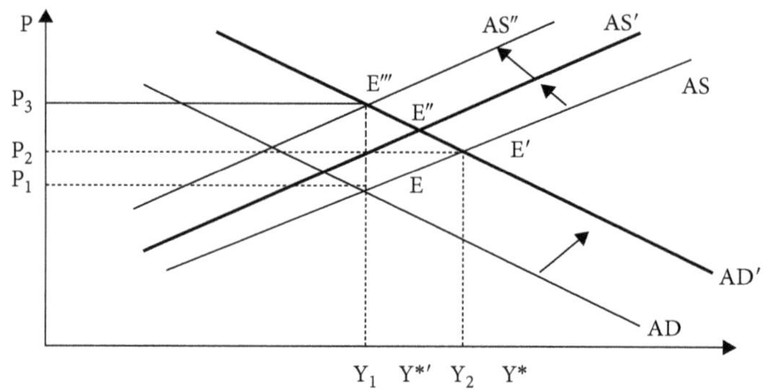

Figure 3.18 AS-AD equilibrium and shifts under different policy scenarios

In Figure 3.18, the initial equilibrium is at point E where the two schedules intersect. If the initial conditions are not in equilibrium, the usual adjustment mechanisms will drive the economy to that point. It is worth noting that the initial equilibrium level of income Y_1 may be below Y* (that is, the level of income ensuring full employment and the maximum potential output). Using this framework we can simulate the impact of supply and demand shocks on the equilibrium level of income and prices as well as determine the extent to which economic policies can mitigate the impact of negative shocks and control the inflationary impact of favourable shocks. The following three subsections consider possible policy scenarios.

Effects of an expansionary monetary policy

Suppose that the central bank adopts an expansionary monetary policy aiming at stimulating a stagnant economy, as Y_1 is below Y*. As seen above, such policy causes a rightward shift of the money supply curve, reduces interest rates, causes a rightward shift of the LM curve and hence—given the IS-LM framework and an unchanged P—a rightward shift of the AD curve to AD′ (Figure 3.18). Given the intermediate AS schedule slope depicted above (that is neither of the neoclassical or Keynesian type), this leads in the short run to a new equilibrium level E′ in which both national income and price level are higher than in the previous equilibrium, as $Y_2 > Y_1$ and $P_2 > P_1$. In the shift from E to E′, prices have risen because the expansion of output and employment have led to wage increases that are in turn transferred by firms on to the price of final goods. In this case—given the slope of the AS schedule (which has elasticities $\Delta Y/Y{:}\Delta P/P > 1$ and $\Delta P/P{:}\ \Delta Y/Y < 1$)—an expansionary monetary policy has a greater impact on the income level than on the price level.

Let us consider now what happens over the medium run. If $Y_2 < Y^*$ there are no further adjustments. But in the case where Y^* is at the level $Y^{*\prime} < Y_2$ (that is, the new level of income is higher than that of full employment), according to relation (3.31) wages will rise at a fast rate, because there is over-employment. As in the case of any other price-shock, such an accelerated increase in wages causes a leftward shift of the AS curve, which determines a new equilibrium level E″ characterized by a higher level of prices and a lower output level. In the long run, wages and prices rise further and thus the AS schedule shifts further to the left to AS″ until it reaches the initial full employment level of income, Y_1. Therefore, if the starting point is one of full employment, and if wages are flexible, in the long run an expansionary monetary policy does not produce real effects but only an increase in inflation. This does not occur if $Y_1 < Y^*$.

Effect of a decrease of autonomous demand

The starting point is $Y_1 = Y^*$. Let us suppose that private investment will be reduced as a result of a worsening of private sector expectations concerning future sales. An autonomous reduction of investment (not due to an increase of the interest rate) has the effect of reducing planned expenditure, shifting the IS curve to the left, and lowering the income and interest rate equilibrium level in the IS-LM framework. This in turn causes a leftward shift of the aggregate demand from AD to AD′ and to a new equilibrium in E′ < E (Figure 3.19) characterized by lower prices, P_2, and income level, Y_2.

This entails an increase in unemployment. But assuming wages are flexible, the rise in unemployment triggers a drop in wages. This will shift the supply curve to AS′, determining in this way a new equilibrium in E″ which is characterized by the same initial level of

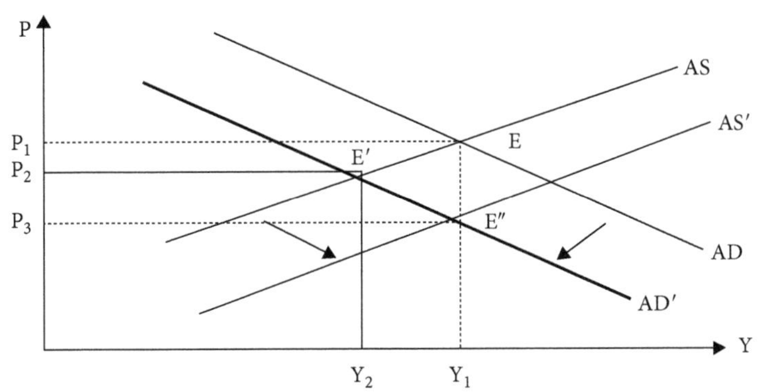

Figure 3.19 Impact of a reduction in autonomous demand in the AS-AD model

full employment income, Y_1, but lower prices, P_3. No changes occur if wages are downward inflexible and the economy remains in the equilibrium E′.

Effect of an exogenous supply shock

Let us suppose that a developing country is hit by a climatic shock (that is more common and of greater intensity than in the developed countries), or by a shock due to a sudden increase in the prices of imported goods such as energy, or by a disarticulation of the economy caused by a problematic transition to a market economy, as observed in the former communist countries of Europe during the 1990s. The immediate effect of such a shock is to increase parameter a (measuring labour productivity) and, as consequence, cause a shift of the AS schedule to the left (Figure 3.20), leading to a change in equilibrium from E to E′. The new equilibrium is characterized by a lower aggregate supply and higher prices. What happens once the shock has produced its immediate effects? If wages are downward flexible, in the long run the economy will gradually return to the initial equilibrium E, albeit at a lower wage level. If wages are downward sticky, the long-term equilibrium will remain in E′.

However, the policymaker may want to adopt accommodating monetary or fiscal policies to offset the effect of the supply shock on the price and income levels. This objective could be achieved, for example, through an expansionary public expenditure policy that would cause a rightward shift of the AD curve to the new equilibrium point E″. At this point the initial income level is restored, although at a higher price level (Figure 3.20). The solution to this dilemma (more inflation and less unemployment, or the opposite solution) varies from country to country given differences in local conditions.

However, with the introduction of neoliberal policies in the 1980s, the policy emphasis has shifted to combating inflation (with the objective of facilitating production and market exchange) and has delegated the solution of the unemployment problem to supply-side measures. Thus, if price stability is the key policy objective, the central bank may choose to introduce inflation targeting. This is a monetary policy regime by which the central bank sets an explicit inflation target (generally 2 per cent) for the medium term and announces it

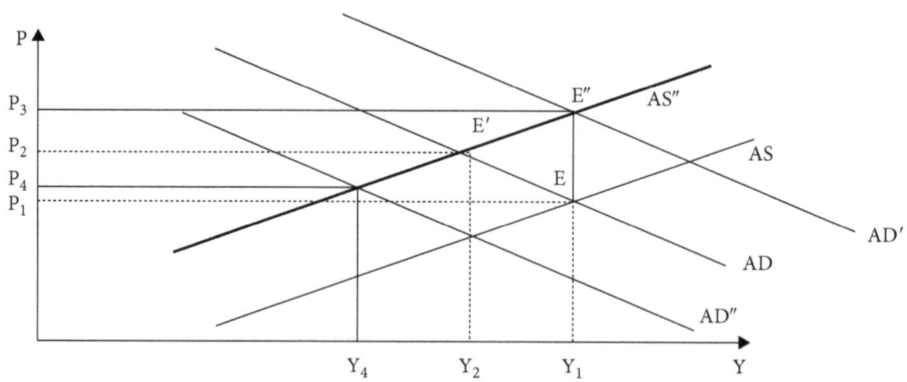

Figure 3.20 Impact of an exogenous shock and of alternative policy responses in the AS-AD model

to the public. The monetary authorities of New Zealand, Canada, and the United Kingdom have adopted this strategy since the 1990s. To reach its inflation target, the central bank raises the interest rate, based on econometric evidence of its impact on the price level. However, such a gradual increase in interest rates would, in the short term, cause a leftward shift of the AD to AD″. In the AS-AD framework this would indeed reduce inflation by depresssing aggregate demand but it would also lead to a further decline in the equilibrium level of income to Y_4 . Whether it would stimulate production cannot be captured in this framework, and this conclusion remains controversial, especially in developing countries suffering from structural inflation (see Chapter 14).

Differences of interpretation of the impact of policies when relying on a dynamic AS schedule

The impact of policy and exogenous shocks have been illustrated in this section within a framework of wage and price setting relations derived from a static AS schedule. It is, however, necessary to mention the results obtained with a dynamic AS schedule based on a Phillips curve linking the variation over time in the unemployment rate to the rate of inflation (and not to the price level). In the advanced countries, this dynamic adaptation has become necessary since the early 1960s, as the price level P has no longer declined as it did in the past during years of economic contraction (Blanchard, 2009, Figure 8.4). Indeed, inflation has become persistent, while economic agents have changed the way they form their expectations about it. Indeed, in the United States, since 1960 inflation has also risen in years of economic contraction, entailing a continuous rise in the price level P. To illustrate this situation, let us go back to relation (3.33a). We now replace the ratio between the current level of economic activity and its potential (Y/Y*) with the unemployment rate U and obtain

$$P = \frac{a(1+z)}{1-\lambda p_m} \varepsilon\, U \tag{3.33b}$$

By differentiating this expression totally over time (Blanchard, 2009, chapter 8) one obtains $\pi = (1+z)/(1-\lambda p_m) - \varepsilon u$, where π is the rate of inflation (i.e. the change in the price level P over time), u is the variation over time in the rate of unemployment, and z, λ, and p_m are, respectively, the mark-up, the amount of raw materials per unit of output, and the price of imported raw materials relative to the domestic price level. a is assumed not to change over time.

This transformation is important as it emphasizes that a policy-induced contraction will not reduce the price level (as indicated for instance in Table 14.2 for the developing countries) but may reduce its rate of increase, that is, the rate of inflation. The latter is, however, unlikely to turn into deflation. The results reported in Table 14.2 therefore have to be interpreted in light of this change of formulation of the AS. In fact, most would agree that, with the modification presented in this subsection, one should expect a decline in the rate of inflation rather than outright deflation which is what is suggested by a decline in the price level P indicated in Table 14.2 and the figures presented above. The reader should be aware of the limitations of the AS-AD model used above when inflation has become persistent and agents have modified the way they formulate their expectations about it in relation to the past.

Finally, at the end of this long discussion about the simultaneous formation of the income and price level reflecting equilibrium conditions on the money and good markets, Figure 3.21 illustrates how the different models reviewed in this chapter are logically related to each other. The IS and LM curves are respectively grounded in the Keynesian cross and the theory of preference for liquidity. In its turn, the simultaneous equilibrium IS-LM is used to derive the AD schedule which, combined with the analysis of aggregate supply, AS is used to derive the model of aggregate demand and supply AD-AS. This model is used to explain short-run income and price fluctuations due to endogenous or exogenous shocks and changes in fiscal and monetary policy.

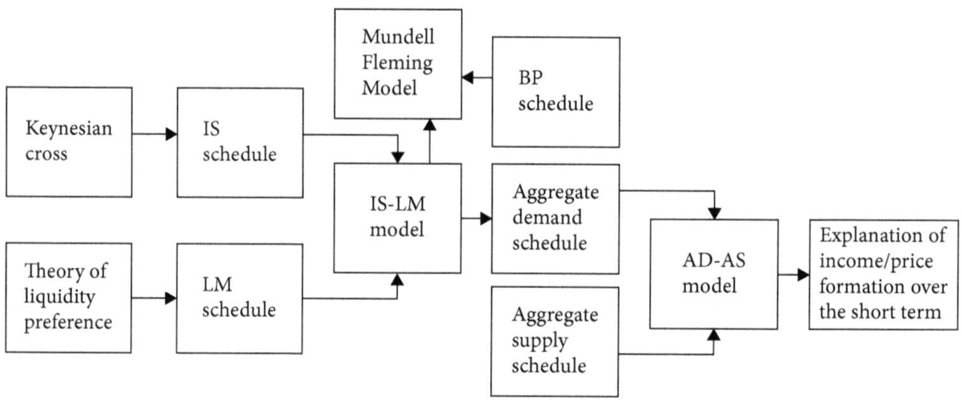

Figure 3.21 Relation between the components of the theory of income formation over the short run

3.7 The Mundell–Fleming model

The Mundell–Fleming model is an extension of the IS-LM model to the open economy. It investigates the determination of the equilibrium level of income and interest rate in the short run under open economy conditions, that is, when the commercial and financial transactions with the rest of the world significantly change the functioning of the macroeconomy, especially in small, open economies. The model also helps to explain the impact of fiscal, monetary, and exchange rate policies under open economy conditions.

While the mechanisms of income formation analysed so far allow for the simultaneous equilibrium in the good and money markets, the Mundell–Fleming model also ensures the simultaneous equilibrium of the external accounts. As in the IS-LM model, the Mundell–Fleming model assumes fixed prices. Concerning the exchange rate, the analysis is first conducted under a flexible exchange rate regime and then under a fixed exchange rate regime. In both cases, the capital account is assumed to be open. However, before introducing the Mundell–Fleming model, it is necessary to derive the balance of payments (BP) schedule that ensures the equilibrium of the external accounts.

Derivation of the BP schedule

The balance of payments (BP) is composed of the current account balance (CA) that includes the trade balance, that is the difference between exports (X) and imports (M) of goods and services, as well as the invisible balance of transactions for services, tourism, net royalties, returns on foreign investments, inflows/outflows of profits and migrant remittances, international aid, and unilateral transfers. In symbols, the current account can be represented in simplified form as CA = X – M. The BP also includes the capital account balance (KA), that is, the difference between capital inflows (KI) and capital outflows (KO). Exports are a positive function of the trading partners' income called 'income of the rest of the world' (Y_{RW}) and of a competitiveness index equal to the ratio of international to domestic prices P_f/P_d multiplied for the inverse of the exchange rate 'e' (the amount of foreign currency needed to buy one euro or other reference currency). In turn, imports (M) are a positive function of the average propensity to import m and of the level of income of the country analysed (Y), and a negative function of the competitiveness index just mentioned. To these variables, are added those exogenous flows C_0 (such as unrequited inward and outward transfers) which are independent from the economic cycle and price competitiveness.

The capital account balance equation takes the form KA = KI – KO. Capital inflows (KI) are a positive function of the domestic interest rate, r, a negative function of the foreign interest rate, r_{RW}, and a positive function of the expectations of appreciation of the exchange rate ($\Delta e^{fc/€}{}_{exp}$), namely the changes in the quantity of the foreign currency needed to buy one euro. Capital outflows (KO) depend positively on the foreign interest rate (r_{RW}), negatively on the domestic interest rate, r, and on the expected depreciation or appreciation of the exchange rate ($\Delta e^{fc/€}{}_{exp}$). Furthermore, some capital movements (K_0) depend on exogenous factors, as in the case of loans or grants from the World Bank and the United Nations and other types of unconditional balance of payments assistance.

In symbols, the CA and KA can therefore be written as follows:

$$CA = X - M = C_0 + \chi Y_{RW} - mY + \gamma(P_f/P_d.e^{fc/€}) \quad \text{where } \chi,\ m,\ \gamma > 0 \tag{3.34}$$

$$KA = KI - KO = K_0 + \alpha r - \beta r_{RW} + \lambda \Delta e^{fc/€}{}_{exp} \quad \text{where } \alpha,\ \beta,\ \lambda > 0 \tag{3.35}$$

The equilibrium condition of the BP is that CAB + KAB = 0 or combining equations (3.34) and (3.35) that

$$C_0 + \chi Y_{RW} - mY + \gamma(P_f/P_d.e^{fc/€}) + K_0 + \alpha r - \beta r_{RW} + \lambda \Delta e^{fc//€}{}_{exp} = 0$$

from which it is possible to derive relation (3.36) which links r and Y as shown below:

$$r = \frac{m}{\alpha}Y - \frac{C_0 + \chi Y_{RW} + \gamma(P_f/P_d e^{fc/€}) + K_0 - \beta r_{RW} + \lambda \Delta^{fc/€}{}_{exp}}{\alpha} \tag{3.36}$$

Equation (3.36) is the locus of all pairs of values of Y and r that allow the overall balance of payments to be in equilibrium. In this equation, the variables C_0, K_0, Y_{RW}, r_{RW}, P_f/P_d, $e^{fc/€}$, and $\Delta e^{fc/€}{}_{exp}$, are shift variables—they are included in the constant (which can be either

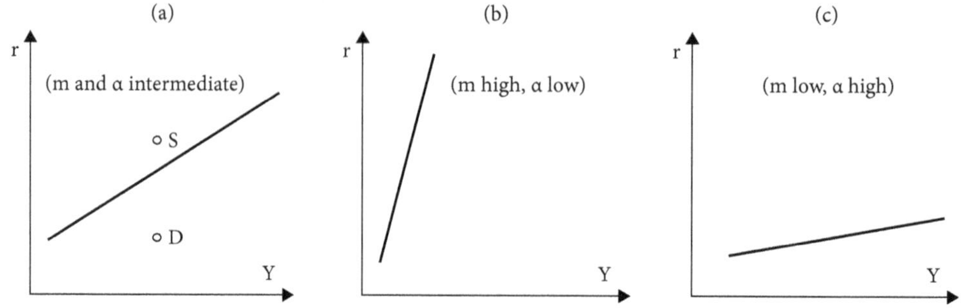

Figure 3.22 Slope of the BP schedule in relation to the import propensity and the elasticity of capital flows

positive or negative) of the linear function $r = f(Y)$ which has a positive slope since both m and $\alpha > 0$ (see Figure 3.22a). All points that do not lie on the BP line indicate an absence of equilibrium. The points above the BP line (such as, for instance, point S in Figure 3.22a) indicate there is a surplus in the overall BP. In fact, for any given income Y, r is higher than its equilibrium level that lies on the BP and will therefore generate additional inflows of capital, so that $BP > 0$. In contrast, point D identifies a deficit of the BP, as the interest rate r is lower than its equilibrium rate and does not attract enough capital to ensure balance of payments equilibrium.

In the real world, the positive relationship between Y and r is easy to explain: in fact, a surge in income Y leads to an increase of imports equal to mY (and—*ceteris paribus*—to a worsening of CA) which requires that r increases enough to generate an offsetting capital inflow in the KA to restore the equilibrium of the BP schedule. The variables that explain the slope of the BP are indicated in parts (a), (b), and (c) of Figure 3.22.

Let us discuss the two theoretically extreme cases, unobserved in reality, but useful for understanding the behaviour of the BP. When the movements of financial capital are completely insensitive to interest rates, that is, when there are administrative barriers and stiff capital controls, or when capital flows are taxed in various ways, α tends to 0, and m/α tends to ∞, so that the BP schedule is vertical. In this case, BP will have to be located at the level of income which ensures the equilibrium of the external accounts.

If, instead, capital flows are infinitely elastic with respect to the interest rate, then α tends to ∞, m/α tends to 0, and the BP is parallel to the x axis. This is the case of perfectly integrated financial markets characterized by complete information, the absence of uncertainty and no transaction costs, a situation not too dissimilar from that observed in the financial markets of the North Atlantic. In this case, the BP is positioned in a way that ensures that the domestic interest rate, r ,equals the world rate, r_{RW}, since even a small difference between them would generate a huge capital inflow or outflow.

Lastly, it is important to assess how the position of the BP varies in relation to changes in the shift variables which enter the constant term of the BP function, that is, C_0, K_0, Y_{RW}, r_{RW} , $P_f/P_d\, e^{fc//€}$, $\Delta e^{fc/€}{}_{exp}$. For this purpose we use equation (3.36) to determine analytically the movements of the BP. First, if C_0 and/or K_0 increase (due for example to an increase in aid flows or to a rise of autonomous capital inflows), the constant term decreases and the BP schedule moves to the right. Furthermore, if the income of the rest of the world increases, the BP curve of the country under analysis shifts to the right (as the constant term decreases) indicating that higher levels of income in the rest of the world generate an increase of the country's exports and therefore the possibility of reaching a higher level of income for any given rate of interest. A similar effect is observed if the exchange rate $e^{fc/€}$ depreciates (less foreign currency, fc, for one €), generating greater incentives to export, thus leading, for any level of the interest rate, to a higher income level Y. The opposite effects are observed if the interest rate of the rest of the world (r_{RW}) increases, thus causing an outflow of funds so that the constant term of equation (3.36) increases. This leads to a lower income Y (which means fewer imports and thus a rebalancing of the current account) and therefore the BP will shift to the left. Finally, an expected future appreciation of the exchange rate (that is, a positive $\Delta e^{fc/€}{}_{exp}$) also entails a rightward shift of the BP, as agents expect to obtain more fc in the future when they will re-exchange the euros purchased today at a lower fc/€ rate.

Formulation of the Mundell–Fleming model

The Mundell–Fleming model constitutes an important theoretical guide to assessing the impact of macroeconomic policies in an open economy. The basic hypothesis is that the three curves, IS-LM-BP, are expected to reach a simultaneous equilibrium in the plane (r, Y) through adjustments in r and Y. The IS-LM equilibrium, in fact, does not guarantee an equilibrium in the external accounts which will be reached either with a shift in the exchange rate (when this is flexible) or by variation in the money supply (in the case of a fixed exchange rate). The Mundell–Fleming model can be written as follows:[13]

$$Y = c(Y - T) + I(r) + G + NX(1/e^{fc/€})^{14} \quad IS \tag{3.37}$$

$$MS/P = l_0 + l_1 Y - l_2 r \quad LM \tag{3.38}$$

$$CA + KA = 0 \quad BP \tag{3.39}$$

where the three equations (3.37)–(3.39) show the equilibrium in the market for goods, money balances, and international transactions. In the Cartesian plane (Y, r) these three equations take the following analytical form:

$$r = \frac{G + I_0 - cT + NX/e^{fc/€}}{h} - \frac{1-c}{h}Y \qquad IS \tag{3.37bis}$$

$$r = [l_0 - MS/P]/l_2 + (l_1/l_2)Y \qquad LM \tag{3.38bis}$$

[13] There are several formulations of such model.

[14] It must be noted that the IS in equation (3.37) represents an extension of the IS described earlier, in which net exports denominated in foreign currency were missing. These therefore need to be converted into national currency by dividing them by the exchange rate $e^{fc/€}$. Obviously, if $e^{fc/€}$ rises (more foreign currency for one euro) the value of net exports expressed in the national currency (euro in this case) drops.

$$r = (m/a)Y - [C_0 + \chi Y_{RW} + \gamma(P_f/P_d.e^{fc/€}) + K_0 - \beta r_{RW} + \lambda \Delta e^{\$/€}{}_{exp}]/\alpha \qquad BP \qquad (3.39bis)$$

where the first is decreasing in Y and the other two are increasing in Y. The IS will be more negatively inclined the higher is the marginal propensity to consume c and the greater is the elasticity of investments, h, with respect to the interest rate. Moreover, as shown in Section 3.5, the IS schedule shifts rightward as a result of expansionary fiscal policies and currency devaluation, whereas the opposite occurs in the case of contractionary fiscal policies and exchange rate appreciation.

In its turn, the LM has a positive slope which becomes steeper for higher values of the elasticity of money demand for current transactions (l_1) and flatter for rises in the elasticity of money demand for speculative purposes (l_2). The LM shifts to the right when (a) the money supply, MS, increases (that reduces the constant term in the square parenthesis) due to an autonomous rise in money supply decided by the monetary authorities, and (b) the balance of payments has positive value, which leads to money creation from abroad. Finally, as noted above, the BP slope becomes steeper in line with increases in the propensity to import m and of the extent of restrictions to capital movements α. The shifts of the BP were illustrated above.

When these three schedules intersect at the same point, there is a simultaneous equilibrium in the goods, money, and international transactions' markets. This equilibrium is the starting point for evaluating the effects of changes in fiscal and monetary policies in an open economy.

As noted in Section 3.5, the IS-LM equilibrium is reached with endogenous changes in r (interest rate) and Y (national income). However, in the short run, the internal equilibrium does not automatically lead to external equilibrium. The initial disequilibrium generates, after some time, an adjustment through changes in money supply or exchange rate (if this is flexible) that will lead to a long-run equilibrium. For instance, in cases where there is a fixed exchange rate regime, if the BP is negative, the money supply will decrease (due to additional euro outflows to pay for the excess of imports over exports or to the outflow of domestic capital). This will determine a contraction in money supply and, as a result, an increase in the interest rate, which will reduce output and imports, thus returning back to an equilibrium point characterized by a lower level of income Y and r. If we assume instead a flexible exchange rate regime, a negative BP will lead to an exchange rate devaluation (more euros for a unit of foreign currency fc), which would be expected to improve net exports and thus lead to a rightward shift of the IS schedule.

Impact of an expansionary fiscal policy under a flexible exchange rate regime

Let us assume that the economy starts from point A in Figure 3.23 in which all three markets are in equilibrium, and that the policymaker wishes to assess the impact of an expansionary fiscal policy. The latter causes a rightward shift of the schedule IS(e) to IS′(e) leading to a new IS-LM equilibrium point in B, in which both the equilibrium level of income (Y) and the interest rate are higher. The impact on the external accounts is not uniquely determined *ex ante*: a higher Y generates more imports, while a higher r leads to

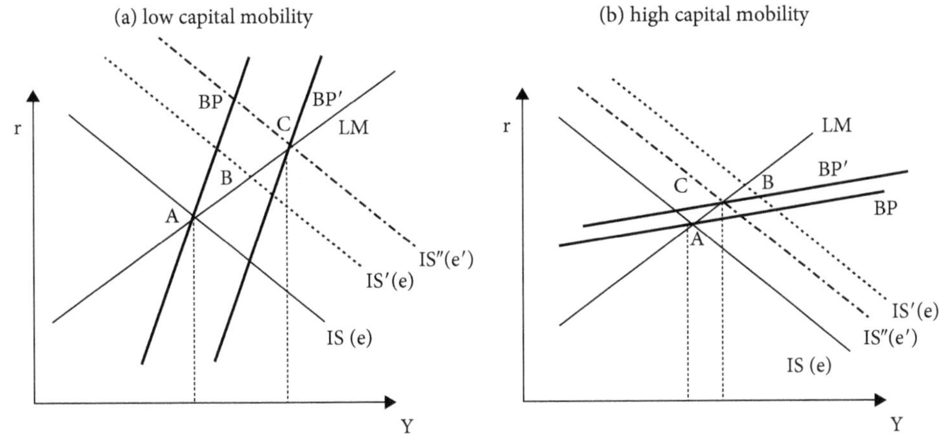

Figure 3.23 Impact of an expansionary fiscal policy under a flexible exchange rate regime in the IS-LM-BP model

an upsurge in net capital inflows and an improvement in the KA. The net effect will depend on m and the degree of international mobility of capital α (low in Figure 3.23a and high in Figure 3.23b). In the first case, the rise in imports prevails, leading to a short-run equilibrium point B located beneath the BP curve that reflects a balance of payments deficit. This will cause a currency devaluation from e to e′ that will shift the IS′(e) to the right to the IS″(e′). Because of the higher exchange rate it will also determine a rightward shift of BP, leading to a long-run equilibrium C characterized by higher values of both Y and r. Different results are obtained in cases of high capital mobility, as the effect of increased capital inflows prevails over the surge in imports determined by the increase in income.

In such a case the new equilibrium point B is located above the BP, thus corresponding to a surplus of the balance of payments. This will entail an appreciation of the exchange rate that will lead to a contraction (leftward shift) of IS′(e) to IS″(e′). Moreover, the exchange rate appreciation will determine an upward shift of the BP (as its constant term rises), reaching a new long-run equilibrium in point C. In this case, however, the impact on income (Y) and interest rate (r) is much smaller than it is when capital movements are restricted, due to the automatic correction generated by the increase of r, which attracts capitals from abroad. This situation appreciates the exchange rate, discourages exports, increases imports, and subsequently slows down the expansion of Y. In the case of complete capital mobility—when the BP schedule is completely flat—an initial fiscal expansion will move the IS to the right (to IS′) and raise Y and r. The increase in the latter, however, will generate large capital inflows which appreciate the exchange rate (a change which worsens the trade balance) and determines a shift of the IS curve to the left (IS″, that is equal to the initial IS). The BP curve does not shift because it is flat. Therefore, in this case, an expansionary fiscal policy generates only temporary effects which will vanish in the long run. In fact, with perfect international financial integration, there is only one rate r (the worldwide one) which guarantees the simultaneous equilibrium of the goods, money, and foreign exchange markets.

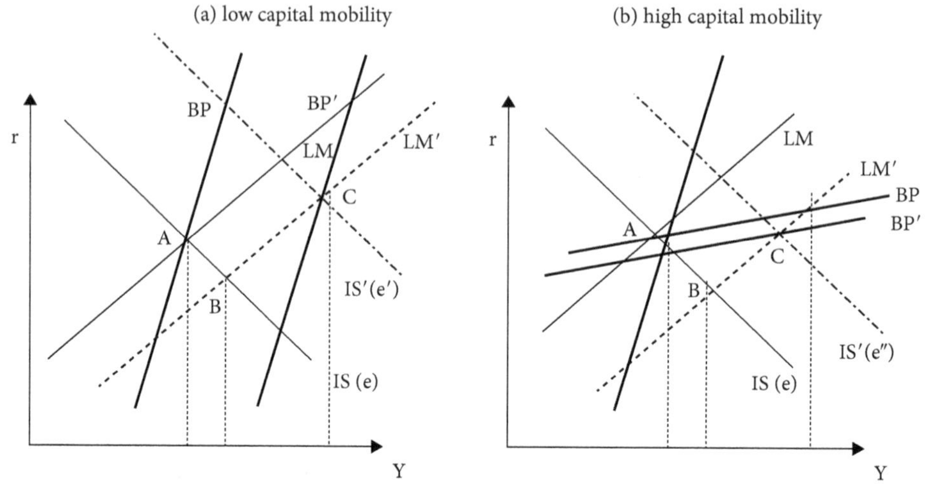

Figure 3.24 Impact of an expansionary monetary policy under a flexible exchange rate regime in the IS-LM-BP model

Effects of an expansionary monetary policy under a flexible exchange rate regime

In this case let us start again with three markets in equilibrium in point A (Figure 3.24). If capital flows are somewhat restricted, an expansionary monetary policy causes LM to shift to LM′ and the new short-term equilibrium of the economy is in point B, which is characterized by a higher level of income and a lower interest rate. This new equilibrium, however, worsens the external accounts because an increase in income will raise imports and depress net exports while the fall of r will trigger an outflow of funds. Point B is in fact below the BP schedule, thus denoting a deficit in the external accounts, in situations of both low capital mobility (Figure 3.24a) and high capital mobility (Figure 3.24b). Such an imbalance in the external accounts leads to a spontaneous exchange rate depreciation that causes the IS to shift rightward as exports rise following devaluation. Moreover, an exchange rate depreciation also causes the BP to shift rightward from BP to BP′. As a result, in cases of both low and high capital mobility, the effect of an expansionary monetary policy over the long term is to move the economy to point C, in which the income level is higher than in A and B, but with a higher level of the interest rate than at the short-term equilibrium point B.

Effects of an expansionary fiscal policy under a fixed exchange rate

Let us consider now the case of an economy with a fixed exchange rate. Although the number of countries adopting such a regime has declined (see Table 15.1 and the related discussion), there are still several nations adopting it.

In all countries with a fixed exchange rate regime, imbalances in the external accounts modify a country's monetary base. If there is a surplus, those who hold extra foreign

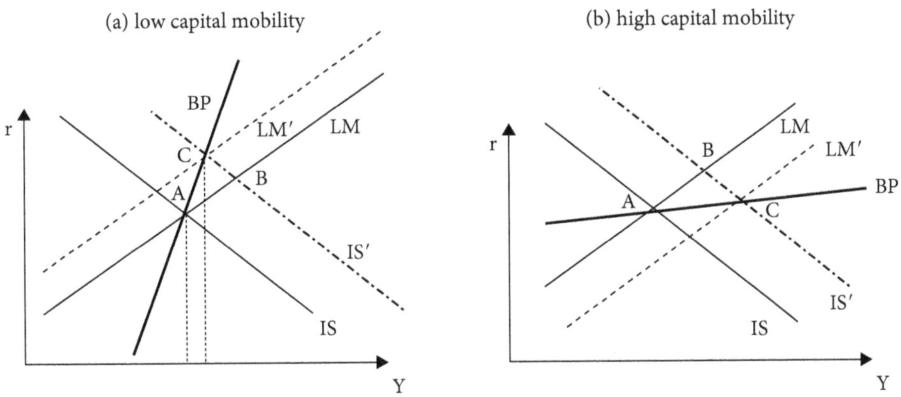

Figure 3.25 Impact of an expansionary fiscal policy under a fixed exchange rate regime in the IS-LM-BP model

currency will convert it into local currency (euros) causing an increase in the demand for euros that will raise the monetary base at a constant rate of exchange. If there is a deficit in the external accounts, the monetary base decreases because those who need to buy foreign currency (e.g. dollars)—to pay for imports or to shift their capital abroad—will supply euro to the central bank (via the commercial banks) in exchange for dollars.

Let us now assume a situation of equilibrium in point A, and imagine that the government introduces an expansionary fiscal policy. As usual, the analysis is conducted in cases of both low and high capital mobility. In the first case, an expansionary fiscal policy causes the IS to shift rightward to IS′. This leads to a short-run equilibrium in point B and income Y correspondingly increases along with the interest rate. An increase in Y, however, worsens the external accounts because it triggers an increase in imports, while the increase in r will not trigger a substantial inflow of capital due to low capital mobility (Figure 3.25a). The import effect thus prevails and the economy's new short-run equilibrium, B, is characterized by a deficit in the external accounts (B is located below the BP). This implies a contraction of the monetary base, with effects similar to those caused by a reduction in the money supply by the central bank. The result is that the LM shifts leftward to LM′ where the long-term equilibrium C is reached at an income level that is slightly higher and at an interest rate that is considerably higher than that at equilibrium A.

When capital mobility is high (Figure 3.25b), the capital inflows triggered by the increase in r prevails over the increase in imports. There will be then a surplus in the balance of payments (as point B is above the BP). This will result in an expansion of the money supply and therefore a shift of the LM to the right to LM′ until a new long-run equilibrium is found in C (Figure 3.25b). Contrary to what is observed in Figure 3.25a, this equilibrium is characterized by a substantially higher income Y and a slightly higher interest rate.

In conclusion, the effect on the equilibrium level of income of an increase in public spending under a fixed exchange rate regime is strongly expansionary if capital mobility is high but limited in a case of low capital mobility. If no capital movements are allowed, the equilibrium level of income does not change.

Effects of an expansionary monetary policy under a fixed exchange rate regime

Let us finally consider the case of an economy in which the three markets are in equilibrium in point A. An expansionary monetary policy triggers a rightward shift of the LM schedule to LM′. In cases of both high and low capital mobility, this will lead to a new equilibrium at point B where the short-term equilibrium income Y is greater than the initial level while the interest rate is lower. However, the external accounts are in deficit (B is below the BP schedule) because of both higher imports and higher capital outflows due to the decrease of r (Figure 3.26). The deficit is sustainable in the short term but leads to a gradual reduction of the monetary base, as agents sell domestic currency to buy the foreign currency needed to pay for imports and finance capital outflows. A monetary contraction in turn leads to a leftward shift of the LM (from LM′ to LM″ = LM), causing the economy to return to the initial level of equilibrium, A. Symmetrical effects occur if a restrictive monetary policy is enacted. In conclusion, this analysis shows that under a fixed exchange rate regime, a monetary policy generates some temporary effects but that is completely ineffective in the long term.

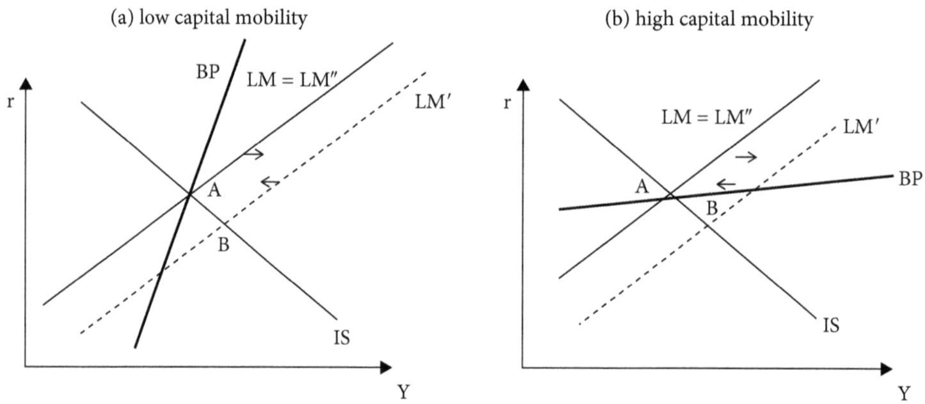

Figure 3.26 Impact of an expansionary monetary policy under a fixed exchange rate regime in the IS-LM-BP model

This chapter has focused on the models of income and interest rate formation over the short and medium term according to standard models in use in developed economies. Table 3.4 summarizes the different effects that fiscal and monetary policies have on the equilibrium level of income and the interest rate, both over the short and medium term, that is three–five years) according to the IS, LM, IS-LM, and IS-LM-BP models. As one can see the results are quite different. The choice of the appropriate analytical model is therefore crucial to determining the likely effect of fiscal and monetary policy. Obviously, more complete models, such as the IS-LM-BP offer a more comprehensive representation of the economy and may therefore be preferred to simpler models, not least because all advanced countries are open economies.

Table 3.4 Comparison of the impact of expansionary fiscal and monetary policies according to the IS, IS-LM, and IS-LM-BP models

		IS-LM-BP		IS-LM	IS
		Flexible Exchange Rate	**Fixed Exchange Rate**		
Expansionary fiscal policy	Low capital mobility	+ Y, + r short term ++ Y, ++ r long term	+ Y, + r short term + – Y, ++ r long term	+ Y + r	+ Y
	High capital mobility	+ Y, + r short term + - Y, + – r long term	+ Y, + r short term + – Y, + – r long term		
	Perfect capital mobility	+ Y, + r short term = Y, = r long term	+ Y, + r short term ++ Y, = r long term		
Expansionary monetary policy	Low capital mobility	+ Y, – r short term ++ Y, – + r long term	+ Y, – r short term = Y, = r long term	IS-LM + Y – r	LM – r
	High capital mobility	+ Y, – r short term ++ Y, – + r long term	+ Y, – r short term = Y, = r long term		
	Perfect capital mobility	+ Y, – r short term ++ Y, = r long term	+ Y,– r short term = Y, = r long term		

Note: a + and a – indicate a positive and negative change. ++ and – indicate a very positive and very negative change.

Source: Own elaboration.

3.8 Concluding Remarks

This long chapter has illustrated the models of Keynesian inspiration and those produced by the neoclassical synthesis (IS-LM, AS-AD, and IS-LM-BP) that have been used over a long period to determine the equilibrium level of income, interest rate, and price level (or rate of inflation) over the short term, and to estimate the impact of the introduction of fiscal, monetary, and exchange rate policies and of exogenous shocks. As shown in Table 3.4, the choice of model is non-trivial, as the results of the models differ both qualitatively and quantitatively. Their results also vary in relation to the numerical values and stability of the parameters of the equations that are included in these macro models. Such parameters and the specifications of the consumption, investment, and money demand functions reflect the real-life conditions of the developed countries considered. Also, as discussed in the initial part of the chapter, the success of expansionary macroeconomic policies depends on the simultaneous availability of underutilized productive resources (labour, capital stock, key intermediate inputs, foreign exchange, and so on) and the stability of the parameters of the behavioural equations included in such models. Finally, different doctrinal orientations and the influence of variables not included in these models may modify the conclusions of the impact of policy changes.

References

Agénor, P. R. and P. Montiel (1998), *Development Macroeconomics*, 2nd edn. Princeton, NJ: Princeton University Press.

Besley, T. J. (1993), 'Savings, Credit, and Insurance', in H. B. Chenery and T. N. Srinivasan (eds), *Handbook of Development Economics*, vol. 3, pp. 2123–207. Amsterdam: Elsevier.

Blanchard, O. (2009), *Macroeconomics*, 5th edition. Prentice Hall, NJ: Pearson Education Inc.

Blanchard, O. and D. Leigh (2013), 'Growth Forecast Errors and Fiscal Multipliers', *American Economic Review*, 103 (3): pp. 117–20.

Dornbush, R. and S. Fisher (1985), *Macroeconomics,* New York: McGraw-Hill Inc.

Herndon, T., M. Ash, and R. Pollin (2013), 'Does High Public Debt Consistently Stifle Economic Growth? A Critique of Reinhart and Rogoff', Working paper n. 322, Amherst MA: Political Economy Research Institute.

IMF (2010), *World Economic Outlook: Risk, Recovery and Rebalancing*. October. Washington, DC: International Monetary Fund.

Irons, J. and J. Bivens (2010), 'Government Debt and Economic Growth: Overreaching Claims of Debt "Thresholds" Suffer from Theoretical and Empirical Flaws'. Briefing Paper n.271. Washington, DC: Economic Policy Institute.

Nuti, D. M. (2014), 'Austerity versus Development', in G. W. Kolodko (ed.), *Management and Economic Policy for Development*, pp. 202–20. Hauppauge, NY: Nova Science Publishers.

Ostry, J. D., P. Loungani, and D. Furceri (2016), 'Neoliberalism: Oversold ?', *Finance and Development*, Washington, DC: International Monetary Fund.

Reinhart, C. M. and K. S. Rogoff (2010), 'Growth in a Time of Debt', *NBER Working Paper* No. 15639, Washington, DC.

Sachs, J. and F. Larrain (1993), *Macroeconomics and the Global Economy*. Upper Saddle River, NJ: Prentice-Hall.

UNCTAD (2011), *Trade and Development Report*, Geneva: UNCTAD.

Suggested further reading

Blanchard, O. and D. Leigh (2013), 'Growth Forecast Errors and Fiscal Multipliers', *American Economic Review*, 103 (3): pp. 117–20.

Ostry, J. D., P. Loungani, and D. Furceri (2016), 'Neoliberalism: Oversold?' *Finance and Development*, June 2016. Washington, DC: International Monetary Fund.

Sachs, J. and F. Larrain (1993), *Macroeconomics and the Global Economy*, Upper Saddle River, NJ: Prentice-Hall.

PART II

ECONOMIC STRUCTURE AND LONG-TERM GROWTH IN DEVELOPING COUNTRIES

4

Genesis of Development Macroeconomics and National Accounts in Developing Countries

This chapter discusses the reasons for the late attention paid to development macroeconomics in low-income countries, the data, conceptual and accounting problems encountered in measuring economic aggregates therein, the conventions and practices used to overcome these problems, and the impact all this has on the estimation of the main macroeconomic aggregates and the evaluation of the impact of public policies.

4.1 Genesis of Development Macroeconomics in Low- income Countries

Until the 1970s, more precisely until the 1973 and 1978 oil shocks, demand-side macroeconomics received limited attention in developing countries. This attitude was justified by the widespread belief that these economies were supply-constrained owing to limited stocks of physical and human capital, technology, and infrastructure. Hence, in such countries, the main focus of analysis was the accumulation of stocks of production factors, rather than the management of aggregate demand and macroeconomic stabilization. This viewpoint was disputed, however, by some economists who adopted a less radical stance on the relevance of demand-side economics in developing countries.

A widespread opinion was that the equilibrium level of income did not depend on the level of aggregate demand, as the overall degree of utilization of the productive resources was considered high, if changing from sector to sector. Such a general proposition was articulated into four specific points: to start with, the physical capital was scarce and for this reason was fully utilized. Second, open involuntary unemployment was limited, as people could not afford to be out of work due to the absence of unemployment benefits. All labour was fully or partially employed or under-employed, even if at low wages and with low productivity. In addition, especially in agriculture, the disguised unemployment was barely spatially mobile and was unwilling to move for fear of losing the security and support provided by the local family and community. A rise in the demand for workers following a fiscal stimulus was therefore not easily matched by an increase in labour supply. Third, the supply of raw materials, inputs, and financial capital was not sufficiently elastic to respond to an increase in aggregate demand. In India, for instance, there was an acute scarcity of intermediate inputs such as steel, cement, and glass. Fourth, the income elasticity of demand for food grains was high, so that a rise in money income generated by a fiscal stimulus was expected to be spent mainly on food grains. Yet, the food supply was inelastic due to its dependence on the weather, lack of irrigation, and shortage of improved seeds and fertilizers which, taken altogether, made it difficult to raise food supply over the

The Macroeconomics of Developing Countries: An Intermediate Textbook. Giovanni Andrea Cornia, Oxford University Press (2020).

DOI: 10.1093/oso/9780198856672.001.0001

short term in response to an increase in demand. In this case, the most likely result of a food demand increase was for its price to rise. The general opinion was that Keynesian policies could not work effectively under these conditions. However, not everyone agreed with these claims. As noted by Myrdal in his 1968 seminal contribution, these claims were based on an improper perception of reality. It was indeed common that underdevelopment and widespread poverty were accompanied by massive labour underutilization, a low usage rate of industrial capital that—despite its scarcity—could fall as low as 25–30 per cent, and—in countries with inefficient land institutions (such as *latifundia*)—low land utilization. In some of them, the underutilization of industrial capital has persisted for years (Table 4.1).

Table 4.1 Utilization rate of productive capacity by sector, Uzbekistan, 2001

Product/sector	Equipment usage rate	Product/sector	Equipment usage rate
Carpets	86.6	Silk	46.4
Oil products	83.8	Chemical fertilizers	45.2
Coal	71.9	Chemical fibers	37.2
Electric cranes	68.4	Margarine	36.8
Beer	57.7	Cars	35.7
Flour	54.4	Plastic	20.4
Shoes	53.3	Tractors	16.0

Source: Personal communication of the Ministry of Macroeconomics and Statistics of Uzbekistan.

Yet, things have gradually changed. During the last thirty to forty years many developing countries have recorded a considerable output growth in both industry and agriculture. The potential for increasing the supply of raw materials and intermediate products has also improved significantly thanks to microeconomic and sectoral interventions that reduced the incidence of chronic coordination problems. As aggregate supply became more elastic, there was a reconsideration of the applicability of demand-side Keynesian macroeconomics. Some authors remarked, for instance, that discarding the Keynesian approach as altogether inoperative in underdeveloped countries was like throwing away the baby with the bath water, and that the Keynesian multiplier can also work well in developing countries if fiscal expansion is carefully designed and implemented. In fact, some of these countries often suffered from excess capacity in several industries due to a deficiency of aggregate demand.

Meanwhile labour became more mobile following urbanization and internal and international migration, so that the formerly disguised unemployed workers were transformed into involuntary open unemployed workers crying out for jobs. In turn, in Asia and Latin America the short-term supply of food grains became more responsive to demand changes thanks to the spread of the Green Revolution. Indeed, several developing countries now have the capacity of increasing supply in agriculture and consumer goods industries in response to fiscal stimuli without causing inflationary pressures. If anything, several low-income countries are now caught in an under-consumption trap due to lack of demand caused—*inter alia*—by a skewed distribution of income.

A second factor which explains the limited attention paid to demand-side macroeconomics in developing countries until the 1970s was the conviction of many Western economists that these countries were not too different from the developed nations

(Stiglitz et al. 2006). As a result, if an analysis of the impact of macroeconomic policies were needed, then the mainstream tools and models used in advanced nations could be used without problems. There was no need, in other words, to develop a macroeconomics for developing countries, as standard models were considered to be fully applicable there.

However, with the recurrent macroeconomic problems faced by several poor countries, there has been increased questioning of the extent to which standard models can be used to analyse the macroeconomic problems of some 150 developing countries. In 2010 these 150 countries produced 30 per cent of world GDP, or 45 per cent if China and the other transition economies are included.

From the 1950s, the answer to this question became increasingly negative and a structuralist macroeconomics started taking shape. The two oil crises of 1973 and 1978; the 1980s Latin American debt crisis and subsequent 'lost decade' (see Chapter 16); the macroeconomic disequilibria recorded during the transition to a market economy by the former socialist countries; the frequent financial crises recorded in emerging countries; and the intensification of global financial and trade contagion lead to frequent and acute crises. These crises exhibited features different from those observed in developed countries, and often caused macroeconomic problems ignored by standard models.

It is important to note that the macroeconomic peculiarities of developing countries—and the need to develop structuralist macro models—are not due to differences in economic aggregates, although one should not ignore the measurement problems encountered in this area, as discussed in this chapter. Nor are they dictated by differences in the rationality of economic agents and governments. Alternative models are needed because of differences in the structure and functioning of markets and public institutions, and because several problems currently affecting some developing countries (such continuing rapid population growth) are no longer relevant and discussed in the developed countries. These problems concern in particular: a considerable institutional weakness; a high degree of vulnerability when hit by internal and external shocks; the dualism of many markets that renders traditional one-sector macro models less useful; differences in behavioural relationships; the direction of causality linking economic variables; the limited effectiveness of standard policy interventions; a limited ability to introduce corrective measures over the short term (in developing countries the mechanisms of economic policy transmission are weak); and different trade-offs between policy objectives. While in industrial countries the key trade-off has long been between inflation and unemployment, this is less often the case in developing countries which are characterized by overall economic and social underdevelopment. In these countries, the key trade-off is between macro stability and long-run economic and social development.

Finally, if it is true that there exist structural differences between the macroeconomics of high- and low-income countries that require the development of ad hoc analytical models for the latter group, to what extent are the problems observed in the 150 or so developing and transitional economies sufficiently homogeneous to be treated as part of a unified body of theory? The relevant literature suggests that such a unified approach should focus methodologically on the choice of a broad structuralist-institutionalist approach whose specificities will vary somewhat across five or six groups of prototypical developing countries. These groups may be, for example: small open economies exporting raw materials; economies with a rigid food supply; mining economies affected by the Dutch Disease; countries with a high external debt; economies witnessing a radical institutional change; and so on. Despite the structural differences existing between them, all these groups of prototypical developing countries do share some common problems.

4.2 The Informal Economy and National Accounting Issues in Developing Countries

The developing countries adopt the SNA standard developed by the Statistical Commission of the United Nations. The accounting framework across these nations is therefore the same and it consists of: accounts for production, uses, and distribution of GDP; external accounts (current account balance, capital account balance, overall balance of payments, and foreign exchange reserves); and wealth accounting by typology of agent (households, non-financial sector, financial sector, and the state); and type of assets. Notwithstanding this unified approach, the SNA theoretical framework does not easily fit the situation of poor countries for the reasons to be set out below.

A widespread self-consumption

Self-consumption, whereby producers are the consumers of most of their output, is widespread, especially in rural areas. Only a small proportion of output is marketed to pay for the purchase of market inputs, school fees, a few consumer goods, funeral ceremonies, taxes, and so on. Self-consumption of agricultural output is particularly widespread in countries where rural and credit markets and storage facilities are poorly developed. Self-consumption concerns not only food, but also housing, personal care, some consumer durables, and investment goods. As a matter of fact, the poor—and often the non-poor—build their homes with local materials as a lack of cash prevents them buying market inputs and services for their construction. Even investment goods (e.g. farm tools) and personal services (such as health and the care of children) are often produced within the household, especially during the dead season, when farmers dig irrigation canals, level the land, repair old tools, or produce new ones. While these investment goods could be bought on the market, and thus enter the calculation of GDP, they are instead produced through the direct application of surplus labour by their users, who utilize no or minimal market inputs. Except for food, self-produced and -consumed goods are generally neglected in the calculation of GDP.

A not uncommon resort to bartering

Goods and services are often exchanged not for cash and on the basis of monetary prices but in exchange for other goods and according to bilateral barter prices which cannot be aggregated for lack of a common metrics, thus making it difficult to include their value in the estimate of GDP. The monetization of the economy improves economic efficiency by reducing search, information, and transaction costs, while barter exchange increases them. Monetization reduces search costs because of the simultaneous double coincidence of wants. Conversely, in a barter economy the meeting of those who want to purchase a good and those who produce it is more difficult. The information costs are therefore higher since, given n goods, there are n (n − 1)/2 prices to be assessed, while in a market economy there are only n prices. Transaction costs, in turn, are generally smaller in a monetized economy, as banks (through their subsidiaries) reduce charges for payments in remote areas.

Unilateral unremunerated transactions

In this case, an individual may donate her labour or provide a service to another individual (for instance, by helping during the harvest or the construction of a house), thus generating value added, but without expecting anything in return, except—in some cases—the right of receiving in the future similar help if a need arises. In such cases, one speaks of implicit contracts of reciprocity. Also unremunerated transactions escape inclusion in the calculation of GDP.

In developed countries, these three types of accounting problems (self-consumption, barter exchange, and unilateral unremunerated transactions) do exist, but are marginal and are therefore safely ignored in the calculation of GDP. This cannot be done in developing countries (especially the Least Developed Countries) where such transactions are common and relevant for the functioning of the economy and the well-being of households. If one accepts that it is practically impossible to include them into the GDP production account, then one will be dealing with macroeconomic aggregates and models that cover only the monetized sector of the economy. However, in very poor countries especially, this would result in a lot of essential transactions being ignored and GDP and well-being would be underestimated.

Evaluating the contribution to GDP of self-consumption, barter exchange, and unilateral unremunerated transactions is complex. How many and how relevant are such transactions? How could they enter the calculation of GDP? Food self-consumption (whch can reach 80 per cent of total household food consumption in parts of the rural Sahel) is generally imputed as income-in-kind. In contrast, self-produced services and housing are generally ignored, thus causing an underestimation of GDP and a possible overestimation of its rate of growth when the relative size of the monetized economy grows and the division of labour and market exchange become more common. Also, what value can be assigned to transactions with no market price to allow them to be included in the calculation of total GDP? How many of these transactions represent production, consumption, or both? Which unit prices should be used to include them in overall GDP? Theory suggests that such transactions should be imputed by means of shadow prices, but these are difficult to determine and the market spot prices used in their place are hardly defensible from a theoretical point of view. For example, if a farmer produces 300 kg of millet for self-consumption, should one include this amount multiplied by its shadow price in the estimate of the agricultural value added? As noted, the latter is usually proxied by the spot price of millet observed in local markets. But this convention is theoretically incorrect, as the market price may change if the 300 kg of self-consumed millet were sold on the market and subsequently re-purchased by the farmer who produced it.

Besides the problems met in the calculation of GDP, the presence of a large non-monetized sector must be noted for other reasons. This sector is, in fact, fairly unresponsive to interest and exchange rate changes, public spending, and taxation, as it operates mostly outside the monetized circuit and therefore responds weakly to monetary, fiscal, and exchange rate stimuli. The impact of macroeconomic policy is therefore less pronounced than in the formal sector and the way its transmission mechanisms work are not well known. The policy impact depends in particular on the links existing between the non-monetized, the informal, and formal sectors. Assessing correctly the overall impact of macroeconomic policies requires a detailed modelling of the relationship between these three sectors.

A large monetized sector with unrecorded transactions

A significant proportion of monetary transactions in the urban and rural areas of low-income countries takes place in the so-called informal sector. In this sector all transactions are liquidated with cash but with no track record of them. There are therefore no administrative documents to estimate how many goods and services were produced and exchanged. In semi-developed and developed economies (such as the transition economies) informality is often explained by the wish to evade taxes and social security contributions and by the fragility of micro-enterprises unable to bear the cost of formalization (see Chapter 8). Moreover, the prices of goods and services in these markets are more variable than in the formal sector and equilibrium prices are seldom observed in local markets. As a result, the prices and quantities of these transactions (which are needed to estimate GDP) are difficult to determine. In addition, the measurement of output and the assessment of the impact of macroeconomic policies requires the use of indirect methods, the launch of sectoral studies, or the estimation of the volume of production by means of satellites or on the basis of the consumption of electricity and other essential market inputs.

4.3 Statistical Errors in the Estimation of Economic Aggregates and the Impact of Policies

High temporal-spatial price volatility

Even ignoring the problem of inflation caused by structural rigidities or monetary factors, the prices of goods—needed to aggregate the quantities of different goods and services to be included in GDP—are unstable across regions and over time. For example, in rural areas the price of agricultural products (net of transport costs) are generally low, while those of manufactured goods are high.

A strong temporal and spatial price variability affects the estimation of real macroeconomic aggregates. These are always first estimated at current prices and then converted into constant prices by using some price deflators. For example, if the GDP at current prices increased over the prior year by k per cent and its price deflator grew at h per cent, the GDP growth rate at constant prices should rise by (k−h) per cent. However, when inflation is high (more than 50 per cent a year), the estimation of the h deflator is generally affected by a rising and often unavoidable absolute error. But an error of 2–3 per cent in its estimation entails a high risk of overestimating or underestimating the real GDP growth rate.

A large volume of mixed-incomes

There are also major difficulties in estimating the distribution of GDP among production factors. The types of incomes accruing to the economic agents are the same as in the developed countries, that is, wages, rents, interest, profits, and other capital incomes (mixed incomes). However, their shares in the total income differ substantially from those of formal economies. In developing countries many people are self-employed: they work as artisans, micro-entrepreneurs, small farmers or tenants who earn mixed-incomes remunerating their labour (through wage earnings), their entrepreneurship (through profits), and ownership of non-reproducible production factors (through land rents). Yet, the precise nature and tax treatment of such incomes are difficult to determine, as it is unclear whether they constitute wage income or other types of incomes. The same agents who earn these mixed incomes rarely know their precise amount, let alone their composition. For this reason, the estimation of the factorial distribution of income between wages, profits, rents, capital income, and so on turns out to be very tentative. In national accounts, mixed incomes are usually estimated on the basis of sample surveys or as a residual after subtracting officially recorded wages from the total national income.

Relative weight of public and private transfers

In the advanced countries the difference between gross market income and disposable income is large (25–40 percentage points) owing to large public transfers to households in the form of non-contributory pensions, social assistance, child allowances, unemployment benefits, and so on. This rarely happens in developing countries which—instead—exhibit significant transfers within extended family networks or groups characterized by strong social, ethnic, or religious ties (Table 4.2).

The value of such transfers varies from country to country owing to differences in social norms and average incomes but can reach up to 30–40 per cent of poor families' total income (Table 4.2). However, the effectiveness of these arrangements is limited by the fact that such transfers may entail implicit reciprocity contracts and constitute only in part a genuine redistribution between rich and poor belonging to the same network. In addition, such transfers may exclude some of the poor who are often perceived as network members

Table 4.2 Frequency of private transfers in selected countries

Country	Families making money transfers	Families receiving money transfers	
		All families	Poor families
Jamaica (1997)	13.1	53.0	65.0
Nepal (1996)	17.4	44.7	55.3
Panama (1997)	15.5	37.8	40.9
Russian Federation (1997)	23.7	25.2	31.5
Bulgaria (1995)	15.0	17.0	21.4

Note: the values in the table are the percentage of total households in each category.

Source: World Bank (2001).

with a high probability of default, as they may not be able to ensure reciprocal transfers to other network members in the future.

A final remark concerns the accounting rules used to register such transfers. Transfers are not in fact considered as 'negative income' for the donors and 'positive income' for the recipients, but rather as consumption for donors and loans (that are not included in the definition of income) for recipients. If this is true, private transfers will not be included in the income of people who receive them, but instead constitute a debt. This affects the estimation of the size distribution of income.

The importance of migrant remittances

In several developing countries, factors income from abroad represents a major contribution to GDP, household income, and foreign exchange. Factors income from abroad generally consists of migrant remittances, although profits, rents and even illicit proceeds are included under the same label. Remittances are very important in the small low-income economies of Central America, the Caribbean, and economies in transition. In Tajikistan, Guyana, Kyrgyzstan, and Haiti they respectively account for 42, 40, 32, and 30 per cent of GDP. Remittances exceed 20 per cent of GDP in the Philippines, Bangladesh, Moldova, Albania, Nepal, Lesotho, Samoa, Armenia, and Gambia. Even in large economies, where they represent a modest percentage of GDP, remittances play an important role in supporting the balance of payments. For instance, in India an estimated US$70 billion remittances account for 23 per cent of all foreign currency earnings. In Mexico they account for at least 30 billion US dollars, which however represent only 2.5 per cent of GDP (Figure 4.1).

However, some remittances escape official registration as they are transferred through informal channels rather than through banks or money transfer operators for fear they could be taxed, confiscated, or stolen, or to avoid having them converted into national currency at unfavourable rates in countries with multiple exchange rates. There are in fact a number of incentives not to declare this source of income. Its value is therefore estimated in national accounts in a tentative way, despite the fact that remittances may affect the macroeconomy by causing a real exchange rate appreciation, an increase in imports, and the dollarization of the economy.

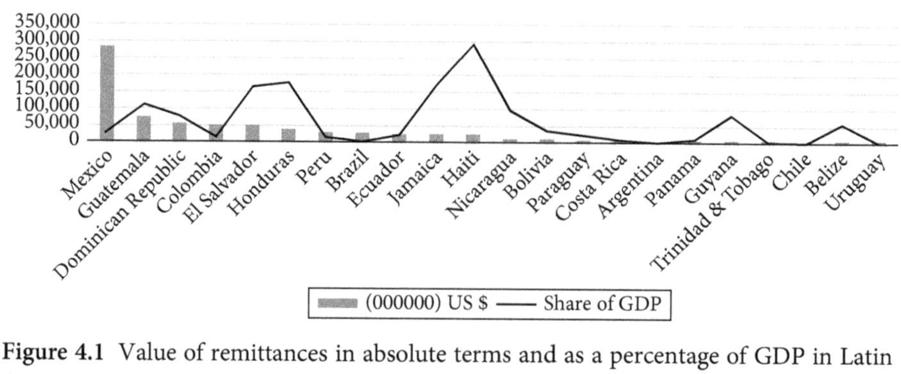

Figure 4.1 Value of remittances in absolute terms and as a percentage of GDP in Latin America, 2016

Source: Own elaboration on World Development Indicators (accessed on 6 February 2018)

For all these reasons, remittances are often underestimated and are included in national accounts with a considerable margin of error. The existing estimates suggest that official remittances represent approximately half of the total. The issue is not easy to clarify even in fairly advanced countries. In Turkey, for instance, the aggregate data show a 50 per cent decline of remittances between 2002 and 2006. Yet, survey data show an increase over the same period, possibly due to rising incentives to use informal channels, or changes in registration procedures. Early on, such monies were recorded as remittances, but more recently they have been accounted as tourist inflows (Clemens and McKenzie, 2014). In low-income countries, remittances are often considered as a key countercyclical stabilizer (Chami et al., 2009). This conclusion is, however, a highly contentious issue; some of the emigrating countries have narrowly diversified distribution of migrants by country of destination, a fact that may reduce their ability to rely on remittances as a macroeconomic countercyclical device (Balli and Rana, 2015).

4.4 Accounting Problems in Estimating the Uses of GDP

Estimating the various components of GDP (private consumption, government spending, investments, exports and imports, changes in stocks) is often affected by an important margin of error for the reasons outlined in the following four subsections

Changes in inventories

Changes in inventories are important in pastoral and mining economies, but are usually ignored. While in advanced countries inventories amount to less than half a per cent of GDP, and can thus be included into investments or ignored without causing too many problems, in developing countries the sudden accumulation or decumulation of inventories can strongly affect the estimate of GDP. For example, in Somalia in 1998 neglecting the accumulation of camels, goats, and sheep led IMF staff to estimate a negative growth rate of GDP, while alternative estimates (that took into account the increase in cattle and camel stocks) concluded that GDP had moderately increased. In contrast, the decline in cattle stock that occurred in Mongolia during the 1990s as a result of two consecutive harsh winters was taken into account when estimating the level of the (sharply declining) GDP.

Self-consumption and consumption volatility

Another feature of private consumption in poor countries concerns its high volatility. While in advanced countries most households manage to stabilize their well-being over time through consumption smoothing, this option is not available to many in poor countries because incomes are highly volatile and access to financial markets to sustain consumption over the short term is foreclosed. Thus, the variations in consumption from one period to the next make it difficult to estimate current consumption on the basis of the consumption of the previous year. Likewise, current investments in developing countries with a large agricultural sector and a sizeable excess labour supply tend to be underestimated because—as mentioned above—part of the investments in irrigation, land terracing, reforesting, and construction of houses and utensils are generally made through the direct application of surplus labour during the dead season. It should be noted that these investments (like digging large irrigation canals) can be a non-negligible component of GDP. During the Mao Tze Tung era, for example, such activities helped to increase markedly agricultural production in China. But, as their estimate is highly problematic, these investments are ignored when estimating total investments.

Unrecorded exports and imports

In many developing countries—especially those with long and leaky borders or characterized by high levels of corruption—the estimation of imports and exports (for which there is in principle double entry accounting, one in the country of origin and one in the destination) is often unreliable. This is due to the existence of substantial parallel imports and exports. The reason why these flows follow informal channels has to do with the existence of import quotas and tariffs, trade taxes, multiple exchange rates, and the obligation to surrender the foreign currency earned to the national foreign exchange office. Informal export earnings also remain undeclared because they may derive from illegal or criminal transactions (e.g. the billions of dollars of drugs exported). Even in fairly developed Poland, parallel exports in the early 1990s were sizeable, as shuttle traders informally exported all sorts of consumer goods worth 2 billion US dollars to neighbouring Germany, so as to avoid filing an income tax declaration. Such transactions were thus not recorded in the trade balance or as taxable income.

Whatever the reasons behind the avoidance of official channels, parallel transactions with foreign countries are not directly included in national accounts and must—every year—be estimated in some way, albeit with a high margin of error. It is therefore difficult to have accurate statiistics of the level of real exports and currency reserves of several developing countries, as the foreign currency holdings are distributed between the central bank, the private sector, and households.

Overall GDP estimation issues

As a result of all this, the estimation of the GDP's production, uses, and distribution is prone to substantial errors, which alter perceptions of the impact of macroeconomic policy, especially if such errors do not offset each other. The GDP growth rate in developing economies should therefore always be interpreted as an estimate characterized by a confidence interval of at least one percentage point.

In conclusion, in developing countries the definition of national account aggregates is theoretically more problematic than in the advanced economies, while their measurement is far less precise and requires a reliance on somewhat arbitrary conventions. The use of costly sample surveys for the estimation of economic aggregates is often impracticable due to the limited resources allocated to this activity. As matter of fact, more than anywhere else, the central statistical offices try to make use of routine data collected for other purposes by government agencies and international organizations. This is the case for the data on industrial and agricultural production (used to estimate GDP and other economic aggregates), data on tax revenue (which can help to estimate the distribution of income), and data on import tariffs and export taxes which help to estimate the trade balance.

4.5 Concluding Remarks

In the past, demand-side macroeconomics has received only limited attention from the policymakers of developing countries and by the theorists of the Classical Development Theory. As these economies were mainly seen as constrained on the supply side, demand management policies were thought to be of little use if not a source of inflation due to a variety of rigidities and coordination failures. Yet, these supposedly supply-constrained low-income countries often exhibit a low degree of utilization and productivity of all production factors, not only in terms of unskilled labour but also of physical capital, skilled labour, and, in some countries, land.

A major policy objective consists, therefore, in removing the obstacles to the utilization of such latent resources. This requires dealing with the handicaps characterizing these countries, including their institutional weakness and distortions, greater vulnerabilities to shocks, and frequent coordination problems. The limited effectiveness of macroeconomic policies in these countries also has to be factored in as their pervasive dualism sharply reduces their impact in part of the economy. To overcome these problems, it is necessary to get a clear understanding of the structure of these economies, deal with the conceptual and measurement problems encountered in the assessment of macroeconomic aggregates, and develop dualistic macroeconomic models reflecting the behaviour of the economic agents in the formal and informal sectors.

References

Balli, F. and F. Rana (2015), 'Determinants of risk sharing through remittances', *Journal of Banking and Finance*, 55: pp. 107–16.

Chami, R., D. Hakura, and P.,= Montiel (2009), 'Remittances: an automatic output stabilizer?' *IMF Working Paper* 09/91, Washington DC: International Monetary Fund.

Clemens, M. A. and D. J. McKenzie (2014), 'Why don't remittances appear to react to growth?', *World Bank Policy Research Working Paper* No. 6856. Washington, DC: The World Bank.

Myrdal, G. (1968), *The Asian Drama: an Enquiry into the Poverty of Nations*. New York: Pantheon Books.

Stiglitz, J., J. A. Ocampo, S. Spiegel, R. Ffrench-Davis, and D. Nayyar (2006), 'Why Is Macroeconomics Different in Developing Countries?', in J. Stiglitz, J. A. Ocampo, S. Spiegel, R. Ffrench-Davis, and D. Nayyar (eds), *Stability with Growth*,. Initiative for Policy Dialogue. Oxford: Oxford University Press.

World Bank (2001), *World Development Report 2000/2001: Attacking Poverty*. Washington, DC: World Bank; and New York: Oxford University Press.

Suggested further reading

Myrdal, G. (1968), *The Asian Drama: an Enquiry into the Poverty of Nations*. New York: Pantheon Books.

Stiglitz, J., J.A. Ocampo, S. Spiegel, R. Ffrench-Davis, and D. Nayyar (2006), 'Why Is Macroeconomics Different in Developing Countries?', in J. Stiglitz, J. A. Ocampo, S. Spiegel, R. Ffrench-Davis and D. Nayyar (eds), *Stability with Growth*, Initiative for Policy Dialogue. Oxford: Oxford University Press.

5

Long-term Growth and Inequality in Economies Relying on Land and Natural Resources

This chapter examines the long-term economic prospects of developing countries whose growth depends on agricultural commodities, mining, and oil extraction. It analyses the causes of the slow and unstable long-term growth of such countries, including those due to the Dutch Disease. It then presents a simple Solow-type model of long-term growth for such economies, and historical evidence of how public policy can moderate or offset the problems linked to productive specialization.

5.1 Resource Abundance and its Impact on Short- and Long-term Growth

Countries endowed with abundant natural resources relative to other production factors tend to grow more slowly over the long term than other types of economy (Sachs and Warner, 1995). The literature also shows that resource-abundant countries are more likely to suffer from greater instability (Erten and Ocampo, 2012) and growth collapses than resource-poor countries. Small (and therefore little diversified) resource-rich countries are particularly affected by such problems. Other challenges frequently faced by these countries concern their macroeconomic management, the development of human resources, and income inequality. In extreme cases, these problems are compounded by political-economic tensions leading to political instability or even to 'greed wars' for the control of natural resources, particularly point resources such as mines and oil wells.

In the mid-1990s, resource rents accounted on average for a share of GDP ranging between 13 and 21 per cent (Auty 2001). Resource rents have, however, risen in several developing countries during the boom in world energy and metal prices recorded during the 2000s (Table 5.1). As an extreme case, in 2010, 75.6 per cent of the Congo Republic's GDP originated from oil extraction and related activities.

5.2 Causes of the Economic Problems Faced by Resource-Rich Countries

Falling and historically unstable terms of trade

The structuralist analysis—and in particular the Prebish–Singer hypothesis (Prebish, 1950)—explained the slow growth of resource-rich countries on the basis of the secular

The Macroeconomics of Developing Countries: An Intermediate Textbook. Giovanni Andrea Cornia, Oxford University Press (2020).

DOI: 10.1093/oso/9780198856672.001.0001

Table 5.1 Evolution of the share of natural resource rents on GDP in sub-Saharan Africa, 1990–2010

Country (a) % share > 20%	1990	2000	2010	Country	1990 (b) % share 10–20%	2000	2010	Country	1990 (c) % share 5–10%	2000	2010
Angola[a]	30.5	42.3	46.9	B. Faso	3.5	3.3	10.5	Côte d'Ivoire[a]	3.0	4.5	6.4
Chad[a]	4.5	5.9	38.4	Burundi	9.5	9.3	10.9	Ethiopia	6.5	10.1	6.4
Congo DR	16.0	21.1	31.8	Cameroon[a]	11.3	12.7	9.0	Ghana	4.4	5.4	8.9
Congo Rep.[a]	46.0	75.6	66.4	G. Bissau	10.1	11.2	4.8	Malawi	6.7	5.9	3.9
Eq. Guinea[a]	12.6	67.0	46.0	Guinea	18.3	10.0	18.2	Mozambique	8.6	4.5	8.7
Gabon[a]	34.7	50.7	50.0	Liberia	—	16.7	11.0	Sierra Leone	12.6	7.7	3.5
Mauritania	11.6	12.3	18.0	Mali	2.4	2.9	12.3	Tanzania	8.3	2.7	7.9
Nigeria[a]	47.5	46.9	27.7	South Africa	6.3	2.2	9.9	Uganda	9.7	6.7	5.8
Zambia	19.3	4.4	25.8	Sudan	—	12.8	17.6	Zimbabwe	3.2	2.4	9.9
Average	24.7	36.2	42.7	Average	7.7	9.0	11.6	Average	7.0	5.5	6.8

Note: Data for another thirteen countries with a share of natural resource rents of less than 5 per cent shows mixed trends.
[a] Refers to oil producers, IMF Economic Outlook Classification.

Source: Own elaboration on World Development Indicators.

decline of their international terms of trade, that is, the ratio of the price index of commodity exports P_X relative to the price index of industrial imports P_I. In this view, world commodity prices fell relative to the prices of industrial goods due to increasing use of synthetics (that shrank the raw material content of industrial goods) and the low-income elasticity of the demand for primary commodities in advanced economies. This phenomenon has also been attributed to the 'fallacy of composition', that is, the decision of many developing countries (often encouraged by the World Bank) to increase their exports of the same commodities in an attempt to benefit from what they perceived was their comparative advantage in international trade. Such a policy, and the impact of technological changes that affected the demand and supply of given commodities, often resulted in a global commodities glut and a fall in their long-term price trend (top part of Figure 5.1) and in their super-cycles (bottom part) that benefited consumers in developed countries. Meanwhile, the prices of industrial goods exported by the latter continued to rise due to the oligopolistic labour markets prevailing in developed countries. This implied that productivity gains in such countries were captured by firms and workers in the form of higher wages and profits, and were not translated into a decline in the price of manufactured goods.

The empirical evidence broadly supported the structuralists' claims until the end of the twentieth century, except on the occasion of the oil shocks of 1973 and 1978 (Figure 5.1). Yet, the recent rise of the Asian economies, and in particular the rapid growth of China since 2000, has overturned this conclusion, as the prices of primary commodities have risen quickly since around 2000 (Figure 5.2) while the price of Chinese manufactured exports has declined. However, since the crises of 2008 and 2013, the price of oil and metals have again declined substantially. As for the future, the commodity price booms that lasted until 2011 (Figure 5.2) is likely to continue only if China, India, and other large developing countries are able to de-link from the slow-growing OECD countries.

A second problem arises in the long-term fluctuation (or 'super-cycles' of 10–20 years) in the price of metals, oil, and cash crops due to changes in demand, prices, new discoveries, and resource depletion, as shown in Figure 5.2. Such fluctuations, especially

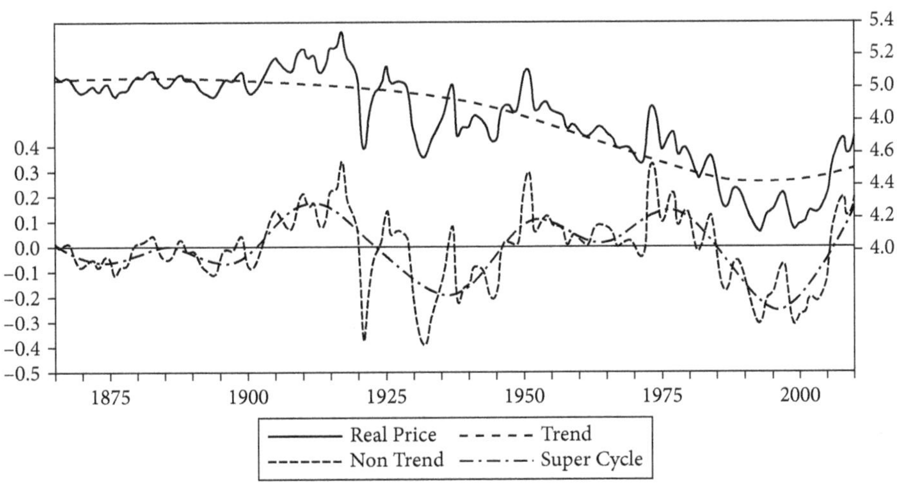

Figure 5.1 Real non-oil commodity price index, 1875–2010

Source: Erten and Ocampo (2012)

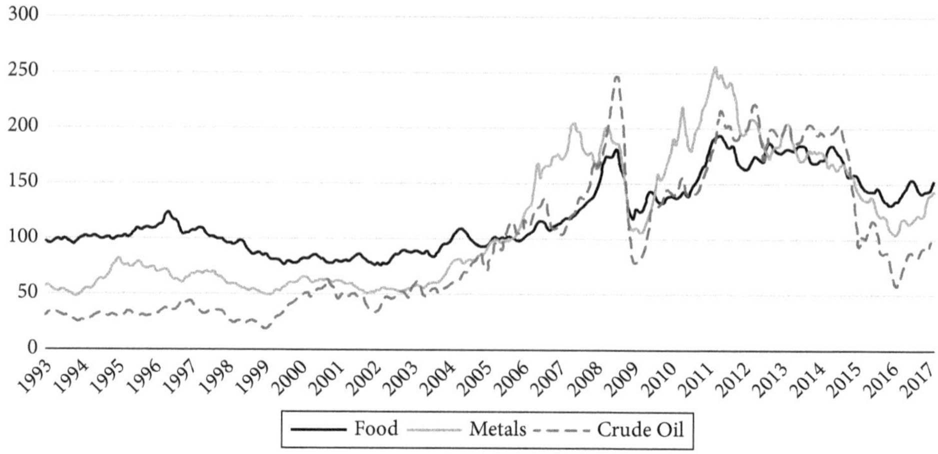

Figure 5.2 World price index for food, metals, and crude oil, 1993–2016 (2005 = 100)
Source: Own elaboration on the IMF' World Economic Outlook (downloaded on 20 June 2016)

those due to the super-cycles documented in Figure 5.1, cause long-term uncertainty, growth instability, fluctuating revenue and public expenditure on essential items, and protracted economic stagnation.

Nature of the production process in the resource sector

In the resource sector, particularly in oil extraction and mining, production requires a considerable amount of capital and little labour. This reduces the demand for unskilled and semi-skilled workers, lowers their wage rate, and so discourages investment in education, a key determinant of long-term growth (see Chapter 2). In addition, the volatility of commodity prices may force poor families to pull children out of school in years of low prices, wages, and labour demand. In this way, transitory shocks can cause permanent damage to the educational opportunities of the poor and raise the long-term polarization of educational attainments.

In addition, the growth of the resource sector does not endogenously lead to broad-based development as mines and oil fields are often located in enclaves characterized by limited forward and backward linkages with the rest of the economy. Equipment used in this sector is in most cases imported, and so are the Western goods consumed by the highly skilled expatriates managing its production, while the processing of raw output tends to occur overseas. Most of the local labour force is made up of unskilled and semi-skilled labour, so that the distribution of income is skewed in favour of capital owners, who in many cases are multinational corporations that remit most of their profits abroad, and of highly skilled (mostly) expatriate workers. This unequal distribution of income generates a limited demand for locally produced goods. Even the fiscal linkage is weak, as extractive firms and plantations have little incentive to pay domestic taxes to improve the socio-economic infrastructure as they function as a 'state within the state' that provides the goods (energy, water, and security) needed for their enclaves to function. As a result, the economy tends to remain specialized in one or a few primary sectors, and profits may be reinvested in the same sector and not in the downstream processing of primary commodities, other sectors, and public infrastructure. There are of course exceptions. Chile for instance, exports mainly smelted and refined copper bars rather than copper ore.

Dutch Disease effects

The Dutch Disease syndrome provides a third explanation for the weak long-term performance of resource-abundant countries. Corden and Neary (1982) described this phenomenon in formal terms. Their model considers a small open economy comprising a tradable resources sector (e.g. oil, gas, or metals), a non-resource tradable sector (e.g. manufacturing and agriculture), and a non-tradable sector comprising real estate, construction, and local services. The nominal exchange rate is fixed. A boom in the resource sector sharply increases the inflow of foreign currency and generates three effects: an increased spending effect, a change in the relative prices of tradables (T) in relation to non-tradables (NT), and a transfer of production factors across sectors. For instance, following the discovery in 1994 of three large offshore deposits of hydrocarbons in Azerbaijan, the value added share of the oil sector rose between 1995 and 2000 from 16.4 to 27.3 per cent of GDP while that of non-oil manufacturing fell from 13.2 to 6 per cent. Similar, if less pronounced, effects were observed for the sectoral distribution of employment.

A large inflow of export proceeds generates increased absorption of both T and NT goods. In an open economy, an increase in the demand for T does not increase their domestic prices (these are determined by the international market) and any excess demand for T over domestic production is satisfied by increasing imports. In contrast, increased spending on NT (e.g. real estate) drives up their price as supply is generally rigid in the short term as shown, for instance, by the housing price bubbles that invariably accompany an increase in commodity prices and export proceeds in resource-rich economies. The increase in the price of NT raises the overall rate of inflation and—given the stability of the nominal exchange rate—causes an appreciation of the Real Exchange Rate (RER) that, as shown in Chapter 15, can be written as the ratio P_T/P_{NT}. This makes the production and export of manufactured and agricultural goods less competitive, while their imports may rise. An appreciation of the RER will also reduce at the margin the rents of the booming tradable resource sector without, however, reducing its output, as precious primary commodities such as oil are exported by a limited number of countries that enjoy large trade margins. In turn, the rise in the price of NT in relation to that of T will cause a shift of labour and capital from manufacturing and agriculture towards this sector. The output of NT will then rise relative to that of T.

The deindustrialization caused by the Dutch Disease reduces long-term growth in relation to economies with no resources, as the contraction of manufacturing reduces the economy-wide externalities, cross-sectoral spillovers and learning-by-doing typically generated by this sector. The effects of deindustrialization on long-term growth will be particularly severe once the mineral and energy deposits are exhausted, as no new sectors were developed during the resource boom years. Resource booms are not harmful if the increase in revenue from resource exports is sustainable over the long term (as in some Gulf States), if the state taxes the commodity rents and invests them in new sustainable industries, and if appropriate macroeconomic policies are introduced to control the appreciation of the RER.

Dutch Disease effects can also be generated by sudden and large inflows of migrant remittances, foreign aid, foreign direct investment (FDI), and portfolio flows. In all these cases, the countries concerned experience—as noted above—a spending effect, an increase in NT prices in relation to T prices, an appreciation of the RER, and a decline of tradable non-resource exports. Since the late 1990s, migrant remittances to developing countries have become a major source of hard currency, greater than Official Development Assistance (ODA) and loans and portfolio flows combined (Figure 5.3). While the trend in global remittance flows rises steadily (Figure 5.3), at the country level it can fluctuate considerably from year to year depending on changes in the economic conditions in the countries of destination. In years of large inflows, remittances have been observed to generate Dutch Disease effects that are, however, generally less pronounced than in oil countries, whose export proceeds exhibit sharper year to year fluctuations.

In addition, large and sudden increases in foreign aid have been associated in several cases with an increase in absorption, rises in the NT price, and an appreciation of the domestic currency. In these cases, while the trend in the aggregate world Official Development Assistance (ODA) is stable, there have been big shifts in its cross-country allocation when large emergencies or institutional changes occur. In this regard, a study by Fielding and Gibson (2013) of twenty-six sub-Saharan African countries finds considerable heterogeneity of the impact of aid inflows on the real exchange rate and output. In most cases, aid inflows caused a RER appreciation, but the size of the effect varied in relation to a country's propensity to invest in fixed capital and the quality of its institutions, both of which mitigated real appreciation. Aid inflows caused greater real exchange rate appreciation in countries with a fixed nominal peg (such as those belonging to the CFA Franc zone and small economies pegged to the South African Rand) than in countries with a more flexible nominal exchange rate. Due to these findings, aid packages should include measures to ensure some exchange rate flexibility, to increase the propensity to invest part of the incoming aid to improve productivity in both the T and NT sectors, and to enhance the quality of institutions.

As for the impact of FDI, the extent of the Dutch Disease effects depend crucially on the sector they target. In most of Latin American and sub-Saharan Africa (but not in East Asia), FDIs have generally targeted the oil and mining sectors. In this case, the effects are similar to those described in Corden and Neary (1982). More favourable effects are

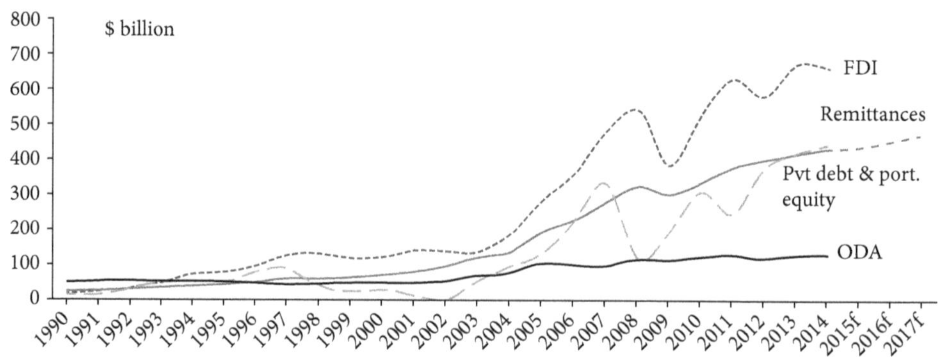

Figure 5.3 Flows of FDI, remittances, portfolio flows and ODA to developing countries, 1990–2017

Source: World Bank (2016)

observed if FDI targets manufacturing or agriculture. In turn, portfolio inflows are a main source of exchange rate instability and economic disruption, as they enter–exit the domestic economy over the short term for speculative purposes (see Chapter 15).

Impact of Dutch Disease on inequality and growth

As noted, in the resource sector production generally requires a considerable amount of capital (whose ownership is highly concentrated, often in the hands of foreign companies), highly skilled workers remunerated at international pay scales, and a relatively modest amount of unskilled labour. The resulting intra-generational functional and dimensional distribution of market income is therefore, by definition, highly unequal. In addition, *ex ante* uncertainty about future commodity prices may reduce investment in education. The wage premium of skilled workers will therefore remain high. Inequality is also affected through other channels. For instance, whenever income is more equally distributed in the labour-intensive manufacturing and agriculture sector than in the non-traded sector, inequality may rise due to a shift of workers to the NT sector caused by the relative rise of P_{NT} prices. Inequality may also be exacerbated by the political-economy effects discussed in Sections 2.5 and 2.6. Econometric analyses of the determinants of income inequality in Latin America and sub-Saharan Africa confirm that the share of output and exports originating from the resource sector correlate positively with inequality (Cornia, 2014, 2016).

The distribution of disposable income may be less skewed if resource rents accrue to the state in the form of royalties or revenue originating from the taxation of profits of state-owned or private companies, and if such rents are redistributed to low-income groups in the form of cash transfers and social services. Chile, Norway, and Botswana are good examples of such a policy approach. But this is not the general rule. Thus, high inequality associated with a large resource sector may be a further factor depressing long-term growth as suggested by most of the literature on the inequality–growth nexus. Indeed, most theories—and empirical evidence—show that high inequality is associated with slower growth owing to incentive problems, political economy effects, financial instability, and a lower provision of public goods (see Chapter 17). A second effect of a high dependence on resource rents concerns the impact on the intergenerational distribution of income. If all the proceedings from the extraction of oil or metals are consumed by the current generation, this will penalize the future ones, as oil and mineral deposits are finite.

An additional explanation of slow long-term growth in resource rich countries is that manna from heaven leads to laziness and sloth. Fiscal laziness is common in resource-rich countries. For instance, in a study on taxation and inequality for the 2000s, Cornia et al. (2011) found that most resource-dependent Latin American countries (Ecuador, Mexico, Peru, and Venezuela) postponed much needed tax reforms to reduce their dependence on non-tax revenue linked to the exploitation of natural resources. Such non-tax revenue is highly volatile, and a fall in commodity prices may impose the adoption of harsh adjustment measures affecting long-term growth and social cohesion. Ecuador's inability to make timely upward adjustments to the tax/GDP ratio illustrates this point. The country relies on tax and non-tax revenue linked to oil extraction for about a third of its budget. During the five years boom that drove oil prices to a 10-year high in 2008, the country did not save any of the related windfall profits or introduce tax reform. After the price of oil fell to a five-year low in 2016, the government was forced in 2017 to cut public spending by 15 per cent. This entailed—*inter alia*—a reduction in the number of planned new schools and police stations and additional borrowing from multilateral lenders.

Domestic policy failures may also negatively affect the level and efficiency of investment and the quality of the workforce due to the state's excessive dirigisme and its long-term reliance on primary products. This implies that resource-rich countries industrialize when wages are higher than in competing resource-poor countries. Without strong policy restraint, rents can thus lead to inferior institutions, rent-seeking competition among factions, high horizontal inequality, corruption, and—in heterogeneous societies with weak social capital—greed wars.

Political economy effects

Auty (2006) illustrates two political economy models of growth followed respectively by resource-rich and resource-poor countries: the Staple Trap Model (STM) linked to high natural resource rents, and the Competitive Industrialization Model (CIM) associated with low resource rents. In the latter, which was followed, for instance, by the East and South East Asian Tigers, the smaller the rents relative to GDP, and the more broadly spread among agents and regions, the greater the probability of engendering a developmental state that will actively promote industrialization. Indeed, low rents limit the period of dependence on commodity exports and force policymakers to nurture industrialization even at a relatively low level of GDP per capita. In its early stages, the development of manufacturing is labour-intensive, faces competition from other producers, and generates positive economic and social externalities. It also leads to rapid urbanization that accelerates the demographic transition that lowers population growth. In turn, the slowing of population growth reduces the dependency rate and so raises—*ceteris paribus*—the rate of saving and investment. The CIM's demographic transition also has the effect that, at some point, wages rise and force firms to diversify into capital- and skill-intensive sectors that strengthen the resilience of the economy to shocks. Finally, in this model, wage and income inequality tends to be low, as the rapid absorption of surplus labour raises the wages of unskilled workers, while the rapid accumulation of human capital supported by the developmental state slows an increase in the skill premium when the economy shifts to highly-skilled industries.

In STM countries, a non-developmental state focuses on capturing resource rents and does little to diversify output, promote competitive industrialization and shift production to labour-intensive manufacturing. The result is that human and social capital are accumulated more slowly than in resource poor countries. In addition, the incentive to invest in the rural sector is scarce at best for economic and political-economy reasons. Nigeria offers a good example of an STM development path. Until the discovery of oil and gas, the country was a net food exporter and had developed an embryo of a manufacturing industry; after the discovery of oil it became a net importer of food and manufactured goods. If reliance on primary exports lasts for many years, competitive industrialization will be postponed indefinitely. Indeed, surplus rural labour persists, unskilled wages remain low, and the government uses the rents to create industrial jobs directly and inefficiently, instead of nurturing industrialization by creating public goods such as human capital and infrastructure. Consequently, diversification occurs under the guidance of a bloated government bureaucracy and protected capital-intensive industry depending on state subsidies financed with resource rents. The expansion of such activities absorbs a large share of available resources, so that the economy-wide rate of investment is reduced and GDP grows slowly. Despite this, the elites benefiting from the rents are likely to block reforms, as they find it politically preferable to sustain transfers to the parasitic sector by taxing capital and profits in the commodity sector. But this depresses incentives in the primary sector and erodes its competitive diversification, so the economy becomes increasingly vulnerable to shocks and growth collapses.

Oil- and gas-rich states enjoy the highest resource rents among the developing countries, which allows them to reduce taxation. This weakens the demand for representation and democratic accountability that is associated with taxation. As noted, as GDP growth decelerates over the long term, competition for rents intensifies and government interventions increase. The collision between the patronage system that sustained the government and encouraged shrinking rents renders the political state brittle as rents are concentrated in the hands of a few key groups and repression is used to maintain control. In extreme cases (as in Angola in the 1980s and early 1990s), resource rents may cause 'greed wars' between national factions. Governance and social capital are also eroded by the decline of rents. This increases corruption as public sector revenues and real wages decline, so that public officials use their discretionary power to extract bureaucratic rents. Atomized corruption, in turn, undermines the integrity of the legal system, raises transaction costs, and may push governments to maintain their authority by resorting to repression.

5.3 A Neoclassical Long-term Growth Model in Countries Dependent on Non-reproducible Resources

As shown *inter alia* by Table 5.1 a considerable number of developing countries from Africa, the Middle East, and Latin America specialize in the production and export of agricultural and mineral commodities. In these countries, good farmable land and/or mines and oil fields are key production factors. With the growth of the rural population and workforce, the land/man ratio remains constant as long as it is possible to extend the land frontier. After that, as discussed in Chapter 7, people move to less fertile lands with lower productivity. For instance, in Niger (13 million inhabitants in 2015) unstoppable population growth pushed every year 70,000–80,000 families to the semi-arid lands of the Sahel which are exposed to severe wind and water erosion and to the risk of desertification.

Likewise, in land-scarce Ethiopia, land/man ratios have been declining over the last twenty years in spite of extensive state-sponsored migration from the densely populated High Lands to the low density Oromoland. Yet, once such options are exhausted, in the absence of steady technological improvements (as observed in the case of the Green Revolution) the decline in the land/man ratio leads to a decline in output per capita and GDP growth per head.

Similarly, in countries where growth depends on the exploitation of mines and oil fields, sooner or later the problem of their exhaustion and of the related fall in output and GDP per capita will arise. There are numerous historical examples of how the exhaustion of mineral resources led to long-term stagnation and decline, as in the case of the exhaustion of *guano* deposits in Peru during the nineteenth century or of oil fields in Argentina during the last ten years. While the discovery of new mines, oil fields, and natural resources can delay the onset of economic decline but, given that the (known and unknown) mining resources—and land resources—are by definition finite, the risk of long-term economic decline cannot be avoided.

How can we model the long-term growth of Y under such circumstances that are typical of several developing countries? To keep things manageable, let us develop an extension of the Solow model, that is a Cobb–Douglas production function homogeneous of degree one in which the production factors include the amount of land (T) and the stock of mining/oil resources (R).

$$Y = K_t^{\alpha}\, R_t^{\beta}\, T_t^{\gamma}(A_t\, L_t)^{(1-\alpha-\beta-\gamma)} \tag{5.1}$$

where α, β, and γ are the marginal productivity of capital, mining resources, and land, where $0 < \alpha + \beta + \gamma < 1$, and where technical progress, A, affects in particular the productivity of labour, L. As discussed in Chapter 2, the growth rate over time of K is given by s−d (savings minus depreciation rate), that of L by n (the growth rate of the labour force), and that of A by λ (the exogenously given rate of technical progress). Land T is assumed to be fully utilized (a situation that will be reached sooner or later) and its growth rate is therefore zero, while that of mining resources R is $r = -\mathbf{b}$ (with $b > 0$), that is, the stock of available natural resources declines every year at a rate b.
Taking the logs of equation (5.1), one obtains

$$\ln Y_t = \alpha \ln K_t + \beta \ln R_t + \gamma \ln T_t + (1 - \alpha - \beta - \gamma)(\ln A_t + \ln L_t) \tag{5.2}$$

One can now differentiate totally both sides of this expression with respect to time, remembering that the time derivative of the log of a variable is the variable's growth rate. By differentiating equation (5.2) with respect to time, one thus obtains:

$$\mathbf{g} = \alpha\, \mathbf{k} + \beta\, \mathbf{r} + \gamma \mathbf{t} + (1 - \alpha - \beta - \gamma)(\boldsymbol{\lambda} + \mathbf{n}) \tag{5.3}$$

which is similar to the Solow decomposition discussed in Chapter 2. In this formulation, it is necessary to recall that the growth rate of farmable land (**t**) is zero (as it is already fully used) and that of natural resources (**r**) is equal to −**b**. Remembering that, if the economy is on a balanced growth path, **g** and **k** must be equal (see Chapter 2) and that the growth rates of land and resources are given above, it is possible to derive the 'balanced growth path' growth rate of this type of economy as shown in (5.4)

$$\mathbf{g} = \frac{(1 - \alpha - \beta - \gamma)\ (\boldsymbol{\lambda} + \mathbf{n}) - \beta\mathbf{b}}{1 - \alpha} \tag{5.4}$$

while the growth rate of output per worker (**g***) is the difference between **g** and **n**. In symbols:

$$\mathbf{g}^* = \frac{(1 - \alpha - \beta - \gamma)\ (\boldsymbol{\lambda} + \mathbf{n}) - \beta\mathbf{b}}{1 - \alpha} - \mathbf{n} = \frac{(1 - \alpha - \beta - \gamma)\boldsymbol{\lambda} - \beta\mathbf{b} - (\beta + \gamma)\mathbf{n}}{1 - \alpha} \tag{5.5}$$

This equation shows that the steady state growth rate of output per worker g^* (that with a simple transformation can be turned into the growth rate of GDP per capita, which is the main focus-objective of many policymakers) can be positive or negative. Indeed, it depends on a positive factor (the first term of the numerator, which is driven by the rate of technical progress λ) and two negative terms, that is, the rate of decline of natural resources b (which is negative—see equation (5.5)) and the growth rate of the labour force n.

The difference in the numerator of (5.5) is divided by $(1-\alpha)$ which is always positive as $< 0\ \alpha < 1$, so the rate of growth of output per worker g^* basically depends on whether the technical progress grows faster than the rate of exhaustion of natural resources and the growth of the labour force, a result which is intuitive. This model represents quite well the Malthusian traps (as observed in some Sahelian countries) in which the rapid growth of the population and labour force (n) may cause g^* to turn negative. Only a high value of λ can solve the problem. As noted, new discoveries of oil and minerals in high demand (gold, copper, and rare earths) can temporarily raise the amount of natural resources per worker and even reduce the parameter 'b' for several years (so that the term '$-$b' in equation (5.5) becomes less negative). This will accelerate the rate of growth per worker, until these new resources are exhausted. In virtuous cases, the temporary acceleration of growth due to new discoveries offers the opportunity to invest in R&D and contribute to an increase in the annual rate of technological progress λ that has been shown in Chapter 2 to guarantee perennial positive steady state growth. However, as discussed earlier in this chapter, in practice resource *bonanzas* have been shown to often generate pernicious political-economy effects and macroeconomic distortions. Converting this manna from heaven into technological progress and a meaningful capital accumulation has turned out to be politically complicated.

The historical evidence broadly confirms the results generated by this neoclassical model. Nordhaus (1992) calculated a GDP growth reduction of a quarter of a percentage point for the United States due to land and resource exhaustion, that is, a smaller value than the rate of technical progress (which ranged between 1–2 per cent a year). However, the Indian stagnation of the 1960s and 1970s or the decline of food output per capita of the 1980s and 1990s in many sub-Saharan African countries (where land quality and quantity and resource use per worker diminished, and the rate of technical progress remained negligible) are examples of situations of 'resource constrained growth'. The spread of the Green Revolution experienced by India since the 1970s and 1980s however helped to increase λ substantially so as to offset the fall in land and resources per capita. In Africa the discovery of new oil fields and mining sites—as well as some increase in agricultural productivity in countries that experienced the maize revolution triggered by the adoption of improved seeds—help to explain the growth acceleration of 1995–2008. At the same time, however, many developing countries have been increasingly affected by the perverse effects of climate change (floods, droughts, frost, locust infestation, rises in sea levels, and so on) that reduced the quality and productivity of land, capital, and labour included in equation (5.1). Such changes are also likely to affect the nature of technical progress λ in the resource sector and short-term growth (see Chapter 14).

The conclusions of equation (5.5) apply in particular to countries where agriculture (Table 5.2) or mining are dominant, such as Burundi and Uganda in the first case and Angola and Congo in the second. Yet, with structural change and urbanization, land becomes a less important source of growth. In contrast, oil and mineral resources remain

Table 5.2 Percentage of rural population in selected African countries, 1990–2009

Country	1990	2000	2010	2017
South Africa	47.9	42.6	39.2	34.2
Botswana	58.1	46.8	43.7	42.0
Ruanda	84.6	85.0	76.4	69.3
Niger	84.5	83.8	82.4	80.1
Uganda	88.9	87.9	85.5	83.2
Burundi	93.7	91.7	89.3	87.3
Sub Saharan Africa	72.9	69.1	64.7	61.2

Source: World Bank staff estimates https://data.worldbank.org/indicator/sp.rur.totl.zs based on United Nations Population Division (2014).

central to the growth process even in countries with high GDP per capita, such as Norway, Australia, South Africa, and the United Arab Emirates.

5.4 Policies to Moderate the Problems of Resource-rich Countries

There are, of course, virtuous examples of resource-rich countries that handled the above problems through well-designed policies, as in the case of Botswana, Malaysia, Chile, and other countries that diversified their output and export baskets. The policies they followed are briefly reviewed in this section.

The immediate policy objective is to avoid the appreciation of the real exchange rate and the related decline of manufacturing output and exports. A first step (especially if most of the *bonanza* inflows accrue to the Government) is to adopt a policy of fiscal restraint. This can be done by investing some of the resource windfalls in offshore funds, so that only part of them immediately enters the national economy. Such offshore funds can have different objectives, that is, reducing volatility, saving resources for future generations, or creating sovereign investment funds to acquire the foreign assets needed to diversify the economy.

For instance, in 1985 Chile created a Copper Stabilization Fund (renamed in 2006 Economic and Social Stabilization Fund or ESSF) to reduce the impact of the fluctuation of copper prices on government revenue and exchange rate volatility. In years of high prices (relative to a long-term benchmark set by law) the additional export proceeds are placed in the ESSF, whose monies are re-injected into the national budget in years of low copper prices, thereby smoothing public expenditure and reducing the risk of depreciation of the nominal exchange rate. For instance, in the global recession year of 2009 the government drew US$9 billion from ESSF with the effect that the country recovered swiftly from the world crisis of that year. In contrast, whenever the inflow of rents accrues mainly to private actors, fiscal policy may choose to constrain absorption by freezing the additional public expenditure generated by a surge in *bonanza*-related revenue. This moderates the rise of aggregate demand, especially for NT goods, while an increase in public spending targeted at improving the efficiency of transport, logistics, rural roads, education, and skills formation would help to improve the long-term potential supply of the economy (Brahmbhatt et al. 2010).

In turn, saving funds aim to reduce intergenerational inequality. In Norway, the government set up an intergenerational Government Pension Fund that absorbs every year around 10 per cent of GDP. The returns on this growing fund will be spent in perpetuity by the government to the benefit of future generations. Timor Este's oil fund is an example of how a Least Developed Country has successfully saved temporary windfall gains for future generations. In turn, sovereign wealth funds have been created in oil-rich countries with the purpose of diversifying the economy over the long term. The fiscal rules adopted for the management of such funds are obviously key for their success, although the optimal solution depends on the actual needs and development level of a country. For instance, in poor countries, such funds should save only a limited part of the windfall income as there is an urgent need to invest in badly needed pro-poor and pro-growth projects in the fields of human capital formation, infrastructure, and antipoverty programmes. With the gradual development of the country, the share of the rents saved may be increased.

Additional fiscal policies are needed in nations affected by large swings in oil and metals prices. As noted, such countries are frequently affected by a fiscal laziness that tends to postpone *sine die* much needed reforms to broaden the tax base and increase revenue collection and reduce public expenditure procyclicality (Frankel et al. 2006). Raising the yields of direct and value added taxes to international standards and removing tax allowances and privileges ought in fact to be introduced during periods of *bonanza*. Last, institutional reforms are needed to ensure transparency in the management of resource rents. The literature surveyed in Ndikumana (2014) indicates in fact that at least 8 per cent of petroleum rents earned by oil-rich African countries with weak institutions ends up in tax heavens located in advanced countries.

A second approach is to reduce exchange rate volatility. This approach may be adopted in countries where the windfall rents accrue mainly to private agents and consists in sterilizing the related increase in money supply by issuing state bonds that curtail the money in circulation and so reduce absorption, NT inflation, and RER appreciation. Other approaches to sterilization consist of administrative measures that reduce the amount of money in circulation. This can be achieved, for instance, by encouraging domestic entities to invest abroad, asking banks to shift their deposits to the central bank, or, in the case of destabilizing portfolio inflows, introducing capital controls (see Section 15.13).

Third, over the medium term resource-dependent economies have to diversify and avoid re-primarization. This can be facilitated by the creation of sovereign investments funds. A few mid- to high-income countries such as Chile and the Gulf States managed to allocate some of the resources of the investment funds to the diversification of the economy and to increase the export of non-resource tradable goods characterized by positive learning-by-doing externalities.

Policies for the management of natural wealth can also help to control the impact of resource abundance on inequality. For instance, the state can use part of the rents to finance human capital formation and increase transfers to the poor. In the 2000s, Bolivia and other Latin American countries redistributed part of their resource rents by expanding secondary education (especially for the children of low-income households), non-contributory pensions, and introducing well-targeted subsidies to the poor. Such an approach reduced both inter- and intra-generational inequality (Cornia, 2014).

5.5 Concluding Remarks

Strange as it may seem, the historical evidence shows that developing countries endowed with natural resources, especially 'point resources' like oil wells and mines, grow more slowly over the long term than countries without resources. This problem arises from the intrinsic characteristics of production in the resource sector, and from the fiscal laziness and political economy problems observed in most of the countries with these resources. The intrinsic economic features of the resource sector concern the instability of its international terms of trade, its enclave nature, high inequality, Dutch Disease problems, and political-economic tensions for the control of natural resources. In addition, natural resources are by definition finite and their exhaustion (that may be compensated for years or decades by new discoveries) entails a slowing down of GDP growth that can only be offset by an increase in technical progress, without which economic growth stagnates. However, during the recent period of high commodity prices, most resource economies have experienced a strong reprimarization of their output and exports, and a decline of the weight of manufacturing.

The chapter has shown that public policy may help to prevent or moderate such problems. Policies that have helped to overcome them, facilitated diversification, and reduced the volatility and appreciation of the real exchange rate include the sterilization in offshore funds of part of the export's windfall rents (as observed for instance in Chile), the adoption of a countercyclical fiscal policy, the creation of saving funds for future generations (as observed for instance in Norway), and the creation of sovereign funds to invest in new sectors and technologies.

References

Auty, R. (2001), *Resource Abundance and Economic Development.* Oxford: Oxford University Press.

Auty, R. (2006), 'Patterns of rent-extraction and deployment in developing countries: implications for governance, economic policy and performance', UNU-WIDER Working Paper 16/2006, Helsinki: World Institute for Development Economics Research.

Brahmbhatt M., O. Canuto, and E. Vostruknutova (2010), 'Dealing with Dutch Disease', Number 16, The World Bank, Poverty Reduction and Economic Management (PREM) Network.

Corden, M. and J. P. Neary (1982), 'Booming Sector and Dutch Disease Economics: A Survey', *Economic Journal*, 92: pp. 826–844.

Cornia, G. A. (2014), *Falling Inequality in Latin America: Policy Changes and Lessons.* Oxford: Oxford University Press.

Cornia, G. A. (2016), 'An Econometric Analysis of the Bifurcation of Within-country Inequality Trends in Sub-Saharan Africa, 1991–2011', UNDP Working Paper Series on Inequality N.4. New York: UNDP Regional Bureau for Africa.

Cornia, G. A., J. C. Gomez-Sabaini, and B. Martorano (2011), 'A New Fiscal Pact, Tax Policy Changes and Income Inequality'. UNU-WIDER Research Paper 70/2011, Helsinki: World Institute for Development Economic Research.

Erten, B. and J. A. Ocampo (2012), 'Super-cycles of commodity prices since the mid-nineteenth century', DESA Working Paper No. 110, New York: United Nations.

Fielding, D. and F. Gibson (2013), 'Aid and Dutch Disease in Sub-Saharan Africa', *Journal of African Economies*, 22 (1): pp. 1–21.

Frankel, J. A., C. A. Végh, and G. Vuletin (2013), 'On Graduating from Fiscal Procyclicality', *Journal of Development Economics*, 100: pp. 32–47.

Ndikumana, L. (2014), 'Capital Flight and Tax Havens: Impact on Investment and Growth in Africa', *Révue d'Economie du Developpement*, 2014 (2): pp. 113–41.

Nordhaus, W. D. (1992), Lethal Model n.2: The Limits to Growth Revisited, *Brookings Papers on Economic Activity*, n.2: pp. 1–43, Washington, DC: The Brookings Institute.

Prebisch, R. (1950), 'The Economic Development of Latin America and Its Principal Problems', *Economic Bulletin for Latin America*, 7: pp. 1–12.

Sachs, J. D. and A. M. Warner (1995), 'Natural Resource Abundance and Economic Growth', NBER Working Paper No. 5398. Washington, DC: National Bureau for Economic Research.

United Nations Population Division (2014), *World Urbanization Prospects: 2014 Revision*. New York: United Nations.

World Bank (2016), Migration and Remittances Factbook 2016, http://siteresources.worldbank.org/INTPROSPECTS/Resources/334934-1199807908806/4549025-1450455807487/Factbookpart1.pdf

Suggested further reading

Auty, R. (2001), *Resource Abundance and Economic Development*. Oxford: Oxford University Press.

Persson, T. and G. Tabellini (2000), *Political Economics: Explaining Economic Policy*. Cambridge, MA: MIT Press.

Prebisch, R. (1950), 'The Economic Development of Latin America and Its Principal Problems', *Economic Bulletin for Latin America*, 7: pp. 1–12.

Sachs, J. D. and A. M. Warner (1995), 'Natural Resource Abundance and Economic Growth', NBER Working Paper No. 5398. Washington, DC: National Bureau for Economic Research.

6

Growth in Dualistic Economies with a Rigid Food Supply

This chapter analyses the growth prospects of developing countries with a dualistic economy that consists of an important agricultural sector and a manufacturing sector the growth of which is influenced by supply rigidities in agriculture. The chapter begins by examining the sources of supply rigidity in agriculture. It then discusses the Kalecki (1976) dual economy model which suggests that—in a closed economy—the rigidity of food supply is a source of rising food prices and overall inflation that may frustrate Keynesian expansionary policies to reduce unemployment in a demand-constrained manufacturing sector.

6.1 Sources of Food Supply Rigidity in Developing Countries

In developing countries, several markets, including the food market, are affected by rigidities of various kinds that significantly hamper the attempts of policymakers to increase effective demand and employment. Figure 6.1 illustrates two non-neoclassical and non-Keynesian situations in which the supply schedule is fairly elastic (left-hand side) or rather rigid (right-hand side). In the first, an increase in aggregate demand generates a modest impact on prices and a sizeable increase in output, while the opposite is true in the second.

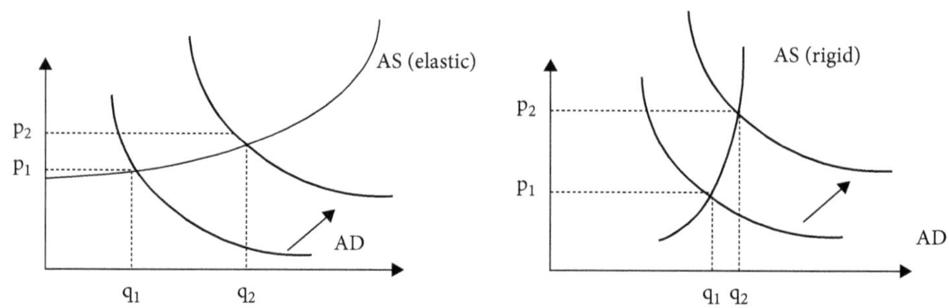

Figure 6.1 Adjustment to a demand shock when the supply curve is elastic or rigid
Source: Cornia and Martorano (2017)

The rigidity of the food supply schedule and, in some cases, of the supply of manufacturing goods assumes particular importance in the early phases of development given the close connection between agriculture and urban-based activities. Agriculture provides wage goods (food) to the urban workers whose real wage depends, given a fixed nominal wage, on the price of food. It also supplies raw materials to urban manufacturing firms. Rural areas likewise represent a main outlet for the domestic production of industrial consumer goods and intermediate inputs, such as tools and fertilizers, used in agriculture.

The Macroeconomics of Developing Countries: An Intermediate Textbook. Giovanni Andrea Cornia, Oxford University Press (2020).

DOI: 10.1093/oso/9780198856672.001.0001

Such a close relationship is critical in the early phases of development when any increase in incomes due to an exogenous shock or a fiscal stimulus is consumed in large part by food. The main factors explaining the rigidity of the food supply schedule are summarized in the following four subsections.

Limited modernization of agriculture when farmland per agricultural worker falls

The limited availability of farmland, accompanied by insufficient technical innovation, is an obstacle to raising output and yields per hectare. Boserup (1981) and Hayami and Ruttan (1985) assumed that, if the rural population grows and the farmable land per rural household falls to 0.2–0.5 hectares, one will observe an endogenous shift to the commercialization of agriculture and higher input-intensity farming. However, as shown by the failure of most of African agriculture to modernize, this outcome is not guaranteed because of the lack of improved technologies for specific crops (such as millet, sorghum, and cassava), and due to limited access to credit, insurance, foreign exchange, extension services, and the other factors discussed in the next three subsections. In all these cases, any increase in income per capita due to higher prices for non-agricultural exports or a fiscal stimulus generate higher imports and inflation.

As noted in Chapter 4, the development thinking of the early years after a country's independence assumed that underemployed rural workers were not willing to migrate to areas with greater amounts of available land for fear of losing the support provided by their families and village communities. A greater demand on labour to grow more food was thus not easily matched by an equivalent increase in its supply. Also, the supply of intermediate inputs and financial capital was not sufficiently elastic to respond to an increase in food demand. Other structural factors limiting the elasticity of food supply were lack of irrigation, and a shortage of improved seeds and fertilizers. Taken altogether, these factors made it difficult to raise substantially the food supply over the short-term in response to a policy driven increase in food prices. A study by Beynon (1989) found that in sub-Saharan Africa the agricultural supply elasticities of an increase in food prices over the short- to medium-term were very low, lying between 0.2 and 0.4, and that large price increases were needed to increase food supply significantly.

Infrastructural, climatic, and terms of trade effects

For a large part of traditional agriculture, yearly food output increases slowly and in an unstable way because of insufficient roads, siloes, and markets, and continued dependence on climatic factors. For instance, in Ethiopia in 2012–13, there were only 78 kilometers of roads per 1,000 square kilometers, despite significant efforts by the government in this area over the previous decade. Under these conditions, an increase in food demand is likely to raise either prices or imports rather than food supply. In this case, the leakage of a fiscal stimulus (that is, more imports) tends to be high and the Keynesian multiplier low. Furthermore, in view of the high relative share of food purchases in total consumption, these rigidities tend to push upward overall inflation. Rigidities in food supply may also be observed whenever an increase in food demand is accompanied by adverse changes in the

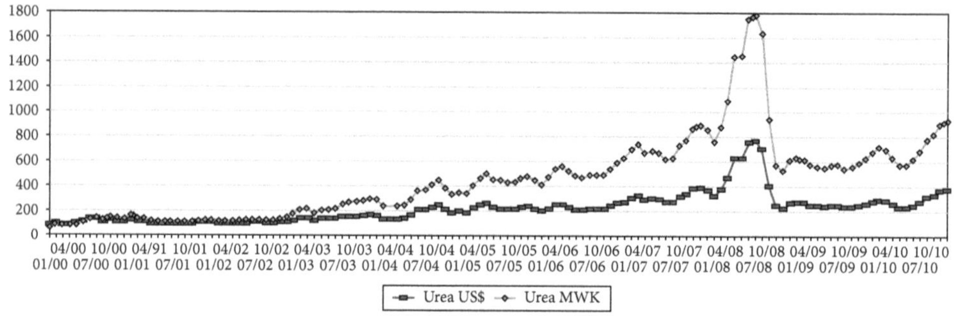

Figure 6.2 Trends in the urea price in US dollars and Malawian kwacha, 2000–2010
Source: Cornia and Martorano (2017)

domestic or international terms of trade. This may be due to a variety of factors, including an increase in the dollar prices of essential imported items (such as oil from which urea is derived), a devaluation of the exchange rate, or both, as illustrated in Figure 6.2.

Institutional factors and distributional conflicts

A slow supply response may also be due to institutional factors. Property rights regimes are not well established in many developing regions. Many farmers do not have land titles certifying their ownership of the land they farm either because of the lack of a cadastre or because the land has been assigned to them in the context of a communal land tenure system which has gradually evolved into an informal private property regime. As a result, their land cannot be bequeathed to their children, sold, or mortgaged. Data from Rwanda show that parcels that could not be bequeathed were much less likely to be improved in any manner, exhibited low productivity, and were unlikely to raise output following a price increase (Migot-Adolla et al., 1991). (However, during the last decade, the government of Rwanda has issued property titles to a large number of small farmers.) Likewise, customary land tenure systems are characterized by substantial risks and transaction costs that lower the expected returns of potential buyers. The lack of clear property rights also hampers access to credit and reduces the possibility of boosting land productivity. In all these cases, the supply elasticity due to an increase in food demand is reduced.

A second institutional factor affecting the supply elasticity of output in labour-surplus agriculture concerns the distribution of land among *latifundia*, capitalistic farms, and small farmers. There is ample empirical evidence showing that (if the access to inputs does not vary across different types of farms) smallholders exhibit higher yields per hectare than large farms. Lower relative yields are typical of *latifundia* owned by absentee landlords who do not behave like profit-maximizing agents but rely for the management and cultivation of their land on middleman who supervise casual labour paid a low wage. Large units of this type thus face a double agency problem, that is, between the absentee landlords and the middleman managing the land and between the latter and the casual labourers. This situation increases labour shirking and monitoring costs and raises production costs to a level higher than in small farms, where the owners and the workers are generally the same people and where there are strong incentives to respond to increases in food demand and prices. High land concentration and precapitalist institutions thus reduces the elasticity of aggregate food supply.

Lack of incentive goods

In rural areas, the availability of incentive goods (manufactured products such as bicycles, candles, soap, radios, sewing machines, oil lamps, clothing, drugs, and so on) may be limited and even have a completely rigid supply schedule. Let us consider the case of an agricultural economy in which farmers produce wheat for self-consumption ($q^{w\text{-}sc}$) and market sale ($q^{w\text{-}s}$) and in which the supply of an incentive good, bicycles for instance, is completely rigid because of limited domestic output and an autarkic trade regime. In such a context, the production function of wheat for sale in the market is quite realistically the following:

$$q^{w-s} = \lambda h^{w-s} \tag{6.1}$$

where $q^{w\text{-}s}$ is the quantity of wheat produced for the market, λ the hourly labour productivity in volume terms, and $h^{w\text{-}s}$ the number of working hours per day dedicated to market production. The welfare function of small farmers and agricultural labourers takes the form:

$$WF = \alpha q^{w-sc} + [\beta\,(q^{w-s}\cdot\, p^{w'})/p^{b}] + \,\gamma\,(10 - q^{w-s}/\lambda) \tag{6.2}$$

in which the first term is the utility deriving from self-consumption of wheat ($q^{w\text{-}sc}$, assumed to remain constant); the second $(q^{w\text{-}s}\ p^{w})/p^{b}$ is the utility deriving from the consumption of bicycles, which have a unitary cost p^{b}, bought by selling wheat on the market; and the third $(10 - q^{w-s}/\lambda)$ represents leisure time, that is, the hours remaining after the reproduction of the workforce (eight hours for sleeping and eating) and after producing wheat for self-consumption (h^{w} equal to six hours). Thus, under normal conditions, the hours that can be assigned to leisure or market production are 10 (24 – 8 – 6). α, β, and γ are subjective weights assigned by the small farmers and farm labourers to each welfare component, where $\beta>\gamma$ because bicycles are highly valued in rural areas. However, the supply of bicycles in rural areas is constant, due to the distance from factories and the urban bias of public policy:

$$q^{b} = c \tag{6.3}$$

so that $\delta q^{b}/\delta p^{b} = 0$. Given this analytical framework, let us now suppose that the government increases the official purchase price of wheat from $p^{w'}$ to $p^{w''}$. According to the standard assumptions of supply models, an increase in wheat prices should lead to an expansion in wheat supply from $q^{w\text{-}s'}$ to $q^{w\text{-}s''}$, which entails an increase in the working hours of farmers for market production from $(h^{w-s'} = q^{w-s'}/\lambda)to(h^{w-s''} = q^{w-s''}/\lambda)$ as well as an increase in their money incomes (Figure 6.3).

With the increase in monetary incomes, farmers will demand more bicycles. However, considering the complete rigidity of their supply, the increase in demand (represented by the rightward shift of the demand schedule from D′ to D″) will generate an increase in the price of bicycles from $p^{b'}$ to $p^{b''}$, while the number of bicycles purchased (q^{b}) will remain exactly the same. This situation will certainly lead to a welfare loss among the farmers. Indeed, in equation (6.2), the first two terms remain unchanged, while the third decreases

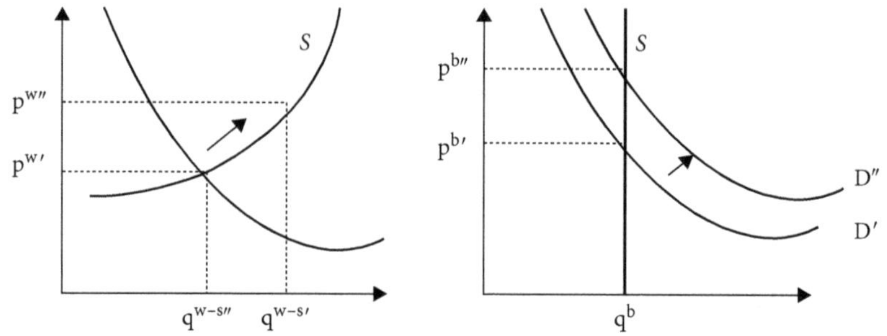

Figure 6.3 Traditional response to an increase in government procurement prices of wheat under a rigid supply of incentive goods

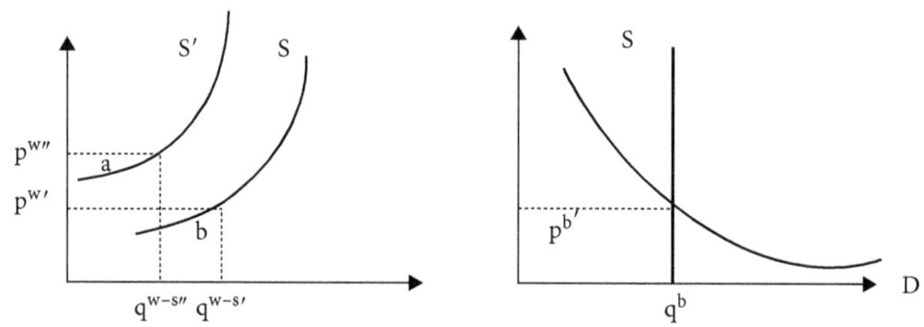

Figure 6.4 Rational response to an increase in the government procurement price of wheat, given a rigid supply of incentive goods

as $(10 - q^{w-s'}/\lambda) > (10 - q^{w-s''}/\lambda)\cdot$ Indeed, to produce a greater amount of wheat, farmers will have to reduce their leisure time.

This solution is clearly irrational. What, then, will be their response to the increase in the public procurement price of wheat? Contrary to the behaviour predicted by the standard model, if faced with a price increase for the purchase of bicycles in rigid supply, the farmers will reduce their wheat supply, which will fall from $q^{w-s'}$ to $q^{w-s''}$ as shown by a leftward shift in the supply schedule from S to S′ (Figure 6.4). This will allow the farmers to earn the same amount of money as before (since rectangle 'a' is equal to rectangle 'b') and be able to buy the same number of bicycles (the demand, supply, and price of which remain unchanged).

This type of response will improve the welfare of the farmers, considering that, while the first two terms of equation (6.2) remain unchanged, the third will increase because, in this case, $q^{w-s''} < q^{w-s'}$ so that $(10 - q^{w-s'}/\lambda) < (10 - q^{w-s''}/\lambda)\cdot$ In short, the farmers obtain the same number of bicycles as before by working less (as wheat now fetches a higher price) and can therefore devote more time to leisure.

6.2 Kalecki's Dual Economy Model

Following Ros (2013), this section discusses the Kalecki (1976) model, which focuses on the structural constraints characterizing the agriculture of developing countries.

These constraints and rigidities may frustrate Keynesian attempts to eliminate industrial unemployment by means of fiscal or monetary stimuli aiming to increase investments and employment in urban manufacturing. This happens because the agricultural sector is supply constrained, that is, it has a rigid food supply. Indeed, an increase in food demand following a fiscal stimulus generates an increase in food prices that erodes the urban real wage, the demand for manufactures and employment in urban manufacturing.

Let us consider the case of a closed economy with fixed nominal wages. The economy has two sectors, agriculture and manufacturing. Agriculture produces only food (a key wage-good in both sectors), operates under competitive conditions, and employs wage-earning agricultural labourers rather than sharecroppers or self-employed small farmers. Manufacturing operates under imperfect competition as only one firm produces each manufactured product. Both sectors exhibit flexible prices, while nominal wages are—as noted—fixed. The monetary wage in manufacturing (W_M) is a multiple l of the agricultural wage (W_A). In symbols:

$$W_M = 1\,W_A \tag{6.4}$$

where l > 1 is a sort of wage premium for the higher human capital of manufacturing workers.

Food production (A) is a function f of a fixed amount of land (T) and labour (L_A), while the manufacturing output (M) is a function g of labour and capital. In symbols:

$$A = f\,(L_A,\ T) \qquad M = g\,(L_M,\ K_M) \tag{6.5}$$

In turn, labour demand and employment in agriculture ($L_A{}^d$) is a function h of the ratio between agricultural wages (W_A) and prices (P_A) and of the fixed amount of land available:

$$L_A{}^d = h(W_A/P_A, T) \tag{6.6}$$

Hence, by substituting (6.6) into (6.5), the agricultural supply is a function j of the ratio between wages and food prices and of the available land, and takes the form $A = j(W_A/P_A, T)$.

In turn, given the price of food, $P_{A,}$ the product wage in manufacturing (i.e. the number of kilogrammes of food that can be purchased with $W_{M,}$) can also be expressed as the ratio of the relative wage (W_M/P_M), divided by the domestic terms of trade ($TOT = P_A/P_M$), as shown below:

$$W_M/P_A = (W_M/P_M)/(P_A/P_M) \tag{6.7}$$

In the agricultural sector, households buy only food because it is assumed that their wage is lower than a critical consumption threshold $C_A{}^*$ below which workers buy only food. In contrast, industrial workers allocate their money to food and manufactured goods. In this sector as well, $C_A{}^*$ is the food consumption threshold below which all of a manufacturing wage is consumed only on food. The total expenditure on food is therefore equal to:

$$P_A C_A = W_A L_A + P_A C_A{}^* L_M \tag{6.8}$$

Food prices depend on the overall food demand by agricultural and manufacturing workers and the degree of rigidity of food supply. Food demand in agriculture is completely inelastic. In manufacturing, prices follow a mark-up rule by which firms add a profit z to production costs, given the units of output k produced with one unit of labour costing W_M

$$P_A = d\,(W_A L_A + W_M L_M) \qquad P_M = (1 + z)\,(W_M/k) \tag{6.9}$$

The food surplus, AS, is the total food supplied by agriculture to the manufacturing sector. It is equal to food production (see equation (6.6)) minus the amount of food consumed by the agricultural workers:

$$AS = h\,(W_A/P_A,\ T) - W_A\,L_A \tag{6.10}$$

Food market equilibrium is verified when the production of food is equal to total food consumption or when AS equals the demand for food by the industrial workers:

$$AS = C_A{}^{*}L_M \tag{6.11}$$

The food surplus AS depends positively on the total food output and on the terms of trade $TOT = P_A/P_M$ so that an increase in food prices caused by supply rigidities increase the food surplus (Ros 2013).

Indeed, an increase in P_A relative to P_M stimulates food production as the product wage in agriculture W_A/P_A falls and raises the incentives to increase the agricultural output and agricultural surplus.

The initial labour market equilibrium is such that the total labour supply is equal to the labour demand in agriculture and manufacturing plus unemployment:

$$L^d{}_A + L^d{}_M + U = L \tag{6.12}$$

Given the existence of unemployment in manufacturing, the policymaker may decide to introduce a fiscal stimulus (by raising, for example, public investment) or monetary stimulus (by reducing, for instance, the interest rate) to increase employment L_M in this sector in order to reach full employment. To study the effect of these measures, we represent the initial food market equilibrium conditions as the equality between the agricultural surplus and the food demand of manufacturing workers.

In Figure 6.5, the food supply schedule in agriculture (AA) is somewhat elastic. Food supply rises, therefore, with an increase in the price of food P_A relative to that of manufactures P_M (which is the domestic terms of trade TOT). This means that an increase of investments and labour demand in manufacturing raises employment in this sector from L_{M1} to L_{M2} (but not to $L_{M\text{-full employment}}$). However, the surge in food prices P_A relative to P_M raises TOT from TOT_1 to TOT_2. With constant P_M and rising P_A, overall inflation accelerates. Reaching full employment in manufacturing ($L_{M\text{-full employment}}$) would therefore require accepting an increase in food prices and the domestic terms of trade TOT that may put into motion an overall inflationary spiral. These are effects that are not contemplated by a standard Keynesian model in which the elasticity of supply (including food supply) is assumed to be high. A high food supply rigidity may thus become a main cause of inflation, as argued by the structuralists.

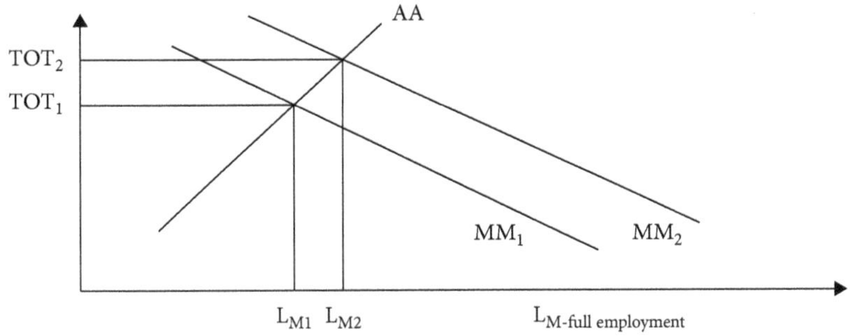

Figure 6.5 Kalecki dual economy model with a semi rigid food supply schedule

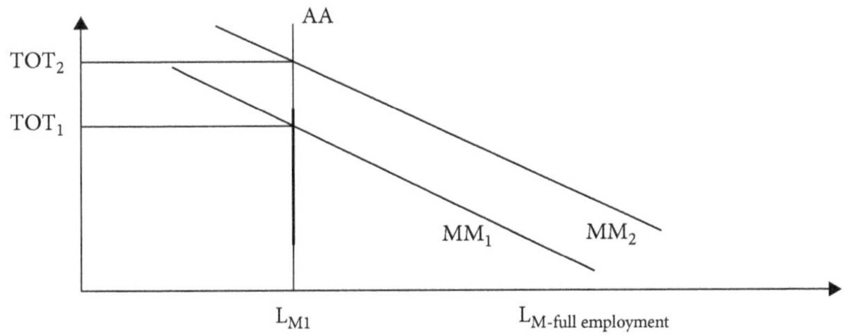

Figure 6.6 Kalecki dual economy model with a completely inelastic food supply schedule

In case the agricultural supply schedule AA is completely rigid (that is, vertical), the only effect of an increase in investment in manufacturing is to raise P_A and TOT (Figure 6.6). There are no effects on manufacturing employment. The reason why the demand for manufactured goods and the level of manufacturing employment in the AA–MM_2 equilibrium remains the same as in the AA–MM_1 equilibrium is that the additional expenditure on manufactured goods due to higher investment and employment in industry following a fiscal stimulus is accompanied by a decline in the consumption of such goods by the industrial workers already employed in this sector. Indeed, confronted with higher food prices P_A, and given an inelastic food demand and a stable nominal wage, these workers reduce their consumption of manufactured goods.

In this case, food prices rise (while industrial prices do not change) and so does overall inflation, while manufacturing output and employment L_M stagnate. Keynesian demand management measures are therefore unable to eliminate the existing structural unemployment in manufacturing because of the rigidity of food supply. Furthermore, because of the increase in inflationary pressures and frequent attempts to stabilize inflation through measures that are likely to generate an output contraction, fiscal and monetary stimuli may give rise to stop-and-go GDP cycles.

A reduction in the structural unemployment associated with food supply rigidity therefore requires the introduction of structural measures such as an intensification of farming techniques (for instance by means of improved extension services), an improvement in rural infrastructure, the introduction of clear property rights removing the fear of land confiscation, the reduction of land concentration through the redistribution of that part of large estates that is underused, temporary compensation for adverse international terms of trade effects, a greater provision of incentive goods in rural areas, and other structural measures.

What happens if the key assumption of Kalecki's model about the stability of nominal wages is abandoned because of the action of trade unions or other factors? In this case, an increase in food prices P_A will trigger an increase in the wage rate and in inflation that will erode the real wage. Ros (2013) argues that there is a minimum threshold wage in terms of food (an inverse function of unemployment) until which a real wage contraction is tolerated by workers, but beyond which a wage increase becomes unavoidable. He shows that the value of this threshold wage depends on the level of industrial employment and the agricultural TOT. Yet, the conclusions of the Kalecki model may differ from those obtained under open economy conditions, as the increased food demand following an expansionary fiscal policy can be satisfied by increasing food imports. In this case, one would avoid an increase in domestic food prices but then has to finance rising food imports (see Section 3.7).

6.3 Concluding Remarks

Despite the preponderance of the agricultural labour force in many developing countries (as in the case of sub-Saharan Africa), food supply has increased slowly over the long term and even more slowly over the short term. Such near complete food supply rigidity is due to a multiplicity of structural (i.e. non-price) factors including: land scarcity in a context of a traditional agriculture that has not benefited from technological modernization; a lack of public goods such as roads and storage facilities to commercialize food crops; increases in international input prices (for fertilizers and other imported inputs); institutional distortions, such as high land concentration, or uncertain property rights over the land; and a lack of incentive goods. The evidence also shows that where such structural obstacles have been removed, the elasticity of food supply has increased and facilitated the process of industrialization.

In this regard, the Kalecki model presented in this chapter has shown that—in a closed economy with fixed nominal wages and an inelastic food demand—a rigid food supply may frustrate in part or *in toto* Keynesian attempts to reduce unemployment in manufacturing (and, by extension, the urban modern sector) by means of fiscal and monetary policies. Indeed, given the rigidity of food supply, an expansionary policy and the creation of new manufacturing jobs may lead to an increase in food demand and food prices. In turn, the additional demand for manufactured goods by the new industrial workers is offset by the drop in demand by previously employed workers who now have to pay higher food prices. Given these circumstances, Keynesian policies appear to be unable to solve structural problems due to the rigidity of food supply. Structural reforms are needed instead.

References

Boserup, E. (1981), *Population and Technology*. London: Basil Blackwell.

Beynon, J. G. (1989), 'Pricism versus Structuralism in Sub-Saharan African Agriculture', *Journal of Agricultural Economics*, 40 (3): pp. 323–35.

Hayami, Y. and V. Ruttan (1985), *Agricultural Development: An International Perspective*. Baltimore: Johns Hopkins University Press.

Kalecki, M. (1976), *Essays on Developing Economies*. Hassocks, UK: Harvester Press.

Migot-Adholla, S., P. Hazell, B. Blarel, and F. Place (1991), 'Indigenous Land Rights Systems in Sub-Saharan Africa: A Constraint on Productivity?' *The World Bank Economic Review*, 5, (1): pp. 155–75.

Ros, J. (2013), *Rethinking Economic Development, Growth and Institutions*. Oxford: Oxford University Press.

Suggested further reading

Beynon, J. G. (1989), 'Pricism versus Structuralism in Sub-Saharan African Agriculture', *Journal of Agricultural Economics*, 40 (3): pp. 323–35.

Ros, J. (2013), *Rethinking Economic Development, Growth and Institutions*. Oxford: Oxford University Press.

7

Rapid Population Growth and Long-term Development

This chapter reviews population trends over the last few hundred years and population projections to the end of the century. It then discusses the five stages of the demographic transition, and different neo-Malthusian and non-Malthusian theories of the relation between population growth and economic development. It emphasizes in particular the effects of rapid population growth on resource availability, human capital formation and population quality, capital accumulation, employment, wages, and income inequality.

7.1 Long-term Population Dynamics

Up to 2017, around 108 billion people have lived on our planet (Roser and Ortiz-Espina, 2017). Around 10,000 BC the world was inhabited by 3–5 million people. Their number then grew slowly, reaching 295 million by AD 1000 as their high fertility was kept in check by a high incidence of epidemics, famines,[1] wars, and natural disasters. With the onset of the industrial and scientific revolution of the mid to late eighteenth century (when the world population was almost stable at around 800 million), the survival rate in the now developed countries improved, and by 1850 the world population exceeded one billion. While the world population growth rate remained below one per cent until 1800 (Figure 7.1), since about 1920 it accelerated to reach 2.1 per cent in 1972.

This was the highest annual growth rate ever recorded. Since then, the world population growth rate has systematically decreased (Roser and Ortiz-Espina, 2017) and the 2015 medium variant projections of the United Nations Population Division suggests it will fall to 0.1 per cent in 2100. There remain however large differences in regional growth rates (Table 7.1). As a result, in 2015 the world population reached an estimated 7.35 billion, of which 1.25 billion (growing at 0.1 per cent a year) resided in the developed countries and 6.01 billion (growing at 1.40 per cent) in the developing ones (United Nations Population Division, 2015). By 2100, the world population is expected to reach 11.2 billion (Table 7.2).

The slowdown of world population growth since 1972 has been characterized by considerable differences in regional growth rates (Table 7.1). While the developed

[1] 70 million people died during the famines of the twentieth century. The main famines of this period include that of 1930–32 due to the forced collectivization of the land of the *Kulaks* in Ukraine and Russia that killed 6–8 million people and caused a major birth deficit; the Great Bengal famine of 1943, and that due to the Big Leap Forward of 1958–62 in China. During the latter, 30–33 million people perished while the birth rate dropped. Its impact was so important that the growth rate of the world population fell from 1.9 to 1.35 per cent a year. During the last thitry years, the number of famines has declined because of improvements in early warnings and transport systems and the expansion of relief operations by the World Food Programme and other agencies. During the last two decades, famines have generally occurred on the occasion of complex humanitarian emergencies, ethnic conflicts, and wars.

The Macroeconomics of Developing Countries: An Intermediate Textbook. Giovanni Andrea Cornia, Oxford University Press (2020).

DOI: 10.1093/oso/9780198856672.001.0001

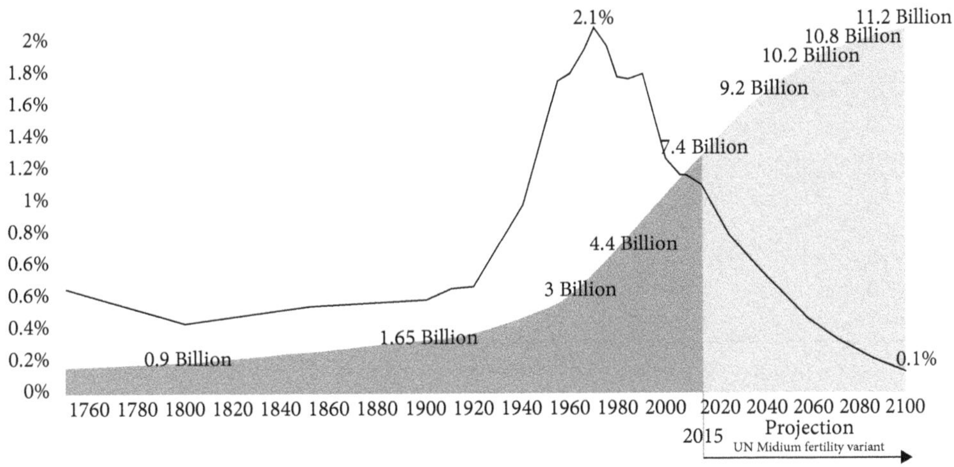

Figure 7.1 World population total and growth rate, 1750–2100
Source: Roser and Espina (2017)

Table 7.1 Annual percentage rate of natural population growth, 1950–2015 by main region and for prototypical countries

	1950–5	1960–5	1970–5	1980–5	1990–5	2000–05	2010–15
World	1.77	1.92	1.96	1.78	1.54	1.24	1.18
Developed	1.18	1.03	0.65	0.47	0.23	0.07	0.10
Developing	2.04	2.29	2.43	2.18	1.89	1.52	1.40
SS Africa	2.19	2.51	2.72	2.89	2.62	2.49	2.60
-Niger	2.86	2.94	2.84	3.02	3.36	3.71	4.02
Asia	1.91	2.11	2.30	1.97	1.68	1.24	1.04
-China	1.91	1.87	2.29	1.48	1.24	0.59	0.54
-India	1.68	2.04	2.23	2.28	1.99	1.69	1.30
L. America	2.71	2.87	2.58	2.30	1.87	1.56	1.19
Europe	1.03	0.94	0.54	0.35	0.03	−0.16	−0.03
-Bulgaria	1.10	0.85	0.64	0.26	−0.25	−0.11	−0.57
-France	0.63	0.68	0.52	0.39	0.34	0.36	0.35
N. America	1.51	1.31	0.64	0.67	0.68	0.54	0.43
Oceania	1.51	1.56	1.47	1.24	1.20	1.07	1.04

Source: Own compilation based on United Nations Population Division (2015 and 2017).

countries have almost reached a stationary population and several of them have experienced a demographic decline for roughly twenty years, the population is still expanding substantially in South Asia, a few Latin American countries and, especially, sub-Saharan Africa. The two extremes of the distribution of natural population growth rates in Table 7.1 (4.02 in Niger and- 0.57 in Bulgaria) underscore these differences in stark terms. Due to the expected persistence of such differentials, the regional composition of the world population will evolve substantially in the future (Table 7.2). The main changes will concern a shrinkage of the population share of the advanced economies and a rise of that of sub-Saharan Africa.

Table 7.2 Population projections and percentage shares in parenthesis, Medium Variant, 2015–2100

	2015	2030	2050	2100
World	7349 (100)	8501	9752	11,213 (100.0)
Africa	1186 (16.1)	1679	2478	4387 (39.1)
Asia	4393 (59.8)	4923	5267	4889 (43.6)
Europe	738 (10.0)	734	707	646 (5.8)
Latin America	634 (8.6)	721	784	721 (6.4)
North America	358 (4.9)	396	433	500 (4.5)
Oceania	39 (0.5)	47	57	71 (0.6)

Note: Population figures are in millions.
Source: As Table 7.1.

7.2 Population Growth during the Five Stages of the Demographic Transition

The natural population growth rate (PGR) is the difference between the birth rate (BR) and the death rate (DR), both for 1,000 people. The BR depends in turn on the total fertility rate (TFR) and the 'population momentum', that is influenced by the share of women of reproductive age in the total population. The evolution of population growth in the course of economic development is illustrated by the Demographic Transition Model (DTM) that was inspired by the historical experience of Europe after the industrial revolution (see later). As noted, the only variables that directly enter the DTM are BR and DR. However, several policy and behavioural factors explain the evolution of these two variables. According to the household economics model (Becker, 1981) the TFR reflects the demand for children as consumption goods or investment goods. Neoclassical consumer theory assumes that an individual with given preferences for a range of goods tries to maximize the satisfaction derived from consuming such goods subject to her income constraint and the relative prices of all goods. Children are considered a special kind of consumption good (e.g. a source of joy and satisfaction for the parents) so that the number of children procreated is a rational parental decision that also takes into account the preferences for and price of other consumption goods. Thus, if other factors are held constant, the desired number of children can be expected to vary directly with household income (although this may not be true, for reasons discussed later, in both poor and rich societies), and inversely with the price of children (that is, the cost of raising a child) relative to the price of other goods. In symbols, these relationships can be formalized as follows:

$$D_c = f(Y/c,\ P_c,\ P_x,\ t_x) \quad \text{with} \quad x = 1,\ 2, \ldots\ n \qquad (7.1)$$

where D_c is the demand for surviving children (reflecting the desired family size after taking into account the level of child mortality rates—which is high in developing countries), depending on the level of household income per capita (Y/c), the price of children P_c (that is, the cost of raising a child, including the opportunity cost of the mother's time), the prices of all other goods (P_x), and the consumer preferences for goods relative to children (t_x). Under standard neoclassical conditions, this implies that:

an increase in household income increases the demand for children; the higher the price of children, the lower the quantity demanded; the higher the prices of other goods relative to that of children, the greater the quantity of children demanded; and the stronger the preference for other goods relative to children, the lower the demand for children.

A household's choice of having a child may depend also on the demand for children as investment goods. Children are in fact considered a source of cheap labour and support for their parents in old age. Their procreation depends on the absence of institutions (e.g. social assistance and old age pensions) or incompleteness of markets to insure oneself against old age, disease, accidents, death of the spouse, unemployment, or crop failure. Obviously, the demand for children as investment goods is influenced by the level of child mortality (the higher it is, the lower is the probability that a child will survive until the old age of the parents), the risk that the children will not earn enough in the future to support the parents, and the risk that children may migrate and remit to the parents only small or no monies. In this framework, $p > 0$ is the probability that each child will survive, will not be poor, migrate, or otherwise be unwilling to look after their parents in old age. In turn, $q > 0$ is the minimum acceptable level of probability (desired by the parents during their reproductive life) that their children will provide for them in old age. Given all this, the number 'n' of children that will be generated has to ensure that the following inequality is satisfied:

$$1 - (1 - p)^n > q \tag{7.2}$$

where $(1 - p)$ is the probability that each child will not look after their parents. If p falls, $(1 - p)$ will rise, and the only way to satisfy the above inequality is to increase n. Note that, given q, if p increases (because of a fall in child mortality, outmigration, and an improvement in the future living conditions of children), n can fall and still satisfy inequality (7.2). Likewise, the development of social pensions for the elderly has the effect of reducing q (the desired probability to be assisted by one's own children in old age). Given p, a reduction in q will entail a decline in n. This decline in fertility may, however, not occur immediately—giving rise to a discrepancy between collective conditions and individual choices. This may be due to incomplete information by the parents who have not observed or internalized the decline in child mortality or rising incomes, as they make their decisions based on adaptive expectations. This may also happen because of the presence of negative externalities that make the fertility considered optimal from the parents' perspective but sub-optimal in terms of collective choices. Indeed, while parents may evaluate their private costs and benefits of having an additional child in the way just discussed, the social cost of each additional child includes not only the private cost but also the collective cost (in terms of social services to be provided by the state, congestion costs, and lower future wages). In brief, the decline in fertility may be stalled by imperfect information or the discrepancy between private and collective costs/benefits of having an additional child. Beyond weak public policies and traditional social norms, sub-Saharan Africa's stalled demographic transition may also be explained by such problems.

The Beckerian model, however, assumes the rationality of all agents, and ignores the impact of traditional values and social norms (such as polygamy, the extended family, and the low social status of women) that may prevent a decline in fertility. In addition, in ethnically divided societies, decisions are taken by the extended family or the communities who may value other factors, for example the size of their group relative to that of other ethnic groups. Becker's model also ignores the availability of contraceptives, a factor that may make achieving the desired number of children more feasible.

At the aggregate level, the demand for children can be represented in similar ways but introducing a few additional variables into the model discussed above. To start with, there is a need to take into account social norms and values, that are time invariant in a micro context but not in cross-sectional and time series analyses. Economic development (proxied by the average Y/c) is an important factor explaining BR and DR in different societies and era. Yet, its distribution across households (measured for instance by the Gini index) is also important, as in unequal societies poor families have a higher demand in relation to the mean for children as investment goods. In addition, a rising Y/c reduces DR especially among children, because of a general improvement in living conditions, greater access to food and other basic necessities such as good quality health services, and the availability of fresh water supply and sanitation. TFR and BR are also equally affected by economic development. A rise of Y/c generally entails (if with considerable variation across countries) a greater coverage of social assistance schemes for the elderly, as well as an increase in the level of education of women and their participation in the labour force, that is, factors that increase the opportunity cost of having a child.

Cultural-political changes leading to their emancipation may also prompt women to have fewer children. In addition, with economic development people gain better access to birth control. In contrast, in rich societies with a low TFR of 1–1.5, a rising age at marriage, the high cost of childcare, the revolution of rising consumption expectations (driven by advertisements and changes in values) reduce the demand for children while the DR rises because of population ageing. As a result, the natural rate of increase of the population may become negative, further increasing the ageing and old-age dependency rate in these countries. This is a major problem for advanced societies, but will not, however, be discussed here.[2]

The evolution of the population growth rate (PGR) can thus be formalized in a simple simultaneous dynamic macro model with time lags of various duration (ignored below) in which BR and DR affect economic development (Y/c), and vice versa:

$$\text{PGR} = \text{BR} - \text{DR} \tag{7.3}$$

$$\text{BR} = \text{f}\,(\text{TFR}) \tag{7.4}$$

$$\begin{aligned}\text{TFR} = \text{f}\,(&\text{DR, Y/c, Gini index, women education/status,}\\ &\text{old age pensions, spread of birth control})\end{aligned} \tag{7.5}$$

$$\begin{aligned}\text{DR} = \text{f}\,(&\text{TFR, Y/c, Gini income, health coverage,}\\ &\text{female education, age structure of the population})\end{aligned} \tag{7.6}$$

$$\text{Y/c} = \text{f}(\text{PGR, pop density, K, HC, L}, \lambda, \text{environmental conditions}) \tag{7.7}$$

[2] The reader interested in this topic may consult the literature on ageing and development. See, for instance, Vos et al. (2009)

As noted at the beginning of this chapter, the evolution of BR and DR and their interaction with economic development can be illustrated by the Demographic Transition Model. This suggests that a country's population growth goes through five stages that exhibit—with variations from region to region—different levels of BR and DR. As the latter two variables change in relation to economic development and to each other, their impact greatly affects a country's total population. In this model, a country will progress from one stage to the next of the demographic transition thanks to changes in social and economic forces and policies that affect BR and DR. The changes occurring during the five stages are as follows:

Stage 1 is characterized by high fertility and high mortality (see Figure 7.2). This situation was observed before the industrial revolution in Europe and at independence in many developing countries. In Stage 1 both birth rates and death rates are high (around 40 per thousand). As a result, natural population growth is low, although it may swing due to wars, famines, pandemics, or natural disasters. Why are both rates so high? Historically, high birth rates are observed in subsistence agriculture societies that make use of unskilled manual labour in a backward land-abundant agriculture where the main production factor is labour. Larger families mean a larger workforce, and a way to increase production.

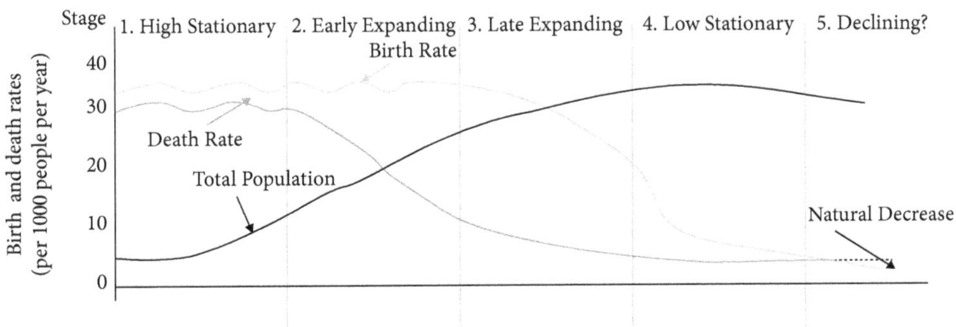

Figure 7.2 Birth and death rates per 1000 and total population level during the five stages of the demographic transition

Source: Own elaboration on https://www.population education.org/content/what-demographic-transition-model

High DR, the security of parents in old age, the low status of women and lack of job opportunities outside the family farm are additional factors explaining high fertility. As noted earlier, families plan their desired family size and opt for high fertility rates as they know that a high proportion of their offspring (up to 350 per 1000 live births in pre-industrial Europe, around 150 in present day poor countries) will not reach age 5 due to inadequate health care, low parental education, limited access to food during the lean season, and lack of potable water and sanitation. Thus, high average TFR and PGR are a response to a high DR among children as shown in Figure 7.3.

During stage two fertility remains high, while mortality experiences an initial fall (Figure 7.2). Unlike in Europe, where the DR fell because of a general improvement in living conditions, in most developing countries its decline (especially among those under 5 years of age) was due to the diffusion of modern public health measures such as antenatal and perinatal care, vaccination, oral rehydration, and penicillin and, in recent times, progress against malaria, AIDS, and tuberculosis. Death rates have also fallen due to the diffusion of female education, improved gender equality, gains in food production, and an increase in incomes. However, this decline in the death rate was not always accompanied by a timely drop in birth rates, as parents did not internalize right away the changes in survival rates among children or abandoned norms rewarding high fertility. The result is rapid population growth. Most countries that are today in Stage 2 come from sub-Saharan Africa. In 2010–15, Niger was the country with the highest rate of natural population growth in the world (Table 7.1) due to a birth rate of 49.8/1,000 and a death rate of 9.6/1,000. With the transition from Stage 1 to 2 its population growth rate rose from 1.86 in 1950–55 to 4.02 in 2010–15. Niger it is a good example of Africa's stalled demographic transition (Canning et al., 2015) caused by unsatisfactory gains in the field of agriculture, literacy, and educational and work opportunities for women. With no changes, and if its current population growth is sustained, Niger's population will double every fourteen years.

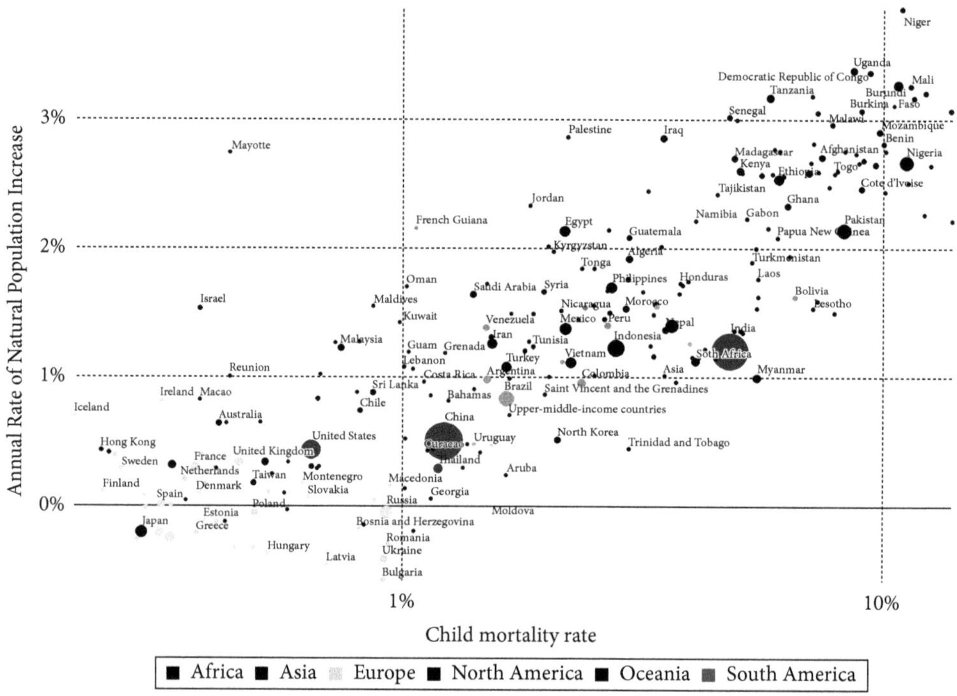

Figure 7.3 Cross-country relation between the under-5 mortality rate and population growth rate, 2015

Source: Adapted from UN Population Division (2017) and https://ourworldindata.org/grapher/child-mortality-vs-population-growth

During Stage 3 one observes a further decline in mortality, and the beginning of a decline in fertility (Figure 7.2). During this period, birth rates start decreasing gradually, usually as a result of improvements in economic conditions and women's status, and greater access to contraception. This is the stage that—towards its end—records a sizeable decline in population growth but its speed and time frame has varied considerably from country to country. Some countries went through a rapid transition with falls in birth rates of more than 40 per cent, while others exhibited a much slower decline. Different patterns of demographic transition have been observed. In Europe fertility fell due to the perceived high cost of marriage and having children. In contrast, in most developing countries, death rates fell first due to the diffusion of Western medicine while fertility fell due to the drop in the demand for children generated by economic development, the spread of social assistance, and an increase in female education and employment that raised the opportunity cost of having a child. In addition, in middle income developing countries, women may pursue advanced education and so are likely to plan for smaller families. The development of social security arrangements for the elderly (which, for example, greatly improved in Latin America during the last twenty years) also reduced the desired family size. Finally, in sub-Saharan Africa the rapid decline in mortality recorded over 2000–15 has not yet been accompanied—with some exceptions—by a decline in fertility.

During this phase, population continues growing slowly until the fertility rate reaches 2.1 births per woman of fertile age. Countries making the transition to Stage 3 generally enjoy economic growth and social stability. A moderate population growth provides significant advantages for a country as it reduces the young-aged dependency ratio and generates the demographic dividend analysed by Bloom and Williamson (1998) for the East Asian Tigers. This dividend is due to an increased supply of workers (born during Stage 2), a decline in births, increased savings, faster human capital formation, and growing domestic demand. The demographic dividend emerged in East Asia and the United States around 1970, and has been seen in India since 2000. Much of Africa has not yet enjoyed such a dividend due to persistently high BRs despite falling DRs. According to Canning et al. (2015), rather than enjoying a demographic dividend, sub-Saharan Africa may now be facing a demographic disaster.

During Stage 4, both the BR and DR are low, population growth falls and remains stable at a low level. The total fertility rate decreases until it reaches replacement level (2.1 births per woman of fertile age) or falls below it. Countries in this group generally have a strong economy, high level of education, and universal healthcare coverage. They have also completed the migration from rural to urban areas, and expanded job opportunities for women. Population slowly reaches its stationary state, while the dependency rate remains stable (or may rise due to population ageing). Argentina, Brazil, most of Europe, the East Asian economies, and the United Stares are in this group.

During Stage 5 one observes a further fall in fertility and a rise in mortality (Figure 7.2). Fertility rates fall below replacement level, and the share of the elderly rises, due to improvements in healthcare, and may exceed that of the youth. Countries in Stage 5 experience a negative natural population increase (as observed in much of Europe, the countries of the former Soviet Union, and East Asia) that is generally compensated for by replacement migration. In this stage the demand for 'children as consumption goods' falls due to their perceived high cost relative to other goods, a longer duration of education, and greater employment opportunities for women. Declining birth rates can also be linked to public policies (as China's One Child Family Policy) or epochal events, such as the dramatic fertility fall and mortality rise caused by the psychosocial stress and growing uncertainty experienced in the former communist countries of Europe during the difficult transition to a market economy in the 1990s. Whatever the reason, all these countries have for years experienced a negative natural population increase. In Germany, the DR has outpaced the BR rate since 1972. Yet, immigration and the time lag associated with demographic momentum, kept total population from declining. In Italy the natural rate of increase of the population started falling in 1990–95 (−0. 1 per cent) to reach −1.1 per cent in 2010–15. However, also in Italy, immigration stabilized the resident population at around 59 million. Keeping this value constant over the next three to four generations requires a continuous inflow of migrants. As a result, in 2100 a third of the resident population of Italy will be made of descendants of immigrants or of recently immigrated people.

7.3 Population Growth and Economic Development

While the role of population policies has seldom been discussed in the context of pro-poor growth (Klasen, 2003), the relationship between population growth and economic development has been a recurrent theme in economic analysis since at least 1798 when Thomas Malthus published his famous '*An essay on the population principle*'. Different schools of thought come to different conclusions about the population-development nexus, although, in recent times, the majority of scholars agree that fertility rates that are too high or too low hamper growth.

Classical and neo-Malthusian theories

The Malthusian and Ricardian theories emphasized the limited amount of land available to grow food and a lack of technical innovation in agriculture. Malthus's model is rather simple. It assumes a fixed quantity of land. An expanding population increases food production in a linear way. In contrast, the population rises exponentially. Both hypotheses are reasonable over the short–medium term, as observed in many countries. Beyond a given equilibrium point, the population grows faster than food production, and this will reduce the amount of food that each individual can consume, ultimately resulting in disease, starvation, and conflicts over food. In this model the only way to avoid such negative outcomes is refraining from having many children. Ricardo also considers the amount of land as finite, but additionally he assumes that the first land put under cultivation is the most fertile. Population growth will induce the cultivation of marginal lands characterized by declining yields per hectare, with the effect that food production will grow in a concave way while population increases exponentially. However, neither Malthus nor Ricardo foresaw the enormous technological advances (such as the Green Revolution) that raised massively land productivity and food output or the health innovations that reduced the toll of infectious diseases. These advances enabled the world's population to grow from 1 billion in 1798 to 7.4 billion today.

Nevertheless, the essential insight that population growth constitutes a potential threat to economic development remained influential and affected the international development agendas, especially in the 1950s and 1960s, a period marked by unprecedentedly rapid population growth in many developing countries. During these years, neo-Malthusian economists such as Lester Brown and initiatives such as that of the Club of Rome, as well as the environmentalists, emphasized—again by means of sophisticated mathematical models—the inability of the planet to support a fast rising population. This inability is not just because of the challenges involved in increasing food production but because of rising pollution levels, the greenhouse effect, the exhaustion of a number of minerals and fuels, and a loss of biodiversity. Some of these predictions (about the impact of the greenhouse effect, the loss of biodiversity, and irreversible loss of forest cover) are beyond questioning, while others are controversial. For instance, while there are still one billion food-insecure people, at the global level there are no immediate signs of food penury. The main problem is the distribution of income, purchasing power, and food consumption both within and between countries.

Theories negating a negative relation between population and economic growth, or positing a positive relation between them

The Classical Development School and the modernization theories of the 1950s and 1960s emphasized the role of capital and skilled workers in promoting growth but ignored the population issue that was implicitly assumed to be growth-neutral (see Section 2.5). During the 1970s numerous empirical studies, utilizing an increasing amount of comparable international data, failed to detect a robust relationship, either positive or negative, between national population growth rates and per capita income growth. For instance, Easterlin (1967) suggested that the existing knowledge of his time did not allow any general conclusion about the impact of population growth given the developing countries' diversity in terms of birth rates, population density, and GDP growth rates. He accepted some of the points made by the population optimists and pessimists (see the following paragraph), but suggested that the pessimistic view may have been exaggerated.

In turn, population optimists such as Simon (1981) and the Unified Growth Theory discussed in Chapter 2 suggest that population growth promotes development, as it increases the supply of young workers and human capital. However, when land/man ratios decline population pressure triggers endogenously an induced technical and institutional innovation, leading to a shift towards modern farming techniques and changes in land tenure systems from communal to private. Population growth also increases the size of the domestic market. The related increase in production would generate economies of scale in manufacturing and a more efficient use of infrastructure and social services. It also leads to a diversification of production, and—after a time lag—to a demographic dividend. In turn, the pro-natalist neo-Marxists have argued that some developing regions (such as today's Central African Republic, Congo, and Kazakhstan) are underpopulated, and their idle arable land could yield large increases in agricultural output if more people were available to cultivate it. Some note that several African countries had in the distant past larger populations than after independence, and that their depopulation resulted from the slave trade, compulsory military service in colonial armies, confinement to reservations, and the forced labour policies of former colonial rulers.

Non-Malthusian theories positing a negative relation

In the 1990s the neutrality of population growth with respect to economic development was questioned in several respects. Analyses of the East Asian miracle of the 1960s and 1970s suggested that there was a negative association between population growth and economic performance. When fertility rates decline over a sustained period of time (as in Stage 3; see Section 7.2) the size of the working age population grows relative to that of children and youth, leading to a situation of 'many working arms' and 'fewer mouths to feed'. Such a change in the age structure generates a window of opportunity during which a country can raise its level of savings, investments, and income per capita. Likewise, in contrast to assessments conducted in the first decades after World War II, analyses conducted since the 1990s on cross-sectional data (see for instance Birdsall and Sinding, 2001) found a negative correlation between population growth and economic development (Figure 7.4). Recent meta-analyses concluded that this negative relationship emerged on

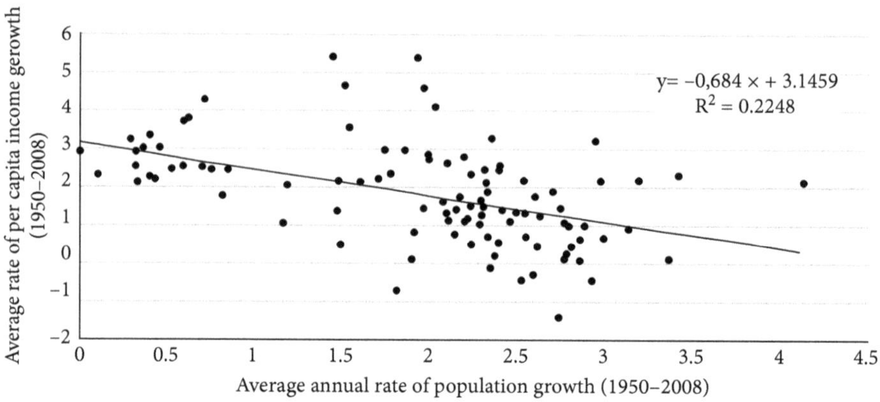

Figure 7.4 Average annual rate of population growth and average per capita income growth, 1950–2008

Source: https//www.theige.org/blog/is-populationgrowth-good-or-bad-for-economic-development/

the basis of post-1980 data, and that its strength increased over time. The channels through which the negative effects of rapid population growth are transmitted to economic development are reviewed hereafter.

To start with, rapid population growth in poor countries diverts to consumption scarce resources that could be saved and invested in physical and human capital, thereby placing a drag on economic development. In Solow's model (see Chapter 2) the steady state growth of total output ($\Delta Y/Y$) and output per capita (($\Delta y/y$) are respectively equal to

$$\Delta Y/Y = \lambda + n \text{ and } \Delta y/y = \lambda + n - p \tag{7.8}$$

while the growth decomposition of the Mankiw et al. model yields similar results, that is

$$\Delta y/y = \lambda + \alpha k + \beta hc - p \tag{7.9}$$

where n, p, k, and hc are the annual growth rate of the workforce, population, capital stock, and human capital, and λ is the rate of technical progress. In relation (7.8) when $n > p$ (as during Stage 3 of the demographic transition) economic growth accelerates. In contrast, whenever $n < p$ (as in Stage 2) growth per capita decelerates, as the income allocated to physical and human capital formation declines. Likewise, in relation (7.9) the growth of income per capita falls in relation to the current level of p. These conclusions, however, must be put into perspective, as—in the real world—savings also depend on other factors, such as the distribution of income among households, the share of public savings in the total (that can be increased even in periods of fast population growth), and other variables.

An effect of a rapid population growth, p, ignored by the models mentioned above concerns its impact on non-renewable resources (see Chapter 5). In countries with a large population and high density (as, at the time of writing, parts of South Asia and sub-Saharan Africa) an increase in population growth leads to a sharp fall in the land/man ratio and falling yields per hectare, as incomplete credit, insurance, and input markets hamper the technological shift assumed to occur endogenously by the population optimists. As for communal forests, pasture land, fisheries, and water sources, population pressure may lead to a 'tragedy of the commons'. For instance, in Malawi, a population growth of 2.5–3 per cent a year reduced the average farm size to 0.23 ha by 2009, not enough to feed a family. In turn, forest cover dropped to 32 per cent of its initial value. Similar arguments may be put forward concerning the international public goods (falling air quality, ozone layer), although population growth is only one factor contributing to such problems. As for minerals and fuels, increased demand due to population growth provokes an increase in their prices and may lead to a faster exhaustion of these resources.

A third negative effect concerns urban congestion. Fast population growth and rural–urban migration lead to the creation of mega-cities that are characterized by huge unhealthy slums and an increase in the marginal cost per capita for water supply, transport services, and housing. Limited urban space also generates negative externalities (for transport costs and time, pollution, and urban land rent) and frustrates the efforts of policymakers to introduce reasonable urban planning. Despite the growth of incomes that generally accompanies urbanization, death rates can increase among marginal populations due to the unavoidable delays in developing costly urban infrastructure: subways, water mains, and in-house piped water that are far more expensive than the buses and communal water stands used in villages and small cities.

Fourthy, rapid population growth may affect its quality, that is, its health, nutrition, and education. During Stage 2 the child population increases exponentially together with the demand for food and health and education services. Public expenditure in these areas does not generally increase as quickly, while most large families have limited private resources per child to invest in these areas. Poor households will therefore suffer from reduced and/or lower-quality access to such services. As a result, their children generally achieve lower educational scores than the children of smaller families. An increase in population quantity thus tends to reduce its quality. Thus, strong demographic pressure may exacerbate the population 'quality–quantity trade-off'. Food security may also be threatened by rapid population growth, as in the case of sub-Saharan Africa, and in India before the onset of the Green Revolution. In Africa south of the Sahara, rising food imports and food aid point to the inability of the region to feed itself. The United Nations Intergovernmental Panel on Climate Change (2014) ranks Africa as the most vulnerable region in this area due to its low adaptive capacity. Climate change in this region is linked not only to agricultural losses but also to violent clashes related to control over food, as illustrated in a study of more than 78,000 armed confrontations between 1980 and 2012 in the Sahel (O'Loughlin et al. 2014).

Fifth, the arrival on the labour market of large cohorts of unskilled workers without a parallel increase of capital stock and farmable land squeezes wages at the lower end of the distribution, and raises land rents and the capital share. Furthermore, much of the workforce remains unemployed or under-employed. For instance, 53 million of Africa's 200 million young people aged 15–34, are not in stable employment. Of these 40 million are not working, 18 million are still looking for a job while the remaining 22 million have given up (African Development Bank, 2012). If the demands of this population are not met, the region may face socio-political destabilization. Low wages and limited employment also lower the opportunity cost of having children among the poor and so increases their fertility rate. To exacerbate the problem, a fall in the wages of working male adults often leads to an increase in labour market participation—at very low wages—by women and children, with negative effects on their well-being.

For all the reasons given above, the negative consequences of rapid population growth fall most heavily on the poor because they are the ones who are made landless, suffer most from cuts in government health and education programmes, and bear the brunt of environmental damage. In addition, the data confirm that the poor have higher fertility than better-off families. This perpetuates poverty but also exacerbates inequality as—given the same family income—higher fertility reduces the income per capita of poor families.

Finally, high population growth is likely to raise international migration and/or political instability. Many consider the increase in international migration, both legal and illegal, to be one of the effects of developing countries' population boom. Although many factors (such as differentials in income and opportunities) spur emigration, as in the case of the low-fertility Eastern Europeans moving to Western Europe, an excess of job seekers due to rapid population growth over job opportunities is surely one of them. The cost of international migration falls on both recipient countries (often developing countries themselves, but increasingly so developed countries) that have to integrate the new arrivals, and on the countries of origin who may suffer from a brain drain. It is not surprising, therefore, that this issue has recently taken on political importance in North America and Europe.

7.4 Concluding Remarks

This chapter has reviewed the main population trends by main regions between 1950 and 2100 and discussed the determinants of population growth at the micro and macro level. In the latter case, these include income per capita, income inequality, education, availability of old age pensions, the age structure of the population, the spread of birth control measures, and social and religious norms affecting the status of women. It has then discussed the demographic transition model inspired by the experience of the industrialized countries of Europe and followed during the post-World War II period by the majority of the developing countries. However, by the standards of this model, the demographic transition has now stalled in several countries of sub-Saharan Africa and some of South Asia. If this phenomenon continues, by 2010 the distribution of world population by the main regions will be strongly affected, and so will the growth pattern of the countries witnessing persistent rapid population growth.

Several theories of the relation between rapid population growth and economic development have been proposed during the last two centuries. Their conclusions differ substantially according to the model utilized and the period covered by these analyses. The more recent analyses suggest that, starting from the 1980s, such relation has become—*ceteris paribus*—negative. The pathways through which GDP growth is being affected include: low wages and a slow growth in income per capita, rising inequality (as the poor families exhibit a higher fertility than the middle class and the elites), mounting pressure on land and non-renewable resources, urban congestion and rising costs to provide fresh water, housing, and transport services. High population growth also exacerbates the trade-off between population quantity and quality as state authorities and households can allocate only limited resources to the health, nutrition, and education of each child and youth. In developing countries with continuing high population growth rates, the adoption of suitable population policies would thus promote medium-term growth and reduce—*ceteris paribus*—income inequality.

References

African Development Bank, OECD Development Centre and UNDP (2012), *African Economic Outlook*. Abidjan, Paris, and New York: OECD.

Becker, G. (1981), *A Treatise on the Family*, Cambridge, MA: Harvard University Press.

Birdsall, N. and S. W. Sinding (2001), 'Population Matters—Demographic Change, Economic Growth, and Poverty in the Developing World', in N. Birdsall, A. C. Kelley, and S. W. Sinding,(eds), *Population Matters: Demographic Change, Economic Growth and Poverty in the Developing World*. Oxford: Oxford University Press.

Bloom, D. E. and J. G. Williamson (1998), 'Demographic Transitions and Economic Miracles in Emerging Asia', *World Bank Economic Review*, 12: pp. 419–55.

Canning D, S. Raja, and A. Yazbeck (eds) (2015), *Africa's Demographic Transition: Dividend or Disaster?* Washington, DC: AFD and World Bank,

Easterlin, R. A. (1967), Effects of Population Growth on the Economic Development of Developing Countries', *The Annals of the American Academy of Political and Social Science* 369: pp. 98–108.

Klasen, S. (2003), 'In Search of the Holy Grail: How to Achieve Pro-Poor Growth?', in B. Tungodden and N. Stern (eds), *Towards Pro Poor Policies. Proceedings from the Annual Bank Conference on Development Economics-Europe*. Washington, DC: The World Bank.

O'Loughlin, J., A. M. Linke, and F. D. W. Witmer (2014), 'Effects of temperature and precipitation variability on the risk of violence in sub-Saharan Africa, 1980–2012' *Proceedings of the National Academy of Sciences*, 111 (47): pp. 16712–17.

Roser, M. and E. Ortiz-Ospina (2017), *World Population Growth*, published online at OurWorldInData.org. https://ourworldindata.org/world-population-growth/.

Simon, J. L. (1981), *The Ultimate Resource*, Princeton, NJ: Princeton University Press.

United Nations Intergovernmental Panel on Climate Change (2014), *2014 Report*. New York: United Nations.

United Nations Population Division (2015 and 2017), *World Population Prospects: 2015 and 2017 Revisions*. New York: United Nations.

Vos, R., J. A. Ocampo, and A. L. Cortez (2009), *Ageing and Development*. London: Zed Books.

Suggested further reading

Boongarts, J. and J. Casterline (2013), 'Fertility Transition: Is Africa Different?' *Population and Development Review*, 38 (Suppl 1): pp. 153–68.

Mason, A. (2001), *Population Change and Economic Development*. Stanford, CA: Stanford University Press.

8

Long-term Growth in Developing Countries with a Large Informal Sector

This chapter examines the features of the informal sector that is an important component of the economy of most developing countries. It also analyses the causes of high rates of informality, the economic efficiency of the informal sector and its impact on aggregate growth. To this end, it presents the Loayza model that posits a negative link between informality and the rate of growth.

8.1 Definition, Size, Composition, and Features of the Informal Sector

The developing countries, particularly the Least Developed Countries, are characterized by a high degree of economic informality that generally declines with an increase in GDP per capita (Figure 8.1). In these countries, most small farmers are self-employed on subsistence plots or work as landless casual labourers. Even today, in several sub-Saharan African countries, employment in agriculture and rural non-agricultural activities accounts for 70 per cent of the total. Such informal sector units typically operate at a low level of organization and with no separation between labour and capital providers.

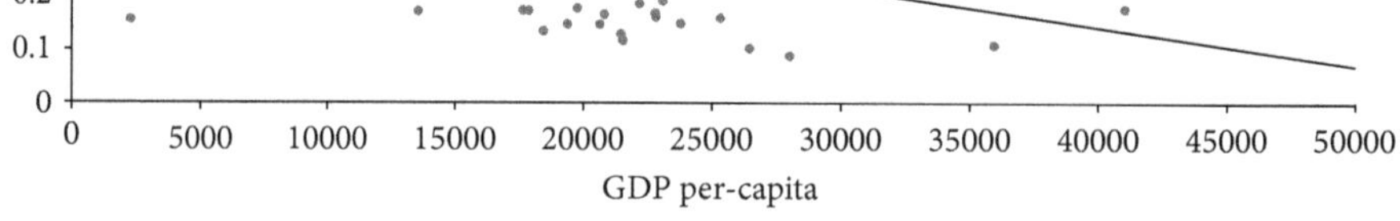

Figure 8.1 GDP per capita and percentage share of the informal economy in the total GDP
Source: Elgin and Oztunali (2013)

In the urban informal sector, people are mainly employed in small manufacturing units (producing clothing, cooking utensils, processed food, furniture, metal utensils, handicrafts, and similar goods), construction (building small houses and kiosks), and informal services (taxis and local transport, car repairs, personal services, hairdressing, restaurants, and street selling). Street vendors make up a large share of the informal urban sector in total employment, ranging from 50 to 90 per cent in India and selected Asian and African

The Macroeconomics of Developing Countries: An Intermediate Textbook. Giovanni Andrea Cornia, Oxford University Press (2020).

DOI: 10.1093/oso/9780198856672.001.0001

countries. Informal sector units typically employ family members and only rarely have a few paid workers. The sector makes extensive use of local raw materials and produces mainly for local markets.

Informal micro firms employ simple technologies and unskilled workers connected by relations of casual employment, kinship, and personal or social ties rather than formal contractual arrangements. They also lack a legal organization, do not separate personal and firm accounts, are not registered, and do not provide written contracts to the non-family workers they may hire. While some informal activities are illegal, the majority of them are perfectly legal, although they are unregistered, and so escape most forms of taxation and formal sector rules. Figure 8.2 suggests that they are more common among households in the bottom three quintiles of income per capita.

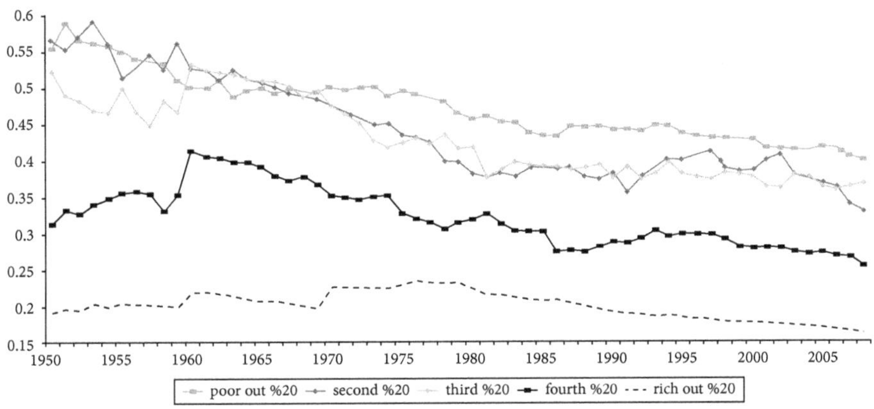

Figure 8.2 Average informality by income quintile, 141 countries, 1950–2009
Source: Elgin and Oztunali (2013)

However, the top end of the informal sector includes microenterprises that employ five or more non-family workers either permanently or for short periods. These Small and Medium Enterprises (SMEs), which are effectively informal sector units that have grown in size, can exhibit an efficient production organization in the agro-industrial sector and in industries where economies of scale in production, procurement, and marketing are limited. SMEs can also achieve an efficient scale of production at a comparatively low level of output. They can additionally present a few advantages in relation to larger firms. Given their low physical and human capital and input intensity of production, they have a low output per worker. Yet, in view of the limited inputs they use, their total factor productivity is not necessarily low. Likewise, their greater employment intensity per unit of output compared with large firms contributes to a faster growth of employment and a better distribution of income in areas with a large labour surplus. And given a much lower investment per worker relative to large firms, they can develop more quickly in regions with low savings. In addition, their reliance on family labour improves production incentives and reduces labour shirking and monitoring costs in relation to bigger firms. Finally, SMEs exhibit greater flexibility and adaptability than big firms in responding to changes in local market conditions. The low entry barriers and low operational costs in sectors such as food preparation, repairs, retail trade, and transport imply that a large number of small units producing or selling almost identical products, as in the fruit and vegetable markets, feed strong competition within these sectors. When this is true, a key policy dilemma is to find ways to help micro firms to graduate into the SME group.

In middle-income countries especially, the informal sector is very heterogeneous. It includes both small low-productivity firms offering some kind of livelihood to people with no better job opportunities, as well as highly skilled people working in modern services (finance, insurance, modern transport, tourism, and government services). Yet, data on eleven middle-income African countries show that their combined value added share accounts for only 12–31 per cent of GDP, while that of informal services (commerce, restaurants, hotels, transport, and community and personal services) ranges between 12–42 per cent of total informal services.[1] In the poorest countries, these imbalances are much greater. In contrast, in the advanced economies, one finds highly trained and well-remunerated self-employed professionals, such as engineers, architects, freelance journalists, and lawyers.

Various studies by the World Bank confirm that, despite its low value added per worker, in low-income, developing countries the informal economy contributes significantly to GNP, consumption (up to 40 per cent of the total), employment, and income generation. It also represents a means of survival for individuals lacking proper jobs and social insurance (Benjamin et al., 2014). The contribution of the informal sector to non-agricultural GDP ranged between 27 and 41 per cent in countries in sub-Saharan Africa, while, in Asia and Latin America, it accounted for 31 and 29 per cent, respectively. In India, the unorganized sector accounts for 62 per cent of GDP, 93 per cent of the total workforce, and 83 per cent of non-agricultural employment. However, the cross-country comparability of these figures is low, because the criteria used to gauge the extent of informality vary across countries. Nonetheless, while the weight of the informal sector is substantial, there is not much evidence that it contributes to aggregate growth. However, firm-level surveys only capture a subset of the vast informal sector. For this reason, there may be some empirical justification for the difference of viewpoints about the growth benefits generated by the informal sector.

8.2 Interaction between the Formal and the Informal Economy

There are important backward and forward linkages between formal and informal sector activities. A substantial proportion of the goods and services produced by the latter are consumed within the sector itself, but another share competes with goods produced by formal manufacturing and services. Informal sector firms may also produce semi-finished inputs for the formal sector at prices below formal sector rates. This may raise the savings in the formal sector and—given certain conditions—promote physical and human capital accumulation. Positive implications for growth may follow.

So, the informal and formal segments of the economy work in part independently, in part in cooperation, and in part in competition. Furthermore, the urban informal sector works as a sponge that absorbs urban surplus labour unable to find employment in formal manufacturing and services. Given the low rate of urbanization and high population growth rate observed in sub-Saharan Africa, rural–urban migration is likely to accelerate, and most new urban migrants will have no choice but to seek jobs in the informal sector.

[1] 10-Sector Database, Groningen Growth and Development Centre, Faculty of Economics and Business, University of Groningen, Groningen, the Netherlands. https://www.rug.nl/ggdc/productivity/10-sector/.

These formal–informal sector relations also change in the course of the business cycle. During recessions, the informal sector behaves counter-cyclically and absorbs labour expelled from the formal sector because of firm failures and employment cuts. Thus, during formal sector crises, such as the 1997 South East Asian crisis, the informal sector expands. In Indonesia, there was even urban–rural return migration. Symmetrically, when manufacturing, utilities, construction, and modern agriculture expand, the size of the informal sector shrinks.

Changes in technology and macroeconomic policy also affect the size of the urban informal sector. For instance, the diffusion of highly divisible and increasingly more affordable new investment goods, such as cell phones, computers, and solar panels, allows firm size to be reduced in industries with limited economies of scale in production (Kaplinsky 2014). In turn, the trade and financial liberalization of the 1980s and 1990s triggered an expansion in informal activities. Indeed, to resist import penetration, formal sector firms relocated to low-wage countries or increased the subcontracting to informal sector firms. Likewise, the liberalization of the capital account and the increased inflow of foreign funds appreciated the real exchange rate, pushing formal firms to cut wage costs by informalizing (Taylor 2004). Changes in tax policy may also affect the spread of the informal sector. For instance, the shift to simpler tax instruments (such as Mexico's *Monotributo*) lightened the administrative and tax burden of micro firms and SMEs, some of which could graduate into the formal sector.

8.3 Causes of Informality

There are at least three theoretical explanations for the high degree of informality observed in several developing countries. The most obvious is the limited volume of private and public savings to finance an adequate accumulation of physical and human capital and public infrastructure. Given the limited substitutability of capital with labour in production, the solution to this problem requires a continued mobilization of savings over many years. A second explanation for the high degree of informality is the dualism of factor markets. Quite independently of the amount of investible resources available to the economy as a whole, formal and informal sector firms experience different levels of access to the markets for credit, insurance, technology, urban space, industrial inputs (such as water and electricity), and skills. Besides being subject to administrative norms that are often complicated for their size, informal sector firms are generally unable to come up with loan collateral. For this reason have no chance of obtaining commercial bank credit, the cost of which is a fraction of the interest rates they have to pay in the informal credit market. The same dualism is observed for the access to insurance, urban land, and industrial inputs.

A third explanation is proposed by Loayza (1997), who argues that in countries with weak institutions and tax rates exceeding the optimal level, many formal sector firms move to the informal sector to escape what they think is excessive taxation. This shift, however, correlates negatively with the growth rate of the economy, a conclusion that is supported by econometric evidence for Latin American countries. Overall, a large informal sector hampers economic growth because it reduces tax revenue, makes use of public services it did not pay for, and in this way crowds out the availability of such services for the higher productivity and tax compliant formal sector firms.

8.4 How does Informality Affect Economic Growth?

As noted, despite its substantial contribution to GDP, in many developing countries there is limited evidence that informal sector enterprises contribute to its growth over time. For some authors, a sizeable informal economy impedes economic growth. But there are also alternative views, backed by the historical experience of now advanced countries (such as Italy) and of emerging economies where micro firms and networks of micro firms have gradually developed into dynamic SMEs.

Informal sector firms as victims of over-regulation

The view of informal sector firms as victims of over-regulation is based on the pioneering work of De Soto (1989), who emphasized that unofficial firms are potentially efficient although, in practice, they are constrained by excessive fiscal and regulatory requirements that hamper their growth and impede their formalization. In his most quoted example, De Soto argues that in New Jersey it takes two weeks to start a business, while in Peru it takes a year and the payment of bribes. Simplified fiscal and regulatory reform and a reduction of entry barriers to formalization, supplemented by easier access to credit and other inputs, would thus facilitate the move of such firms into the formal economy. A second crucial assumption of this viewpoint is that there are no fundamental differences between formal and informal firms, and that the substantial productivity gap existing between registered and unregistered firms is due to marked differentials in the use of modern technologies and in the capital intensity and scale of production. As a result, the administrative formalization of informal firms due, for instance, to simplified regulatory reforms may not necessarily lead to substantial productivity gains over the short term unless the dualism of factor markets is eliminated or reduced.

Informal sector firms as a burden to the economy

According to the view of informal sector firms as a burden to the economy, unofficial firms are a threat to formal sector firms and an obstacle to overall economic growth. Not only does the small scale of informal firms lead to inefficient production, but it also generates an incentive to remain small to avoid detection by public authorities. As a result, the absence of investible profits for their technological upgrading confines informal firms to a low productivity trap that adversely impacts overall growth. Indeed, informal firms operate about 50 per cent below the average productivity level of formal firms in the same sector. Second, the advantage enjoyed by informal firms because of tax evasion and regulatory non-compliance gives them an unfair edge over formal firms, thereby allowing them to impinge on the formal sector's market share. Formal firms are thus exposed to unfair competition, which reduces their incentive to invest, expand, and improve productivity. In addition, the reduction of tax revenue due to the existence of a large informal sector may induce more stringent taxation of the formal sector and may consequently fuel further expansion of the informal sector. Proponents of this view call for stronger fiscal and regulatory enforcement as well as reforms to curb informality. This view is opposed by De Soto, as several firm-level surveys do not provide much evidence to support the view that the practices of informal firms are a substantial obstacle to the operations of formal sector firms.

The dual economy view

According to the dual economy view, informal firms are perceived to be considerably different from their formal sector counterparts as they are less efficient and operate in traditional sectors with little capital and obsolete technologies. Formal and informal firms coexist and operate in segmented markets with different degrees of access to inputs, and differences in the consumers they target. Hence, informal firms are not viewed as a threat to the formal sector, but, at the same time, they are seen as not contributing much to growth. As the informal sector provides subsistence to millions of poor people, any fiscal and regulatory amendments that are potentially costly to informal firms are discouraged. Yet, proponents of this view support policies that create new formal firms rather than formalize the informal ones. Informality would diminish with growth and the transfer of labour to the new formal sector. Survey data yield results that are consistent with this view because informal firms differ considerably from formal firms. De Soto (cited in Loayza 1997) shows, for instance, that in 1988 Peruvian informal firms borrowed from non-institutional lenders at a nominal monthly rate of 22.0 per cent, while formal sector firms borrowed at 4.9 per cent from the banking sector. Likewise, in Bangladesh, in 1998 informal firms obtained credit from moneylenders at 48–100 per cent a year, while formal sector firms borrowed from commercial banks at 12 per cent. At the same time, informal firms were found to bear a smaller labour cost because of their non-compliance with labour laws and reliance on family labour.[2]

8.5 The Loayza Model on the Impact of Informality on Growth

As noted above, Loayza (1997) shows that there exists a negative relation between the size of the informal sector and the rate of growth of GDP. His theoretical prediction is supported by empirical evidence for the Latin American countries. A large informal sector has a negative impact on economic growth because it reduces tax revenue and therefore negatively affects government spending on public goods such as infrastructure and public services. In addition, informal sector firms make use of public services and so crowd out their availability for more efficient and tax-paying formal sector firms.

The Loayza model emphasizes the costs and benefits of being informal, but ignores some important aspects of informality such as the size of firms, their capital per worker, and the segmentation of the labour market that have been mentioned in Sections 8.2–8.4.

In Loayza's model, the economy is made up of agents endowed with a different starting level of a combined measure of physical and human capital. Such agents operate a

[2] In developing countries, the labour market is strongly dualistic. In the formal sector, wages may be set through collective bargaining, while workers benefit from some form of social protection and minimum wages. These conditions do not apply to the informal sector, where oligopolistic demand–supply relations prevail, and labour protection is not enforceable. However, there are some real-life exceptions. For instance, Kristensen and Cunningham (2006) show that, in nineteen Latin American countries, the formal sector minimum wage represents a reference wage for the informal sector, thus overturning the prior conclusion. This may not be true, however, in countries with greater underemployed labour.

technology that exhibits constant returns to capital to produce a single good, which can be either consumed or invested. Unskilled labour is not a production input. The overall production function is given by

$$Y_i = A\,(G/Y)^{\alpha}\,k_i \text{ with } 0 < \alpha < 1 \tag{8.1}$$

where Y_i and k_i are the output and capital of economic agent i; A is an exogenous productivity parameter; G is the flow of public services; Y is the total output of the economy; and α is the elasticity of output with respect to G/Y.

In this model, economic agents can choose to belong to the formal or informal sector. The first pay a proportional income tax rate (τ) that is used in part to finance the provision of public services (G), in part for the enforcement system, while part may be wasted on unproductive public activities. Informal firms may instead pay a proportional fraction (π) of their income as a penalty for non-compliance. Such monies are used to help to finance the government's enforcement system, but not for growth-promoting public services (G), to which informal agents have access only up to the share (δ) because of their unregistered status. Given all this and the sector to which the economic agent *i* belongs, the net-of-tax or penalty income of the agent is given by

$$Y_i^F = (1 - \tau)\,A(G/Y)^{\alpha}\,k_i \tag{8.2}$$

$$Y_i^I = (1 - \pi)\,A(\delta\,G/Y)^{\alpha}\,k_i \text{ with } 0 < \tau, \delta \text{ and } \pi < 1 \tag{8.3}$$

where the superscripts F and I refer to the formal and informal sector, and the parameter δ is the share of public services utilized by the informal sector. The size of the informal sector in total production is $I = Y^I/Y$, while the public expenditure on growth-enhancing activities G is

$$G = \phi\,(q,\ \lambda)\,(\tau,\ Y^F) \tag{8.4}$$

where the first term is a function measuring the share of taxes collected on formal sector activities used to fund G, while the rest is used unproductively. The function depends positively on parameter q, a proxy for the quality of public institutions and thus of public spending, and negatively on parameter λ, that is the strength of the enforcement system, as a stronger enforcement system absorbs resources that could be spent on G. Overall, the function ϕ (q, λ) is positive.

The ratio of public services to total production is then given by

$$G/Y = \phi\,(q,\ \lambda)\ [(\tau\,(1 - Y^I/Y)] \tag{8.5}$$

which shows that, for any given q, λ, and τ, an increase in the size of the informal sector (that does not pay taxes) reduces the share of Y that can be allocated to growth-enhancing activities. In turn, the effective penalty rate (π) depends on the ability to detect and punish informal activities, that is, on the strength of the enforcement system (λ) and on the public dissatisfaction with the spread of the informal sector, I. However, as noted, a strengthening of the enforcement system absorbs fiscal resources. The generic function $\pi = \pi(\lambda, I)$ can be written in explicit multiplicative terms as $\pi = \lambda I$.

Given that the economic agents can move freely between the formal and informal sectors, the equilibrium between the rates of return on capital in the two sectors (that is derived by equalizing the right hand side of equations (8.2) and (8.3)) is given by:

$$(1 - \tau)\ A(G/Y)^{\alpha} = (1 - \pi)\ A(\delta G/Y)^{\alpha} \tag{8.6}$$

Remembering now that π can be written as λI, after dropping the terms that appear on both sides of equation (8.6), it is possible to write

$$(1 - \tau) = (1 - \lambda I)\ \delta^{\alpha} \tag{8.7}$$

from which one may derive, through simple changes, the equilibrium size of the informal sector as

$$I = (\delta^{\alpha} + \tau - 1) / \lambda\delta^{\alpha} \tag{8.8}$$

Equation (8.8) shows that the size of I depends positively (after a given threshold) on the tax rate (τ), as a high τ raises the incentives to evade taxes, and on the share of public services accessible by the informal sector (δ). At the same time, the size of I depends negatively on the enforcement capacity of the tax administration (λ) and the elasticity (α) with which Y increases following a rise of G/Y· *A*n increase in institutional quality q (not included in (8.8)) is also likely to lead to a decline in I.

One can now relate in the Loayza model the growth rate of Y (y) to the tax rate (τ) in the context of an optimal taxation model in which such a relation has an inverted U shape. We then compare this relation with that identified by the Barro–Sala-i-Martin (B-SM) optimal tax policy model in which there is congestion in the use of public services, but no tax-evading informal sector. The analytical demonstration is omitted here, but Figure 8.3

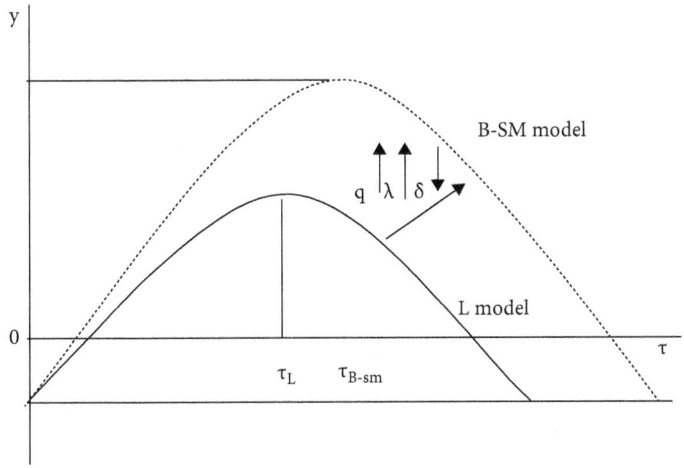

Figure 8.3 Relation between tax rate and GDP growth rate in the Loayza model in relation to the Barro–Sala-i-Martin model in the context of an optimal taxation model relating the growth rate of output to the tax rate.

Source: Own elaboration of Figure 1 in Loayza (1997)

shows that in the Loayza model the optimal tax rate (τ_L) and y are lower than the corresponding rates identified in the B–SM ($\tau_{B\text{-}SM}$) model. As discussed above, this is because the informal sector pays no taxes (while the eventual fines it has to pay are not used for growth-enhancing activities), crowds out a share, δ, of public expenditure, G, and has lower capital productivity relative to the formal sector (see equation (8.3)).

Figure 8.3 shows in particular that the concave (τ, γ) function shifts to the right (more rapid growth) with an increase in q (the quality of public institutions) and in λ (the enforcement strength). But the latter is costly to improve, so the effect of an increase in λ may also generate the opposite effect, suggesting that the effect of an increase in λ is ambiguous *ex ante*. In turn, an increase in δ (the share of public services appropriated by the tax-evading informal sector, which is less productive than the formal sector) reduces the rate of growth.

8.6 Measures to Improve the Productivity of the Informal Economy

The main obstacles to the development of informal firms and SMEs are the lack of credit, skills, technology, space, and access to water and electricity as well as the obligation to comply with complicated administrative and tax norms. Policy responses generally focus on breaking up the informal sector, while preserving its job-creation and income-generating potential, by investing in integrated urban local development activities (International Labour Office 2007). This entails investing in human capital formation (for example, through apprenticeship courses); facilitating access to improved technology and credit through bank-assisted credit unions and microcredit institutions, especially among women (as done in Bangladesh by the BRAC Bank); the titling of public land used for productive purposes; improved supply of water and power; and affirmative policies that enhance social protection for informal sector workers. However, to see these measures implemented, the informal sector needs to become politically organized and strive to consult with the government to frame policies in its favour.

Long-term preventative measures that support capital accumulation and the modernization of agriculture, construction, and manufacturing also need to be introduced. If these sectors develop rapidly, there will be fewer people engaged in livelihood activities in the informal sector. Likewise, there is a need to help develop modern services. While waiting for long-term policies to yield their results, governments and aid agencies should aim to upgrade the productivity of informal firms. The informal sector is heterogeneous (it comprises micro firms and better-structured SMEs). A disaggregation of its composition is therefore needed before planning the most suitable interventions. The development of government services, infrastructure, and utilities often entails an increase in public spending and so requires an increase in tax revenue. But, possibly, the most important policy intervention should focus on the creation of a de-repressed, accessible, and regulated financial and insurance sector. The experience of Japan in the 1960s and of Latin America in the 2000s may represent a blueprint for action in low-income developing countries. During the early phases of its development, Japan reached a high coverage of formal banking services by relying on a widespread network of post offices. This reform helped to raise saving deposits and provide credit to productive sectors all over the country. Having previously over liberalized the financial sector without increasing the supply of credit to the economy and experiencing considerable financial instability, Latin America introduced reforms in the 2000s that enhanced the capitalization, funding, and supervision of banks. It also introduced stricter prudential regulation of financial systems, enhanced risk-assessment mechanisms in large banks, developed appropriate legal and accounting frameworks, and reduced currency mismatches (Rojas-Suarez 2010).

8.7 Concluding Remarks

Most development models (such as the Lewis and Kalecki models) assume a modern urban sector populated by formal manufacturing and service firms. However, the reality of developing countries, especially the low-income ones, is quite different, as the urban labour market is dominated by informal sector firms. To increase the efficiency of the unorganized sector it is necessary to understand the origins of informality, the diffusion of which can be alternatively (or simultaneously) attributed to low savings and capital accumulation, a dualism of input markets that penalizes small firms, or the desire to escape what is perceived as excessive taxation. The reality varies considerably across countries: in some areas informal firms may be victims of administrative over-regulation and excessive taxation. Their formalization and overall GDP growth may therefore require a reduction in entry barriers and ad hoc taxes. In other countries, informality may be the result of the deliberate decision of economic agents who choose to remain small to avoid excessive regulation and taxation. By doing so, however, they may generate unfair competition for formal sector firms that may be forced to reduce their output and investments, with negative effects on aggregate growth. In this case, stricter regulation and enforcement are the recommended policy. The dualism of input markets may also be a source of informality that can be reduced by improving the functioning of such markets.

The Loayza model formally analyses the impact of informality within the context of an optimal taxation growth model. It shows that, compared to an economy with only formal firms, overall growth declines in line with the spread of informal firms which do not pay taxes and so reduce public spending on pro-growth externalities. Additionally, at the same time, they use part of the existing public infrastructure, thus reducing its availability for formal sector tax-paying firms. The quality of public institutions (that reduces the share of taxes wasted) and the strength of tax enforcement (that reduces tax evasion by informal units) limit the decline of growth in relation to the scenario of an economy with only formal firms. The model does not discuss, however, the dualism caused by low savings and investment in low-income economies.

References

Benjamin, N. with K. Beegle, F. Recanatini, and M. Santini (2014), 'Informal Economy and the World Bank', Policy Research Working Paper 6888, May 2014, Washington, DC: The World Bank,.

De Soto, H. (1989), *The Other Path: The Invisible Revolution in the Third World*. New York: Harper and Row.

International Labour Office (2007), 'Upgrading Work and Enterprises in the Informal Economy: Organizing for Voice and Participation', Geneva: http://www.ilo.org/public/portugue/region/eurpro/lisbon/pdf/forum_session2.pdf.

Kaplinsky, R. (2014), *Innovation for Pro-Poor Growth: from Redistribution with Growth to Redistribution through Grow* in G. A. Cornia and F. Stewart (eds), *Towards Human Development: New Approaches to Macroeconomics and Inequality*. Oxford: Oxford University Press.

Kristensen, N. and W. Cunningham (2006), 'Do Minimum Wages in Latin America and the Caribbean Matter? Evidence from 19 Countries', Policy Research Working Paper 3870, Washington, DC: World Bank.

Loayza, N. (1997), 'The Economics of the Informal Sector: A Simple Model and Some Empirical Evidence from Latin America', Policy Research Working Paper, Washington, DC: World Bank.

Rojas-Suarez, L. (2010), 'The International Financial Crisis: Eight Lessons for and from Latin America', Working Paper 202, Washington, DC: Centre for Global Development.

Taylor, L. (2004), *External Liberalization, Economic Performance and Distribution in Latin America and Elsewhere*, in G. A. Cornia (ed.), *Inequality, Growth, and Poverty in an Era of Liberalization and Globalization*. Oxford: Oxford University Press.

Suggested Further Reading

De Soto, H. (1989), *The Other Path: The Invisible Revolution in the Third World*. New York: Harper and Row.

Elgin, C. and O. Otsunali (2013), *Institutions, Informal Economy, and Economic Development*, Working Paper 2013/3, Department of Economics, Istanbul: Bogazici University.

International Labour Office (2007), Upgrading Work and Enterprises in the Informal Economy: Organizing for Voice and Participation, Geneva. http://www.ilo.org/public/portugue/region/eurpro/lisbon/pdf/forum_session2.pdf.

9

Balance of Payments-constrained Growth

This chapter illustrates the features of the external sector of commodities-exporting and investments-importing developing countries. It discusses in particular the value of the price and income elasticities of commodity exports and compares them with those of capital goods and key intermediate inputs exported by the industrialized countries. It then illustrates the Thirlwall model which shows that unfavourable values of such import and export elasticities may reduce their rate of growth of GDP compatible with a balance of payments equilibrium.

9.1 Structural Features of the External Sector of Developing Countries

Several developing countries are affected by a strong external vulnerability that reduces their long-term growth and increases their short-term instability. This depends on the features of their exports and imports. With rare exceptions, the developing countries tend to be open economies with trade/GDP ratios greater than 50 per cent. This exposes them to a rapid transmission of the volatile global business cycle through a fall in the volume of world demand and prices of the goods they export, and increases in the global supply of commodity exports due to new discoveries and other shocks discussed in this chapter. As a result, the prices of primary commodities are affected by high volatility, as shown in Figure 9.1 for metals (left panel) and oil (right panel).

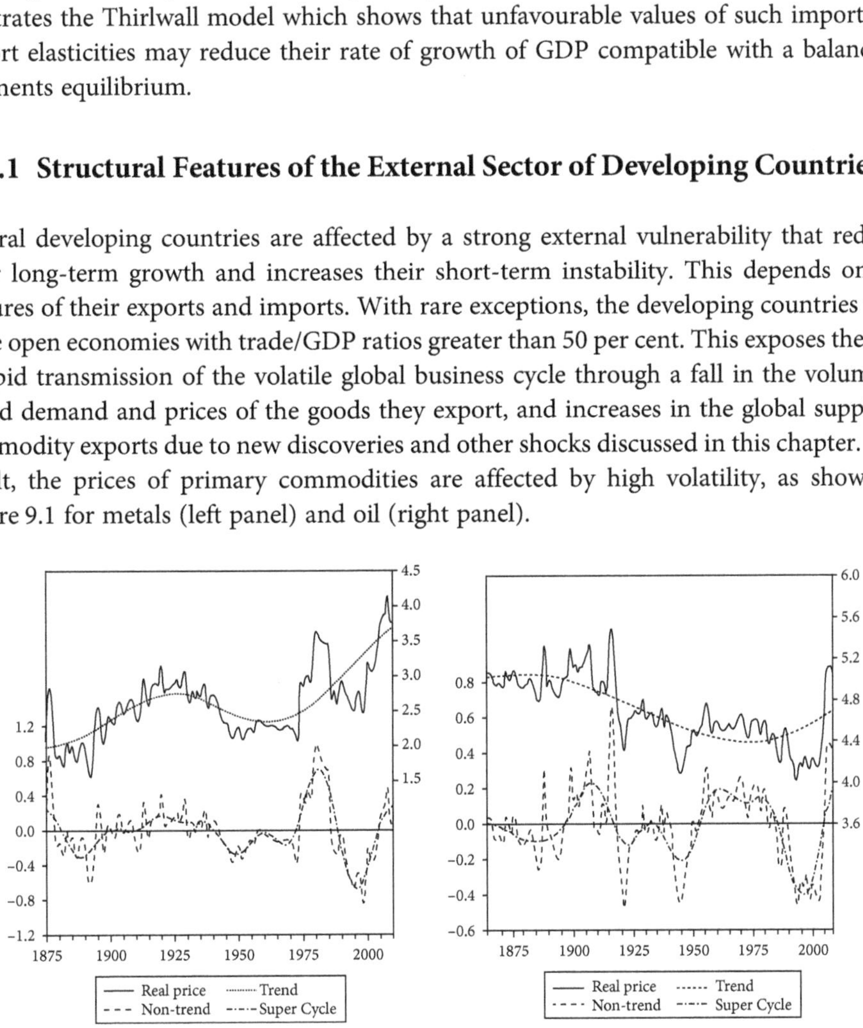

Figure 9.1 Long-term super-cycles of the real prices of metals and oil, 1975–2002
Source: Erten and Ocampo (2012)

One of the reasons behind the external vulnerability of most developing countries is that they are price takers, as they have limited control of the world prices of the goods they

The Macroeconomics of Developing Countries: An Intermediate Textbook. Giovanni Andrea Cornia, Oxford University Press (2020).

DOI: 10.1093/oso/9780198856672.001.0001

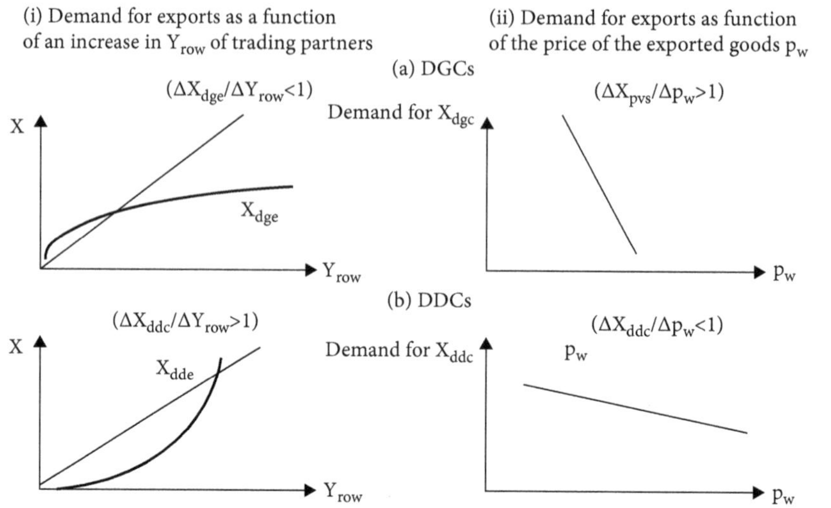

Figure 9.2 Export elasticity with respect to world growth (left) and export prices (right) 'for developing countries (DGCs) and developed countries (DDCs).

export and import. Indeed, their share of exports (X_i/X_t) and imports (M_i/M_t) in total international trade is generally small. Only sixteen developing countries have an X_i/X_t index greater than 10 per cent in the three-digit Standard International Trade Classification (SITC). This means that their aggregate demand is much more exposed to exogenous price shocks than that of economies that control a higher share of the world market of both imports and exports. Furthermore, with the exception of China, Brazil, and few countries in South East Asia, developing countries exhibit a high degree of export concentration by type of goods sold abroad and countries of destination.[1] As a result of the above, over the short term the international terms of trade of developing countries fluctuate markedly. This entails, for example, that the standard open economy macroeconomic model of income determination used for the advanced countries (as the Mundell–Fleming model that assumes exogenous international terms of trade) cannot be satisfactorily used for many developing countries.

The trade shocks affecting the current account balance of developing countries—that is, an increase in import prices, fall in export prices, contraction of world demand for their exports, and increased protectionism in the countries of destination for their exports[2]—are amplified by the unfavourable values of the price and income elasticities of demand for their exports (Figure 9.2). Figure 9.2a(i) for the developing countries shows that the income elasticity of demand for their exports following a 1 per cent increase in the income of the rest of the world (Y_{row}) is smaller than 1. This is because the developing countries often export inferior goods (e.g. agricultural commodities) the demand for which rises

[1] An index that measures export concentration is the Herfindal–Hirshman index that takes the form $HH = \Sigma\, sh_i^2$, where Σsh_i is the share of the export item 'i' in a country's total exports. Assuming that the total number of exported goods is equal to n, HH ranges between 1/n (maximum diversification, that is, when the sh_i are all equal to 1/n and $HH = n.1/n^2$) and 1 (when the sh_i are all zero except one, in which case the HH index is equal to 1) (see Agenor Montiel 1998).

[2] Here we neglect the long-term effects on the developing countries due to the dematerialization of production in developed countries and the substitution of some raw materials with synthetic products.

slowly following an increase in the income of the rest of the world. Likewise, Figure 9.2a(ii) shows that developing countries face a high price elasticity of the demand for their exports, as markets for colonial goods are almost saturated and as the developed countries often produce almost perfect substitutes of such goods. In turn, Figure 9.2b(i) for the developed countries illustrates the opposite situation. Indeed, the demand for the exports of these countries has a high income elasticity. Indeed, developing countries increasingly need investment goods and new technologies imported from the industrialized countries to sustain their development. Likewise, Figure 9.2b(ii) shows that such exports have low price elasticity, as developing countries seldom produce domestic substitutes of such goods. As a result of such differences in export and import structure and in price and income elasticities, the aggregate demand in developing countries is prone to a greater number of exogenous shocks than that of less dependent economies. These include developed countries that have diversified export/import structures by commodity groups and countries of destination, and economies controlling a bigger share of the world market of the goods they export. What needs to be underscored here is that the vulnerability of many developing countries to exogenous shocks raises the volatility of their exports, imports, currency reserves, tax revenue, and budget deficit, causing not only a balance of payment crises but also a budgetary crisis, a rise in inflation, and—likely—an increase in the public debt (Figure 9.3).

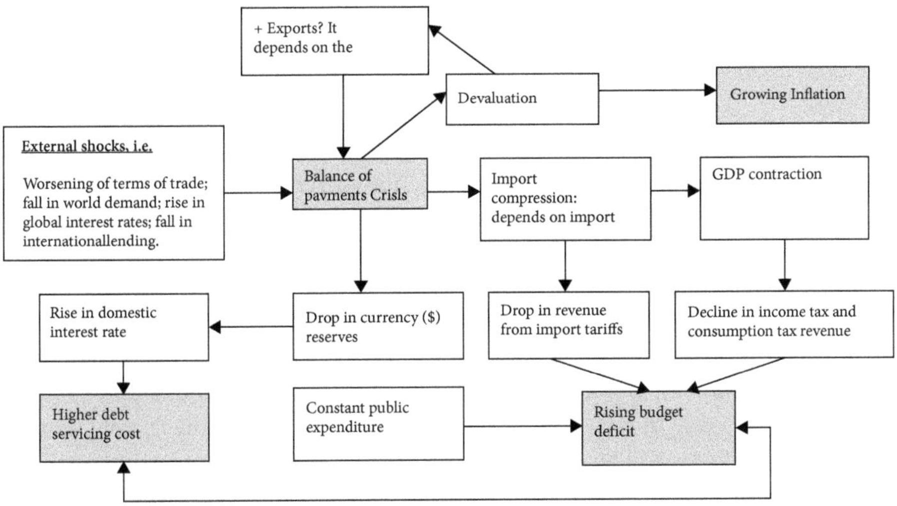

Figure 9.3 Representation of the macroeconomic impact of an external shock in developing countries

9.2 Current Account Balance and Growth: The Thirlwall Model

Supply-side growth models of Keynesian and neoclassical inspiration often assume a closed economy with no demand constraints. In a way, it is assumed that the Say Law applies, that is, that each supply generates its own demand. But in many low-income developing countries the ultimate constraint to growth is a narrow domestic market coupled with a shortage of foreign exchange due to a low world demand and prices for their exports. With the surge in commodity prices observed during the 2000s, this has become less true than before for countries exporting valuable commodities (see Figure 5.2), but lack of foreign exchange remains a problem for countries exporting less valuable items.

In a small–medium sized developing country, especially, exports have often been a major driver of GDP growth, as in the case of the Asian Tigers in the 1950s, 1960s, and 1970s. As noted, several low-income countries are heavily dependent for their development on the importation of investment goods and intermediate inputs. In turn, their exports are still exposed to external shocks affecting both demand and supply. These have, however evolved, favourably during the last decade[3] but have become more volatile since 2008 (see Figure 5.2).

As noted above, the income elasticity of demand for the commodities exported by developing countries and demanded by the rest of the world is generally lower than that for manufactured goods exported by the developed countries.[4] The income elasticity of demand is greater than one if the product is buoyant, and less than one if it is an inferior good such as traditional agricultural commodities, the world demand for which may be almost saturated. The Thirlwall (1979) model explores such a situation in a formal way. It concludes that—if the long-run balance of payments equilibrium on the current account is a requirement for growth, and if the real exchange rate stays relatively constant—the long-run growth of a country can be approximated by the ratio of the growth rate of exports to the income elasticity of their demand for imports.

Derivation of the Thirlwall model

The 1979 version of the Thirlwall model states that no country can grow over the long term faster than the rate consistent with equilibrium in the current account balance, unless it can finance ever-growing current account deficits with a steady inflow of FDI and rising external indebtedness. However, the empirical evidence shows that dependence on capital inflows cannot be sustained over the long term. Indeed, there is a limit to the sustainability of a country's rising foreign debt/GDP ratio, beyond which financial markets get nervous, the country spread rises, and the risk of a financial crisis mounts (see Chapter 10). The simplest way to model growth within a balance of payments constrained framework, therefore, is to start with the equilibrium condition of the current account of the balance of payments. The next step is to specify the export and import demand

[3] The Prebish–Singer theorem maintained that the terms of trade (the ratio of the index of the prices of exports divided by the index of the prices of imports) experienced a secular deterioration as commodity prices tended to increase at a slower rate than those of manufactured goods. Since countries of the periphery specialized in the production of raw materials and the developed ones in the production of industrial goods, the worsening of the international terms of trade (P_x/P_m) meant that in order to maintain the trade balance in equilibrium, so as to continue importing a constant amount of capital goods and intermediate inputs needed for their growth, the peripheral countries needed to export increasing volumes of commodities. This hypothesis has been tested empirically numerous times, especially after breaks due to rises in commodity prices. Recently, Arezki et al. (2013) examined the secular trend and the short-run volatility for twenty-five commodities starting as far back as 1650. These authors used panel data stationarity tests that allow for multiple structural breaks. Their results show that, after allowing for structural breaks, the series are stationary. The results of tests of the Prebisch–Singer hypothesis about the secular decline in the price of commodities are mixed, but with a majority of commodities showing a negative trend.

[4] The income elasticity of demand of a given good is the ratio between the percentage changes in demand divided by a one percentage increase in the income of the rest of the world.

functions and since, import growth is a function of domestic income growth (a good proxy of GDP), solve the model for its growth rate consistent with the long-run equilibrium in the current account of the balance of payments.

In this approach (Thirlwall, 1979), the current account equilibrium in domestic currency is given by

$$P_{dt}\,X_t = P_{ft}\,M_t\,e_t^{nc/\$} \tag{9.1}$$

where X_t and M_t are the volume of exports and imports, P_{dt} is the domestic price of exports in national currency; P_{ft} is the US dollar price of imports, and $e^{nc/\$}$ is the nominal exchange rate, that is, the amount of national currency needed to buy a US dollar.

By taking the logs of equation (9.1), one obtains:

$$\log P_{dt} + \log X_t = \log P_{ft} + \log M_t + \log e_t^{nc/\$} \tag{9.2}$$

Then, by differentiating totally equation (9.2) with respect to time, one obtains with equation (9.2a) the dynamic equilibrium relation of the current account of the balance of payments:

$$\mathbf{p}_{dt} + \mathbf{x}_t = \mathbf{p}_{ft} + \mathbf{m}_t + \mathbf{e}_t^{nc/\$} \tag{9.2a}$$

where the lower case bold letters are the growth rates over time of the relevant variables.

Relying on standard demand theory, we now specify the export demand function (which includes the variables that explain exports) expressed in a multiplicative form and assuming constant elasticities α, δ, and ε:

$$X_t = (P_{dt}/\,e_t^{nc/\$})^{\alpha} P^{\delta}{}_{ft}\,Z^{\varepsilon}{}_t \tag{9.3}$$

where X_t, P_{dt}, P_{ft}, and $e_t^{nc/\$}$ have been defined above, Z_t is the level of world GDP, $\alpha\ (<0)$ is the own price elasticity of exports), $\delta\ (>0)$ is the cross elasticity of demand for exports, and $\varepsilon\ (>0)$, Z is the income elasticity of demand for exports. Also, in this case, we take the logs of the above relation and then differentiate it totally with respect to time, obtaining relation (9.4) where also in this case the lower case bold letters are growth rates over time of the relevant variables:

$$\mathbf{x}_t = \alpha\mathbf{p}_{dt} - \alpha\mathbf{e}_t^{nc/US\$} + \delta\mathbf{p}_{ft} + \varepsilon\mathbf{z}_t \tag{9.4}$$

One must now write the equation that explains the developing country imports M. According to standard demand theory, the quantity of imports demanded is a function of the price of imports (measured in domestic currency by multiplying their US dollar price P_{ft} for the exchange rate), the price of import substitutes (P_{dt}) and the domestic GDP (proxied by Y):

$$M_t = (P_{ft}\,e^{nc/\$}{}_t)^{\beta} P_{dt}{}^{\gamma} Y_t{}^{\pi} \tag{9.5}$$

where $\beta\ (<0)$ is the own price elasticity of imports, $\gamma\ (>0)$ is the cross elasticity of demand for imports and $\pi\ (>0)$ is the income elasticity of demand for imports.

Also in this case, by taking the logs of equation (9.5) and then differentiating it totally with respect to time, one obtains:

$$\mathbf{m}_t = \beta\,\mathbf{p}_{ft} + \beta\mathbf{e}_t^{nc/US\$} + \gamma\mathbf{p}_{dt} + \pi\mathbf{y}_t \quad (9.6)$$

where the bold letters indicate rates of change over time. At this point, one can substitute the results of equations (9.4) and (9.6) that explain the growth rate of exports and imports, into equation (9.2a) obtaining:

$$\mathbf{p}_{dt} + (\alpha\mathbf{p}_{dt} - \alpha\mathbf{e}_t^{nc/US\$} + \delta\mathbf{p}_{ft} + \varepsilon\mathbf{z}_t) = \mathbf{p}_{ft} + (\beta\mathbf{p}_{ft} + \beta\mathbf{e}_t^{nc/\$} + \gamma\mathbf{p}_{df} + \pi\mathbf{y}_t) + \mathbf{e}_t^{nc/\$} \quad (9.7)$$

and solve (9.7) for $\mathbf{y}_t$, that is, the rate of growth of income Y_t (that proxies GDP) which ensures the dynamic equilibrium of the balance of payments in the current account:

$$\mathbf{y}_t = \frac{\mathbf{p}_{dt}(1 + \alpha - \gamma) - \mathbf{p}_{ft}(1 - \delta + \beta) - \mathbf{e}_t^{nc/\$}(1 + \alpha + \beta) + \varepsilon\,\mathbf{z}_t}{\pi} \quad (9.8)$$

Remembering the signs of the elasticities, that is: $\alpha < 0$, $\gamma > 0$, $\delta > 0$, $\beta < 0$, ε and $\pi > 0$, Thirlwall argues that equation (9.8) suggests some plausible findings.

- By itself, an improvement in the real terms of trade (or real exchange rate) $(\mathbf{p}_{dt} - \mathbf{p}_{ft} - \mathbf{e}_t^{nc/US\$}) > 0$, will raise—*ceteris paribus*—the growth rate of Y ($\mathbf{y}_t$) consistent with the balance of payments equilibrium;
- Domestic inflation in developing countries ($\mathbf{p}_{dt}$) will lower their growth rate consistent with the balance of payments equilibrium in the current account if the sum of the own price elasticity of demand for exports (α) and the cross elasticity of demand for imports (γ) is greater than unity, that is, if $1 < (\alpha - \gamma)$ (remember that α is negative)·
- World inflation ($\mathbf{p}_{ft}$) will improve the developing countries growth rate consistent with the balance of payments equilibrium provided the sum of the own price elasticity of demand for imports (β) and the cross elasticity of demand for exports (δ) is greater than one, that is, if $\delta + \beta > 1$ (remember that β is negative).
- Devaluation of the nominal exchange rate, ($\mathbf{e}^{nc/US\$}$), will improve the growth rate $\mathbf{y}$ if $\alpha + \beta > 1$, that is, provided the sum of the own price elasticities of demand for imports and exports is greater than 1, as suggested by the Marshall–Lerner condition (see Section 15.5). However, a once and for all devaluation of the currency cannot permanently raise the GDP growth rate compatible with the balance of payments equilibrium. To raise the balance of payments equilibrium growth rate ($\mathbf{y}_t$) permanently, the policymaker needs to introduce continuous devaluations, a decision that may not be desirable for a variety of reasons (see Chapter 15).
- Faster growth of world income ($\mathbf{z}_t$) raises the GDP growth rate compatible with balance of payments equilibrium. The extent of this growth acceleration depends crucially on the income elasticity of demand for a country's exports ε. This depends on its export structure, as discussed in Section 9.1.

- The developing countries' growth rate consistent with the balance of payments equilibrium is inversely related to its import propensity π. As noted, in these countries, growth is often dependent on the import of investment goods, key inputs, food, and energy. The greater this dependence, the lower the growth of GDP.

Computing the balance of payments equilibrium growth rate from equation (9.8) requires being able to count on a large amount of information about the value of the elasticities; this information is not always readily available and may change over time. However, if one assumes—as is usually done—that the own price elasticities of demand for imports and exports are equal to the cross elasticities (that is, that $\beta = \gamma$ and $\alpha = \delta$), it is possible to simplify relation (9.8) by replacing β in lieu of γ in the first round parenthesis of equation (9·8) and α in lieu of δ in the second round parenthesis, while remembering that α and β have a negative sign (so that these parameters become positive if they are preceded by a negative sign). One obtains in this way relation (9.9):

$$y_t = \frac{(1 + \alpha + \beta)\ (p_{dt} - p_{ft} - e_t{}^{nc/\$}) + \varepsilon\, z_t}{\pi} \tag{9.9}$$

Assuming now that $\alpha + \beta = -1$ (as both parameters are negative), or if relative prices measured in a common currency ($p_{dt} - p_{ft} - e_t^{nc/US\$}$) do not change over the long run (which means the terms of trade measured in a common currency are broadly stable and that, by implication, their growth rate is equal to zero), then the growth rate of GDP consistent with the equilibrium of the current account of the balance of payments becomes:

$$y_t = \varepsilon\, z_t/\pi \tag{9.10}$$

and, given that the term $\varepsilon\, z_t = x_t$, it is possible to further simplify the result of the model as follows:

$$y_t = x_t/\pi \tag{9.11}$$

This result basically states that the growth of GDP compatible with equilibrium of the current account depends on the growth rate of exports divided by the own import elasticity of income. Policy wise, the model suggests that y_t can be accelerated by speeding up the rate of growth of exports through structural measures enhancing their competitiveness, export promotion policies, and upgrading their quality. y_t can also be accelerated by reducing the appetite for imports through WTO-compatible import substitution policies. Indeed, over the long term (i.e. several decades) the developing countries ought to try changing their output, export and import structures, moving away from their historically determined colonial specialization on inferior goods, and developing the production and export of superior goods.

How well does the evidence about the actual growth experience of countries fit the growth rate computed by the Thirlwall model? The model suggests that a country cannot grow faster than its overall balance of payments equilibrium growth rate for long, unless it runs down its currency reserves, receives substantial FDI every year, or systematically borrows abroad. But even substantial capital inflows, that is, of 3–4 per cent of GDP, make little empirical difference to the growth predictions of the basic model, as the observed growth rates are generally lower than those predicted by the model.

But there are also factors that prevent a country from growing as fast as allowed by $\mathbf{y_t}$ and force it to accumulate currency reserves. This may be the case when the $\mathbf{x_t}$ is so high that a country does not have the capacity to absorb all exports earnings due to structural bottlenecks and time delays in developing new sectors, as is often the case in oil exporting countries. So, $\mathbf{y_t}$ may be seen as a sort of upper bound of the actual growth rate of GDP.

In conclusion, Thirlwall's model belongs to a group of models inspired by the export-led development strategy successfully followed in the 1960s and 1970s by Japan, Taiwan, and South Korea and more recently by China and Vietnam. At the same time, in many commodity exporting countries, trade liberalization led to premature deindustrialization and the 're-primarization' of output and exports, that is, a greater export dependence on primary commodities that, as shown in Figure 9.2, tend to have a low income elasticity and high price elasticity. In addition, it is clear that an export-led growth strategy focusing on primary commodities cannot be followed by all developing countries, as this may lead to a problem of 'fallacy of composition', that is, a glut of primary commodities on the world market that depresses their price.

In a more recent article Thirlwall (2013) suggests that for all these and other reasons the adoption of an export-led growth strategy and the liberalization of international trade have not lived up to their promises in terms of the balance of payments, growth, poverty reduction, and the distribution of income. As a result, both economic theory and the historical and contemporary evidence all provide arguments for selective industrial protection in developing countries.

9.3 Concluding Remarks

Since the early 1960s many developing countries have shifted from an import-substitution growth pattern to an export-led development strategy. Considerable success was achieved in several instances, especially in East Asia. Yet, in the countries that still export non-oil primary commodities, the long-term growth of GDP compatible with the equilibrium of the current account balance remains strongly influenced by the unfavorable structure of their exports and imports. In particular, it is influenced by the differences between their price and income elasticities of imports and exports. These in turn are influenced by the objective features of these countries that evolve slowly and are at times still dependent on their prior colonial experience. Practically all non-oil commodity exporting developing countries are small price-taker open economies with high export/GDP ratios and exports concentrated in a narrow range of primary commodities with a low income elasticity and high price elasticity of exports. In contrast, the income elasticity of their imports is very high and the related price elasticity is low. In addition, world commodity prices tend to fluctuate widely and—before the rise of China—fell in relation to the prices of manufactured goods exported by industrialized economies.

In these economies, trade diversification towards exports with more favorable import and export elasticities is necessary if the countries are to exit their commodity trap. The Thirlwall model formally confirms this conclusion, by showing that the rate of growth of

GDP depends on the growth rate of exports (which would be more stable if the basket of goods sold abroad became—*ceteris paribus*—increasingly more diversified) and on their import propensity. The latter may decline if the import dependence on a broad range of manufactured goods is reduced in an efficient way.

References

Agénor, P. R. and P. Montiel (1998), *Development Macroeconomics*, 2nd edn. Princeton, NJ: Princeton University Press.

Arezki, R., K. Hadri, P. Loungani, and Y. Rao (2013), 'Testing the Prebisch–Singer Hypothesis since 1650: Evidence from Panel Techniques that Allow for Multiple Breaks', IMF Working Paper WP/13/180 Research Department. Washington, DC: International Monetary Fund.

Erten, B. and J. A. Ocampo (2012), 'Super-cycles of commodity prices since the mid-nineteenth century', UN DESA Working Paper No. ESA/2012/DWP/110. New York: United Nations.

Prebisch, R. (1950), 'The Economic Development of Latin America and Its Principal Problems, *Economic Bulletin for Latin America*, 7: pp. 1–12.

Thirlwall, A. P. (1979), 'The balance of payments constraint as an explanation of international growth rate differences', *Banca Nazionale del Lavoro Quarterly Review*, 32 (128): pp. 45–53.

Thirlwall, A.P. (2013), 'The Rhetoric and Reality of Trade Liberalization in Developing Countries', *Rivista Italiana degli Economisti (The Journal of the Italian Economic Association)*, 2013 (1): pp. 3–24.

Suggested further reading

Erten, B. and J. A. Ocampo (2012), 'Super-cycles of commodity prices since the mid-nineteenth century', UN DESA Working Paper No. ESA/2012/DWP/110. New York: United Nations.

Kaplinsky, R. (2016), 'Revisiting the Revisited Terms of Trade: Will China Make a Difference?', *World Development*, 34 (6): pp. 981–95.

10

External Financing, Gap Models of Growth, and the Macroeconomics of Relying on Foreign Resources

This chapter reviews the factors responsible for the strong dependence of developing countries on foreign capital and aid. It then discusses a family of models, some of which were developed after the debt crisis and recession of the 1980s and 1990s. Such models aim to determine the amount of foreign loans and grants required to reach a preset rate of growth of GDP. It finally assesses the macroeconomic and growth impact of high dependence on foreign finance.

10.1 Structure of Credit and Foreign Exchange Markets

Firms in developing countries have a weak cashflow (amortization provisions plus net profits), a fact that reduces their liquidity and self-financing capacity. They must therefore finance themselves almost completely with domestic bank loans and advances from moneylenders. Their production costs depend much more on the level of interest rates than is the case for firms operating in developed countries—they can count on a greater self-financing capacity and lower domestic borrowing costs.

The cause of all this is the fact that financial markets are incomplete and distorted. Indeed, poor countries are characterized by low monetization, high informalization, and low financial intermediation proxied, for example, by the ratio M2/GDP, where M2 is the sum of cash in circulation, current account deposits, and saving accounts. As a result, their money multiplier (e.g. 2–3) is typically lower than that of industrial countries (for the derivation of the money multiplier see footnote 8 in Chapter 3). Thus, the effects of monetary policy are weaker than in countries with a higher M2/GDP. In addition, the credit market is strongly dualistic. The formal sector is dominated by commercial banks that are exposed to asymmetric information about the solvency of potential borrowers and the risk of adverse selection. They therefore protect themselves from the default risk by demanding collateral for loans. However, this approach excludes the poor from this market as they do not have collateral to offer as a guarantee. In some of the urban and peri urban areas and in most rural areas, it is the informal credit sector that dominates the scene. The lenders in this sector are generally less exposed to the risk of adverse selection as they live in the same areas as the borrowers and can therefore informally assess their default risk. Moneylenders (such as cereals wholesalers and large landowners), however, behave like local oligopolists. The loans they grant carry high interest rates, have a short maturity and are generally used to finance working capital and not new investments. The impact of

The Macroeconomics of Developing Countries: An Intermediate Textbook. Giovanni Andrea Cornia, Oxford University Press (2020).

DOI: 10.1093/oso/9780198856672.001.0001

monetary policy on the informal credit market depends largely on the relations that link them to the formal sector. Thus, an analysis of the overall impact of a given monetary shock requires modelling the relations existing between these two markets. In addition, in some developing countries the formal banking sector still remains subject to financial repression involving high reserve ratios, restrictions on interest rates, and an administrative allocation of credit which further limit the impact of monetary policy. Some of these problems have persisted despite the financial liberalization of the 1980s and 1990s, while other problems (such as financial instability) have appeared.

In turn, the public sector often borrows domestically to cover the difference between an inertial public expenditure and a highly unstable revenue that is affected by changes in the world prices of the primary goods the country exports and by the difficulties met in taxing agriculture and the informal sectors. Whenever the domestic bond market is lacking or is too narrow and the interest rate on public bonds is too high, governments borrow abroad in hard currency at substantially lower interest rates.

Because of all this, the firms and governments of many developing countries have become net importers of financial capital in its various forms. However, dependence on foreign capital exposes the developing countries to several risks, such an increase in the Libor/Euribor rate and in the country's risk premium, a drop in the volume of foreign loans and foreign aid, financial contagion, and a depreciation of the exchange rate that increases the national currency cost of debt servicing. These events reduce the net transfer of resources from abroad while—in the case of a large foreign public debt—devaluation curtails public expenditure and drains currency reserves.

Despite these problems, many developing countries continue to depend on foreign capital and aid for their growth. A family of 'gap models' has thus been gradually developed to determine the volume of foreign savings needed to achieve a GDP growth target pre-set by the policymaker. Gap models are rather compact and describe the macroeconomy of developing countries through highly stylized relationships of the balance of payments, production, fiscal balance, and banking system. As noted by Taylor (1994), despite their simplicity, these models have substantially influenced the macroeconomic policy debate since the 1970s.

The gap models have evolved from direct observation of the lack of various resources which constrain economic growth. In an empirical investigation of the factors which retarded growth in fifty developing countries, first Chenery and Strout (1966), and then Bacha (1990) and others identified the following factors as main constraints to growth.

(a) A skills gap: indeed insufficient technical knowledge hinders the absorption of new investment and new technologies even in the presence of an abundant supply of savings and investment goods. Such a gap is normally filled by bilateral and multilateral technical assistance programmes or through long-term investments in human capital and technical skills.
(b) A savings gap: a lack of savings does not permit the financing of the accumulation of physical capital needed to reach pre-set growth objectives. A solution to this problem has to be found in an increase in foreign savings, the mobilization of latent domestic savings, or redistributing income towards classes with a higher marginal propensity to save.

(c) A foreign exchange gap: the lack of hard currency does not permit the machinery and equipment needed to reach a given growth objective to be imported, regardless of the availability of domestic savings denominated in national currency.
(d) A fiscal gap: as noted in Chapter 3, the mainstream emphasizes the 'crowding out' of private investment caused by the rise of interest rates due to the issuing of state bonds to finance public investments. However, the empirical evidence shows that in many developing countries public investment may generate a 'crowding in' of private investment. The need to increase the supply of public goods is certainly more pronounced in poor countries with limited transport and telecommunication infrastructure, markets, and educational systems. The 'fiscal gap' caused by an increase in public spending could be covered by foreign capital, higher taxes, or, when these alternatives are non-viable, through the monetization of the budget deficit and the related inflation tax. By reducing the real value of unindexed domestic financial assets such as cash and bonds, the monetization of the deficit allows the government to appropriate part of private savings.

Three observations are necessary at this point before discussing the various gap models. The first is that the factors that constrain growth in these models coincide only in part with those discussed in Chapter 2 on long-term growth models for industrialized countries. These models emphasize the role of labour, physical and human capital, and technological capacity, but ignore the limiting effects that the lack of foreign exchange and fiscal revenue have on aggregate investments, and the role of inflation in appropriating a part of private savings through seignorage. Thus, the logic of gap models of growth is quite different from that of the models used in advanced countries. Second, except for technical skills, in this type of model all gaps can be filled and growth stimulated by an increase in foreign savings received by the government. In fact, a rise in foreign currency inflows directed to the government (which is assumed to invest these funds) simultaneously reduces the fiscal, foreign exchange, and savings gaps. All this reflects the thinking of the 1980s and 1990s, according to which most development problems were seen to depend on the availability of foreign aid and loans. Third, in these models, while these gaps are in equilibrium *ex post*, they always differ *ex ante*. The *ex post* equilibrium is reached through a series of macroeconomic adjustments discussed below.

Indeed, in the case of the two-gap model, given the relation of the uses of GDP ($Y = C + I + X - M$), it is possible to derive—given $Y - C$[1] $= S$—the following relation

$$I - S = M - X[= F] \tag{10.1}$$

whcih shows that the savings gap ($I - S$) is equal to the foreign exchange gap ($M - X$) which is covered by foreign financing, F. In turn, the equalization of the relationships surrounding the uses of GDP and the income utilized by the main economic actors (firms, families, and the state) $Y = C$[2] $+ S + T$ (see Chapter 1) yields

$$C + S + T = C + G + I + X - M \quad \text{where} \quad X - M = F \tag{10.2}$$

[1] In this case, C comprises both private consumption and public consumption.
[2] In this case, C refers only to private consumption.

and allows us to obtain with a simple manipulation:

$$(S - I) + (T - G) = F \tag{10.3}$$

in which the first term is the savings gap, the second the fiscal gap, and F is the foreign exchange gap, which is to be covered by the foreign financing, F. It is important to underscore that these are *ex post* identities that do not tell us anything about the *ex ante* gaps. In fact, the economic agents make their *ex ante* decisions independently from one another on the basis of different information and decisional criteria. Decisions about consumption are made by families, those about investments and exports by firms, and those about taxation and public expenditure by the government. It is difficult to imagine that these three gaps are in equilibrium *ex ante* as described in equations (10.2) and (10.3). There is nothing strange therefore if $(I - S)^P \neq (M - X)^P$ where the superscript ^{P} stands for planned (or *ex ante*). The gap models study, in fact, which of the various gaps becomes more binding for growth before other gaps start constraining it, and which are the adjustments and interactions between gaps that take place, so that the three *ex ante* gaps became equally binding *ex post*.

10.2 The One-gap Model: the Revised Minimum Standard Model

While the IMF models exhibit a relatively well-developed monetary sector, the same cannot be said about the real sector. Yet, it is clear that as soon as a country has stabilized inflation, the budget deficit, and the balance of payments (that is, objectives that often entail a contraction of GDP but also an increase in foreign exchange reserves and some restoration of macroeconomic credibility), the most important task is to re-start the growth process. The question then arises: 'Are all the resources necessary for the planned economic recovery available?' And, in particular, 'Are there enough savings to finance the investments needed to reach a preset growth target?' The RMSM model, for a long time in use at the World Bank, tries to respond to this question, by calculating the amount of autonomous savings, that is, the savings that are needed (beyond those generated by the expected growth) to reach a given GDP growth objective (say, 5 per cent a year). Autonomous savings have to be mobilized domestically by the government or received from abroad. In a sense, the RMSM model can be defined as a 'one gap model'. The model includes five simple equations:

$BP = X^* - m(Y_{t-1} + \Delta Y) + F$	balance of payments	(10.4)
$I = \nu\Delta Y$	production function	(10.5)
$I = (Y - C) + (mY - X^*)$	investment – savings equilibrium	(10.6)
$S = Y - C$	domestic savings	(10.7)
$S = Sa + sY$	savings composition	(10.8)

where BP is the total balance of payments, X* the exogenously given exports (as their level is set by the international market), Y is the national income (or GDP), m the import coefficient,

F the net transfer of resources from abroad, v the incremental capital–output ratio, S the aggregate savings, Sa the autonomous saving, and s the average propensity to save.

What is the volume of savings which allows a given growth of GDP to be achieved (Agénor and Montiel, 1999)? To this end, it is necessary to compute the quantity of investments, I, which is required to generate an output increase ΔY. Let us recall from the Harrod –Domar production function that $Y = K/v$, where v is the average capital–output ratio, that is, the amount of capital needed to produce a unit of output. At the margin we have that $\Delta Y = \Delta K/v$ or $\Delta Y = I/v$ where v is the Incremental Capital/Output Ratio (ICOR) which is assumed in this case for simplicity to be equal to the average capital–output ratio. It is possible to rewrite the relation in equation (10.5) as $I = v\ \Delta Y$.

Recalling from the national accounts that $I = (Y - C) + (mY - X^*)$ where X^* are the fixed exports, one can compute the volume of savings needed to finance the output increase ΔY. To do so, one equalizes the terms on the right-hand side of relations (10.5) and (10.6), thus obtaining:

$$v\ \Delta Y = (Y - C) + (mY - X^*) \text{ or} \tag{10.9}$$

$$v\ \Delta Y = S + (mY - X^*) \tag{10.9b}$$

Remembering now that $Y = Y_{t-1} + \Delta Y$, one can derive the relation that measures the total amount of savings needed to finance the growth target ΔY by replacing in the round parenthesis above $Y_{t-1} + \Delta Y$ in lieu of Y, so as to obtain:

$$S = X^* - mY_{t-1} + (v - m)\Delta Y \tag{10.10}$$

which shows that S is a growing function of ΔY, given that the difference between v and m is always positive, as the first term is markedly bigger than the second (3–4 versus 0.2–0.4).

Recalling then from equation (10.8) that savings, S, is a linear function of income, Y, so that some savings will be endogenously generated by achieving the preset GDP growth target, by substituting in (10.10) the value of S (i.e. $S_a + sY$ that can also be written as $S_a + sY_{t-1} + s\Delta Y$) and, by solving for S_a, one obtains the value of the autonomous savings which have to be mobilized by the public authority or received from abroad to achieve the growth objective ΔY. In symbols, the autonomous savings are equal to:

$$S_a + sY_{t-1} + s\Delta Y = X^* - mY_{t-1} + (v - m)\,\Delta Y, \tag{10.11}$$

or

$$S_a = X^* - (m + s)Y_{t-1} + [(v - (m + s))\,\Delta Y \tag{10.11b}$$

which shows that the amount of required autonomous savings increases in parallel with the growth target ΔY and the incremental capital–output ratio v, and falls for an increase in m (as more resources are imported), s (the saving propensity out of Y), and Y_{t-1} (the initial level of output).

10.3 The Two-gap Model

The two gaps model was developed by Chenery and Bruno (1962) and was later refined by Chenery, Strout, Bacha, and others. The two gaps considered are the savings–investment gap and the export–import gap. Let us start by deriving the two equations which describe the two gaps.

The savings gap

From the national accounts on the uses of Y, one can derive the relation:

$$I = (Y - C) + (M - X) \tag{10.12}$$

while the balance of payments account can be written as:

$$M - X = F - J \tag{10.13}$$

where the traditional relation $M - X = F$ (the net foreign financing) is written as $F - J$ to underscore the effect of the variable J. This is the transfer abroad of the net income generated by foreign assets in the form of profits on FDI and interest payments on foreign loans. In the 1980s and 1990s the volume of profit remittances and, especially, the interest payments on foreign loans absorbed considerable resources. The outflow of J is normally included in the overall current account balance but in specific cases, such as the debt crisis of the 1980s in Latin America, interest payments on the foreign loans and profit remittances should be treated separately given the high value such a variable may take. For instance, during the Latin American debt crisis J grew substantially, so much so that $F - J$ became negative.[3] In fact $F - J$ measures the 'net transfer of resources *from* or *to* abroad', meaning that such a variable may become negative.

Substituting in lieu of $M - X$ its equivalent value $F - J$, equation (10.13) becomes:

$$I = (Y - C) + (F - J) \tag{10.14}$$

showing that investments are equal to the sum of domestic savings $(Y - C)$ and foreign savings $(F - J)$ net of interest payments on the foreign debt and the outflow of profit remittances. When the national income is at its potential level Y^*, and C is given exogenously, this relation measures the level of investment constrained by saving that is called IS. In this model, the increase in national output (ΔY) is a function of the investment

[3] In the 1980s Latin America recorded a negative net transfer of resources from abroad $(F - J)$ owing to the strong rise of international interest rates on the dollar loans it had contracted in the 1970s, the halt on new loans (with the exclusion of involuntary lending consisting in the forced rescheduling of old debts), and the reimbursement of some of the outstanding debts. With the introduction of the Brady Plan in 1989, voluntary lending resumed and, in this way, the net transfer of resources to the developing countries again became positive. The situation further improved in the 2000s with the cancellation of the multilateral debt of many low-income countries under the Highly Indebted Poor Countries Initiative (HIPC), and the repayment of the official and commercial debt by middle-income countries. For instance, in Latin America, the average gross foreign public debt/GDP ratio fell from 42 to 20 per cent between 2002 and 2007.

constrained by saving IS divided by the ICOR ν, that is, $\Delta Y = IS/\nu$ or $IS = \nu\Delta Y$. IS can thus be written as:

$$IS = (Y^* - C) + (F - J) \tag{10.15}$$

Thus, IS is the 'maximum achievable investment constrained by the availability of savings'. It depends on a constant $(Y^* - C)$ and on the variable net amount of foreign savings received $(F - J)$. If Y is disaggregated into the income of the state (T) and of families and firms (Y_p), if total consumption C is broken down into private consumption (C_p) and government consumption (G), and recalling that $S_p = Y_p - C_p$, then equation (10.15) can be rewritten as:

$$IS = S_p + (T - G) + (F - J) \tag{10.16}$$

where—by assuming fairly realistically that all capital flows are received by the government that is therefore responsible for the reimbursement of all the foreign debt and the payment of interests J—it appears that the investment level constrained by savings depends on private savings (S_p), the primary surplus of the state budget (excluding the payment of interest on the foreign debt), and the net resource transfers from/to abroad $(F - J)$, where J has been defined above. Assuming now that the variables on the right-hand side are exogenous and that Y_p is at the level of full employment $Y_p{}^*$, equation (10.17) describes the determinants of the maximum achievable investment IS constrained by savings:

$$IS = S_p{}^* + (T - G) + (F - J) \tag{10.17}$$

Given that $\Delta Y = IS/\nu$, relation (10.17) permits the maximum achievable growth on the basis of domestic and foreign savings to be measured. One can thus represent equation (10.17) in the Cartesian plan $(F - J, IS)$ as a linear function where the constant term is $S_p{}^* + (T - G)$ and the variable term is $(F - J)$. When used alone, and given $S_p{}^* + (T - G)$, this relation allows us to compute by difference the amount of $(F - J)'$ needed to reach a given growth objective $\Delta Y'$ and the related level of required investment $IS' = \Delta Y'\nu$.

The foreign exchange gap

Let us start from relation (10.13) $M - X = F - J$. The overall imports M can be divided into M_k (imports of capital goods) and M_0 (other imports) so that $M = M_k + M_0$. One defines then the variable 'exports minus other imports' $E = X - M_0$, and write M_k as a share q of the overall investment, that is $M_k = q\,I$ (where $0 < q < 1$). Substituting these values into equation (10.13) one obtains $qI - E = F - J$ from which—by assuming that E cannot exceed a maximum potential level E*—one obtains

$$IE = \frac{1}{q}[E^* + (F - J)] \tag{10.18}$$

where IE is the maximum achievable investment constrained by the availability of foreign exchange. The latter depends on the volume of exports minus other imports (E*) and the resource transfer from abroad (F − J). In this case, it is also possible to represent equation (10.18) in the Cartesian plan (F − J, IE) as a linear relation. Additonally in this case, given a growth objective ΔY, one can compute the additional level of foreign resources $(F - J)'$ needed to reach a given growth objective.

It must be noted, however, that the functions IS and IE have different slopes and intercepts as shown in Figure 10.1. Indeed, the slope of the IE is greater than one (given that $q < 1$), while that of the IS is equal to one. As for the intercepts, $Sp^* + (T - G)$ is generally greater than E*/q, although in extreme cases this may not be true. Figure 10.1 shows also that up to point $(F - J)'$ investments (and, thus, growth) are constrained by a lack of foreign exchange and beyond such point by a lack of savings. This leads to the well-known empirical finding of Chenery and Strout that in poor countries investment and growth are hindered more by a lack of foreign exchange than of savings. This means that an increase in foreign transfers has a greater impact in poor than middle-income economies.

Figure 10.1 also shows that if $(F - J) = (F - J)'$ the two *ex ante* gaps are equally constraining. No adjustments are therefore necessary to ensure that the two *ex post* gaps coincide.

However, if $(F - J)'' > (FJ)'$ the lack of savings is more constraining than that of foreign exchange (as $I - S > X - M$) and therefore adjustments will be needed to reach an *ex post* equilibrium. The most plausible adjustment is that the country will not be able to export all E* demanded by the world economy because, given that on the IS schedule the installed capacity is fully utilized, investments are insufficient to increase production, in order for the IS to shift downwards. This will entail the introduction of export quotas that—as shown in Figure 10.1—entail a lowering of E*/q and thus a rightward shift of IE until the point where the two gaps coincide.

Finally, Figure 10.1 shows that if $(F - J)''' < (F - J)'$, the foreign exchange gap is more constraining than the savings gap. Therefore, investments and output (on the ordinates—not included to avoid overloading Figure 10.1) will be smaller than those achievable with the available savings. In this case, the adjustment needed to reach an *ex post* equilibrium between the two gaps consists in a fall of investment and output below the potential Y*, to

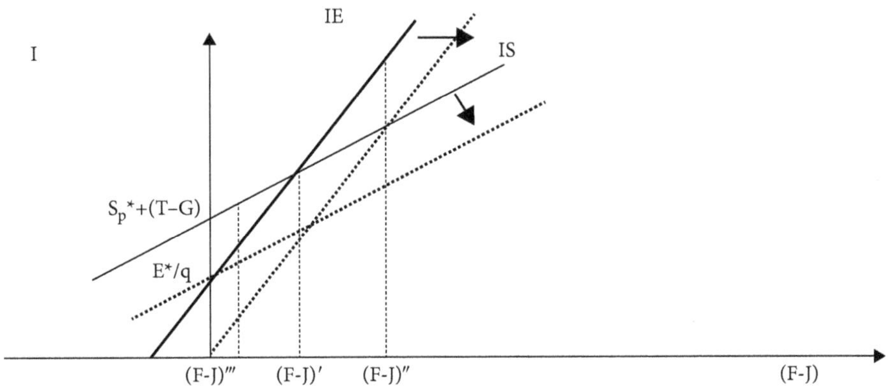

Figure 10.1 Maximum feasible investment according to the availability of foreign exchange (IE) and savings (IS)

be achieved, for instance, through the rationing of foreign exchange. The fall of investments and output will negatively affect the constant term which will decline—causing a downward shift of the IS (the dotted line in Figure 10.1) thus creating unused capacity. Bacha (1990) argues, however, that—especially for middle-income developing countries—the constraint represented by a lack of foreign exchange is a short-term problem that is likely to change over the medium term. Indeed, the surge in non-utilized capacity could lower the wage rate, stimulate foreign competitiveness, and raise E*, given that the country may now capture a greater share of world trade. This entails an upward shift of IE until the two gaps coincide.

Summing up, the two-gap model identifies the amount of foreign resources (F – J) needed to reach a given investment and growth objective. It must be noted that while the foreign resource transfers affect both gaps (as well as the fiscal gap, see later), they have different impacts on the savings gap and foreign exchange gap. The model therefore illustrates the adjustments that may take place to ensure that the two *ex post* gaps coincide.

This modelling approach has been criticized for its high degree of aggregation. Indeed, the saving and foreign exchange gaps vary considerably from sector to sector. Furthermore, by focusing almost exclusively on the volume of foreign resources, the solution of internal problems to development is neglected. Lastly, in recent years this family of models has captured less well the real-life circumstances of a growing number of emerging countries. In these countries, the net transfer of resources from abroad is dominated not so much by flows of aid and official loans but by FDIs and portfolio investments which are highly sensitive to changes in interest rates, exchange rates, and expected devaluations. However, as noted by Taylor (1994), despite their simplicity, these models continue to play a relatively important role in the calculation of the required volume of foreign transfers needed in low-income economies to reach a given growth target.

10.4 The Three-gap Model

The three-gap models were developed in the 1980s and 1990s by Latin-American economists who stressed that the debt crisis that began in 1982 following the sharp rise in US interest rates led to a massive increase in the volume of public funds that had to be allocated to the servicing of the foreign public debt (see Section 10.7). Often, public funds were also used for the servicing of private debt that had been guaranteed (often retrospectively) by the state. All this entailed a strong compression of primary public expenditure on social and economic services and public investments in infrastructure, both of which were and still are badly needed in these countries. Indeed, in economies still lacking schools, roads, markets, telecommunication systems, harbours, and so on, a decline in public investment entails a reduction of private investment due to falling net returns on private capital due to stagnation of public infrastructure. Increasingly, overall investment and growth were being hindered by a lack of expenditure on public investment.

This fiscal gap was covered in some cases by an increase in foreign transfers (F – J) which, however, became increasingly more costly, with the effect of pushing J upwards. Once this and other approaches were foreclosed, countries made use of seignorage (monetary emission to cover the deficit) and of the attendant inflation tax that reduced the real incomes and savings of holders of national unindexed financial assets such as cash, current account deposits, and government bonds. In this way, the state captured a proportion of private savings, in order to raise public savings and investments. Yet, as is well known, beyond a certain threshold, seignorage yields declining revenue from the inflation tax. Thus, such an approach to the financing of public investments may generate negative effects as, beyond the threshold, an increase in the monetary base reduces real incomes, increases volatility, and leads to a flight from the domestic currency.

The fiscal gap

To formalize analytically the fiscal gap one can recall from equation (10.16) that $I = S_p + (T - G) + (F - J)$, and break down overall investment into private and public investment ($I = I_p + I_g$) to obtain:

$$I_g = (S_p - I_P) + (T - G) + (F - J) \tag{10.19}$$

from which it appears that public investment is equal to the balance of private saving net of private investment, plus public saving, plus foreign saving (which is assumed to be received solely by the government). If one assumes then the existence of a crowding in effect, it is possible to write $I_p = k^* I_g$ where $k^* > 0$ is the maximum crowding in effect of public investment on private investment. However, as noted by Bacha (1990), such effect tends to diminish with a rise of inflation for the reasons illustrated above. If one then assumes that there is no domestic bond market on which the government could finance the deficit $(T - G)$ (due in part to outlays on public investment), then an expansion of the monetary base (ΔH) remains the sole alternative way to finance the public deficit. This is tantamount to saying that the monetization of the deficit is the only way to appropriate—through seignorage[4] and the ensuing inflation—the net balance of private saving over investment $(S_p - I_p)$. However, seignorage (and the government capacity of appropriating $S - I_p$) is an inverted U-shaped function of the inflation rate p and of the propensity to hold assets in domestic currency, as suggested by equation (10.20):

$$S_P - I_P = \Delta H/p = f(p, h) \tag{10.20}$$

Given the shape of the relation between monetary emissions, inflation, and seignorage, an initial increase of ΔH first has a positive effect on seignorage (as p increases marginally), but its further expansion negatively affects the revenue it generates (Figure 10.2).

By substituting equation (10.20) into (10.19) and recalling that $I/(1 + k^*) = I_g$ one can derive IT, that is, the maximum investment achievable on the basis of the availability of government budget funds,

$$IT = (1 + k^*)[f\ (p, h) + (T - G) + (F - J)] \tag{10.21}$$

[4] Seignorage accounted on average for 3 per cent of GDP over the period 1975–85 in the developing countries and for 1–3 per cent in the industrialized countries (Sachs and Larrain, 1993). Over 1992–96, it has declined with rare exceptions to around 2 per cent of GDP (Agenor and Montiel, 1999).

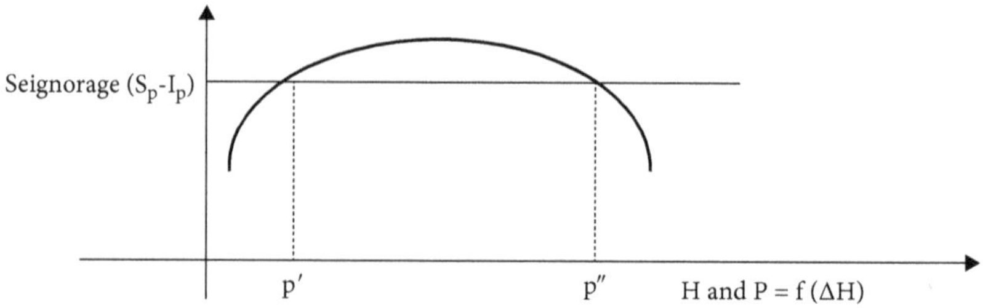

Figure 10.2 Relation between inflation and revenue generated by the inflation tax

Tthis relation can also be plotted on the Cartesian plane (F − J, IT) as a straight line with constant $(1 + k^*)$ [f (p, h) + (T − G)] and slope $(1 + k^*)$, where k^* is the '*crowding in*' coefficient. In such a relation the first term in square parenthesis is positive over the price interval between 0 and p′, but negative from p″ onward, while between p′ and p″ other constraints (not discussed hereafter) dominate. Thus, an expansion of public investment funded with monetary emission has a 'crowding in' effect on private investment up to p′ but a 'crowding out' effect beyond p″.

Interaction between the savings gap and the fiscal gap

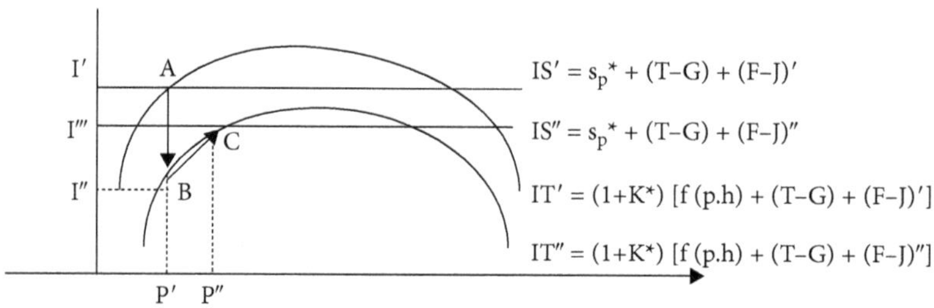

Figure 10.3 Interaction between the fiscal and savings gaps following a drop of foreign resources

Having formalized this new gap, it is now possible to study how it interacts with the other two gaps, taken one at a time, and then simultaneously. Let us first consider the interaction between the fiscal and savings gap by representing their schedules not in the usual plane (F − J, I) but in that (p, I) which allows us to represent directly the positive and then negative effect on overall investment of the monetization of the budget deficit. In contrast, the IS constraint is invariant in relation to the rate of inflation and is therefore represented by a line parallel to the horizontal axis with a constant equal to $Sp^* + (T - G) + (F - J)'$ (Figure 10.3). With foreign transfers equal to $(F - J)'$ the equilibrium is at point A. On its left is the fiscal gap which constrains investments (and growth), while on its right it is the savings gap which becomes constraining.

Let us examine now what happens in case of a reduction of foreign transfers from $(F - J)'$ to $(F - J)''$. Both schedules move downward but the IT schedule falls by more than the IS as $\Delta (F - J)$ is multiplied by $(1 + k^*) > 1$. If the policymaker wants to avoid an increase in inflation, the fiscal gap becomes binding and investment thus falls to I″, while part of the installed capacity becomes idle (B is below IS). Obviously, all this entails a reduction of investment and growth.

The government can tackle the drop in investment and growth in various ways. If it raises the primary surplus (T − G) by an amount equal to the drop of (F − J) the two schedules would return to the initial equilibrium in A. But such a measure, which would replace the fall of foreign transfers with a rise of the primary surplus, as observed after the South Korean crisis of the 1980s, entails cutting public expenditure or raising taxes and may be opposed by various lobbies. An alternative, followed for instance in Brazil, consists in increasing the monetary emissions to finance public investments. This would entail climbing along the IT″ schedule until one arrives at the new equilibrium point C, which is characterized by a higher investment level I‴(and thus greater growth of GDP than in B) but at the cost of higher inflation.

Interaction between the foreign exchange gap and the fiscal gap

To study this interaction, it is necessary to plot on the Cartesian plane (F − J, I) the two relations that illustrate the maximum feasible investments made possible by the availability of foreign exchange and fiscal resources (Figure 10.4). The position of the two schedules in this plane is not uniquely determined, as it depends on the relative magnitude of the slopes of the two schedules $1/m$ and $(1 + k^*)$. Their relative position depends on the type of country analysed. In the case of a large semi-developed country (e.g. India, China, or Brazil) which has the capacity to produce investment goods and a large share of public investment in the total, m (the import contents of investments) is likely to be small (0.2–0.3) while k is likely to be large (1.0–1.5). In this case, $1/m > (1 + k^*)$ and therefore the IE schedule has a steeper slope than the IT. In contrast, in the case of a small country where the state plays a limited investment role (as in Chile), m is likely to be big and k small, and therefore $1/m < (1 + k^*)$, which means that IT has a steeper slope than IE (Figure 10.4). Similar comparisons can be made for the constant terms, for which it is generally true that $1/m\ E^* < (1 + k^*)\ [f\ (p,\ h) + (T - G)]$

Let us suppose for the case discussed hereafter that $1/m > (1 + k^*)$, and that the initial equilibrium A corresponds to an inflow of foreign resources $(F - J)'$ and an investment

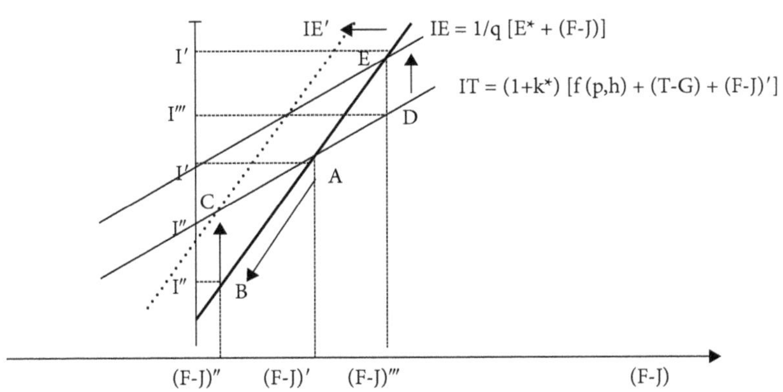

Figure 10.4 Interaction between the foreign exchange and fiscal gaps

level equal to I′. Let us now assume that—as a result of a rise in the interest rate on the foreign debt—$(F - J)''$ declines, making the foreign exchange binding and reducing the investment level to I″ through a series of measures rationing and controlling the access to foreign exchange. This is intended to reduce investment activities no longer compatible with the fall of the net foreign transfers. Public investment is the first to decline and to drag down also private investment. The new equilibrium is at point B which entails a major increase in idle productive capacity. At this point, much depends on whether, following the fall of investment from I′ to I″, wages, land, and real estate rents drop. Should this be the case, E* would rise and thus the constant term of the IE would shift leftwards until it reaches the new equilibrium point C corresponding to a level of investment I″*, which is smaller than I′ but bigger than I″.

What happens in the case of a positive shock, that is, of an increase of foreign transfers to $(F - J)'''$? In this case the schedule IT becomes binding while leading to a higher investment level I‴ and more rapid growth. Such growth is, however, inferior to that obtainable on the basis of the availability of foreign exchange. This means that part of the additional transfers would be accumulated in the form of foreign exchange reserves of low productive value. In order to avoid such a phenomenon, the policymaker could decide to liberalize imports or set an upper limit on exports, but such measures would meet considerable resistance by the domestic producers of import-competing goods and by the exporters. On the other side, donors consider such an accumulation of reserves as a positive achievement, as they think that this will exempt them from having to provide further financial assistance in the future.

On the other side, the increase of foreign exchange reserves will entail an expansion of the monetary mass. This, in turn, will cause a surge in inflation that, assuming the economy is still is on the favourable (left) side of the concave inflation–seignorage curve, would raise forced private savings, by raising the term f(p,h). This will determine an upward shift of the IT until it reaches a new equilibrium point E, characterized by a higher level of investment $I'^{V.}$ Thus, investment and growth would rise but at the cost of higher endogenous inflation caused by the increase of the monetary mass as a result of the higher inflow of foreign aid and loans received by the government.

A similar result (in terms of investments and growth) that avoids a surge in inflation could be reached if, parallel to the increase of (F – J), the government raised the primary surplus (T – G). This could be done, for instance, by raising taxes, a measure which would sterilize the increase of the monetary supply caused by the increase of (F – J), and so contain inflation while at the same time raising public saving. Analytically, an increase of (T – G) would result in an upward shift of the IT schedule which would find a new equilibrium in E, always at a higher level of investment, unaccompanied however by an increase in inflation. From a political economic perspective, this means that increasing the primary surplus when receiving additional financial transfers from abroad would permit an increase in total investment with no inflation.

10.5 The Macroeconomics of Foreign Aid and Finance

The previous sections have suggested that the developing countries suffer from multiple resource gaps and are characterized by a low self-financing capacity for both private and

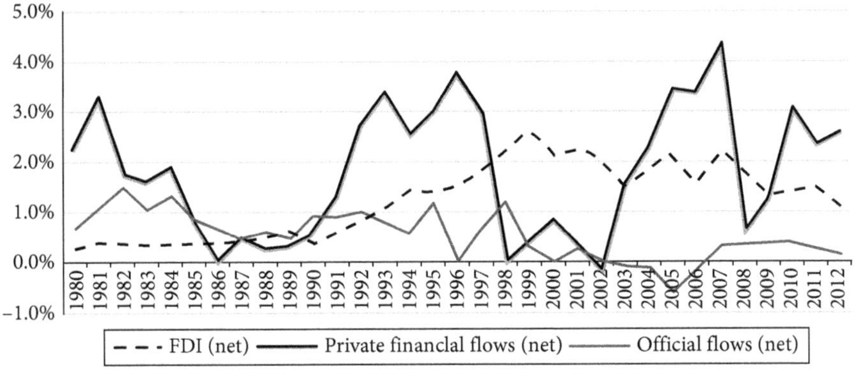

Figure 10.5 Capital flows to emerging and developing countries, 1980–2012
Source: Ocampo (2015)

public investments.[5] They are therefore under pressure to finance investments in physical and human capital with foreign resources. The natural corollary of this premise is that promoting capital inflows to poor countries should represent a priority of governments and the international community. Although not undisputed, the idea that the development of poor countries requires externally financed investments is indeed a *leitmotif* of more than sixty years of development thinking (Easterly, 2006). The Big Push theory (see Chapter 2) is the most telling example of such aid-based development paradigms. The Washington Consensus approach of the 1980s and 1990s assigned to aid and international capital injections an essential role for the development of poor countries. A similar emphasis is also found in the Millennium Development Goals Strategy, 2000–15. This is why the integration of international capital markets has been a pillar of the macroeconomic reforms promoted by the international agenda since the 1990s (see Table 2.7). Indeed, private capital flows to developing countries surged in that decade and, up to now, have remained substantially higher than in previous decades (Figure 10.5).

But how effective has foreign capital been in promoting investments and economic growth, as suggested by the gap models discussed in this chapter? The answer varies depending on the type of financial flows considered, that is bank loans, grants, FDI, portfolio flows,[6] official development assistance, and other concessional lending from public institutions. Indeed, not all international capital flows have the same potential to fill in the foreign exchange gap of developing countries. The varying development benefits of these flows stem from differences in terms of their source, purpose, time profile, reversibility, volatility, obligations, spillovers they generate and their complementarity with local resources.

Conclusions about the effectiveness of foreign resources in triggering investment and growth in poor countries depends on the level (microeconomic or macroeconomic) of the assessment. Addison et al. (2017), for instance, suggest that most microeconomic evaluations of the impact of aid on the economic and social sector show positive results. These tend to vanish or are no longer statistically significant, however, in macroeconomic evaluations where the composition of aid and capital flows and many other macro variables blur the picture.

[5] This section draws in part on Addison et al. (2017).

[6] Portfolio flows include transactions in equity and debt securities, such as bonds, notes, money market instruments, and financial derivatives.

Portfolio flows and bank lending

Portfolio flows (short-term speculative flows) and bank lending show a high degree of reversibility and procyclicality (Figure 10.5) and are difficult to predict, while bank loans and investment in debt securities raise a country's level of indebtedness. In addition, speculative flows may prefer investment in sectors—such as finance, insurance, and real estate—with low labour intensity and limited impact on capital accumulation in the traded sector. Such flows are also highly concentrated in high- and middle-income countries and hardly represent a solution to the saving and foreign exchange gaps of poor countries. For these reasons, despite the standard efficiency arguments attributed to these flows (diversification, efficient allocation of capital, disciplining effect on domestic macro policies, increased competition, and so on), financial liberalization and the increasing volume of portfolio flows may not be the best option to help the poorest countries to fill their foreign exchange and savings gap. Such flows entail, in fact, substantial instability and there is no evidence they accelerate the growth of GDP (Prasad et al., 2003; Ostry et al., 2016). They may also reduce the autonomy of monetary policy (due to the 'impossible trinity', see Chapter 15) and are often associated with negative distributive effects. Indeed, the poor may be harmed not only during a reversal of such financial flows, but also during periods of massive inflows and liquidity expansion because of the Dutch Disease effects they generate (see Chapter 5). Furthermore, the empirical evidence shows that surges of portfolio inflows increase the chance of financial crises during which income inequality worsens (Ostry et al., 2016). The evidence therefore seems to point to a mounting costs–benefits ratio associated with short-term portfolio inflows. From this evidence, there is a growing conviction about the need to regulate them, including by introducing capital controls when necessary (Ocampo, 2015; see also Chapter 15).

Foreign direct investment

Despite the 2008–9 global financial crisis, over the last decades foreign direct investment (FDI) has become the largest external financial flow to developing economies (UNCTAD, 2017; see also Figure 5.4). The FDI going to developing countries has also increased, possibly as part of the restructuring of global production along value chains, albeit they are less stable and common relative to other external resources of finance such as ODA and remittances (UNCTAD, 2017). FDI are more oriented to the long term, are more stable than portfolio flows, and in several cases contribute to long-term growth. They are therefore more likely to be an engine of growth in recipient countries, helping to fill the foreign exchange and savings gaps of developing countries without increasing indebtedness. However, FDI do not provide a free lunch either, because they generate at times sizeable outflows of profits and dividends, and often entail (especially in the initial years) massive imports of equipment and semi-finished products, as shown in Table 10.1 in the case of Malaysia over 1980–92.

Despite these caveats, the economic literature generally identifies several elements of the growth and development potential of FDI in recipient countries. Examples include direct contributions to capital accumulation, the transfer of technology, knowledge, skills, and improved managerial and legal practices, overall productivity gains due to the exposure of

Table 10.1 Direct effects of FDI on Malaysia's balance of payments, 1980–1992

	Net Inflow of FDI (1)	Exports by foreign firms (2)	Imports by foreign firms (3)	Trade balance of FDI firms (4) = 2 − 3	Outflows of profits, rents, dividends and royalties (5)	Net effect (6) = 1+4+5
1980	2033	9066	11,191	−2124	−142	−233
1981	2914	9094	11,599	−2505	−2576	−2167
1982	3263	10,344	13,349	−3005	−2691	−2433
1983	2926	11,483	13,251	−1768	−3202	−2044
1984	1869	14,255	15,671	−1416	−3445	−2992
1985	1725	13,496	15,884	−2388	−3084	−3747
1986	1262	13,894	14,489	−595	−2341	−1674
1987	1065	19,492	18,464	1028	−4115	−2022
1988	1884	24,863	22,352	2511	−4088	307
1989	4518	33,606	28,778	4828	−5509	3837
1990	6300	41,822	39,694	2129	−6444	1985
1991	9600	50,284	53,865	−3581	−7125	−1106
1992	10,500	56,847	55,960	888	−7641	3747

Note: The figures are in millions of ringgit.

Source: Chang Hooi Eng (1998).

local industry to competition, the development of infrastructure, exports growth among domestic firms, and participation in international production networks through backward and forward industrial links. At the same time, several factors can reverse the potential positive effects of FDI. The first risk is the crowding-out of less efficient national firms, especially in low-income countries with a thin industrial base and credit market. An increase in FDI may thus depress domestic savings and investment. Moreover, countries with weak institutions and a poor justice system, low financial development, limited human capital, and lack of complementarity between local and foreign-owned firms may not be well positioned to exploit these benefits. Similarly, the sectoral composition of FDI can impact economic outcomes in host countries. For instance, FDI in extractive activities generates less development benefits than FDI in the manufacturing sector.[7] Finally, although to a lesser extent than portfolio flows, FDI also remains predominantly concentrated in a few emerging economies and bypasses poor countries in need of external capital. In short, as noted by Addison et al. (2017), private external sources are unlikely to fill the savings and foreign exchange gaps in poor economies and to allocate funds to investment that generates high social returns due to positive externalities, the development of merit goods, and the allocation of funds to sectors with delayed returns over the long term and high upfront capital costs.

Official Development Assistance

Official Development Assistance (ODA) consists of mission-oriented public flows. By its nature, ODA has a greater ability to finance fragile economies, human capital formation,

[7] For the problems entailed by an abundance of natural resources, see Chapter 5.

and projects with long gestation periods but high social returns. ODA flows are also less volatile and procyclical than private flows. Thus, foreign aid is a prominent instrument used by the international community to assist poor countries in the achievement of their development goals. In the context of a Harrod–Domar model, foreign aid can be seen as a source of additional saving and under the two- and three-gap models, foreign aid simultaneously helps to reduce the fiscal, foreign exchange, and savings gaps. Finally, the analyses of the informal sector and of the urban–rural migration of the 1970s, and the recent growing awareness of the need to reduce poverty and unemployment in developing countries have shifted the focus of aid policies from capital accumulation to poverty reduction and basic needs (Tarp, 2000).

Despite its potential role for promoting growth in developing countries, foreign aid has been the object of severe criticism. High hopes have been accompanied by big disappointments, especially in terms of its macroeconomic impact. In some cases, the more radical critics have pointed at the negative effects induced by aid dependence and perverse incentives. If a consensus has been reached on the positive effect of aid at the micro level, the role of foreign aid in fostering aggregate growth is much more controversial. Referring to the contrast between positive rates of return in projects and the insignificant or low rates of return at the macro level, Mosley (1986) introduced the concept of the micro–macro paradox in the impact of aid, a notion that the aid literature has periodically revived. The existing meta-analyses and literature surveys on the macro level aid–growth nexus have come to contrasting conclusions, even if, over the last ten years, a convergence to a cautious positive view is emerging. According to Doucouliagos and Paldam (2015), forty years of research up to 2004 showed that aid has not been effective in promoting accumulation or growth, although more recent evidence supports the existence of a small positive effect. Mekasha and Tarp (2013) reach a more favourable conclusion. In their view, the effect of aid on growth is positive and statistically significant, thus giving plausibility to the inclusion in gap models of foreign savings as a determinant of growth. This issue is sensitive, and empirical analysis encounters data and econometric difficulties in reaching definite conclusions, and it is likely that the aid–growth and aid–development debate will continue.[8] At the same time, there is a broad consensus that aid has shortcomings and cannot be the main solution for all development goals. Thus, the most useful question is probably not whether aid is beneficial for development but when does it not work.

10.6 Domestic Political Economy and Donor Policies

The aid literature identifies several factors that can hinder aid effectiveness and limit the potentially positive role of foreign aid. In the following subsections, the main explanations for the failure of aid to reach its stated objectives are briefly reviewed.

[8] Themes include the endogeneity of aid, establishing the direction of causation (does aid affect growth or do donors allocate aid flows according to growth rates in potential recipient countries?), creating a counterfactual to aid, interactions with other determinants of growth and development, choosing the time horizon necessary to detect an impact on growth, and tackling any overestimation of flows in data released by donors.

Aid to governments may engender perverse effects on their behaviour

The critics of aid have highlighted different ways in which foreign aid can induce people and governments to follow strategies with limited short-run political and/or economic costs, but with negative long-run effects. In particular, foreign aid can reduce incentives to collect taxes and undermine governance because the amount of aid-related revenue received by the government is not affected by efficiency considerations. Reliance on aid as a substitute for domestic revenues creates a moral hazard in state–society relations, which reduces the accountability of government and the participation of citizens to political life. This may impair the quality of development policies. Furthermore, as in the case of resource rents, aid flows may encourage rent seeking. These arguments, however, forget that, in many cases, it may improve domestic revenue mobilization or the quality of national policies. Foreign aid, may be used, for instance, to support the government's fiscal capacity-building, or to introduce incentives to strengthen tax collection, without which no additional aid will be provided. In general, whether there is complementarity or substitutability between aid and domestic tax revenue is a matter for empirical investigation. Its outcome depends, among other factors, on the type of aid, the objectives of donors, and aid conditionality. Aid may also cause a Dutch Disease. In this case, large and sudden aid inflows may lead to an appreciation of the real exchange rate that undermines the competitiveness of the tradables sector. However, the evidence in this regard is mixed. Indeed, aid-induced Dutch Disease effects may not occur in cases of humanitarian aid to import food, shelter, and drugs, or if aid is used to finance public goods or to import goods that enhance the productivity of the traded-goods sector.

Bad governance and limited capacity to absorb aid in recipient countries may reduce its impact

That bad governance in recipient countries and a limited capacity to absorb aid may reduce its impact is the classical argument introduced in the 1990s by proponents of liberal policies who argued that aid works only in a liberal macroeconomic policy environment (Burnside and Dollar, 2000). This shift in emphasis marked the beginning of the aid selectivity and performance-based allocation of ODA by major donors. This stance carries the risk, however, of generating an adverse selection of aid recipients. Indeed, the poorest and most fragile states and countries with weak institutions are less likely to apply sound policies, and so they risk becoming aid orphans. Also, Burnside and Dollar's contribution has been disputed for methodological and data weaknesses, while several scholars and aid agencies have suggested adjustments in aid conditionality and allocation criteria to reduce the negative effects of aid selectivity. This strand of the literature, however, has played an important role in recognizing that local governments, elites, and their policies are crucial in mediating the impact of aid programmes.

Donor policies and aid effectiveness

Whenever the donors' primary rationale for ODA allocation are former colonial ties, commercial penetration, and geopolitical considerations, it is not surprising that foreign aid generates only limited impact in promoting development in poor countries (Bertoli et al., 2007 and the references cited therein). For instance, it is no mistake that, in 2015, Afghanistan and Turkey were the first recipients of aid provided respectively by the United States and the European Union. Donor policies may also reduce the incentives to monitor whether aid is wasted or reaches the target groups. Donors can also adopt practices that reduce the actual value and scope of the aid they provide, as in the case of tied aid, while they raise aid volatility whenever they shift aid allocations from one country to another. This causes difficulties in poor countries that had planned to finance long-term investments with ODA. Aid fragmentation and duplication is another disturbing feature of the behaviour of ODA donors. Also, many bilateral and multilateral donors require an administrative capacity and coordination that is not available in many developing countries. In all these cases, aid is not therefore consistent with the logic of the gap models.

10.7 The Foreign Gap, and the 1980s Debt Crisis

In many historical instances, borrowing from abroad made sound economic sense. For instance, the development of the railway systems of the USA, Argentina, and other Western offshoots in the nineteenth century was financed by bonds issued in London and long-term loans from European banks. Yet, this has not been the general rule, and in the 1980s the developing countries (especially those of Latin America and sub-Saharan Africa) experienced a debt crisis that had no precedent other than the Great Depression of the 1930s. The crisis of the 1980s led to a lost decade in terms of GDP growth, income inequality, and social well-being. For instance, the average regional GDP growth rate over the 1980s fell by three points in relation to the 1970s in Latin America and by two points in South East Asia (Sachs and Larrain, 1993).

As shown by Figure 10.5, the 1970s expansion of global finance coincided with the massive recycling of petrodollars generated by the oil price hikes of 1973 and 1978. Faced with such oil price increases, most oil-importing developing countries did not opt to introduce contractionary macroeconomic policies but chose to finance their growing external deficits by borrowing petrodollars at variable interest rates from the international banks. By borrowing heavily, these countries managed to grow at a relatively rapid pace during the second half of the 1970s but did not anticipate the possible adverse effects of such large debt accumulations at variable rates, and of a decline in the international prices of their exports. As a result of this policy stand, by 1982 the accumulated debt of developing countries had reached US$562 billion. In Latin America 65 per cent of such debt was negotiated at floating interest rates (Sachs and Larrain, 1993). On the other hand, the oil producing countries lacked a banking system capable of absorbing and lending the large balance of payments surpluses that had been generated by the tripling of the oil price. Such surpluses were therefore deposited in the main international banks and recycled as petrodollars that were lent to oil importing countries. However, in their efforts to maximize profits, these banks often relaxed the standard prudential norms required for the concession of credits. Loans were available at low or even negative real interest rates, and some major banks lent more than 100 per cent of their capital (Sachs and Larrain, 1993). Few worried about the rapid increase in the foreign debt of developing countries (that in some cases used such resources to finance public and private consumption rather than productive investments) as interest rates were low and the world prices of the commodities exported by borrowing countries were high. In addition, the syndicated loan system through which much of the lending operated provided a false sense of security. In turn, in the poor African countries 96 per cent of the lending was public or publicly guaranteed as it was granted by the governments of industrialized countries or international organizations.

So, while the nineteenth-century US and Argentinean railway companies were able to repay their debts, by the early 1980s it had become increasingly evident that the international recession of 1979–82 caused by the sharp increase in US interest rates put the countries that had borrowed heavily in dollars at variable rates—particularly Brazil, Argentina and Mexico—in a situation where they could not repay their foreign debt. Indeed, the strong increase in US interest rates introduced by the US Federal Reserve to fight inflation were quickly transmitted to the interest rates charged by the international banks for loans to developing countries. In addition, the world recession that followed the rise in US interest rates lowered the demand and prices of the commodities exported by the debtor countries. This reduced their ability to service their foreign debt. The appreciation of the dollar made servicing the foreign debt even more difficult. Some countries' foreign debt often exceeded the sustainable threshold of 200–250 per cent of exports and interest payments exceeded the alarm threshold of 20–25 per cent of export earnings. In Latin America, for instance, by 1981–82 interest payments had already risen to 30 per cent of export earnings.

The resulting debt crisis threatened the economic prospects of developing countries and the financial stability of large banks in rich countries. However, the adjustment burden of this crisis fell entirely on the developing countries. These countries seldom defaulted on their foreign debt obligations and, to service the interest payments on their foreign debt, adopted highly contractionary policies that depressed imports of essential items, economic growth, and social expenditure while the surplus of the trade balance realized through these import compressions was used to service the interest on the foreign debt. With no new capital inflows (that fell as a whole from US$38 billion in 1981 to 3 billion in 1983) and substantial outflows to service foreign debt, the North to South resource transfer of resources became negative. Large-scale defaults were avoided only by the repeated intervention of the IMF and, in the case of large countries, by the introduction of various US-backed plans such as the Baker and the Brady Plans. Later on, the debt overhang of low income countries was sharply reduced by the introduction of the Highly Indebted Poor Countries initiative that mostly benefited the African nations.

10.8 Concluding Remarks

The narrowness and distortions of their financial markets, and the limited capacity to mobilize latent domestic savings has forced many developing countries to become chronically dependent on foreign resources for the financing of their capital accumulation. Meanwhile, with the spread of financial globalization, access to foreign loans has become much easier. The one-gap model (that measures the shortage of autonomous savings), two-gap model (that emphasizes the lack of both savings and foreign exchange) and three-gap model (that also includes the shortage of fiscal revenue) were developed to determine the amount of foreign resources needed to achieve a preset GDP growth target that could not be financed on the basis of domestic savings alone. Indeed, an inflow of foreign funds fills both the saving and foreign exchange gaps and, if the funds are received by the government, it also fills the fiscal gap. Given the negative transfer of resources to developing countries that characterized the 1980s, such models highlight the risks of an over-dependence on volatile external finance. Despite their simplicity, such models illustrate the macroeconomic adjustments that are necessary when the inflow of foreign funds increases or contracts.

What does the empirical evidence say about the effectiveness of foreign finance in promoting growth in recipient countries? Several evaluations suggest that countries with a higher share of domestic savings in total savings grow faster than those depending to a considerable extent on foreign finance. The impact of a dependence on foreign finance is also affected by its composition. Portfolio flows and bank lending do not generate any perceptible growth improvement but they do increase economic instability. FDI may generate better results but this depends on their sectoral composition and whether they are greenfield investments or acquisitions of local firms. Finally, the impact of foreign aid is characterized by the 'micro–macro paradox' outlined in Section 10.5. Yet, the latest evaluations suggest that over the last decade the impact of aid seems to have been somewhat more favourable. This is true, in particular, if opportunistic behaviours by both donor and recipient countries are controlled.

References

Addison, T., O. Morrissey, and F. Tarp (2017), 'The Macroeconomics of Aid: Overview' *The Journal of Development Studies*, 53 (7): pp. 987–97.

Agénor, P. R. and P. Montiel (1999), *Development Macroeconomics*, 2nd edition. Princeton, NJ: Princeton University Press.

Bacha, E. (1990), 'A Three Gap Model of Foreign Transfers and the GDP Growth Rates in Developing Countries', *Journal of Development Economics*, 32: pp. 279–96.

Bertoli S., G. A. Cornia, and F. Manaresi (2007), 'Aid Effort and Its Determinants: A Comparison of the Italian Performance with other OECD donors' *Moneta e Credito, Banca Nazionale del Lavoro Quarterly Review*, 60 (242): pp. 271–321.

Burnside, C. and D. Dollar (2000), 'Aid, Policies and Growth' *American Economic Review*, 90 (4): pp. 847–68.

Chang Hooi Eng (1998), *Foreign Direct Investment: A study of Malaysia's Balance of Payments Position*. Malaysia: Pelanduk Publications.

Chenery, H. and M. Bruno (1962), 'Development Alternatives in an Open Economy: the Case of Israel' *Economic Journal*, 72 (285): pp. 79–103.

Chenery, H. and A. S. Strout (1966), 'Foreign Assistance and Economic Development' *American Economic Review*, 56: 679–733.

Doucouliagos, C. and M. Paldam (2015), 'Finally a breakthrough: The recent rise in the size of the estimates of aid effectiveness', in B. M. Arvin and B. Lew (eds), *Handbook on the Economics of Foreign Aid*, pp. 325–49, Cheltenham: Edward Elgar.

Easterly, W. (2006), 'Reliving the 1950s: the big push, poverty traps, and take-offs in economic development' *Journal of Economic Growth*, 11: pp. 289–318.

Mekasha, T. J. and F. Tarp (2013), 'Aid and growth: What meta-analysis reveals' *The Journal of Development Studies*, 49: pp. 564–83.

Mosley, P. (1986), 'Aid effectivenesss: Te Micro-Macro Paradox', IDS Bullettin, 17 (2).

Ocampo, J. A. (2015), 'Capital account liberalization and management', *WIDER Working Paper* 2015/048, Helsinki: World Institute for Development Economics Research.

Ostry, J. D., P. Loungani, and D. Furceri (2016), 'Neoliberalism: Oversold?' *Finance and Development*, Washington, DC: International Monetary Fund.

Prasad, E., K. Rogoff, S. J. Wei, and M. A. Kose (2003), 'Effects of Financial Globalization on Developing Countries: Some Empirical Evidence'. IMF Occasional Paper 220. Washington DC: International Monetary Fund.

Sachs, J. and F. Larrain (1993), *Macroeconomics and the Global Economy*. Upper Saddle River, NJ: Prentice-Hall.

Tarp, F., ed. (2000), *Foreign Aid and Development: Lessons Learnt and Directions for the Future*. London: Routledge.

Taylor, L. (1994), 'Gap Models' *Journal of Development Economics*, 45: pp. 17–34.

UNCTAD (2017), 'World Investment Report 2017'. Geneva: UNCTAD.

Suggested Further Reading

Arndt, C., S. Jones, and F. Tarp (2010), 'Aid, growth, and development: Have we come full circle?' *Journal of Globalization and Development*, 1 (2): article 5.

Bacha, E. (1990), 'A Three Gap Model of Foreign Transfers and the GDP Growth Rates in Developing Countries' *Journal of Development Economics*, 32: pp. 279–96.

Mekasha, T. J. and F. Tarp (2013), 'Aid and growth: What meta-analysis reveals' *The Journal of Development Studies*, 49: pp. 564–83.

Tarp, F., ed. (2000), *Foreign Aid and Development: Lessons Learnt and Directions for the Future*. London: Routledge.

Taylor, L. (1994), 'Gap Models' *Journal of Development Economics*, 45: pp. 17–34.

11

Institutions, Investment, and Growth in Developing Countries

This chapter discusses the nature and impact of formal and informal political and economic institutions. It highlights their interaction and their impact on growth, inequality, and political stability. It places special attention on the institutions that build the market and facilitate economic exchange and on the public organizations mandated with their enforcement. It then discusses their impact on growth and macroeconomic stability.

11.1 What Do We Mean by Institutions?

The term institutions refers to those non-traditional factors, which are often ignored in mainstream economic analyses, that influence in a significant way the behaviour of economic agents: the GDP growth and pattern, and the distribution of income. According to North (1990):

> Institutions are the rules of the game in a society or, more formally, are the humanly devised constraints that shape human interaction.... In consequence they structure incentives in human exchange, whether political, social, or economic. (North 1990, p. 3)

One normally distinguishes between political and economic institutions. These are, however, closely inter-related while both are strictly dependent on the political power of the dominant social groups (Acemoglou et al. 2005). In brief, one could say that the nature of the political power (democratic, autocratic, or colonial) determines the main political institutions that in turn markedly influence the choice of economic institutions consistent with the interests of the dominant class. The institutional approach is essential to understanding the politics and political economy of any country's development path. This is particularly true in developing countries where the institutional setup is still evolving for the reasons discussed in this chapter.

To a large extent, institutions are endogenous as they emanate not so much from the choice of a neutral and enlightened policymaker, but from the power struggle between social classes and the nature of the political system that emerges from such a struggle. Changes in class composition can, however, endogenously change economic institutions, as observed in Latin America over 2002–15, a period during which growth accelerated and inequality fell. The key analytical challenge consists in the identification of the factors that led to changes in class alliances and political dominance during this period, a period which experienced a strengthening of democracy and a fall in inequality that correlates with the political orientation of the incumbent governments (Table 11.1).

The Macroeconomics of Developing Countries: An Intermediate Textbook. Giovanni Andrea Cornia, Oxford University Press (2020).

DOI: 10.1093/oso/9780198856672.001.0001

Table 11.1 Inequality trends by the ideological orientation of the incumbent governments, Latin America, 2002–2010

Political orientation of incumbent government	Total multi-year change in the Gini index under different incumbent governments	Average yearly change in the Gini index under different incumbent governments
Radical left	−3.59	−0.42
Social democratic	−3.21	−0.54
Centrist	−1.79	−0.20
Centre-right	−1.01	−0.08

Source: Cornia (2014).

Economic institutions are also path-dependent, as they generally evolve slowly. In order to understand why some institutions persist and others do not, Acemoglu et al. (2005) posit a framework that is rooted in the past distribution of resources and preexisting political institutions. As noted above, these two factors determine the *de jure* political power, which in turn defines this period's economic institutions and future political institutions. Likewise, the current economic institutions determine the next period's distribution of resources and this cycle repeats itself. In contrast, North (1990) attributes institutional change to the work of political entrepreneurs, such as political parties, which weigh the expected costs of altering the existing institutional framework against the benefits they can derive from a change in both formal and informal institutions.

In many developing countries, the current pace and stability of growth, macroeconomic equilibrium, and distribution of income have been influenced by the adoption of a foreign-financed development strategy based on the export of commodities (see Chapter 9), as well as by the asset concentration inherited from the colonial era. In both Europe and much of Asia, high asset concentration was determined by the then prevalent feudal systems. In contrast, in East and Southern Africa and Latin America, a high asset concentration was the result of the dispossession by colonial rulers of the land and natural resources of indigenous populations. This led to the development of institutions that perpetuated the privileges of a tiny agrarian and commercial oligarchy until well after World War II thanks to the diversification of the land and mining assets of the oligarchs into industrial and financial assets. Evidence from sub-Saharan Africa supports the hypothesis of a close relationship between current inequality and past property rights regimes over land and mines. At the time of the independence of countries in West and Central Africa which had abundant land then, land ownership was communal and land allocations were made by village heads in an egalitarian manner. These countries were characterized by a near absence of large-scale properties and of a landed gentry. Even today, the Gini index of the distribution of consumption per capita of these nations is substantially lower than that of the *white-settler* economies of Eastern and Southern Africa where estates and mines are owned by the descendants of colonial rulers or of their indigenous successors (Table 11.2).

A key issue concerns the persistence of path-dependence over time. Indeed, the relationship between initial asset concentration and subsequent income inequality may be eroded by the withering away of the agricultural share in GDP (Klasen et al., 2018). Yet, such a relation may survive if dualistic financial markets lend only to the rich, if human

Table 11.2 Gini coefficient of land concentration by type of land tenure system in sub-Saharan Africa

Countries with a dominant communal land tenure system	Land Gini	Countries with a dominant white-settlers dualistic land tenure system	Land Gini
Burkina Faso (1993)	39.1	Liberia (1971)	68.1
Mali (1960)	45.1	Uganda (1991)	57.4
Niger (1980)	31.2	Tanzania (1960)	70.0
Senegal (1960)	46.7	Zambia (1971)	69.9
Guinea (1989)	45.2	South Africa (1960)	64.3
Sierra Leone (1970)	42.4	Swaziland (1971)	83.5
Côte d'Ivoire (1974)	41.5	Madagascar (1970)	80.4
Ghana (1970)	53.0	Mauritius (1930)	74.2
Togo (1961)	45.2		
Cameroon (1972)	40.7		
Gabon (1974)	40.2		
Congo (Zaire) (1970)	53.2		
Ethiopia (1977)	42.4		
Mozambique (1999)	36.8		
Average	43.0	Average	70.9

Source: Frankema (2005).

capital remains insufficient and unequally distributed, and if political democratization and mass education are postponed. Yet, even a return to democracy or a revolution are no guarantee that growth will pick up and inequality fall, as demonstrated in the case of the recent political liberalization in the former Soviet Republics, where inequality widened markedly during the transition before stabilizing at rather high levels (Gruen and Klasen 2012). But path-dependence may break down because of growing conflicts between old and new elites. Indeed, history provides counterexamples to the thesis that a unified oligarchic interest creates a smooth transition between agrarian and industrial-financial dominance, asset inequality and growth patterns. Indeed, sooner or later, the new industrial elites may find themselves involved in a power struggle with the rural elite. In Chile, for instance, a peasant-industrialist alliance overcame the opposition of the agrarians to land reform. Generally speaking, a transformation in the composition of a country's élites weakens path dependence.

External factors may also affect path-dependence. The gains in the international terms of trade experienced in Latin America during the globalization of 1870–1914 exacerbated the income inequality inherited from the colonial period as globalization raised the returns to land that benefited a tiny class of large landowners. However, the effects of gains in terms of trade are themselves endogenous to the political orientation of incumbent governments. This depends on a host of factors, including the birth of new political actors, such as the Argentinean *cartoneros* and the new indigenous movements that have emerged in the Andean Region. For example, while, over 1870–1914, gains in the terms of trade exacerbated inequality, econometric evidence for the years 2002–13 comes to opposing conclusions. Indeed, the distribution of income during this period was influenced by the region's political 'left turn', by the related increased taxation of land and mining rents, and the redistribution to the poor of part of such rents through the creation of new redistributive institutions (Cornia, 2017).

Demography also affects path dependence and the degree of income inequality. In the once land-abundant communitarian nations of West and Central Africa, rapid population growth over the last four decades has altered farming systems and land distribution. Initially, the growing demand for food was satisfied by extending the surface of good land under cultivation. At a later stage, in view of the inability of countries to modernize farming techniques, rapid population growth accelerated the migration to marginal lands characterized by low yields and frequent food crises. In bad years, the land of smallholders unable to feed their families was informally sold to an emerging class of medium-size farmers. This promoted land concentration and added to the proletarization of a segment of the rural labour force.

11.2 Economic Institutions: Legal Systems and Market Rules

Economic institutions can be divided into constitutions; legal systems and norms regulating production, trade, and other economic activities; public and private organizations that ensure the enforcement of the above norms; informal institutions that affect the adherence (or less) to legal norms and their practical application. It should be noted immediately that these institutions vary strongly across countries and—even more so—between advanced economies and developing countries. In addition, institutions vary markedly among developing countries themselves and this institutional heterogeneity affects differentially the agents' behaviour, the functioning of the macroeconomy, growth, and the distribution of income. This implies that in many developing countries the aggregate supply curve AS is steep and policy credibility limited. As a result, growth and distribution may be affected unfavorably. The main objective of the policymaker concerning economic institutions therefore ought to be building and regulating an efficient market by establishing fair rules in the following six areas.

(a) Market entry and ease of doing business, so as to avoid the exclusion of some firms and an inefficient and unfair market segmentation based on race, class, religion, caste, region, and other discriminatory criteria. This segmentation is inefficient and unfair, as in the case of the Indian labour market. Such segmentation lowers the ease of doing business especially in South Asia and sub-Saharan Africa (Table 11.3). Thus, norms that aim at equalizing market opportunities must remove those hurdles that are discriminatory, reduce economic incentives, discourage entrepreneurship, production, and exchange by delaying market entry or making it more

Table 11.3 Average regional rank of the 'ease of doing business' index, 2016

Region (no. of countries)	Regional rank	Region (no. STET)	Regional rank
OECD—High income (32)	25.9	MENA (25)	107.0
Europe–Central Asia (25)	50.1	Latin America/Caribbean (33)	108.1
East Asia and Pacific (12)	95.7	South Asia (8)	123.5
		Sub-Saharan Africa	145.5

Note: a high value of the regional rank indicates problems in building efficient formal market institutions.
Source: Own elaboration on World Bank http://www.doingbusiness.org/rankings (accessed 27 October 2017).

expensive, or by requiring applicants to obtain many costly permits. Whenever these segmentations were inherited from the colonial or pre-capitalist past, the pursuit of growth and equity should focus on either their elimination or transformation into inclusive institutions.

(b) Market exit for those producers or intermediaries who generate tensions, defaults, and inefficiencies because of their incompetent or fraudulent behaviour. For this reason, the legal systems have introduced institutions such bankruptcy, which temporarily or permanently excludes from the market incompetent or corrupt entrepreneurs who are a source of disturbances, uncertainty, and market disruption. In many countries simple bankruptcy entails a five-year ban from the market, more in cases of fraudulent bankruptcy.

(c) Ensuring free competition. It is well known that regulated market competition determines better social outcomes, as it reduces the prices of goods and stimulates greater innovation compared to monopolies and oligopolies. For this reason, the policymaker introduces anti-monopolistic norms and laws on the abuse of a dominant market position. Their actual application, however, is complex and less stringent in developing countries with underdeveloped regulatory bodies.

(d) Regulating natural monopolies. Whenever there are important economies of scale or case of natural monopolies or of institutions not subject to competition (such as the stock market), it is necessary to introduce rules that prevent the formation of distorted and misleading price signals, that may generate turbulence, crises, and inefficiency. This regulatory role is played by public supervisory authorities. In many low-income developing countries and in the slowly evolving transition economies of Central Asia, legislation on the regulation of market behaviour in the above areas is weak or absent.

(e) Security of property rights. The legislation that institutes, guarantees, and enforces property rights has a strong influence on the investment rate and growth. Clear legislation in this area provides a secure time horizon for investors, including foreign investors who can be the source of innovation, modern management techniques, and finance, which many developing countries need. A lack of secure property rights and fear of confiscation discourage investment and growth. It is important to emphasize that property rights take many forms: private property regimes (as in most of the OECD), cooperative property rights (as in the Chinese town and village enterprises), communitarian property rights (as in parts of West Africa), and state property rights (as in the former Soviet Union). While legal systems may differ, it is important that property rights are clearly specified and that norms ensure the respect and security of whatever property regime exists.

(f) A well developed and regulated financial system. Clear norms on property rights and market competition do not ensure a country's prosperity in the absence of financial markets where money can be borrowed to finance current production and new investments. As noted in Chapter 10, the weakness of financial markets is particularly acute in developing countries where local firms have a low self-financing capacity.

The financial sector is particularly exposed to the risk of asymmetric information, adverse selection and moral hazard, as observed in the case of the conflicts of interest—which have surfaced dramatically during the last decade on occasion of the fraudulent defaults of Enron, Parmalat, and US banks issuing sub-prime mortgage loans. Hence, the proper functioning of the financial sector crucially depends on the existence of detailed prudential rules, which must prevent and prohibit conflicts of interest inside and outside financial sector firms, and assign to the central bank the task of carrying out adequate surveillance of the credit system. As seen recently, this has for years been a sore point in the European Union and the United States.[1]

Financial crises have also become more frequent in developing countries (see Figure 2.3). Devastating crises took place in Thailand and the rest of South East Asia in 1997, Russia and its trading partners in 1998, Argentina in 2001–02 and so on. The quality of financial institutions has thus become even more crucial for macroeconomic stability and growth during the past twenty years of globalization, international financial integration, and global financial contagion. A survey by Kunt and Detragiache (2005) shows that—on the one side—the probability of being hit by a banking-financial-currency crisis increased as a result of the liberalization of the financial sector but that—on the other side—such risk can be reduced by establishing appropriate institutional and regulatory systems. The second conclusion, however, remains controversial. For instance, during the 2000s only Latin America was spared by the contagion of the 2008 US financial crisis, thanks to the introduction of stronger regulatory rules (Rojas Suarez, 2010).

(g) Public goods and social norms. A proper functioning of the economy also requires social consensus. Some developing countries have long tolerated, for cultural and historical reasons, high levels of inequality and poverty. For both intrinsic and utilitarian reasons it is, however, necessary to introduce norms ensuring a socially acceptable income distribution. Social norms can help to establish clear criteria to guarantee job opportunities and social transfers to those who are unable to earn a sufficient income, whether temporarily or permanently. The lack or weakening of such norms can cause high economic and social costs, political tension, and crime. For example, highly unequal countries such as Nigeria and Guatemala, where the strong inequality of the primary distribution of income and limited redistribution are characterized by uncertain property rights and some of the highest homicide rates in the world and—until recently—by unstable growth.

11.3 Public Organizations that Enforce the Rules of the Game

Most of the legal norms and regulations discussed in Section 11.2 are implemented by various branches of public administration, whose efficiency influences the degree to which they are effectively enforced. A key aspect of state administration concerns the effectiveness of its interventions in economic and social areas. While there are various theoretical

[1] In the United States, the Sarbanes–Oxley Act that was adopted in the aftermath of the Enron crisis of 2001–2, the new Frank-Dodd and Consumer Protection Act adopted in 2010 after the 2008 US financial collapse, as well as the new Basel 3 requirements about banks' capital adequacy, stress tests and market liquidity risks introduced in 2013 have all attempted to tackle the problem of financial instability by imposing stricter rules and higher penalties against possible offenders, but may not be sufficient to avoid the repeat of the financial crisis of 2008–2011 that led to a new Great Depression in Europe.

models of the state (that is, libertarian, liberal, or interventionist), the empirical evidence shows that, in all cases, there is a need for a 'minimal state' which mediates between the various social groups, thereby generating a basic political consensus (that helps to avoid conflicts) and agreement on the economic rules of the game (that helps to reduce crime and the insecurity of property rights). This preempts the adoption of Darwinian non-market behaviours, such as violent expropriation, hoarding, black marketeering and so on. In fact, the minimal state represents a kind of social glue that provides services not supplied by the market, including security at the local level, an efficient administration, and a minimum of redistribution through subsidized access to education, health, and public infrastructure. The collapse of the minimal state has often led not only to a rise in production and transaction costs, but also to civil wars. In order to exert its functions, the minimal state needs resources that are generated by taxation, royalties, and other means, and an efficient and honest public administration. A few aspects of public administration that can weaken the minimal state are discussed in following subsections.

Red tape

Oppressively complex and time-consuming bureaucratic procedures, and low administrative efficiency raise business costs by increasing the time and fees for registration and licensing needed to establish and run a business. As noted in Chapter 8, such problems are not uncommon in developed countries but are pervasive in many developing countries, including in fast growing China.

Indexes of such inefficiency include the ease of doing business (Table 11.3), the number of permits and time needed to set up a company, the time required to clear goods through customs, the time/permits necessary to enlarge existing plants, the number of inspections carried out by public officers, the complexity of the tax regime for small firms, and so on. Delays, uncertainty, and inconsistency between norms, low productivity, and the lack of incentives for civil servants (who are often so poorly paid that they have to take a second job or ask for bribes) increase the time needed to run a business, raise transaction and production costs, and discourage investment and economic activity.

Bureaucratic rents and corruption

In a number of cases, administrative inefficiency is combined with the corruption of the public administration. In some countries, the civil service is conceived not as an institution aiming to provide public goods to all citizens, to facilitate the development of productive activities, and to redistribute income and services in favour of the poor, but rather as a source of bureaucratic rents, that is, a power position that allows resources to be extracted from those who need permits and authorizations or have to undergo controls. Under these circumstances, public jobs are often 'sold' at a price proportional to the rents each civil servant can extract from consumers and entrepreneurs. Getting a traffic police job in some Central Asian countries, for example, used to cost around $2,000, that is, much less than that of a provincial prefect (that used to cost around $300,000) as the former can extract only modest rents through fake fines that he keeps to himself, while the latter has ample opportunities to make big money by controlling building permits and public works, and by selling the jobs of the civil servants under his authority. As many state employees are paid little, more than being blatant corruption, this behaviour is a critical reflection of an inefficient institutional setup that burdens citizens and firms rather than the Treasury. The problems of corruption have been theorized in a different way by Bates (1983) when discussing the neo-patrimonial rent-seeking states of sub-Saharan Africa. In his view, in carrying out their tasks, public officials do not seek to maximize the collective well-being, but rather their rents. This kind of corruption is most prevalent where the administrative norms are complex and the legislator is granted ample discretionary power to decision-making officials who use it to their advantage.

Finally, one should also mention the 'big corruption' that also affects several developed countries (Japan, Italy, Spain, France, etc.). This corruption is in most cases a 'tax' imposed on firms executing big public contracts. It is levied for the personal enrichment of corrupt high level civil servants or—more frequently—for the financing of Pharaonic initiatives that promote the visibility of political parties. This practice is also common in developing countries. A World Bank study, for example, indicates that all big construction and industrial works entrusted to multinational contractors in developing countries entailed the payment of bribes to key political parties and figures (Kenny, 2007).

While it is clear that corruption leads to higher costs for firms and to moral hazard, one may ask whether bribes stimulate investment and growth. Bribes—it is argued by some—speed up the granting of permits; they avoid those bureaucratic hurdles that prevent the implementation of large projects, which, in the end, stimulate growth and reduce the costs borne by firms. Thus, it is argued, it is preferable to pay bribes to carry out the planned investments on time rather than seeing them abandoned due to red tape and corruption. Empirical analyses show, however, that corruption depresses investment and—less markedly—growth (Mauro, 1995).

Tax administration

One of the key branches of the public administration is tax administration. This branch is particularly exposed to the risk of corruption, and yet it is charged with the task of generating—in the least distortionary and most equitable way—the resources necessary for the proper functioning of the state, or at least for the functioning of the minimal state. An inefficient tax administration threatens growth if it is unable to finance essential activities with tax revenue, and force the government to finance them instead with potentially inflationary monetary emissions, risky international borrowing, or distortionary ad hoc excises that negatively affect the allocation of resources and post-tax income distribution.

In many developing countries tax collection faces objective problems due to the dominance of hard-to-tax agriculture (whose cadastre is often missing) and informal sector activities (see Chapter 8). The trend toward the informalization of the economy observed in developing countries during the last thirty years may have eroded the provision of public goods and the functioning of the 'minimum state'. As shown in Table 11.4, however, there are significant cross-country variations in revenue collection, suggesting that there is room for improvement.

Empirical analyses have allowed the hypothesis about the negative growth impact of a sharp decline in tax revenue to be tested. For example, Table 11.5 shows that a decline in tax

Table 11.4 Indexes of efficiency of the tax administration in selected transition economies, 1998

Country	VAT			Social security contributions			Direct taxes on corporations		
	Statutory tax rate	VAT/ GDP	E/S ratio[a]	Statutory tax rate	SSC/ GDP	E/S ratio	Statutory tax rate	DTC/ GDP	E/S ratio
Check Rep.	22	7.1	0.40	47.5	15.2	0.94	39.0	3.4	0.23
Kazakhstan	20	3.5	0.21	32.0	6.2	0.68	30.0	2.4	0.15
Kyrgyzstan	20	5.6	0.34	37.0	5.9	0.68	30.0	1.1	0.06
Russian Federation	20	7.2	0.43	39.5	9.9	0.71	35.0	4.2	0.33
Tajikistan	20	1.5	0.09	38.0	1.6	0.31	40.0	1.2	0.04
Uzbekistan	17	6.1	0.42	43.0	6.7	0.61	37.0	7.9	0.47
Average EU15	—	—	0.45	—	—	0.88	—	—	0.24

Notes: [a]The E/S (effective/statutory) tax ratio measures the efficiency of tax administration. It is obtained by dividing the actual tax revenue by its theoretical value calculated on the basis of the tax legislation. A value of E/S smaller than 1 may be due to tax rebates, delays in liquidating taxes, tax avoidance, tax evasion, and inefficiencies of the tax administration.

Source: Schaffer and Turley (2001).

Table 11.5 Growth regression results for a panel of transition economies

Equation number/Number of observations/ Variables	1 N=28	2 N=28	3 N=28	4 N=28	5 N=17	6 N=17
Constant	5.23	4.96	5.55	5.71	5.91	6.07
Initial economic distortions as % of GDP	−0.01	−0.01	−.010	−0.01	−.001	−.001
1987 PPP GDP per capita, as % of US GDP	−0.01	−0.02	−0.01	−0.01	−0.02	−0.01
War dummy variable (1, 0)	−0.63	−0.58	−0.40	−0.40	0.26[c]	0.27[c]
Decline of revenue/GDP ratio 89–91 to 93–96	−0.01	−0.01	−0.01	−0.01		
Index of economic liberalization		(0.07)		(−.40)		(−.05)
Log Inflation, (geometric mean 1990–95)			−0.12	−0.14	−0.12	−0.14
Informal economy as % of GDP in 1994					−0.02	−0.02
Corrected R^2	0.75	0.75	0.85	0.84	0.92	0.91

Note: The dependent variable is log GDP1996/GDP1989. The parameters in parentheses are not significant at the 5 per cent probability level.

Source: Cornia and Popov (2001).

revenue—which varied considerably among the transition economies during the period studied—caused a statistically significant slowdown in growth, as shown by the negative value of the parameter of the variable 'decline of the revenue/GDP ratio between 1989–91 and 1993–96'. Similarly, an increase in the informal economy also affected economic performance.

Police and judicial system

These institutions have been created to ensure—*inter alia*—stable and balanced growth in the economy. Their task is to ensure the respect of property rights, contract enforcement, and the security of citizens and firms. As a matter of fact, an efficient and independent police and judicial system reduce risks and transaction costs for firms, especially for small and medium sized enterprises that are unable to look after their own safety in the same way as large firms. Yet, in many developing countries, effective reliance on the police and legal system is not always possible, either because such organizations have limited resources or because their staff are not hired on a merit basis and are not paid adequately, with the result that they are easily corruptible.

11.4 Political and Economic Institutions, Investment, and Growth

What does the empirical evidence show about the relation between institutions, growth, and inequality in developing countries? For ease of exposition, we discuss the impact of institutions under two broad headings: political institutions and economic institutions.

Impact of political institutions

Political institutions are defined as the political structures (constitutions, strong or weak democracy, electoral systems, dictatorship, etc.) which affect the functioning of the political system, the behaviour of economic agents, the stability and credibility of public policies, and—as a result—economic and social performance. Table 11.6 summarizes the findings of the literature on the economic impact of political institutions. It shows that—with the exception of cases characterized by extreme political violence—the relationship between democracy, investment, and growth is not as simple as one may think. In contrast,

Table 11.6 Relationship between political institutions and growth based on objective indicators

Institutional framework	Indicator	Result	Related literature
Democracy	Gastil Index	No relationship with growth but positive relationship with investments	Kormendi and Meguire (1985)
	Gastil Index	Not robust relationship with growth and investments	Levine and Renelt (1992)
Government stability	Revolutions and coups	Positive relationship with growth and investments	Barro (1991)
	Revolutions and coups	No robust relationship with growth; positive relationship with investments	Levine and Renelt (1992)
Political violence	Political assassinations	Negative relationship with growth and investments	Barro (1991)
Volatility of the policies adopted by central governments	Standard deviation of monetary policies	Negative relationship with growth and investments	Kormendi and Meguire (1985)

Note: The synthetic Gastil index includes political rights, civil liberties, and electoral arrangements.
Source: Moers (1999).

the link between the stability of governments and growth is less controversial. The evidence seems to suggest in fact that long-lasting governments (whether democratic or not) are more likely to introduce irreversible and credible policies that may improve aggregate development though not necessarily inequality, as observed post-1991 in authoritarian but fast growing Uzbekistan and post-1978 China. For example, by sustaining the announced monetary policies, governments in these countries allow economic agents to predict the future economic environment in a less uncertain way.

Democracy spread massively after the fall of the Soviet regime, to stabilize during the early twenty-first century (Figure 11.1). Its relation with income inequality (which influences growth) is the subject of several studies that show that such a relationship is negative but weak, indicating that the introduction of 'procedural democracy' (free elections, press freedom, separation of powers, etc.) does not necessarily lead to a fair society. This result may depend on the fact that the terms 'democracy' and 'authoritarian regimes' refer to highly heterogeneous categories, not easily represented by synthetic indexes such as the Freedom House Index used in Figure 11.1.

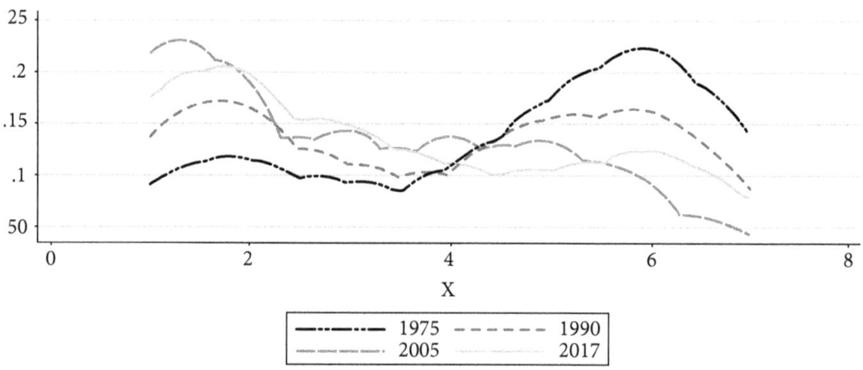

Figure 11.1 Frequency distribution of the Freedom House democracy index in 100 countries, 1975–2017

The recent shift to a 'true democracy' in some regions is, however, worth noting. For instance, what explains the adoption of more progressive economic and social policies during the 2000s in Latin America, South East Asia, and some African nations? A key factor was the return to democracy after years of authoritarian or military rule. Indeed, if political power is concentrated in the hands of authoritarian elites, the political system tends to adopt unequalizing policies (Robinson, 2010). For instance, during the Chilean military dictatorship (1973–90), inequality rose sharply as the regime liberalized foreign trade (a measure that raised the skill premium), introduced labour reforms biased against workers and unions, lowered taxes on wealth, capital gains, profits, and luxuries, and introduced sweeping educational reforms that favoured private schools and educational inequality. A second factor was a steady shift towards the election of regimes more sensitive to social equity (Figure 11.1).

Genuine (as opposed to procedural) democracy, greater electoral participation and its consolidation over time may reduce the concentration of power and facilitates the transition towards non-clientelistic policies. In contrast, the adoption of neutral or regressive policies in the Asian economies in transition has been influenced by the different evolution of their political systems. In turn, in the economies that emerged from decades of state dominance and a very compressed income distribution (as in the former Soviet bloc), the policies followed in the 1990s and 2000s were influenced by the desire to reduce the role of the state in the economy, eradicate the past spirit of forced egalitarianism, and replace the principle of equalizing outcomes with that of equalizing opportunities.

In contrast, the political evolution of Latin America and parts of South East Asia has differed. In the former (once the symbol of authoritarianism, inequality, inflation, and slow growth), the political landscape witnessed a steady shift towards democratization and, from the late 1990s, a drift in political orientation towards progressive centre-left regimes (Figure 11.2). Matters of social justice and economic development were at the core of the identity of the parties supporting such regimes. The new regimes' concern for poverty and inequality, market failures, and strengthening of state institutions emerged in stark contrast to the neoliberal emphasis on shrinking the state and the self-sustained role of markets promoted during the liberal experiment of the 1970s, 1980s, and 1990s.

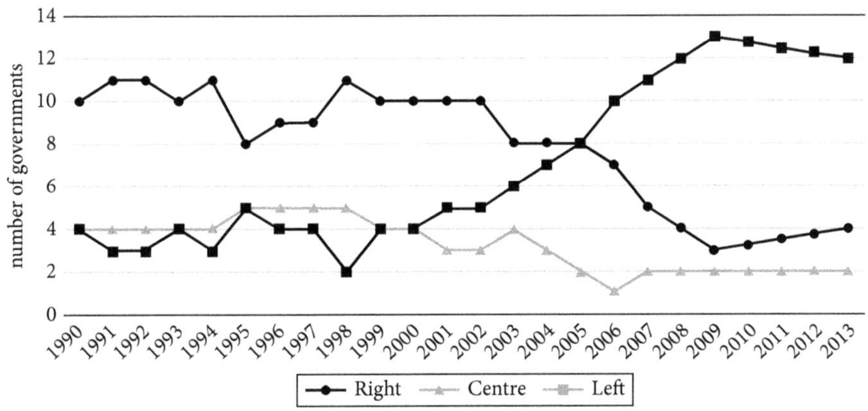

Figure 11.2 Changes in the political orientation of 18 Latin American governments, 1990–2013
Source: Cornia (2014)

Overall, the evidence of a broad panel of developed and developing countries show there is a negative relation between the extent of democracy (proxied by the Freedom House Index) in the 1990s and the level of the Gini coefficient of the distribution of income in the 2000s.

Impact of economic institutions

The empirical evidence so far shows that—on average—there is a positive relationship between institutional and economic development. If these findings are confirmed, the theoretical models and empirical analyses of growth for developing countries can no longer neglect the institutional variables. For instance, it is plausible that—by ignoring the impact of institutions—the aggregate growth models overestimate the potential output that can be produced on the basis of the traditional production factors. Rodrik (1995), for example, found that labour productivity in South East Asia during the period 1960–94 was explained by the GDP per capita in 1960, the average number of years of schooling of the labour force and an index of the quality of public institutions. Many other studies (some of them summarized in Table 11.7) indicate that the institutional quality of a country is positively correlated with growth.

Table 11.7 Results of the analyses of the relationship between institutions and growth

Institutional characteristics	Indicator's components	Results	Related literature
Efficiency of public administration	Judicial system, red tape, corruption	No robust relation with growth; positive relation with investments	Mauro (1995)
Security of property rights	Expropriation risks, 'rule of law', the quality of public admin. and corruption	Positive relation with both growth and investments	Knack and Keefer (1995)
Government's credibility	Laws and policies, stability, security of property rights, personal security and corruption	Positive relation with both growth and investments	Brunetti, Kisunko, and Weder (1997)
Social capital	Trust, strength of civil society	Positive relation with both growth and investments	Knack and Keefer (1997)

Source: as Table 11.6.

11.5 Informal Institutions

Countries with similar economic structures, legal frameworks and administrations often apply legal provisions in different ways, sometimes by adhering literally to legal prescriptions, and at other times by applying them in a limited way. This depends on the culture inherent to informal institutions. Douglass North (1990), the father of the neo-institutionalist school, has suggested that differences in informal institutions markedly affect formal institutions and economic performance.

Understanding a country's growth and macroeconomic dynamics, therefore, requires distinguishing between formal and informal institutions. The first are those established by the legal system. Most of the literature on the rule of law and institutions suggests that these have an important role to play in guiding economic development. Yet, in many developing countries, formal institutions are perceived in a negative way due to corruption, high legal costs, and lengthy waits to issue a resolution (Fandl, 2008). As a result, informal institutions are frequently relied upon to establish property rights, litigate disputes, enforce contracts, regulate labour relations, and address other legal and social issues. Informal institutions can contribute to development if they are linked to formal enforcement systems or fill a void in the field of property recognition, contract enforcement, and labour and social protection.

While some of these informal norms are eventually absorbed by formal legal systems, the overall existence at any point in time of a two-track institutional system raises questions about which will prevail, the efficacy of macroeconomic policies under such circumstances, and long-term development. Informal institutions are common for firm ownership and property rights, and the relationships between firms and external investors. In China and some states of India, substitutive informal institutions replace ineffective formal arrangements, and are critical in creating a corporate governance leading to enhanced domestic and foreign investment (Estrin and Prevezer 2011). In contrast, Russia is characterized by competing informal institutions whereby various informal mechanisms of corporate governance associated with corruption and clientelism weaken the functioning of formal institutions and generate uncertainty about their applicability In turn, Brazil is characterized by accommodating informal institutions which circumvent restrictive formal institutions and reconcile varying objectives between actors in formal and informal institutions (Estrin and Prevezer 2011).

One key area where informal institutions are important is that of land property rights. Since the 1990s, the problems related to land scarcity has increased in most sub-Saharan Africa due to population growth, conflicts between farmers and herders, the weakening of customary institutions, limited land reform, and the purchase of land by foreign investors. Since the mid-1990s some West African governments have introduced new tenancy reforms for the protection/registration of customary land rights, land market liberalization, and a small number of land redistribution programmes. However, implementation of these provisions was generally slow. While formal state controls over the land remain widespread, the new tenancy reforms allow some land transfers. In Rwanda, for instance, nine million plots were registered, enabling small farmers to invest in them and increase productivity.[2] In turn, in countries exhibiting high administrative costs for official land titling, local communities developed a simple system of informal registration of property rights recognized by local administrators.

Social protection is another areas where informal institutions play an important role. In developing countries dominated by traditional societies, informal arrangements dominate as formal mechanisms still have limited coverage in most cases. Informal institutions have socially shared rules, which are unwritten and yet are known by all the inhabitants of a country. Social protection relies on household savings, the extended family, communal insurance and local-level redistributive mechanisms. The extended family is a main source of survival for the elderly and family members in need. Food security and labour exchanges (that ensure that essential tasks are carried out even during the illness of a household) are typically organized at community level. Such mechanisms work well to offset the effects of idiosyncratic shocks and are less affected by problems of asymmetric information and adverse selection than formal mechanisms. But they work poorly in cases of covariant shocks.

11.6 Measurement Issues Concerning the Impact of Institutional Variables

The definition and measurement of the quality of formal institutions are still at an early stage. Even when theoretical concepts are defined in a rigorous way, the measurement of the quality of formal institutions is carried out by means of proxy variables or—worse—by the judgement of experts who are unconsciously and unavoidably biased one way or another. These proxy variables (generally collected for other purposes) are used to reduce the cost of research, given the high price of information derived from ad hoc surveys, such as the *Latino Barometro*.[3] Furthermore, in some cases, such as those concerning the extent of corruption, the people interviewed have no incentives to disclose their conduct.

[2] http://blogs.worldbank.org/developmenttalk/land-rights-and-the-world-bank-group-setting-the-record-straight
[3] http://www.latinobarometro.org/lat.jsp)

Be that as it may, to measure the degree of institutional development, the World Bank[4] and independent research centres have developed an array of synthetic and sector-specific governance and institutional indexes (see Alonso and Garcimartin 2008, chapter 4, for a compilation and analysis of the problems of the synthetic indexes of institutional quality). Among the main indicators are: the Institutional Composite Index (ICI), that comprises the cancellation of contracts by central government; the risk of expropriation; the quality of bureaucracy; the extent of corruption; and the legal tradition. One may ask, however, what is the rationale for the selection of these five variables and the exclusion of others that might have been plausibly included in the ICI. Thus, often the variables selected have some plausibility but lack a clear theoretical basis. Other synthetic measures are the Freedom House Index, Polity IV Project, International Country Risk Guide, the Database on Political Institutions, and so on. Examples of sector-specific indexes (Voice and Accountability, Political Stability, Government Effectiveness, Regulatory Quality, Rule of Law, Control of Corruption, Transparency International, and so on) are included in the World Bank's Worldwide Governance Indicators project. Many of the other indicators are included in the Quality of Government Dataset that is publicly available online (http://qog.pol.gu.se/data).

Identifying the causal effect of formal and informal institutions on various developmental outcomes, while at the same time taking into account the impact of informal institutions on formal institutional quality, is a challenging econometric issue. The relationship between institutions and economic outcomes was initially studied empirically by means of cross sectional analyses or macro panels making use of the OLS estimator for regressions that mostly took the following form:

$$Y_{i,\,t+n} = \alpha + \beta\ FI_{i,\,t} + \chi\ II_{i,\,t} + \delta\ C_{i,\,t} + \phi Y_{i,\,t-1} + \varepsilon_{\iota,\,t} \tag{11.1}$$

where $Y_{i,t+n}$ is the level of GDP per capita (or other impact variable) at time $t+n$ and in country i, $FI_{i,t}$ is an index of the quality of formal institutions in country i, $II_{i,t}$ an index of the spread of informal institutions, $C_{i,t}$ a set of control variables, $Y_{i,\,t-1}$ the level of GDP per capita in the year preceding the start of institutional change, $\varepsilon_{\iota,t}$ an error term, and α, β, χ, δ, and ϕ parameters to be estimated.

However, this approach is fraught with problems. A key issue concerns the direction of causality between institutions and economic performance. If it is true that good formal institutions may facilitate the development of a country, one may also surmise that growth itself may modify the influence of informal institutions on the functioning of the formal ones, as noted in Section 11.5 by Estrin and Prevezer (2011) in the case of China, India, and Brazil, and by North's (1990) general observation that formal institutions tend to be shaped over time by informal institutions. Attempts to solve this problem normally rely on the instrumental variable approach (see Acemoglu et al. 2005). Problems also arise due to the inability to account for unobservable and missing variables affecting both institutions and economic outcomes. The most difficult task, however, is probably the correct econometric estimation of the parameters α, β, χ, δ, and ϕ as the OLS estimator assumes that the variables measuring institutions (FI and II) and the error term (ε) are uncorrelated.

[4] http://siteresources.worldbank.org/INTLAWJUSTINST/Resources/IndicatorsGovernanceandInstitutionalQuality.pdf -and the literature reviewed therein.

But in several cases these variables are instead closely correlated. There are, in other words, one or two problems of endogeneity (also depending on whether II is included in equation (11.1)). Such problems may be due to the omission in equation (11.1) of key explanatory variables, errors in the measurement of FI and II, or reverse causation. In the latter case it is possible to estimate the true relationship between Y, FI, and II using instrumental variables. This involves the identification of an instrumental variable Z (or Z and W if we deal with both formal and informal institutions) which is correlated with institutions but not with ε. In the first case, this formally requires that: $(\mathrm{corr}, Z, FI) \neq 0$, while $(\mathrm{corr}, Z, \varepsilon) = 0$. If these conditions are met, one then first estimates the relation $\hat{FI} = \mu + \zeta Z + \omega$ by means of the TSLS approach. If ζ is significantly different from zero, $\hat{FI}$ is used instead of FI (and II^ instead of II when the two instrumental variables Z and W are used simultaneously) in the initial regression.

An alternative and promising, but data-intensive, approach consists in carrying out natural experiments. That involves collecting long-run data on institutional and economic changes in initially similar pairs of countries, then comparing by means of the diff-in-diff methodology the dynamics of investments, growth, and inequality experienced by them after years of different institutional evolutions. The success of this procedure depends on the fact that the initial conditions of the two countries are similar and that the institutional change is exogenous, that is, unrelated to their economic, cultural, or geographic features. An interesting example of this approach concerns the 'Korean experiment', that is, a comparison between institutions and economic development in South versus North Korea (Acemoglu et al. 2005).

11.7 Concluding Remarks

In many developing countries formal political and economic institutions are still evolving and informal institutions regularly play a key role in determining the rules of the game prevailing in a given country. Informal institutions are often relied upon to guide the political system and solve issues of property rights, contract enforcement, and social protection. However, most economic analyses of long-term growth neglect the impact of formal and informal institutions. The large statistical residual of all growth regressions may thus be due in part to such neglect that is due in turn to difficulties in modelling institutions and the limited availability of objective information. As for the relation between economic and political institutions, the main theoretical models assume plausibly that the economic policies followed by a country are influenced by its path-dependent political structures and economic institutions. Current economic policies are, in turn, seen as a key source of future political arrangements.

Political institutions comprise constitutions, legal systems, and the nature of democracy (whether procedural or substantial). Most quantitative analyses have established a positive link between indicators of political development and growth. Yet, these results have to be read *cum grano salis* due to the limited informational content of the indicators used in trying to summarize—in a few relatively simple categories—highly heterogeneous situations. Formal economic institutions are concerned with the rules that build the market, and in particular with setting norms about the entry and exit of firms to and from the market, market competition, protection of property rights, regulation of the financial sector, provision of public goods, and social protection. They also focus on the efficiency of organizations charged with the implementation on such norms. Econometric analyses suggest a positive relation between the development of economic institutions and growth. While these conclusions seem broadly plausible, issues of econometric specification, the neglect of informal institutions, and uncertainties about the direction of causation may cloud the picture. Analytical approaches focusing on comparisons of the growth performance of initially similar countries that followed different institutional trajectories are more promising but are very data-intensive. More analytical efforts need to be carried out in this field in the future.

References

Acemoglu, D., S. Johnson, and J. A. Robinson (2005), 'Institutions as a Fundamental Cause of Long-Run Growth', in P. Aghion and S. Durlauf (eds), *Handbook of Economic Growth*, 1st edition 1, vol. 1, ch. 6, pp. 385–472. Amsterdam: Elsevier.

Alonso, J. A. and C. Garcimartin (2008), *Collective Action and Development: The Role of Institutions* (in Spanish). Madrid. Editorial Complutense and ICEI.

Bates, R. (1983), *Essays on the Political Economy of Rural Africa.* Cambridge: Cambridge University Press.

Cornia, G. A. (2014), *Falling Inequality in Latin America: Policy Changes and Lessons.* Oxford: Oxford University Press.

Cornia, G. A. (2017), 'Is Latin America's recent income inequality decline permanent or temporary?' in P. Bergjeijk and R. van der Hoeven (eds), *Sustainable Development Goals and Income Inequality*, Cheltenham: Edward Elgar.

Cornia, G. A. and V. Popov (2001), *Transition and Institutions: The Experience of Gradual and Late Reformers.* Oxford: Oxford University Press.

De Soto, H. (1989), *The Other Path: the Invisible Revolution in the Third World.* New York: Harper and Row.

Engerman, S. L. and K. L. Sokoloff (2005), 'Colonialism, Inequality and Long Run Paths of Development'. NBER Working Paper 11,057, Cambridge, MA: National Bureau of Economic Research.

Estrin, S. and Prevezer, M. (2011), 'The role of informal institutions in corporate governance: Brazil, Russia, India, and China compared', *Asia Pacific Journal of Management*, 28 (1): pp. 41–67.

Fandl, K. J. (2008), 'The Role of Informal Legal Institutions in Economic Development', *Fordham Intl Law Journal*, 32, (1): pp. 1–31.

Frankema, E. (2005), The Colonial Origins of Inequality: Exploring the Causes and Consequences of Land Distribution, Discussion Papers n. 119, Göttingen: Ibero-America Institute for Economic Research of Georg-August-Universität.

Frankema, E. (2009), 'The colonial roots of land inequality: geography, factor endowments, or institutions?', *The Economic History Review*, 63 (2): pp. 418–51.

Gruen, C. and S. Klasen (2012), 'Has the transition improved well-being?' *Economic Systems*, 36 (1): pp. 11–30.

Kenny, C. (2007), 'Construction, Corruption, and Developing Countries', Policy Research Working Papers No 4271, Washington, DC: The World Bank.

Klasen, S., G. A. Cornia, R. Grynspan, L. F. e Lopez Calva, and N. Lustig (2018), 'Income Inequality and Social Progress', in *International Panel on Social Progress, 'Redesigning Society for the XXI Century'*, Cambridge: Cambridge University Press.

Kunt, D. A. and E. Detragiache (2005), 'Cross-country Empirical Studies of Systemic Bank Distress', World Bank Policy Research Working Paper 3719, Washington, DC: The World Bank.

Mauro, P. (1995), 'Corruption and Growth' *Quarterly Journal of Economics*, 110 (3): pp. 681–712.

Moers, L. (1999), 'How important are institutions for growth in transition countries?' https://papers.tinbergen.nl/99004.pdf.

North, D. (1990), *Institutions, Institutional Change and Economic Performance.* Cambridge: Cambridge University Press.

Robinson, J. (2010), 'The Political Economy of Redistributive Policies', in L. F. Lopez Calva and N. Lustig (eds), *Declining Inequality in Latin America: a Decade of Progress?* Washington DC: Brookings Institution Press, and New York: UNDP.

Rodrik, D. (1995), 'Getting Interventions Right: How South Korea and Taiwan Grew Rich', *Economic Policy*, 20: pp. 55–107.

Rojas Suarez, L. (2010), 'The International Financial Crisis: Eight Lessons for and from Latin America', Working Paper 202, Washington, DC: Centre for Global Development.

Schaffer, M. and G. Turley (2001), 'Effective versus statutory taxation: measuring effective tax administration in transition economies', Working Paper No 62, London: European Bank for Reconstruction and Development.

Suggested Further Reading

Acemoglu, D., S. Johnson, and J. A. Robinson (2001), 'The colonial origins of comparative development: An empirical investigation', *American Economic Review*, 91: pp. 1369–401.

Mauro, P. (1995), 'Corruption and Growth', *Quarterly Journal of Economics*, 110 (3): pp. 681–712.

North, Douglass. C. (1990), *Institutions, Institutional Change and Economic Performance*, New York: Cambridge University Press.

12
How do Neoclassical Growth Models Behave in Low-income Countries?

This chapter discusses the extent to which the neoclassical growth models developed for the advanced economies are able to reproduce the developing countries' long-term growth path, convergence with the advanced countries, and steady state equilibrium. To do so, the chapter assesses first whether the hypotheses at the basis of the original Solow model are verified in a prototypical developing country. It then lists the factors that explain the lack of convergence between the GDP per capita of developing and developed countries predicted by the Solow model, and the problems faced by low-income countries in exiting low-level equilibrium poverty traps. It then presents modified Solow models characterized by multiple equilibria that fit the situation of less developed countries.

12.1 The Original Solow Model with a Single Steady State Equilibrium

The original Solow model (see Chapter 2) relies on a number of assumptions that are often not verified in developing countries. To start with, in such models all factor markets exist, are in equilibrium, and there is no discrimination in accessing them by agents with different capital endowments. Also, there is no risk or, if it exists, it can be insured. The distribution of wealth (capital and savings) and the ownership of factors of production do not affect performance. Because of this, all agents have similar saving rates and a similar capital per worker. At the same time, the concavity of output per worker leads all countries to converge in the long run to the same steady state growth. However, Banerjee and Duflo (2004) cite the work of Mankiw et al. (1992) that shows that the correlation between the growth rate of GDP over 1960–92 and the log of its initial value is small (0.0943) and positive while standard convergence theory predicts it is negative. In addition, the theoretical literature suggests that—due to their high rate of return on many projects—developing countries should have high investment/GDP ratios (including in the form of FDI). Yet, this is rarely observed. What, then, explains the lack of convergence, low investment/GDP ratios, and lower than expected productivity per worker typical of many developing countries?

The failure of convergence (the rapid growth of the Asian countries since 2000 has modified in part such a conclusion for this region but not for others) may be due to the failure to construct an aggregate production function on the basis of heterogeneous microeconomic production functions reflecting the different economic circumstances of agents who—for the reasons discussed below—are not able to adopt profitable technologies that are potentially available to them. A general reason behind all this is the dualism or

The Macroeconomics of Developing Countries: An Intermediate Textbook. Giovanni Andrea Cornia, Oxford University Press (2020).

DOI: 10.1093/oso/9780198856672.001.0001

complete heterogeneity of production conditions faced by different groups of agents. This is due to the government's failure to provide all producers with a standard set of services, including access to infrastructure, water, electricity, and human capital, and to the dualism of the credit and insurance markets (see Chapter 8). For instance, Banerjee and Duflo (2005) indicate that in Kerala and Tamil Nadu informal sector producers borrowed from rural moneylenders at annual interest rates averaging 52 per cent, well above what was charged by commercial banks to formal sector firms. This underscores the co-existence of high and low production opportunities in the same industry.

While these authors surmise that rates of return in sectors where agents borrow at such high interest rates must be substantial, they also emphasize that borrowing conditions are not uniform, and that market forces are far from equalizing them across agents. Credit market failures are thus pervasive and a cause of investment misallocation. Even greater distortions are observed in the insurance market, which systematically fails to insure even the risk borne by poor farmers planting high-yielding but risky varieties.

Investment in physical capital relative to GDP in developing countries are lower than in industrialized countries (China is an obvious exception). This is even truer for investment in human capital that is mainly financed by the government. Private investment on the human capital of one's own children does not always rest on the perspective of reaping high returns later in life. In turn, the access to technology varies across firms because of differences in the scale of production, dualism in accessing technology, and its cost and appropriateness for many agents for whom labour-saving technologies are not in line with their factor endowments. Similar considerations concern institutional failures, particularly in terms of the ability of the state to coordinate investment decisions and provide protection for property rights. Summing up, all this can explain large variations in production conditions across firms that operate in different environments, exhibit large productivity differentials and suffer from sectoral, technological, and product misallocations due to various factor market imperfections. Finally and crucially, the original Solow model assumes that the growth rate of the labour force and the savings rate remain constant over the long term, while these assumptions are unrealistic in developing countries. Thus, the above micro distortions explain the failure of the original Solow model to represent correctly aggregate production conditions and long-term growth in developing countries.

12.2 A Modified Solow Model with Multiple Steady State Equilibria

Because of the real-life differences between developed and developing countries in terms of growth of the labour force, saving rates, and other production conditions, Sachs et al. (2004) identified situations in which the original Solow model needs to be amended to capture the reality of developing countries, so as to illustrate analytically the factors behind the persistence of poverty traps in South Asia, sub-Saharan Africa, and Central America, and identify a threshold of capital per worker beyond which the modified Solow model behaves as in its original formulation. Three different situations that cause the persistence of low-level equilibrium poverty traps due to violations of the assumption of the basic model are illustrated in the following three subsections.

Poverty traps due to production inefficiencies

Let us recall that in the original Solow model the production function $y = k^{\alpha}$ is concave (due to decreasing returns to increasing capital per worker k), but with an initial steep slope which indicates a high efficiency of capital per worker at low levels of k. The production function mirroring the efficiency of capital rises more rapidly than the straight line of the investment function , i.e. the amortization of the existing capital per worker and the increase in investments needed to accommodate the new entrants in the labour force (Figure 12.1, left panel). The faster savings rise than investments allows the investment per worker to be expanded, generating rapid growth of GDP at the beginning of the growth process, as happened in the now industrialized countries during the first half of the twentieth century. Now, let us consider a backward economy, with a low initial endowment of capital per worker, poor public infrastructure, and a low level of coordination among different private agents due to la ack of infrastructure and human capital, and weak public institutions. Under these circumstances, the country exhibits several production inefficiencies that make the production schedule grow slowly and in a convex way so as to remain below the $(n + d)k$ schedule until a minimum threshold of capital per worker ($k_{threshold}$) is reached. As a consequence, until the savings per worker remains below $(n + d)k$, production will not take off. Only beyond $k_{threshold}$ are the predictions of the original Solow model verified, and the economy reaches the steady state at the level of capital per worker k_{ss} and a high level of output per worker y_{ss} (Figure 12.1, right panel). Below such a steady state the model will converge to an income level of pure subsistence that coincides with the origin of Figure 12.1, which, however, is not necessarily equal to zero. The amended Solow model exhibits multiple equilibria in this case; two stable equilibria i corresponding to the origin and of k_{ss}.and an unstable equilibrium correspondingto $k_{threshold}$.

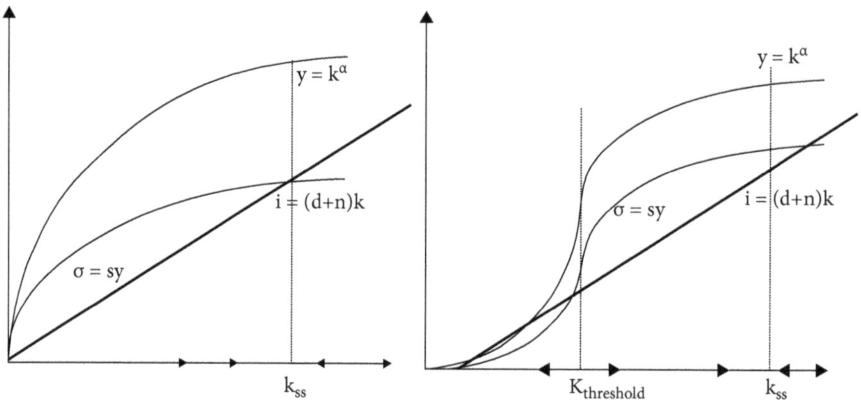

Figure 12.1 Behaviour of the original Solow model and its modified version in case of production inefficiencies below a minimum threshold of capital per worker

Poverty traps due to low savings at low levels of output per worker

Even assuming that the economy is sufficiently efficient from the start, there is a second situation in which the Solow model does not lead to a high-income steady state equilibrium corresponding to a level of capital per worker, k_{ss}. This is observed when the economy does not generate a volume of savings that will ensure adequate capital accumulation. In all cases in which household incomes are sufficient to satisfy only basic needs or the banking system is unable to mobilize latent domestic savings, the economy does not generate a level of savings greater than the amortization of the existing capital plus the new investment required by the rise in the number of workers. For instance, the trend in domestic saving/GDP over 1950–95 in India (Figure 12.2) illustrates in part this situation—the ratio ranged between a low 10–15 per cent between 1950 and 1970 (a period of slow growth of GDP per capita), and shifted to substantially higher values in subsequent years, when GDP growth started to accelerate.

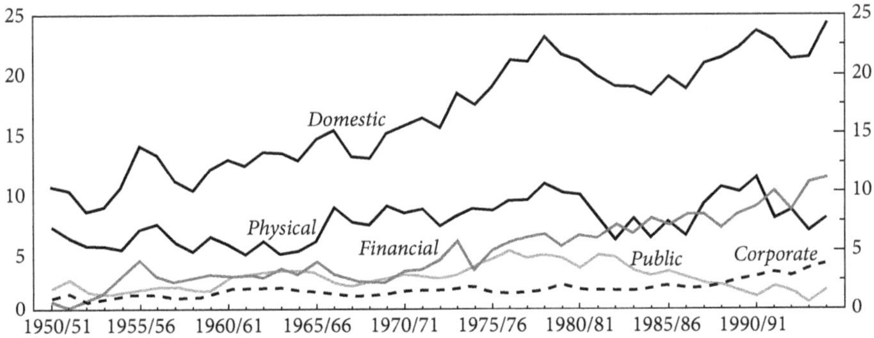

Figure 12.2 Saving/GDP ratio, total, and by component, India, 1950–1995
Source: Muhleisen (1997)

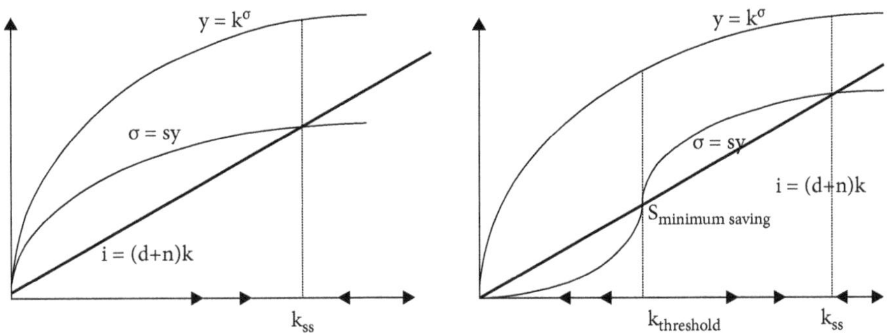

Figure 12.3 Behaviour of the original Solow model and of its modified version in case of insufficient savings below a minimum threshold of capital per worker

Additionally, in this case, the economy converges to a level of mere subsistence and is unable to exit the poverty trap in which it finds itself (Figure 12.3). Obviously, there are historical examples (such as China and the Soviet Union) where savings rose at a low level of GDP and capital per worker. This was achieved by the government—if at high social cost—by compressing the incomes and consumption of the workers. This compression of private consumption, however, did allow the minimum savings needed to finance the $k_{threshold}$, to be reached, beyond which the usual dynamics of the original Solow model started operating, eventually leading to the high income steady state characterized by a capital per worker k_{ss}.In this situation, the modified Solow model exhibits multiple equilibria. In rare cases, the increase in capital accumulation occurred thanks to a Big Push financed by FDI and foreign aid.

Poverty traps due to the persistence of rapid population growth

Low-level equilibrium poverty traps persist over time also when the growth rate of the population rises for many years in a convex fashion and not in a linear fashion (Figure 12.4, right panel). Table 12.1 illustrate the case of two countries, Bangladesh and Kenya, where population growth increased in the initial phase and started slowing down only since 1975–80 and 1990–95 to become broadly stable at 1.2 and 2.7 per cent, respectively.

It is well known that the total fertility rate is higher in underdeveloped societies than in the advanced ones, given that—in the absence of social security—children represent a cheap source of labour and a support for parents during their old age (see Chapter 7). It is equally true that high birth rates are accompanied by high child mortality (which peaked in the past at 300 deaths per thousand live births during the first five years of life). In this case, with income increasing from conditions of widespread poverty, a child and overall mortality decline gives rise—given the stability of the birth rate—to an increase in the growth rate of population and—with a lag—in the number of workers, n. This raises (n + d)k more rapidly than in the initial years. Thus the modified Solow model will reach a first steady state equilibrium at a low level of income corresponding to $k_{low\ income}$ (Figure 12.4). Only when the birth rate declines (that is, when the country completes the first demographic transition) will the economy return to a growth rate of the overall population and of workers, n, lower than that of the first phase. This will cause a reduction of the slope of (n + d) and, as a consequence, convergence towards the new steady state $k_{threshold}$ (Figure 12.4). Such equilibrium, however, is unstable, given that on its left i is greater than σ (making the economy converge towards the low-income steady state, therefore leaving the country in a poverty trap), while on its right σ is greater than i (making the economy converge to the high-income steady state corresponding to k_{ss}). However, moving from the low-income equilibrium to the high-income equilibrium turns out to be problematic and is feasible only thanks to policy measures or exogenous shocks which lower the growth rate of the population or raise the savings rate. In the absence of such shocks, the country will return to the low-income equilibrium (Figure 12.4). Iin this scenario as well, the modified Solow model exhibits multiple equilibria, with two stable steady state equilibria and an unstable one.

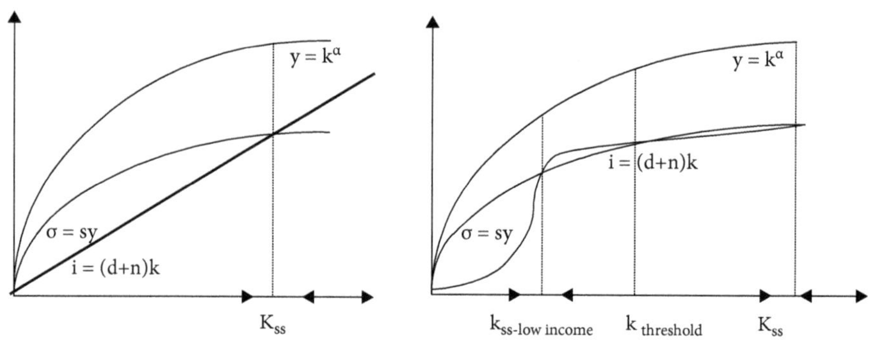

Figure 12.4 Behaviour of the original Solow model and of its modified version in case of a rapid increase of the labour force below a minimum threshold of capital per worker

Table 12.1 Rise and slowdown of the population growth rate in Bangladesh and Kenya, 1950–1955 to 2010–2015

	1950–1955	1955–1960	1960–1965	1965–1970	1970–1975	1975–1980	1980–1985	1985–1990	1990–1995	1995–2000	2000–2005	2005–2010	2010–2015
Bangladesh	2.12	2.70	2.94	3.06	1.84[a]	2.67	2.69	2.61	2.23	2.06	1.73	1.18	1.16
Kenya	2.77	2.99	3.19	3.38	3.62	3.75	3.78	3.49	3.12	2.80	2.73	2.74	2.66

Note: During this quinquennium the country fought the Independence War and was affected by two famines.

Source: https://esa.un.org/unpd/wpp/Download/Standard/Population/.

12.3 How to Exit Poverty Traps: Africa's Persistent Poverty and the Big Push

Despite the GDP growth acceleration of the last twenty years and talks about Africa's Renaissance, much of the region still witnesses a high incidence of poverty, especially in rural areas. Simulations on the number of countries that will not be able to reach Sustainable Development Goal number 1 (complete poverty eradication) by 2030 shows that 90 per cent of them are from this region (Cornia 2018). The challenges facing Africa have been considered by Sachs et al. (2004). They argue in the context of a modified Solow model that much of the region is caught in a low-level equilibrium poverty trap and needs a Big Push à la Nurske (1953) to move to a high-income per capita steady state equilibrium. Such a Big Push would consist—*inter alia*—of eliminating existing coordination failures, increasing labour productivity by raising capital accumulation (financed by growing domestic savings and foreign aid) and pro-active population policies. Reliance on large inflows of foreign aid, however,, remains controversial (Chapter 10) and foreign public aid has in any case increased slowly over the last decade (see Figure 5.4). Private foreign aid, however, increased rapidly but is generally allocated to specific social sector activities.

Sachs and colleagues (2004) attribute the persistence of mass poverty in several African countries to the factors discussed above, but in particular to low agricultural productivity, isolation, and a high burden of disease. A Big Push supported by foreign aid (to complement insufficient domestic savings and the shallowness of domestic financial markets) needs to promote—*inter alia*—a Green Revolution, develop the transport infrastructure, and intensify efforts at disease control. In doing so, there is a need to increase capital per worker to a threshold beyond which the original Solow model starts operating.

12.4 Concluding Remarks

The standard neoclassical growth models (of Solow and Mankiw et al.) are a poor fit with the reality of developing countries and do not replicate their conclusions concerning the saving/investment rates, conditional or unconditional convergence towards a single steady state, and GDP growth over the initial phases of development. This is caused by the incompleteness of credit and insurance markets that impede all economic agents, big and small, to count on adequate endowments of production factors. In fact, in developing countries many agents are unable to adopt some profitable technologies, potentially available to them, because of the incompleteness of the factors market and inadequate infrastructure. The agents' production functions are therefore heterogeneous, and this poses a major statistical and substantial problem in building an aggregate production function fitting the data. In addition to production inefficiencies, low savings and rapid labour force growth in the early phases of development lead to a situation where long-term growth is characterized by the persistence of poverty traps and multiple equilibria, some at a very low level of output and income per capita. This situation has for years characterized several countries in sub-Saharan Africa.

According to some commentators, getting out of such poverty traps requires a major multisectoral investment effort (a Big Push) driven by foreign aid or—as in the case of the Soviet and Chinese Revolutions—a compression of wages and rural incomes that has in the past created large social costs. In brief, the standard neoclassical long-term growth models need major adjustments to capture the reality of developing countries. Even better, they need to be replaced by structuralist models reflecting the conditions on the ground.

References

Banerjee, A. and E. Duflo (2005), 'Growth Theory through the Lens of Development Economics' in P. Aghion and S. N. Durlauf (eds) *Handbook of Economic Growth*, Vol 1B, Amsterdam: North Holland.

Cornia, G. A. (2018), Eradicating poverty by the year 2030: Implications for Inequality, Population Growth and Food Prices (and Faster Growth?). CDP Discussion Paper 40. New York: UN-CDP.

Mankiw, N. G., D. Romer, and D. N. Weil (1992), 'A Contribution to the Empirics of Economic Growth', *Quarterly Journal of Economics*, 107 (2): pp. 407–437.

Muhleisen, M. (1997), Improving India's Saving Performance, IMF Working Paper 97/4. Washington, DC: International Monetary Fund.

Nurske, R. (1953), *Problems of Capital Formation in Underdeveloped Countries.* New York: Oxford University Press.

Sachs J. D., J. W. McArthur, G. Schmidt-Thaub, M. Kruk, C. Bahadur, M. Faye, and G. McCord (2004), 'Ending Africa's Poverty Trap', *Brookings Papers on Economic Activity*, 1: pp. 117–216.

Suggested Further Reading

Snowdon, B. (2009), 'The Solow Model, Poverty Traps, and the Foreign Aid Debate', *History of Political Economy* 41 (annual suppl.).

Walton, M. (n.d.), 'The Big Push: What does it mean and does it make sense for Ethiopia?' Teaching Notes PED1. http://www.michaelwalton.info/wp-content/uploads/2011/08/Big-Push-Ethiopia.pdf

PART III

DEMAND MANAGEMENT AND SHORT-TERM GROWTH

IS-LM and AS-AD in Developing Countries

13

Short-term Behavioural Equations for Developing Countries

This chapter discusses the behavioural relations for consumption, investment, and money demand that fit the reality of developing countries. It then compares them with those discussed in Chapter 3 for the advanced economies, showing that their inclusion in the IS-LM and AS-AD models often modifies the impact of policy changes and endogenous shocks in relation to those obtained in the advanced economies.

13.1 The Consumption and Saving Functions in Developing Countries

As in the advanced economies, in developing countries private consumption is the main component of aggregate demand. And, also, in poor countries, the impact of a fiscal stimulus depends crucially on the value of c, the marginal propensity to consume. However, the consumption/saving functions formulated for the developed countries neither correctly identify c nor include several variables that are relevant in poorer countries (but not in the advanced economies) to determine the aggregate level of consumption. Thus, there is a need to identify the structural differences between developed and developing countries that influence consumption and savings behaviour, and write functions that fit the conditions prevailing in these countries. Finally, we need to evaluate the impact of these alternative behaviours in the context of models dealing with the formation of the equilibrium level of income over the short term.

Theoretical problems of standard consumption models when applied to developing countries

Let us recall (see Chapter 2) that the basic assumptions of the consumption/saving model used for the developed countries are as follows. The consumer optimizes the distribution of consumption over her lifecycle, which means that current consumption does not depend on current income but on permanent or life-cycle income. This implies that a consumer does not face liquidity constraints and can shift her consumption flows forwards and backwards by means of an efficient financial market. This allows the consumer to accumulate savings during her working life and to borrow or make use of her saving in periods of low current income, such as during their youth, old age, and periods of uninsured unemployment. A further assumption is that there is no uncertainty about future income flows while risky events can be insured, thus entailing that the time horizon over which

The Macroeconomics of Developing Countries: An Intermediate Textbook. Giovanni Andrea Cornia, Oxford University Press (2020).

DOI: 10.1093/oso/9780198856672.001.0001

agents optimize the allocation of life-cycle consumption is their life expectancy. Current consumption also depends on the time preference rate, which is assumed to remain constant over time and is typically lower than in developing countries, and on the interest rate, an increase of which determines a forward shift in consumption, and a decrease the opposite effect. And, finally, public spending on health and education replaces private consumption, since it is a near perfect substitute for it and, in this way raises private savings.

What is the situation in most developing countries? Shifting resources backwards and forwards over time is mostly impossible because financial markets are lacking, incomplete, or imperfect. Moreover, in all cases where financial repression prevails, the real interest rate tends to be negative (thus entailing a high cost for consumption smoothing), whereas the liberalized financial markets have a positive real interest rate but a high default risk. Lastly, to the extent that the formal credit market is lacking in most rural areas, consumers have to depend on moneylenders who lend at high interest rates and only for short periods. This means that many consumers in developing countries are liquidity constrained and therefore their current income is more important than life-cycle income in determining current consumption.

Similar considerations apply with regard to the uncertainty of future income flows and the time horizon over which the economic agent intends to optimize her consumption. In developing countries, future income streams are more uncertain than in advanced economies. Indeed, climatic shocks and fluctuations in domestic and international prices, as well as the inability to insure against such events, make future incomes uncertain and unstable. Macroeconomic aggregates and inflation are also less stable. This means that, with greater uncertainty about the future, the time horizon for planning consumption and savings/investments is shorter and more uncertain.

The effect of an interest rate change on consumption differs from that observed in advanced countries. Contrary to the hypothesis made for the latter, in poor countries an increase in the interest rate has a modest impact on the consumption level. This is because the time preference rate is high (at least for people on low incomes), and almost always greater than the interest rate, despite the fact that this is also generally quite high. For many people in poor countries, private consumption is likely to stem from subsistence needs rather than from the intertemporal marginal rate of substitution between present and future consumption. Nevertheless, if we consider the consumption behaviour of the richest 20 per cent of the population (who have a lower time preference rate than the poor), an increase in the interest rate may raise savings and reduce consumption. Thus, the overall level of consumption is influenced by the distribution of income.

Lastly, in developing countries, an increase in public expenditure does not greatly impact private expenditure—therefore, there is no 'crowding out' effect between G and C—as the goods provided by the public sector are complementary to rather than substitutes for those supplied by the private sector.

Statistical problems encountered in the measurement of income and consumption

The econometric estimation of the parameters of the consumption/saving function is fraught with several conceptual and statistical problems. To avoid reaching misleading conclusions, we therefore have to correct the data for these biases. The most important of them concern the overestimation of consumption and underestimation of income. In many surveys on household income and consumption, the latter is greater than the former for the bottom 6–7 household deciles. This anomaly concerns not only the poor—for whom one could formulate a theoretical explanation of this phenomenon—but also the middle class. This is due to the following facts and statistical conventions:

(a) First, the prices used to compute the household income, including the goods produced for self-consumption, are the producer prices P_p, whereas the prices used to compute the value of self-consumed goods are the consumer prices P_c. The mismatch between consumption and income in surveys is thus explained in part by the fact that, generally speaking, P_p is smaller than P_c. In addition, the reference period used to estimate consumption and production are not the same. This may lead to differences in recall errors that grow in size when the survey's questions concern distant consumption and income flows.

For example, in most surveys the questions about consumption refer to the previous week (for the consumption of food) or month (for less frequently consumed items), thus entailing only small recall errors. In contrast, in order to avoid the bias due to the effect of seasonality, survey questions about income generally refer to the previous year and so unavoidably cause greater recall errors.[1] As for the impact of price changes over time, the evaluation of consumption and income is carried at current prices without correcting for price increases at various points in time. Consumption is assessed at the prices of the last week or month while incomes are evaluated at the prices of the previous year, which, in high inflation countries, are generally significantly lower than current prices.

(b) The underestimation of self-consumption. Household surveys generally underestimate the level of income and consumption-in-kind of households operating outside of the monetary sphere (see Chapter 4). This is due to the non-imputation among the income stream of various goods and services, such as housing, health services, and land improvements that are self-produced and consumed but are not recorded in surveys. A second problem concerns the shadow prices used for the imputation of self-consumed food. Standard practice is to use spot market prices at the time of the survey. But these may differ from the shadow equilibrium prices that would be observed if all self-consumed goods and services were traded on the market. Thus, these imputed values suffer from an indeterminate bias that needs to be taken into account case by case.

(c) Price differences between the rural and urban sector. In developing countries the rural sector accounts for 40–80 per cent of employment and 25–40 per cent of GDP, with the urban sector accounting for the rest. Economic analyses are often carried out by means of two sector models. However, the comparison between the two sectors is undermined by non-negligible statistical problems. The first is the underestimation of income and consumption in rural areas as mentioned above. The second is that the prices of goods and

[1] That the differences in reference periods can be a major source of error is shown by the lively debate on the decline of poverty in India during the last two decades of the twentieth century. In this case, the shortening of the reference period in the Indian National Sample Survey led to a statistical increase in measured consumption that implied a more rapid decline of poverty in the 1990s (i.e. years dominated by liberal policies) with respect to the 1980s (i.e. years of interventionist policies). However, after correcting for this change, the 1990s poverty decline was seen to have been no faster than in the 1980s, and might even have been slower.

services vary significantly between rural and urban areas. In rural areas, food and housing prices are lower than in urban areas. At the same time, rural prices of industrial goods are significantly higher than in towns. Although these two effects offset each other, proper comparisons between the two sectors ought to be carried out using the same set of prices for a common basket of goods.

13.2 Aspects of Consumption Behaviour Ignored in the Standard Models

Household size and structure

The consumption/savings model used for the industrialized countries assumes a representative household consisting of father, mother, and one to two children.[2] However, in developing nations household size is generally greater (six to seven people, on average). Second, the household structure differs from that of a classical mono-nuclear family prevailing in developed countries. In fact, in low-income countries the household is often multi-generational (particularly so in rural areas, less so in urban areas) and in several cases people live in an extended family in which people are related by distant kinship relations. In some areas of Africa, the Middle East, and South Asia one also finds polygamous families, while many countries of Latin America comprise a large number of single parent families headed by the mother. Third, the typical developing country household is characterized by a higher overall dependency rate, which means that each active adult has to provide for a greater number of dependants than in advanced countries.

These demographic and cultural differences affect the consumption/saving behaviour of households. Let us consider the case of two households with the same per capita income but different demographic structures. What are the effects of these differences on the consumption and saving behaviour? First, if the elderly live in a multi-generational family that provides for them, their need to save for their old age is reduced and therefore the household propensity to consume rises. As a result, current income becomes more important than life-cycle income in determining overall consumption. Second, the larger the extended family, the higher its ability to insure against idiosyncratic risks (such as illness or job loss) that are not otherwise insurable and that would require self-insurance by accumulating precautionary savings in the form of jewellery, livestock, and cash. Also in this case, therefore—given the same income per capita—people living in large extended families have a higher marginal propensity to consume than those living in smaller families.

Third, the age composition of the household generates relevant effects on consumption behaviour. Let us remember that the consumption function estimates the value of the average family's consumption per capita in relation to the average family's income per capita. Yet, in order to reach the same level of consumer satisfaction, a 3-year-old child

[2] In Part I, 'savings' refers to 'household financial savings'. This definition is, however, incomplete. A more comprehensive definition includes (a) overall financial savings, that is, the savings of households, firms (i.e. undistributed profits), the state (investments in infrastructure), and the rest of the world; (b) public and private expenditure on human capital; (c) minus the exhaustion of nonrenewable resources (soil, minerals, energy sources, forests, and so on); (d) investments created through the direct application of surplus labour.

needs a lower expenditure than a man of 40 years or a woman of 30. To address this issue, it is possible to introduce equivalence scales that determine the ratio between the consumption of several age/gender groups with respect to that of the household head who is most often an adult male. As an example, the OECD uses the following consumption equivalence scales: first adult = 1, other adults = 0.8, the elderly = 0.6, children 5–15 years = 0.5, children of less than 5 years = 0.3.[3] Using these equivalence scales, one can express family size in units of equivalent adults[4] and calculate the income and consumption per adult equivalent. This means that given the same income per capita, the well-being of a typical family in a developing country is reached at a lower level of average consumption per capita than that of a family of an advanced country which comprises mainly adults and only few children. Therefore, given the same income and consumption per capita, a family with many children is likely to have a higher savings rate and a lower propensity to consume.

Fourth, given the same family income per capita, a family with a greater number of members may reach the same levels of well-being at a lower consumption per capita because of economies of scale in consumption. In particular, when expenditure on housing, consumer durables, and services used by several family members grows as a share of the total, it is possible to achieve similar levels of consumer satisfaction and well-being at a lower expenditure per capita, as the same couch, stove, fridge, and radio can simultaneously meet the needs of several people.

The above considerations allow the construction of a function of consumption per capita (C/c) in which the main determinant is the current disposable income per capita (YD/c). The second explanatory variable is household size (HS). This parameter takes a negative sign to capture the effects of economies of scale in consumption and a high share of children in the family, and a positive sign when belonging to an extended family reduces the need to save for retirement and insure against idiosyncratic shocks. The joint effect of these factors is indeterminate and varies from place to place:

$$C/c = \alpha + \beta\ YD/c \ \pm\ \chi\ HS \tag{13.1}$$

Fifth and last, let us compare the behaviour of different families (by type and number of members) with the same overall household income. An analysis by the OECD Development Centre assesses the relationship between family type and consumption/saving decisions in China, Indonesia, Ghana, and Côte d'Ivoire on the basis of surveys that also provide data on the frequency distribution of various family types (Table 13.1). The study concludes that—*ceteris paribus*—an extended family tends to consume more than a nuclear family since the number of inactive people is greater and because this type of family acts as an insurance device for its members, as discussed above.

In turn, in polygamous families the propensity to consume is higher than in nuclear families. There are several reasons for this. Whenever inheritance norms of a deceased father establish that his assets have to be divided among only male offspring, competition develops between polygamous wives to procreate male children who will support them in

[3] Another equivalence scale considers the number of equivalent adults to be equal to the square root of the number of family members.

[4] From a theoretical point of view, the determination of country-specific equivalence scales requires detailed data on household expenditures and the use of complex econometric analyses.

Table 13.1 Percentage distribution of household types in four countries, early 2000s

Country	Location	Extended family	Nuclear family	Monogamous family	Polygamous family	Incomplete family
Côte d'Ivoire	Urban	53	31	62	21.0	16
	Rural	43	50	48	44.0	8
	Total	47	42	54	35.0	11
Ghana	Urban	18	45	60	3.0	37
	Rural	17	54	63	8.0	29
	Total	17	51	62	6.0	31
Indonesia	Urban	28	60	86	2.3	12
	Rural	21	68	87	2.3	11
	Total	23	65	86	2.3	11
China	Rural	8	89	96	0.0	4

Note: The sum of the values by line does not add up to 100 because some families are included in two columns. The sum of columns 1 and 2 is equal to that of columns 3 and 4. Adding the incomplete families, one obtains 100 per cent.

Source: de Laiglesia and Morrisson (2008).

their old age. This raises their fertility rate and worsens the overall dependency ratio of the family that—for any given overall family income—reduces savings. These families not only show a lower savings rate but also lower expenditure on the health and education of children. Part of this neglect is due to the fact that the polygamous husband 'buys' wives (a cheap source of labour, the producers of future labour force, and a sign of prestige) and 'sells' daughters who are seen as an asset. Finally, given the same overall level of household income, the propensity to consume is higher in single-parent incomplete families (which are mostly headed by women, as frequently observed in Latin America), than in complete ones. This is because the dependency rate of the former is greater than that of the latter; despite the smaller consumption needs of children, a lack of adult time may push the lone parent to purchase services (including oversight of the children) that are not provided by the missing parent.

Place of residence

Another important theoretical determinant of consumption/saving behaviour in developing countries is the place of residence. The poorer rural sector has traditionally been considered to have a higher propensity to consume and a lower propensity to save. Indeed, in most development models, the rural sector plays an ancillary role in relation to the urban sector which is considered the growth engine of the economy (see the Lewis model discussed in Chapter 2).

However, empirical evidence shows that this is often not true as the rural propensity to consume from both permanent income (YDP) and transitory income (YD –YDP) is lower. The reason for this difference is that the share of transitory income in rural areas is higher than in urban areas. Indeed, rural areas are more prone than urban areas to weather, price, and other shocks. As a result, as income instability is greater, precautionary savings tend to be higher than in urban areas.

Second, the residents of rural areas (both self-employed people and wage earners) are less exposed to advertising and the penetration of the consumption patterns of advanced countries that are spreading in urban areas. In the latter the number of supermarkets and shopping centres has been increasing rapidly even in poor countries, while advertising promotes lifestyles and consumption models, even among the poor, similar to those of the local middle-upper class. In contrast, rural residents have fewer contacts with richer foreigners, while distance and traditional values hinder the spread of consumerism and reduce the impact of the imitation effect. Furthermore, in many cases, industrial consumer goods are not readily available in rural areas (see Chapter 6). Therefore, even the propensity to consume from permanent income is likely to be lower in rural areas. These considerations allow the following consumption functions to be written for the urban and rural sectors where the β coefficients are the propensity to consume from the permanent (YDP) and transitory (YD-YDP) income:

$$C_u = \alpha + \beta_{1u}\, YDP_u + \beta_{2u}(YD_u - YDP_u) \quad \text{where} \quad \beta_{1u} > \beta_{2u} > 0 \tag{13.2}$$

$$C_r = \alpha + \beta_{1r}\, YDP_r + \beta_{2r}(YD_r - YDP_r) \quad \text{where} \quad \beta_{1r} > \beta_{2r} > 0 \tag{13.2a}$$

and where

$$YDP_u/YD_u > YDP_r/YD_r \text{ and } \beta_{1u} > \beta_{1r},\ \beta_{2u} > \beta_{2r}$$

Income composition

A third aspect of the consumption/saving function ignored in developed countries concerns the composition of total family income. In rural areas, consumers and producers are often the same people (as in the case of smallholders) and their consumption/investment decisions are taken simultaneously. When the farmer or micro-entrepreneur is the owner of her means of production—and can therefore assess concrete investment opportunities by postponing consumption—she may decide at the same time whether to consume or invest her self-employment income (SE) on her small farm or firm. Furthermore, the small farmer and entrepreneur are partly obliged to maintain a high level of investment because of the narrowness of the rural or informal credit market. In contrast, people who receive a wage (W), interests (I), or transfers (T) do not have the possibility of choosing simultaneously between consumption and direct investment and thus have a higher propensity to consume. In this case, in fact, a reduction in consumption determines a rise in financial savings whose returns are uncertain due to bank instability and inflation. In view of all this, the aggregate consumption function also depends on the national income composition as indicated below:

$$C = \alpha + \zeta\, SE + \chi\, W + \delta T + \varepsilon\, I \text{ where } \zeta < \chi,\ \delta,\ \varepsilon \tag{13.3}$$

Finally, the impact of inflation on savings depends on the presence or absence of indexation mechanisms. Whenever these are lacking or weak, it is likely that the propensity to consume increases, especially for the purchase of durable goods which could be used as a hedge against inflation.

In conclusion, in developing countries, the specification of the consumption function uses current rather than life-cycle income, and permanent income rather than total income. It also takes into account the urban or rural origin of total income, and the composition of total income by type. It emphasizes the importance of family size, family composition between active and dependent members, and the type of family, including whether it is polygamous or monogamous. Variations in the interest rate do not have a perceptible impact on consumption while public consumption is a complement (and not a substitute) for private consumption. Finally, it includes among its determinants the inflation rate, even though the empirical evidence about its effects is ambiguous.

Table 13.2 summarizes the results of an econometric analysis comparing the sign of several determinants of saving behaviour in developed and developing countries. It shows that the signs and size of the parameters for developing countries often differ from those expected on the basis of the standard theory or estimated for developed countries.

In view of this analysis it appears that the impact of fiscal or monetary policies on aggregate demand varies according to the family characteristics illustrated in this section. Long-run growth models also need to take into account the income differences across sectors since—as argued above—an increase of rural incomes seems to have—*ceteris paribus*—a greater impact in terms of aggregate saving formation.

13.3 The Investment Function

In advanced countries, the investment function includes alternatively or simultaneously the following arguments: the expected increase in demand (ΔY); the user cost of capital, that is, the interest rate and amortization, to which it is possible to add more detailed models of the tax rate on profits, the expected technological progress, the level of profits and/or sales; and Tobin's 'q'.

In developing countries, the formulation of the investment function is influenced by the structural characteristics of these countries (Agénor-Montiel, 1999, 95–102), starting with the segmentation of the credit market. The formal sector is usually dominated by financial repression (that is, a r_f below its equilibrium level, and a credit allocation often favouring state-owned agencies) while the informal sector is characterized by a high interest rate, r_i, due to its oligopolistic nature, lack of loan collateralization, and greater default risk. A neoclassical representation of this situation is offered by Figure 13.1 but there are alternative ways of modelling such relation. Figure 13.1 shows that—when starting from a situation of equilibrium in both markets, financial repression causes a fall in the formal interest rate and the volume of credit it provides. The people excluded from such markets are unloaded onto the informal credit market and so cause an increase in its credit demand and interest rate $r_{i\text{-}repr}$. The liberalization of the repressed interest rate generates symmetric effects. The macroeconomic impact of monetary policy, and in particular of interest rate policy, thus depends on the relative weight of these two sectors and on the linkages between them.

However, the conclusions to be drawn from Figure 13.1 depend on assumptions that are not always plausible. The first is that the agents excluded from the formal credit market can easily switch to the informal one. This may not be possible given the structural differences

Table 13.2 Signs of the parameters of the saving function expected on a theoretical basis and estimated econometrically for advanced and developing countries

Signs	**Income trend**	**Wealth**	**Income growth***	**Transitory income**	**Real interest rate**	**Inflation**	**Family size**	**Dependency rate**
Predicted by theory	+	–	–	+	+	+ or –	+	–
Estimated, for developed countries	+	ns	+ (high)	+	–		Ns	+
Estimated for, poor countries	–	–	+ (low)	+	Ns	Ns	+ (low)	–

Notes: ns = not significantly different from zero.
* Refers to income growth over the previous five years.
Source: Muradoglu and Taksin (1996).

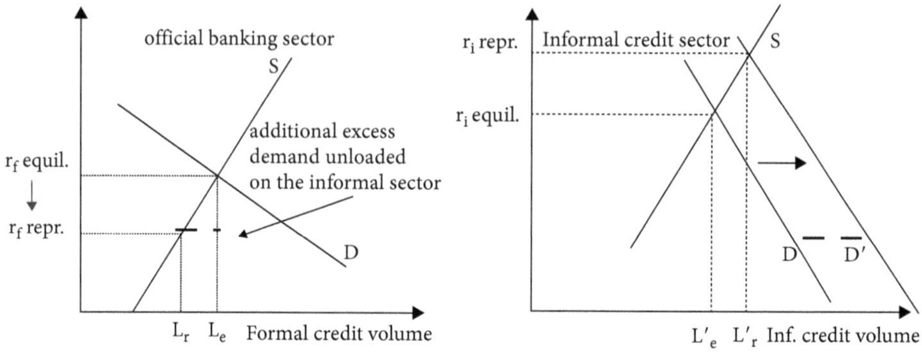

Figure 13.1 Links between the official and informal credit markets

between the two sectors. It may even be plausible to assume that the two markets are completely disconnected. Second, the informal credit sector might not have the ability to supply a greater volume of loanable funds which, according to Figure 13.1, would rise from L'_e to L'_r if there is financial repression in the formal sector. As a matter of fact, the supply of funds to the informal sector may be completely rigid, unless there are lending agreements between risk-averse formal sector banks and poorly financed informal sector entities—such as microcredit schemes—which, however, are better placed to assess loan risks among informal borrowers. Except in this case, the availability of loanable funds in the informal sector may be completely rigid. Financial repression and a fall in the formal sector interest rate, r_f, and an increase in the demand for credit in the informal sector would only raise informal interest rates.

In developing countries, therefore, the credit market needs to be modelled in a dualistic way by introducing both r_f and r_i, the respective volumes of credit granted by the two sectors, and the interrelation between the two markets. A further consideration concerns the elasticity of demand for investible funds with respect to the formal and informal interest rates. Such demand—particularly in the informal sector—is inelastic as firms have limited cashflow and therefore a weak self-financing capacity. Little empirical evidence, however, is available in this regard.

Second, in poor countries the absence or narrowness of the stock exchange make the 'Tobin q' an irrelevant explanation of investment decisions. Even where it exists, the stock exchange lists and trades actively only a limited number of securities. Third, most developing countries are markedly dependent on the import of investment goods and essential intermediate inputs. This makes investment decisions strongly reliant on the costs of and accessibility to foreign exchange at the official rate or at the expensive parallel market rate. In such a context, a devaluation of the exchange rate is likely to depress investment, particularly in the non-tradable sector, while an exchange rate appreciation generates the opposite effect. Investments often boom before an announced devaluation, while immediately afterwards they stagnate.

The relationship between public and private investments is generally more important in developing than in advanced countries. In the former, public infrastructure (roads, airports, telecommunication networks, electrical grids, schools, research, and so on) are generally underdeveloped and this imposes significant costs on private producers.

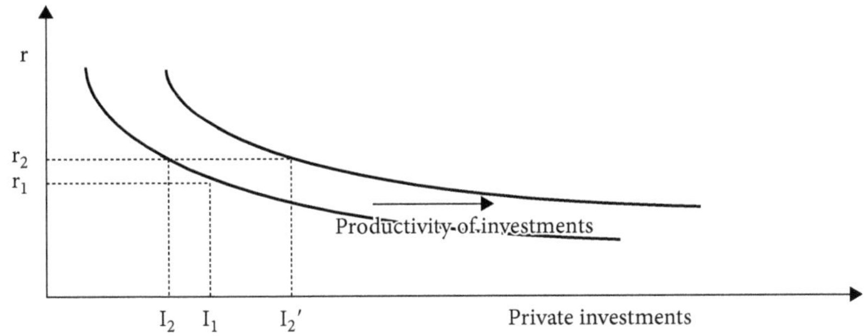

Figure 13.2 Public investment, the interest rate and crowding in effects

The conventional analysis for the developed countries suggests that an increase in public investment crowds out private investment due to the increase in interest rates caused by the issuance of state bonds to finance them (Figure 13.2).

However, whenever public investments (IPu) substantially raise the rate of return on private investment, one observes a crowding-in effect, by which private investments (IPr) increase and, all else being equal, growth accelerates, as shown by equation (13.4) and Figure 13.2. This effect obviously depends on the composition and quality of public investment.

$$\mathrm{IPr} = \mathrm{a} + \mathrm{b\ IPu}\ +\ \mathrm{c}[\mathrm{X}] \tag{13.4}$$

In Figure 13.2, for example, an increase in public investments causes an increase in the interest rate from r_1 to r_2 but simultaneously causes a shift to the right of the marginal productivity of private investments. Without this effect, the investment would decline from I_1 to I_2 while, thanks to it, it increases to I'_2. Studies cited in Agénor and Montiel (1999) indicate that a public investment of one dollar in infrastructure generates an increase in private investment equal to US$0.25, while public investment in other sectors would lead to a decrease in private investment equal to US$0.30. And a study by Calderon and Serven (2004) shows that raising the level of public infrastructure in Argentina to the level of Costa Rica (the regional leader) would generate—*ceteris paribus*—an increase in its GDP growth rate by 1.7 per cent a year, due—*inter alia*—to a strong crowding-in of private investment. Finally, macroeconomic instability does affect investment intentions. Instability can be proxied by the budget deficit, instability of the real exchange rate (Larrain and Vergara, 1993), the variability of the inflation rate, and a high public debt/GDP ratio—especially if its foreign component is high. A worsening of such indicators increases uncertainty, the risk of recession and higher future taxes, and thus may cause a delay or decrease in current investments.

As noted when discussing the consumption function, given the same income per capita, agricultural households and small business owners are likely to exhibit a higher rate of saving and investment than wage and profit earners and higher than people receiving wages, transfers, or other types of income. Thus—*ceteris paribus*—an egalitarian distribution of assets favouring small producers can increase the rate of saving and investment (Birdsall et al., 1996). Finally, in developing countries the level of aggregate demand influences investment demand more than in advanced countries where there might be greater spare capacity. However, when making investment decisions, firms in developing countries have to compare the expected price of their future output (P) not only with the wage rate (W) but also with the cost of foreign currency ($e^{nc/\$}$), that is, the amount of national currency, nc, required to buy a US dollar, as most investments are imported.

In conclusion, the investment function in developing countries is more complex than in advanced ones. Equation (13.5) summarizes the relevant variables explaining private investment, where the symbols have the meanings outlined above.

$$IPr = f(Y,\ r_f,\ r_i,\ e^{nc/\$},\ P,\ W/P,\ e^{nc/\$}/P,\ IPu) \tag{13.5}$$

13.4 The Money Demand Function

In advanced countries the standard money demand function includes among its determinants the interest rate r and income Y. The situation of developing countries is more complex for the reasons alluded to in the introduction of this chapter and due to factors discussed hereafter. To start with, given the underdevelopment of the financial sector (as suggested for instance by a low M2/GDP ratio, the number of banks per 100,000 people and the amount of bonds in circulation), the volume of deposits and credit granted by the banking sector is comparatively limited. In addition, developing countries are characterized by strong financial dualism, a fact that weakens the response of the economy to changes in monetary policy. Changes in the central bank discount rate, r_b, do not generally produce important effects on money demand. Furthermore, in financially repressed systems the nominal interest rate does not change for long periods while for most economic agents what matters is not r_f, but r_i. The latter is not, however, easily observable and there are hardly any time series to estimate econometrically its impact on the demand for money. The decisions of policymakers will thus depend on the way r_b, r_f. and r_i interact with each other. For instance, in Figure 13.1, the relation between the formal and informal interest rate appears to be inverse, but different alternatives can be put forward. In view of this, most models attempting to introduce the nominal interest rate into the money demand equations lead to unsatisfactory results, except perhaps in countries where the degree of financial repression is lower and the informal credit sector comparatively smaller. Generally speaking, the elasticity of the money demand of firms with respect to r is close to zero and in most cases its estimates are not statistically significant.

The rate of inflation is generally higher in developing economies. While low inflation does not affect the demand for money, higher inflation erodes the real value of money balances and thus determines a decrease of real money demand. It is therefore necessary to introduce the rate of inflation into the money demand equation in order to take into account the high opportunity cost of holding liquid assets.

High inflation also leads to currency substitution and dollarization. Currency substitution is a widespread problem in developing countries. It can take different forms, such as the accumulation of hard currency in cash by households or firms, the opening of foreign currency accounts at national banks (now allowed in an increasing number of countries), or the opening of foreign accounts abroad. The degree of currency substitution and the increasing demand for dollars (rather than for the national currency) depends on several factors. These include the level of inflation, limited opportunities to diversify financial assets, the capping of the domestic interest rate on deposits, the level of international interest rates, political instability, the risk of financial asset confiscation, and low conversion costs from national to international financial assets and vice versa. As shown in Figure 3.1 in Agénor and Montiel (1999), the demand for foreign currency often reaches 30–40 per cent of the total demand for money even under relatively normal situations. In countries affected by hyperinflation, rising demand for foreign money determines a near complete currency substitution and a flight from the national currency.

The consequences of currency substitution are well analysed: over the short term an increase in the demand for foreign currency generates upward pressure on the domestic interest rate (which must rise to increase the attractiveness of national financial assets) and on the exchange rate (which tends to depreciate) and downward pressure on the currency reserves of the central bank. These events may lead to severe economic crises and a total flight from the national currency. Even under less dramatic conditions, the impact of currency substitution on the real economy can be remarkable, especially in case of its third type of substitution. The first effect is due to the reduction of investible funds (that will no longer be intermediated by the domestic financial system) and a capital accumulation slowdown. Second, the government ability to tax decreases and this increases the government necessity to borrow abroad or to turn to monetary emissions.

The money demand by firms also depends on the need to import intermediate inputs and investment goods whose national currency cost is—as seen above—influenced by the exchange rate. In view of this, the money demand function for a developing country may take the following form:

$$MD/P = f\ [(Y,\ P,\ (e^{nc/\$} - e^{nc/\$*})] \tag{13.6}$$

which reflects the situation of an economy under pressure where Y, P, and ($e^{nc/US\$} - e^{nc/US\$*}$) are the real income, the rate of inflation, and the deviation of the market exchange rate from a reasonable shadow exchange rate $e^{nc/\$*}$. When ($e^{nc/US\$} - e^{nc/US\$*}$) increases, there is a flight from the national currency and MD/P falls. Alternatively, in situations of limited currency substitution, it is possible to decompose the total money demand in household money demand (DM/P_h) and firms money demand (MD/P_f).

$$MD/P_h = f\ (Y,\ r) \tag{13.7}$$

$$MD/P_f = f\ (wN/P,\ e^{nc/\$}\, mY/P,\ r) \tag{13.7a}$$

For firms, money demand is also a function of the real wage bill (wN/P, where w is the nominal wage rate, N the number of workers, and P the price level) and import costs denominated in US dollars multiplied by $e^{nc/\$}$. If $e^{nc/\$}$ rises (as in the case of a devaluation) the demand for money increases. The interest rate (r) also affects the demand of money by firms in a negative way.

13.5 Concluding Remarks

Consumption, investment, and money demand behaviour in developing countries share some common elements with those observed in developed countries. But the structural differences characterizing the economies of poor countries require the introduction of additional variables that are not relevant in advanced countries. The overall effect is that the behavioural relations in these three areas differ perceptibly from those of the industrialized countries. Introducing such specific equations into the IS-LM model and, indirectly, the AS-AD model for developing countries has important implications for determining the equilibrium levels of income, interest rate, and price level. A second difference concerns the informational base used to estimate such relations in developing countries, as data for several variables are only scantily available while the macro picture may be blurred by a number of measurement biases.

As for the consumption function, the main differences concern the adoption of current or permanent income instead of life-cycle income; the impossibility to shift incomes over time due to the incompleteness of financial markets; the inability to foresee future income streams; a high time preference and rate of inflation; and the impact of household size and structure, place of residence, and income composition. In addition, public consumption is seen as a complement (rather than a substitute) for private consumption. The determinants of investment differ even more on account of the dualistic nature of the credit market, the impact of the exchange rate on the domestic cost of imported investments, and the crowding-in effect of public investment on private investment. Finally, the money demand function includes new arguments, such as the rate of inflation and the exchange rate's black market premium, while the interest rate is statistically non-significant, as firms have a small self-financing capacity and therefore have to borrow even if the interest rate is high.

References

Agénor, P. R. and P. Montiel (1999), *Development Macroeconomics*, 2nd edition. Princeton, NJ: Princeton University Press.

Birdsall, N., T. C. Pickney, and R. H. Sabot (1996), 'Why Low Inequality Spurs Growth: Savings and Investment by The Poor', Working Paper 327, Washington, DC: Inter-American Development Bank Office of the Chief Economist.

Calderon, C. and L. Serven (2004), 'The Effects of Infrastructure Development on Growth and Income Distribution', WPS 3400, Washington, DC: The World Bank.

de Laiglesia and Morrisson (2008), *Household Structures and Savings: Evidence from Household Surveys*, Paris: OECD Development Centre.

Larrain F. and R. Vergara (1993), 'Investment and Macroeconomic Adjustment: The case of East Asia', in L. Serven and A. Solimano (eds.) *Striving for Growth after Adjustment.* Washington DC: The World Bank.

Muradoglu, G. and F. Taksin (1996), 'Differences in Household Savings Bahaviour: Evidence from Industrial and Developing Countries', *The Developing Economies*, XXXIV (2): pp. 138–53.

Suggested Further Reading

Birdsall, N., T. C. Pickney, and R. H. Sabot (1996), 'Why Low Inequality Spurs Growth: Savings and Investment by The Poor', Washington, DC, Working Paper 327, Inter-American Development Bank Office of the Chief Economist.

Calderon, C. and L. Serven (2004), 'The Effects of Infrastructure Development on Growth and Income Distribution', *Working Papers Series* 3400, Washington, DC: The World Bank.

Ray, D. (1998), *Development Economics.* Princeton, NJ: Princeton University Press.

14

IS-LM and AS-AD with Behavioural Equations for the Developing Countries

This chapter discusses the IS-LM and AS-AD models for developing countries, as was discussed for the developed countries in Chapter 3.[1] However, while the basic components of such models are similar to those used for the industrialized countries, their analytical specification is markedly different, as they rely on the behavioural structural equations discussed in Chapter 13. As a result, the effects of exogenous shocks and government macroeconomic policies often differ from those derived for the developed countries on the basis of the conventional IS-LM and AS-AD models.

14.1 Aggregate Supply

As argued in Chapters 4 to 13, it is useful to reiterate that the specification of the behavioural equations that enter the IS-LM and AS-AD models for developing countries is influenced by the real-life functioning of the markets for production factors and final goods, and by the different reactions of entrepreneurs and workers to changes in price signals. The models for developed countries assume that factor and product markets are competitive but in developing countries such markets are characterized by several distortions.

The goods market tends to be oligopolistic and practises *mark-up* pricing. The market for non-traded goods (NT) is comparatively narrow and there is little competition, and the traded goods (T) may not be greatly exposed to international competition due to the ISI-inspired trade policies that protected them in the past. In many countries this situation has, however, gradually changed since the 1990s (see Table 2.7). In turn, the labour market includes a unionized sector that pays comparatively high salaries in the manufacturing and public sectors and in multinational corporations, and a large informal sector characterized by oligopolistic relationships or, especially in agriculture, by the dominance of wage norms barely ensuring the reproduction of the labour force (Ray, 1998). In the latter case, low wages, assumed to remain constant over the short term, are the general rule.

Intermediate inputs are often imported from abroad, given that in the early stages of industrialization firms do not invest heavily in vertically integrated sectors. The aggregate supply therefore crucially depends on the exchange rate $e^{nc/\$}$ that may exhibit a single or multiple rates. In turn, in the credit market working capital is financed by bank credit due to the firms' limited cashflow and reliance on equity capital, as only a few companies are able to raise risk capital through the emission of stocks. Thus, bank credit and the bank

[1] This chapter draws in part on Jha (2003)

The Macroeconomics of Developing Countries: An Intermediate Textbook. Giovanni Andrea Cornia, Oxford University Press (2020).

DOI: 10.1093/oso/9780198856672.001.0001

lending rate, r_f, are key determinants of the total cost of production. Finally, the rate of utilization of productive capacity is often low, so that high values of Y/Y^* (the ratio between effectively used capacity and its potential) are seldom a source of inflation. As in Jha (2003), we can therefore write the supply function for a typical developing country as follows:

$$Y = f\ (P,\ r_f,\ w,\ e^{nc/\$})^2 \tag{14.1}$$

or its inverse $P = g(Y, r_f, w, e^{nc/\$})$, where P is the price level, Y the real output, w the wage rate, $e^{nc/US\$}$ the exchange rate and r_f the interest rate charged by banks.[3] In view of the strong underutilization of existing productive capacity, in the short run it is likely that the AS schedule be elastic, that is, resembling the Keynesian supply schedule. It is well known, however, that over the medium and long term various structural factors (poor transport and telecommunication infrastructure, discontinuity of the investment function, incomplete financial markets, and so on) render this schedule more rigid (Figure 14.1).

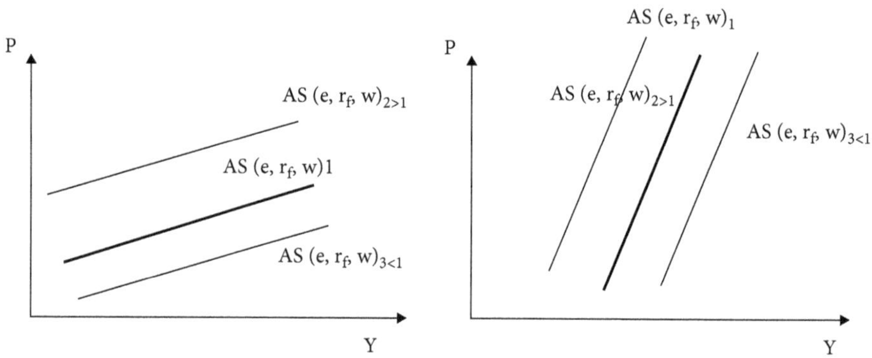

Figure 14.1 AS schedule over the short term and long term in a typical developing country

Given that the AS derived from equation (14.1) takes the following explicit linear form $P = (\alpha_2 r_f + \alpha_3 w + \alpha_4 e^{nc/\$} - \alpha_0)/\alpha_1 + Y/\alpha_1$, an increase in the values of $e^{nc/\$}$, r_f, and w entails a rise of the constant term and a leftward shift of the aggregate supply schedule, while their decrease has the opposite effect. In developing countries, climatic shocks are particularly pervasive and, as noted, shift the AS schedule to the left. Floods and droughts reduce land and labour productivity. This pushes upward the value of w per unit of output, and possibly generates an increase in r_f due to greater demand of credit for climate adaptation and prevention activities, and $e^{nc/\$}$ due to mounting needs to rely on imports to compensate output losses. Labour productivity may also be reduced by climatic shocks that cause the spread of diseases and food shortages. Additionally, in such cases, we see an adverse impact on w, r_f, and $e^{nc/\$}$ that causes a leftward shift of the AS schedule. In long-term growth models (see for instance Chapter 5) the effect of adverse climatic changes on land, labour, and capital productivity is stronger and longer lasting.

[2] Compare (14.1) with the aggregate supply schedule for industrialized countries, that is, $P = [a(1+z)/(1-\lambda)p_m]w_{-1}[1+\varepsilon(Y/Y^* - 1)]$, which shows that the main cost components are wages and, to a lesser degree, primary commodities.

[3] If (14.1) is written in linear form, $Y = \alpha_0 + \alpha_1 P - \alpha_2 r_f - \alpha_3 w - \alpha_4 e^{nc/\$}$ that can easily be transformed into $P = Y/\alpha_1 + (\alpha_2 r_f + \alpha_3 w + \alpha_4 e^{nc/\$} - \alpha_0)/\alpha_1$

14.2 Aggregate Demand

Let us recall that the AD schedule is the locus where all its points reflect the simultaneous equilibrium of the IS and LM schedules, and where changes in the price level P are obtained by letting this variable vary in the LM schedule. For the developing countries, it is necessary to derive such an equilibrium on the markets for goods and money balances by using the specific behavioural functions for private consumption, investment, money demand, public expenditure, and net exports that fit the reality of developing countries discussed in Chapter 13.

Derivation of the LM schedule

To derive the LM, let us recall again the characteristics of developing countries' money markets (Chapter 13). With a low M2/GDP, the financial sector is underdeveloped and dualistic. High inflation reduces the demand for domestic currency and raises the demand for foreign currency. The economy has a low degree of monetization, and the non-monetized sector is little affected by changes in official interest rates and the compulsory reserve ratios that concern the commercial banks. Open market operations of the central bank are rare and, due to financial repression, commercial banks may be obliged to purchase public debt at artificially low interest rates.

In such a context, the definition of the money supply requires that the main accounting relations of the central bank (Table 14.1) are first illustrated. This can be written as follows:

$$\Sigma_t \, BP + \Sigma_t \, BD = RE + CU \tag{14.2}$$

where $\Sigma_t BP = FA$, is the algebraic summation over time of the surpluses and deficits of the balance of payments. Such a summation is equivalent to the net foreign exchange reserves (FA) of the central bank (Table 14.1). In turn, $\Sigma_t BP$ equals the net domestic assets (DA), that is, the summation over time of the government budget deficits and surpluses BD financed—*inter alia*—with state bonds purchased by the central bank. And finally, RE are the compulsory and voluntary reserves deposited by the commercial banks at the central bank. In this way, all the elements of equation (14.2) are included in the balance sheet of the central bank that takes the form shown in Table 14.1. (see Jha 2003).

Table 14.1 Schematic representation of the balance sheet of the central bank

Assets	Liabilities
(FA) Net foreign assets Foreign exchange reserves Gold	(CU) Currency in circulation in the hands of households, banks, and firms
(DA) Net domestic assets Government bond and securities Loans to commercial banks Others Monetary Base H	(RE) Banking monetary base (equivalent to the compulsory and voluntary reserves of commercial banks deposited at the central bank) Net worth Monetary Base H

As far as the money supply is concerned, let us recall that the nominal money supply MS is equal to the monetary base H multiplied by the money multiplier, mm < 1 (see footnote 8 in Chapter 3), in symbols:

$$\mathrm{MS} = \mathrm{mmH}.$$

In this case, after dropping CU, which is neglected in what follows, $\mathrm{MS} = (\Sigma_t \mathrm{BP} + \Sigma_t \mathrm{BD})/\mathrm{re}$. Indeed, while mm is generally equal to $(1 + \mathrm{cu})/(\mathrm{re} + \mathrm{cu})$, if we neglect cu for simplicity, mm becomes 1/re. In turn, the total real money demand is decomposed into the real money demand of households ($\mathrm{MD_h}$) and of firms ($\mathrm{MD_f}$) and can be written as follows:

$$\mathrm{MD_h} = \mathrm{f}\ (\mathrm{Y},\ \mathrm{r_f}) \tag{14.3}$$

$$\mathrm{MD_f} = \mathrm{f}\ (\mathrm{wN/P},\ \mathrm{e}^{\mathrm{nc}/\$}\ \mathrm{mY/P},\ \ \mathrm{r_f}) \tag{14.4}$$

where the meaning of the above variables was illustrated in equations (13.7) and (13.7a). From an empirical perspective, it must be recalled that the elasticity of $\mathrm{MD_f}$ is about one in relation to wN and $\mathrm{e}^{\mathrm{nc}/\$}\mathrm{mY}$, while it is almost zero in relation to $\mathrm{r_f}$.

Let us now define the equilibrium in the money market, where the nominal money supply is deflated as usual with the price level P in order to express it in real terms, like MD. One obtains the LM schedule for a typical developing country by equalizing the real demand and supply of money as follows:

$$\mathrm{MD} = \mathrm{MS/P} \tag{14.5}$$

which can be written in full as:

$$\mathrm{f}\ [(\mathrm{wN} + \mathrm{e}^{\mathrm{nc}/\$}\mathrm{mY})/\mathrm{P},\ \mathrm{r_f}] + \mathrm{f}(\mathrm{Y},\ \mathrm{r_f}) - (\Sigma_t\, \mathrm{BP} + \Sigma_t\, \mathrm{BD})/\mathrm{re} = 0^4 \tag{14.6}$$

which is a function with three endogenous variables (i.e. the price level, the interest rate, and the income level), which describe the equilibrium in the money market. Rewriting the LM in explicit linear terms yields:

$$\frac{\sum_t BP + \sum_t BD}{re} - \omega_1 Y + \omega_2 r_f - \frac{\lambda_1 wN}{P} - \frac{\lambda_1\ e^{nc/\$} mY}{P} + \lambda_2 r_f = 0 \tag{14.6a}$$

which can be represented in the $(\mathrm{Y}, \mathrm{r_f})$ plane in the form:

$$r_f = \frac{\frac{\lambda_1 wN}{P} - \frac{\sum_t BP + \sum_t BD}{re}}{\bar{\omega}_2 + \lambda_2} + \frac{\bar{\omega}_1 + \frac{\lambda_1 e^{nc/\$}\ m}{P}}{\omega_2 + \lambda_2} Y \tag{14.6b}$$

from which it appears that the variables included in the constant term are shift variables and that an increase in $\mathrm{e}^{\mathrm{nc}/\$}$, that is, a devaluation of the exchange rate, or a rise of in the

[4] The LM for developed countries takes the form $\mathrm{M/P} = \mathrm{f}(\mathrm{Y}, \mathrm{r_f})$. Note the differences with that of a developing country.

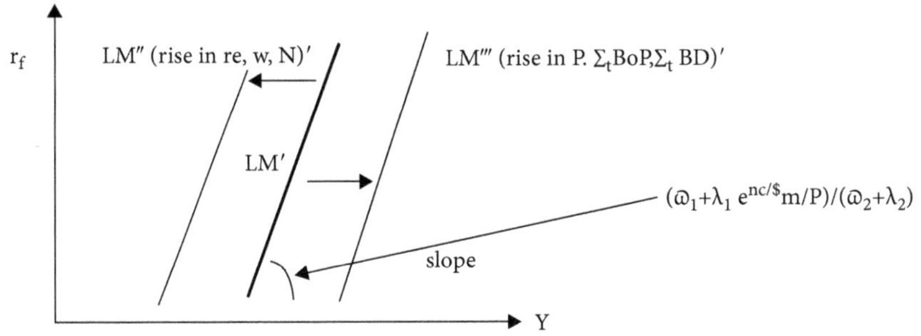

Figure 14.2 LM schedule for a typical low income developing country

import coefficient, m, render the LM more steeply sloping. In such a relation, some variables are given (i.e. they cannot be modified as they refer to the past) for example the summation till time (t − 1) of Σ_{t-1}BP and Σ_{t-1}BD, while the current values of BP and BD are influenced by current changes in $e^{nc/\$}$ and re. The shifts of the LM in relation to the changes of the exogenous variables can be represented as in Figure 14.2.

In this case, an increase of re, w, and N (while leaving the other components of the constant unchanged) causes a leftward shift of the LM. In turn, an increase of P, Σ_tBP $e^{nc/\$}$ Σ_t BD (while leaving the other components of the constant unchanged) causes a rightward shift.

In terms of its slope, in developing countries the LM is likely to be steeper than in developed countries, as the elasticity of the demand for money of firms (λ_2) and households (ϖ_2) in relation to the interest rate is very small. Indeed, the limited monetization of the economy and high inflation imply that money is demanded only for current transactions and not for investments or speculative reasons, so that the interest rate r_f (and, more broadly, monetary policy) affect Y less than in developed nations.

Derivation of the IS schedule

The IS schedule describes the equilibrium between Y and r_f in the goods market. For developing countries the derivation of the IS requires that the behavioural equations for the different components of aggregate demand discussed in Chapter 13 are used. Let us thus recall the following behavioural functions inspired by the structure of the economy of developing countries:

$$\text{Private consumption} \qquad C = f\,(Y,\ Y_{p/a}/Y,\ \tau_y) \tag{14.7}$$

where $Y_{p/a}/Y$ is the percentage of total disposable income received by peasants, artisans, and small entrepreneurs (who have a lower propensity to consume), and τ_y is the income tax rate;

$$\text{Investment} \qquad I = f\,(Y,\ r_f,\ r_i,\ L_b,\ w/P,\ e^{nc/\$}/P) \tag{14.8}$$

where r_f and r_i are the interest rates prevailing in the formal and informal credit market, L_b is the volume of bank credit granted to the economy and w/P and $e^{nc/\$}$/P represent the relative cost of the wage rate and foreign exchange. Both such variables have a negative sign;

$$\text{Public expenditure (assuming no transfers)} \quad G = f\,(w\,N_g,\; I_g) \tag{14.9}$$

where wN_g is the public sector wage bill (that is, the wage rate w multiplied by the number of public employees N_g) and I_g the public investments;

$$\text{Net exports in national currency } NX = X - M = e^{nc/\$}\,[(1-\tau_x)X]\,[e^{nc/\$}\,P_f(1-\tau_x)/P_d] - e^{nc/\$}(1+\tau_m)\,mY \tag{14.10}$$

where we abandon the hypothesis that the domestic price of tradables is equal to their world price. Indeed, in view of the still important role played by trade taxes in developing countries, X and M are corrected by $(1-\tau_x)$ and $(1-\tau_m)$ so as to take into account the effect of export taxes (or subsidies if τ_x takes a negative value) and import taxes τ_m. As X and M are priced in dollars, they must be converted into the domestic currency by multiplying them by the exchange rate $e^{nc/\$}$. Exports are also influenced by the term $[e^{nc/\$}P_f(1-\tau_x)/P_d]$, which is an index of competitiveness equal to the ratio between foreign prices and domestic prices. In contrast, the specification of imports M (the last term of equation (14.10)) does not include the ratio between domestic and international prices. Indeed, X and M are not easily substituted with each other. Exports often include primary commodities and imports are mainly constituted by machinery and intermediate inputs) and therefore a devaluation of the exchange rate does not reduce the demand for imports as these are not replaceable with near perfect domestic substitutes. This means that a change in $e^{nc/\$}\,P_f/P_d$ or τ_m has a limited impact in shifting the demand for such goods from imports to domestic production.

One can now write the equilibrium relation IS as follows:

$$Y = f_c\left(Y,\ \frac{Y_{p/a}}{Y},\tau_y\right) + f_i\left(Y, r_b, r_i,\ \ \frac{w}{P},\frac{e^{nc/\$}}{P}\right) + f_g(wN_g, I_g) + e^{nc/\$}[(1-\tau_y)X]\left[\frac{e^{nc/\$}\ P_f(1-\tau_x)}{P_d}\right] - e^{nc/\$}(1+\tau_m)\ mY \tag{14.11}$$

which, if written in explicit linear terms, takes the following form (after unifying r_i with r_f):

$$Y = \alpha_0 + \alpha_1 Y - \alpha_2\frac{Y_{p/a}}{Y} - \alpha_3\tau_y + \beta_1 Y - \beta_2 r_f\ \beta_3\frac{w}{P} - \beta_4\frac{e^{nc/\$}}{P} + \gamma_1 wN + \gamma_2 I_g + e^{nc/\$}[(1-\tau_y)X]\left[\frac{e^{nc/\$}\ P_f(1-\tau_x)}{P_d}\right] - e^{nc/\$}(1+\tau_m)\ mY \tag{14.11a}$$

from which one can derive the IS in the bidimensional plane (r_f, Y). The IS takes the form:

$$r_f = \left[\alpha_0 - \alpha_2\frac{Y_{p/a}}{Y} - \alpha_3\tau_y - \beta_3\frac{w}{P} - \beta_4\frac{e^{nc/\$}}{P} + \gamma_1 wN/P + \gamma_2 I_g + e^{nc/\$}[(1-\tau_y)X]\left[\frac{e^{nc/\$}P_f(1-\tau_x)}{P_d}\right]\right] - \left[\frac{1-\alpha_1-\beta_1+(1+\tau_m)m}{\beta_2}\right]Y \tag{14.11b}$$

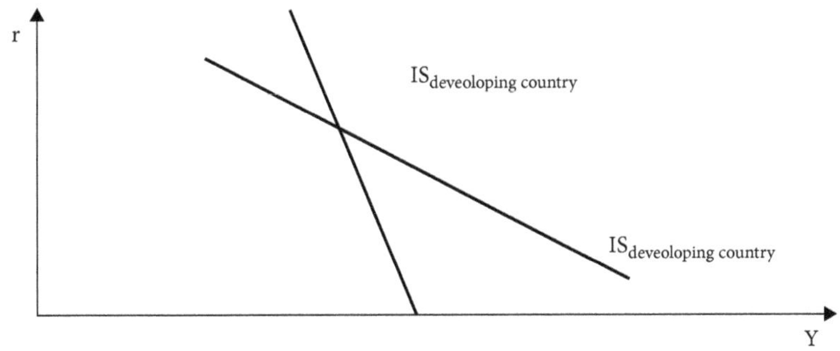

Figure 14.3 IS schedule for developed and developing countries

which shows that r_f is a positive function of the constant (the long square parenthesis) and a negative of function of Y. The variables included in the constant are taken as fixed at a given point in time—while their change entails a shift of IS with unchanged slope $[1 - \alpha_1 - \beta_1 + (1 + \tau_m)m]/\beta_2]$. In developing countries the IS also has a negative slope. Given the low elasticity of investment demand, β_2, in relation to the interest rate (due to the limited self-financing capacity of firms), this relation tends to be inelastic, and the IS therefore has a steep slope (Figure 14.3).[5]

In addition, in developing countries the LM and IS shift following changes in the policy variables included in the constant of equations (14.6b) and (14.11b). By reducing or increasing the numerical value of some of the components of the constants in such equations, one obtains the direction of the shift of the LM or IS and—by extension—of the AD. The impacts of a number of policy changes are illustrated in Figure 14.4.

For instance, an increase in the compulsory reserve ratio (re) (the first row in Figure 14.4) reduces the money supply and increases the interest rate from r_1 to r_2 with the result that the LM shifts to the left (Figure 14.4b). The impact on the IS-LM equilibrium is a fall in the level of income Y (Figure 14.4c), which also explains why the AD shifts to the left because, for the same price level P, Y declines.

In turn, as shown in the second row in Figure 14.4 an increase in public expenditure $(\gamma_1 wN/P + \gamma_2 I_g)$ causes an increase in the constant term and no changes in the slope of planned expenditure, which shifts upwards (see Figure 14.4b) and intersects the schedule 'expenditure = production' at a higher level, leading in this way to a higher Y for each level of r_f. This means that the original IS schedule shifts rightward and so does the AD, because for any price level P the new IS-LM equilibrium generates a higher level of income Y.

Finally, as shown by the third row in Figure 14.4 a devaluation of the exchange rate generates the following effects: in equation (14.8) it reduces I, it raises X (by how much depends on the elasticity of the international demand for the goods exported by the developing country considered), and does not reduce, or only moderately, M which is price inelastic. Thus, both ε_X (the export elasticity vis-à-vis the exchange rate) and ε_M (the import elasticity) are rather small, and their sum is likely to be smaller than one. If this is true, devaluation does not improve the current account balance (NX) and may in fact worsen it. This reduces the overall planned expenditure and causes a leftward shift in the IS (this point is discussed in

[5] Dividing the numerator by a small β_2, one gets a large overall coefficient of Y, which means that r_f will grow a lot in relation to a unitary change of Y.

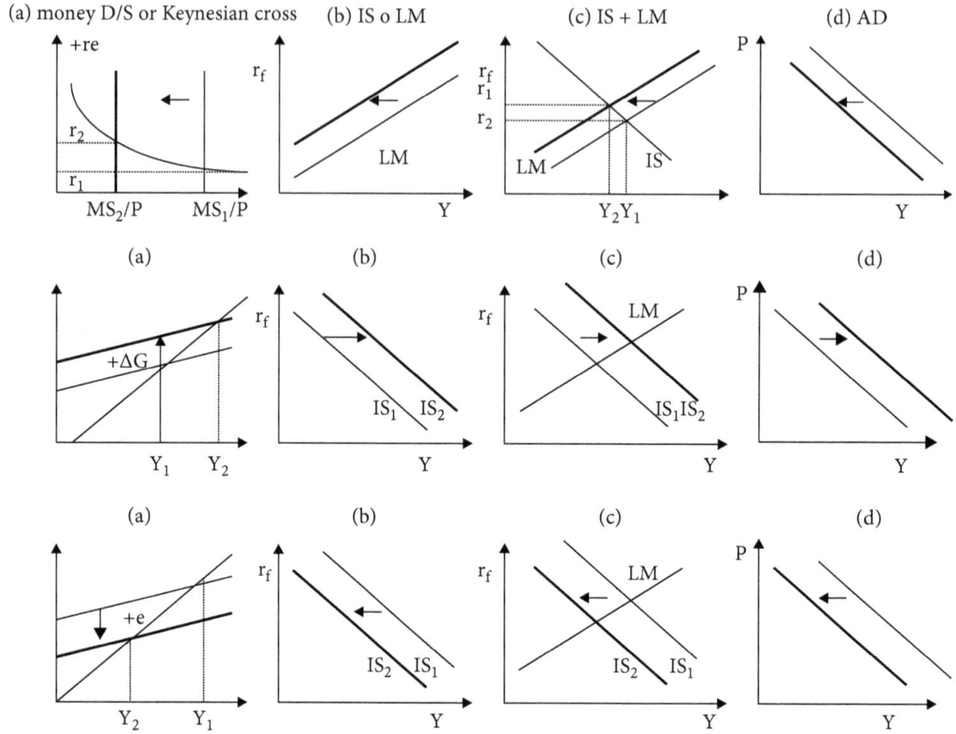

Figure 14.4 Examples of logical sequences to determine the shifts of LM, IS and AD in case of an increase in re, ΔG and $e^{nc/\$}$

detail in Chapter 15). With a stable LM, the leftward shift of the IS generates a lower level of income Y that—given the stability of prices causes a leftward shift also in the AD.

14.3 AD-AS Equilibrium

As mentioned, the aggregate demand schedule represents the locus of points for which there is a simultaneous equilibrium on the goods and money market for any level of P. In addition, for developing countries, the aggregate demand schedule AD combines the variables that enter the definitions of IS and LM—and therefore the behavioural functions that describe private consumption, investments, net exports, and money demand and supply discussed in Chapter 13. AD therefore takes the generic form that includes all variables that are part of IS and LM:

$$Y = f(P, re, Y_{p/a}/Y, r, w, e^{nc/\$}, N_g, I_g, \tau, \tau_x, \tau_m, \Sigma_t BP, \Sigma_t BD) \tag{14.12}$$

and is derived analytically from the IS and LM written with r (i.e. r_f simplified) as a dependent variable:

IS	$r = [\text{constant}] - \text{parameter } Y$	(see 14.11b)
LM	$r = [\text{constant}] + \text{parameter } Y$	(see 14.6b)

By equalizing the right-hand side of the two equations above, the variable r is eliminated. In this way it is possible to represent AD in the bidimensional space (Y, P). The algebraic derivation of AD is cumbersome. Footnote 6 shows how AD is derived in the (simpler) case of developed countries.[6]

By dropping for the sake of simplicity some non-essential variables ($Y_{p/a}$, N_g, τ_y, τ_x, τ_m) in the analysis that follows, the algebraic expression of the AD schedule can be simplified as indicated in equation (14.13):

$$Y = f\ (P,\ re,\ w,\ e^{nc/\$},\ I_{g,\ ,}\ \Sigma_t\, BP,\ \Sigma_t\, BD) \tag{14.13}$$

To obtain analytically the sign of the partial derivatives, we have to go back to analyse the impact of the changes under consideration on the IS and LM schedules (see Figure 14.4). Figure 14.4 provides three examples of this logical chain in situations of a rise in the compulsory reserve ratio (re), an increase in public spending ($+\Delta G$ leading to an increase in BD), and nominal devaluation.

14.4 Simulation of the Impact of Macroeconomic Policies in the IS-LM Model

We are now equipped with the duly simplified AD and AS schedules, that is:

$$AD:\ Y = f(P,\ re,\ w,\ e^{nc/\$},\ I_{g,\ ,}\ \Sigma_t\, BP,\ \Sigma_t\, BD) \tag{14.14}$$

$$AS:\ Y = f\ [P,\ r\ ,\ w,\ e^{nc/\$}] \tag{14.15}$$

and can therefore proceed to a simulation of the impact of exogenous shocks and policy changes, as presented in Section 3.5 for the advanced countries. Inspired by Jha (2003), let us consider the impact of four policy changes, that is, a contraction of the money supply, a reduction in public expenditure, an exchange rate devaluation, and a contraction of real wages. These policies have often been included in the policy package recommended by the IMF to stabilize the macroeconomic imbalances which have affected many developing, transitional, and developed countries during the last thirty years.

Monetary contraction

The tools at the disposal of the central bank to reduce money supply include an increase of the reserve ratio (re) and open market operations, that is, the sale against cash of state bonds held as part of its portfolio. To these one can add administrative measures on the maximum allowed volume of credit that commercial banks can grant to firms

[6] In a developed country (that has simpler behavioural relations than a developing country) the AD is derived by setting the equilibrium between IS and LM, that is, $(G + I_0 - cT+)/h - (1 - c)/hY = [l_0 - MS/P]l_2 + (l_1/l_2)Y$, from which it is possible to extract the function $P = f(Y)$ thanks to a simple but heavy manipulation which leads to $P = 1/\{l_2/MS[l_0/l_2 - (G + I_0 - cT)/h]\} + 1/[(1 - c)/h + l_1/l_2]Y$ where the angular coefficient is negative as a rise in Y (in the denominator) reduces P, as c, h, l_1, $l_2 > 0$ and $c < 1$.

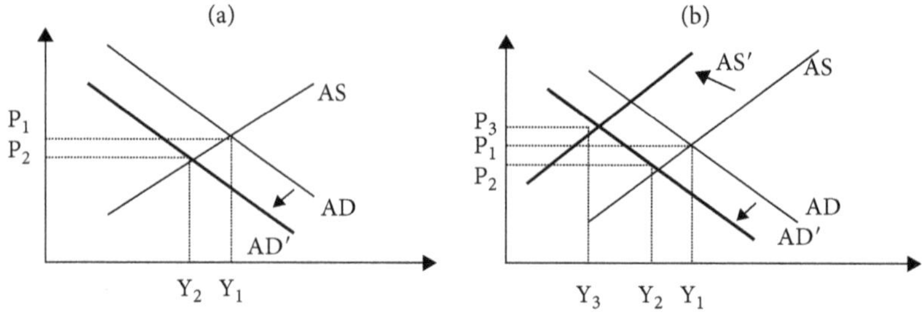

Figure 14.5 Impact of monetary contraction in developed and developing countries

and households. In a developed country the short-term impact of an increase in re (Figure 14.5a) cause a drop in money supply that raises r, that shifts the LM to the left, while it depresses investments and so shifts the IS and AD leftward. With no changes in AS, income and prices fall to Y_2 and P_2.

In developing countries the impact on the AD is the same but that on the AS is a bit more complicated. Indeed, in Figure 14.5b) an increase of re raises r, which in poor countries negatively affects the aggregate supply AS, as financial charges represent an important part of their total cost of production. Their increase causes a contraction of aggregate supply, as shown by the shifts of the AS leftwards to AS′. In conclusion, in advanced countries, monetary contraction entails a fall of Y and P, while in a developing country it entails a bigger fall of Y and an increase (or a smaller decline) of P.

Contractionary fiscal policy

In advanced countries, a cut in public expenditure entails a fall of overall planned expenditure, a leftward shift of the IS schedule, no changes in the LM schedule, and thus a leftward shift of the AD schedule. In developing countries, the leftward shift of the IS also entails a fall in the interest rate, as money supply remains constant but its demand diminishes due to the decline of public expenditure, the budget deficit BD_t, Σ_t BD, and public borrowing. There is therefore a lower crowding out of savings by the state treasury which pushes downward the interest rate. In turn, a drop in the latter shifts the aggregate supply AS to the right (Figure 14.6b), as financial charges represent—as noted—an important component of the production costs borne by firms.

Thus, while in Figure 14.6a fiscal austerity generally leads to a lower level of Y and P (or, more realistically, of its increase, that is the rate of inflation), in developing countries it leads to an expansion of Y and—depending on the extent of the AS shift—to a fall in prices or in the rate of inflation (Figure 14.6).

Exchange rate devaluation

In diversified economies, devaluation leads to a surge in exports, as the higher domestic prices that exporters accrue induce an increase in export supply which is price elastic and is absorbed by the world market (which is characterized by an infinitely elastic demand at the

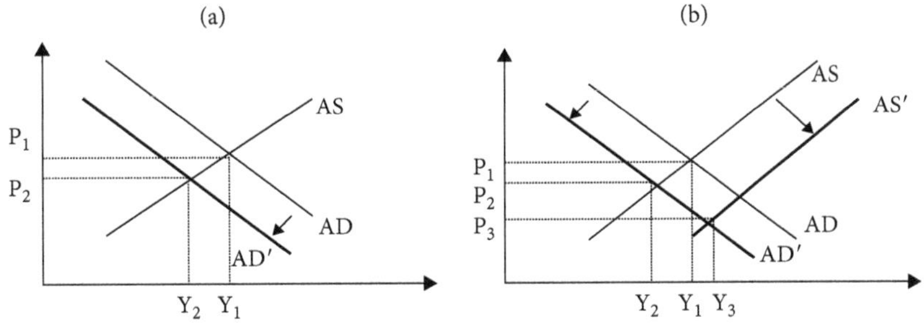

Figure 14.6 Impact of fiscal cuts in developed and developing countries

world equilibrium dollar price). Devaluation also leads to a reduction in imports (that are also price elastic) as—due to their higher cost in domestic currency—they are replaced by perfect domestic substitutes that compete with what are now more expensive imports. As a result, there is an increase in NX, an improvement in the balance of payments and an expansionary impact on domestic production. This entails a rightward shift of the IS schedule and, with no changes in the LM, a rightward shift in the AD (Figure 14.7).

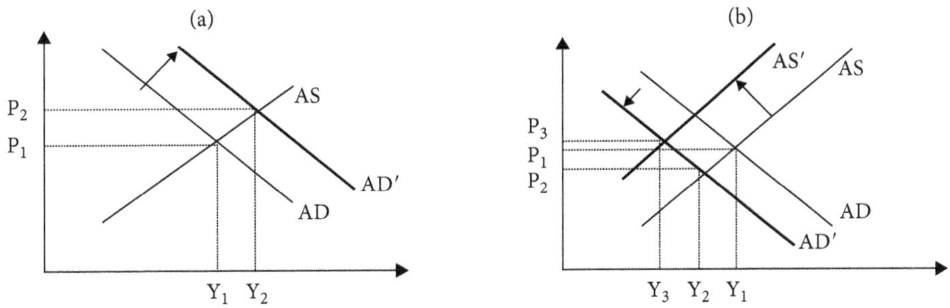

Figure 14.7 Impact of devaluation in developed and developing countries

In developing countries that still depend on the export of agricultural goods and minerals with a comparatively rigid export supply and import goods that cannot be easily replaced with near perfect domestic substitutes, a devaluation may generate different effects. In such countries the sum of the export and import elasticities of devaluation ($\varepsilon_X + \varepsilon_M$) is often smaller than one. And in other developing countries, the export supply is fairly rigid due, for instance, to a poor infrastructure that limits their export potential, especially if the additional supply originates from regions far from harbours and markets.

For instance, one can reasonably surmise from equations (14.8) and (14.10) that an increase in $e^{nc/\$}$ negatively affects investments and—probably—the current account balance. Indeed, difficulties in expanding the supply of exportables, together with an increase in the domestic currency cost of imports mean that NX worsens, causing a contraction of aggregate demand, as discussed in Krugman and Taylor (1978) and analysed in detail in Chapter 15. This negative impact is reflected by a leftward shift in the IS. In addition, the slope of the LM increases (see equation (14.6b)). Indeed, as shown in equation (14.5) a devaluation entails an increase of the production costs of firms which—being unable to finance them with their cashflow—increase their demand for money, push upwards the money demand schedule, and cause a rise in the interest rate. These two effects combine to cause a leftward shift of AD, which reflects a contractionary effect on the level of output and Y.

Such a negative effect is exacerbated by the leftward shift of the AS schedule. As indicated by the aggregate supply function (equation (14.15)), an increase of $e^{nc/\$}$ and r entails an increase of production costs and therefore a leftward shift of the aggregate supply schedule (Figure 14.7b) and therefore a worsening of domestic production and income together with a possible increase in the price level (this depends on the extent of the leftward shift of the AS schedule).

Summing up, while in most advanced nations devaluation increases both Y and P, in poor countries exporting low-value primary commodities the effect of devaluation is to reduce domestic output and income. The effect on the price level depends on by how much the AS schedule shifts to the left.

Reduction of the real wage or of the total wage bill

The objective of reducing the real wage or the total wage bill can be achieved in different ways. First, the government can cut the real wages of state employees, workers of state controlled companies, and people enrolled in public works programmes, for instance by reducing the indexation of wages to inflation. Second, it can set limits to wage increases in private firms and fine those that raise wages beyond a given threshold or that exceed a pre-set total wage bill (as in the case of the early 1990s Polish *popiska*). In advanced countries the effect of such measures may be expansionary, leading to a rise of Y. This is the net result of two opposite effects: on the one side, the reduction of real wages reduces G, but, on the other, it may increase I if the investment function includes profits—which may rise due to the fall of wages. It is possible that the net effect over the short term is a drop of planned expenditure, E, which causes a leftward shift of the IS and also—with no changes in the LM—of aggregate demand AD (Figure 14.8). At the same time, however, a reduction of the average wage entails an expansionary effect on aggregate supply as, in these countries, wages constitute the main component of the total cost of production.

In developing countries, the impact is similar in terms of the likely effects on aggregate demand. A reduction of w, N_g, or both causes a fall of G and C, which causes a leftward

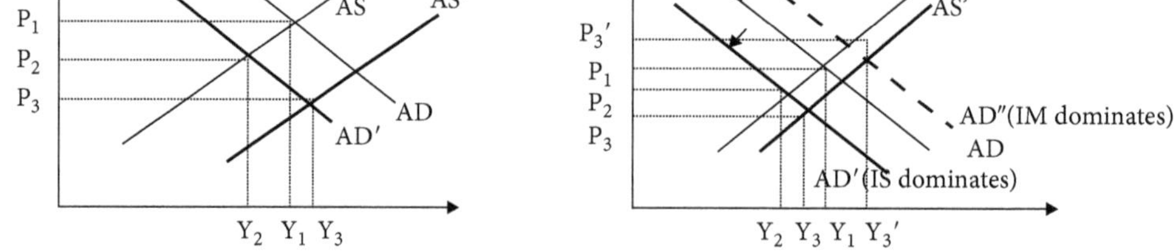

Figure 14.8 Impact of the reduction of real wages in developed and developing countries

shift of the IS schedule. But this also entails a fall in the firms money demand to finance the current wage bill (see equation (14.5)), as well as a reduction of the budget deficit, BD, and in Σ_t BD. These two effects reduce overall money demand, which, as a result, shifts downwards and causes a fall in the interest rate, leading to a rightward shift of the LM. The net effect on AD of these two opposite effects (IS to the left, LM to the right) will depend on specific local conditions. Suppose that the net effect is contractionary and that the AD shifts to the left; but other hypotheses are plausible under certain conditions.

As for the effects on aggregate supply, the smaller financing needs of firms (as both the wage rate and the interest rate have diminished) cause a shift of the AS to the right, generating a moderating effect on the leftward shift of AD on Y. If the fall of aggregate demand had been (graphically speaking) more limited, the country would have experienced a modest impact on the decline of Y. If the effect on the LM is dominant, the AD shifts to the right to AD″. All else being equal, the effect on P is likely to be greater than that observed in a developed country (Figure 14.8b).

Summing up, in advanced countries a policy of wage cuts tends to generate an expansionary effect on Y and a reduction in the price level or in the rate of inflation. In developing nations, in contrast, the impact on Y is negative (even though the expansionary effect on AS reduces the size of such an effect) while prices tend to fall. But the effect on the AD may be expansionary (if the LM effects dominate) thus leading to an overall expansion in national income to Y_3'. This is not the case if the AD shift is dominated by a shift of the IS due to a decline of aggregate demand.

Table 14.2 summarizes the different impact of the same policy measures in advanced and developing nations, showing that there are important differences in results, especially in the case of devaluation. The main point of this long discussion is that the standard AS-AD model incorporating behavioural equations derived from the industrialized countries does not correctly capture the impact of policy changes in developing countries. Thus, before introducing policy changes, it is necessary to specify behavioural relations and structural models reflecting the real economic conditions prevailing in the developing country considered. In the tropics, IS-LM and AS-AD do not necessarily behave in the same way as in temperate climates!

Table 14.2 Comparison of the impact of four policy changes on the income level and prices (or rate of inflation) in developed and developing countries

	Developed countries	Developing countries
Monetary contraction	Y: falls P: falls	Y: falls much more P: rises
Public expenditure cuts	Y: falls P: falls	Y: rises (short term) P falls (most likely)
Devaluation	Y: rises P: rises	Y: falls P: uncertain/rises
Reduction of the real wage or wage bill	Y: rises P: falls	Y: falls moderately if the effect on the IS is dominant Y: rises if the effect on the LM is dominant P: uncertain/falls

Note: P refers to the absolute price level or to the inflation rate.

14.5 Concluding Remarks

In developing countries, explaining short-term fluctuations in the income and price level (or in the rate of inflation when this has become permanent—see Section 3.6) requires developing IS-LM and AS-AD models incorporating behavioural equations reflecting the structural differences of markets in these economies. From a macro perspective, the main differences in outcomes entailed by differences in behavioural equations concern: the negative supply impact of increases in interest rates, as financial charges are a main determinant of the total cost of production; the negative supply and balance of payments effect of devaluation, as poor countries seldom have domestic substitutes for imported capital goods, so that the price elasticity of their imports is low; the increase in money demand caused by devaluation as firms are unable to self-finance the greater cost of imported goods; the stronger impact in developing countries of an increase in money supply caused by the budget deficit and balance of payment surplus; and the near-zero elasticity of the demand for money in relation to a rise in the interest rates, as developing countries' firms have a very low cash flow. Because of all this, the impact of monetary and fiscal contraction, devaluation, and wage cuts on the income and price levels of a country can differ substantially from those observed in developed countries. Thus, to assume that in developing countries the impact of these policy changes is similar to that observed in developed countries is often wrong and may cause unanticipated and costly policy problems.

References

Krugman, P. and L. Taylor (1978), 'Contractionary Effects of Devaluation', *Journal of International Economics*, 8 (3): pp. 445–56.

Jha, R. (2003), *Macroeconomics for Developing Countries*, 2nd edition. London and New York: Routledge.

Ray, D. (1998), *Development Economics*. Princeton, NJ: Princeton University Press.

Suggested Further Reading

Jha, R. (2003), *Macroeconomics for Developing Countries*, 2nd edn. London and New York: Routledge.

Taylor, L. (1987), 'Macro Policies in the Tropics: how Sensible People Stand', *World Development*, 15 (12): pp. 1407–35.

15

Modelling the Open Economy, Devaluation, and the Exchange Rate in Developing Countries

This chapter first examines the limitations of conventional open-economy macro models when applied to developing countries, and presents the Swan–Salter and the three-sector dependent-economy model that better capture the reality of poor countries. It then discusses the impact of devaluation under conditions of closed and open capital account. In this regard, it examines the results of the empirical literature on the contractionary or expansionary effect of devaluation in developing countries. Finally, it reviews the pros and cons of alternative exchange rate regimes, the impossible trinity theorem, and measures to control exchange rate volatility through capital controls.

15.1 Limits of the Conventional Open-economy Models for Developing Countries

The limitations of the standard models discussed in Part I when applied to the developing countries concern also the modelling of macroeconomic changes and shocks under open economy conditions. To start with, such limitations concern the nature of the trade integration and financial dependence (see Chapter 10), although these can in part by captured by the Mundell–Fleming model illustrated in Chapter 2. A second more binding limitation concerns the assumption that an increase in domestic prices is due to domestic factors such as a fiscal expansion or a supply shock and not—as often observed in small, open developing economies—to changes in international prices and in their international terms of trade. Third, most mainstream open economy models ignore the disaggregation of the economy into the traded (T) and not-traded (NT) sectors, and the fact that the NT prices in developing countries are downward sticky. A fourth unrealistic aspect of mainstream open economy modelling concerns the assumption that these countries import a single composite good for which there exist a near-perfect domestic substitute, whose domestic supply increases following a devaluation. This is a poor fit for the situation of developing countries with path-dependent import and export structures. This difference has already been alluded to in Chapter 14 when discussing the impact of devaluation in an AS-AD framework. Fifth, even when the T and NT goods are being treated separately, the standard approach does not break down the traded goods sector into imports and exports, although in developing countries these are structurally very different, especially in the countries affected by the 'dependency syndrome'. Finally, contrary to what is observed in industrialized countries, in many developing countries the impact of devaluation on net exports tends to be negative over the short term and at times even over the long term.

The Macroeconomics of Developing Countries: An Intermediate Textbook. Giovanni Andrea Cornia, Oxford University Press (2020).

DOI: 10.1093/oso/9780198856672.001.0001

15.2 The Mundell–Fleming Model and the Treatment of the Terms of Trade

The approach followed in previous chapters did not explicitly deal with P_X and P_M, that is, the prices of X and M, or, in other words, with the problem of the international terms of trade, which is central to the macroeconomic management of many developing countries. A few additional approaches are presented in this chapter to improve the pertinence and relevance of macro modelling for these countries.

The Mundell–Flemingmodel discussed in Chapter 3 focuses on the international trade of a single composite good and in this way ignores the domestic and foreign prices of imports and exports. For the developing countries, it is therefore necessary to correct this anomaly and to introduce such prices, in order to be able to deal with the key issue of international terms of trade. As noted, the Mundell–Fleming model assumes that all countries produce a single composite good which is an imperfect substitute of a good produced by the world economy and that it is consumed by both a country's citizens and the residents of other nations. It also assumes that the law of one price applies, and that therefore the world price P* of the imported good expressed in national currency P is equal to $P^{*}e^{nc/US\$}$. Likewise, the price P of the domestically produced composite good exported to the rest of the world is equal to $P/e^{nc/\$}$. From this, it follows that the international terms of trade z are given by $P^{*}e^{nc/\$/}P$.

In this model, the international terms of trade are endogenous. While P* (the world price expressed in US dollars) is set by the world market, P is determined by the market forces of the country under consideration. This means that changes in the domestic demand of the importing country will influence its domestic production and prices as well as the international terms of trade in ways which depend on the prevailing exchange rate regime (that can alter the international terms of trade) and the supply elasticity of the composite good (see below).

Let us recall that (C + G + I) is defined as absorption (A). One can then write that the balance of payments depends negatively on the level of A (as many resources will be used domestically) and positively on z (as a high value of $P^{*}e^{nc/\$}$ discourages imports). Thus:

$$BP = f(A,\ z) \tag{15.1}$$

If the Marshall–Lerner condition ($|\varepsilon_X| + |\varepsilon_M| > 1$) (discussed in Section 15.7) applies—meaning that the price elasticities of the demand for M and X are not low—the equilibrium condition on the goods market is as follows:

$$Y = A + f(A,\ z) \tag{15.2}$$

where output Y is equal to absorption A plus net exports NX = BP which depends on absorption and changes in the terms of trade z.

Given this framework, what happens when the domestic demand for such a composite good rises following, for instance, the adoption of an expansionary fiscal policy? The effect depends on the supply response, that is, whether it leads to an increase in prices or in supply. Over the short term, it is reasonable to assume that the capital stock, K, is constant and that an increase in aggregate supply depends to a large extent on an increase in labour supply. In this respect, we can distinguish three situations. If we assume a neoclassical labour market characterized by full employment, a rise in domestic demand leads to a surge in the domestic prices, P, a fall in the terms of trade, ($z = P^*e/P$), as the domestically produced composite good costs more than the imported one, and a worsening of the balance of payments (see Section 15.1).

In contrast, if one assumes a Keynesian labour market characterized by involuntary unemployment with an infinitely elastic labour supply schedule, an increase of A will generate an increase in the labour supply that will not affect P, the terms of trade and the balance of payments.

If one assumes a positive but not infinitely elastic supply of labour, we will have both an increase in the supply of the composite good, some rise of its domestic price, P, a fall of z, and some worsening of the balance of payments. Thus, in this case the worsening of the balance of payments depends on domestic factors, an outcome that is plausible in the standard model for large advanced economies. Naturally, if the world price, P*, rises even faster than P, z increases, the balance of payments improves, and the national product Y grows.

15.3 The Swan–Salter Model of a Dependent Economy with Exogenous Terms of Trade

Before discussing this new topic, it is necessary to introduce a short methodological clarification about the various concepts of exchange rate, to aid the reader to understand this section. Indeed, with the term 'exchange rate' we may refer to: (a) the nominal exchange rate $e^{nc/\$}$ that is the quantity of national currency (nc) exchanged for one US$; (b) the real exchange rate, rer (or $rer_t^{nc\$}$), that is the nominal exchange rate doubly deflated with the domestic inflation rate and US inflation rate, i.e. $rer_t = e^{nc/\$}{}_t P_t^*/P_t$. It is expressed as an index number with the real exchange rate in the base year equal to 100. Let us consider for instance the nominal exchange rate ($e^{nc/\$}$) of the Peruvian peso/US$ over 2005–08, and take into account inflation in Peru and the United States so as to obtain the rer that—in Table 15.1—does not change in 2006, depreciates in 2007, and appreciates in 2008.

In the two sector model of Swan and Salter, the real exchange rate is given by $z = P_T/P_{NT}$. How does one arrive at such a formulation? Let us remember with Krugman

Table 15.1 Examples of hypothetical changes in the real exchange rate

Year	Nominal exchange rate (pesos/$)	Index of inflation in Peru	Index of inflation in the United States	Real exchange rate ($rer_t = e^{nc/\$}{}_t P^*/P$)	Real exchange rate index (peso/US$) (2000 = 100)
2005	10	100	100	10	100 (base value)
2006	12	120	100	12 × 100 : 120 = 10	100 (stability)
2007	15	140	105	15 × 105 : 140 = 11.3	113 (devaluation)
2008	16	180	106	16 × 106 : 180 = 9.4	94 (appreciation)

and Obstfeld (1988) that in a small open economy P_T is determined by the world market ($P_T = e^{nc/\$}P_T^*$), while the price of non-tradable P_{NT} is determined by domestic demand and supply, with the latter often being quite rigid. The analytical demonstration of why the real exchange rate, z, is equal to P_T/P_{NT} begins with the exchange rate theory (based on Purchasing Power Parities (PPP)), which states that the nominal exchange rate (for instance between the Chinese yuan and the US$) is given by the ratio of the price level in the two countries, that is, $e_{PPP}{}^{c/US\$} = P_c/P_{us}$. In both China and the United States the overall price level is the weighted average of the T and NT prices. In symbols, in China $P_c = \alpha P_c{}^{NT} + (1-\alpha)\, P_c{}^T$ where α is the share of the NT sector in GDP while in the United States we have a similar relation, i.e. $P_{US} = \beta P_{US}{}^{NT} + (1-\beta)\, P_{US}{}^T$ Given all this, one can write that $e_{PPP}{}^{c/US} = [\alpha P_c{}^{NT} + (1-\alpha)P_c{}^T]/[\beta P_{us}{}^{NT} + (1-\beta)P_{us}{}^T]$. One can now divide the numerator of this expression by $P_c{}^T$ and the denominator by $P_{us}{}^T e^{c/\$T} = P_c{}^T$ where $e^{c/\$T}$ is the PPP exchange rate for the tradable goods. In this way we obtain $P_c/P_{us} = e^{c/\$T}[\alpha P_c{}^{NT}/P_c{}^T + (1-\alpha)]/[\beta P_{US}{}^{NT}/P_{US}{}^T + (1-\beta)]$. In the next step one factors out $e^{c/US\,T} = P_c/P_{us}[\beta P_{us}{}^{NT}/P_{us}{}^T + (1-\beta)]/[P_c{}^{NT}/P_c{}^T + (1-\alpha)]$ from which it appears that, given the overall price level in the two countries, the Chinese real exchange rate appreciates if its NT prices rise in relation to its T prices.

We now return to the conclusions of Section 15.2 about the effects of an expansionary fiscal policy in a one-sector economy. Such conclusions depend entirely on the fact that P—the price of the composite good exported by the developing country—is influenced by changes in domestic absorption. This makes the international terms of trade $P^*e^{nc/\$}/P = z$ endogenous (P^* and $e^{nc/\$}$ are exogenous but P is endogenous and thus the composite variable is endogenous). But the overwhelming majority of developing countries are price-takers and their decisions do not affect P^* in a relevant way. If P is taken as exogenous (in the sense that it strictly depends on P^*), then changes in domestic economic conditions should not affect P, given that, at such a price level, the world market is characterized by an infinitely elastic demand. The only role of the domestic conditions is to determine the production exceeding domestic demand which could be exported, influencing the balance of payments but not the international terms of trade.

A model that better captures the conditions of several developing countries and that exhibits exogenous terms of trade, is the Swan–Salter model. In this model the economy comprises two sectors, the non-tradable sector (NT) where the NT goods can be sold only on the domestic market and the tradable sector (T) whose goods can be sold domestically and abroad. The T goods include both exportable goods (exports plus the goods which could be exported but are sold on the domestic market) and importables. In this model, exportables and importables are treated as a single traded good. The prices of T goods are determined by the world market. The prices of NT goods are set by domestic demand and supply and are downward sticky. The international terms of trade P_X/P_M are exogenously given and assumed constant. The fundamental price of the economy is the real exchange rate which is equal to the domestic terms of trade $z = P_T/P_{NT}$ with the prices of both goods written in national currency and with $P_T = P^*{}_T e^{nc/\$}$. Finally, the production functions for Y_T and Y_{NT} are based only on the labour employed (equations (15.3)), while the demand for labour, n, in both sectors varies inversely to the relative wage rate. While the nominal wage rate, w, is the same in both sectors, the relative wage rate (i.e. the nominal wage rate divided by the price level in each of the two sectors) varies, as shown by equation (15.4). Indeed, by substituting equation (15.4) into equation (15.3), it appears that the output in the two sectors depends on their relative wage expressed in terms of w/P_T. One obtains (see Agénor Montiel, 1999, 48–51):

$$\text{production } Y_T = f(n_T), Y_{NT} = f(n_{NT}) \tag{15.3}$$

$$\text{labour demand } n_T = h(\omega)\ n_{NT} = h(z\ \omega) \text{ where } \omega = w/P_T \tag{15.4}$$

$$\text{production in reduced form } Y_T = g(\omega), Y_{NT} = g(z\ \omega) \tag{15.5}$$

where labour demand and production in reduced form in the two sectors are both expressed as functions of the relative wage $\omega = w/P_T$ prevailing in the T sector. Indeed, $z = P_T/P_{NT}$, $z\ \omega = w/P_T$. $P_T/P_{NT} = w/P_{NT}$. Absorption in each of the two sectors (see equations (15.6)) depends on the overall absorption, A, and on z, that is, the ratio of the prices of the two sectors. For instance, a high P_T increases z, and so discourages the absorption of T goods and encourages that of NT goods.

$$\text{sectoral absorption } A_T = k_T(A,\ z) \quad A_{NT} = k_{NT}(A,\ z) \tag{15.6}$$

In turn, total absorption A is the sum of the absorption in the two sectors:

$$\text{total absorption } A = A_T + z^{-1} A_{NT} \tag{15.7}$$

Finally, the equilibrium on the T market is realized when the difference between the supply and demand of T goods is zero, as in equation (15.8):

$$\text{external equilibrium} : BP = g(\omega) - h(A,\ z) \tag{15.8}$$

while the internal equilibrium on the NT market is verified when the domestic demand and supply of such goods equal each other:

$$\text{internal equilibrium} : E_{NT} = g(z\ \omega) - h_{NT}(A,\ z) \tag{15.9}$$

Let us examine now the impact of a fiscal expansion in the context of this model under the assumption that the economy is characterized by full employment. The impact of such a policy is that absorption exceeds the national income, as output cannot increase because all the labour is employed. The increase in income will trigger a surge in the absorption of both tradables (a_T) and non-tradables (a_{NT}), in proportions that vary in relation to the value of z. Under these circumstances, while P_T does not increase because it is set internationally, P_{NT} rises and in this way generates an incentive to NT firms to increase output—as P_{NT} rises while w is constant—and attract workers from the T sector. However, higher NT prices discourage demand in this sector. Meanwhile the real exchange rate $z = P_T/P_{NT}$ appreciates (as P_T remains constant while P_{NT} rises), thus causing a reduction of exports and an increase in imports, that worsen the balance of payments. In short, together with an increase in overall absorption A, one observes an appreciation of the real exchange rate, a worsening of the balance of payments, and an increase in labour absorption, output, prices, and excess supply in the NT sector.

How can the policymaker tackle such a situation which is characterized by both an external imbalance (that is, a deficit of the balance of payments) and an internal imbalance (that is, excess production of NT goods)? A contractionary fiscal policy can help in two ways: first, it reduces the domestic demand of imports and exportables, and so it releases a greater amount of tradable goods which can be sold abroad. But this measure will worsen the internal equilibrium as the fiscal contraction also reduces the absorption of NT goods. The worsening of the internal equilibrium is due to the fact that P_{NT} prices do not decline, despite a fall in demand, as they are assumed to be downward sticky. In brief, the fall of domestic demand for tradables is not accompanied by the expansion of that for non tradables, leading to a situation of underutilization of resources. A contractionary policy, in other words, improves the external equilibrium but worsens the internal equilibrium.

Contractionary measures therefore need to be accompanied by a second measure, that is, the devaluation of the nominal exchange rate $e^{nc/\$}$. This aims—through a rise in the real exchange rate, $z = P_T/P_{NT}$(as $P_T = P^* e^{nc/\$}$), to reduce the internal demand of tradables (which becomes more expensive after the devaluation), so as to free part of them for their exportation, and to shift domestic demand towards the NT goods which, after devaluation, have become relatively less costly than the T goods. At the same time, the increase of P_T relative to P_{NT} shifts labour from the NT to the T sector which can now increase production, while the NT sector reduces it. Thus, devaluation moderates or offsets the overall economic contraction due to public expenditure cuts by expanding exports of T and by reducing their domestic absorption, as T goods are now more expensive in national currency. Thus, the balance of payments improves thanks to the fiscal cuts that reduce absorption and because of the devaluation that increases exports. Nominal devaluation also increases the demand for NT goods (that are now cheaper than T goods) while it reduces its supply as labour moves back to the T sector. So, devaluation helps to re-establish both external and internal equilibrium.

15.4 A Three-sector Model of Dependent Economy

The Salter–Swan model describes in a more realistic way the two-sector economies of developing and developed countries. However, also this model does not allow to capture the impact of changes in the international terms of trade. In the Salter–Swan model, in fact, imports and exports are merged into a single category of tradables that are assumed to be imperfect substitutes of each other, they are in other words the same type of goods, and—precisely for this reason—the international terms of trade between the prices of imports and exports are ignored and remain constant.

Such an assumption is not realistic. and does not help an understanding of the macroeconomic changes of developing countries hit by changes in the international terms of trade. Such changes are linked to their path dependent trade specialization that reflects their factors endowment and colonial history. It is therefore necessary to develop a model in which the exportables are not consumed (or only in part) at the national level and are mainly exported, a reasonable hypothesis in the case of agricultural and non-oil extractive products. Furthermore, the international terms of trade, $tot = P_X/P_I$, are exogenous as they are determined by the world market while the real exchange rate,

$z = P_I/P_{NT}$, is endogenous (as P_{NT} is endogenous).[1] Lastly, let us recall that the law of one price establishes that $P_I = P_I{}^* e^{nc/\$}$ and $P_X = P^*{}_X e^{nc/\$}$. In contrast, P_{NT} is set by the domestic market.

Similarly to equation (15.5), one can represent the supply side of the economy through three reduced form production functions which show that output depends inversely on the relative wage of each sector. After some simple manipulation[2] these can all be written as a function of $\omega = w/P_I$, that is, the nominal wage standardized by the price of imported goods. One can then write:

$$Y_I = g\ (\omega),\ \ Y_X = g\ (\omega/tot) \qquad Y_{NT} = g\ (z\ \omega) \tag{15.10}$$

where a rise in the relative wage rate in each sector causes a drop of the sectoral output. Thus, the equations (15.10) suggest that, if the external terms of trade, tot, deteriorate (for instance, if the world price of the exported commodities falls), the production of Y_X will fall as tot falls and therefore ω/tot rises. In turn, an increase of the price of imported products, P_I, will push z upwards (as $z = P_I/P_{NT}$) and therefore cause a decline of Y_{NT}. The only sector which may expand is Y_I, given that an increase of P_I reduces the relative wage of the sector, a fact which lowers its relative wage. Summing up, the export sector contracts, the NT sector also contracts, while the sector of importables expands (assuming they are produced or producible in the developing country considered). The last conclusion is not true when the importable sector is absent or very small. Therefore, a fall in the international terms of trade of many developing countries generates a contractionary effect not only in the export sector but for the economy as a whole.

A second observation concerns the effect on wages and employment in the three sectors. Let us recall that the nominal wage w is linked to ω by the relation $\omega = w/P_I$, and that therefore an increase in the price of the importables reduces ω (the relative wage) in this sector, which will therefore employ additional workers. In the exportables sector, the real wage is equal to ω/tot and therefore a worsening of the international terms of trade, $tot = P_X/P_I$, leads to an increase of its relative wage (ω/tot) so that the sector will therefore employ fewer workers. Lastly, in the NT sector, the relative wage $z\omega$ will rise due to the increase in the price of importables. Therefore, this sector will also expel labour. In the context of a neoclassical model (in which full employment is assumed) the workers expelled from the exportables and NT sectors must be absorbed by the import sector. This labour reallocation takes place through a fall of the relative wage rate.

The third and last observation is that a worsening of the international terms of trade also entails an income effect, as developing countries receive, for instance, fewer dollars per ton of exported coffee. This entails a fall of national income and absorption. As a matter of fact, all three components of A are affected: private consumption, C, falls due to the drop in the incomes of producers, investment, I, falls as the rate of return on traditional exports diminishes, and government expenditure, G, drops because tax revenue contracts, as the revenue generated by *ad valorem* trade taxes falls. The tax revenue decline could be offset

[1] Alternatively, the real exchange rate can be set as follows $z = P_X/P_{NT}$.

[2] Let us recall that $z = P_I/P_{NT}$, that $\omega = w/P_I$ and that therefore $z\,\omega = w/P_I$, $P_I/P_N = w/P_{NT}$. Furthermore, $\omega/tot = (\omega/P_I)/(P_X/P_I) = w/P_X$.

in part by the revenue generated by an increase in tariffs, but the fall of incomes and increase of P_I reduce the demand for imported goods.

In summary, a worsening of the international terms of trade reduces both income and absorption of C, G, and I; redistributes labour demand across sectors assuming a neoclassical world (or increases unemployment if assuming a Keynesian world); and has a differential impact on sectoral wages and production.

15.5 Impact of Devaluation in Developing Countries

Macroeconomic models for developed countries generally show that devaluation has an expansionary impact (Part I). Given a deficit of the current account balance, devaluation would thus determine simultaneously a rebalancing of external accounts and an increase in GDP.

While this conclusion tends to apply also to developing countries with a diversified production structure (as observed for instance on the occasion of the 100 per cent devaluation of the Korean won in 1997), the impact is more complex in backward and less diversified economies characterized by various types of structural rigidities. This section discusses a series of situations commonly observed in developing countries that could reduce, retard, or entirely offset the potential benefits of the devaluation of the nominal exchange rate.

Failure to comply with the Marshall–Lerner condition

A key precondition for an improvement of the current account balance following devaluation is that—to put it simply—exports and imports are sufficiently sensitive to changes in the nominal exchange rate. This condition is codified in precise terms by the Marshall–Lerner condition that is derived analytically hereafter.

Let us define X as the volume of exports and with p_x their price expressed in domestic currency. M is the volume of imports and p_m their price expressed in dollars, while $e^{\$/nc}$ is the exchange rate, that is the quantity of foreign exchange needed to buy a unit of domestic currency.[3] Then assume that the value of the current account balance (CA) priced in dollars is in equilibrium, in symbols:

$$X\ p_x\, e^{\$/nc} = M\ p_m \quad \text{or} \quad CA = X p_x\, e^{\$/nc} - M\ p_m = 0 \qquad (15.11)$$

If we now devalue the exchange rate, making it vary negatively by $\delta e^{\$/nc}$ (as fewer \$ are demanded per unit of national currency). By how much do exports and imports change as a result of such a devaluation, using as a starting point for the demonstration equation (15.11)? The answer, obtained[4] under the assumption that both p_x and p_m do not change, depends on the partial derivatives of X and M, that is:

[3] This formulation of the exchange rate ($e^{\$/nc}$) is generally used in countries with a strong currency, and is the inverse of that used in most developing countries ($e^{nc/\$}$).

[4] The derivative of a product and difference of variables, as $f = x.y - z$, is equal to $f' = x'.y + x y' - z'$.

$$\frac{\delta CA}{\delta e^{\$/nc}} = \frac{\delta X}{\delta e^{\$/nc}} p_x\, e^{\$/nc} + Xp_x - \frac{\delta M\, p_m}{\delta e^{\$/nc}} \tag{15.12}$$

At this point, equation (15.12) needs to be manipulated in order to make this result easier to interpret. To this end, one multiplies the first addend on the right hand side of equation (15.12) for $X/X = 1$, while in the third addend one substitutes in place of p_m the value obtained from equation (15.11), that is $p_m = X\, p_x e^{\$/nc}/M$. After introducing these manipulations in equation (15.12) one obtains:

$$\frac{\delta CA}{\delta e^{\$/nc}} = \frac{\delta X}{\delta e^{\$/nc}} \frac{X}{X} p_x\, e^{\$/nc} + Xp_x - \frac{\delta M\, X\, p_x\, e^{\$/nc}}{\delta e^{\$/nc} M} \tag{15.13}$$

which can be re-written as:

$$\frac{\delta CA}{\delta e^{\$/nc}} = \frac{\delta X}{X} \frac{e^{\$/nc}}{\delta e^{\$/nc}} Xp_x + Xp_x - \frac{\delta M}{M} \frac{e^{\$/nc}}{\delta e^{\$/nc}} Xp_x \tag{15.13a}$$

while, by factoring out $X\, p_x$, one obtains:

$$\frac{\delta CA}{\delta e^{\$/nc}} = Xp_x \left(\frac{\delta X}{X} \frac{e^{\$/nc}}{\delta e^{\$/nc}} + 1 - \frac{\delta M}{M} \frac{e^{\$/nc}}{\delta e^{\$/nc}} \right) = Xp_x\, (\varepsilon_X + 1 - \varepsilon_m) \tag{15.13b}$$

given that $(\delta X/X)\ (e^{\$/nc}/\delta e^{\$/nc}) = \varepsilon_x$ and $(\delta M/M)\ (e^{\$/nc}/\delta e^{\$/nc}) = \varepsilon_m$

It must be noted that the sign of ε_x is negative ($\delta X/X$ is positive as exports should rise as a result of devaluation but $\delta e^{\$/nc}$ is negative as exporters receive a smaller amount of foreign currency for a unit of domestic currency. In turn, the sign of ε_m is positive (given than the changes in δM and $\delta e^{\$/nc}$ are both negative), so that the last result of equation (15.13b) can be rewritten as:

$$\delta CA/\delta e^{\$/nc} = X\, p_x(1 - |\varepsilon_x| + |\varepsilon_m|) \tag{15.13c}$$

For devaluation to succeed, $\delta CA/\delta e^{\$/nc}$ must be negative (as the numerator is expected to be positive while the denominator is negative). It is therefore necessary that the expression on the right-hand side be smaller than zero, that is to say that $Xp_x(1 - |\varepsilon_x| + |\varepsilon_m|) < 0$. Since Xp_x is constant and positive, the only possibility for such inequality to be verified is that $1 - (|\varepsilon_x| + |\varepsilon_m| < 0$, an inequality that can be rewritten as $|\varepsilon_x| + |\varepsilon_m| > 1$. This is the Marshall–Lerner condition.

How often is this condition verified in developing countries? It is seldom verified in little industrialized countries that depend on the importation of energy, semi-finished products, and machinery whose ε_m tends to zero. It is more frequently verified in countries that depend on imports for which there are domestic substitutes or which are characterized by a high ε_m for luxury imports. Thus, the expected contraction of imports in the wake of devaluation depends on their structure. In turn, the value of ε_x depends on the structure of exports: if these originate mostly from sectors with a fairly rigid short-term supply, as in the case of agriculture (especially its subsector producing tea, coffee, cocoa, etc. which grow on shrubs whose output increases only after 3–5 years after planting), then ε_x is low

($\approx 0.1 - 0.2$), at least over the short term. The situation improves if exports originate from a diversified manufacturing sector in which there is spare production capacity. In any case, devaluation raises the domestic price of tradables.

This conclusion is questioned by liberal economists who argue that the rise of the domestic price of tradables due to devaluation opens up new opportunities to diversify the export basket as devaluation makes exporting more attractive. This is also true of exports in sectors where there is not yet a consolidated tradition of production. All this may be true, if there are underutilized production factors characterized by high spatial and sectoral mobility which could smoothly shift from the NT sector or from other less promising T subsectors. This process of labour and capital reallocation can be eased by re-training programmes and new investments. Yet, in several cases, the conditions for labour reallocation are not verified, as observed in adjustment programmes during which devaluation is invariably accompanied by public expenditure cuts and interest rate rises, which depress investment in new sectors, and programmes to increase labour mobility. In these cases, the potentially diversifying effects of devaluation vanish.

In brief, if $|\varepsilon_x| + |\varepsilon_m| < 1$, it is not possible to rule out the possibility that devaluation may worsen the current account balance, leading sooner or later to foreign exchange rationing even for imports of machinery and energy that are essential for current and future growth. As shown in Figure 15.1, where such co-variation between M and GDP is high, a decline in essential imports affects GDP with a short lag

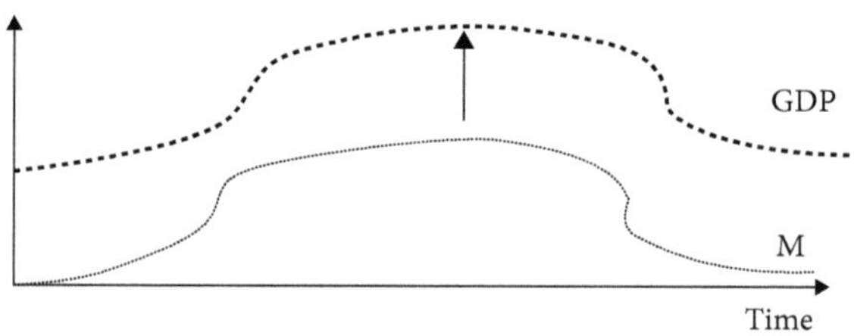

Figure 15.1 Covariation between imports M and GDP

Under these circumstances, it is preferable not to devalue but instead to raise tariffs on unnecessary imports, introduce microeconomic measures aimed at diversifying the economy, improve public infrastructure, subsidize exports, and reduce import dependence over the medium term through WTO-compatible import substitution policies.

Devaluation and J curve effects

Even when the Marshall–Lerner condition is verified, it is not certain that devaluation leads immediately to an improvement of the current account balance. Indeed, in real life the volume of imports and exports adjusts only gradually to the devalued exchange rate. This is largely due to the so-called 'fixity of contracts' which are usually stipulated three to twelve months before the delivery of the goods at the established world price. As a matter of fact, in the short term, X and M are fixed or vary little. This means that, immediately after devaluation, imports will cost more in domestic currency (as Mp_m is divided by a

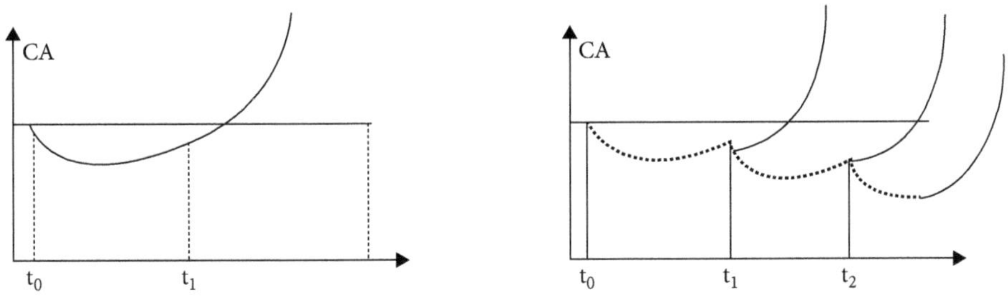

Figure 15.2 J curve effect and J curves build up

devalued (that is, smaller) exchange rate $e^{\$/nc}$)[5] while the price and volume of exports remain constant.[6]

$$CA_{\text{value (in national curreny)}} VA = X\ p_X - M\ p_m/e^{\$/nc} \tag{15.14}$$

Over the medium term, the volumes of both X and M change and therefore the current account balance eventually improves, but over the short term it is common to observe a worsening of the CA. Figure 15.2, left panel, describes graphically this phenomenon—the CA first deteriorates and then improves; this is referred to as the J curve effect.

The message of the J curve is clear: before observing an improvement in the CA, it is practically unavoidable to first experience a temporary worsening. However, it may well be that, because of dissatisfaction with the results recorded during the first months after devaluation, the policymaker may feel that the latter was not sufficiently large to improve the CA and that, therefore, it is necessary to further devalue the exchange rate. But, after the second devaluation, the problems entailed by the fixity of contracts could occur again, pushing the policymaker to introduce several successive devaluations, all of them perceived as unable to improve the CA. One will observe a new J curve being grafted onto the first one—which had just started to trend upwards. And this process may be repeated several times. As a result, the time trend of the CA takes the shape of a 'run-up of J curves' (Figure 15.2, right panel). In brief, one has to be patient to see devaluation produce its effects.

Devaluation and pass-through effects

A devaluation of the domestic currency makes exports more attractive for national producers, as the domestic price of exported goods rises. However, this may not happen if the intermediaries who sell the country's exports on the world market (priced in dollars) decide to pocket part or all of the difference of domestic prices between before and after the devaluation, raising their profit margin, but at the same time removing the incentive for

[5] $e^{\$/nc}$ is equal to the quantity of US$ needed to buy a unit of the domestic currency.

[6] In this case we assume that the domestic price of exports remains unchanged, that is, that the effect of devaluation, which lowers the price of exports in US dollars, leads over the medium term to an increase in export volumes without modifying the domestic currency prices of T goods. Another hypothesis, when assuming an infinitely elastic world demand for our exported goods, is that as a result of devaluation exporters will align domestic prices to US dollar prices, multiplied by the devalued exchange rate, causing a rise in the domestic prices of T goods. Often, the post-devaluation domestic currency prices of exported goods are to be found in between the two extremes discussed above.

producers to increase their output. Thus, if the pass-through of devaluation to domestic producers is zero or minimal (due to the increase in the intermediaries' profit margin), the supply of exports will not increase, while at the same time imports will be more expensive. Also, in this case, the current account balance, CA, will not improve and output may contract due to the increase in the domestic cost of imports.

Devaluation and expectations of further devaluations

At times, the devaluation of the domestic currency may not be completely credible, giving rise to expectations of further devaluations. Such a lack of credibility affects the behaviour of importers and exporters. Importers will try to speed up to the maximum possible extent the payments of foreign invoices, as—if the exchange rate were devalued again—their imports would cost more in domestic currency terms. In turn, exporters will try to delay the conversion into domestic currency of their foreign exchange earnings, as they expect that the national currency will depreciate. If the economic agents act in this way, the current account balance will deteriorate over the short term. And—as a result of this deterioration—there might be a further devaluation of the exchange rate, giving rise to self-fulfilling predictions of devaluation. At times, such expectations of further devaluations are influenced by the worsening of the capital account balance which may follow the devaluation. Devaluation may thus lead in this way to a vicious circle.

15.6 The Structuralist Critique: Devaluation, Distributive Effects, and GDP Contraction

In an often cited article, Krugman and Taylor (1978) have argued against the universal conclusion that devaluation triggers an expansionary growth effect (in the presence of underutilized resources) or a price rise (in case of full employment). They underline in particular that such a debate ignores the distributive effects of devaluation, and that these could cause a contraction of GDP even in the presence of an improvement of the current account balance. This may be due to three factors, which are discussed in the following three subsections.

Devaluation in the presence of a deficit of the current account balance

Let us assume that the current account balance is in equilibrium, the international terms of trade, P_x/P_m, are constant, and exporters benefit from devaluation as the pass-through is not reduced. In the short run, that is, before the volumes of X and M change, devaluation leaves things in equilibrium, as the increase in domestic currency prices concerns imports and exports equally. While there is a redistribution of income from the consumer of imported goods to exporters, the overall national income does not change. However, even if the Marshall–Lerner condition applies, in all cases in which the value of exports is lower than that of imports, the devaluation of the exchange rate may worsen the current account balance and induce a fall in GDP. Indeed, whenever $X p_x < M p_{m}/e^{\$/nc}$, the price increase will be felt more strongly for imports than for exports. There will therefore be a negative income effect in the country analysed and a positive income effect abroad. The reason is that household income, after paying for the imported goods which are now more costly, will decline. This income effect will reduce the aggregate demand for domestically produced goods and will therefore have a contractionary effect on output that will rise in proportion to the deficit of the current account balance. In the short term, there will be both a worsening of the current account balance (which will change over the medium term if $|e_x| + |e_m| > 1$) and a contraction of GDP.

Impact of devaluation on the distribution of income

Even when the current account balance is in equilibrium, devaluation can generate a contractionary effect on aggregate demand and output for the following reason. If money wages are sticky or fixed over the short–medium term, the rise in domestic prices of imported goods and exportables sold on the domestic market caused by devaluation erodes the real wage and real money supply, while it will raise profits in the export sector.[7] If the propensity to save of profit recipients is greater than that of wage-earners, then aggregate demand will drop in the short term, triggering a contractionary output effect.

These conclusions can be exacerbated if the asset concentration is high. Indeed, if the asset distribution is highly unequal and exports originate mainly from large agricultural farms such as *latifundia* relying on wage labour (instead of from small peasant farms) or capital intensive firms, devaluation shifts the distribution of income in favour of profits and rents. This is the case, for instance, of the exports of cocoa in Côte d' Îvoire and tea in Kenya or of the exports of capital-intensive mining companies. In fact, while devaluation raises the domestic prices and volumes in the tradable sector, nominal wages remain constant due to an infinitely elastic labour supply. Meanwhile real wages decline due to the rise of the domestic prices of tradable goods induced by devaluation. If—as noted above—the saving propensity of profit and rent earners is greater than that of workers, there will be a contractionary effect, the magnitude of which grows in proportion to the difference between the two saving propensities and the extent of asset concentration in the export sector.[8]

Devaluation and the shift of income from the private sector to the government

Whenever a country relies on *ad valorem* import taxes, devaluation redistributes income from the private sector to the state treasury. Indeed, in the short term (when M and p_m

[7] This is not true if wages are fully and instantaneously indexed. This is, however, seldom the case, and even in a case of full *ex post* indexation, the wage earners always lose some of their purchasing power between two indexations.

[8] Naturally this contractionary effect can be partly offset whenever the devaluation leads to a medium-term expansion of X—once the J-curve effects are over.

remain constant), the domestic currency value of $Mp_m/e^{\$/nc}$ rises due to the devaluation of $e^{\$/nc}$ (which falls, pushing upward $Mp_m/e^{\$/nc}$). The revenue generated by the *ad valorem* import tax T_m[9] also increases and this contributes to reduce the net income of households while increasing the revenue accruing to the treasury. The same effect occurs if the income tax on profits and rents in the export sector is progressive, generating additional tax revenue as compared to the pre-devaluation situation while, at the same time, reducing real household incomes. Thus, whenever the tax system has such features, devaluation causes a transfer of income from households to the state treasury. If the government and the households had the same short-term propensity to consume, nothing would change in terms of the level of the overall aggregate demand (as the drop of C would be compensated by an increase in G). However, over the short term, the government has a propensity to save equal to one,[10] and this reduces over the short-term aggregate demand and the level of GDP.

All this has led Krugman and Taylor (1978, 454–5) to argue that, while the role of devaluation in correcting medium-term balance of payments disequilibria cannot be ignored, it is equally true that the short-term adjustments of the CA achieved by means of devaluation may be costly in terms of reduced output, even in the presence of an improvement of the current account balance. If this structuralist analysis is correct, and it must be underscored in this regard that it depends on a number of restrictive assumptions, the policymaker would be faced with a *trade-off* between an improvement of the CA on the one side and GDP stagnation on the other. This has led these authors to suggest that instead of devaluing, governments may choose to finance the short-term deficit of the current account by borrowing abroad while trying to improve the medium-term export performance by removing the structural rigidities that constrain export expansion by means of subsidies, preferential credit arrangements, investments in infrastructure, and import substitution policies.

15.7 Evidence on the Impact of Devaluation on the Current Account Balance

The prior discussion suggests that in developing countries the impact of devaluation is not necessarily expansionary and that its results depend on the characteristics of each country and the circumstances leading to the exchange rate devaluation. The empirical literature offers some evidence based on the experience of several countries (Kamin and Klau, 1997): first, devaluation is not expansionary, and can even be contractionary over the short term, but tends to be neutral or expansionary over the long term. For instance, during episodes of macroeconomic stabilization in twenty-eight Latin American countries, real devaluation reduced GDP over the short term and started to produce its anticipated effects only after two or more years, a finding that raises thorny questions about the political sustainability of such a measure.

[9] This would not occur if the taxes on imports were not calculated *ad valorem* but on the import volume.

[10] Over the medium term, the government generally has a higher propensity to consume than the households. However, short-term unexpected revenue increases lead to a rise of public savings, given that all new expenditures have to be authorized by parliament-approved modifications of the budget law that take place only rarely.

However, from a methodological perspective it is not clear whether the GDP contraction observed over the short term was due to devaluation as such—or to the prior recession which led to the decision to devalue the currency. This is a problem of attribution of causality. Subsequent studies have suggested that most results of cross-sectional analyses on the effects of devaluation are subject to important restrictions, given that they do not always distinguish the short-term effects from the medium–long-term effects. They also do not adequately control for the influence of those shocks that simultaneously cause economic contraction and—as a response to it—devaluation, leading at times to spurious correlations. Furthermore, several analyses do not sufficiently emphasize the differences in results between regions, even though it is well known that the overall policy approach and the results of devaluation have—historically—varied considerably across regions. In addition, such analyses do not explicitly consider the possibility of reverse causation, that is, that slow growth may trigger a devaluation. These authors have therefore carried out a panel regression analysis with regional dummies and separated out the short- and long-term effects of devaluation. Their results show that devaluation does not engender a contractionary effect in the long run—which means that the current account balance can be improved without loss of output and employment. However, they also find that devaluation can be contractionary over the short term. This effect was more pronounced in Latin America than in East Asia and the industrialized countries.

15.8 Devaluation under Open Capital Account Conditions

The analyses presented so far have exclusively focused on the impact of devaluation on the current account, while neglecting that on the capital account. However, during the last three decades, liberalization of the capital account (see Table 2.8) has led to a situation in which the fluctuation of the exchange rate and the effects of devaluation are—to a large extent—determined by capital account considerations. Two notable effects of devaluation concern macroeconomic credibility and the effects on unhedged foreign exchange liabilities.

When aiming to restore confidence as part of an overall macroeconomic strategy, including appropriate monetary and fiscal policies, devaluation of a managed exchange rate to a level perceived by the markets to be close to its equilibrium level may have an expansionary impact, as it is likely to stimulate new inflows of foreign capital. However, if devaluation is perceived as a measure dictated by panic and not capable of restoring confidence, it will trigger capital outflow and further self-fulfilling devaluations. In countries where the exchange rate policy pivots around a fixed peg (which was supposed to remain stable for decades), nominal devaluation entails a major loss of credibility by the monetary authority, which may generate a loss of confidence among foreign investors and a reversal of capital flows.

In developing countries where domestic agents (banks, government, firms, and households) have short-term unhedged hard currency exposures, devaluation raises the domestic currency cost of servicing foreign debt, leading to compression of other types of public and private expenditures. All this generates deflationary effects. As far as firms with uninsured foreign debts are concerned, devaluation can have devastating effects on their balance sheets, making it impossible for them to reimburse overdue loans, or causing a profit compression which reduces their investments.

In case of company bankruptcies, other components of aggregate demand (e.g. private consumption) will also decline. In turn, households who borrowed in hard currency at lower interest rates to finance the purchase of housing face similar problems, as devaluation raises the domestic currency cost of servicing monthly repayments of hard currency loans in proportion to the devaluation of the exchange rate. These households may become unable to service their mortgage and face repossession of their houses by the lending domestic banks. If the latter are affected by a large increase in non-performing hard currency loans, and are forced to repossess the real estate assets received as collateral, they will face a rising risk of bankruptcy: indeed, the value of an increasing number of repossessed assets will decline because of a glut in supply. This is what happened in Eastern Europe during the 2008–09 crisis, but it has also been seen in well managed economies such as Finland where there was a major banking crisis in 1991–93. This resulted in many bankruptcies, housing repossessions, an 18 per cent fall in GDP and a rise in unemployment of similar proportions as the devaluation of the Finnish Markka made it impossible for many households and firms to service their Deutsche mark or US dollar loans. Thus, contrary to the standard case, if countries have large unhedged hard currency exposure, devaluation tends to be contractionary, while an appreciation of the exchange rate tends to be expansionary as it reduces the domestic currency cost of reimbursing foreign debt. The exchange rate appreciation may, however, negatively affect exports over the medium term. In addition, the relative lack of liquidity affecting the banking sector in the aftermath of a large devaluation and the increase in defaults and housing repossessions hamper the financing of exporting firms that may, in principle, profit from devaluation. This was the experience of Indonesia in 1997–98 in the aftermath of the Asian crisis and the huge devaluation of the rupiah. Furthermore, on the occasion of the 1997 Indonesian and Thai crises, large dollar exposures led to a temporary over-devaluation of the exchange rate which caused several negative effects on the real economy, as the domestic currency costs of imported investment goods and essential intermediate inputs skyrocketed.

While single agents may insure themselves by means of derivative contracts, the effects described above *de facto* narrow the choices of policymakers who fear that devaluation may cause large capital account problems, defaults, and a contraction of the real economy. Thus, rather than correcting current account imbalances by devaluing the exchange rate, some countries prefer to raise interest rates, in order to reduce domestic activity and imports, and thereby improve the position of the trade balance. Alternatively, they may dollarize. This decision, however, may cause deflationary effects and lead to output and employment losses greater than those occurring due to a hypothetical devaluation.

15.9 Exchange Rate Regimes in Developing Countries

In a world economy ever more integrated through flows of trade and finance, the exchange rate plays a key policy role. The choice of an exchange rate regime suitable to a country's domestic conditions therefore constitutes one of the key macroeconomic decisions of every developing country. In general terms, it can be argued that such choice has a triple objective: promote the growth of exports and the real economy; prevent the collapse of the exchange rate when faced with speculative attacks in financially integrated economies; and prevent the instability of capital movements.[11]

Until the early 2000s, the dominant viewpoint concerning the choice of the exchange rate regime was that, to reach these three objectives, developing countries had to choose between one of the two 'corner solutions', that is, a hard peg or a free float, while avoiding intermediate regimes. However, the discussion that follows shows that this theoretical stance is not supported by empirical evidence of the relative efficiency of alternative exchange rate regimes adopted *de jure* or *de facto*. As a result, since the early 2000s a growing number of developing countries has adopted intermediate managed regimes (Table 15.2), as neither corner solutions enabled them to reach the three objectives mentioned above. In contrast, advanced countries have increasingly adopted free floating regimes. The main features and principal advantages and disadvantages of the major exchange rate regimes are reviewed hereafter.

Table 15.2 Share of alternative exchange rate regimes, 1970–1979 to 2009–2016

	1970–1979	1980–1989	1990–1999	2008–2011	2009–2016
Fixed	84.8	68.4	46.6	12.7	13.0
Managed	11.0	22.5	26.4	39.3	42.5
Free float	4.3	9.1	27.0	38.1	35.0
Others	—	—	—	9.9	9.5

Note: The data in the table refer to period averages in per cent.
Source: Excerpted from Ghosh et al. (2004) for the first three columns and from the IMF AREAER database for the last two.

Fixed peg regimes

After the collapse of the Bretton Woods system in 1971, fixed peg regimes have steadily declined and now represent only around 13 per cent of all exchange rate arrangements (Table 15.2). The main types of fixed pegs regimes are: dollarization, currency boards, and traditional fixed pegs.

With dollarization, the dollar, euro, or other strong currency becomes a country's legal tender. In small developing countries prone to external shocks and lacking a real monetary base (that is, an adequate production of tradable goods), dollarization has the advantage of avoiding the free fall and high volatility of the exchange rate; of eliminating exchange rate risk in international trade and financial transactions; and of ensuring policy credibility. For instance, El Salvador and Ecuador use the US dollar as their legal tender. In turn, the currency used in Kosovo and Montenegro is the euro. In addition, fifteen countries of West and Central Africa are part of the CFA franc currency area that is pegged to the euro. The main problems of this approach are that the dollarized country completely loses control of

[11] Other policy objectives which are often assigned to the exchange rate policy are control of inflation and equilibrium of the external accounts.

its exchange rate and monetary policy which have to follow passively those of the anchor country. This can be especially damaging if the currency of the anchor country appreciates. In addition, with a loss of control over these two policy instruments, the policymaker can tackle external shocks and re-establish its competitiveness only by reducing the domestic cost of production—that is by cutting wages, diminishing corporate taxes, and reducing the costs of electricity and other utilities. This adjustment approach is labelled 'internal devaluation' and has been applied over 2008–10 by the Baltic countries that had earlier adopted the euro as their legal tender (Purfield and Rosenberg, 2010). However, cutting domestic production costs is often a slow process, and one likely to meet political and labour opposition. It requires a strong government and the cooperation of trade unions to accept the wage compression and rise in unemployment inherent in the macroeconomic approach to stabilization typical of dollarized countries.

The problems entailed by dollarization become especially severe when the business cycles of the anchor country and the dollarized country are not synchronized. This is a common occurrence, given that developing and advanced countries tend to be hit by different types of booms and shocks. For instance, GDP will contract whenever the anchor country raises interest rates to control the overheating of its economy, while the dollarized country may need to cut them to fight a recession. Lastly, with dollarization the central bank no longer plays the role of lender of last resort (as it cannot print money), a role which must therefore be assumed by the fiscal authority.

In the case of currency boards, the national currency is the legal tender. This, however, is linked at a fixed and unchangeable parity set by law to an anchor currency. The domestic monetary base in circulation must be supported by a high proportion (or identical amount) of deposits denominated in the currency of the anchor country at the central bank. In extreme cases (as in Estonia prior to its entry into the euro in early 2011), the currency board did not allow the government to issue public debt instruments, which meant that public expenditure had to be equal or lower than current government revenue. The proponents of this approach underscore that this regime guarantees credibility, transparency, low inflation, and (by eliminating the risk of devaluation) low interest rates. While these constitute important advantages, especially in countries (such as those of Latin America and the European economies in transition) that previously experienced episodes of fiscal populism, hyperinflation, and a steady slippage of the exchange rate.

But currency boards also present considerable problems. To start with, the central bank must hold a huge amount of highly liquid foreign reserves. Second, external shocks cannot be tackled by devaluing the exchange rate while the central bank cannot print money and play the role of lender of last resort. Furthermore, such a system does not work well in the absence of a rigorous fiscal policy (which was lacking, for example, in Argentina in the 1990s) or when the adoption of the currency board entails an initial appreciation of the real exchange rate and a drop in exports, as has been observed in several Latin American countries in the past. Such appreciation threatens the sustainability of the currency board itself. Currency boards can also cause savings disincentives due to the high liquidity of the banking system, and demand a flexible labour market facilitating the compression of the wage rate to absorb external shocks, especially if these do not affect the anchor country, without incurring a large increase in unemployment.

In the traditional fixed peg regimes, the nominal value of the national currency is set at a given parity in relation to a single reference currency or to a known or undisclosed currency basket, in which the share of each currency is generally proportional to the share of trade of each trading partner in the total. This approach reduces the volatility of the exchange rate while at the same time it leaves the fiscal, monetary, and exchange rate policy in the hands of national policymakers. In particular, such an approach leaves open the possibility of devaluing in response to large shocks. In addition, contrary to the two prior regimes, a fixed peg regime does not automatically impose restrictions on the fiscal and monetary policy and thus provides a partial solution to the problem of inter-temporal consistency of economic policies. Yet, its credibility is strictly dependent on the supporting measures adopted in the fiscal and monetary domain and on past macroeconomic management. In addition, the adoption of such a regime could cause an initial appreciation of the real exchange rate which, in the presence of free capital movements, could become the object of speculative attacks.

Intermediate (or managed) regimes

Intermediate (or managed) exchange rate regimes include the crawling peg, target fluctuation bands, and dirty floats. With the adoption of a crawling peg, the nominal exchange rate fluctuates according to a predetermined rule set in relation to the anchor currency or to an anchor currencies basket. Such a rule may entail, for example, that the nominal exchange rate depreciates by a pre-determined amount or—more frequently—by the inflation differential vis-à-vis the anchor country or countries. In this way it leaves the real exchange rate unchanged. This regime (in some cases dubbed 'stable and competitive real exchange rate' (SCRER)) is often followed in countries that try to reduce inflation gradually by leaving the real exchange rate unchanged, in order to avoid penalizing exports and growth prospects (Rodrik, 2003; Frenkel, 2008). In a world with free capital movements, however, such an approach may become the object of speculative attacks, and its stability then depends on the credibility of the accompanying fiscal, monetary, and capital control measures (Williamson, 2003).

With the introduction of target fluctuation bands, the nominal exchange rate fluctuates freely within a preset band ranging between +/− 2.5 and, at most, +/− 5/10 per cent, of the central parity. When the exchange rate reaches the upper or lower limit of the fluctuation band, the central bank intervenes in the foreign exchange market by buying or selling hard currency to support the central parity. In cases of extreme shocks, the monetary authority may reset the central parity. Such a system assigns some role to the currency market in balancing the effect of external shocks, but could become the object of speculative attacks as by itself it does not constrain fiscal and monetary policies which—if they are perceived as inconsistent with the exchange rate policy—may affect the credibility of the latter.

With the 'dirty float' (i.e. a managed exchange rate with discretionary interventions) the exchange rate is determined by the currency market, and not by a fixed parity, with or without fluctuation bands. Indeed, the public authorities intervene in the currency market by buying and selling hard currency to influence the exchange rate without being constrained by any pre-determined rule. In many cases, such a regime targets a predetermined inflation rate. The system does not by itself constrain the monetary and fiscal policies which, as noted, are generally used to target inflation.

Floating exchange rates

A regime of floating exchange rates is generally adopted by countries with a strong currency that is rarely affected by large fluctuations. These countries respond to shocks by letting the currency freely adjust in the currency market, thus eliminating the need to accumulate large foreign exchange reserves at the central bank. However, this regime does not provide an anchor to expectations about the future value of the exchange rate, and can therefore discourage international trade. In developing countries, a free floating regime is prone to the risk of over-devaluations, imported inflation and new devaluations, especially when the fiscal and monetary policy is inconsistent, setting in motion an 'inflation–devaluation–inflation' spiral. For low income countries competing on the world market for the export of the same type of primary products, a free float represents an intrinsically unstable system which pushes these countries to introduce competitive devaluations which affect negatively trade relations. Lastly, a free float can lead to costly over-devaluations or a free fall of the exchange rate, with devastating effects on the balance sheets of the entities with large unhedged foreign currency liabilities.

15.10 Relative Efficiency of Alternative Exchange Rate Regimes

Table 15.3 presents a comparative assessment of the growth, inflation, and balance of payments performance of various types of exchange rate regimes declared to the IMF by the member states (*de jure exchange rates*) or classified as 'effective' by IMF staff (*de facto exchange rates*).[12]

Table 15.3 Performance of different types of exchange rate regimes, 1970–2001

Classification	Fixed peg or similar	Limited flexibility	Managed exchange rate	Floating exchange rate	Free falling
	Average annual inflation rate				
Classification *de jure*	38.8 (2)	5.3 (1)	74.8 (3)	173.9 (4)	n.a.
Classification *de facto*	15.9 (3)	10.1 (2)	16.5 (4)	9.4 (1)	443.3 (5)
	Average annual growth rate of GDP				
Classification *de jure*	1.4 (3)	2.2 (1)	1.9 (2)	0.5 (4)	n.a.
Classification *de facto*	1.9 (3)	2.4 (1)	1.6 (4)	2.3 (2)	−2.5 (5)
	Exports + Imports as % of GDP				
Classification *de jure*	69.9 (2)	81.0 (1)	65.8 (3)	60.6 (4)	n.a.
Classification *de facto*	78.7 (2)	80.3 (1)	61.2 (3)	44.9 (5)	57.1 (4)
Overall score, *de jure*	7 (2)	3 (1)	8 (3)	12 (4)	—
Overall score, *de facto*	8 (2)	4 (1)	11 (4)	8 (2)	14 (5)

Note: The numbers in parentheses indicate the rank of the exchange rate regime.
Source: Adapted from Reinhart and Rogoff (2003).

[12] The *de facto* exchange rate is identified by IMF analyses of changes in reserve levels and interest rates, that is, measures that suggest the existence of interventions to support the exchange rate in spite of its supposed free fluctuation.

Table 15.3 shows that the countries which adopted limited flexibility regimes (crawling pegs with a pre-established rule and target oscillation bands) show a better performance in terms of growth, inflation, and foreign trade than other regimes. Such a conclusion also broadly holds when adopting a *de facto* classification, even though the distance in performance between the various regimes becomes smaller. Furthermore, the ranking of inflation performance changes slightly. However, the most important point to note is that, when moving to the *de facto* classification, the countries that adopted a free floating exchange rate achieved results that were no worse than those achieved with a fixed peg. These results provide only limited empirical proof (and must therefore be interpreted with an element of caution) as they refer to heterogeneous countries and concern average values over long periods of time characterized by marked differences in capital mobility.

Be that as it may, a review of the literature by Helleiner (2014) suggests that exchange rates typically matter much more than other trade policies (such as trade barriers, preferential country treatment, aid for trade, and so on) at least over the short- to medium-term. Indeed, real exchange rates vary far more than trade taxes, subsidies, and trade barriers. Among the various exchange rates, Rodrik (2003) suggests that while there is no unique solution, a managed, stable, and competitive real exchange rate promotes employment in the tradable sector (where the poor are often employed), kick-starts growth, generates equitable effects, and strengthens the current account balance.

15.11 Objectives of Alternative Exchange Rate Regimes

What should be the long-term objectives of the exchange rate policies discusssed above? The answer varies from case to case, but several general considerations apply. Indeed, one can distinguish three main policy objectives and related approaches. The first (the Nominal Anchor Approach) is recommended by those who believe that the exchange rate should mainly be an anchor against inflation. The second (the Real Targets Approach) assigns to the exchange rate the role of achieving equilibrium of the balance of payments. The third (the Real Exchange Rate Stability Approach) aims to preserve a real and competitive exchange rate.

The Nominal Anchor Approach

The main objective of the Nominal Anchor Approach is price stability, that is, low inflation, especially low imported inflation. In view of the strong constraints they impose on monetary policy (Section 15.10), fixed peg regimes allow policymakers to pursue a policy of financial integration and exchange rate stability. As noted, however, in all these cases public policy cannot influence the level of domestic output through variations of the exchange rate. When the latter is fixed, a deficit of the balance of payments leads to a drop in money supply and a slowdown in inflation, as shown by the Mundell–Fleming model (see Chapter 3).

This approach presents some advantages, especially for small open economies with high import/GDP ratios. However, such benefits must be compared with the initial appreciation of the real exchange rate which follows the adoption of the fixed peg due to the slow convergence of the domestic inflation rate to that of the anchor country. Over the long term, such initial real appreciation may lead to the collapse of the exchange rate regime due to the slow growth of output caused by the appreciation of the real exchange rate. Other problems concern the need to accumulate huge foreign exchange reserves, to unload onto the labour market and the treasury the asymmetric shocks which may hit the economy, and the lack of synchronization of the country's business cycle with that of the anchor country.

The Real Target Approach

The Real Target Approach aims to achieve one of the two key objectives of macroeconomic policy: internal equilibrium (low inflation and budget deficit) and external equilibrium (no deficit of the balance of payments). These objectives are pursued through an appropriate fine-tuning of fiscal-monetary and exchange rate policies, with the latter focusing on the external equilibrium.

A floating exchange rate allows policymakers to achieve the objective of financial integration and an independent monetary policy, as the effects of decisions concerning M and r, as well as changes in Y are unloaded onto the exchange rate, which may become somewhat volatile, with possible effects on the real economy. Such a regime should also allow an interest rate policy different from that of the world reserve country, the United States, to be adopted. Yet, the empirical evidence shows that—with the exception of a few large industrialized countries—in most developing countries the domestic interest rates closely follow those of the United States, independently of their exchange rate regime, thus suggesting that even the real target approach does not allow countries to conduct an independent monetary policy.

The Real Exchange Rate Stability Approach

The Real Exchange Rate Stability Approach underscores the fact that the instability of the real exchange rate is not due to changes in macroeconomic fundamentals (which the policymaker can control by means of the usual policy instruments) but to expectations about its future value. For this reason, a completely free floating exchange rate could generate damaging effects on the growth of exports, output, and employment. The objective of stabilizing the real exchange rate could be reached by manipulating the domestic interest rate, but this approach may have negative effects on the real economy. For this reason, the policymaker focuses instead on credibly stabilizing the real exchange rate and expectations about its future value. An exchange rate regime which permits such an objective to be achieved is the BBC (basket, band, and crawl) regime. In this approach—which belongs to the class of intermediate regimes discussed above—the policymaker of a developing country first sets the nominal exchange rate in relation to a basket of the currencies of the main trading partners on the basis of the PPP approach. Subsequently, the nominal exchange rate is allowed to fluctuate within a pre-determined band so as to neutralize small shocks. The policymaker may, however, alter the central exchange parity by devaluing/appreciating it in case of large shocks which could raise inflation and trigger a substantial change in the real exchange rate—with negative effects on the tradable sector.

Sustaining a Stable and Competitive Real Exchange Rate (SCRER) is an essential component of the development strategy of the roughly one hundred small and medium-sized developing countries which sell only part of their output on their narrow domestic market. A competitive exchange rate encourages firms to sell an important share of their traditional and new tradable goods on the world market, and subsequently invest in new equipment and employ new workers. The evidence shows that the growth take-off of many developing countries coincided with the adoption of a competitive real exchange rate (Rodrik, 2003).

The need to sustain a competitive exchange rate is thus essential in developing countries to reduce widespread poverty and deal with strong fluctuations in export receipts caused by changes in international terms of trade or climatic shocks, which could lead to devastating over-devaluations whenever the exchange rate fluctuates freely. These countries cannot count on a strong demand for their financial assets denominated in domestic currency and would therefore benefit little from the financial credibility and disciplining effect supposedly associated with fixed peg regimes.

Maintaining a competitive real exchange rate and avoiding its real appreciation are therefore an essential component of a policy relying on the promotion of exports, investments, and growth. Capital inflows could, in principle, augment the overall investment rate. However, they may also cause a real appreciation which would be mainly determined in the market for financial assets. Which policies can prevent real appreciation? The Williamson (2003) menu includes measures that control/limit capital inflows, and that offset their effects on the expansion of domestic money supply.

Among the first, one should include the Chilean-style compulsory deposit for a year (or similar period) on non-interest bearing central bank accounts of a share (say, 50 per cent) of the capital inflow, regardless of the maturity of the domestic securities purchased. The first group of measures also includes limits on domestic banks' dollar exposure and borrowing abroad to lend money to firms in the non-tradable sector, and the removal of all tax incentives and subsidies for foreign investors.

In turn, the measures aiming to offsett the expansion of money supply generated by speculative capital inflows include the demand that state-controlled domestic financial institutions shift their deposits from commercial banks to the central bank (as observed in the past in Singapore), and the sterilization of capital inflows through the issuance of state bonds. However, sterilization can be quite costly. Indeed, the interest rate paid by the central bank on the domestic bonds it issues to sterilize dollar inflows is higher than the interest rate (corrected for the expectation of exchange rate variations) on US bonds in which the central bank invest the sterilized dollar inflows. The central bank can also raise the compulsory reserve ratio of commercial banks with large foreign deposits, liberalize capital outflows, and encourage the domestic financial institutions (e.g. pension funds) to invest part of their deposits abroad, as observed in the past in Chile.

15.12 The Impossible Trinity

The Impossible Trinity Theorem (Mundell, 1963) states that it is impossible to pursue simultaneously policies of a fixed exchange rate, free capital movements, and an independent monetary policy characterized by interest rates differing from the world rate. Such a theory is based on the uncovered interest rate parity condition which states that, in the absence of interest rate spreads (measuring country risk), arbitragers will ensure that a country currency will depreciate or appreciate vis-à-vis another currency for an amount equal to the difference between their nominal interest rates. Under a fixed exchange rate, the model implies that the two countries' nominal interest rates will be equalized, with the interest rate of the country with a fixed peg adjusting to that of the anchor country. This implies that the pegging country has no ability to develop an autonomous monetary policy and set its nominal interest rate independently. The only way a country could have both a fixed exchange rate and an independent monetary policy is to prevent arbitrage in the foreign exchange rate market by introducing capital controls.

What happens if a country tries to pursue all three policy objectives at once? Let us consider the case of a nation with a fixed exchange rate and open capital account that introduces an expansionary monetary policy to stimulate its slow growing economy. The ensuing increase in domestic money supply leads to a fall in the domestic interest rate below the world rate. Due to the fixing of the exchange rate, domestic agents may shift their financial assets abroad after converting their domestic currency into hard currency, depressing the level of the central bank's and commercial banks' reserves. Likewise, foreign economic agents may borrow in the country's pegged currency, sell the borrowed currency for hard currency at a fixed exchange rate, and then lend these moneys abroad at a higher interest rate. Also in this case, the level of domestic currency reserves would decline. With no capital controls, domestic and foreign agents may do this on a massive scale. As the nation has a fixed exchange rate, it will defend its pegged rate and sell its hard currency reserves to buy back its national currency. But, the international markets will continue to sell domestic currency until the pegged country's foreign exchange reserves are depleted, a fact that will cause a breakdown of the fixed peg and a devaluation of the currency.

The fixed peg may also break down in the opposite situation, that is, when a country has higher interest rates than the world rate. Given the stability of the exchange rate, this will attract speculative capital from abroad to benefit from the interest rate differential. As long as the trade balance is positive, the policymaker can afford to adopt a fixed peg, free capital movement, and an independent monetary policy. But if the trade balance deteriorates, the foreign investors perceive that the currency reserves will soon be exhausted. They will therefore convert their portfolios of domestic bonds into dollars and exit the country. Given the volume of these transactions, currency reserves at the central bank may be quickly exhausted and the country will have to abandon the fixed peg and devalue. This sequence of events occurred in 1997 in Thailand when its currency, the bath, was pegged to an appreciating US dollar.

Given the limitations imposed by the Impossible Trinity, which options concerning the exchange rate, capital controls, and an independent monetary policy can be pursued by developing countries? There are three possibilities, illustrated in Figure 15.3: option 'a' relies on a stable exchange rate and free capital flows, but not on an independent monetary policy that has to follow that of the anchor country; instead, in option 'b' the country adopts an independent monetary policy and free capital movement but no stable exchange rate; and third, in option 'c' the country chooses a stable exchange rate and an independent monetary policy but no free capital movements that will need to be controlled. After the numerous financial crises of the 1990s, 2000s, and 2010s (Figure 2.3) this last option is becoming increasingly more common.

The prior conclusions concerning a surge of free capital inflows under a fixed exchange rate and with an independent monetary policy need not apply universally or may apply

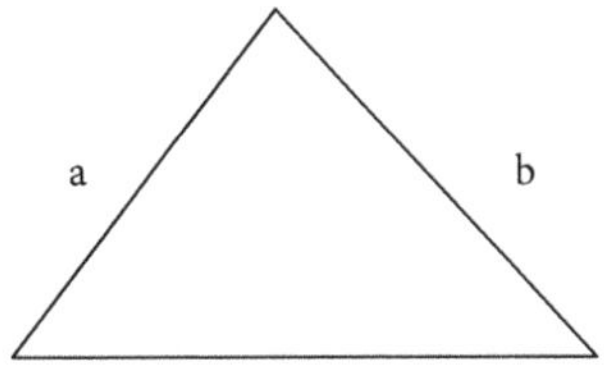

Figure 15.3 Pairs of policy options under the impossible trinity scenario
Source: Oxelheim (1990)

only in part. Taylor (2008) distinguishes three situations, depending on how the capital inflows are modelled. In the first scenario, the increasing demand for domestic bonds linked to capital inflows would normally be associated with a reduction in the domestic interest rate. However, the interest rate may increase if the inflows are preceded or accompanied by a contractionary monetary policy or by a strong increase in economic activity which generates a growing demand for money. Thus, the domestic monetary policy would no longer be independent, but would result in a rise rather than a fall in the interest rate.

In the second scenario, the receiving country's interest rate (which is generally much higher than that of the originating country of the capital inflows) may not be affected because of a 100 per cent sterilization of the capital inflows. Indeed, the central bank and the commercial banks may issue an increasing level of domestic bonds and securities to mop up the increase in money supply caused by the capital inflow. This results in an increase of the foreign assets in the domestic banking sector but also in a surge in the volume of its domestic bond liabilities. In this case, a 100 per cent sterilization of the inflows leaves domestic interest rates and the fixed exchange rate unchanged in spite of free capital movements, thus contradicting the conclusions of the Impossible Trinity. Yet, sterilized interventions through open market sales of government securities or central bank bills prevent the domestic–international interest rate differential from narrowing and may even attract further inflows. In addition, sterilization has significant quasi-fiscal costs (see Section 15.9). Other measures to control the domestic money supply in the presence of an increase in capital inflows are discussed at the end of Section 15.11 and include an increase in the reserve ratio of commercial banks as observed in several countries of Asia and Pacific (Hossain and Chouwdhury, 1998).

Finally, in a third modelling of the impact of capital inflows, Taylor (2008) assumes that the exchange rate is endogenous and is allowed to float, thus coming to the same conclusions as the Impossible Trinity Theorem, that shows (as in Thailand in 1997) that the exchange rate will appreciate as a result of an increasing demand for domestic currency in exchange for US dollars, until a crisis erupts.

In conclusion, the first modelling approach suggests that an interest rate increase after a capital inflow may be due to a restrictive monetary policy and high level of economic activity. In the second approach there should be a degree of automatic and policy-driven sterilization after the inflow. The last approach shows that capital inflows lead to an appreciation of the exchange rate, in this case coming to a conclusion in line with the Impossible Trinity Theorem. Taylor notes that—during the last three decades of the twentieth century—policymakers operated somewhere amongst these three options.

15.13 The Case for Stabilizing the Exchange Rate through Capital Controls

The negative impact of uncontrolled capital movements

The Bretton Woods Agreement of 1944 was influenced—*inter alia*—by the criticism of the liberal financial order that had prevailed until the early 1930s. Capital movements were in fact seen as a key source of financial instability and a contributor to the collapse of the world economy in the 1930s. The Agreement strongly defended the countries' rights to manage their capital accounts (Ocampo, 2015). In other words, cross-border capital movements should not have been allowed to disrupt the policy autonomy of states to fix interest rates according to domestic priorities such as the search for full employment. The liberal financial order was also seen as incompatible with the search for stable exchange rates, which were essential for the reconstruction of international trade in the post-war years (Ocampo, 2015). The liberalization of cross-country capital flows resumed in the United States in 1974 and then spread to the rest of the advanced economies in the subsequent fifteen years (Table 2.8). This new bout of financial liberalization coincided with the recycling of petrodollars after the oil price hikes of 1973 and 1978. At the theoretical level, the liberalization of international capital flows was justified by the benefits it would have generated in terms of a better world allocation of global savings, the disciplining effect on the macroeconomic policies of countries receiving the inflows, and the portfolio diversification of investors in both developed and developing countries (see Chapter 10). Such a shift in policy gathered considerable consensus, and in 1997 the IMF attempted (without succeeding) to include capital account openness among its Articles of Agreement (Ocampo, 2015).

A major problem of portfolio flows and short-term bank lending turned out to be their extreme pro-cyclicality, which impacted the exchange rates volatility and the growth rate of GDP (Prasad et al., 2003). Even when capital flows were not the main cause of the crises, they played a central role in their propagation. Figure 10.5 illustrates the four boom–bust cycles of external financing experienced since the mid-1970s in emerging and developing countries due to a number of factors: the recycling of petrodollars; the large Mexican borrowing and ensuing crisis; the global financial expansion of 2003–07; and the massive expansion of liquidity by the central banks of major countries in response to the sub-prime loans crisis and collapse of Lehman Brothers (see Table 3.3). Given their relatively small share in global finance, emerging and developing countries are particularly sensitive to even small ripples in the financial markets of developed countries. The increasing use of derivatives has become an additional source of volatility. Although the accelerated growth of derivative markets has helped to reduce micro-instability, the creation of new hedging techniques that allow individual agents to cover their risks might have increased systemic macro-instability.

Countercyclical capital account regulations

The regulation of international capital flows is justified by the needs to broaden the policy space to introduce countercyclical monetary and exchange rate policies, and to correct financial market failures. During booms, capital account regulations allow policymakers to undertake contractionary monetary policies to avoid the appreciation of the exchange rate and the adverse effects on the tradable sector. During crises, they create room for expansionary monetary policies while avoiding capital flights, excessive exchange rate depreciation, inflation, and a rise in the debt/GDP ratio.

As in the case of domestic prudential regulations, the capital account regulations are price-based or depend on administrative controls. As already noted, the latter include prohibitions or ceilings on certain types of capital flows, derivatives, or net exposure in foreign currency by domestic banks; minimum stay periods; and restrictions on non-residents' purchases of domestic securities. In turn, price-based regulations include unremunerated reserve requirements on capital inflows and taxes on capital inflows or outflows that make them less attractive.

The capital account regulations may concern capital inflows, capital outflows, operations of the financial sector, and regulations on the use of foreign exchange (Ocampo, 2015). The first and second of these cover regulations across six types of financial assets, the third relates to different forms of discrimination between residents and non-residents (including granting the non-residents the right to hold domestic accounts), as well as limits on residents' capacity to borrow and hold accounts abroad. Finally, foreign exchange regulations concern restrictions on their domestic use, that is, lending locally in such currencies, purchasing locally issued securities denominated in foreign currency, limits on foreign exchange indebtedness, and managing the net foreign exchange exposure of domestic financial institutions. A policy such as this has been followed in Colombia for decades.

Figure 15.4 illustrates the frequency with which capital account regulations were introduced by fifty-one emerging and developing economies between 1995 and 2012. While most countries reduced regulations until the eruption of the Thai–Asian financial crisis of 1997, since then the trend has reversed. The most frequently used regulations were foreign exchange-related, followed by capital outflow restrictions, capital inflow restrictions, and financial sector regulations.

How effective are capital account regulations? Most of the literature is based on analysis of the individual countries that applied such regulations (Ostry et al., 2012). This literature

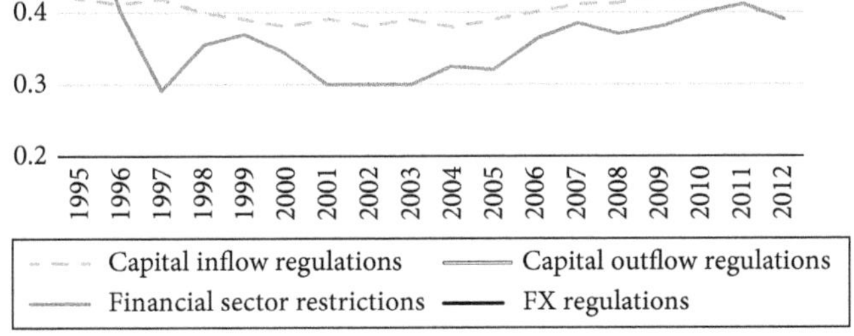

Figure 15.4 Frequency of introduction of different types of capital controls
Source: Erten and Ocampo (2013)

shows that capital account regulations lengthen the maturity of external debt obligations, increase monetary policy autonomy, and partly delink the effects of capital inflows on interest and exchange rates. Yet, so far, capital account regulations have generally acted as temporary speed bumps rather than permanent restrictions. Traditional administrative regulations may be better at reducing inflows than market-based regulations, as shown by the case of Malaysia in the mid-1990s. Similarly, the high tax on outflows introduced by Malaysia in 1998 is generally considered to have been very effective. Overall, there is significant evidence that these measures improve the composition of capital movements towards less reversible flows and increase monetary independence without sacrificing exchange rate objectives. The work by the IMF (Ostry et al., 2012) and other institutions has shown that countries with such regulations in place before the onset of the recent global financial turmoil were able to mitigate the contraction of GDP during the crisis.

To conclude this section, it is useful to take stock of the recommendations of Gallagher et al. (2012) concerning the desirable features of capital control regulations. In their view, these measures should be seen as a permanent part of a countercyclical macroeconomic policy aimed at smoothing financial booms and busts, and not as a temporary measure to be adopted in an emergency situation (see Chapter 18). They should also be seen as cheaper alternatives to the costly accumulation of foreign exchange reserves by means of the sterilization of capital inflows. Capital controls should adjust to new situations when investors try to circumvent them through mis-invoicing trade flows, derivative operations, and FDIs that are in fact debt flows, and should apply to both capital inflows and outflows. The last measure is a strong deterrent of undesirable inflows. Price-based regulations are more market neutral, but—as noted—the quantity-based ones may be more effective in nations with relatively closed capital accounts and weak central banks. The authors also note that the full burden of managing capital flows should not only fall on the receiving developing countries, but also on the source countries that ought to regulate excessive outflows of short-term capital, conscious of the negative global spillover effects of a crisis in developing countries triggered by their own weak policies on capital movements.

15.14 Concluding Remarks

The weakness of the external sector is a key factor conditioning long-term growth in many developing countries. Yet, the open economy macroeconomic models developed for advanced economies ignore several problematic features of the external sector of developing countries and, as such, cannot be satisfactorily used to provide policy guidance in these countries. Such models assume, in fact, that a country trades a single composite good, and so they ignore the composition of the economy between traded and non-traded goods and the impact of changes in the domestic terms of trade. Even more crucially, they ignore changes in the prices of imports and exports and the issue of changes of international terms of trade. And adverse changes in the ratio between domestic and foreign prices are always attributed to the introduction of domestic expansionary measures or to shocks. Changes in the international terms of trade, however, are in most cases determined by changes in world prices as, with rare exceptions, developing countries are small, dependent price-takers. To correct these modelling inadequacies, it is necessary to develop two- and three-sector macro models including non-tradables, exports, and imports. A second area of difference between developed and developing countries concerns the impact of a devaluation of the nominal exchange rate. While in advanced countries this is generally expected to improve growth and the trade balance, the situation is more complex in developing countries where devaluation may be contractionary (at least over the short term) and worsen the trade balance. This may be due to noncompliance with the Marshall–Lerner condition, J curve effects, pass through problems, lack of credibility, and distributive effects linked to the structure of such economies. As its impact may vary from one developing country to another, the policymaker should assess *ex ante* the pros and cons of devaluation. The latter is also problematic in countries that have received capital inflows under a hard peg exchange rate regime. Under this type of regime, devaluation entails a loss of credibility and increases the cost of servicing foreign public and private debt, with devastating effects on firms' and households' balance sheets and the allocation of government expenditure.

In the 1970s nearly all developing countries pegged their exchange rate to the dollar or the currency of their former colonial rulers. This type of exchange rate regime has declined substantially (but is still in operation in West and Central Africa), as there was a shift to different kinds of intermediate regimes allowing greater flexibility. Countries with a fixed exchange rate faced—and still face—the 'Impossible Trinity' problem, that is, an inability to pursue at the same time an independent monetary policy and free capital movements. The evidence shows that countries simultaneously pursuing these three policy objectives may witness a collapse of the exchange rate.

The choice of the optimal exchange rate is influenced by the economic structure of each developing country. For instance, for very small monocultural primary commodity exporters, dollarization may be the least costly approach. But in many small–medium developing countries with a narrow domestic market, a stable and competitive real exchange rate can be an important determinant of an increase in exports and the growth rate of GDP. Possible speculative attacks against this exchange rate regime can be moderated by means of temporary or permanent capital controls—that is, measures that are in any case often needed to prevent international financial crises. Indeed, while capital controls were gradually dismantled in the past, since the Thai–Asian crisis of 1997 they have become increasingly accepted from a theoretical perspective and are being introduced in a growing number of countries—with the blessing of the IMF.

References

Agénor, P. R. and P. Montiel (1999), *Development Macroeconomics*, 2nd edn. Princeton, NJ: Princeton University Press.

Frenkel, R. (2008), 'The Competitive Real Exchange Rate Regime, Inflation and Monetary Policy', *CEPAL Review*, 96: pp. 191–201.

Gallagher, K., S. Griffith-Jones, and J. A. Ocampo (2012), 'Capital Account Regulations for Stability and Development: A New Approach', in K. Gallagher, S. Griffith-Jones, and J. A. Ocampo (eds), *Regulating Global Capital Flows for Long-Run Development*. Boston: Boston University, Pardee Center for the Study of the Longer Range Future.

Ghosh, A., A. M. Gulde, and H. Wolf (2004), *Exchange Rate Regimes: Classification and Consequences*. Cambridge, MA: MIT Press.

Helleiner, G. (2014), 'Trade, Exchange Rates ad Global Poverty: Policies for the Poorest', in G. A. Cornia and F. Stewart (eds), *Towards Human Development: New Approaches to Macroeconomics and Inequality*. Oxford: Oxford University Press.

Hossain, A. and A. Chowdury (1998), *Open-Economy Macroeconomics for Developing Countries*, Cheltenam and Northampton, MA: Edward Elgar.

Kamin, S. B. and M. Klau (1997), 'Some Multi-Country Evidence on the Effects of Real Exchange Rate on Output'. Working Paper No.48. Basel: Bank for International Settlements.

Krugman, P. and M. Obstfeld (1988), *International Economics*. Glenview, IL: Scott, Foresman and Company.

Krugman P. and L. Taylor (1978), 'Contractionary Effects of Devaluation', *Journal of International Economics*, 8 (3): pp. 445–56.

Mundell, R. A. (1963), 'Capital mobility and stabilization policy under fixed and flexible exchange rates', *Canadian Journal of Economics and Political Science*, 29 (4): pp. 475–85.

Ocampo, J. A. (2015), 'Capital account liberalization and management', WIDER Working Paper 2015/048. Helsinki: World Institute for Development Economics Research.

Ocampo, J. A. (2017), *Resetting the International Monetary (Non) System*, WIDER Studies in Development Economics. Oxford: Oxford University Press.

Ostry, J. D., A. R. Ghosh, M. Chamon, and M. S. Qureshi (2012), 'Tools for Managing Financial-Stability Risks from Capital Inflows', *Journal of International Economics*, 88 (2): pp. 407–21.

Oxelheim, L. (1990), *International Financial Integration*. Heidelberg. Springer Verlag.

Prasad, E. S., K. Rogoff, S.-J. Wei, and M. A. Kose (2003), 'Effects of Financial Globalization on Developing Countries: Some Empirical Evidence'. Occasional Paper 220. Washington, DC: International Monetary Fund.

Purfield, C. and C. Rosenberg (2010), 'Adjustment under a Currency Peg: Estonia, Latvia and Lithuania during the Global Financial Crisis 2008–09', IMF Working Paper 10/2013, Washington, DC: International Monetary Fund.

Reinhart, C. and K. Rogoff (2003), 'A Modern History of Exchange Rate Arrangements: A Reinterpretation'. Mimeo, Washington, DC: International Monetary Fund.

Rodrik, D. (2003), 'Growth Strategies', Working Paper 2003–17, Linz: Department of Economics. Johannes Kepler University.

Taylor, L. (2008), 'A foxy hedgehog: Winne Godley and macroeconomic modelling', *Cambridge Journal of Economics*, 32: pp. 639–63.

Williamson, J. (2003), 'Exchange Rate Policies and Development', Working Paper for the Initiative for Policy Dialogue. New York: Columbia University.

Suggested Further Reading

Krugman, P. and L. Taylor (1978), 'Contractionary Effects of Devaluation', *Journal of International Economics*, 8 (3): pp. 445–56.

Ocampo, J. A. (2015), 'Capital account liberalization and management', WIDER Working Paper 2015/048. Helsinki: World Institute for Development Economics Research.

Rodrik, D. (2003), Growth Strategies, Working Paper 2003–17, Linz: Department of Economics. Johannes Kepler University.

PART IV

SPECIFIC MACROECONOMIC PROBLEMS FACED BY DEVELOPING COUNTRIES

16
Macroeconomic Stabilization in Developing Countries

This chapter discusses the issue of macroeconomic stabilization in developing countries, an issue that has generated considerable theoretical and political controversy. It presents the theory behind monetary models of stabilization in a closed and open economy which have inspired adjustment programmes supported by the IMF, the concrete measures adopted as part of this stabilization approach, and their pitfalls. Mention is also made of the criticism attracted by such an approach. The final section analyses the relation between orthodox stabilization and the incidence of poverty.

16.1 A Frequent Recourse to Macroeconomic Stabilization

Macroeconomic stabilization (a term used interchangeably with 'adjustment') has become a central component of the macro management and political economy of developing countries and transitional economies in the 1980s and 1990s, and of the developed nations since the onset of the 2007–08 sub-prime crisis and the 2010–14 European sovereign debt crisis. During the 1960s and 1970s the IMF initiated some twenty to thirty country stabilization programmes every year. However, with an increasingly more integrated and financialized world economy characterized by unstable commodity prices (Figure 5.2), the rapid spread of financial contagion among countries, and recurrent financial crises (Figure 2.3), the number of macroeconomic stabilization programmes has tripled. Nowhere has this issue been more important than in the fragile low-income countries. The rising frequency and cyclicality of IMF stabilization programmes is well illustrated by the fact that over 2008–12 (that is, in the aftermath of the sub-prime crisis) around fifty stabilization programmes were initiated every year. The emphasis on contractionary stabilization, typical of IMF conditionality, has unavoidably entailed a neglect of structural reforms and rekindled a heated debate. Only in 2008–09 did the IMF support policies based on an expansionary stabilization (Table 3.3). Macroeconomic stabilization has the objectives discussed in the following three subsections.

Budget equilibrium or a small deficit as percentage of GDP

Budget equilibrium entails that total public expenditure (PE) and tax and non-tax revenue (T) balance out or that the former exceeds the latter by just few percentage points of GDP. The achievement of this objective is meant to avoid an excessive accumulation of debt, pressure on interest rates and prices, and an erosion of macroeconomic credibility. However, realizing such an objective through the traditional monetary approach (see

The Macroeconomics of Developing Countries: An Intermediate Textbook. Giovanni Andrea Cornia, Oxford University Press (2020).

DOI: 10.1093/oso/9780198856672.001.0001

Sections 16.1 and 16.2) has often engendered recessions that raised unemployment and poverty, as argued by Cornia et al., (1987), Stiglitz (1998), Jha (2003), Chand (2006), Ostry et al. (2016), and many others. Similar problems (and related criticism) have arisen in the aftermath of the stabilization of the sub-prime and European sovereign debt crises of the late 2000s and early 2010s (Jolly et al., 2012; Ostry et al., 2016).

In the conventional IMF approach, budget equilibrium can be achieved through public expenditure cuts and increases in user fees (that is, charges for the utilization of public services) or, less frequently (especially in the past), by increasing tax revenue. The past preference for cutting public expenditure was due to political-economy difficulties, as well as to the longer time required to raise revenue from direct taxes[1] and to introduce VAT. The time needed to reduce public expenditure is generally shorter, although it is not politically easy to cut legislated expenditures which are already in the disbursement pipeline—unless the government shifts from the approved budget to a cash budget by delaying approved payments.

The greater preference accorded to public expenditure cuts to reduce the budget deficit depends also on the fact that—according to mainstream economics—an increase in taxation entails efficiency costs. Such costs are the sum of a lower demand for consumer goods due to higher taxes, the greater administrative costs borne by the tax administration, and the erosion of incentives caused by the rise in tax rates. The cost of raising a dollar through higher taxes is estimated at 1.50–1.80 US$ in the advanced nations and 2.00–3.00 US$ in developing countries. Indeed, direct taxation may reduce the net returns to labour and capital, and cause an erosion of the incentives of workers and investors who might reduce their supply of labour and new investments. In turn, an increase in indirect taxation would reduce the consumer surplus more than the increase in government revenue generated by the tax increase, causing a welfare deadweight loss. How large these effects are is, however, a matter for empirical investigation. The answer depends on the initial level of taxation, and the composition of the additional revenue raised. There are examples (e.g. Uruguay in 2008) of moderate increases in direct taxation from low levels that did not generate any of the above mentioned efficiency costs.

Another reason behind the preference accorded to user fees rather than to general taxation in mainstream adjustment programmes is the supposed informational advantage of consumers in relation to the state. Households, in fact, are expected to have better knowledge about the type of public services they want to consume and—for this reason—are willing to pay for them with user fees and similar charges. This situation is preferable—it is argued—to that in which all citizens are subjected to general taxation, the revenue of which is then used by the government to provide free services, the mix and distribution of which among citizens is determined by the state itself without precise knowledge of consumers' preferences. Indeed, so goes the argument, it is not easy for the policymaker to identify citizens' preferences and demands, resulting in oversupply of one type of services and undersupply of another. However, with the introduction of substantial user fees, the poor are excluded from accessing basic public goods and services, a fact that entails for them a welfare loss and negative aggregate effects on long-term growth.

[1] This is not true in the case of excises, sale taxes, and import tariffs, which are, however, regressive and inflationary.

Limit the accumulation of public debt and a rise of the debt/GDP ratio

Beyond a given threshold (the precise value of which is still hotly debated), an accumulation of public debt to finance and an expansionary adjustment policy may entail a redistribution of well-being between present and future generations. In addition, mainstream supporters argue that when the public debt/GDP ratio exceeds 90 per cent (see Section 3.4), its servicing (the term $r\ PD_{t-1}$ in equation (16.1)) may become explosive, cause macro crises, and slow down long-term growth. Indeed, if either the public debt, PD_{t-1}, or r are very high, the budget deficit, BD, becomes explosive even if the primary deficit (T-PPE) is positive, that is, when tax revenue exceeds the primary public expenditure, PPE, which is total public expenditure excluding interest payments. Indeed, the increment of the public debt, ΔPD (that is equal to the budget deficit BD) can be written as follows

$$\Delta PD = BD = T - PPE - r\ PD_{t-1} \tag{16.1}$$

There are therefore two alternative conditions required to stabilize the value of the public debt ($\Delta PD = 0$), that is:

$$\text{(i)} \quad (T - PPE) = r\ PD_{t-1} \quad \text{or} \quad \text{(ii)}\ r \rightarrow 0 \tag{16.2}$$

The first condition entails that—when the interest rate on the public debt is high—the primary surplus ($T - PPE$) must be equal to the expenditure on interest on the public debt, PD. A high primary surplus, however, may squeeze other types of productive and pro-poor expenditures. Alternatively, public debt can be stabilized if the interest rate tends to zero, an unrealistic assumption in developing countries. The latter approach to the stabilization of the public debt has been followed, however, in Japan where there is a public debt/GDP ratio of around 220 per cent but an average interest rate on the public debt of around 0.10 per cent. In some cases, controlled or moderate inflation helps to reduce the PD/GDP ratio. Public debt is, in most cases, denominated in constant nominal terms while GDP and T are expressed in current prices and therefore increase in line with inflation. Also in developed countries the public debt is mostly not indexed to inflation, whose target rate is generally agreed to be around 2 per cent. This means that every year 2 per cent of its nominal value is eroded by inflation.

Low inflation and a sustainable deficit of the balance of payments

The first objective is pursued to avoid modifying excessively the relative price ratio p_i/p_j between the goods i and j, as this could cause uncertainty, reduce real money supply, and, in extreme cases, a flight from the national currency and dollarization, that is, all factors which may entail a recession. Of course, the meaning of 'high' and 'low' inflation varies depending on the characteristics of each economy. Generally speaking, in the developed countries the target inflation rate is set at 2 per cent. Recently, however, there have been suggestions this this could be raised to 4 per cent, so as to widen the monetary authorities' room for manoeuvre when they are aiming to reduce the policy rate during periods of stagnation.

In the past, for the developing countries characterized by various rigidities, the IMF's Research Institute placed an acceptable inflation rate at around 10 per cent. However, Bruno and Easterly (1998) found that, contrary to the findings of the new growth literature on the negative long-run relation between inflation and growth, there is no cross-sectional correlation between the long-run averages of these two variables. Their examination of discrete high-inflation episodes suggests that growth falls sharply during such crises but recovers rapidly provided inflation remains below 40 per cent. This result was obtained, however, during years characterized by a lower financial integration than at present.

As for the current account balance, the objective is to achieve, over the short term, deficits that are sustainable on the basis of the existing foreign exchange reserves, expected export earnings, and the financing of international lenders. In practice, the short-term deficit of the current account is financed in good part with debt-creating capital inflows. However, the long-term equilibrium of the total balance of payments must necessarily be achieved on the basis of the equilibrium of the current account balance, as there is a limit to the accumulation of foreign debt.

16.2 Monetary Approach to Stabilization

This section considers two simple models of monetary inspiration, which show that inflation (in a closed economy) or the worsening of the balance of payments (in an open economy) depend on an excessive expansion of credit to the economy and money supply. These models have been in use for many years but are often criticized by the monetarist school itself for their simplicity. However, more complex models (such as the DSGE models discussed in Section 1.4) are difficult to operate and do not guarantee to generate better results.

The closed economy model

In the closed economy model, real money demand (MD) depends positively on Y (the income needed for current transactions) and negatively on r (the opportunity cost of keeping money in liquid form for speculative and prudential reasons). In turn, the nominal money supply (MS) depends on the product of the monetary base, H, and the money multiplier, mm.[2] The real money supply is obtained by dividing the nominal money supply MS by the price level P. In symbols:

[2] The money multiplier, mm, is equal to the money supply, MS, divided by the monetary base, H. By substituting in the place of MS and H their components, one obtains: $mm = (CU + D)/(CU + RE)$ where CU is the amount of financial assets held in cash by households and firms, D is that deposited in bank accounts, and RE the compulsory (rr) plus voluntary reserves held by commercial banks at the central bank. By dividing the numerator and denominator of the right hand side by D one obtains $mm = (cu + 1)/(cu + re)$ where $cu = CU/D$ and $re = RE/D$. It must be noted that $re = f\ (Y, r_p, r_a, rr, cu, r_d, \sigma)$, in which mm depends negatively on the active interest rate, r_a (the interest rate paid to banks by households and firms); positively on r_d, i.e. the discount rate charged by the central bank for loans it grants to commercial banks; positively on rr, i.e. the compulsory reserve ratio set by the central bank; positively on cu, i.e. the percentage of cash reserves retained by families in relation to their financial assets; positively on σ, i.e. the variance of withdrawals and deposits from current accounts; and positively on Y. Given this, an increase in rr and r_d increases the denominator of $(cu + 1)/(cu + re)$ and thus reduces mm.

$$\text{real money supply} \qquad MS/P = mm \;\; H/P \tag{16.3}$$

$$\text{real money demand} \qquad MD = f\;(r,\;Y) \tag{16.4}$$

The model rests on restrictive assumptions such as full employment of resources (meaning that an increase in money supply cannot generate a rise in output), a stable money multiplier, its independence vis-à-vis the increase in the monetary base ΔH, and a stable r. The equalization of money demand and supply is given below for fixed values of r_0 and Y_0:

$$\begin{aligned} MS/P &= MD \\ mm.H &= f(r_0,\;Y_0).P \end{aligned} \tag{16.5}$$

Now, given the invariance in this model of the function f, an expansion of the monetary base ΔH can only lead to an increase in the price level from P to P′. In symbols:

$$mm\;(H+\Delta H) = f(r_0,\;Y_0).P' \quad \text{where} \;\; P' > P \tag{16.6}$$

In conclusion, an increase of the monetary base raises the price level under restrictive hypotheses that are rarely verified in real life. From this, the policy conclusion is that a reduction of inflation entails a curtailment of the monetary base, H. Which other variable of equation (16.6) could be modified by the policymaker to avoid an increase in inflation from P to P′? If the assumption about the stability of the money multiplier, mm, were relaxed, one might think that the increase in P could be avoided or reduced by raising the discount rate, i_d (that influences the bahaviour of households and firms) and increasing the reserve ratio, rr, of commercial banks, in this way reducing the money multiplier. Yet, it would be peculiar to expand on the one side the monetary mass by ΔH while at the same time reducing mm by means of the measures mentioned above. In addition, it is easier for the policymaker to intervene on the monetary base rather than on the money multiplier, which varies less in absolute terms, and depends also on the response of households and firms to an increase in the discount rate.

The open economy model: the monetary approach to the balance of payments

The monetary approach to the balance of payments (MABoP) has long inspired IMF stabilization programmes. It is based on the following assumptions: the economy is in equilibrium; there is full employment of all production factors; prices are flexible both upward and downward; markets are efficient; the exchange rate is fixed; and exports and capital movements are constant. Let us now recall from Table 14.1 that the balance sheet of the central bank allows the following relation to be written: $H = DA + FA$ where H is the monetary base, DA are the domestic assets of the central bank (i.e. claims on commercial banks, state bonds, and other claims on state institutions), while FA are its foreign assets (gold, foreign exchange, foreign bonds, and other foreign assets).

As always, in equilibrium one has $MS/P = MD$ or, in explicit terms, $mmH = f\;(r,\;Y)P$. Now, by substituting $(DA + FA)$ in lieu of H, one obtains:

$$FA = [f(r,\ Y)\ P]/mm - DA \qquad (16.7)$$

and given that, by definition, the yearly deficit or surplus of the balance of payments equals the variation of the foreign assets of the central bank, that is $BP = \Delta FA$, by writing equation (16.7) in first differences one obtains:

$$BP = (X^* - M + K^*) = \Delta[P\ f(r,\ Y)]/mm - \Delta DA \qquad (16.8)$$

where K^* and X^* refer to net capital inflows and exports, and M to imports (the first two are assumed to be constant).

Equation (16.8) shows that BP depends positively on the increase in nominal money demand $\Delta[P.f(Y, r)]$ that causes a rise in interest rates and reduces household expenditure, part of which is satisfied by imports. Such a measure therefore improves the BP through a decline in imports. In turn, BP depends negatively on the volume of additional credit granted to the economy (ΔDA).

In such a framework the disequilibrium of the foreign accounts is due to excessive monetary expansion and not, for instance, to an exogenous fall in export prices or a rise in import prices. Given that the new position of the balance of payments, BP', following a rise in ΔDA is not sustainable on the basis of the existing foreign exchange reserves and expected net foreign exchange inflows, that is, X^* and K^*, the political economy of stabilization implies that the policymaker and the IMF follow a standard procedure. First, they have to set a sustainable (less negative) value of the balance of payments $BP''>BP'$ which can be financed over the medium term on the basis of existing reserves, expected export earnings, aid flows, and net foreign lending. If this sustainable value is negative (as it is in all cases), the IMF finances the foreign exchange gap for a few years. As a second step, the IMF estimates the increase in money demand $\Delta f(r, Y)$. This is treated as an exogenous variable—a somewhat problematic assumption, given that money demand depends on Y, which in turn depends on ΔDA. At this point, one can solve equation (16.8) for the value of ΔDA which is consistent with BP''. Determining a sustainable level of ΔDA thus becomes the main policy problem at hand. In symbols, the value of ΔDA is determined as follows:

$$\Delta DA = \Delta[P.\ f\ (r,\ Y)]/mm - BP'' \qquad (16.9)$$

In conclusion, the sequence of events portrayed in this type of policy approach is as follows: one starts from a situation of equilibrium. The adoption of expansionary credit policies raises money supply, reduces r, and increases consumption and investments, part of which are satisfied with an increase in imports. As exports and capital inflows are assumed to be fixed, the increase in imports leads to a deterioration of the current account balance. Even in situations where production factors are not fully employed, the increase in domestic demand will leak in part to the import sector. To restore equilibrium in the current balance, it is necessary to reverse this process and reduce ΔDA, that is, the credit expansion to the economy.

What are the main theoretical limitations of the MABoP approach? To start with, it ignores the effects of monetary expansion on income and prices that—as noted—are assumed as constant, while in real life they are always affected to some degree by monetary expansion. Furthermore MABoP assumes that the worsening of the balance of payments is due to an excessively expansionary monetary policy, while in many cases it is due to an exogenous drop in foreign demand, a worsening of the international terms of trade, or an endogenous rise of public expenditure unaccompanied by a parallel increase of revenue. Therefore, although these external shocks also generate an *ex post* imbalance in monetary aggregates, the MABoP approach tends to cure the symptoms and not the real cause of the problem, and does not therefore necessarily engender the expected results, or it generates them—after additional cuts in credit ceilings—at high costs in term of lost production, unemployment, and poverty. Indeed, in terms of its economic impact, such an approach tends to cause an *overkill*, that is, a decline in GDP, investments, and employment far greater than predicted by the IMF country programme developed to reach a given balance of payments objective. At the same time, the current account balance systematically improves faster than projected (Table 16.1), as the fall in Y curtails imports more than expected while exports do not change. In addition, the increase in prices is systematically underestimated, suggesting that the monetary explanation of inflation is incomplete.

Table 16.1 illustrates these problems vividly in the case of the European economies in transition which simultaneously stabilized their macroeconomy, liberalized prices, and transformed their economic structure. All these changes were well known to the IMF economists who computed the planned results reported in Table 16.1. Chand (2006, Table 3.2) provides additional evidence of the *overkill*, while Blanchard and Leigh (2013) come to similar conclusions about the effects of fiscal cuts during recent IMF-supported adjustment programmes. In the latter study, the source of the *overkill* is attributed to the systematic underestimation of the negative Keynesian multipliers operating during IMF-supported stabilization programmes.

Table 16.1 Planned and observed results of IMF stabilization programmes in Eastern Europe, early 1990s

Country	GDP (% change)	Inflation (CPI) (% change)	Average wage (% change)	Convertible current account (billions of US$)
Hungary (1991)				
- planned results	−3	31	0	−1.2
- real life results	−8	32	20	0.3
Poland (1990)				
- planned results	−5	94	0	−3.0
- real life results	−12	249	160	0.7
Poland (1991)				
- planned results	3	36	0	−2.7
- real life results	−8	60	54	−2.2
Czechoslovakia (1991)				
- planned results	−5	30	17	−2.5
- real life results	−16	54	14	0.2
Bulgaria (1991)				
- planned results	−11	234	146	−2.0
- real life results	−23	339	142	−0.9
Romania (1992)				
- planned results	0	104	0	−1.7
- real life results	−12	223	124	−1.3

Source: Bruno (1994).

So, what causes the *overkill*? The contraction in domestic credit to the economy ($-\Delta DA$) generates, as planned, an initial recession and a fall in Y and imports. But this income contraction is exacerbated when firms cut their investments in what they perceive is a declining economy (Chand, 2006), as suggested by the accelerator investment function discussed in Section 3.2. As a result, despite stringent domestic bank credit ceilings, primarily aimed at the government, the banks find themselves excessively liquid for lack of borrowers of reasonable quality. In addition, due to the contraction of Y, the money multiplier, mm, also declines (see footnote 2 on the determinants of mm). The overall money supply thus falls. In the context of Fisher's exchange relation, $PY = MV$, such a contraction is observed even in relation to a declining Y so that, to maintain equilibrium, money velocity is seen as rising, providing a false signal the economy is overheating and justifying possible additional cutbacks in credit ceilings. This is particularly the case if prices have risen more than projected by the stabilization programme, which is what happens in many instances, as shown for instance in Table 16.1. This is due to a large extent to the concomitant devaluation of the nominal exchange rate that is not included in the MABoP model but that in practice takes place in most adjustment programmes. The remedy, of course, would have been to provide the credit freed up by the non-borrowing private sector to the government so that at least the overall credit ceilings would be maintained and aggregate demand sustained.

This explanation emphasizes the impact of monetary contraction, and fits well the discussion of the pros and cons of the MABoP model analysed in this section; but it is incomplete. Indeed, the stabilization programmes of monetary inspiration always include a sizeable compression of public expenditure that by itself causes, as planned, a decline in national income and imports. Also—where the exchange rate regime allows it—a devaluation of the nominal exchange rate is also introduced (see Section 16.3). In countries that are part of a currency union, such as Greece and the African countries that are members of the CFA franc zone, whose money supply is influenced by super-national considerations, the emphasis shifts from cuts in credit ceilings to direct restraints of government expenditure and an improvement of the primary surplus that can be as or more deflationary than a credit contraction. In these countries, fiscal restraint becomes the tool of choice for the stabilization programme. Finally, the financial programming approach does not fit too well with contemporary open-economy macroeconomics in which capital movements and credibility play a key role. Lacking a comprehensive theory, the standard approach has thus reverted to prescriptions on how much credit ceilings, the budget deficit, and government expenditure should be cut. As noted above, however, the decline in income and imports caused by fiscal contraction is in many cases greater than projected because of the systematic underestimation of the negative Keynesian multiplier during contractionary stabilization, as highlighted by Blanchard and Leigh (2013). Given the uniformity and frequent poor performance of the traditional stance, more expansionary approaches to macroeconomic stabilization have been proposed by Stiglitz et al. (2006) and other authors (see Section 18.3).

16.3 Specific Stabilization Measures Introduced in the Context of MABoP

The MABoP model provides a road map to macroeconomic stabilization in case of large deficits of the balance of payments and state budget or of strong inflation. In real life, the most common reason to request IMF assistance and the launch of a stabilization programme is a worsening of the current account balance as this may—*inter alia*—threaten the international payments system. In this regard, it must be underscored that in most cases an orderly macroeconomic stabilization cannot be avoided, that delays in introducing it are often costly, and that a market-driven spontaneous adjustment generally entails higher costs than in case of an adjustment programme guided by the policymaker and benefiting from some international assistance.[3] Yet, while there is general agreement on the need to stabilize the economy, views differ on how to design and implement such stabilization measures. For instance, an IMF stabilization programme typically includes the measures discussed in the following two subsections, but alternative approaches may also be pursued.

Expenditure reducing measures

Measures taken to reduce expenditure diminish the level of domestic absorption, aggregate demand, and national income as they cut private and public consumption and imports. Such measures include slower growth in the nominal money supply (which entails a fall of the real money supply) achieved by controlling the growth of the monetary base, H; the imposition of credit ceilings; and reducing the money multiplier, mm. Cutting the volume of credit to the economy also entails reducing the purchase of state bonds by the central bank, limiting the treasury's withdrawals from its current account at the central bank, reducing the credit ceilings to commercial banks, raising commercial banks' compulsory reserve ratios, and/or raising the central bank discount rate.

Expenditure reducing measures also include cutting the budget deficit, which is achieved by compressing the real volume (more rarely, the nominal value) of current public expenditure for subsidies, salaries, current purchases, maintenance, and investments. As noted earlier, reducing the budget deficit through an increase in tax pressure is less common, although improvements in this area have been realized during the last fifteen years in many developing countries. In a way, explicit public expenditure cuts seem to be superfluous, given that the central bank will already have reduced the purchase of state bonds and other forms of credit with which the government finances the budget deficit. Yet, fiscal cuts could be needed in countries where the budget deficit may be financed by issuing state bonds on the domestic market or where the central bank is allowed by law to cover part of the deficit with monetary emissions, as tended to happen in several European countries until about twenty-five years ago.

In view of the preponderance (up to 90 per cent) of wages in total public expenditure, a reduction of the budget deficit entails a reduction of the real public sector wage bill. Where possible, private wages may also be cut. There are various mechanisms to cut real wages. One of them consists in modifying their indexation to inflation from *ex ante* to *ex post*, to reduce its frequency, or to under-index wages to inflation. With this approach, most of the cost of the macroeconomic adjustment is unloaded onto the real wage. More rarely, one observes a reduction of nominal wages, in view of the psychological effect and opposition this could generate. These expenditure reducing measures cause a drop in the demand for domestically produced and imported goods.

[3] Countries characterized by high income inequality and class polarization tend to delay macroeconomic stabilization and therefore often suffer greater GDP losses.

This approach has been criticized when the deficit of the current account balance is caused by exogenous international shocks. Indeed, under these circumstances, equilibrium of the current account could be achieved by means of selective measures, such as temporary tariffs, quantitative trade restrictions, or export subsidies. This would reduce the external deficit without inducing a recession, such as that caused by a contraction of credit to the economy and public expenditure cuts. This alternative approach is likely to be viable, for instance, whenever imports compete with domestically produced goods whose competiveness would be improved by the introduction of tariffs. But it is more problematic in the case of imports of essential intermediate inputs and investment goods for which there are no domestic substitutes. Furthermore, the introduction of trade protection may trigger retaliatory measures from trading partners. Lastly, if the increase in tariffs becomes permanent, domestic firms may be affected by an erosion of their incentives to compete. Despite these caveats, such alternative measures are viable, especially when a worsening of external conditions may threaten the national economy, as foreseen by the IMF Articles of Agreement.

Expenditure switching measures

Expenditure switching measures aim to enhance export incentives to improve the balance of payments. They include a devaluation of the nominal and real exchange rate; subsidies and pricing policies supporting the export sector; measures to increase the mobility of production factors from the non-tradable to the tradable sector (such as infrastructural improvements); training in new skills; and a reduction in interest rates. In case the country under consideration is in a situation of full employment, the reduction of the balance of payments deficit demands the reallocation of resources towards the tradable sector. For instance, in an African economy the tradable sector includes mainly agriculture and mining, while the non-tradable sector broadly coincides with urban activities (real estate, services, and so on). There is therefore a need to change the domestic terms of trade (as shown by the Swan–Salter model), so as to strengthen the tradable sector.

The devaluation of the real exchange rate is seen by many as the tool of choice[4] to reduce the deficit of the current account balance. Indeed, devaluation compresses imports (as it makes them more costly in domestic currency terms) while—at the same time—it stimulates exports. In all those cases in which devaluation generates these effects, it also triggers an expansionary effect on the equilibrium level of income. However, to generate these positive effects, devaluation must fulfil the Marshall–Lerner condition and other requirements discussed in Chapter 15. If these are not met, devaluation not only may not improve the balance of payments but it may also generate a contraction of GDP.

One of the often ignored problems of devaluation is that (in developing countries and some developed ones) production factors are often fairly immobile. Their reallocation from the declining to the potentially expanding sector is often made difficult by various structural rigidities. For instance, it may not be possible to redeploy sector-specific

[4] In contrast, the expenditure reduction measures unavoidably have a contractionary effect, which is often distributed in a regressive manner. They can therefore be considered as a negative instrument of macro stabilization.

industrial machinery for the production of different goods; workers too need sector-specific training before transferring to new industries. In addition, the regions where the new tradable industries are being created may be far from those where the declining sectors are located, while the availability of housing, social services, credit, and social insurance needed to facilitate the transfer of labour may be inadequate. Furthermore, the reallocation of labour is possible only if it is accompanied by new investment. But, as noted above, during recessions and standard macroeconomic stabilization programmes, it is precisely private investment that contracts most for the reasons discussed above.[5] In view of this, the policymaker may try to ease this complex transfer of productive resources from one sector to another by launching retraining courses and public investment meant to raise the efficiency of private investments.

Another way to ease the reallocation of resources among sectors is to encourage household savings, but the increase in interest rates invariably introduced as part of the standard stabilization programmes also raises the cost of borrowing by firms and households. The IMF rightly advises that interest rates be raised in countries characterized by financial repression and negative real interest rates, but also—more arguably—during periods of recession. Higher interest rates are supposed to increase a country's credibility and attract portfolio investments, but at the same time they depress domestic investment. Finally, mainstream stabilization ensures that—if a country with a balance of payments crisis accepts the IMF conditions—the latter coordinates a financial support package which includes not only new IMF money but also some foreign debt cancellation, and financing from the World Bank, the regional development banks, and members of the Paris club of public creditors and of the London club of private creditors.

16.4 Polak's Model of Orthodox Stabilization, Poverty, and Alternatives

Inspired by Chand (2006), this section presents the Polak (1957) model, the basic framework of which goes back several decades. Its longevity underscores its operational simplicity and the importance of the intuition which constitutes its main attraction. As discussed in Section 16.2, the model is used to determine the extent of the credit contraction under macroeconomic stabilization, and is a key element of IMF financial programming. Hereafter we also explore the impact of the application of the Polak model on growth and the incidence of poverty.

Analytical formulation

The model includes the following four equations (Polak, 1998).

$$M_0 = \frac{1}{v}Y \qquad \text{money demand} \tag{16.10}$$

[5] A change of the sectoral distribution of investments is more likely during periods of growth, during which time investments increase more rapidly than GDP, due to the functioning of the accelerator mechanism and due to positive expectations.

$$M = mY \qquad \text{import function} \tag{16.11}$$

$$\Delta M_0 = \Delta DA + BP \qquad \text{internal and external sources of money creation} \tag{16.12}$$

$$BP \equiv X - M + K \qquad \text{balance of payments} \tag{16.13}$$

where M_0 is money demand, v is the velocity of circulation, M imports, m the import propensity, BP the local currency value of the variation of the level of international reserves (which is equal to the value of the balance of payments), DA the stock of domestic assets of the banking system, X exports, and K net capital inflows. All variables are expressed in nominal domestic currency.

Equation (16.10) describes money demand, which is stable over time, while equation (16.12) illustrates the two main sources of money creation, that is, the expansion of bank credit and purchase of state bonds (ΔDA), and the increase in money supply due to the net inflow of foreign exchange. To simplify the exposition, it is assumed that the parameters m and v are constant. The exchange rate does not appear in the model and is treated as an exogenous variable. The effects of its variations are mirrored by changes in the values of exports, capital inflows, and the import coefficient.

At this point, following Chand (2006), it is possible to derive from the four relations (16.10)–(16.13) equations for the growth of GDP and the balance of payments. To this end, by expressing equation (16.10) in first differences, one obtains $\Delta M_0 = \Delta Y/v$, which allows the ΔM_0 so obtained to be equalized with that of equation (16.12) obtaining in this way,

$$\frac{1}{v}\Delta Y = BP + \Delta DA \tag{16.14}$$

while with a series of manipulations described in the footnote,[6] from equation (16.13) it is possible to derive equation (16.15) which measures the growth of nominal income:

$$\frac{\Delta Y}{Y_{-1}} = \frac{1}{(1+mv)}\left\{\left(\frac{\Delta(K+X)}{M_{0-1}}\right) + \left(\frac{BP_{-1}}{M_{0-1}}\right)\right\} + \frac{1}{(1+mv)}\left(\frac{\Delta DA}{M_{0-1}}\right) \tag{16.15}$$

[6] Let us start from the following relation (see equation (16.14) in the main text)
(1) $1/v\ \Delta Y = BP + \Delta DA$
and recalling that $BP = X - M + K$ can be rewritten as $BP = BP_{-1} + \Delta K - \Delta M + \Delta X$ one obtains
(2) $1/v\ \Delta Y = [BP_{-1} + \Delta(K+X) - \Delta M] + \Delta DA$
and recalling again that $M = mY$ and that $Y = Y_{-1} + \Delta Y$, one obtains
(3) $1/v\ \Delta Y = BP_{-1} + \Delta(K+X) - mY + mY_{-1} + \Delta DA$
Dividing everything by mY_{-1}, one then obtains
(4) $1/mv.\ \Delta Y/Y_{-1} = BP_{-1}/mY_{-1} + \Delta(K+X)/mY_{-1} - Y/Y_{-1} + 1 + \Delta DA/mY_{-1}$
while decomposing the numerator of the third addendum Y in its components $Y = Y_{-1} + \Delta Y$, one obtains
(5) $1/mv.\ \Delta Y/Y_{-1} = BP_{-1}/mY_{-1} + \Delta(K+X)/mY_{-1} - 1 + \Delta Y/Y_{-1} + 1 + \Delta DA/mY_{-1}$
By simplifying and factoring out, one then obtains
(6) $(1+mv)/v.\ \Delta Y/Y_{-1} = BP_{-1}/mY_{-1} + \Delta(K+X)/mY_{-1} + \Delta DA/mY_{-1}$
and multiplying on the right- and left-hand side by mv, and recalling that (16.10) says that $M_0 = Y/v$, then $1/M_0 = v/Y$ and $1/M_{0-1} = v/Y_{-1}$ one then obtains, after dividing both sides by $(1+mv)$, equation (16.15) in the text.

in which the left-hand side is the growth rate of nominal income (GDP) which is a positive function of the exogenous value of exports, capital inflows, the 'initial conditions' of the balance of payments (BP_{-1}), and the increase in the volume of credit to the economy, ΔDA. All variables are standardized by the value of the monetary base of the prior year (M_{0-1}), to emphasize the role of money supply.

One can now derive the relation which describes the determinants of the balance of payments. To this end, one can substitute relation (16.15) into equation (16.14), thus obtaining[7] the following expression:

$$\frac{BP}{M_{0-1}} = \frac{1}{(1+mv)}\left(\frac{\Delta(K+X)}{M_{0-1}} + \frac{BP_{-1}}{M_{0-1}}\right) - \frac{mv}{(1+mv)}\left(\frac{\Delta DA}{M_{0-1}}\right) \tag{16.16}$$

which shows that the balance of payments is a positive function of exports, capital inflows, and the initial conditions, but also—as expected—a negative function of the increase in the volume of domestic credit. Equation (16.16) also shows that the greater the net capital inflows and exports, the less restrictive needs to be the monetary policy required to meet a given objective $(BP/M_{0-1})^*$. Furthermore, in the model there are two constant exogenous parameters, that is, m and v. However, it is evident that if m tends to zero (as in case of complete autarky), $mv/(1+mv)$ tends to zero and hence the last term on the right-hand side can be neglected, indicating that under autarky the monetary policy has no effects on the balance of payments. In turn, if m tends to one (as in case of total trade integration) $mv/(1+mv)$ tends to $(v/1+v)$, that is, a value which comes close to one.

A comparison between equations (16.15) and (16.16) underscores the existence of a typical policy trade-off, that is, a conflict between policy objectives. In fact, while in equation (16.15), a credit expansion ($\Delta DA/Mo_1$) positively affects the growth of incomes, in equation (16.16) it worsens the balance of payments. Indeed, an increase in income, Y, entails not only an increase in domestic consumption, but also in imports and therefore a *ceteris paribus* deterioration of the balance of payments.

As explained in Section 16.2, in order to stabilize BP one must first set the value of the balance of payments deficit $(BP/M_{0-1})^*$ which can be sustained over the medium term (including on the basis of financing provided by the IMF and other institutions) and solve equation (16.16) for the value of $(\Delta DA/M_{0-1})^*$ that is compatible with such a policy objective. One can therefore substitute the value of $(\Delta DA/M_{0-1})^*$ so obtained in the last terms of equation (16.15), obtaining the growth rate of nominal income $(\Delta Y/Y_{-1})^*$ consistent with the monetary expansion $(\Delta DA/M_{0-1})^*$. In symbols one obtains (simple demonstration omitted):

$$\left(\frac{\Delta Y}{Y_{-1}}\right)^* = \frac{1}{mv}\frac{[\Delta(K+X) + BP_{-1}]}{M_{0-1}} - \frac{1}{mv}\left(\frac{\Delta BP}{M_{0-1}}\right)^* \tag{16.17}$$

[7] Let us start from $1/v\ \Delta Y = BP + \Delta DA$ from which one can derive $\Delta Y = v\ BP + v\ \Delta DA$. By substituting in lieu of ΔY its value derived from equation (16.14) $\Delta Y = Y_{-1}/(1+mv)[BP_{-1}/M_{0-1} + \Delta(K+X)/M_0 -1 + \Delta DA/M_{0-1}]$, one obtains $vBP = Y_{-1}/(1+mv)[BP_{-1}/M_{0-1} + \Delta(K+X)/M_{0-1}] - v\ \Delta DA$ where by dividing both sides by Y_{-1} and recalling that $v/Y_{-1} = 1/M_{0-1\ s}$, one obtains formula (16.16) reported in the text.

Impact of conventional stabilization on poverty

At this point, , one can ask how does the poverty rate ($H = N_p/N$, i.e. the number of people, N_p, with a per capita income below the poverty line, z, divided by the total population, N) change when the policymaker decides to improve the balance of payments, BP. To this end, let us remember that a change over time in the poverty rate can be precisely decomposed into the change of four variables.

The first variable is changes over time in the poverty line $\Delta z/z$ (where z is the value of $\Sigma p_i q_i$, where q_i are the normative quantities of those goods—food, clothing, heating, drugs, and so on, necessary for survival and a minimal quality of life—which are included in the poverty basket while p_i are their domestic prices which may vary over time). In developing countries that depend on imports to cover the consumption of goods that enter the poverty basket a correct determination of the poverty line, z, must specify separately the quantity of imported q_{jf}, as their domestic price is equal to $p_{jf}\, e^{nc/\$}$, where p_{jf} is the world price of the imported item i and $e^{nc/\$}$ is the exchange rate. In such a case, the precise formulation of the poverty line is $z = \Sigma_i\, p_i\, q_{id} + \Sigma_j\, e^{nc/\$} p_{jf}\, q_{jf}$ where the first term on the right-hand side is the cost of the domestic component of the poverty basket while the second is its foreign component. In such a formulation it is evident that the poverty line rises in line with the devaluation of the exchange rate, and that this effect is more pronounced for high values of the ratio ($\Sigma_j\, e^{nc/\$} p_j\, q_{jf}/z$). Lastly, it must be observed that where the law of one price applies, the developing country under consideration is a price taker, and there are no restrictions to the export of basic tradable goods consumed on both the domestic and international markets (as in the case of food), a devaluation causes an increase of the poverty line that is also due to the rise of the price of exportables, that is, domestically produced traded goods even if they are not exported. In this case, the poverty line has to be formulated as $z = \Sigma_i\, p_{iNT}\, q_{iNT} + \Sigma_j\, e^{nc/\$} p_{jT}\, q_{jT}$. As many of the items entering the poverty line are tradables (food, medicines, kerosene, etc.), under the three circumstances mentioned above, the value of the poverty line is much more dependent than in the prior case on changes in world prices and the exchange rate. However, this effect does not arise (or does so only through a surge in the domestic price of imported inputs such as fertilizers) in developing countries where the goods that enter the poverty basket are exchanged on local markets but not on the world market.[8]

The second variable that enters the decomposition of poverty changes over time is the growth rate of the population, $n = \Delta N/N$, which varies only modestly over the short term. The third variable is the growth rate of income ($\Delta Y/Y_{-1}$) and the fourth variable describes the changes in the distribution of income. These can be proxied for instance by changes in the Gini or Theil coefficients.

On the basis of these considerations, one can thus decompose the change in the poverty rate into:

$$\Delta H/H_{-1} = \acute{\eta}_{Hz}[\Delta z/z_{-1} + n - \Delta Y/Y_{-1} + \Delta\, \mathrm{Gini}] \quad (16.18)$$

[8] This is the case of *teeff,* tubers, *and quinichua* that are a basic staple in Ethiopia, Equatorial Africa, and Bolivia.

At this point, one can replace, in lieu of $\Delta Y/Y_{-1}$, the value that is consistent with an improvement in the balance of payments $(\Delta Y/Y_{-1})^*$ (see equation (16.17)) and obtain:

$$\frac{\Delta H}{H_{-1}} = \acute{\eta}_{Hz}\left\{\frac{\Delta z}{z_{-1}} + n - \frac{1}{mv}\frac{[\Delta(K+X)+BP_{-1}]}{M_{0-1}} - \frac{1}{mv}\left(\frac{\Delta BP}{M_{0-1}}\right)^* + \Delta Gini\right\} \quad (16.19)$$

From equation (16.19) it appears that a change over time in the poverty rate depends negatively ($\Delta H/H_{-1}$ grows) on: (a) how ambitious is the balance of payments objective $(\Delta BP/M_{0-1})^*$. In this regard, equation (16.19) describes analytically the trade-off between poverty incidence and the speed of improvement of the balance of payments; (b) the changes in the poverty line (due for instance to a rise in the prices of essential goods); (c) the population growth rate; (d) an eventual worsening of the income distribution (proxied for instance by the Gini coefficient) during macroeconomic stabilization; (e) the change in import dependence measured by the import coefficient m. If m increases, the third element on the right-hand side falls more rapidly than the fourth given that, generally speaking, $\Delta(K+X)+BP_{-1}>\Delta BP^*$; (f) an increase in the velocity of the circulation of money, v, which would cause an increase in available means of payment, with effects similar to those of a credit expansion. v is endogenous, as it reflects the behaviour of the agents. In contrast, the poverty rate falls ($\Delta H/H_{-1}$ falls) due to an increase in exports, a rise of capital inflows K, and how favourable the initial conditions of the balance of payments BP_{-1} are.

What is missing in this analytical framework? A possible devaluation of the exchange rate $e^{nc/\$}$ which, as noted, is not explicitly included in the Polak model. How can one then measure the poverty impact of devaluation in this model? To answer this question one has to ask which variables of equation (16.19) could be influenced by devaluation. The possible effects are the following: to start with, $\Delta z/z_{-1}$ may increase (and thus $\Delta H/H_{-1}$ rise) because of the higher cost of the imported items entering the calculation of the poverty line, or if devaluation triggers a widespread increase in inflation, including the prices of the domestic items that enter the poverty basket. Second, with devaluation, the import coefficient, m, should decline (and $\Delta H/H_{-1}$ drop) but, as explained earlier, this depends on ε_M (the elasticity of imports in relation to a devaluation of the exchange rate). If essential imports have no domestic substitutes, devaluation will affect m only modestly. Third, a devaluation may cause a decline of private K (and a rise of $\Delta H/H_{-1}$), as foreign investors are hesitant to convert hard currency into national currency, fearing that the devaluation is not credible and that it will be followed by further devaluations which would reduce the future dollar value of their investments. Yet, if most capital inflows are of an official nature (that is, if they are supplied by the IMF, the World Bank, and bilateral donors) the impact would be the opposite. Fourth, X may rise (and $\Delta H/H_{-1}$ fall), but this effect depends on ε_X (the export elasticity of devaluation), as discussed in Chapter 15. Finally, the effect of devaluation on the Gini coefficient is undetermined *ex ante*, and varies with factors such as: the dependence on imports of goods consumed by the poor (in this case poverty and inequality will likely worsen); on whether low-income employees are working in the traded sector (poverty would fall because of a possible increase in job opportunities) or non-traded sector (the opposite); on the concentration of productive assets (poverty would rise if it is high), and so on. Furthermore, as shown in Chapter 15, devaluation could negatively affect the distribution of income (and have contractionary effects) due to the structural impact described therein.

Measures to offset the negative impact of orthodox stabilization on growth and poverty

Given the comprehensive analytical framework provided by equation (16.19), we ask now, together with Chand (2006), how can the policymaker moderate the impact of a balance of payments stabilization on growth and poverty? Some of the measures discussed in this subsection affect both growth and poverty, others concern only poverty. To start with, such measures could pivot around a less ambitious and more gradual improvement of the balance of payments, ΔBP^*. As shown by equation (16.19), the more ambitious this objective is (for instance, achieving a balance of payments surplus of 1 per cent of GDP starting from a deficit of 4 per cent), the greater the increase in poverty. It is thus necessary to follow, where possible, a gradual stabilization approach supported by greater foreign financing. Equation (16.17) shows that such an approach would allow a higher growth rate of income, $\Delta Y/Y_{-1}$, to be sustained with beneficial effects on the incidence of poverty. It is also likely that a gradual stabilization would prevent a worsening of the Gini coefficient, which in developing countries is likely to rise in the face of sharp GDP contractions. The empirical evidence shows in fact that, *ceteris paribus*, in poor countries the Gini coefficient worsens during the contractionary phases of the business cycle due to the downward flexibility of wages, the modest coverage of social security arrangements, and the limited diffusion (at least till a decade ago) of social assistance schemes (public works, social pensions, training schemes, and so on) aiming to support households' incomes during difficult periods.[9]

A second measure to offset the impact of adjustment on poverty is to consider carefully the changes of the import coefficient, m, entailed by devaluation and the trade liberalization which often accompanies macroeconomic stabilization. As seen in Chapter 15, devaluation generates effects which vary from country to country depending on the elasticities ε_X and ε_M. If ε_M is small, devaluation tends to raise the national currency value of the import coefficient, m. This effect is accentuated in instances of rapid trade liberalization that displaces domestic production with imports. In this case, it is evident that macroeconomic stabilization needs to be accompanied by a moderate devaluation, a postponement, or only gradual trade liberalization, and the introduction of temporary import restrictions, such as tariffs and non-tariff barriers on competing imports, and export subsidies. It is equally important to assess the impact of devaluation on exports and capital movements and to introduce corrective measures if necessary. As noted in Chapter 15, the impact of devaluation on exports depends on ε_X that reflects structural economic factors that change only over the medium term. Yet, the value of ε_X may be enhanced over the short term with export-promoting measures such as VAT reimbursement, de-taxation of exporting firms, direct subsidies, and microeconomic measures improving the functioning of the export infrastructure.

Particularly in developing countries with a large foreign debt, devaluation tends to generate devastating effects on the capital account, public finance, firms' default risk, and

[9] The situation is different in developed countries where, while profits drop during recessions due to lack of demand, the wage bill remains broadly unchanged as wages are downward sticky, firms hoard labour to avoid future screening and selections costs (for interviews, travel, trial period, training courses, and so on) when the economy recovers, and because social security offsets to a large degree the wage loss of fired workers. The liberalization of the labour market and the ensuing precarious nature of labour over the last two decades have changed this conclusion in part.

the banking system. Indeed, devaluation raises the domestic currency cost of servicing the foreign debt of the state, firms, and households. In addition, especially if it is perceived as non-credible, devaluation could lead to a drop in capital inflows, K, which could even become negative. To avoid these effects, it will be necessary to identify an acceptable devaluation of the exchange rate, and freeze at a bearable level the cost of servicing the foreign debt through automatic standstills, debt rescheduling, and other debt management measures. In a situation with capital market tensions, it may be necessary to introduce controls on capital outflows by residents and non-residents.

It is likewise essential to consider the effect of devaluation on the poverty line, z. In an open economy, devaluation triggers an increase in the price of the tradable goods included in the poverty basket as these often increase more rapidly than the rate of inflation, at which rate nominal incomes, Y, are assumed to grow. This may have a greater negative impact than measures that aim to liberalize foreign trade, for example the removal of restrictions to the exportation of key goods such as food, as observed during the IMF adjustment programme introduced in India in 1991. Also, if devaluation raises domestic food prices, wholesalers may hoard food in the expectation of further price rises.

The offsetting measures that could be introduced under such conditions include caps on unjustified price rises, the obligation of wholesalers to sell stocks of hoarded food on the open market, and the promotion of selective low-cost imports to break expectations of further domestic price rises. Such offsetting measures may also include restricting the export of essential goods for which the domestic price is lower than the world price (as observed in Argentina for the export of beef during the increase in world food prices of 2009), and introducing explicit subsidies on the production of essential items. These subsidies could be financed by taxing the windfall profits realized by exporters or owners of foreign assets whose domestic currency value rises in line with devaluation, or adopting a preferential exchange rate for the importation of essential goods such as drugs.

As for the impact on income distribution, the policymaker may aim to offset the adverse changes induced by macroeconomic stabilization and devaluation. Interventions in this field are many and obviously vary depending on the specific impact of the stabilization measures introduced. Some of them are mentioned hereafter as mere examples (see Chapter 18 for further details). For instance, if the impact of stabilization and devaluation are felt on the labour market, the policymaker might launch measures to support employment and wages such as public works programmes, minimum wage increases, microcredit schemes, and training in new skills to stimulate self-employment in small businesses. In contrast, if the impact occurs via the state budget, the policymaker may adopt measures that enhance the level and incidence of progressive taxation and public expenditure. And if the effects of stabilization manifest themselves mainly through changes in relative prices, the policymaker could consider introducing some of the measures mentioned above such as multiple exchange rates and a more gradual trade liberalization.

16.5 Concluding Remarks

Since the 1980s macroeconomic stabilization and structural adjustment have replaced, to a considerable extent, the development programmes followed by poor countries to modernize their economies and grow (see Section 2.5). Stabilization focuses on reducing the budget and current account deficits, contain the rise of public debt and reduce inflation. Official macroeconomic stabilization programmes benefiting from external support are preferable to market-led, spontaneous adjustments that tend to be costly. While stabilization programmes were also common in the 1960s and 1970s, their number has increased massively as a result of the oil crises of 1973 and 1978, the 1982–85 world recession, the international debt crisis of the 1980s, and o the many financial crises that have followed since the 1990s. In the near totality of cases, stabilization and structural adjustment programmes were carried out with the financial and technical support of the IMF. The analytical models at the basis of the IMF approach are of monetary inspiration and aim first of all to stabilize the balance of payments. As their impact tends to be recessionary and regressive, their multiplication has thus generated a heated debate about the overkill they generate and its impact on poverty and inequality. A main criticism of the standard approach concerns the assumption that balance of payments crises are always the result of excessive domestic credit expansion and that, therefore, the return to equilibrium entails a monetary contraction supported by the inflow of funds. Yet, the balance of payments crises of developing countries are often due to exogenous deteriorations of their international terms of trade and a fall in demand for their exports. These may be tackled by means of selective trade protection, export subsidies, and other targeted measures. A second criticism concerns the persistent underestimation of the negative output multipliers induced by the monetary and fiscal contraction that are at the basis of the overkill problem.

Within the context of the MABoP model, it is analytically and empirically evident that there is a trade-off between the speed of stabilization of the balance of payments and the incidence of poverty. Indeed, rapid stabilization tends to depress GDP, affect in an unpredictable way the exchange rate, and increase the incidence of poverty. Poverty, however, can be moderated by a more gradual approach to stabilization, gradual trade liberalization, limited devaluation, the provision of export subsidies, the reimbursement of VAT on exports, control of the prices of essential goods entering the poverty basket, and distributive measures supporting the incomes of low-income groups.

References

Blanchard, Olivier and Daniel Leigh (2013), 'Growth Forecast Errors and Fiscal Multipliers', *American Economic Review*, 103 (3): pp. 117–20.

Bruno, M. (1994), 'Stabilization and Reform in Eastern Europe: A Preliminary Evaluation', in O. Blanchard, K. A. Froot, and J. D. Sachs (eds), *The Transition in Eastern Europe*, Vol I, Cambridge, MA: National Bureau of Economic Research.

Bruno, M. and W. Easterly (1998), 'Inflation crises and long run growth', *Journal of Monetary Economics*, 41: pp. 3–26.

Chand, S. (2006), 'Can Monetary Approaches to Stabilization be Pro-Poor?' in G. A. Cornia, (ed.), *Pro Poor Macroeconomics: Potential and Limitations*, Geneva and Basingstoke: jointly published by UNRISD and Palgrave Macmillan.

Cornia, G. A., R. Jolly, and F. Stewart (1987), *Adjustment with a Human Face: Protecting the Vulnerable and Promoting Growth*, Oxford: Oxford University Press.

Jha, R. (2003),*Macroeconomics for Developing Countries*, 2nd edn. London and New York. Routledge.

Jolly, R., G. A. Cornia, D. Elson, C. Fortin, S. G. Jones, G. Helleiner, R. van der Hoeven, R. Kaplinsky, R. Morgan, I. Ortiz, R. Pearson, and F. Stewart (2012), *Be Outraged: there are Alternatives*. Mimeo.

Ostry, J. D., P. Loungani, and D. Furceri (2016), 'Neoliberalism: Oversold?', *Finance and Development*, Washington, DC: International Monetary Fund.

Polak, J. J. (1957), 'Monetary Analysis of Income Formation and Payments Problems', *IMF Staff Papers*, 6, pp. 1–50. Washington, DC: International Monetary Fund

Polak, J. J. (1998), 'The IMF Monetary Model at Forty', *Economic Modelling*, 15: pp. 395–410.

Stiglitz, J. (1998), 'More Instruments and Broader Goals: Moving towards the Post-Washington Consensus', *Annual WIDER Lecture* n.2. Helsinki: World Institute for Development Economics Research.

Stiglitz, J., J. A. Ocampo, S. Spiegel, R. Ffrench-Davis, and D. Nayyar (2006), *Stability with Growth: Macroeconomics, Liberalization, and Development*, Oxford: Oxford University Press.

Suggested further reading

Cornia, G. A., R. Jolly, and F. Stewart (1987), *Adjustment with a Human Face: Protecting the Vulnerable and Promoting Growth*. Oxford: Oxford University Press.

Polak, J. J. (1998), 'The IMF Monetary Model at Forty', *Economic Modelling*, 15: pp. 395–410.

Stiglitz, J., J. A. Ocampo, S. Spiegel, R. Ffrench-Davis, and D. Nayyar (2006), *Stability with Growth: Macroeconomics, Liberalization, and Development*. Oxford: Oxford University Press.

17
Internal and External Liberalization, Inequality, Growth, and Poverty

This chapter illustrates a general framework to analyse the impact on inequality, growth, and poverty of the internal and external reforms introduced in the developing and developed countries during the last three decades. It then discusses the main theories concerning the relation between inequality and growth. This debate has acquired considerable relevance with the adoption in 2015 by the United Nations General Assembly of the Sustainable Development Goals strategy that focuses—*inter alia*—on eradicating poverty by 2030 and on reducing income inequality to tolerable levels.

17.1 Economic Reforms and their Impact over the Last Three Decades

The macroeconomic reforms discussed in this chapter have been introduced with increasing frequency from the 1980s. As already noted, their rapid spread was due to the growing instability resulting from the gradual surge of inflation in the developed countries during the 1970s,[1] and from the US monetary contraction of 1982 when the US Federal Reserve raised the policy rate by ten points over a short period of time. This measure generated a major recession over 1982–85 in the OECD countries that spread rapidly to developing countries. The oil shocks of 1973 and 1978, the increased borrowing of petrodollars by the developing countries during the 1970s, and the 1982–85 recession led to an explosion of balance of payments deficits and an accumulation of foreign debt in many developing countries that dominated policymaking for the whole of that decade (for more details see Section 10.7). The period was also characterized by increasing criticism of the growth and inequality performance of the countries that had followed Import Substitution Industrialization policies. Such criticism led to the spread of the neoliberal economic approach that shifted the focus of government policy from full employment to the control of inflation and the achievement of macroeconomic equilibrium. This policy approach—that was and still is referred to as the Washington Consensus (WC) and Augmented Washington Consensus (AWC)—includes three sets of measures: macroeconomic stabilization; the liberalization of domestic markets; and the liberalization of international transactions.

[1] In those years the OECD published an important study on the 'narrow path of non-inflationary growth' which showed that the search for growth and full employment was becoming increasingly difficult because of the surge of inflation in the US and other advanced economies. The debate on the causes of such acceleration of inflation juxtaposed analyses à la Philips–Lipsey with those that emphasized the collapse of the Bretton Woods Agreement caused by the loss of competitiveness and higher inflation experienced in the United States that could no longer be tolerated under a fixed exchange rate regime. Such analyses emphasized as well the macroeconomic impact of the Vietnam War.

The Macroeconomics of Developing Countries: An Intermediate Textbook. Giovanni Andrea Cornia, Oxford University Press (2020).

DOI: 10.1093/oso/9780198856672.001.0001

Macroeconomic stabilization

As noted in Chapter 16, although it was implemented during the late 1960s and the 1970s, macroeconomic stabilization has become a dominant policy objective during the last three decades. In developing countries, the characteristics of stabilization programmes have gradually evolved over time, as the traditional one-year IMF Standby Agreements (SBA) were gradually replaced or accompanied by programmes of longer duration and with a more structural nature. For example, the IMF introduced the Extended Fund Facility (EFF), the Enhanced Structural Adjustment Facility (ESAF) and, starting from the 2000s, the Poverty Reduction and Growth Facility (PRGF) and its successor, the three-pronged Poverty Reduction and Growth Trust. As noted in Chapter 16, all of these programmes of macroeconomic stabilization include a monetary and fiscal contraction, an interest rate increase, and the devaluation of the exchange rate. Their logic, theoretical underpinning, specific policy measures, and economic and social impact were discussed in Chapter 16 to which the reader is referred.

Liberalization of the domestic markets and international transactions

Liberalization measures dominated the scene in the 1980s and 1990s and consisted in removing obstacles to entry into the market for consumer and investment goods. They also focused on the liberalization of domestic markets of production factors, for example dualistic labour markets and repressed financial markets (Table 2.7), as well as the reform of taxation and social transfers inspired by optimal taxation theory, the introduction of user-fees and targeting of public benefits on the 'deserving poor'. Finally, particularly in the economies in transition, there was also a drive towards the privatization of public assets such as land, factories, and public utilities.

Since the beginning of the 1990s, the liberalization of international trade picked up speed. Tariff rates were reduced and unified (Table 17.1), quantitative restrictions to international trade were eliminated, and full convertibility of current account transactions

Table 17.1 Trend in average regional import tariff rates, 1982–1990 to 2002–2010[a]

Region	1982–1990	1991–1997	1998–2002	2002–2010
South America	40.0	19.0	12.2	10.6
Central America and Mexico	46.6	18.1	8.8	7.2
Sub-Saharan Africa	26.7	24.9	14.5	13.2
MENA	29.7	21.9	17.3	16.2
South Asia	62.9	52.9	20.8	14.9
East and South East Asia	20.3	16.7	7.6	6.9
Asian economies in transition	44.5	38.9	15.5	12.5
Eastern Europe and Central Asia	.....	11.0	9.0	6.0
Advanced economies	8.5	7.1	3.3	4.2

Note: The data in the table refer to period averages.

[a] It is still unclear whether the 2019 trade war between the US and China will lead to an abandonment of the free trade policies followed over the last three decades.

Source: Own calculations on the Economic Freedom Dataset.

such as exports and imports was introduced. FDIs were liberalized together with short-term portfolio flows (Table 2.7, bottom panel). Other international transactions were also reformed, if much more slowly, as in the case of technology transfers (codified in the TRIPS agreement) and trade in services (negotiated under the GATS agreement).

17.2 Impact of the Economic Reforms on Growth, Income Distribution, and Poverty

Figure 17.1 describes the relationships between initial conditions, macroeconomic policy changes, growth, income inequality, and poverty. A first point to note is that the changes in the policies mentioned above affect at the same time both growth and income distribution that, in turn, affect poverty. Second, in most cases, it is not possible to establish *ex ante* in theoretical terms whether the effects of a policy are positive or negative, as they largely depend on a country's initial conditions in the economic area (A) and in the field of income and assets distribution (B). For instance, in economies with a large labour surplus in agriculture, the liberalization of output prices tends to generate positive effects on growth and poverty alleviation where an efficient smallholder agriculture prevails but negative effects on income inequality and neutral effects on growth where *latifundia* are dominant.

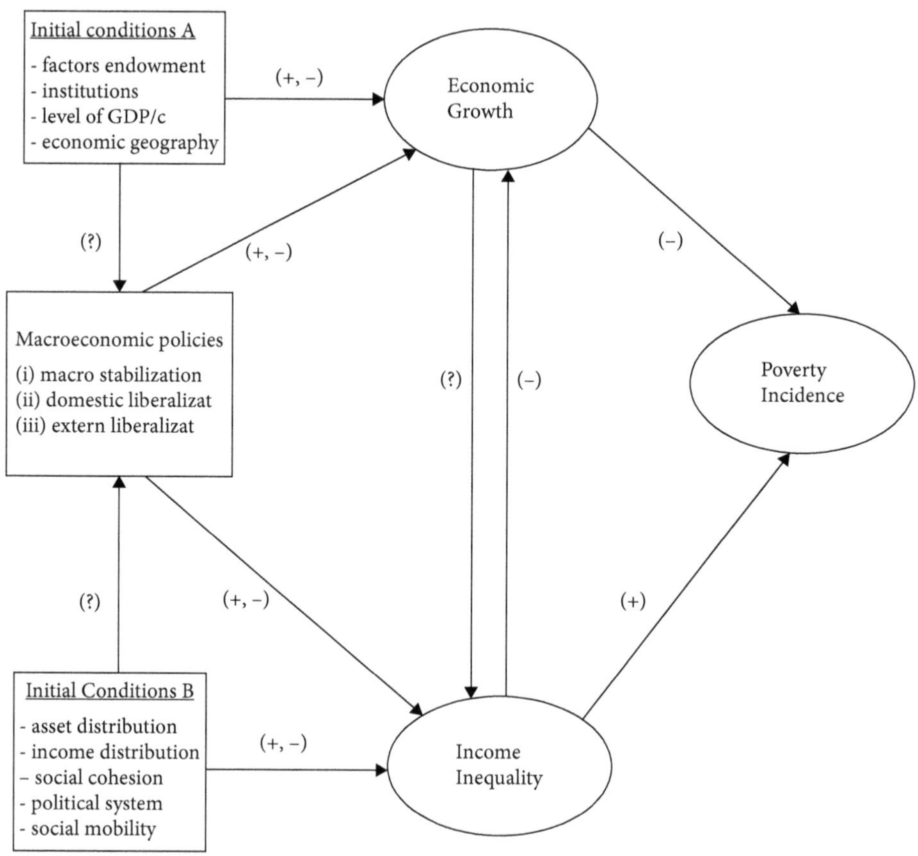

Figure 17.1 Relationship between poverty, growth and inequality, and their determinants

Likewise, the effects of an exchange rate devaluation on income inequality vary depending on whether the tradable sector produces labour-intensive or capital-intensive goods. The same is true in the case of an egalitarian privatization of state assets (such as that carried out in the Czech Republic in the 1990s) but not if privatization is highly unequal (as in the case of the oligarch-dominated Russian privatization). Thus, the distributive impact depends not so much on privatization per se but on the choice of the approach followed.

Third, it is necessary to underscore that the specific macroeconomic policies adopted are often endogenous, that is, they depend on the initial conditions prevailing in a country during the years in which they were designed. For instance, it is argued that the Russian privatization model (which consisted in distributing 50 per cent of the stock of state companies in equal proportions between factory workers and directors) was the only possible model in view of the enormous power that factory directors had acquired during the communist period.[2] If this is true, the achievement of given objectives in the fields of growth, inequality, and poverty does not require so much, or not only, changes in macroeconomic policies but also changes in the institutional setup of the economy. Accepting such a viewpoint has important implications for policy design and the political struggle. Fourth, it must be emphasized that while macroeconomics directly affects both growth and inequality, these two variables also strongly affect each other. However, while the view concerning the negative impact of inequality on growth is generally accepted both theoretically and empirically (this point is discussed in detail at the end of this chapter) this is not the case for the impact of growth on inequality. Indeed, such impact depends more on the pattern of growth rather than the rate of growth. Finally, as suggested by Bourguignon (2003), assuming lognormality of the distribution of income, the poverty headcount ratio (PHR) is a function of GDP per capita, the Lorenz curve, and the poverty line z, in symbols:

$$\text{PHR} = f\,(\text{GDP}/c, \text{Lorenz}, z) \tag{17.1}$$

In turn, the Lorenz curve can be parametrized by means of synthetic inequality indexes such as the Gini coefficient, Theil coefficient, inter-decile ratio, coefficient of variation, P90/P10 ratio, and average logarithmic deviation, that is, indexes that summarize the degree of inequality of a given Lorenz curve. All this means that—if the poverty line z is assumed to remain constant—the percentage variation over time of the PHR (i.e. PHR*) becomes a function of the growth rate of GDP per capita (GDP/c*), of the percentage variation over time of the Gini index (Gini*) and of a negligible interaction term IT:

$$\text{PHR}^* = -\alpha\,\text{GDP}/c^* + \beta\,\text{Gini}^* + \text{IT} \tag{17.2}$$

In this regard, it must be noted that the elasticity of PHR in relation to the growth of GDP per capita (α) and to that of the Gini coefficient (β) varies substantially in relation to the initial ratio between the poverty line z and the level of GDP per capita, and to the level of the Gini coefficient. For instance, as shown in Table 17.2, in middle-income countries with

[2] The remaining 50 per cent initially remained in the hands of the state but was later transferred to the red directors as part of the infamous 'loans for shares agreement'. With this agreement, the directors-turned-oligarchs loaned monies (which were never returned) to the Russian state, which needed to cover a huge budget deficit it could no longer monetize, in exchange for the remaining 50 per cent of the stock of state companies (which was never returned to the state).

Table 17.2 Poverty elasticities of growth and income inequality

	Poverty elasticity of growth (PHR*/GDP/c*)				**Poverty elasticity of inequality (PHR*/Gini*)**			
z/GDP per capita	Gini Index				Gini Index			
	0.3	0.4	0.5	0.6	0.3	0.4	0.5	0.6
0.33	−3.9	−2.1	−1.3	−0.8	5.2	3.3	2.4	2.0
0.50	−2.8	−1.6	−1.0	−0.7	2.5	1.7	1.3	1.2
0.67	−2.0	−1.2	−0.8	−0.5	1.2	0.9	0.8	0.8
1.00	−1.2	−0.8	−0.5	−0.4	0.2	0.2	0.3	0.4

Note: z is the absolute poverty line. A country with a z/GDP/c of 0.33–05 has a middle level of income, while one with values between 0.67 and 1 is poor.

Source: Son and Kakwani (2003).

a low z/GDP per capita and a high Gini (such as those of Latin America), the poverty elasticity of inequality (PHR*/Gini*) is greater than the poverty elasticity of the growth of GDP per capita (PHR*/GDP/c*). This means that the PHR declines faster owing to a 1 per cent distributive improvement than to a 1 per cent growth of GDP per capita. The opposite is true in poor developing countries (such as the rural economies of West Africa) with a high z/GDP/c and a low Gini index, as in these countries the PHR declines only slightly or not at all in the absence of economic growth.

For each macroeconomic policy, and for all policies taken simultaneously, the impact on growth can be written in general terms as:

$$\text{GDP/c} = \kappa\,\text{MacroPolicy} + \mu\,\text{ICA} - \lambda\,\text{Gini} \tag{17.3}$$

or, in first differences,

$$\Delta\text{GDP/c} = \kappa\,\Delta\text{MacroPolicy} + \mu\,\Delta\text{ICA} - \lambda\,\Delta\text{Gini} \tag{17.3a}$$

where κ, μ, and λ are parameters reflecting the influence of the relative variables. Whenever economic policy is endogenous to the initial conditions A and B, in symbols Macropolicy $= \gamma$ICA $+$ vICB, equation (17.3) becomes

$$\Delta\text{GDP/c} = (\kappa\gamma + \mu)\,\Delta\text{ICA} + \kappa\varpi\,\Delta\text{ICB} - \lambda\Delta\text{Gini} \tag{17.4}$$

17.3 Concepts of Income and the Shape of Alternative Distributions of Income

Income concepts

To assess the distributive impact of macroeconomic reforms it is necessary to first define precisely the income concepts and their distributions used in the analysis, as both vary considerably. There are two main types of income distribution: the first is the functional distribution of income, that is, the distribution of the total output among production factors (land, capital, labour). The latter allows the calculation of the labour share, capital

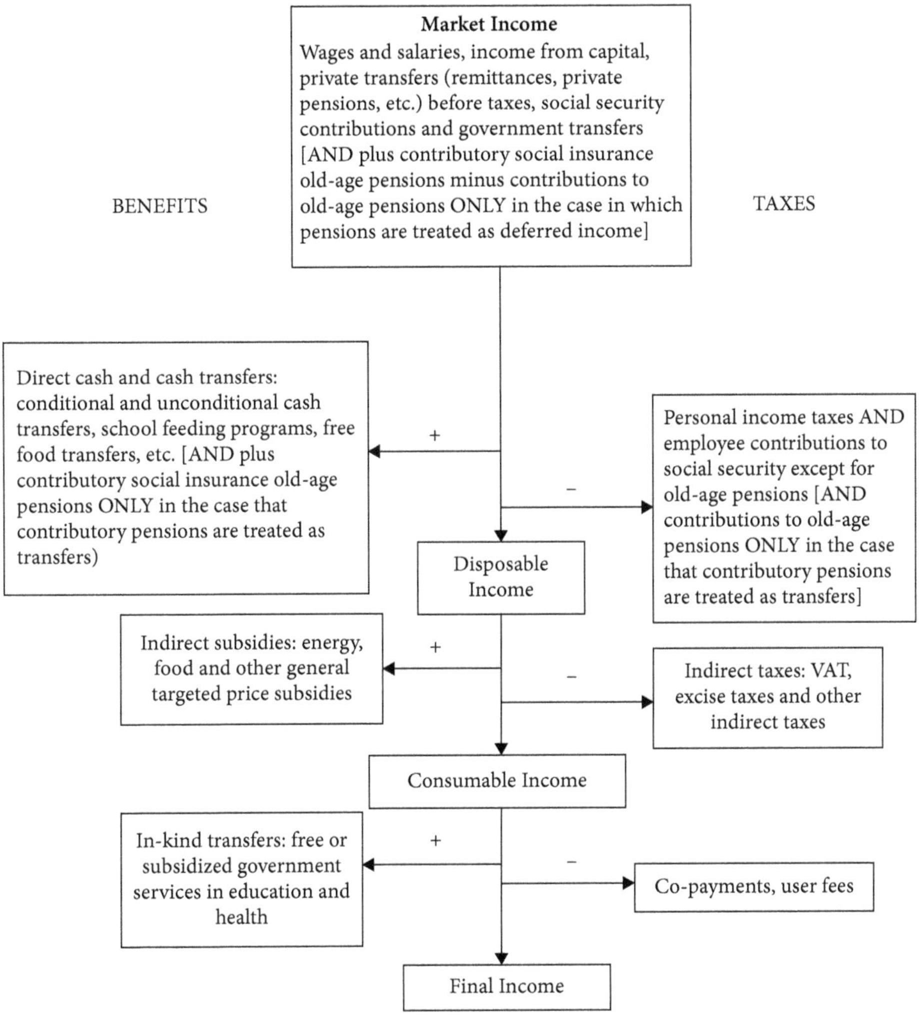

Figure 17.2 Definition of alternative income concepts and factors affecting their distribution
Source: Lustig et al. (2013)

share, and so on. The second concept of income distribution refers to the dimensional distribution of income, that is, the distribution of the total and of each type of income by percentile of the total income. It allows the computation of synthetic inequality indexes (such as the Gini coefficient) of the distribution among households of total income and of its components. For both the functional and dimensional distribution of income five concepts of income can be distinguished: gross market income; net market income; disposable income; post fiscal income; and final income (see Figure 17.2).

The distribution of gross market income (also called the primary income, or market income) refers to the distribution of gross national income among factors of production (capital, labour, land, entrepreneurs, etc.) before the payment of direct taxes and social security contributions.[3] Let us recall that the parameters of the neoclassical production function α, β, and γ represent the marginal productivity of such factors and—according to

[3] Gross market income also includes private transfers which are, in a way, considered as earned income.

this theory—their fair factorial income shares of the national product, although in reality these depend on several structural factors (see Chapter 2 and the chapters in Part II). The distribution of gross market income (before taxes and transfers to households) among types of income is the most unequal. It can be written as:

$$Y = (W + P) + I + R + \Pi + SE \tag{17.5}$$

where the first element on the right-hand side is the remuneration of labour (W for wages and P for contributory pensions—that are considered as a deferred wage). The next three variables are the remuneration of financial capital (I), land and other rents (R), and profits (Π). The last variable, SE, is the remuneration of self-employed workers who earn a mixed income rewarding their labour, capital, and entrepreneurship. In many developing countries, (W + P) and SE account for around 70 per cent of gross national income (Y), while the remaining 30 per cent is absorbed by capital incomes such as profits, interest, and rents of various types.

The distribution of net market income (also called secondary distribution of income) refers to the distribution of gross market income after the payment of direct taxes and social security contributions, T, by households. These are payable on each type of market income, and $T = T_{w-p} + T_{se} + T_i + T_r + T_\pi$ is the sum of direct taxes and social security contributions collected by the state treasury and national social security agency. The sum of the net value of each type of income is equal to the net market income, as shown by equation (17.6):

$$(Y - T) = (W + P - T_{w-p}) + (SE - T_{se}) + (I - T_i) + (R - T_r) + (\Pi - T_\pi) \tag{17.6}$$

It is obvious that, if direct taxation is progressive, as it mainly is, the distribution of net market income will exhibit more equitable income shares of the various production factors compared to those of gross market income. Moreover, the dimensional distribution of each type of income will also improve, since high income taxes are generally paid by high-wage earners and contributory pensioners and by recipients of high interest, rents, and profits.

Third, the distribution of net disposable income, YD (also called the tertiary distribution), refers to the distribution of net market income after the transfer of public cash benefits to households. Since cash transfers (social assistance, non-contributory benefits, social pensions, child allowances, conditional-cash transfers, etc.) are (or should be) mainly targeted on low-income groups, the distribution of disposable income, YD (equation (17.7)), is expected to be more equitable than that of net market income. Indeed, if one decomposes the total income of the poorest household decile, it is possible to see that cash benefits constitute up to 30–50 per cent of total income in developed countries and 10–30 per cent in developing countries. In symbols:

$$\begin{aligned} YD = (Y - T + TR) = (W - T_{w-p} + TR_{w-p}) + (SE - T_{se} + TR_{se}) \\ + (I - T_i + TR_i) + (R - T_r + TR_r) + (\Pi - T_\pi + TR_\pi) \end{aligned} \tag{17.7}$$

where $\Sigma T > \Sigma TR$, given that part of tax revenue is used by the government to provide goods and services in kind such as general administration, health, and education. This is especially true in developing countries. If transfers are added in a single term (TR), and assuming that

90 per cent of the income from self-employment, SE, is labour income and 10 per cent is capital income (indicating both of them with the symbol ′ which indicates that they are net of taxes), and considering then that the incomes I, R, and Π (from interest, rents, and profits) can be grouped into a single group of capital incomes, K, one can now write:

$$YD = W' + K' + TR \tag{17.8}$$

This relation indicates that net disposable income is composed of labour income, capital income, and social transfers. The dimensional distributions of these three types of income differ considerably among each other. In terms of their degree of inequality, the Gini index or the concentration coefficient (also named the quasi-Gini index as it ranges between −1 and 1) of transfers, T, ranges between −0.20 and 0.20, that of wages and self-employment income between 0.30 and 0.40, and that of capital incomes between 0.60 and 0.80.

Fourth, it is important to compute the distribution of post-fiscal income by subtracting from the distribution of net disposable income indirect taxes (VAT, excises, other sales taxes, import duties and export taxes, taxes on financial transactions, duty stamps, and so on). These are paid not on the basis of the gross income of the household but when purchasing goods or when making use of public services provided by the state administration subject to co-payments. From these indirect taxes and duty stamps, we subtract the indirect subsidies received by the households, for example purchases of basic items at subsidized prices in special state stores, such as the Indian Public Distribution System (PDS) that provides food items at below market prices to people of low incomes. Indirect taxes are generally slightly or markedly regressive, while indirect subsidies are generally well targeted and progressive but absorb only a small share of GDP. The net effect probably varies, but it is unlikely that, in the absence of large PDS-type programmes, the distribution of post-fiscal income has a much lower Gini than that of net disposable income (Figures 17.2 and 17.3).

Fifth, the distribution of final income refers to the post-fiscal income to which have been added government in-kind transfers in the form of free or subsidized education, health, and housing, minus co-payments (such as user fees) for the utilization of such services.[4] Generally speaking, in most developing countries public expenditure on primary and secondary education, primary health care, and communal water and sanitation services is progressive, while that on university education, hospitals, and urban piped-water systems tends to be regressive. In the developing countries of Latin America, the distributive effect of public social expenditure tends to be progressive, especially in highly urbanized countries—such as Brazil, Argentina, and Uruguay—where the possibility of extending public services to most of the population is greater than in low-density or remote rural areas.

Summing up, Figure 17.3 helps us to understand why, in middle-income developing countries, taxation can reduce the Gini coefficient of the distribution of gross income by only 1–2 percentage points, as in these countries income taxes are paid by only 20–30 per cent of households. Instead, cash benefits tend to improve the distribution of net income markedly, for example by 4.2 Gini points in Argentina and 2.1 in Brazil. The distribution of post-fiscal income after considering indirect taxes and subsidies hardly changes the distribution of income (e.g. the Gini changes by one point in Bolivia and 0.2 points in

[4] One can also define the concept of final income as disposable income plus government in-kind subsidies in the form of free or subsidized services in education, health, and housing minus co-payments.

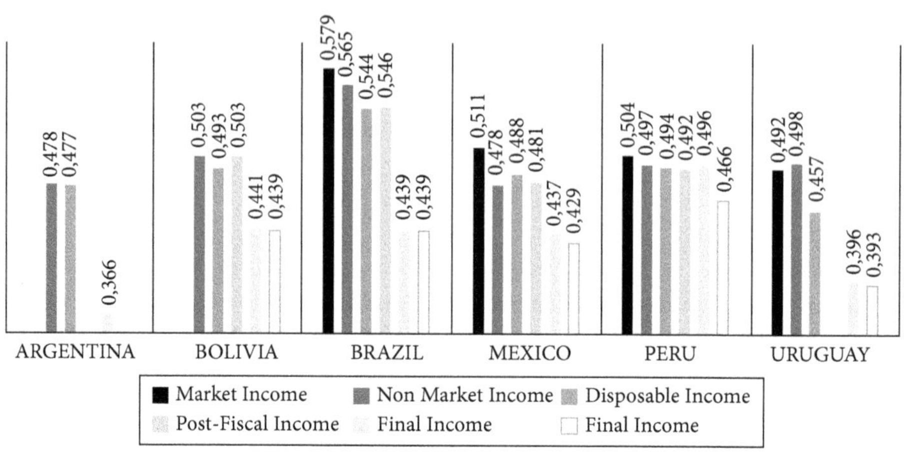

Figure 17.3 Gini coefficient according to different concepts of income distribution in six Latin American countries, 2008, 2009, and 2010

Source: Own elaboration on Lustig et al. (2013)

Brazil) due to the regressive nature of still dominant indirect taxes and the limited scope of indirect subsidies. A major redistributive effect is generated instead by the provision of services in kind (which reduce the Gini coefficient of post-fiscal income by more than 10 Gini points in Brazil and 4.4 in Mexico).

Alternative distributions of income

The dimensional distribution of income—whether gross, net, disposable, post fiscal, or final—measures the distribution of total household income per capita (or of each of its components, such as wages, transfers, and capital incomes) by percentiles of total household income per capita. The dimensional distribution may be represented graphically in several ways (Figure 17.4). The first distribution (going from left to right) is the frequency (or density) function, which exhibits the level of household income per capita on the horizontal axis and the absolute number (or relative percentage) of individuals with such income per capita on the ordinates. It can also be represented through the cumulative Pareto distribution, which has the income level per capita on the horizontal axis and the cumulative percentage of population with an income per capita below a given level on the ordinates. This function is the integral of the density function. In turn, the Penn Parade exhibits the income earners arranged in ascending order on the abscissas and their absolute income on the ordinates. Finally, the Lorenz curve presents the cumulative percentage of

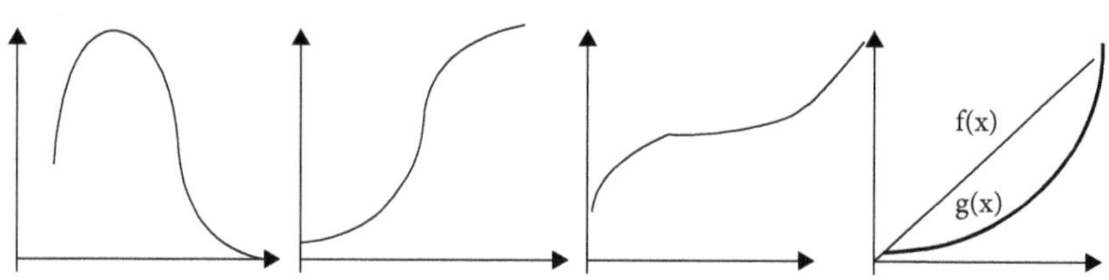

Figure 17.4 Shape of the density function, Pareto distribution, Penn's Parade and Lorenz curve

income earners on the abscissas, and the cumulative percentage of income accruing to them on the ordinates (Figure 17.4). Each of these distributions is particularly fit for specific types of analyses (see Section 17.4).

There are many indexes that summarize the size distribution of income. The most commonly used are: the Gini coefficient which varies between zero and one; the interdecile ratio (that is, the ratio between the income share of the richest 10 per cent of the population and that of the poorest 10 or 40 per cent) which has an indeterminate range of variation but is particularly helpful to illustrate the income polarization between the rich and the poor; and the Theil coefficient, which does not have a predefined range of variation but is perfectly decomposable.

17.4 Sources of Change in the Distribution of Disposable Income

Let us suppose that we have constructed the distribution of the total net household disposable income per capita by means of the Lorenz curve and measured its degree of inequality by means of the Gini coefficient. Now, at each point in time, the Gini coefficient (which can be represented as $G = [\int f(x) - \int g(x)]/\int f(x)$[5] is equal to the sum of the concentration coefficients (which vary between -1 and 1) of each category of income (C_{it}) weighted by its share of income (sh_{it}) from wages, capital incomes, and transfers in total disposable income, that is:

$$G_t = \Sigma_i\, sh_{it} C_{it} \qquad \text{given } \Sigma_i\, sh_{it} = 1 \tag{17.9}$$

By differentiating over time, equation (17.9), the change in the Gini index ($\Delta G = G_{t+1} - G_t$) can be decomposed as follows:[6]

$$\Delta G = \Sigma_i \Delta sh_i\, C_{it} + \Sigma_i \Delta C_i\, sh_{it} + \Sigma_i \Delta sh_i\, \Delta C_i \tag{17.10}$$

or, when specifying in full all income components, as follows:

$$\begin{aligned}\Delta G = {} & (\Delta sh_w\, C_{wt} + \Delta sh_k\, C_{kt} + \Delta sh_{tr}\, C_{trt}) + (sh_{wt}\Delta C_w + sh_{kt}\Delta C_k + sh_{trt}\Delta C_{tr}) \\ & + + (\Delta sh_w \Delta C_w + \Delta sh_k \Delta C_k + \Delta sh_{tr} \Delta C_{tr})\end{aligned} \tag{17.11}$$

This decomposition shows that a change over time in the distribution of the total net household disposable income per capita is due to three factors, that is, changes in the income shares of labour, capital, and transfers, sh_i, between t and t + 1, each weighted by their concentration coefficients in the base year t, C_{it}; changes in the concentration coefficients of each type of income (wages, rents, transfers) weighted by their respective shares of income in the base year t, sh_{it}; and an interaction term ($\Sigma_i \Delta sh_i\, \Delta C_i$) equal to the product of the change of the concentration index multiplied by the changes of income shares, both between time t and t + 1. This term is usually neglected as it is very small.

[5] The functions f(x) and g(x) are those shown for the Lorenz curve in Figure 17.4.

[6] This result is obtained by using the general formula for the differentiation of a function over time. For instance, if $c = ab$, the time differentiation produces the following result: $\Delta c = a\Delta b + b\Delta a + \Delta a\Delta b$.

Thus, changes in economic policies can influence the overall distribution of income if they modify the percentage shares of the various types of income. The income distribution will evolve in a more equitable way if the share of social transfers and wages increases at the expense of that of capital income. For instance, if the government taxes financial rents and allocates the revenue collected to the poorest households in the form of social transfers, the share of the unequally distributed rents in total income decreases, while that of progressive social transfers increases. If, in contrast, the capital share increases due to a rise of interest rates which benefits the rentiers, there will be a *ceteris paribus* worsening of the overall distribution. Economic reforms can likewise modify the degree of inequality of the distribution of each income component (wages, rents, and transfers) and of the overall income distribution if their concentration coefficients change. For example, a rise in the Gini coefficient of the distribution of wages due to a fall in minimum wages is likely to entail a deterioration of the overall size distribution of income. Likewise, if a reform of social transfers targets them accurately on the poor, then their distribution will improve and so will the overall income distribution.

The next sections evaluate the impact of the policy reforms of the last three decades on the distribution of total income, keeping in mind the analytical framework of equations (17.10) and (17.11), namely the possibility that these policies may alter the shares of the components of total income (Δsh_w, Δsh_k, Δsh_{tr}) or their dimensional distribution (ΔC_w, ΔC_k, ΔC_{tr}).

17.5 Liberalization of the Labour Market

The reforms adopted in this field since the1980s and 1990s promoted wage flexibility, the abolition of several labour regulations, a reduction of the coverage of minimum wages, and a weakening of unionization and collective bargaining. The impact of these measures was often exacerbated by the removal of controls on capital inflows and outflows This was a decision that increased the bargaining power of firms when negotiating wage settlements with unions and governments, as emphasized by the literature on 'footloose capital and immobile labour', according to which the liberalization of capital movements tends to erode the direct and indirect wage. The impact of labour market reforms varies according to the type of measures introduced and the initial conditions.

Liberalization of a dualistic labour market with a small formal sector

Economies such as Zimbabwe or India today are characterized by a dualistic labour market, with a small but highly unionized formal sector (absorbing around 10–20 per cent of the workforce). The unionized labour succeeds in imposing in the formal sector a regulated minimum wage, W_{fr}, that is higher than the equilibrium wage, W_{fe}. In turn, the informal sector is characterized by neoclassical demand–supply relations in the presence of a large surplus labour, or by oligopolistic, exploitative labour relations. There is no open unemployment, while the regulated minimum wage cannot be enforced in the informal sector.

The informal sector absorbs the excess labour force which fails to find employment in the formal sector. It is assumed that within both the formal and informal sectors all workers receive the same wage. Due to the introduction of minimum wages in the formal sector, the labour demand by firms drops. As a result, the supply of labour to the informal sector will rise from LS′ to LS and the related wage fall to W_{ir} that is lower than the equilibrium wage, W_{ie} (Figure 17.5). Given these initial conditions, the inequality of the distribution of wages will be a function of the wage differential ($W_{fr} - W_{ir}$) and the corresponding share of employment in the two sectors.

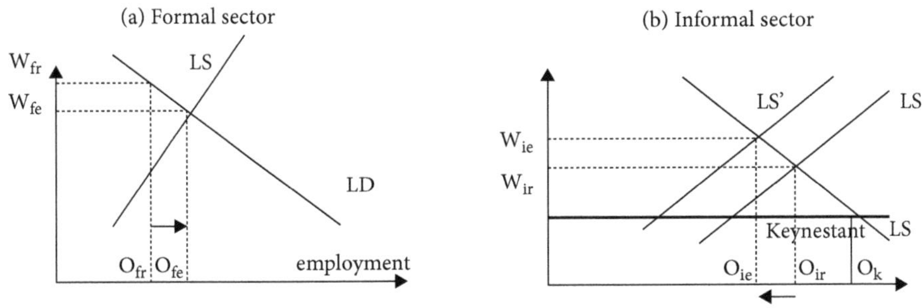

Figure 17.5 Impact of wage liberalization in a dualistic labour market

What happens if the formal sector minimum wage is abolished? In this model, its abolition lowers the formal sector wage and raises the informal wage (Figure 17.5), while the employment effects are symmetric, as the labour supply to the informal sector declines and labour absorption in the formal sector rises. In this case, the abolition of minimum wages in the formal sector reduces the wage gap between the two sectors and reduces overall wage inequality.

These conclusions, however, depend on assumptions that may not be validated in a developing country context. In a poor country, for instance, the supply of labour is probably infinitely elastic (as shown by the bold Keynesian schedule parallel to the x-axis in Figure 17.5). Therefore a transfer of informal workers to the formal sector due to the abolition of a minimum wage in the formal sector would not raise informal sector wages, thus generating a smaller impact on the wage gap as the difference ($W_{fr}-W_{ir}$) would decline by less. Second, the realism of the hypothesis about the intersectoral mobility of supposedly homogeneous workers is questionable. In some cases, this transfer may not be feasible because of location or lack of specific training for informal sector workers. Finally, formal sector minimum wages may also have an impact in the informal sector. For instance, Kristensen and Cunningham (2006), studying nineteen countries in Latin America and the Caribbean, found cliffs in the cumulative wage distribution around the level of minimum wages for both formal and informal workers. This suggests for these countries the existence of a 'lighthouse effect', as the minimum wage of the formal sector becomes a reference wage (a lighthouse) also for wage setting in the informal sector. The neoclassical assumptions that the minimum wage is applicable only to formal workers would then fall and—in this case—the abolition of minimum wages may also affect informal sector workers, generating uncertain distributive effects.

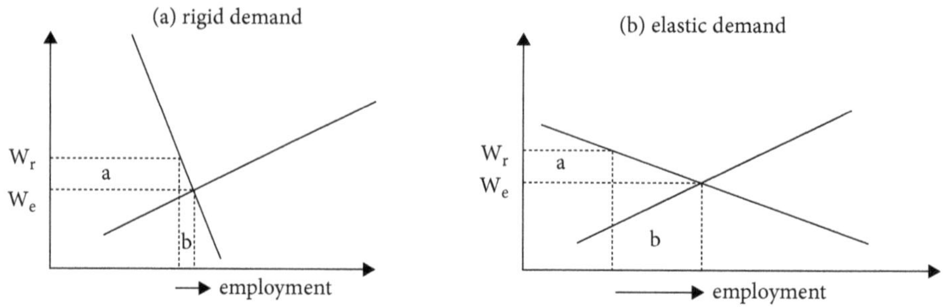

Figure 17.6 Impact of liberalization in labour markets with different elasticities of labour demand

Wage liberalization in a unified labour market

The liberalization of a regulated wage set by means of collective bargaining or government norms (Figure 17.6) generates an increase in employment, a fall in unemployment, and a drop in the wage rate from w_r to w_e. If it is assumed that Y remains constant, the effect on the functional distribution of income depends on the elasticity of labour demand. In case of inelastic labour demand, wage liberalization leads to a decrease of the total wage bill (as, in Figure 17.6a, as $b < a$). and to a likely deterioration of the functional distribution of income. In this case, the increase in the wage bill due to an increase in employment less than compensates the drop in the total wage bill caused by the drop in the wage rate.

Conversely, if the labour demand is elastic (near w_r), wage liberalization leads to an increase of the wage bill (as $b > a$) and—assuming a constant Y—to an improvement in the functional distribution of income and of the Gini of the total income distribution. Less clear is the impact on growth. In a static neoclassical framework characterized by full employment, growth may not increase but there will be a substitution between labour (as activity rates will rise) and capital. More likely, in Figure 17.6b there will be an increase of production (and therefore a positive growth effect) given a possible increase in investment that will accompany rising activity rates and greater employment, with ambiguous distributive effects.

Wage liberalization with heterogeneous workers

A liberalization of wages generally involves a de-compression of the wage distribution that—after liberalization—is likely to correlate more than before with the human capital and experience of the workers. In the past, the inequality of the original wage distribution was reduced by collective bargaining or, as in the former transition economies, by a socialist distributive rule. In this case, the *ex ante* impact of wage liberalization on the distribution of earnings is undetermined because it depends on two opposite effects: an unequalizing effect due to greater wage dispersion (Figure 17.7), and an equalizing effect due to the creation of new jobs. When the wages of low- to medium-skilled workers fall, there may be a rise in demand for their labour. In this case, the equalizing effect is due to the fact that previously unemployed workers received no salary.

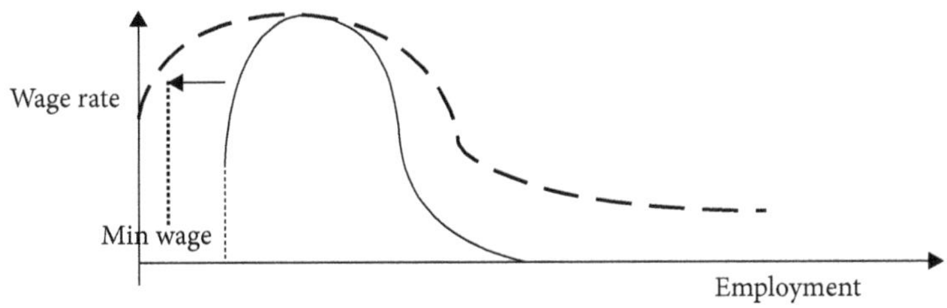

Figure 17.7 Impact of labour market liberalization on the distribution of wages in a labour market with heterogeneous workers

The empirical evidence shows that the first effect has prevailed in many cases and that wage inequality rose in many developing countries and transition economies that liberalized wage setting. In Eastern Europe, the fall of minimum wages in relation to the average level and in absolute terms was closely correlated with the observed increase in earnings inequality. Likewise, Behrman et al. (2000) show that in eighteen Latin American countries wage differentials widened in the 1980s and 1990s after the liberalization of the labour market. Symmetrically, Keifman and Maurizio (2014) show that the labour reforms introduced in this region during the 2000s (that is, a reintroduction of collective bargaining, a tighter enforcement of labour laws, and an increase in minimum wages) reduced the inequality of the distribution of hourly wages.

17.6 Domestic Financial Liberalization

In the developing countries, the liberalization of domestic finance has been one of the key reforms of the 1980s and 1990s. Even deeper changes have affected the advanced countries since 1994, when the Glass–Steagall law was repealed in the United States. Reform of the financial sector in low-income countries was inspired by the objective to abolish the financial repression inherited from the first three decades after World War II. Financial liberalization was expected to lead to low but positive market-determined real interest rates, a financial deepening measured by a rise of deposits and M2/GDP, greater competition among domestic and foreign banks, a decline in spreads, an expansion of credit to the private sector, and the creation of stock markets, that is, measures that were expected to improve financial intermediation, the savings rate, investment, employment, growth, and income distribution.

However, the empirical evidence suggests that while this reform generated positive growth and distributive effects in the 1990s in the OECD countries and some developing economies (for instance, Mauritius), in the majority of low-income countries the impact was negative. This negative impact was due, in particular, to an increase in financial instability, an excessive rise in interest rates, the persistence of high spreads, and the limited and poorly allocated increase in the volume of credit. How can this discrepancy between theoretical expectations and the empirical evidence be explained?

A first problem has been poor policy sequencing. In many cases, financial liberalization was introduced in the presence of large budget deficits that—after liberalization—had to be financed with the sale of state bonds on the domestic market. Because of the novelty and low credibility of the new securities, the limited depth of the new bond markets, and the considerable volume of bonds issued, interest rates rose dramatically in both nominal and real terms. This increase in interest rates was rapidly transmitted to the rest of the financial sector, with the effect of shifting the distribution of income in favour of depositors belonging to medium- to high-income groups. Second, contrary to expectations, financial liberalization did not succeed—especially in the 1980s—in raising competition within the domestic financial sector. While the balance sheet of banks improved in most cases, their privatization transformed them into private oligopolies, as suggested by the sharp increases in real interest rates and spreads. The entry into the domestic market of foreign banks failed to improve competition, given that—due to asymmetric information problems—these banks focused on a few low-risk customers, ignoring the credit demands of small producers, who continued to rely on informal credit at much higher interest rates. Third, financial liberalization was introduced with no prior strengthening of the regulatory and supervisory capacity of central banks and of the public bodies in charge of supervising the banks and the stock market. Just the opposite. In many cases, the usual prudential norms (such as the ratio between own means and deposits) that have to be satisfied for the opening of new banks and carrying out financial transactions were loosened beyond any reasonable level. Thus, in many cases financial deregulation led to an increase in financial instability, with negative distributive and growth effects.

The financial deregulation of the last twenty-five years in the OECD countries has generated even more pronounced unequalizing effects therein and in developing countries affected by financial and real contagion. In this case, excessive leverage and risk taking eroded banking regulation and prudential and accounting norms about non-performing loans. Furthermore, the unchecked proliferation of derivatives and other 'over the counter' (i.e. unrecorded) contracts generated boom-and-bust credit cycles that affected inequality. The analyses of Keynes, Minsky, Schiller, Stiglitz, and others about the inherent instability of financial markets have emphasized the dangers of an all-out internal and external financial liberalization and the need for efficient regulation that does not repeat the mistakes of the past financial repression. For instance, Moss (2010) has related bank failures and financial reforms in the United States from 1864 to 2006, showing the connection between turning points in regulatory approaches and changes in inequality proxied by the income share of the top 10 per cent. In this regard, Figure 17.8 suggests that the magnitude of the recent financial crisis reflects the failure of the regulatory philosophy of the past two decades. In his view, the financial collapse of 2007–09 was not an accident but rather a mistake driven by the faulty post-1994 US regulatory approach.

An additional triggering factor of the recent wave of financial crises was the loosening of banking and financial regulation of the 1980s and 1990s that allowed the creation of off-balance-sheet and shadow financial institutions to that escape the control of central banks. This increased leverage and contributed to a long series of financial and banking crises. However, unlike in the OECD and European transition economies, the developing countries have recently, including in 2008–09, experienced fewer financial, sovereign debt, and banking crises. One reason for this crisis avoidance was the expanded role played by the IMF. Another factor was the banking reforms implemented in several developing countries. For instance, as argued by Rojas-Suarez (2010), during the 2000s many Latin American countries (which had experienced many financial crises in the past) enhanced the capitalization, funding, and supervision of their banking systems; encouraged the development of local capital markets; introduced a stricter prudential regulation of financial systems; enhanced risk-assessment mechanisms in large banks; developed appropriate

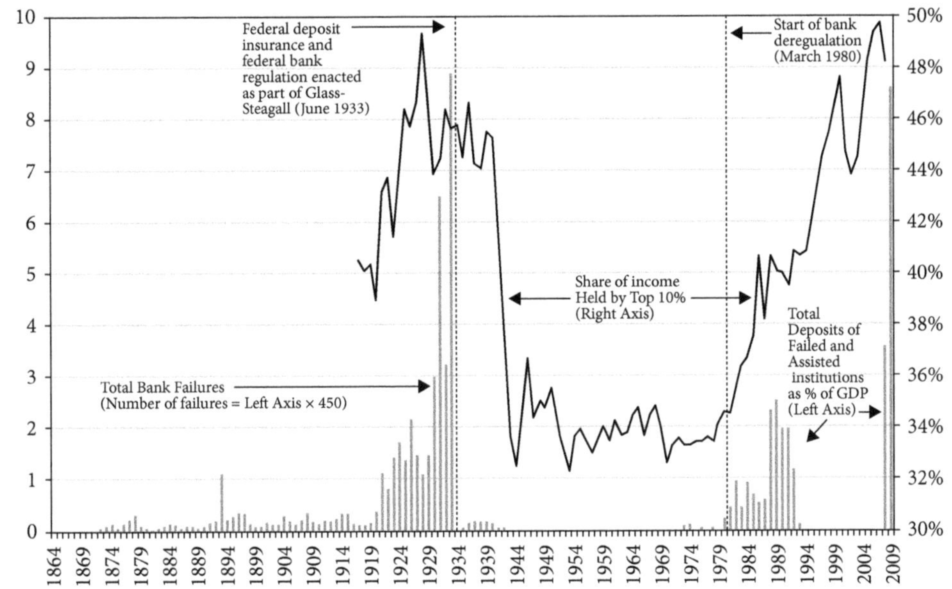

Figure 17.8 Bank failures, regulation and inequality in the United States, 1864–2009
Source: Moss (2010)

legal, judicial, and accounting frameworks; and assigned a broader role to state banks in financing economic activity during crises.

A final reason for the limited success of orthodox financial liberalization was the persistence or worsening of credit discrimination of small and medium-sized enterprises. Certainly, repressed financial systems allocated credit in unfair and inefficient ways. However, financial liberalization did not solve this problem (see Chapter 8) and in several cases it worsened it. On the one hand, the allocation of preferential credit at subsidized interest rates to small firms and agriculture was often discontinued. On the other, the rigid adoption of risk minimization and profit maximization objectives at the level of each bank branch led to the closure of many rural banks and a sharp decline in the volume of credit allocated to agriculture. For example, in India, the financial liberalization of 1991 eliminated almost entirely the obligation of the major banks to allocate a share of their lending to agriculture and small firms.

The net result of these changes was strongly unequalizing, given that it increased the share of national income allocated to the payment of interest, that is, a type of income that is characterized by a high Gini index. In developing countries, the incidence of tax revenue (used to pay the interest on public debt) is roughly proportional, while state bonds are mainly owned by high income people. Domestic financial liberalization has thus lead to a substantial increase in the rate of return on such financial assets, an increase in the share of GDP allocated to capital income and—*ceteris paribus*—an overall worsening of income distribution.

17.7 Reform of Taxation and Social Transfers

During the 1980s and 1990s, the tax systems of developing countries evolved towards simplification (by eliminating inefficient taxes, exemptions, and tax privileges) and lower progressivity (by reducing the top tax rates and by substituting direct taxes with non-graduated indirect taxes). However, while tax progressivity was reduced everywhere, leading to higher vertical inequality, a strong emphasis was also placed on reducing horizontal inequality among people in the same income bracket by eliminating tax exemptions, holidays, deductions, and special tax regimes. The net impact of these two changes differed from country to country, depending on the relative weight given to the two measures. The empirical evidence suggests, however, that in most cases the rise in vertical inequality dominated the broadening of the tax base, so that overall tax revenue and progressivity declined. For example, an analysis of the impact of tax reform in Latin America in the 1980s and 1990s (Morley, 2000) concluded that the reforms moved the tax burden from the rich to the middle class and the poor. And in Pakistan, the introduction of such tax reform increased the tax burden on the poor by 7.4 per cent between 1987–88 and 1997–98, while it reduced it by 15.9 per cent for the richest households. Finally, a study of the tax reforms introduced in thirty-five developing countries since the mid-1970s (Chu et al., 2004) concluded that the revenue/GDP ratio fell on average by one percentage point between the 1980s and 1990s (while it had increased by 1.6 points between the 1970s and 1980s). Chu and colleagues also found that the importance of direct taxes in the total fell, along with the overall progressivity of taxation. The impact of such reforms on growth remains controversial. Yet, when the reduction of the tax/GDP ratio takes place from an already low level of taxation, it is likely that it exacerbates the government's inability to finance those public goods that are essential for long-term growth.

However, the situation changed in the 2000s thanks to a more pragmatic approach to policy reform and the IMF and donors' encouragement to raise tax/GDP ratios. The new approach is inspired by the search for greater tax equity and the principle of 'fiscal exchange' according to which governments can raise taxes if, at the same time, they increase the quantity and quality of services provided to a broad spectrum of the population. The specific changes introduced by the new approach included a rise in revenue generated by income and wealth taxes, particularly corporate income tax (Cornia et al. 2014). To do so, many Latin American governments eliminated a long list of exemptions, deductions, and tax holidays introduced in the 1980s and 1990s to attract foreign investments that did not, however, yield the desired effect. Presumptive taxation was also strengthened. Several Latin American countries also introduced a surrogate tax on financial transactions. As a result, tax/GDP ratios rose, and tax progressivity improved, as shown in Table 17.3.

The reform of income transfers was generally less important, given their modest volume in most developing countries, especially the low-income ones. In these countries the available resources for social assistance are used to finance consumer subsidies for food, kerosene, drugs, public works, and, since the 2000s, non-contributory minimum pensions or social assistance benefits for the poor. But recently, Chile, Brazil, Mexico, and other Latin American countries have developed a broad system of conditional and non-conditional cash transfers targeted on the poor, which over 2005–08 have generated an average regional decline of the Gini coefficient of 2.2 points (Cornia, 2014). In turn, social insurance benefits (unemployment subsidies, old age and sickness pensions, and family allowances) remain available only to formal sector workers (that is, 10–20 per cent of the workforce) and are in any case included in the gross income (see Figure 17.2).

In contrast, the reforms of social insurance transfers instituted during the 1990s in most transition economies consisted in reducing their volume, duration, and eligibility

Table 17.3 Changes in the Reynolds–Smolensky index for Latin American countries, 1990s and 2000s

	1990s	2000s	2000s–1990s
Argentina	−1.95	1.90	3.85
Brazil	−0.70	0.42	1.12
Chile	−0.80	0.27	1.07
Costa Rica	−0.98	1.24	2.22
Ecuador	−0.70	0.70	1.40
El Salvador	−1.40	−0.75	0.65
Guatemala	−0.77	1.20	1.97
Honduras	−2.87	−0.10	2.77
Nicaragua	−5.20	0.17	5.37
Panama	−0.69	0.91	1.60
Uruguay	−0.20	1.10	1.30

Note: the Reynolds–Smolensky index is the difference between the Gini coefficient of the gross distribution of income and that of disposable income. A negative value of the index denotes a regressive taxation, a positive value a progressive one. For instance, Argentina experienced a drop of the Gini index by 3.85 points due to the impact of the tax measures introduced in the 2000s.

Source: Cornia et al. (2014).

Table 17.4 Share of income transfers in total income in selected transition economies, 1989–1994

	1989	1991–1992	1993–1994
Hungary	26.1	28.2	26.7
Slovenia	10.9	—	20.4
Romania	12.5	9.3	7.8
Bulgaria	21.9	21.6	19.0
Moldova	11.3	—	8.3
Ukraine	16.1	11.2	—

Source: UNICEF (1994 and 1995).

(Table 17.4), that is, measures that entailed a reduction in the transfer share in a declining total income. These measures also targeted previously universal transfers on the poor. While the first measures had a regressive impact (since the concentration coefficient of transfers is lower than that of other types of income), the second can in principle be progressive, especially when the targeting is done by means of objective criteria.

In terms of the transfers in kind for health, education, and housing, IMF aggregate data suggest an improvement in their progressivity. The preference assigned to certain types of social transfers (e.g. old-age pensions) affected the overall progressivity of public policy in this area. Data reported for selected transition economies in the 1990s (Table 17.5) suggest, in fact, that the concentration coefficient of various types of social transfers varies considerably. For instance, family allowances, unemployment benefits, and social assistance have a concentration coefficient ranging between −0.3 and 0.2, while sickness benefits and old-age pensions have a concentration coefficient varying between 0.1 and 0.4. The overall impact of the reform of social transfers thus varied from country to country depending on the policy mix followed.

Table 17.5 Changes in the concentration coefficients of social transfers, Eastern Europe, 1989–1993

	Unemployment subsidy and sick pay	Pensions	Family benefits
Bulgaria 1992	6.1	—	−4.1
Bulgaria 1993	10.6	—	−5.0
Hungary 1989	19.8	19.9	−15.2
Hungary 1993	−11.3	19.9	−15.2
Poland 1990	−14.7	13.7	−16.2
Poland 1993	−8.6	33.6	−11.8

Source: Cornia (1996).

17.8 Liberalization of Foreign Trade

These reforms were introduced on a priority basis in the 1980s and 1990s in almost all developing countries. Contingents and other quantitative restrictions were converted into tariffs, while these were lowered and unified within a relatively narrow band (Table 17.1). In addition, direct and indirect export subsidies were reduced or removed (except for the costly subsidies granted under the European Common Agricultural Policy and similar US and Japanese support schemes), the real exchange rate was devalued and full convertibility was introduced for all current account transactions. What was the impact of these reforms on inequality and growth? To answer this question, let us first examine what mainstream theory says in this regard, and then compare the theoretical predictions with the empirical evidence.

The theoretical rationale for trade liberalization is provided by the Hecksher–Ohlin theorem, a pillar of neoclassical trade theory, and by its Stolper and Samuelson corollary. The above theorem refers to a situation of 2 × 2 × 2, that is, trade between two countries producing two goods with two factors of production (capital and labour). Both countries use the same technology that remains constant over time. The model also assumes there are no economies of scale, markets are efficient, and the balance of payments is in equilibrium. The theorem shows that free trade leads to greater production specialization in the sectors of the two trading countries that utilize more intensely the production factors with which they are endowed. This leads to an increase in national income in both countries as a result of a more rational sectoral allocation of production factors. In the case of developing countries with a strong supply of unskilled labour, trade liberalization shifts production from the non-tradable and import-substituting sectors towards the labour-intensive tradable sector. This increases the demand for unskilled workers, raises their relative wage in comparison to better paid skilled workers and therefore improves the distribution of wages and income. In turn, the Stolper–Samuelson corollary shows that trade liberalization leads to a convergence in the prices of the two goods to that of the most competitive producer. Trade liberalization also equalizes the price of production factors to an intermediate value of their initial prices of the two trading partners. It will also generate an improvement in income distribution in countries endowed with unskilled labour, and a deterioration in those engaged in the production of goods requiring large amounts of capital, land, and skilled labour.

The predictions of the Hecksher–Ohlin theorem have been roughly validated in the European countries and the United States during the globalization of 1870–1914. Such globalization led to greater integration among the New and Old Worlds, thanks to policies of liberalization and globalization, which—*inter alia*—cut import tariffs. As a result, the trade/GDP ratio rose, there was a convergence in the prices of final goods among the trading countries, and in the wages and GDP per capita of the New and Old Worlds. Finally there was an increase in the wage/rental ratio (an index of the functional distribution of income) in Europe (which was endowed with a large amount of unskilled labour). Meanwhile this ratio fell in the United States due to an increasing demand for land to produce cereals, which raised land rents and encouraged increased immigration from Europe of many unskilled workers, leading to depressed unskilled wages.

The predictions of the Hecksher–Ohlin model and of its corollary have also been confirmed by the trade liberalization in the first wave of Asian Tigers, which specialized in the export of labour-intensive goods, thereby generating rapid growth and distributive improvements. Likewise, a study by Bourguignon and Morrison (1989) on the determinants of inequality in thirty-five small and medium-sized developing countries concluded that the gradual abolition of trade tariffs on manufactured products reduced the income share of the richest 20 per cent of the population and improved that of the poorest 60 per cent. An equally important empirical literature, however, comes to opposite conclusions. Helleiner (2014) suggests that the econometric evidence on the relation between trade policy, growth, and poverty alleviation is inconclusive. A comprehensive meta-analysis of the empirical studies in this field (Koujianou-Goldberg and Pavcnik, 2007) indicates that there is a negative relation between trade openness and income inequality. So, how can such a discrepancy between the theoretical predictions of the Hecksher–Ohlin theorem and contradictory empirical evidence be explained?

17.9 Alternative Explanations of the Distributive Effects of Trade Liberalization

One of the reasons why the Hecksher–Ohlin theorem is often unable to explain the changes caused by trade liberalization is that it is based on a restrictive $2 \times 2 \times 2$ framework. Its generalization is impossible in a real world where trade takes place among many countries, exchanging a variety of goods produced by a variety of production factors. In addition, the assumptions on which such a model is built (constant technology, full employment, factors of mobility, and so on) are seldom or never verified in real life. While the general principle of comparative advantages remains plausible, a formal extension of the model or the abandonment of some key assumptions on which it is based do not allow to reach the same conclusions about the efficiency and equity of trade liberalization, as illustrated by the examples discussed in the following subsections.

Production factors intensity and income distribution

Many developing countries export goods that incorporate not unskilled labour, as such, but instead land, mining endowments, and skilled work. This comparative advantage drives them to intensify the use of such factors, whose remuneration is distributed in an unequal way. In addition, although agricultural exports may have a strong unskilled labour content, it is not evident that the remuneration of this factor increases as a result of trade liberalization. This remuneration depends on the shape of the unskilled labour supply curve and on the degree of land concentration. For example, an increase in exports of land-intensive agricultural products has an equalizing effect if the land is distributed equitably (as in Costa Rica), if it involves a widespread increase in farm incomes, a reduction of the rural–urban income gap, and a fall in overall inequality. However, the same effect cannot be observed in Paraguay and Guatemala, where trade liberalization would benefit mainly large landowners. In addition—even in the case of egalitarian land distribution—the overall inequality impact of trade liberalization will be favourable only if the increase in output, employment, and wages in agriculture more than compensates the loss of jobs and incomes in the formerly protected sector that collapsed because of trade liberalization.

Trade liberalization in countries exporting commodities whose prices are subject to shocks

The static and dynamic advantages of international trade are less evident in nations specialized in the export of raw materials (tropical beverages, vegetable fibers, minerals). This sector is characterized by a number of problems. The global demand for these goods had been stagnant until the early 2000s, as the demand for them was almost saturated. The rise of China and other emerging economies has since changed things. But these economies remain vulnerable to strong shocks in world prices and volumes, such as that of 2008–09. In all these cases, price shocks reduce the trade/GDP ratio, despite the liberalization of their trade regime. When commodity prices fall, not only does the value of exports decreases, but so does that of imports, as well as the trade/GDP ratio. In this case, trade liberalization leads to a decline in employment and incomes in the protected sector, without generating a corresponding increase in the export sector (see the three-sector model of a dependent economy in Section 15.3). In addition, as already noted, the reallocation of labour from the declining sector to the export sector faces a number of obstacles (see Chapter 16).

Third-party effects

The limitations of the 2 × 2 × 2 Hecksher–Ohlin model are particularly evident when trade takes place among more than two countries, whose comparative advantages and export potential change over time as a result of the decisions of third countries to change their trade policy. Country A, for example, may have a comparative advantage in the production of unskilled labour-intensive goods in relation to country B (which is endowed with capital and skilled labour), but not in relation to country C, which—however—has not yet liberalized its trade regime. If the latter decides to open up to international trade, this is likely to generate a negative distributional impact on A by affecting its comparative advantage in labour-intensive goods. In particular, the prediction that as a result of trade liberalization A will record an improvement in its income distribution thanks to an increase in labour-intensive exports to B will not be verified, since A's exports to B will be displaced by exports from C to B. The best example of this situation is offered by the decision of China (and other low-wage economies such as Indonesia, Bangladesh, and India) to participate in an increasingly active way in international trade since around 2000. This has undoubtedly lowered the international price of labour-intensive goods, but it has also eroded the previous comparative advantages of the middle-income countries of Latin America and South East Asia vis-à-vis the OECD countries.

Trade liberalization and imports of skill-enhancing investment goods

As noted, a key assumption of the Hecksher–Ohlin model is that the production technology of the countries participating in international trade does not change over time. This is not realistic and leads to erroneous conclusions. Indeed, by generating export revenues in hard currency, trade liberalization improves the access of all trading countries to previously inaccessible technologies and sophisticated capital goods. This skill-enhancing trade effect increases total factor productivity, the rate of return on assets, the demand for skilled workers, their wages, and the share of capital income in the total. At the same time, it will reduce the demand for unskilled workers. These two effects worsen the overall income distribution. This is one of the channels through which trade liberalization pushed up the Gini index of many Latin American countries in the 1980s and 1990s (see Table 2.5). In all these cases, the countries importing modern technologies face a trade-off between microeconomic efficiency (and possibly growth) and income inequality. In dynamic terms, it is possible that the growth benefits outweigh the costs due to a worsening of inequality. The new technologies may reduce the importing country's technological backwardness, attract FDI and modernize the economy. Short-term compensatory measures would, however, be required to offset the negative effects on income inequality. But these are seldom introduced because of their fiscal cost.

Protectionism in trading partners and interaction between trade and capital account liberalization

Another assumption of the Hecksher–Ohlin model is that liberalization takes place simultaneously in all the trading partners. But this is not always true, as shown by the case of developing countries' exports of agricultural and low-tech goods. For them, liberalization has led to an unsatisfactory export performance, not only due to their domestic problems but also because of persistent protectionism in their trading partners. Developing countries' exports towards the OECD countries, for example, have for many years had to overcome trade barriers four times higher than those applied on their imports, This is because the advanced nations have only slowly modified their policy of subsidizing their agricultural sectors and dumping agricultural goods onto the world market at a fraction of their production cost.

Meanwhile, as noted by Taylor (2004), the liberalization of capital movements has often led to an appreciation of the real exchange rate which reduced the competitiveness of national exports and shifted domestic demand towards cheap imports and away from domestic production. This pushed the domestic producers of exportable goods to cut costs by firing formal sector workers and relying on offshoring or sub-contracting to informal sector firms. These decisions reduced the demand for or the wage of unskilled workers and increased the inequality of the distribution of wages.

17.10 Capital Account Liberalization

The domestic financial liberalization of the 1970s and 1980s was followed in the 1990s by the liberalization of international capital movements (see Section 15.13). In developing countries, this reform was expected *ex ante* to generate an increase in overall savings, and an improvement in their capital accumulation, employment, and production. All these measures were expected to generate positive distributive effects. In addition, the liberalization of the capital account was expected to lead to a portfolio diversification of national investors, a disciplining of macroeconomic policies in developing countries that needed to attract foreign capitals, and an improvement of the global allocation of world savings, by allowing foreign capital to flow to low-income countries with higher rates of return on investments.

In a growing number of countries, however, this reform worsened income distribution and slowed growth. Indeed, the disciplining effect of liberalization on tax policy, public spending, and labour markets was in most cases regressive (as discussed in this chapter) In addition, the appreciation of the real exchange rate induced by the capital inflows triggered—as noted—a shift of production towards the non-tradable sector as well as an increase in sub-contracting and wage cuts in the tradable sector (Taylor, 2004).

The liberalization of capital movements also caused increasing instability, as indicated by the frequency and severity of financial crises in recent years (Figure 2.3). Several analyses have pointed to the relationship between capital account liberalization, financial crises with real effects, and income distribution, particularly in countries with weak labour institutions and social protection mechanisms. In Latin America and Asia, for instance, financial crises pushed up inequality in 73 and 62 per cent of the cases, respectively, while Finland, Norway, and Spain, which also experienced banking and financial crises in the early to mid-1990s, did not suffer an inequality surge thanks to their social protection institutions. Partial equilibrium analyses show that over the short term financial crises affect first the skilled workers of sectors such as finance, insurance, and real estate. Yet, general equilibrium analyses over the medium and long term show that the social groups most affected by financial crises are the poor who are hit by a generalized fall in labour demand, a decline in wages and higher inflation for wage goods. An empirical analysis on Latin America in the 1990s (Behrman et al., 2000) concludes that external financial liberalization was the component of the overall WC package with the strongest negative distributional impact.

17.11 Overall Impact of the Reforms

The analysis of the distributional and growth impact of the various WC reforms has mostly been carried out on the basis of partial equilibrium analyses (that is, assuming *ceteris paribus* conditions for the rest of the economy). This approach has serious limitations, as the various reforms interact with each other and may, in this way, generate different impacts from those due to the reforms considered individually. For example, domestic financial liberalization (which—as noted—has entailed financing the budget deficit through the issuing of bonds on the domestic market) can have a particularly perverse effect if it is introduced before the budget deficit has been stabilized. Similarly, the impact of adopting a managed exchange rate depends on the control of capital movements. And so on. Given the seven policy reforms considered here, there are at least $21 = (7 \times 6)/2$ possible interactions between two policy reforms and an even greater number of interactions between three or more reform measures.

The effects of these interactions could be analysed *ex ante* from a theoretical perspective or by means of large, cumbersome, and costly computable general equilibrium models. As an alternative, regression analysis has been used to try to solve this problem by estimating the simultaneous impact of all policy changes on the distribution of income, including by considering a few key interactions between policy measures. By adopting this approach, Behrman et al. (2000) analysed the impact of six types of reform (trade liberalization, liberalization of capital movements, domestic financial liberalization, tax reform, privatization, and reform of the labour market) on the wage distribution of eighteen countries in Latin America between 1980 and 1998. The study found that the overall package of macroeconomic reforms inspired by the Washington Consensus generated a significant regressive effect over the short term, the intensity of which, however, tended to disappear over time. The study also suggested that the three reforms with the greatest adverse effect on equality were domestic financial reform, the liberalization of capital movements, and tax reform. The liberalization of foreign trade did not cause positive or negative impacts, probably because it generated opposing effects which may have offset each other. However, as noted above, the assessment by Koujianou-Goldberg and Pavcnik (2007) shows that trade liberalization also tends to adversely affect inequality. Similar empirical results were identified during twenty-one reform episodes covering eighteen developing countries and Russia. In this study, Taylor (2000) shows that inequality rose in thirteen cases, remained constant in six and improved in two (El Salvador and Costa Rica) where, during a period of external liberalization, there was a surge in the employment of low-skilled workers in the export sector.

In conclusion, the empirical evidence suggests that of the six components of the Washington Consensus package, the liberalization of the capital account had the greatest negative distributional impact, followed by domestic financial liberalization, tax reform, and the deregulation of the labour market. Privatization generated effects that varied according to the approach followed. The effects of trade liberalization were less marked and varied somewhat from country to country.

17.11 Relationship between Income Inequality and Economic Growth

The analysis in this chapter so far has shown that the macroeconomic reforms introduced over the 1980s, 1990s, and 2000s under the auspices of the Washington Consensus generated, in several cases, an increase in inequality and a slowdown in growth and poverty alleviation.[7] The above analysis has also emphasized that in many cases this unsatisfactory result depended not only on the macroeconomic policies and structural reforms introduced but also on adverse initial conditions. As illustrated in Figure 17.1, the impact on poverty reduction has also been influenced by the impact of (often rising) inequality on growth, a topic that is discussed hereafter. In contrast, the impact of growth on inequality has been ambiguous, as it has depended on the pattern of growth adopted, and for this reason it is ignored in the following discussion.

Theories positing a positive relation between inequality and growth

Theories positing a positive inequality–growth relation emphasize the different propensities to save of workers and capitalists and among workers with high and low wages. Such theories suggest that a polarization of the income distribution accelerates growth and employment creation, and is therefore also favourable for the poor over the medium–long term (see Kaldor, 1966 for a critique of such approach). Two arguments generally support this position. To start with, if national income is distributed between wages (W) and capital incomes (Π) and if $S = S_W + S_\Pi$ that is, total savings are equal to the savings of wage earners and recipients of capital income, the total savings amount to:

$$S = s_1 W + s_2 \Pi \qquad (17.13)$$

where it is assumed that s_2 (the propensity to save out of capital income) is greater than s_1 (the propensity to save out of wages). If this is true, then shifting a share of national income Y from W to Π results in an increase in overall national savings S. A second argument supporting the view that an unequal income distribution increases the rate of growth is related to the supposed greater saving propensity of high wage earners, as suggested by the Keynesian savings function presented hereafter, according to which the average propensity to save is higher for people with high wages (see Section 3.1):

$$s_1 = -\alpha + \beta W \qquad (17.14)$$

Thus, if the total wage bill is distributed in a way that is more unequal, the total savings originating from wages increases. A third argument in favour of an unequal distribution of income emphasizes the fact that investments often require a large amount of savings while the imperfections of financial markets make the access to credit problematic for small and medium-sized firms. In view of all this, the achievement of a given investment target requires that a substantial share of national income and savings is concentrated in the hands of a few capitalists or of the state, which are the only ones able to generate the resources needed for sizeable investments. These three arguments suggest that an unequal distribution of income does increase the volume of domestic savings and the savings rate. Given a Harrod–Domar model in which it is assumed that $I = S$ (see Chapter 2), it follows that higher inequality increases overall savings, S, and the savings rate, s, and that this raises the rate of growth of GDP (g) as indicated in equation (17.15):

[7] For a recent review of the relation between inequality and growth see Klasen et al. (2018).

$$g = s/\nu - \delta \tag{17.15}$$

in which g depends on s = S/Y, the capital/output ratio ν, and the amortization rate δ.

Objections about the high distributional costs to be borne by the poor to promote economic growth in this way find an answer in the observation that if g is high enough, at time t + 1, the poor will also enjoy higher incomes, consumption, and utility U (see equation (17.16)) than in the case of a more egalitarian initial distribution of income[8] (as in equation (17.17)), a situation expressed below in symbols:

$$U(\text{poor})_{t+n}{}^{(\text{high } \Pi/\text{Y and Gini w})}{}_{t} > U(\text{poor})_{t+n}{}^{(\text{low}\Pi/\text{Y and Gini w})}{}_{t} \tag{17.16}$$

$$U(\text{rich})_{t+n}{}^{(\text{high } \Pi/\text{Y and Gini w})}{}_{t} > U(\text{rich})_{t+n}{}^{(\text{low } \Pi/\text{Y and Gini})}{}_{t} \tag{17.17}$$

If this is true, then the policymaker is faced with two trade-offs, one between equity and growth, and the other between present and future income, consumption, and utility.

In the past, these conclusions influenced the decisions of policymakers. However, despite their intuitive nature, the empirical evidence in their support depends on the time horizon of the analysis and the type of data used. While the Keynesian saving theory is tested successfully on micro surveys at one point in time, this is not the case for tests conducted on long-term macroeconomic time series. Indeed, other variables such as an increase in M2/GDP linked to the spread of the banking infrastructure, the diffusion of sales by instalments, and the wealth effect due to capital gains have reduced the savings rate of many income groups over time. In addition, in developing countries other factors (such as income composition, the rural–urban structure of the economy, and opportunities for direct investment) play a role in determining the overall rate of saving and investment. Moreover, even if one accepts that greater inequality leads to higher savings, before concluding that the latter lead to faster growth, one must agree with the specification of the investment function in the Harrod–Domar model, that is I = S. As noted in Chapter 2, I = S ignores other relevant determinants of investment and is rarely observed in real life (see the investment theories discussed in Chapter 13).

The Kuznets's inverted U curve (Figure 17.9) also posits (indirectly) a positive relation up to a given income level between the level of inequality and income per capita (proxied by the share of workers in the modern sector). The Kuznets curve does not illustrate a theory of the relationship between inequality and growth, but it is discussed here because it constitutes one of the classical analyses of the relation between growth and inequality. The Kuznets (1955) model essentially suggests that an increase in inequality is inevitable in the early stages of development, as is its decline in more affluent societies.

In a backward and dualistic economy, growth depends on the transfer of labour from the backward sector B, where productivity and wages are low, to the advanced sector A where wages and productivity are high (see Section 2.5). In this model, there are no other ways to grow such as, for instance, a parallel increase in productivity and wages in both

[8] This is not true at time t. Other objections relate to the social discount rate and the value of n that allows equation (17.16) to be verified. Obviously, if the social discount rate is high, equation (17.16) is not valid.

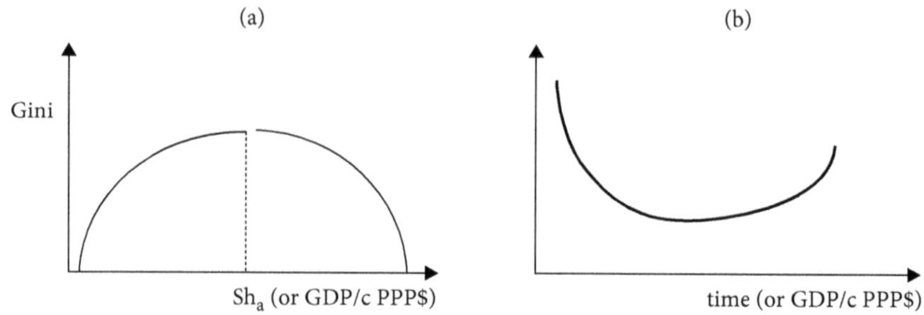

Figure 17.9 Trend of income inequality predicted by the Kuznets curve (a) and observed in real-life in several countries, 1950–2000 (b).

A and in B, as suggested by the model of Fei and Ranis (1964). If one starts from a situation in which all workers are employed in B and receive the same salary, W_b, the Gini coefficient of the income distribution will be equal to zero. With the gradual shift of workers from B to A, overall inequality rises, since the workers in A have a higher productivity and wage (W_a) than the average wage (AW) and the wage paid in B (W_b), which remains constant in this model despite the steady transfer of labour to A. Beyond a certain threshold, with the continuous increase in the share of workers employed in A (Sh_a) and the decline of that of workers engaged in B (Sh_b), inequality starts to decline. When all the workers have moved to A, one returns to a situation of perfect equality as all workers earn the same wage. To derive formally the relation between growth and inequality, we define the average wage, AW (see equation (17.18)), and a measure of wage inequality (equation (17.19)), that is, the weighted average of the distance between AW and W_a and between AW and W_b weighted by the respective employment shares, Sh_a and Sh_b. In symbols:

$$\begin{aligned} AW &= W_a Sh_a + W_b (1 - Sh_a) \text{ where } Sh_a + Sh_b = 1 \\ AW &= W_a Sh_a + W_b - W_b Sh_a \end{aligned} \tag{17.18}$$

$$\begin{aligned} \text{Wage Ineq} &= (W_a - AW)\, Sh_a + (AW - W_b)(1 - Sh_a) \\ \text{Wage Ineq} &= W_a Sh_a - AW\, Sh_a + AW - W_b - AW\, Sh_a + W_b Sh_a \end{aligned} \tag{17.19}$$

Now substituting the value of AW derived from (17.18) into (17.19) and manipulating the equation so obtained, one derives in expression (17.20), a relation that shows that the inequality of the distribution of wages is a second order concave function of Sh_a.

$$\text{Wage Ineq} = 2(W_a - W_b)\, Sh_a - 2(W_a - W_b)\, Sh_a^2 \tag{17.20}$$

In short, at the beginning inequality rises for an increase in the share of modern sector activities, Sh_a, in the total. But beyond the value of Sh_a for which the first derivative of the function (17.20) is equal to zero, inequality falls, giving rise to an inverted-U curve (Figure 17.6a). Yet, despite considerable efforts, the Kuznets curve was successfully tested only on cross-country data in the 1950s/1960s and only if the developed nations, which had at the time a comparatively low inequality, were included in the sample. Data on the evolution over time of inequality for many countries taken individually show different—often opposite—trends than those surmised by the Kuznets curve (Table 2.6 and Figure 17.9b).

The most important critique of the Kuznets model emphasizes the fact that inequality does not depend on some kind of universal iron law but rather on government policies and factos endowment. Piketty (2014) offers a political interpretation of such a supposed iron law that was first presented in 1953 at the peak of the Cold War. In his view, the empirical work of Kuznets acquired an important political dimension. It showed that rapid economic development in countries of the free world would have, sooner or later, been accompanied by a decline in inequality and greater social justice. However, Table 2.6 shows that between 1980 and 2000 inequality rose in 69 per cent of the 105 countries with time series on income distribution, including in most high income economies where—according to the Kuznets curve—inequality should have declined. Piketty concludes his analysis stating that what he describes as the 'fairytale Kuznets curve' was to a large extent developed, or in any case used, for political reasons. Piketty's work also indicates that the Kuznets empirical forecast about falling inequality in the course of development has been contradicted, despite a huge amount of research aiming to confirm it, by the subsequent increase of income inequality in many middle-income and advanced economies.

Theories positing a negative relation between inequality and growth: the median voter model

In this model, (Alesina and Rodrik 1994), a high initial asset inequality penalizes growth since—under democracy—it leads to the election of governments that favour income redistribution financed by an increase in marginal tax rates that discourages private investments and growth. According to this theory, the bigger the distance between the income of the median voter and the average income, the higher is taxation, and the lower are investment and growth. Other versions of the same model emphasize that a strong initial concentration of assets reduces the access to education of the poor, and slows the accumulation of human capital, which is an important determinant of long-term growth. In addition, beyond the impact on lower spending on education, high asset inequality tends to be associated with a slow decline of the total fertility rate, possibly due to the negative impact of low expenditure on female education and family planning. A slow fertility decline leads to rapid population growth and a slow growth of GDP per capita. The policy conclusions arrived at on the basis of this model favour an initial redistribution of assets and the expansion of financial markets to facilitate the private financing of human capital formation, but no income redistribution through taxation because that is regarded as inefficient since it reduces investment and growth.

However, the empirical testing of this class of models is problematic for the following reasons. First, it is not evident that public policies are the result of the electoral process rather than of pressure by lobbies and interest groups with enough resources and connections to affect policy formulation, Second, there is no empirical evidence that—also in democratic regimes—a high initial inequality leads to a greater redistribution. In fact, as shown by the Russian Federation and Latin America during the 1990s, democratic countries with high Gini coefficients were often characterized by low tax/GDP ratios and regressive public expenditure systems (this situation changed in Latin America during the 2000s). Third, there is no empirical evidence of the supposed negative relationship between taxation and growth. If a relationship exists, it is a positive one, as suggested by the Wagner law and by Perotti (1995). Indeed, a well designed and implemented public expenditure on infrastructure financed with additional tax revenue may increase the rate of return on private investment as shown by the case of East Asia and a number of developing countries. Finally, in the original empirical test of such a model, several of the sample countries were not democracies.

Inequality, incomplete financial markets, and decreasing returns to investment

Another explanation of why a strong concentration of assets and income slows down growth focuses on the decreasing returns to investment when capital per worker rises, as assumed for instance in the Solow model (see Chapter 2). In this model, financial markets are incomplete, investments are lumpy and production opportunities are concentrated in the hands of the rich, who are the only group controlling investible funds. Given the impossibility of borrowing, the poor cannot invest in human or physical capital. This situation slows down growth because production functions are non-convex (that is, they are characterized by decreasing returns to rising capital per worker). The underdevelopment of financial markets concentrates savings in the hands of the rich who use them for large investments with decreasing returns, while excluding the poor who would invest in smaller and more productive activities (Aghion et al., 1999). Moreover, also in this case, investment in human capital will remain lower than in the case of a more equitable distribution of income. In short, an unequal distribution of resources and investible funds reduces the average return to investment and growth. Cornia (1985), for example, showed for fifteen developing economies exhibiting rural surplus labour that land yields decreased as the size of the farm increased, and that therefore an unequal distribution of land reduced aggregate output when compared with a situation in which the land was distributed more equitably.

Inequality and the inability of governments to conduct timely stabilization policies

Strong inequality and social polarization may also lead to episodes of macroeconomic populism, such as the adoption of unsustainable fiscal and monetary policies that will require, at some point, the introduction of macroeconomic stabilization. Populist policies are often adopted when the usual approaches to the financing of government activities and the implementation of redistributive programmes (via taxation, labour, and land reforms, and subsidized training of human capital) are precluded by social polarization and the power of lobbies. However, if it is impossible to tax, the government may borrow abroad and so risk a default on its international debt, or pursue a policy of excessive seignorage that triggers, beyond a certain threshold, a surge in inflation. Yet, in a polarized economy characterized by two antagonistic and non-cooperative social groups, the government may be forced to delay the introduction of macroeconomic stabilization. Indeed, each of the two groups may refuse to bear any of the costs of macroeconomic stabilization, hoping that the other bears all or most of them, even if for both groups the gains of stabilization would far exceed its aggregate cost. The time that elapses before the cost of stabilization is unloaded onto the losing social group increases as a function of the inequality of the distribution of income. As suggested by the theory of collective action, a society with a more equitable income distribution has a greater potential to generate the political consensus necessary to quickly introduce macroeconomic adjustment measures and avoid the high costs of delayed stabilization and a growth slowdown.

Inequality and government inability to provide basic public goods

Public choice theory suggests that when income inequality is high, governments (as well as self-interested bureaucracies) are likely to implement suboptimal policies that retard the provision of essential pro-growth public services. A rising divergence of interests and types of public services demanded by the rich and the poor lead to an overall drop in the supply of basic public services essential for growth, such as personal security, contracts enforcement, security of property rights, and human capital formation. Indeed, the rich resist taxation as they perceive that the supply of public services funded by an increase in revenue will bring little benefit to them. In extreme cases, high-income groups support policies that preserve their privileges even at the cost of slow or stagnant aggregate growth. The problem is particularly severe when the concentration of income in the upper deciles is accompanied by widespread poverty at the bottom of the distribution, with no middle class capable of politically challenging inefficient government decisions. The situation of Guatemala in the early 2000s, where the tax/GDP ratio was 8 per cent and the coverage of public services minimal, is a good example of this state of affairs (since 2003 taxation has risen and inequality declined, if modestly).

Inequality and the erosion of social capital and collective action

Social capital (that is, the relations of mutual trust and cooperation, and the informal social norms and networks that improve economic efficiency) has a high economic value. Indeed, it facilitates the diffusion of information and coordinated action among enterprises and households; it reduces the costs of information, transactions, and contract enforcement thanks to the trust existing between the contracting parties; it exerts social control over collective behaviours and deviance; and it encourages the formation of strong informal institutions of collective regulation that enable more efficient functioning of the market (see Chapter 11). Strong pro-growth social capital is often associated with moderate inequality. For instance, in both the United States and Italy the percentage of households participating as volunteers in the work of NGOs is higher in areas with lower inequality. It is equally true, however, that a rapid increase of income inequality may erode social cohesion by increasing the heterogeneity of government services demanded by increasingly different social strata, by raising informational asymmetries in social exchange, by reducing cooperation and efficiency, and by increasing the psychological distance between members of the same community, a fact that reduces trust and increases the costs of transaction and social interaction.

Rising inequality, household indebtedness, financial crises, and further inequality increases

A recent explanation of the rise of inequality focuses on growing financialization, rising household indebtedness and the eruption of unequalizing financial crises. Prior studies by

Keynes, Minsky and Schiller have emphasized the inherent instability of financial markets. Such instability increased after the financial deregulation of the last 20 years. In the United States, the effective Glass-Steagall Act introduced after the financial crisis of 1929 to regulate banking and financial activities was repealed in 1994. Its abrogation paved the way to the financial crisis of 2008. The Dodd-Frank and Consumer Protection Act introduced in 2012 to prevent future financial crises do not have the same regulatory power. In this regard, Khumof and Rancière (2011) have developed a model with two types of agents, the capitalists (5 per cent of the population) who receive capital income from the remuneration of their assets, and the workers (95 per cent of the population) who earn only wages. Following any shock that augments the income share of the top 5 per cent and cuts that of the 95 per cent, the capitalists may choose to invest their extra income in new factories, thus generating additional jobs that raise the incomes of the workers to their prior level. Alternatively, they may invest their extra income in the financial sector, so that the banks can lend these new deposits to the workers who aim at smoothing their consumption by borrowing funds (see chapter 3). During the 2000s, in the United States, such consumption smoothing was facilitated by an accommodating monetary policy, financial liberalization, the development of over the counter derivatives and risky sub-prime loans, and growing balance of payments disequilibria. Indeed, the balance of payments surpluses of OPEC countries, China, Japan, South Korea, and so on were invested in the US financial market, which could count in this way on ample liquidity to lend to the impoverished 95 per cent of the population.

However, the growing indebtedness of the 95 per cent (that fueled rapid economic growth till 2008) reduced the solvency of households that had borrowed and raised the probability of their default. Simulations of different scenarios of the Kuhmof-Rancière model suggest that the probability of a crisis decreases only if the growing profits received by the capitalists are not placed in the financial sector but are reinvested into productive activities which raise labour demand and wages. Such choice would in fact reduce inequality and the need to borrow. If this does not happen, the default risk rises and financial crises may erupt. In turn, such crises are likely to increase income inequality as they generate adverse real effects on GDP, employment and wages.

Theories positing a concave relation between inequality and growth

All theories discussed above have focused on inequality-growth relations that are monotonically increasing or decreasing. Such universal monotonicity, however, seems counter-intuitive from a theoretical perspective. In fact, it is difficult to accept that a 20 per cent increase of the Gini coefficient from 0.20 to 0.24 may cause the same impact on economic performance and social wellbeing than a 20 per cent increase from 0.50 to 0.60. It is therefore possible that the gradient of the inequality growth schedule varies with the level of inequality. One way to explain such non linearity is to emphasize the role of microeconomic and social incentives (Cornia et al., 2004). To prove this, let us define two income distributions. The first is the latent (that is, unobserved) natural distribution of income which reflects the inequality due to differences in human capital, efforts and talent among the population. Such distribution generates fair income shares of the rich, middle class and poor $sh_i^* = [sh_p^*, sh_m^*, sh_r^*]$ The second distribution is the real life distribution of income defined by the observed incomes shares $sh_i = [sh_p, sh_m, sh_r]$. Under conditions of equal opportunities, of an equitable distribution of assets and efficient markets, the natural distribution of income is determined entirely by the individual characteristics of the workers, that is, their different endowments of talent, and their different work effort. Such natural distribution may also allow for a socially accepted under-remuneration of the most talented workers and an over-remuneration of the less talented ones. The sh_i^* are not observed by the policymakers but the agents perceive correctly if their share of real income sh_i is equitable, that is, if on the whole it corresponds to their relative effort, talent and merit.

In practice, however, the real distribution of income $sh_i = [sh_p, sh_m, sh_r]$ reflects not only talent, merit and effort—but also an unequal distribution of assets, educational and employment opportunities, distortions in the markets of goods and productive factors, biased economic policies and discriminatory social norms. Thus, *ceteris paribus*, growth g is influenced by the sum of the absolute value of the differences between the income shares of the natural and real life distributions g is

$$g = f\left(\Sigma \left| sh_p - shp^* \right| + \left| sh_m - sh_m^* \right| + \left| sh_r - sh_r^* \right| \right) \tag{17.21}$$

especially affected when the distances between the two distributions exceeds a given tolerance level (TL) beyond which incentives are affected negatively.

$$\Sigma_i \left| sh_i - sh_i^* \right| > TL \tag{17.22}$$

In this case, some social classes will reduce their supply of labour, entrepreneurship or investments. Workers may also reduce the intensity of their effort and shirk labour. Of course, labour shirking can be offset by hiring supervisors to ensure that labourers work diligently, but this raises the supervision, control and monitoring costs. Alternatively firms can shift to a piece-rate remuneration, but this is not possible in sectors where the workers' output is not easily observable. Therefore, whenever the real-life income distribution is strongly misaligned with the latent one, microeconomic efficiency is affected together with aggregate growth. This is true both in situations characterized by very low and very high Gini coefficients.

As a result, in this model, the relationship between inequality and growth is concave and asymmetric (Figure 17.10): too low inequality, in relation to the latent distribution, reduces growth. In fact, at low levels of inequality the distribution of earnings is much more compressed than that based on talent, merit and effort, and for this reason growth is hampered by a loss of work incentives by labourers who elude their job, adopt opportunistic behaviour and try to live a quite working life. The Soviet pay scales, for example, artificially compressed the distribution of income just above the median wage and so induced risk aversion and lack of initiative in the managers, an erosion of labour discipline among workers and a poor performance among both managers and workers. The same phenomenon may occur when workers have to pay high marginal tax rates, or when social norms impose to them to redistribute an important part of their earned income within the community in which they live, as in the African extended family setup. Growth does not change much in the middle inequality range but worsens a lot when the difference $sh_r\_sh_p$

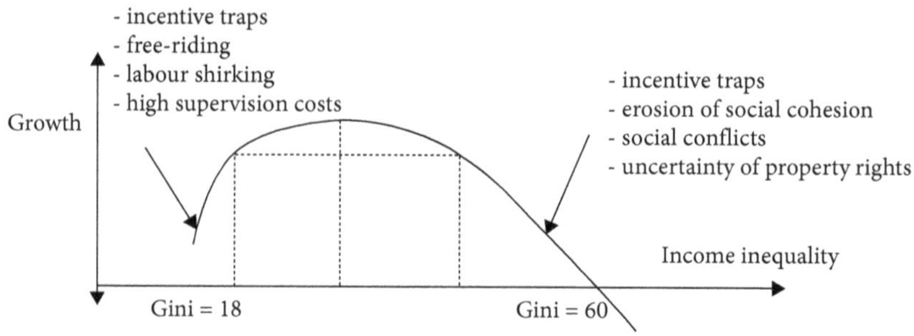

Figure 17.10 Concave relation between income inequality and growth

is very high. In this case the compatibility of working incentives between poor workers and rich asset holders disappears and gives rise to an intensification of strikes, a contraction of labour supply and free-riding and opportunistic behaviours, so that as a result growth becomes negative. Examples of this situation are not uncommon: for example, a strong concentration of land (as in the case of *latifundia*) is generally accompanied by low work incentives, labour shirking and high monitoring costs. As a result, land yields are lower than in small farms operated with family labour. For instance, there is evidence that in India the most unequal sugar cooperatives were less productive than the more egalitarian ones, with differences in per capita output that reached 50 per cent (Cornia 2004).

A highly unequal distribution erodes also social cohesion. In this case, the reaction of the agents whose share of income is perceived to be artificially compressed is to acquire resources through theft, violent action and expropriation, that is, behaviours that significantly raise the costs of enterprise security, contract enforcement and protection of private property. For example, various studies have shown that there is a strong relationship between unemployment-inequality on the one side and crime rate on the other. All this implies (think, for instance, of South Africa) loss of lives, the diversion of resources from productive uses to the control of criminal activities and the flight of FDI and domestic investors.

17.12 Concluding Remarks

Since the beginning of the new millennium, the issues of income inequality and of its impact on poverty and growth has received increasing attention. The reasons for this renewed interest are to be found in the insights generated by new theoretical models, greater data availability, and the emphasis on tolerable levels of inequality placed by the international community with the Sustainable Development Goals initiative, following the rapid increase in income inequality over the last three decades. These decades have witnessed also a proliferation of reforms in the field of stabilization, privatization and the liberalization of domestic and international markets. Questions have therefore arisen about the relationship between such reforms and the concomitant changes in inequality and poverty, and between inequality and growth. To tackle such complex set of issues a few decompositions of the determinants of poverty have been developed. These show that poverty incidence depends on the growth of income and the level of inequality. This suggests that especially in high-inequality, mid-income countries poverty can be reduced rapidly by lowering inequality, while the opposite is true in low-income and low-inequality countries where poverty reduction requires a growth acceleration.

The chapter has also discussed the relation between income inequality and the policy reforms part of the WC package. It has done so by juxtaposing the theoretical predictions of mainstream theories about their impact on inequality and the changes observed in real life. The empirical evidence suggests that international and domestic financial liberalization have had an adverse effect on inequality, followed by the tax reforms introduced in the 1980s and 1990s and the liberalization of the labour market. The evidence on the inequality impact of trade liberalization is less marked and consistent, while the impact of privatization depended on the approach followed. Finally, the chapter has discussed the relation between income inequality and growth by reviewing three groups of theoretical models that suggest a positive, negative and concave relation between these two variables. While the Keynesian models suggest that inequality accelerates GDP growth, most of the new theories come to the opposite conclusion. In turn, the models theorizing a concave relation between inequality and growth are more plausible but are less numerous and well tested than the other two groups.

References

Aghion, P., E. Caroli, and C. Garcia-Penalosa (1999), 'Inequality and economic growth: The perspective of the new growth theories', *Journal of Economic Literature*, 37: pp. 1615–60.

Alesina, A. and D. Rodrik (1994), 'Distributive politics and economic growth', *The Quarterly Journal of Economics*, 109 (2): pp. 465–90.

Behrman, J., N. Birdsall, and M. Székely (2000), 'Economic reform, and wage differentials in Latin America'. RES Working Paper 4235. Washington, DC: Inter-American Development Bank.

Bourguignon, F. (2003), 'The Poverty, Growth, Inequality Triangle', unpublished paper. Washington, DC: The World Bank.

Bourguignon, F. and C. Morrison (1989), *External Trade and Income Distribution*. Paris: OECD Development Centre.

Chu, K. Y., H. Davoodi, and S. Gupta (2004), 'Income Distribution and Tax and Government Social-Spending Policies in Developing Countries', in G. A. Cornia (ed.), *Inequality, Growth and Poverty in an Era of Liberalization and Globalization*. Oxford: Oxford University Press.

Cornia, G. A. (1985), 'Farm size, land yields and the agricultural production function: An analysis for fifteen developing countries', *World Development*, (13) 4: pp. 513–34.

Cornia, G. A. (1996), 'Fancy Models and Hard Facts: Children and Youth During the Transition to the Market Economy in Eastern Europe', in A. Pio (ed.), *From Adjustment to Long-Run Growth*. Milan: Università Bocconi.

Cornia, G. A. (ed.) (2004), *Inequality, Growth and Poverty in an Era of Liberalization and Globalization*. Oxford: Oxford University Press.

Cornia, G. A. (ed.) (2014), *Falling Inequality in Latin America: Policy Changes and Lessons*. Oxford: Oxford University Press.

Cornia, G. A., T. Addison, and S. Kiiski (2004), 'Income Distribution Changes and Their Impact in the Post -Second World War', in G. A Cornia. (ed.), *Inequality, Growth and Poverty in an Era of Liberalization and Globalization*. Oxford: Oxford University Press.

Cornia, G. A., J. C. Gomez Sabaini, and B. Martorano (2014), 'Tax policy and income distribution during the last decade', in G. A. Cornia (ed.), *Inequality, Growth and Poverty in an Era of Liberalization and Globalization*. Oxford: Oxford University Press.

Fei J. C. H. and G. Ranis (1964), *Development of the Labour Surplus Economy: Theory and Policy*, Yale University: A Publication of the Economic Growth Centre.

Helleiner, G. (2014), 'Trade, Exchange Rates ad Global Poverty: Policies for the Poorest', in G. A. Cornia, and F. Stewart, *Towards Human Development: New Approaches to Macroeconomics and Inequality*. Oxford: Oxford University Press.

Kaldor, N. (1966), 'Marginal Productivity and the Macro-Economic Theories of Distribution: Comment on Samuelson and Modigliani', *The Review of Economic Studies*, 33 (4): pp. 309–19.

Keifman, S. and R. Maurizio (2014), *Changes in Labour market Conditions and Policies*, in G. A. Cornia (ed.). *Falling Inequality in Latin America: Policy Changes and Lessons*. Oxford: Oxford University Press.

Klasen, S., G. A. Cornia, R. Grynspan, L. F. Lopez-Calva, and N. Lustig (2018), 'Economic Inequality and Social Progress', in *International Panel on Social Progress 'Rethinking Society for the 21st Century'*, Volume 1. Cambridge: Cambridge University Press.

Koujianou-Goldberg, P. and N. Pavcnik (2007), 'Distributional effects of globalization in developing countries', NBER Working Paper 12885. Cambridge, MA: National Bureau of Economic Research.

Kristensen, N. and W. Cunningham (2006), 'Do Minimum Wages in Latin America and the Caribbean Matter? Evidence from 19 Countries'. World Bank Policy Research Working Paper 3870. Washington, DC: The World Bank.

Kumhof, M. and R. Rancière (2011), 'Inequality, Leverage and Crises', IMF Working Paper, WP/10/268, Washington, DC: International Monetary Fund.

Kuznets, S. (1955), 'Economic Growth and Income Inequality'. *American Economic Review*, 45: pp. 1–28.

Lustig, N. and S. Higgings (2018), 'The CEQ Assessment. Measuring the Impact of Fiscal Policy on Inequality and Poverty', in N. Lustig, (ed.), *Commitment to Equity Handbook. 'Estimating the Impact of Fiscal Policy on Inequality and Poverty'*. Tulane, LA and Washington, DC: CEQ Institute and Brookings Institution Press.

Morley, S. (2000), 'Distribution and growth in Latin America in an era of structural reforms', Paper presented at the Conference on Poverty and Inequality in Developing Countries: A Policy Dialogue on the Effects of Globalization, 30.11–1.12.2000, Paris: OECD Development Centre.

Moss, D. (2010), Comments on bank failure/regulation/inequality chart. www.tobinproject.org/sites/tobinproject.org/files/assets/BankFailures_Chart with Comments_Moss.pdf (accessed 24 February 2016).

Perotti, R. (1995), 'Growth, Income Distribution and Democracy: what the Data Say'. *Discussion Paper* No. 757, New York: Columbia University.

Piketty, T. (2014), *Capital in the Twenty-first Century*. Cambridge, MA and London: Belknap Press of Harvard University Press.

Rojas-Suarez, L. (2010), 'The International Financial Crisis: Eight Lessons for and from Latin America', Working Paper 202, Washington, DC: Centre for Global Development.

Son, H. and N. Kakwani (2003), 'Pro-Poor Growth: Concept, Measurement, and Application', Unpublished paper, University of New South Wales, Australia.

Taylor, L. (2000), *Varieties of Stabilization Experiences: Towards Sensible Macroeconomics in the Third World*. Oxford: Oxford University Press.

Taylor, L. (2004), 'External liberalization, economic performance and distribution in Latin America and elsewhere', in G. A. Cornia (ed.), *Inequality, Growth and Poverty in an Era of Liberalization and Globalization*, pp. 166–96. Oxford: Oxford University Press.

UNICEF (1994), *Eastern and Central Europe in Transition: Crisis in Mortality, Health and Nutrition*. Florence: UNICEF-ICDC.

UNICEF (1995), *Eastern and Central Europe in Transition: Poverty, Children and Policy: Responses for a Brighter Future*. Florence: UNICEF-ICDC.

Suggested Further Reading

Alesina, A. and D. Rodrik (1994), 'Distributive politics and economic growth', *The Quarterly Journal of Economics*, 109 (2): pp. 465–90.

Cornia, G. A. (ed.) (2014), *Falling Inequality in Latin America: Policy Changes and Lessons*. Oxford: Oxford University Press.

Taylor, L. (2004), 'External liberalization, economic performance and distribution in Latin America and elsewhere', in G. A. Cornia (ed.), *Inequality, Growth and Poverty in an Era of Liberalization and Globalization*, pp. 166–96. Oxford: Oxford University Press.

18
Macroeconomic Policies for Growth and Poverty Reduction

This chapter reviews alternative sets of macroeconomic policies to support the achievement of the Sustainable Development Goals (SDGs) to the year 2030. The first goal of this strategy is the complete eradication of poverty by 2030, following its successful halving between 2000 and 2015. While poverty can also be reduced with redistributive and social policies, the accent in this chapter is on preventative macroeconomic measures to be introduced before crises break out, and on macroeconomic policy approaches to be adopted once unavoidable shocks hit a country. Overall, fiscal, monetary, exchange rate, regulatory, and debt management policies are shown to have an important impact on poverty eradication and income inequality.

18.1 Sustainable Development, Macroeconomic Policies, and Poverty Reduction

The issue of poverty reduction became a major, perhaps the major, objective of the global development paradigm agreed by all governments and international institutions on the occasion of the United Nations General Assembly of September 2000, which adopted the Millennium Development Goals (MDGs) for the period 2000–15. The MDGs planned—*inter alia*—a halving by 2015 of the poverty rate of 2000. By 2015 this objective had been broadly achieved on a global scale, because of the stellar performance of China and a few other nations, despite the less satisfactory results achieved by the poor developing countries of sub-Saharan Africa. The emphasis on poverty eradication, and now also on inequality reduction, was reiterated in September 2015 on the occasion of the General Assembly of the United Nations, which brought together also the World Bank, IMF, and OECD, and adopted the Sustainable Development Goals (SDGs) for the period 2015–30. The SDGs contemplate—*inter alia*—fully eradicating poverty by 2030 in all countries, both developing and developed.

The policies promoted by the MDG and SDG strategies to reduce or eradicate poverty emphasize a number of microeconomic and social sector measures (including an enlarged access to health, education, fresh water, housing, decent jobs, social subsidies, foreign aid, and similar programmes) that have been demonstrated to impact poverty and inequality in a perceptible way. However, both the MDG and SDG approaches have been silent on the nature of an overall development strategy, and even more so about the macroeconomic policies, that would help to eradicate poverty. This is a controversial area, as several approaches and policies are followed in different countries and different schools of thought recommend alternative approaches. Be that as it may, the evidence shows that during

The Macroeconomics of Developing Countries: An Intermediate Textbook. Giovanni Andrea Cornia, Oxford University Press (2020).

DOI: 10.1093/oso/9780198856672.001.0001

macroeconomic crises, poverty tends to rise and, in some cases, to become permanent. Indeed, large shocks tend to have a negative effect not only on the short-run level of output but also on short- and long-term poverty incidence. Examples of such shocks include the institutional changes and disorganization experienced by the European economies in transition during the 1990s, large devaluations of the exchange rate, and sharp increases of the prices of imported goods and international interest rates, among other crises of various types. For instance, the Inter-American Development Bank estimated that in Latin America a decline of 1 per cent of GDP per capita caused a 2 per cent increase in the poverty headcount ratio (Lustig, 2000). In turn, ECLAC data on the impact of the 2009–15 crisis confirm that—despite the introduction of pro-active social policies—over 2012–15 the poverty headcount ratio rose from 28.2 to 29.2 per cent, while the number of poor rose from 164 to 175 million (ECLAC, 2015). Thus, while there is broad agreement on social and sectoral measures, the key challenge to improving the effectiveness of the SDG paradigm is to define explicitly the nature of macroeconomic policies that would support the achievement of poverty eradication and the reduction of inequality to tolerable levels by 2030.

Lack of clarity about the nature and role of macroeconomic policies for poverty eradication and the reduction of inequality is, however, a persistent and growing problem. Indeed, over the past three decades the number of macroeconomic crises and economic downturns has increased in frequency and intensity due to the liberalization of international capital flows and greater integration through trade flows and international migration. While such greater integration may also transmit positive growth impulses from one country to another, it can also cause a spread of financial and real contagion and a surge in poverty.

These shocks not only affect output and prices (as shown by the AS-AD model), exchange rates, and interest rates (as shown in the IS-LM-BP model), but also make the achievement of macroeconomic equilibrium more difficult. Indeed, shocks of this nature push the economies into situations where the deficit of the balance of payments, the budget deficit, public debt/GDP ratio, and inflation are no longer at acceptable levels. Macroeconomic imbalances resulting from external shocks tend to be particularly marked in developing countries that have had to accept a slowdown or even a reversal of the progress towards eradicating poverty realized by means of social and sectorial policies. For example, in the OECD countries, a decline of 1 per cent of GDP leads to a fall in tax revenue of 1.8 per cent. However, in Latin America the greater variability of tax revenue (relying more than in OECD countries on the taxation of international transactions and the formal sector, which contracts the most during crises) means that tax revenue drops by 5.8 per cent as a result of a 1 per cent fall of GDP (Lustig, 2000). A fall in tax revenue will, sooner or later, lead to cuts in social expenditure, affecting both poverty and inequality.

If the SDGs are to be achieved, it is therefore essential to design macroeconomic policies that explicitly take into account their impact on poverty and inequality. However, there is no unanimity on the nature of policies that need to be introduced to reduce the risk of macro shocks and the disequilibria resulting from them. A widening of the deficit, for example, may be financed through loans by foreign banks, the issuance of state bonds on the domestic market, or seignorage. Or, as suggested by the orthodox stance portrayed in Figure 18.1, the deficit can be reduced through restrictive fiscal and monetary policies that shift the AD schedule to the left. According to this stance, these measures are necessary as

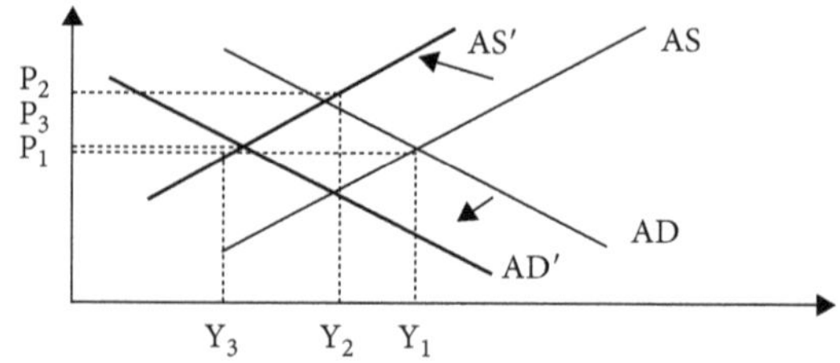

Figure 18.1 Impact of a contractionary policy introduced to reduce the inflationary impact of an exogenous shocks

the persistence of disequilibria could prove detrimental to long-term growth via a loss of credibility and excessive debt accumulation. While in Figure 18.1 an exogenous supply shock may shift the AS to the left and reduce the equilibrium level of income from Y_1 to Y_2, a restrictive macroeconomic policy would cause a shift of the AD to AD′, entailing a further income fall (from Y_2 to Y_3) in order to reduce the price increase to a level P_3, similar to P_1.

An alternative viewpoint is that macroeconomic policy must smooth the business cycle, and avoid marked recessions. The twin deficits should be reduced to acceptable levels. However, this should be consistent with a level of taxation which prevents cuts in the provisions of essential social expenditures and guarantees a tolerable level of inflation (that tends to hurt the poor the most), thereby creating the conditions for long-term growth and poverty reduction. This is all the more necessary considering that in the case of shocks and subsequent macroeconomic imbalances, the pro-cyclicality of financial markets exacerbates the problems caused by exogenous shocks. Thus, fiscal and monetary policy needs to be clearly countercyclical and allow an increase in indebtedness during periods of recession, while generating a surplus and a fall of debt/GDP ratios during boom years.

The viewpoint about the need for macroeconomic austerity is increasingly seen by both its proponents and critics as incapable of ensuring long-term growth and the reduction of poverty and inequality (Rodrik 2006). While the Austerians and the IMF have recently paid greater attention to these issues, there is no explicit attempt to consider them to be as important as macroeconomic equilibrium. Yet, the experience of the past thirty years, and especially that of the 1990s in developing countries and during the period 2008–14 in the developed ones, has shown that growth will remain elusive if macro stability is not accompanied by a countercyclical fiscal and monetary policy, low positive real interest rates, a stable and competitive real exchange rate, and adequate regulation of the financial sector, domestic banking, and the amount/type of foreign indebtedness of the private and public sector. These measures are essential to ensure adequate long-term growth, employment, and adequate expenditure on social programmes for the poor.

In view of all this, a question arises about when should the policymaker intervene to ensure that a pro-poor macroeconomic policy is introduced? Hereafter, a two-step approach is suggested: first, during non-crisis years the policymaker should introduce measures that reduce the risk of being hit by avoidable exogenous shocks. Second, during systemic crises that cannot be prevented through *ex ante* measures, it is necessary to introduce policies that minimize the loss of income of the poor during the adjustment process. Such policies ought, in fact, to maximize the net present value (NPV) of the income streams of the poor during the entire adjustment period, taking into account that their social discount rate is generally higher than that of the non-poor. If such a gradualist approach turns out to be too costly for society as a whole, an approach focusing on minimizing the loss of total output should be followed. At the same time the poor should be compensated for the loss of income incurred during a front-loaded adjustment to the crisis.

18.2 Measures to Prevent Macroeconomic Crises

As noted by Kanbur (1998), it is difficult to identify *ex ante* universal policies for an optimal adjustment to a macro shock, both from the point of view of the poor and of the entire community. The choice of such optimal policies depends on a long list of circumstances which include: the type of sector (T or NT) in which the poor work; the elasticity of the supply of wage goods; the role the government plays in the economy; the level of the foreign debt; and so on. The optimal policy solution therefore varies from country to country. However, some general principles guiding the formulation of a pro-poor macroeconomics and pro-poor growth are valid in fairly general terms, and for this reason are discussed in the following five subsections.

Control of portfolio flows and capital flights

As discussed above, the most problematic component of external liberalization regards the liberalization of portfolio flows. Premature liberalization in the presence of a large budget deficit, weak financial regulation, and lack of competition has proved to be an inexhaustible source of financial instability and macroeconomic and social disasters (see Chapter 17). The benefits implicit in the regulation of portfolio flows are therefore considerable. A first question concerns the composition of capital flows from abroad. Which of these are beneficial to the poor? This may be the case of manufacturing FDI in non-competing sectors, and long-term loans at low interest rates. Most portfolio flows (the purchase by nonresidents of bonds, stocks, derivatives, as well as short-term borrowing in hard currency by the domestic banking sector) may be problematic, especially over the short term, as they are highly volatile and exacerbate financial instability (see Sections 10.5 and 15.3).

This raises the problem of how to control both the inflows and outflows of portfolio capital and how to use capital controls as instruments of countercyclical regulation (Ocampo, 2015). Some measures have aimed to control capital inflows or to offset their effects on the money supply, others are intended to control their outflows during crisis situations (see the detailed discussion in Section 15.13). Among those aiming to control inflows, we include the obligation to deposit part of the inflows on non-interest bearing accounts at the central bank. This measure is tantamount to a kind of Tobin tax applied at the national level, as it reduces the yields on the domestic bonds purchased by foreign residents. Further capital controls include: prudential regulation of the level of foreign indebtedness of domestic banks; the removal of tax and other incentives attracting foreign capital; the sterilization of an increase in money supply due to the inflow of foreign capital; an increase in the compulsory reserve ratio of banks with foreign deposits and external exposures; the substitution—when feasible—of foreign indebtedness with domestic indebtedness; the liberalization and encouragement of capital outflows; the imposition of administrative controls on the inflows and outflows of capitals (as undertaken in Taiwan, Singapore, and Colombia); permanent closure of the capital account to portfolio flows (as in the case of China and to a lesser extent India), or its temporary closure in times of crisis (as in Malaysia). Implementation of the latter two measures requires the (often grudging) cooperation of banks and financial institutions and may not always be effective. However, these two measures often serve as a deterrent and are able to curb the bulk of inflows or illegal outflows.

A final consideration is required at this point. An increase in capital inflows frequently tends to depress domestic savings, causing a substitution of domestic savings with foreign savings, and increasing the dependence on foreign finance. However, an excessive reliance on foreign capital as a source of savings is a lazy and dangerous way to finance new investments, and must therefore be accompanied by greater efforts to mobilize domestic savings, and develop the domestic financial sector. The evidence in this area shows diverging trends. For instance, over 2000–08, Latin America sharply improved its net foreign asset position (currency reserves minus outstanding foreign debt). In contrast, the countries of Eastern Europe experienced a deterioration due to their deliberate policy of borrowing massively from Western Europe. When the latter area was hit by the sovereign debt crisis of 2008–12, East European countries were badly affected due to a sudden halt to capital flows and a major reduction in exports from the region.

The IMF now accepts the introduction of temporary controls on inflows and outflows of capital in times of crisis. In those developing countries that can count on a strong regulatory capacity and the ability to supervise the banking system, these controls have reduced the risk of financial volatility and financial crises. Such a policy, however, is not easy to apply in countries with limited skills in the field of financial regulation.[1]

Banking and financial sector regulation

Until recently, macroeconomics did not deal with the regulation of finance, as this would have been considered as undue interference with the 'good functioning' of the financial markets. Yet, there is now a consensus that macroeconomic performance can be improved through stricter regulation of the domestic financial sector, such as that adopted in some developing regions in the late 2000 and early 2010s, and as suggested by the econometric results of Cornia and Martorano (2012). Indeed, a remarkable feature of the last decade is that—after the early 2000s crises in Turkey, Argentina, Uruguay, and Ecuador—there were fewer significant financial crises in developing countries, including during the 2007–12 global crisis. One of the reasons for this crisis avoidance was the broader role played by the IMF. Since 2008, the IMF has been lending growing levels of resources, with easier access and conditionality, to transition economies and developing nations affected by financial

[1] In absolute terms, low-income countries are less likely to be influenced by fluctuations in capital movements similar to those observed in the emerging economies. However, they are also exposed to such problems as even comparatively modest flows can have a destabilizing effect on their small economies.

contagion. Indeed, between July 2008 and November 2009 the IMF financed no less than nineteen Standby Agreements in developing and transitional countries.

Improvements in domestic banking regulation and financial oversight were also behind the greater financial stability of several developing countries. As noted earlier, in addition to the adoption of countercyclical policies, several Latin American governments enhanced their financial stability by introducing measures reducing banks' currency mismatches; improving the capitalization, funding, and supervision of their banking systems; encouraging the development of local capital markets; adopting a stricter prudential regulation of bank lending; enhancing risk-assessment mechanisms in large banks; creating appropriate legal, judicial, and accounting frameworks; and assigning to state banks a greater role in the mobilization of domestic savings and the financing of economic activity.

Choice of an exchange rate which minimizes the risk of over- and under-shooting

In medium-size developing countries with narrow domestic markets, the main long-term objective of an exchange rate policy is to sustain the growth of the traded sector (both exports and importables) (see Chapter 15). The main objective is, therefore the management of a stable and competitive real exchange rate so as to avoid its excessive volatility or, worse, its collapse.

Until a decade ago, the dominant position was that regimes based on hard pegs or free floats were best suited to avoiding foreign exchange crises. But, as shown by the crises of Thailand in 1997 and Argentina in 2001 (both caused—*inter alia*—by the adoption of fixed pegs), it appears that hard pegs are more prone than other regimes to an appreciation of the real exchange rate and speculative attacks. Thus, with the exception of small economies lacking a real monetary base for which dollarization may be a solution, in other small and medium-sized developing countries a pro-poor and pro-growth macroeconomic policy should—*ceteris paribus*—focus on adopting a stable and competitive real exchange rate, and on stabilizing the expectations about its future value. An example of such an exchange rate regime is the BBC (basket, band, and crawl) approach, in which the real exchange rate is fixed in a competitive manner against a basket of currencies of the main commercial partners. The rate floats freely within a limited bandwidth (see Section 15.11 for more details). This regime allows a broadly constant real effective exchange rate to be sustained, thus leaving unchanged export competitiveness, growth, employment, and poverty reduction Such a regime must, however, be accompanied by consistent fiscal and monetary policies and capital controls aiming to prevent the appreciation of the real exchange rate, and avoid pressures to devalue.

Stabilization funds, fiscal rules, and countercyclical fiscal policy

Public finance in developing countries is particularly fragile due to fluctuations in the volume of demand and international prices of the commodities they export, and to their susceptibility to climatic and economic shocks. Tax revenue (from trade and sale taxes) fluctuates strongly with the business cycle, while international capital markets behave pro-cyclically, and foreign loans are available only during years of expansion.

Several authors have documented how fiscal policy has tended to be more procyclical than in industrialized countries (Frenkel et al., 2013). When government receipts from taxes or mineral royalties rise during booms, governments often cannot resist the political pressure to increase spending in line with the increase of revenue, especially when there exists a genuine need for more government spending in critical social areas. A similar procyclical pattern can be observed in terms of tax policy that, in contrast, has been acyclical in industrialized countries. In turn, during crises, imperfect access to the international credit market and limited domestic financial depth force governments of developing countries to cut public spending and raise taxes, with deleterious effects on long-term growth and employment. The procyclicality of fiscal policy exacerbates recessions during crises and inflationary pressures and the appreciation of the real exchange rate during booms, reducing in this way the effectiveness of macroeconomic policy.

Frenkel et al. (2013) show, however, that a steadily growing number of developing countries, including for instance Chile, and Botswana, have graduated from procyclicality since the beginning of the century. Their number has in fact increased from 8 in 1960–99 to 24 over 2000–09. This increase has been due to the *ex ante* adoption of fiscal rules by which the countries create stabilization funds that set aside resources during booms (thus reducing the inflationary pressures typical of such periods in the NT sector). These funds are then transfered back into the public budget during crises—working as a kind of quasi-automatic stabilizer and intertemporal self-insurance device.

The proper functioning of stabilization funds requires a set of rules concerning the long-term reference price of the exported commodity above which it is justified to set aside resources; how much to set aside; in what kind of financial instruments to invest; the circumstances under which monies from the stabilization fund can be transferred back to the state budget, and so on. One of the essential requirements for the good functioning of stabilization funds is that the rules that govern them must be set by law, and not left to the discretion of incumbent policymakers. Policymakers can often be exposed to the pressures of various lobbies or be tempted to increase public expenditure when elections are approaching. The main problem of stabilization funds is that the long-term trend of the price of the commodity exported could be a random walk with no mean reversion, with the result that—after the commodity price has fallen for several years—the stabilization fund could exhaust its resources and collapse.

Another solution to the problem of instability and procyclicality of public expenditure comes from the *ex ante* introduction of contingency rules. Such rules state that—in the event of unanticipated and/or uninsurable external shocks—governments are not bound by the usual budgetary rules such as, for example, to run deficits of no more than x per cent of GDP. Thus, in the event that such uninsurable shocks occur, governments would be free to increase public expenditure, and allow a widening of the deficit. *Ex ante* contingency rules are particularly beneficial in developing countries with weak automatic stabilizers and where a discretionary countercyclical fiscal policy may be looked upon with suspicion by the IMF and the financial markets.

What explains the ability of some developing countries, to escape the procyclical fiscal policy trap? The literature points to the importance of institutions in determining various aspects of public policy (see Chapter 11). For instance, Frenkel et al. (2013) develop an index of institutional quality (combing investment risk, extent of corruption, law and order, and bureaucratic quality) aiming to explain the decline in the cyclicality of fiscal policy observed in the 2000s. Even after taking into account possible problems of endogeneity, they found a strong causal link running between the quality of institutions and countercyclical fiscal policy. While institutional change is not easy to explain and often occurs only slowly, the payoffs in terms of being able to escape the trap of a cyclical fiscal policy can be substantial.[2]

Global insurance, stabilization, and aid mechanisms to offset the effects of global shocks

The shocks affecting developing countries are of different types: totally exogenous (e.g. tsunamis and droughts), due to poor domestic policies, or caused by international contagion (e.g. that due to the 1997 Thai crisis, the Argentinean crisis of 2001–02, the 2008–09 US sub-prime loan crisis, and the EU sovereign debt crisis of 2010–13). Even countries with a solid macroeconomy and not prone to climatic shocks may thus be hit as innocent bystanders. Now, if a shock originates from the poor functioning of the global economy, logic would dictate (according to the principle that the one who triggers a crisis should pay for the damage it causes) that any solution of the consequent problems should be funded with monies from the countries whose activities caused the damage. For example, the yields of the Tobin Tax on cross-border capital movements could be used to support the business cycle of innocent bystanders whose macroeconomy was affected by financial or real contagion generated by a global financial crisis. Of course, assigning responsibility for a global macro shock is not straightforward, and possible moral hazard problems must be taken into consideration, but such a principle can be defended even if it has not yet been fully accepted.

A weaker version of this principle concerns situation where it is not possible to assign clear responsibility for a global shock to specific speculative activities. Innocent bystanders ought to be compensated on the basis of derivatives and other insurance contracts stipulated *ex ante* and supported with aid flows or low conditionality loans by the international community, for the sake of solidarity and in consideration of the potential damage through contagion to other countries. Loan- or grant-based compensatory mechanisms have been set up in the past by the European Union (e.g. in the case of the Stabex) and the IMF (by means of the former Oil, Food and Compensatory Financing Facility, that was replaced in 2008 by the concessional Exogenous Shocks Facility and in 2010 by the

[2] Persson and Tabellini (2000) developed a comprehensive analysis to explain huge cross-country differences in economic policies and redistribution. Their analysis straddles political science, economics, and the interplay between alternative political institutions (such as different types of democracy, whether parliamentary or presidential, constitutions, and electoral systems, whether proportional or majoritarian) and the reaction of rational individuals, lobbies, and parties. Their aim is to explain how economic policies are influenced by political institutions (that they assume exogenously). Their work is inspired by three main theoretical approaches: the rational expectations in macroeconomics, public choice theory, and political rational choice theory. In their view, differences in political institutions explain to a good extent the observed cross-country variation in monetary and fiscal policy, in particular in the fields of public spending, public debt, pensions, and taxation. The authors wonder, however, whether the observed cross-country differences in such policy areas reflect the preferences of a majority of citizens, the imperfection of political institutions, or differences in the motivation (opportunistic versus partisan) of the politicians. According to their view, suboptimal and ineffective macroeconomic policies depend on the institutional setup of a country, the influence of various lobbies, and political trends, as in the case of electoral cycles.

Standby Credit Facility). Likewise, in 1979 UNCTAD unveiled an Integrated Programme for Commodities aiming simultaneously to stabilize the prices of eighteen primary commodities (excluding oil) by means of a Common Fund financed by all UNCTAD members, and in particular by the advanced countries. The Common Fund (that in the end did not fly politically) was designed to finance the purchase of commodity buffer stocks during periods of declining prices and to sell them during periods of price increases, thus protecting both producers and consumers from large downward or upward variations in the prices of the eighteen commodities.

A key question is how to finance such mechanisms of global insurance and assistance. Attempts have so far emphasized the role of insurance, donations, and global taxes. This is an unresolved problem, but various approaches to the global taxation of capital movements, air flights, TNCs, and other cross-border activities are beginning to be discussed (Atkinson, 2004).

18.3 Measures to Be Adopted in Unavoidable Crises

In many cases, even when the measures discussed above have been successfully introduced, a number of macroeconomic crises will unavoidably occur, hit the developing countries, and potentially raise their poverty and inequality. The question then concerns which macroeconomic policies are most suitable under such circumstances. The main features of this approach are discussedin the next six subsections.

Choice of overall adjustment approach

There are basically two approaches that can be adopted, the pros and cons of which should be compared case by case before making a choice (Stiglitz et al., 2006). The first approach pivots around a defence of the nominal hard peg, interest rate rises, and fiscal austerity. It aims to defend the credibility of the exchange rate in order to induce the foreign capitals to come back thanks to large temporary increases of the interest rate. Such capital inflows would compensate the current account deficit caused by a macro shock and the ensuing crisis. This approach has a modest impact on inflation due to the stability of the nominal exchange rate and the deflationary effect of the interest rate rise. The impact on poverty and inequality will vary, according to the sectors which are most affected by the interest rate rise. Wages and employment in sectors with high profits would remain roughly unchanged, while employment and wages would fall in less efficient firms, leading to adverse distributional and poverty effects. Even if wages do not change, employment is likely to decrease in weak sectors and firms and in those linked to them.

This approach, however, involves significant output losses. The large increase in the interest rate and the public expenditure cuts needed to support the exchange rate are—by definition—contractionary, at least in the short term, and so accentuate the fall of the equilibrium level of GDP caused by the initial shock (Figure 18.1). As a result, the number of bankruptcies increases, employment falls, and poverty rises over the short term. Moreover, it is not certain that the defence of the nominal exchange rate is sustainable. In fact, it is not obvious that a temporary increase in the interest rate can lead to a permanent strengthening of the exchange rate and to the restoration of confidence among foreign investors. Foreign capital may, in fact, not come back if the approach is perceived as non-credible.

Other effects relate to the financial sector. Indeed, a rise in the interest rate will lead to an increase in bankruptcies among domestic firms as well as a rise in the cost of servicing the interest payments on the domestic public debt, a situation that will generate further contractionary effects. In addition, as a consequence of the increase in the interest rate, firms that did not go bankrupt will experience a decline in their net profits and so may relocate abroad, thus causing an additional contractionary effect on output and employment. Third, increasing the interest rate generates—*ceteris paribus*—a reduction in asset prices, with the effect of discouraging companies to invest and employ new workers, thus causing a simultaneous fall in demand and aggregate supply (see Chapter 13). Finally, the increase in bankruptcies and defaults on bank loans may reduce the propensity of banks to grant new loans, thus contributing to a slowdown in investment.

In short, this approach would lead to a sharp rise in domestic bankruptcies, a credit crunch, and the contraction of domestic demand and output without generating a sustainable improvement in the current account balance driven by an increase in exports (Stiglitz et al., 2006). Access to international capital markets would remain broadly unchanged. Of course, these effects vary from place to place, and they will be less serious in developing countries with low public debt, whose firms are financed in large part with their cashflow, and where exports can be increased by a compression of real wages.

The second approach focuses on a devaluation of the nominal and real exchange rate and a fiscal expansion that involves an increase in the budget deficit. These measures will likely generate an increase of domestic output and a surge of exports, possibly resulting from the real devaluation. Both of these measures should compensate for the contraction of output and employment caused by the external shock. Clearly, this approach presupposes the existence of underutilized productive capacity and a high elasticity of export supply that would moderate the impact of the exogenous shock on output, employment, and poverty and that would respond to the increase in domestic demand and exports due to devaluation and fiscal expansion.

This approach, however, would also generate some adverse effects. First higher inflation (due both to the devaluation of the currency and the fiscal expansion), would affect most seriously the poor, especially the urban poor, who hold their financial assets in national currency and not in dollars or other stores of value. In this approach, the poor are more exposed to the erosion of unindexed monetary transfers such as pensions and social assistance, and are likely to be more affected by inflation than the non-poor, as during periods of financial turbulence price rises tend to be more pronounced for wage goods than for luxury goods. Finally, the literature shows that the poor are psychologically more concerned about inflation.

However, the impact of inflation on the poor varies greatly between the rural sector (especially in the little monetized subsistence sector) and the urban sector, and the industries of employment. For instance, the poor would be less affected if they were employed in the traded sector, and be less damaged by the 'fiscal drag' induced by inflation if they worked in the informal sector where they do not generally pay income tax. Furthermore, they would avoid the strong fall in employment that occurs when a monetary approach to stabilization is adopted and an increase in interest rates introduced to curb inflation. In fact, the literature seems to emphasize that the impact on poverty is greater in the case of a contractionary approach that in an expansionary-inflationary adjustment.

The success of this type of adjustment clearly depends on the effectiveness of devaluation in stimulating exports. The limits of devaluation in improving the current account have been illustrated in Chapter 15 to which we refer the reader. Here it is worth illustrating the effects of devaluation on the capital account.

Devaluation could cause adverse effects on the credibility of economic policies, especially if it is perceived to be non-credible and if it generates expectations of further devaluations. The impact of devaluation would be also felt on public and private balance sheets. For the public sector, where dollar debts are mostly uninsured through derivative contracts, devaluation entails higher expenditures for interest payments and the amortization of foreign debt. This entails a compression of the primary expenditure that is likely to generate contractionary effects on long-term growth, and that would damage the poor the most. For firms with dollar exposures, devaluation may cause an increase in the number of bankruptcies, a default on their foreign debt, and their possible exclusion from the international financial market.

In search of the least costly approach

Given the characteristics of these two approaches, the choice of the overall adjustment package will be inspired by the principle of the least costly approach based on the five criteria, discussed in following paragraphs.

The cost of the output decline: this is generally more pronounced in the monetarist approach, which induces a contraction of domestic demand and a stagnation of exports, except in cases where the policymaker is able to compress real wages and other domestic production costs through a so-called 'internal devaluation' (see Section 15.9). Except for rare cases, the Keynesian approach may also generate a contractionary effect on domestic demand given the negative impact of devaluation on the capital account discussed above. However, especially if the banking sector is helped to reorganize swiftly to finance the expansion of exports made possible by devaluation, the foreign component of aggregate demand should recover fairly quickly.

As for the costs relating to inflation: if the defense of the fixed exchange rate is successful, the monetarist approach will generate a smaller increase in prices than the Keynesian approach. The poor would benefit from it, but they would be, at the same time, more affected by the greater contraction of output, employment, and wages typical of the monetary approach.

As for the costs to exports and the balance of payments: over the short term, changes in the current account balance should be more favourable under the Keynesian approach; those related to the capital account balance are uncertain, and probably more favourable if the monetary approach is adopted. Over the long term, however, the equilibrium of the overall balance of payments depends on improvements in the current account balance and therefore, again, the Keynesian approach would be preferable, although—as noted—this will depend on the respect of the Marshall–Lerner condition and on the ability to fix the banking sector quickly to support the new export drive.

As for costs relating to bankruptcies and moral hazard: in the monetary approach, the stability of the nominal exchange rate tends to protect international creditors and causes, at the same time, the failure of domestic firms affected by the increase in the interest rate. This is a source of moral hazard, in the sense that international creditors would not bear any cost for their decisions to lend short-term dollar-denominated loans for which they did not do a due diligence. With the devaluation-based approach, it is likely that defaults will instead affect foreign debts more significantly, while the defaults among domestic firms should be fewer. This would shift the loans default from the domestic to the international sector, thus reducing the moral hazard problem.

Finally, in terms of exclusion from the financial markets: this is definitely smaller in the case of the monetary adjustment than in the Keynesian approach characterized by greater international defaults. However, it is not clear how expensive such exclusion is. The most recent studies, including those by the IMF, indicate that international portfolio flows do not always generate clear positive effects (see Chapter 10), while their effects in terms of increased consumption volatility are clear, and therefore this exclusion may not cause a growth slowdown over the long run. A problem could arise, however, if FDI were discouraged.

By combining these five criteria, it seems that the Keynesian approach is superior (three advantages versus two) in general terms, although this conclusion needs to be verified on a case by case basis, with the possibility that the monetarist approach is preferable in some cases.

Fiscal policy

How large can the budget deficit be during the adjustment period? The mainstream view is that it should be limited to a few percentage points of GDP and that, to achieve this objective, significant deficit reductions (up to 4–5 per cent of GDP or more) may be necessary for the initial years to avoid inflation, loss of credibility, and the crowding out of private investments by bond emissions.

The problem with this position is that there is no evidence that transitory deficits—even of sizeable dimensions—are costly, while there is clear evidence that sharp public expenditure cuts have strong short and long contractionary effects on aggregate demand, employment, public investment, and the welfare of the poor. Moreover, given that tax revenue is endogenously determined by the equilibrium level of income, a rapid reduction of the deficit involves a drop in tax revenue which leads to a new widening of the deficit and a new round of expenditure cuts. Such an approach therefore leads to an illusory adjustment. Under such circumstances, reaching the pre-set target deficit requires the imposition of additional austerity measures over several years. As suggested by Adam and Bevan (2001), deficit reductions of up to 1.5 per cent of GDP a year help to re-establish the fiscal balance with a minimal impact on growth, but larger reductions actually damage the prospects for growth.

In the case of unexpected and uninsurable transitory shocks, especially, it is therefore preferable to allow an increase of the budget deficit for a few years in order to sustain aggregate demand and short-term growth. The deficit will then be gradually reduced in parallel with the recovery of the economy. A further argument in favour of a countercyclical expansion of the deficit, and of its reduction during the expansionary phase of the business cycle, concerns the distribution of the costs and benefits of alternative fiscal adjustment policies. For example, a higher deficit, even if accompanied by some rise in inflation, could harm the poor less than an approach that requires large public spending cuts that would cause an immediate worsening of employment, wages, and income distribution that invariably affects the poor disproportionally.

Approaches to deficit reduction

Once the size of the target deficit has been determined, it is necessary to choose the policies that can help to reduce the current deficit to the target deficit in the least costly way. In this regard, equation (18.1) provides a current prices decomposition of the budget deficit in all its components, allowing the policymaker to assess the costs and benefits of alternative strategies for the reduction of the current budget deficit (BD_t) to its targeted value.

$$\frac{BD_t}{Y_t} = \frac{PPE_t}{Y_t} - \frac{TR_t + NTR_t + FA_t}{Y_t} + (r-g)\frac{NPD_{t-1}}{Y_t} + (r'-g){e^{nc/\$}}_t \frac{FPD_{t-1}}{Y_t} - \frac{\Delta H}{P_t Y_t} \quad (18.1)$$

In the above equation PPE is primary public expenditure, TR, NTR, and FA are tax revenue, non-tax revenue, and foreign aid, NPD and FPD are domestic and foreign public debt, ΔH the expansion of the monetary base, $e^{nc/\$}$ the nominal exchange rate, r and r′ the domestic and international interest rate, g the growth rate of Y (GDP), and P the price level.

The conventional viewpoint is that there is a need to reduce the budget deficit by cutting PPE, not least for the greater technical viability and faster implementation of this measure. But—while cuts are needed in many cases for efficiency reasons—this approach involves problems, especially where large budget cuts may arouse the opposition of influential vocal minorities. This may frustrate or retard the whole stabilization effort. Second, as noted before, large cuts involve a contractionary effect on aggregate demand and short-term growth. In addition, if such cuts fall on the provision of essential public goods (security, law and order, infrastructure, and human capital) they could negatively affect long-term growth. In either case, the growth rate of GDP (g) would contract, tax revenue would fall, and the deficit rise again. From a political economy perspective, it is also important to note that the politically unorganized poor with no voice are likely to be affected more than proportionately from large expenditure cuts, unless governments introduce explicit measures to protect them (see later in this chapter).

Alternatively, the deficit can be reduced with an increase in progressive tax revenue (TR), non-tax revenue (NTR), and foreign aid (FA), or by channelling resources rom Stabilization Funds into the public budget (see Section 18.2). From a macroeconomic point of view it is important to note that a tax increase has a less contractionary effect on aggregate demand than a cut in public expenditure (see the comparison of various multipliers in Table 3.2). Over the medium term, a tax increase introduced during a crisis period may also contribute to supporting spending on under-provided public goods that are essential for long-term growth. In countries with low tax/GDP ratios (as many are in Central America and Africa), increased taxation of the middle class and the rich may also improve the distribution of income compared to the scenario which contemplates a proportional cut in public expenditure. Finally, in developing countries, increased taxation of the rich is desirable from the point of view of the balance of payments, since this group generally has a higher propensity to consume imported goods.

Increasing taxation may, however, be more difficult for technical reasons, especially in developing countries with a large informal sector, and could entail delays in revenue collection. Yet, even in low-income agrarian countries such as Ethiopia, revenue collection has increased substantially during the last two decades, indicating the importance of political commitment to implement such a measure. Some also argue that taxing profits may be counterproductive in the case of footloose capital and firms that could relocate abroad. There are examples, however, of economies which have introduced taxes on corporate profits and financial assets (that were previously exempted), as observed for instance in Latin America where the overall regional tax revenue/GDP ratio rose by 3.5 GDP points between 2002 and 2012 (Cornia 2014). Finally, increasing taxation during crises may also generate longer-term benefits. Indeed, the empirical evidence shows that countries that achieved an adequate tax/GDP ratio were less likely to be affected by macroeconomic instability and budget deficits over the long term.

In countries with a high domestic debt/GDP ratio (NPD), in particular, the budget deficit could also be reduced by lowering the nominal interest rate. The introduction of such a measure, however, must be supported by other monetary measures, and may require the introduction of capital controls since, in liberalized financial markets, agents may shift their savings to countries with higher interest rates. Such a measure would cause a depreciation of the exchange rate, $e^{nc/\$}$, and—as shown by equation (18.1)—raise the domestic currency cost of the interest paid on foreign debt (FPD).

Finally, the deficit could be financed by a controlled expansion of the monetary base, ΔH, beyond that made possible by the increase of the nominal GDP (i.e. real GDP plus the rate of inflation) that does not cause, in principle, any increase in the price level P. Overall, if practised with moderation, seignorage can generate considerable resources without causing an acceleration of inflation (Agénor and Montiel 1999, Figure 1.9). Yet, beyond a given limit, monetary emissions depresses the value of seignorage, do not improve the deficit, and may even make the overall real tax revenue fall because of the so-called Tanzi–Olivera effect. The latter is observed when the real value of the tax revenue collected with a delay of several months is eroded by inflation caused by excessive expansion of the monetary base. For example, with inflation at 100 per cent per quarter and a delay of six months between assessment of taxes and their collection, the real value of the tax collected is reduced by three-quarters.

Another way to reduce the current deficit to the targeted level consists in reducing the stock of domestic public debt (NPD) and foreign public debt (FPD). During crises, the developing countries, especially thel Least developed countries, have great difficulties servicing their public debt, especially the part denominated in foreign currency. In cases of severe and persistent shocks, the policymaker may therefore try to reduce the budget deficit through a series of debt management measures. These include debt standstills, according to which the reimbursement of bonds coming to maturity—and sometimes even the payment of interest—is suspended due to *force majeure*. Debt standstills should become automatic in the event of exogenous shocks such as disasters, financial crises, and the collapse of raw materials prices. In such cases, the reimbursement is postponed—at no cost—to better times. A second measure to reduce current expenditure on debt servicing consists of debt rescheduling. With this measure, the whole reimbursement is redistributed over a longer period of time, thereby easing current obligations. Yet, this measure often entails rising interest rates and commissions and thus raises the costs of debt servicing in the future. Third, 'debt haircuts' and debt securitization could be considered—such as those applied in Latin America as part of the Brady and Baker plans in the 1980s and early 1990s, and in Greece in 2012–13. Such measures consist in exchanging old unsafe bonds with new securities of smaller value but guaranteed by valuable assets and carrying attractive rates. In the early 2000s Argentina adopted a programme of this type in which the old peso debt was exchanged (at 32 dollar cents per peso) for new dollar denominated bonds.

Other debt reduction policies may focus on debt-for-development swaps. In this case, the foreign debt denominated in dollars is cancelled but national governments undertake to use the equivalent value (or part of it) in national currency to develop programmes to combat poverty, promote growth, and protect the environment. If there are no discounts on the face value of the foreign debt, the benefit of such measures is perceived only on the side of the balance of payments and not in the public budget. Finally, countries may reduce their debt service and improve their fiscal account and balance of payments through debt repudiation, or debt cancellation. In both cases, the debt is extinguished (and therefore rDPN and r′DPE are cancelled out, thus improving the deficit). In the first case this is due to a unilateral decision of the indebted country, in the second it occurs with the agreement and on the initiative of the creditors, as in the case of the IMF-managed Highly Indebted Poor Countries (HIPC) programme. The debt repudiation tends to be politically onerous and may result in a loss of credibility for the government and exclusion from international financial markets.

In both cases, it is important to distinguish the effects on the cash deficit from those on the approved budget deficit. While the results of the latter can be considerable, the impact on the cash deficit is often nil, as the debt being cancelled was not being serviced and only fed the accumulation of arrears. But it is also true that a radical debt cancellation allows countries who are not servicing their debt to return to the financial markets from which a large accumulation of arrears had excluded them in the past.

Intersectoral allocation of expenditure cuts and safety nets

Whatever decision is taken in terms of the size of the deficit and of the speed of its reduction, fiscal policy can significantly influence the well-being of low-income groups by means of a progressive and efficient distribution of spending cuts. Proportional cuts across all sectors may be easier to implement from a political economy perspective but they are less efficient. In fact, due to the limited political influence of the low-income groups, programmes which benefit them are often cut more than others. Yet, social and economic efficiency suggest that in crisis situations it is necessary to support or even expand public spending on basic health, primary education, secondary and technical education, personal and social security, public works, essential social transfers, rehabilitation of infrastructure, and essential investments for long-term growth. Indeed, the social rates of return of public spending in these sectors are high,[3] especially for basic interventions. Under such circumstances, supporting priority expenditure requires reducing or postponing non-essential and unproductive expenditures, such as part of military spending, odious debt service, unnecessary investment, and expenditures that can be delayed without damage.

Within the priority areas indicated above, public spending should be focused on programmes with low administrative costs, high intrinsic efficiency, and strong targeting on those persons, areas, and sectors most exposed to the risk of adjustment-related impoverishment. This policy is desirable because it improves the welfare of the poor at a limited cost in terms of public spending. Such an objective could be achieved by establishing clear spending priorities or by assigning earmarked taxes to essential programmes such as child immunization, primary education, the maintenance and rehabilitation of key infrastructure, and so on. If practised on a large scale, however, a policy of earmarked taxes may lead to budget rigidity and a possible political capture of such revenue by the rich. An approach that focuses much of the benefit on low-income groups could also be politically unsustainable—since the middle class (and at times the rich) may oppose programmes from which they derive no benefits. The evidence shows, in fact, that to increase the political viability of efficient priority programmes benefiting the low-income groups, it is often necessary to accept that part of these benefits accrue to the middle class.

Under a crisis situation, public expenditure policy should also consider the possibility of making transfers (in cash or nature) to the poor to moderate the impact of exogenous shocks and of the adoption of recessionary stabilization policies. The principle that social assistance should intensify during times of crisis is now universally accepted. By 2012, there were already some 850 million people worldwide benefiting from social assistance programmes (in particular conditional and non-conditional cash transfers and non-contributory pensions costing between 0.5 and 2 per cent of GDP) that are broadly sustainable from a public finance perspective or were financed by donors. Examples of these efficient programmes include the *Bolsa Familia* in Brazil, *Oportunidades* in Mexico, and minimum social pensions in Southern Africa.

Monetary policy, inflation targeting, and interest rates

Inflation is costly as changes in relative prices reduce the informational power of the price system, and so may cause uncertainty which reduces economic activity and discourages new investments and production. Second, high inflation results in perverse monetary effects as it reduces the real money supply and so generates—*ceteris paribus*—a rise in the interest rate and a decline in production, a fall in the real value of tax revenue, and, in extreme cases, a flight from the domestic currency and dollarization. A third argument in favour of inflation control (which becomes even more necessary in countries with an open capital account and a large foreign debt) is that inflation mostly affects the poor. Most of the literature shows, in fact, that the incidence of the inflation tax is U-shaped, and that

[3] These rates of return do not include the value of lives saved or of other externalities that cannot be evaluated in monetary terms. If these benefits were accounted for, the benefits of such programmes would be well in excess of many other interventions.

it affects most severely the first and last deciles of the income distribution. One therefore needs to bring inflation under control.

To deal with these problems the standard approach consists in achieving a pre-set one-digit inflation rate by means of inflation targeting consisting in a substantial increase in the policy rate of the central bank. But a macroeconomy in favour of growth and poverty reduction must also take into account other types of arguments. As already mentioned in Chapter 16, the empirical evidence compiled by Bruno and Easterly (1998) shows that reducing inflation to below 40 per cent does not lead to faster long-term growth, although it may generate positive effects on poverty for the reasons mentioned above. The empirical evidence also shows that reducing inflation to a single digit in developing countries requires the adoption of recessionary policies (characterized by very high interest rates—and expenditure cuts) that generate high social costs. Furthermore, given the low self-financing capacity of most firms, the low elasticity of their demand for money in relation to an increase in the interest rate, and the mark-up price formation mechanism prevailing in developing countries, a pronounced increase in interest rates tends to cause a rise in costs and prices that may negatively affect aggregate supply.

In developing countries, there exists a trade-off between the extent of inflation targeting and growth. Whenever the objective of reaching a single digit inflation target is pursued with only monetary policies[4] and not through structural policies, the country is likely to experience high 'sacrifice ratios' that is, a high loss of output for a 1 per cent decline in inflation.

A monetary policy aimed at poverty eradication as proclaimed by the first SDG must take this into account, and set less ambitious inflation targets, although these should be no less consistent over the long term. This will, therefore, lead to a policy of positive but comparatively low real interest rates. In the case of the quite common cost-push inflation (see equation (14.1)), this policy should help to contain the increase of prices and avoid a leftward shift of the AS schedule and the related decline in real growth and employment. Monetary policy, by necessity, will have to be more accommodating than under the

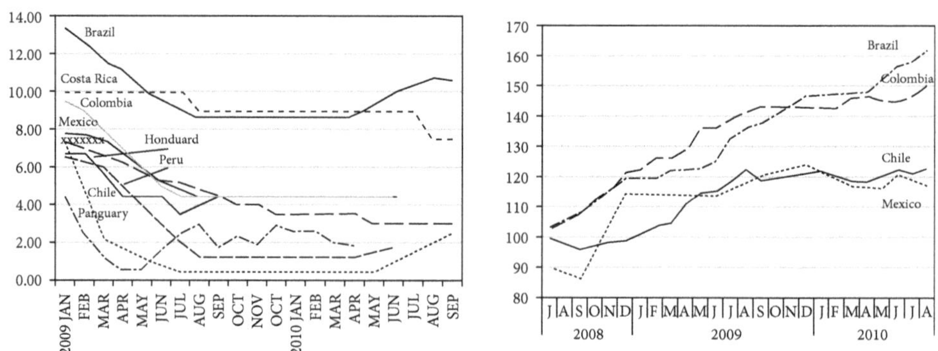

Figure 18.2 Annual monetary policy rate (left) and index number of public banks' lending (right), first half of 2008 = 00

Source: Elaboration on Kacef (2010)

[4] This perhaps explains the use of the exchange rate policy (currency boards and fixed peg or hard peg) as a tool to fight (hyper) inflation as in the case of Argentina and several transition economies.

standard approach. For instance, in several Latin American countries the central bank sharply reduced the policy rate during the crisis of 2008–09 and started raising it moderately towards the end of 2010 in parallel with the recovery of the economy (Figure 18.2, left panel). At the same time, to avoid the credit crunch typical of years of crisis there was a substantial increase in the commercial short- and long-term lending by public credit institutions (Figure 18.2, right panel).

18.4 Intertemporal Aspects and Speed of Macroeconomic Adjustment

The mainstream approach suggests adopting a rapid, front-loaded, adjustment approach. Although it is recognized that such an approach is economically and socially costly over the short term, its proponents believe it makes the economy recover quickly, incurring in this way a smaller total output loss over the entire adjustment period. However, it might be objected that gradual but irreversible cuts (accompanied if necessary by temporary import controls in case of balance of payments problems) may be technically and politically more tolerable than approaches that are more ambitious but socially unsustainable (see Section 16.4). A further argument in favour of a more gradual approach concerns the choice of the optimal time profile of adjustment from the point of view of the poor (see Figure 1 in Lustig, 2000). Which time profile of adjustment is preferable for the poor and the economy as a whole? An adjustment that results in a greater initial contraction but has a higher overall Net Present Value of output over the entire adjustment period, or another that has a lower NPV but a less marked initial contraction? If one assumes a concave utility function $U = f(c)$, with $f'(c) > 0$ and $f''(c) < 0$ for all agents and that the social discount rate of the poor is higher than that of the rich, the ranking of optimal adjustment policies change. In fact, the poor will choose—rationally—a more gradual approach even if this means—for the economy as a whole—a higher loss of output. In this case, the policymaker has two options. The first option is to choose an optimal pro-poor adjustment path. The second is to choose a faster adjustment path which is the best option for the entire country but not for the poor, while compensating the latter for the losses implicit in such approach.[5]

18.5 Concluding Remarks

The emphasis placed since the start of the twenty-first century on the Millennium Development Goals and since 2015 on the Sustainable Development Goals has brought to the fore the issue of which policies and programmes can help to reduce poverty and inequality over the medium term. In this regard, the current debate shows that there is broad agreement among all schools of thought on the nature of social and sectorial policies needed to eradicate poverty by 2030. A similar agreement does not exist, however, about the macroeconomic policies that should facilitate the achievement of this objective. This poses a major problem as an

[5] This conclusion could change, however, if the social discount rate of the poor is reduced by an improvement in the credit and insurance markets, which would allow them to preserve a minimum income even during periods of contraction.

increasing number of macroeconomic shocks linked to the globalization and liberalization of economies and the procyclicality of financial markets can easily set back the advances realized during years of progressive social and sectorial initiatives.

Alternative macro theories compete to explain the business cycle and long-term growth. The vagueness of the macroeconomic prescriptions at the basis of the MDG and SDG strategies therefore needs to be replaced by a consistent package of measures that aim to sustain growth and reestablish the macro balance, but also to eradicate poverty. Such an approach entails first of all introducing in non-crisis years a series of measures that reduce the predisposition of a country's economy to be hit by exogenous shocks or domestic policy mistakes that can cause permanent damage. These measures include the institution of capital controls; a strong regulation of the domestic financial market; the choice of a stable and competitive real exchange rate; the creation of stabilization funds; and the establishment of global insurance mechanisms to compensate countries hit by exogenous shocks. A second set of macroeconomic measures needs to be adopted when—despite the institution of the *ex ante* measures mentioned in this chapter—a developing country is hit by an unavoidable macro shock. Such measures concern the choice of a suitable overall adjustment approach and of a pace of adjustment that avoids large front-loaded contractions. It also concerns the adoption of a countercyclical fiscal and monetary policy; the choice of the most suitable approach to the reduction of the budget deficit; identification of the most efficient and equitable intersectoral allocation of spending cuts; and the identification of feasible debt reduction measures.

References

Adam, C. and D. Bevan (2001), 'Non-linear Effects of Fiscal Deficits on Growth in Developing Countries'. Working Paper, Department of Economics, Oxford: Oxford University.

Agénor, P. R. and P. Montiel (1999), *Development Macroeconomics*, 2nd edn. Princeton, NJ: Princeton University Press.

Atkinson, A. B. (2004), *New Sources of Development Finance*. Oxford: Oxford University Press.

Bruno, M. and W. Easterly (1998), 'Inflation crises and long run growth', *Journal of Monetary Economics*, 41: pp. 3–26.

Cornia, G. A. (2014), *Falling Inequality in Latin America: Policy Changes and Lessons*. Oxford: Oxford University Press.

Cornia, G. A. and B. Martorano (2012), 'Development policies and income inequality in selected developing regions, 1980–2010', UNCTAD Discussion Paper 210, Geneva: UNCTAD.

ECLAC (2015), *Social Panorama of Latin America*. Santiago: Economic Commission for Latin America and the Caribbean.

Frenkel, J. A., C. A.Végh, and G. Vuletin (2013), 'On Graduating from Fiscal Prociclicality', *Journal of Development Economics*, 100: pp. 32–47.

Kacef, O. (2010), PowerPoint presentation at the Conference on Lessons from Recent Economic Management in Latin America for Rich Countries. Pocantico. Rockefeller Foundation, ECLAC and The New School of Social Studies, 2 November 2010.

Kanbur, R. (1998), 'The Implications of Adjustment Programs for Poverty: Conceptual Issues and Analytical Framework', in Ke-young Chu and Sanjeev Gupta (eds), *Social Safety Nets: Issues and Experiences*. Washington, DC: International Monetary Fund.

Lustig, Nora (2000), 'Crises and the Poor: Socially Responsible Macroeconomics', *Economia*, 1 (1): pp. 1–19.

Ocampo, J. A. (2015), 'Capital account liberalization and management', WIDER Working Paper 2015/48. Helsinki: World Institute for Development Economics Research.

Persson, T. and G. Tabellini (2000), *Political Economics: Explaining Economic Policy.* Cambridge, MA: MIT Press.

Rodrik, D. (2006), 'Goodbye Washington Consensus, Hello Washington Confusion? A Review of the World Bank's Economic Growth in the 1990s: Learning from a Decade of Reform', *Journal of Economic Literature*, XLIV: pp. 973–87.

Stiglitz, J., J. A. Ocampo, S. Spiegel, R. Ffrench-Davis, and D. Nayyar (2006), *Stability with Growth: Macroeconomics, Liberalization, and Development.* Oxford: Oxford University Press.

Suggested Further Reading

Atkinson, A. B. (2004), *New Sources of Development Finance.* Oxford: Oxford University Press.

Lustig, N. (2000), 'Crises and the Poor: Socially Responsible Macroeconomics'. *Economia*, 1 (1), pp. 1–19.

Stiglitz, J., J. A. Ocampo, S. Spiegel, R. Ffrench-Davis, and D. Nayyar (2006), *Stability with Growth: Macroeconomics, Liberalization, and Development.* Oxford: Oxford University Press.

Index

Note: Tables and figures are indicated by an italic '*t*' and '*f*', respectively, following the page number.

The manufacturer's authorised representative in the EU for product safety is Oxford University Press España S.A. of el Parque Empresarial San Fernando de Henares, Avenida de Castilla, 2 – 28830 Madrid (www.oup.es/en or product.safety@oup.com). OUP España S.A. also acts as importer into Spain of products made by the manufacturer.

www.ingramcontent.com/pod-product-compliance
Ingram Content Group UK Ltd.
Pitfield, Milton Keynes, MK11 3LW, UK
UKHW051048150926
475595UK00006B/182
* 9 7 8 0 1 9 8 8 5 6 6 7 2 *